COPYRIGHT LAW

ESSENTIAL CASES AND MATERIALS

Third Edition

■ ■ ■

Alfred C. Yen

Associate Dean of Faculty and Professor of Law
Boston College Law School

Joseph P. Liu

Professor of Law
Boston College Law School

AMERICAN CASEBOOK SERIES®

WEST
ACADEMIC
PUBLISHING

American Casebook Series is a trademark registered in the U.S. Patent and Trademark Office.

© West, a Thomson business, 2008
© 2011 Thomson Reuters
© 2016 LEG, Inc. d/b/a West Academic
    444 Cedar Street, Suite 700
    St. Paul, MN 55101
    1-877-888-1330

West, West Academic Publishing, and West Academic are trademarks of West Publishing Corporation, used under license.

Printed in the United States of America

ISBN: 978-1-63459-445-5

To my parents, Karin, Julie, and Stephen

To my parents, Karen, Cate, and Ben

*

Preface

Authors of modern copyright casebooks face interesting challenges. Frequent legislative enactments, the challenges of digital technology, and the increasing commercial value of copyrightable subject matter have rendered the law more voluminous and complex. Standard teaching materials have responded by following suit. Copyright casebooks frequently now measure from 800 to over 1000 pages in length. These lengthy books are impressive and valuable. Teachers can include almost any subject in a syllabus, and researchers can use the books as reference tools.

Unfortunately, the size of modern copyright casebooks creates problems. A 3 or 4 credit course cannot cover all of the material presented. Teachers must therefore skip back and forth in the book, losing the coherent presentation of overarching themes. Numerous squib cases, notes, and questions add potentially valuable nuance and detail, but the flood of information often frustrates, confuses, and overwhelms students.

We have decided to tackle this problem by presenting a compact set of cases and materials focused on copyright's essentials. We believe that students learn most effectively, particularly in an introductory course, when confronted by manageable amounts of reading directed to the major issues being discussed in class. In our experience, comprehension suffers when students confront unduly lengthy assignments. Students may read more, but they absorb less and think less. We therefore think that students will learn more when presented with details in class after they have mastered the basics. Indeed, students who are comfortable with the basics frequently raise advanced topics on their own.

With this in mind, our casebook makes no effort to be truly comprehensive. We do not explore every wrinkle raised by the cases, nor do we analyze the many fascinating and important scholarly articles that now grace the field. The book contains no squib cases, and relatively few string cites. We have edited the cases fairly heavily to keep them "on message," and we have tried to limit ourselves to four notes and questions per case, although we have used more at a few important junctures.

In return, teachers and students get a book of manageable length that keeps the central themes of copyright front and center. First and foremost, the book introduces the doctrines and statutory provisions that matter most to practicing attorneys. At the same time, it permits students to engage with these doctrines and statutory provisions in more depth. We ask students to confront the frustrating ambiguity of copyright's major concepts. The book pushes students to consider whether those ambiguities can be explained or resolved by copyright's effect on the creation and use of socially valuable works, its relationship to basic notions of fairness and justice, or the influence of the legislative process and political power.

Of course, our concise approach risks omitting things that individual teachers may desire. We address these problems by taking advantage of Internet technology. Our TWEN website offers a number of items of interest to those using our book, including a library of audio-visual materials, updates, additional cases and materials, cases from previous editions, links to statutes, and a section where teachers can share their own modules of cases and materials with others. Teachers can thus supplement the essential materials in the casebook with additional materials that are of particular interest to them, without detracting from the focused and compact nature of the casebook.

In this third edition of the casebook, in addition to the standard updates and edits, we have made a number of significant changes to reflect new developments in this dynamic field. Specifically:

- In Chapter Three, we added *Aalmuhammed v. Lee* in the section on joint works. We also reduced *New York Times v. Tasini* to a note and added a new short section on interpreting and drafting transfers and licenses.

- In Chapter Five, we reduced *Bridgeport Music v. Dimension Films* to a textual description. We replaced *Quality King Distributors v. L'anza Research* with the more recent Supreme Court case *Kirtsaeng v. John Wiley & Sons*. In the section on Digital Technology, we deleted *MAI Systems v. Peak Computer*, summarizing it in the text, and added the Supreme Court's decision in *American Broadcasting Co. v. Aereo*.

- In Chapter Six, in the discussion of fair use, we deleted *Kelly v. Arriba Soft* and created a new subsection titled "Aggregative Uses," which includes two new cases: *Bill Graham Archives v. Doris Kindersley* and *Authors Guild v. Google*. In the section on Statute of Limitations, we include a brief discussion of *Petrella v. Metro-Goldwyn-Mayer*.

- In Chapter Seven, we made several changes to the section on the DMCA and ISP Liability, greatly editing down the statutory text, deleting *Perfect10 v. CCBill* and *ALS Scan v. RemarQ Communities*, and replacing the district court opinion in *Viacom v. YouTube* with the appellate court opinion.

- In Chapter Eight, we updated the text to reflect the most recent DMCA rulemaking.

- In Chapter Nine, we deleted *Salinger v. Colting*.

- In Chapter Ten, in the section on the Right of Publicity, we added *Laws v. Sony Music Entertainment*.

Although we believe these new cases better reflect the present state of copyright and will foster good class discussions, we realize that some teachers may still wish to use the old cases. Accordingly, edited versions of those cases from earlier editions are available on our TWEN website.

Like all authors, we owe debts of gratitude to countless people who have discussed our ideas and offered support. Most of all, however, we would like to thank our families and loved ones, who have cheerfully tolerated and encouraged our interest in the subject of copyright.

ALFRED C. YEN
JOSEPH P. LIU
NEWTON, MA

January 2016

Summary of Contents

Table of Contents

———————

Table of Cases

The principal cases are in bold type. Cases cited or discussed in the text are roman type. References are to pages. Cases cited in principal cases and within other quoted materials are not included.

COPYRIGHT LAW

ESSENTIAL CASES
AND MATERIALS

Third Edition

Chapter One

INTRODUCTION

The United States Code contains three major forms of intellectual property: copyright, patent, and trademark. Each has its own distinct subject matter and confers different rights to intellectual property owners. Patent protects useful, novel, and non-obvious inventions. It allows patent holders to prevent others from making, using, or selling the patented invention. Trademark protects words, phrases, or symbols used to designate the source of goods or services. It gives trademark holders the right to prevent others from using a protected mark in ways that confuse the public about the source of competing goods and services. Copyright, the subject of this book, governs various rights in books, musical works, movies, computer programs, and other original works of authorship. It gives copyright owners the exclusive right to reproduce, make derivative works from, distribute, publicly perform, and publicly display their works.

SECTION A. HISTORY OF COPYRIGHT

Let us begin our study of copyright with a brief account of its Anglo-American history. This is important because the arguments and perspectives that shaped copyright over 400 years ago remain vital to this day. The advent of computers and the Internet may give us the impression that the 21st century is fundamentally different from the 16th. However, as the following pages will show, copyright's fundamental issues have remained largely the same.

1. EARLY ENGLISH COPYRIGHT

Many scholars trace the origins of modern copyright to the introduction of the printing press to England. This technology created a new and profitable industry, the printing and selling of books. It also raised the suspicion of the British Crown, for the widespread availability of affordable texts meant that increasing numbers of people would read political and religious challenges to the Crown's authority.

Not surprisingly, the Crown decided to censor the new industry, and it did so by catering to the economic interests of printers and booksellers. In 1557, Queen Mary granted exclusive rights of printing to the Stationers' Company. These exclusive rights gave the Stationers' Company an effective monopoly over the printing industry, for it now had the power to seize and destroy unauthorized presses and books. The Stationers' Company used these powers to enforce the Crown's censorship while enjoying the profits that came with the elimination of rival printers. This state of affairs continued under a combination of royal decrees and legislation until 1694, when the House of Commons ended censorship by deciding not to renew the Licensing Act of 1662.

The end of censorship destroyed the monopoly enjoyed by the Stationers' Company. Its most powerful group, the booksellers, lobbied the House of Commons for new protective legislation on the ground that competition from previously outlawed rival printers would ruin the profitability of the booksellers' business. The House rejected these efforts because it objected to, among other things, the booksellers' role in censorship, the high cost and low quality of printed texts, and the perception that booksellers unfairly profited from the labor of authors. However, this rejection did not mean that monopolies would forever disappear from the printing industry.

In 1710, the booksellers made a new appeal to the House of Commons. This time, however, they tried a new tactic. Instead of claiming that the printing industry would suffer economic loss, they argued that the termination of exclusive rights in printing had removed important financial incentives for the writing of new books. Unless the House of Commons restored some kind of protection against the free printing of texts, the public would suffer because authors would earn insufficient profits from their works and respond by writing less. This plea worked, and the House of Commons eventually passed the Statute of Anne.[1] The Statute, entitled "An Act for the Encouragement of Learning," granted authors the exclusive right to print their works for up to 28 years.

The Statute of Anne was the first Anglo-American copyright statute, and as such, it initially established copyright as a right of limited duration granted by the state for a public purpose. Although intended for the benefit of authors, the Statute of Anne's limited rights protected the interests of the booksellers because booksellers dominated the market for printed works so completely that authors had to sell their exclusive rights to the booksellers if they wanted their works printed at all. However, the Statute of Anne also gave the booksellers less than they desired, for the limited term of exclusive rights meant that the booksellers'

---

[1] 8 Anne, ch. 19 (1710).

monopolies would expire fairly quickly. Indeed, when rival publishers began printing books that had fallen into the public domain, the booksellers returned to Parliament seeking yet another extension of exclusive rights, but they failed.

Undaunted, the booksellers turned to the English courts. In *Millar v. Taylor*,[2] the plaintiff Millar had purchased the rights to James Thomson's poem "The Seasons" and had enjoyed a full term of protection under the Statute of Anne. However, upon expiration of that term, the defendant Taylor began printing the poem, and Millar sued.

The biggest problem with Millar's suit was of course the Statute of Anne, for the expiration of Millar's rights under that law presumably meant that he no longer had any rights in "The Seasons." However, Millar tried a novel argument, contending that English common law protected an author's natural right of property in his literary work, separate and apart from any limited statutory scheme. The King's Bench agreed.

In deciding for Millar, the court borrowed heavily from the philosophy of John Locke, particularly Locke's argument that a person has a property right in his labor. Because, in the court's view, an author's work is peculiarly the product of the author's labor, fundamental principles of justice required recognition of Millar's asserted property rights:

> [B]ecause it is just, that an author should reap the pecuniary profits of his own ingenuity and labour. It is just, that another should not use his name, without his consent. It is fit, that he should judge when to publish, or whether he ever will publish.[3]

According to the court, the Statute of Anne did not limit this common law right of the author, so Millar had to win.

Millar v. Taylor could have drastically altered the basic nature of copyright, for it took the position that basic principles of justice required a perpetual common law copyright right in excess of any rights created by the Statute of Anne. Indeed, if followed by other courts, *Millar* would have reinstated the perpetual monopoly enjoyed by the Stationers' Company under censorship. This did not occur, however, for it took only 5 years for the House of Lords to overrule *Millar* in the case of *Donaldson v. Beckett*.[4]

Donaldson ironically involved yet another dispute over exclusive rights to "The Seasons." After *Millar v. Taylor*, a group of printers including Beckett acquired the common law copyright to the poem. Beckett sued the proprietors of an unauthorized edition of the poem, but the House of Lords ultimately rejected Beckett's claim. This meant that copyright could exist only by statutory decree, and it restored the Statue of Anne's control over the existence and duration of an author's exclusive right to print her works.

---

[2] 98 Eng. Rep. 201 (1769).
[3] 98 Eng. Rep. 252 (opinion of Mansfield, J.).
[4] 1 Eng. Rep. 837 (1774).

2. MODERN U.S. COPYRIGHT

The development of English copyright did not go unnoticed by those in the United States. Madison wrote about the value of copyright in the *Federalist Papers*, and the framers gave Congress explicit authority to pass copyright legislation in the Constitution.[5] Not surprisingly, the first U.S. Copyright statute, passed in 1790, borrowed its basic structure from the Statue of Anne, giving copyrights with initial and renewal terms of 14 years to the authors of "maps, charts, and books."[6]

In 1909, Congress passed a new statute that considerably expanded the scope of copyright. The new statute protected "all writings of an author," and not merely "maps, charts, and books." Additionally, copyright now lasted for a total of 56 years, with authors receiving initial and renewal terms of 28 years each.[7] The 1909 Act governed copyright for over 60 years, providing legal rights that supported the growth of, among other things, the book, music, movie, and television industries. Eventually, however, various forces created momentum for change.

First and foremost, new technologies such as radio, television, and the phonograph created new ways to exploit copyrighted works that the 1909 Act did not fully account for. The profits associated with these uses increased the potential value of copyrights and encouraged holders of existing copyrights to seek longer and broader protection. Second, the 1909 Act contained a number of technical formalities such as the process for renewing copyright that caused inadvertent forfeiture of rights. Third, the emerging globalization of business meant that U.S. copyright holders wanted assurances that other countries would recognize rights already enjoyed under U.S. law. It therefore became desirable for the United States to adhere to the Berne Convention, the leading international copyright treaty. However, the United States could not do so without modifying its copyright law to conform to the treaty's requirements.

In response to these pressures, Congress began the lengthy and politically delicate process of revising the 1909 Act. Every proposed change to the law created potential winners and losers, and the value of copyright-related businesses had become sufficiently large to make lobbying Congress worthwhile. In 1976, after many years of debate and negotiation, Congress managed to pass a new statute (generally referred to as the "1976 Act") that gave new works a single term of copyright that lasted for the life of the author plus 50 years. The 1976 Act also lengthened the duration of existing works to 75 years from publication and began reducing the importance of formalities in copyright. These changes, along with others found in the Berne Convention Implementation Act of 1988, paved the way for the United States to join the Berne Convention in 1989.

---

[5] U.S. Const. Art. I, § 8, cl. 8.
[6] Copyright Act of 1790 § 1.
[7] An Act to Amend and Consolidate The Acts Respecting Copyright § 4, 23.

The 1976 Act is the statute that generally governs U.S. copyright today (although as we will see, works created prior to the 1976 Act may still be governed by the 1909 Act). Congress has, however, amended the 1976 Act many times. Although these amendments are too numerous to summarize here, it is safe to surmise that the future will bring even more amendments to our copyright statute as Congress and its political constituencies respond to the changing economic and technological contexts in which copyright becomes relevant.

3. COPYRIGHT TODAY

At the time of the 1976 Act's passage, most lawyers considered copyright a relatively obscure specialty. However, technology and globalization would soon bring copyright the prominence it enjoys today.

Technology affected copyright by both increasing its commercial importance and facilitating infringement. The proliferation of consumer electronics enabled people to enjoy copyrighted works as never before. Compact disc players, video cassette players, and personal computers created new markets for the sale of works to consumers around the world. Digital technology also led to new, valuable forms of copyrightable subject matter on which entire new industries would rise. For example, the widespread use of personal computers meant that millions of individuals and businesses depended on copyrightable subject matter such as computer software to conduct their daily business. Finally, digital technology, particularly the Internet, made it easy for almost anyone to both reproduce and distribute perfect copies at low cost.

This created opportunities for copyright holders to find new ways of selling and delivering works to consumers, but it also greatly increased the challenges facing copyright holders. New technologies made it much easier for consumers to make and distribute unauthorized copies of copyrighted works. As a result, copyright holders had to confront the possibility that every customer might commit mass infringement by making a single copy of a purchased work and posting it on the Internet for millions to download. In short, technology made copyright more valuable around the world, but it also threatened the security of copyright.

The challenges posed by technology influenced individuals and governments to change the shape of copyright. Within the United States, copyright holders took steps to protect themselves from piracy while exploiting new markets for their works. In some cases, they tried technological solutions such as copy-protection for CDs and DVDs. In others, they successfully sought new legislative enactments such as the Digital Millennium Copyright Act, which increased protection for copyrights, and the Sonny Bono Copyright Term Extension Act, which increased the duration of copyright to the life of an author plus 70 years. Finally, copyright holders filed a number of high-stakes lawsuits that they hoped would curb infringement.

Additionally, many intellectual property producing countries, including the United States, recognized that the sale of copyrighted material had become a very profitable and valuable segment of their economies. Those nations decided that their copyright-based industries could not continue thriving without more protection than that provided by the Berne Convention. They began arguing that a country's failure to protect intellectual property damaged free international trade by subsidizing domestic business over foreign providers of copyrightable subject matter.

Ultimately, these countries pushed for and received stronger international guarantees of copyright protection during negotiations over the General Agreement on Tariffs and Trade (GATT). In 1994, the countries participating in the latest round of GATT negotiations approved the TRIPS agreement ("Agreement on Trade-Related Aspects of Intellectual Property Rights, Including Trade in Counterfeit Goods"). This agreement committed its adopters to minimum standards of copyright protection and created procedures for resolving disputes with countries accused of providing inadequate protection of copyrightable subject matter.

Each of these efforts has proven controversial, for many consumers and businesses worry about the consequences of stronger copyright. For example, consumers enjoy the convenience of digital access to copyrighted works, and stronger copyright implies that the cost of copyrighted works will rise. Similarly, many businesses worry that stronger copyright will cost them money because higher costs will suppress consumer demand for the computers, gadgets, and Internet services that they want to sell. And of course, nations that are net importers of copyrighted materials maintain that larger industrialized nations use copyright to extract monopoly rents from their less wealthy neighbors. Accordingly, there is now great debate about whether the United States, and indeed the world, will gain or lose by increasing copyright protection.

SECTION B. THINKING ABOUT MODERN U.S. COPYRIGHT

The burning question of how copyright affects society's best interest shows that it is important for students to learn both copyright doctrine and policy. Interestingly, the forces that shaped early English copyright are still perhaps the most cogent perspectives from which to study the subject today. The Statute of Anne's stated purpose of encouraging learning indicates that copyright exists as a necessary incentive for the production of valuable works. *Millar v. Taylor* shows how copyright might be a form of property that should belong to authors as a matter of fairness and justice. Finally, the lobbying efforts of the Stationers' Company demonstrate that governments sometimes create copyright rights on behalf of powerful interests who ask for them. Let us take a few moments to illustrate how these perspectives shed light on the basic issues of copyright, namely its existence, scope, and duration.

1. COPYRIGHT AS ECONOMIC INCENTIVE

Courts and commentators alike frequently describe copyright as an economic incentive for the production of works. Support for this view comes from the Constitution, which authorizes Congress to pass copyright legislation "to promote the Progress of Science and the useful Arts."[8]

The intuitive link to economics is simple. Consider an author who wants to sell copies of a book that has taken a year to write. If copyright did not exist, our author would face a problem. If she begins selling copies of the book, others may decide to produce and sell their own copies of the book at prices too low for the author to match. This happens because those who produce competing copies of the book enjoy a significant cost advantage over the author, for the author must bear the costs of writing the book (namely living expenses for a year) and printing copies. By contrast, the author's competitors need only pay for the cost of printing competing copies. This makes it difficult, if not impossible, for the author to sell copies of her book for a profit. Indeed, an author facing this problem might decide not to write the book at all. Things are even worse for someone who produces a work that is very expensive to produce, such as a $200 million movie that can be copied for the price of a blank DVD.

Copyright ameliorates this problem. If an author can enjoin or get damages from those who make unauthorized copies of the author's work, she can eliminate competition from those who would duplicate her work and sell it for a low price. She can then sell her books at a price that compensates her for the time and effort she expended to write the book. In short, copyright helps authors profit from the creation and sale of their works, and society benefits by gaining access to works that would never have been written or distributed.

The benefits of copyright do not come without cost. After all, the ultimate purpose of copyright is not only to provide incentives for the creation of new works, but also to make those works available to the broader public. It is therefore in society's best interest to distribute works as widely as possible. Copyright, however, permits authors to restrict dissemination of their works, and this robs society of the benefits that come from wider distribution. Additionally, the process of authorship itself frequently requires some use of existing works. If copyright becomes too strong and unduly restricts these uses, it can paradoxically hinder the creation of new works. Society must therefore decide the extent to which it will tolerate copyright's costs in exchange for its economic incentives.

It is, of course, possible to describe this intuition in more rigorous terms. Let us begin with the problem of public goods. According to economists, public goods have two characteristics that distinguish them from private goods: non-rivalrousness and non-excludability. Non-

---

[8] U.S. Const. Art. I, § 8, cl. 8.

excludability means that it is difficult for one person to prevent others from enjoying a particular good. Non-rivalrousness means that consumption of a good by one person does not diminish consumption of the same good by another person. These characteristics create an economic explanation for the existence and purposes of copyright.

Lighthouses offer a classic example of public goods. A person who builds a lighthouse enjoys the safety offered by its beacon. However, that person cannot stop other mariners from seeing the beacon and using it as a warning. The lighthouse therefore exhibits non-excludability. Additionally, enjoyment of the lighthouse by one person does not diminish enjoyment by others. An infinite number of mariners can simultaneously use the lighthouse's beacon to steer clear of danger without interfering with similar use by others. The lighthouse therefore exhibits non-rivalrousness. Lighthouses contrast sharply with private goods like apples. A farmer who produces an apple can prevent others from enjoying it simply by retaining possession. Moreover, an infinite number of people cannot simultaneously enjoy an apple. If one person eats it, no one else can.

The subject matter of copyright includes many forms of public goods. Books, movies, computer programs, and music all exhibit considerable non-excludability. An author who has sold a copy of his work can do nothing to prevent others from making their own copies of the work for sale to others. These works also exhibit non-rivalrousness. An infinite number of people can enjoy a book or movie without diminishing the experience of others doing likewise.

Non-excludability and non-rivalrousness explain copyright's existence and limits. As an initial matter, economic theory predicts that an unregulated market economy will under-produce public goods. A farmer who operates an apple orchard can ensure payment from each person who wants to enjoy the apples. By contrast, the author of a book cannot ensure payment from every person who wants to print it or read it. This suggests that the revenue which supports the production of apples will not exist for the production of books and movies, and prospective authors will have insufficient incentives to produce new works. Copyright solves this problem by creating a legal regime that gives profits from the sale of books to authors, thereby creating economic incentives for the creation of new works.

Copyright's ability to create incentives for the production of works does not mean, however, that copyright should be absolute. Non-rivalrousness means that society benefits when a book or movie is distributed as widely as possible, for enjoyment of a work by one person generates social welfare without harming welfare associated with enjoyment by others. Unfortunately, copyright operates by creating artificial scarcity for copyrighted works. A person who holds copyright in a work profits by preventing others from reproducing or using the work. The resulting scarcity eliminates competition and allows the copyright holder to charge an artificially high price for the work. This reduces social welfare in two ways. First, society loses the benefits associated with ordinary consumers who no longer can afford to buy the work. Second, society loses the benefits associated with future authors who might have used an existing work to create a new work (for example, using a poem as lyrics to a song), but cannot afford to pay the necessary royalties.

The foregoing shows that copyright creates social benefits and losses that need to be balanced. Copyright may increase social welfare by encouraging the production of works, but too much copyright will rob society of the benefits that come with wide distribution and use of works. This describes how copyright works and suggests how it might be changed. For example, consider how long copyright should last. If the term of copyright is too short, society may suffer from too little authorship. If the term is too long, society could equally suffer by paying higher prices for limited access to works. Similarly, if the scope of copyright is too narrow (perhaps because infringement includes only complete, literal duplication of a work), authors may receive incentives insufficient to encourage authorship. However, if the scope of copyright is too broad (perhaps because infringement includes even a small quotation from a work), society may lose the benefits associated with small, incidental uses of copyrighted works.

Of course, recognizing the need for balance in copyright does not tell us exactly how to set that balance. Does society benefit more when copyright rights are relatively strong because authors will not produce enough works without strong financial rewards? Or, does society do better with relatively modest copyright rights because smaller financial rewards are sufficient to induce authorship while ensuring widespread distribution and use of copyrighted works at lower cost?

Indeed, is copyright even the best method for encouraging the creation and distribution of new works? Government could stimulate production of works by extending cash grants or tax subsidies to authors. In some cases, being first to the market may provide enough advantage to recoup investments in creative effort. In yet other cases, authors may be able to find other ways (e.g. advertising or giving live concerts) to receive compensation for their efforts. Would these spur production as effectively as copyright with fewer undesirable consequences? These questions arise repeatedly in the construction and interpretation of copyright, and you can enrich your study of the subject by keeping them in mind.

2. COPYRIGHT AS FAIRNESS AND JUSTICE

The economic perspective on copyright offers great insight. Indeed, courts sometimes say that it provides the only perspective from which to understand copyright. The Supreme Court articulated this position in *Sony Corp. of America v. Universal City Studios, Inc.*:

The monopoly privileges that Congress may authorize are neither unlimited nor primarily designed to provide a special private benefit. Rather, the limited grant is a means by which an important public purpose may be achieved. It is intended to motivate the creative activity of authors and inventors by the provision of a special reward, and to allow the public access to the products of their genius after the limited period of exclusive control has expired.[9]

It is not entirely clear, however, that a purely economic perspective provides an adequate foundation for copyright. Courts may say that copyright exists only as an economic incentive, but this does not mean that economics alone explains judicial decisions or legislative enactments in copyright.

To get an intuitive feel for non-economic theories of copyright, ask yourself whether copyright should protect works that authors would have created anyway. For example, copyright protects works that students must write in order to get degrees, such as doctoral dissertations. Copyright also protects works written with no intention of profit, such as private letters, works written by the state (as opposed to federal) government, and art drawn by children at birthday parties. It makes relatively little economic sense to extend copyright to these works because their existence does not depend on copyright. Does this mean that copyright should not protect these works?

A strong proponent of economic copyright theory might respond by arguing that copyright for such works is a mistake. However, courts and Congress have shown no inclination to deny copyright to these works, perhaps because they believe that an author should control the publication of her work and receive any profits from it, even if she would have created the work in the absence of copyright. This implies that copyright exists, at least in some cases, for reasons other than encouraging the creation of works. Indeed, the Supreme Court itself has suggested that copyright is something that authors deserve, and not purely a matter of economic stimulation:

> The economic philosophy behind the clause empowering Congress to grant patents and copyrights is the conviction that encouragement of individual effort by personal gain is the best way to advance public welfare through the talents of authors and inventors in "Science and useful Arts." *Sacrificial days devoted to such creative activities deserve rewards commensurate with the services rendered.*[10]

The notion that authors justly deserve copyright comes from natural law. It begins with John Locke's argument that people have a natural right of property in their bodies and their labor.[11] Authors therefore own the works they create because those works result from their labor. This does not mean, however, that the scope copyright is infinite, for Locke's

---

[9] 464 U.S. 417, 429 (1984).

[10] *Mazer v. Stein*, 347 U.S. 201, 219 (1954) (emphasis added).

[11] *See* J. Locke, *The Second Treatise of Civil Government* § 27, *in* TWO TREATISES OF GOVERNMENT (1698) (P. Laslett ed. 1970).

justification of property from labor contained an important limitation. According to Locke, labor leads to property only when the person acquiring property leaves "enough and as good in common ... to others."[12] Thus, if granting unlimited copyright to authors would worsen the situation of others, society should limit copyright's reach.

Like economics, natural law theory establishes the central role of balance in copyright, particularly when one takes into account the realities of authorship. Unlimited copyright makes sense only if authors truly create everything found in their works. Of course, this is not the case. No matter how gifted, every author borrows from those who preceded her. Authors do not exist apart from society and artistic traditions, even those who seek solitude. They use the ideas and expressions of others, and they frequently work within or in response to defined artistic traditions. This means that even the most original works combine new material with existing material. Indeed, new authorship depends on access to old authorship.

The realities of authorship limit copyright in two ways. First, copyright must not allow authors to claim copyright in things they did not create. Second, copyright must leave future authors access to and use of existing works roughly equivalent to the opportunities enjoyed by previous authors. Natural law therefore supports copyright's existence, but it also supports restraining copyright to ensure access to existing works, perhaps through limits on copyright's duration, restrictions on copyrightable subject matter, and affirmative defenses such as fair use.

Natural law adds richness and depth to our understanding of copyright by connecting it to basic questions of fairness and justice. Obviously, this textbook cannot describe or resolve the complicated philosophical issues raised by natural law and its application to copyright. Nevertheless, it is still very much worth your while to consider whether economics alone offers a sufficiently persuasive account of copyright, or whether the added insight of natural law proves useful.

3. COPYRIGHT AS LEGISLATION

The perspectives offered so far construct copyright as the logical consequence of grand theory. There are good reasons for doing so. If one or two basic theories explain all of copyright, then it becomes easier to make sense of the entire subject. Students no longer have to memorize case after case because they can infer correct results from correct understandings of basic theory. Granted, case law rarely, if ever, organizes itself with such clarity. Nevertheless, the search for clarity offers general themes around which understanding can grow.

A different and interesting way to study copyright eschews the use of grand theory, at least at the substantive level of copyright. Instead of

---

[12] *Id.*

building copyright from first principles of economics or natural law, why not analyze copyright as the product of a legislative process? After all, nothing requires Congress to implement theoretical consistency in its statutes, and this perspective is surely consistent with copyright's origins in the Statute of Anne. Indeed, Congress has amended the 1976 Copyright Act over 20 times since its enactment. This suggests that many provisions of the Copyright Act develop as pragmatic responses to specific problems, and not the enunciation of basic principles that elegantly shape the law.

The discounting of grand theory associated with a legislative perspective on copyright makes sense because Congress writes statutes while being lobbied by those with immediate financial stakes in the shape of copyright. Accordingly, copyright legislation rarely expresses an elegant, theoretically consistent view of the law. Instead, it contains policies and compromises that reflect the interests of those who lobby Congress. This suggests that courts should interpret copyright by implementing the compromises that motivated enactment of the law, even if they appear theoretically inconsistent with other portions of the Code.

The value of this perspective on copyright becomes most apparent when studying the statutory details of copyright. For example, the Digital Millennium Copyright Act contains a few basic statutory schemes that contain a bewildering number of special exceptions. Likewise, § 110 of the Copyright Act limits the basic rights of copyright holders by granting special permission to specific users of copyrighted works in specific contexts. It is tempting, but probably impossible, to understand provisions like these as advancing the promotion of the arts. However, the provisions make sense as the legislative embodiment of compromises between the interests of those who own copyrights and those who use copyrighted works. This does not, of course, mean that the compromises reflect society's best interests, but it does explain why copyright looks the way it does.

SECTION C. STUDYING COPYRIGHT

The foregoing introduction has raised only the most prominent ways of thinking about copyright. The pages that follow will introduce many more perspectives on the subject. You may find yourself frustrated that our legal system struggles to adopt a consistent understanding of copyright. Copyright relies on imprecise terminology that hampers predictability, and it is hard to determine what kind of copyright regime best serves society's interests. Indeed, judges often adopt inconsistent theories of copyright in cases that purport to be consistent with each other. The successful copyright student must therefore be prepared to encounter a certain degree of ambiguity that can be explained, but perhaps never resolved. Nevertheless, the authors of this book hope that you will come to appreciate that copyright's ambiguity, while frustrating, should come as no surprise. After all, our society shares multiple, inconsistent perceptions of copyrightable subject matter, namely literature, movies, music, and art. And, if society cannot find a completely consistent understanding of those things, perhaps it is unreasonable for us to expect courts to do so as well. With that in mind, let us begin a more detailed examination of copyright.

Chapter Two

COPYRIGHTABLE SUBJECT MATTER

The doctrines presented in this chapter define the works protected by the copyright statute. The most relevant statutory provisions are relatively brief. Section 102(a) of the Copyright Act extends protection to "original works of authorship fixed in any tangible medium of expression," while § 102(b) contains the limitation that "In no case does copyright protection for an original work of authorship extend to any idea, procedure, process, system, method of operation, concept, principle, or discovery, regardless of the form in which it is described, explained, illustrated, or embodied in such work."

The brevity of these provisions suggests that the scope of copyrightable subject matter is simple and clear. However, as you will soon discover, it is not. As an initial matter, words like "original" and "idea" have ambiguous colloquial meanings. Additionally, copyright pursues a number of complex policies related to the creation of socially valuable works and public access to those works. Terms like "original" and "idea" may or may not adequately express or balance the many considerations behind these policies. Finally, courts must decide whether it is more important to pursue an ideal, but difficult to understand, definition of copyrightable subject matter, or whether it would be better to settle for a relatively clear definition that leads to a number of undesirable results.

The materials that follow include a number of leading cases and exemplars that illustrate the various doctrines and analytical methods that courts use to define the subject matter of copyright. In reading these cases, keep in mind that copyright law has not always developed in a logical or linear fashion. You will probably wonder from time to time if these cases are truly consistent with one another. Indeed, you may even perceive that individual opinions contain internal conflicts. This may frustrate you. However, ambiguities like this provide important opportunities for you to think about the basic theory, objectives and analytical methods of copyright.

SECTION A. ORIGINALITY

Section 102(a) of the Copyright Act provides:

(a) Copyright protection subsists ... in original works of authorship fixed in any tangible medium of expression .... Works of authorship include the following categories:

    (1) literary works;

    (2) musical works, including any accompanying words;

    (3) dramatic works, including any accompanying music;

    (4) pantomimes and choreographic works;

    (5) pictorial, graphic, and sculptural works;

    (6) motion pictures and other audiovisual works;

    (7) sound recordings; and

    (8) architectural works.

Congress clearly intended to make this list of "works of authorship" non-exhaustive. Accordingly, copyright protection for a work depends on its status as an original work of authorship, and not on its characterization as a literary work, dramatic work, or motion picture.

According to the Supreme Court, "[o]riginal...means only that the work was independently created by the author (as opposed to copied from other works), and that it possesses at least some minimal degree of creativity."[13] This section begins with two important cases decided many decades ago because Congress decided to define copyrightable subject matter in the present Copyright Act by codifying a long line of cases interpreting earlier versions of the statute. These cases introduce basic concepts that influence the definition of copyrightable subject matter to this day, including the constitutional basis of copyright and the nature of copyrightable subject matter.

Burrow Giles Lithographic Co. v. Sarony
111 U.S. 53 (1884)

MILLER, J.

This is a writ of error to the circuit court for the southern district of New York. Plaintiff is a lithographer, and defendant a photographer, with large business in those lines in the city of New York. The suit was commenced by an action at law in which Sarony was plaintiff and the lithographic company was defendant, the plaintiff charging the defendant with violating his copyright in regard to a photograph, the title of

---

[13] *Feist Publications v. Rural Telephone Service Co.*, 499 U.S. 340, 346 (1991).

which is "Oscar Wilde, No. 18." A jury being waived, the court made a finding of facts on which a judgment in favor of the plaintiff was rendered for the sum of $600 for the plates and 85,000 copies sold and exposed to sale, and $10 for copies found in his possession, as penalties under section 4965 of the Revised Statutes. Among the finding of facts made by the court the following presents the principal question raised by the assignment of errors in the case:

> "(3) That the plaintiff, about the month of January, 1882, under an agreement with Oscar Wilde, became and was the author, inventor, designer, and proprietor of the photograph in suit, the title of which is 'Oscar Wilde, No. 18,' being the number used to designate this particular photograph and of the negative thereof; that the same is a useful, new, harmonious, characteristic, and graceful picture, and that said plaintiff made the same at his place of business in said city of New York, and within the United States, entirely from his own original mental conception, to which he gave visible form by posing the said Oscar Wilde in front of the camera, selecting and arranging the costume, draperies, and other various accessories in said photograph, arranging the subject so as to present graceful outlines, arranging and disposing the light and shade, suggesting and evoking the desired expression, and from such disposition, arrangement, or representation, made entirely by the plaintiff, he produced the picture in suit, Exhibit A, April 14, 1882, and that the terms 'author,' 'inventor,' and 'designer,' as used in the art of photography and in the complaint, mean the person who so produced the photograph."

Other findings leave no doubt that plaintiff had taken all the steps required by the act of congress to obtain copyright of this photograph, and section 4952 names photographs, among other things, for which the author, inventor, or designer may obtain copyright, which is to secure him the sole privilege of reprinting, publishing, copying, and vending the same. That defendant is liable, under that section and section 4965, there can be no question if those sections are valid as they relate to photographs.

Accordingly, the two assignments of error in this court by plaintiff in error are: (1) That the court below decided that congress had and has the constitutional right to protect photographs and negatives thereof by copyright. The second assignment related to the sufficiency of the words "Copyright, 1882, by N. Sarony," in the photographs, as a notice of the copyright of Napoleon Sarony, under the act of congress on that subject.

[The Court concluded that the notice of copyright was complete.]

The constitutional question is not free from difficulty. The eighth section of the first article of the constitution is the great repository of the powers of congress, and by the eight clause of that section congress is authorized "to promote the progress of science and useful arts, by securing, for limited times to authors and inventors the exclusive right to their respective writings and discoveries." The argument here is that a photograph is not a writing nor the production of an author. Under the acts of congress designed to give effect to this section, the persons who are to be benefited are divided into two classes—authors and inventors. The monopoly which is granted to the former is called a copyright: that given to the latter, letters patent, or, in the familiar language of the present day, patent-right. We have then copyright and patent-right, and it is the first of these under which plaintiff asserts a claim for relief. It is insisted, in argument, that a photograph being a reproduction, on paper, of the exact features of some natural object, or of some person, is not a writing of which the producer is the author. Section 4952 of the Revised Statutes places photographs in the same class as things which may be copyrighted with "books, maps, charts, dramatic or musical compositions, engravings, cuts, prints, paintings, drawings, statues, statuary, and models or designs intended to be perfected as works of the fine arts." "According to the practice of legislation in England and America," says Judge Bouvier, 2 Law Dict. 363, "the copyright is confined to the exclusive right secured to the author or proprietor of a writing or drawing which may be multiplied by the arts of printing in any of its branches."

The first congress of the United States, sitting immediately after the formation of the constitution, enacted that the "author or authors of any map, chart, book, or books, being a citizen or resident of the United States, shall have the sole right and liberty of printing, reprinting, publishing, and vending the same for the period of fourteen years from the recording of the title thereof in the clerk's office, as afterwards directed." 1 St. p. 124, 1. This statute not only makes maps and charts subjects of copyright, but mentions them before books in the order of designation. The second section of an act to amend this act, approved April 29, 1802, (2 St. 171,) enacts that from the first day of January thereafter he who shall invent and design, engrave, etch, or work, or from his own works shall cause to be designed and engraved, etched, or worked, any historical or other print or prints, shall have the same exclusive right for the term of 14 years from recording the title thereof as prescribed by law.

By the first section of the act of February 3, 1831, (4 St. 436,) entitled "An act to amend the several acts respecting copyright, musical compositions, and cuts, in connection with prints and engravings," are added, and the period of protection is extended to 28 years. The caption or title of this act uses the word "copyright" for the first time in the legislation of congress.

The construction placed upon the constitution by the first act of 1790 and the act of 1802, by the men who were contemporary with its formation, many of whom were members of the convention which framed it, is of itself entitled to very great weight, and when it is remembered that the rights thus established have not been disputed during a period of nearly a century, it is almost conclusive. Unless, therefore, photographs can be distinguished in the classification of this point from the maps, charts, designs, engravings, etchings, cuts, and other prints, it is difficult to see why congress cannot make them the subject of copyright as well as the others. These statutes certainly answer the objection that books only, or writing, in the limited sense of a book and its author, are within the constitutional provision. Both these words are susceptible of a more enlarged definition than this. An author in that sense is "he to whom anything owes its origin; originator; maker; one who completes a work of science or literature." Worcester. So, also, no one would now claim that the word "writing" in this clause of the constitution, though the only word used as to subjects in regard to which authors are to be secured, is limited to the actual script of the author, and excludes books and all other printed matter. By writings in that clause is meant the literary productions of those authors, and congress very properly has declared these to include all forms of writing, printing, engravings, etchings, etc., by which the ideas in the mind of the author are given visible expression. The only reason why photographs were not included in the extended list in the act of 1802 is, probably, that they did not exist, as photography, as an art, was then unknown, and the scientific principle on which it rests, and the chemicals and machinery by which it is operated, have all been discovered long since that statute was enacted. ...

We entertain no doubt that the constitution is broad enough to cover an act authorizing copyright of photographs, so far as they are representatives of original intellectual conceptions of the author.

But it is said that an engraving, a painting, a print, does embody the intellectual conception of its author, in which there is novelty, invention, originality, and therefore comes within the purpose of the constitution in securing its exclusive use or sale to its author, while a photograph is the mere mechanical reproduction of the physical features or outlines of some object, animate or inanimate, and involves no originality of thought or any novelty in the intellectual operation connected with its visible reproduction in shape of a picture. That while the effect of light on the prepared plate may have been a discovery in the production of these pictures, and patents could properly be obtained for the combination of the chemicals, for their application to the paper or other surface, for all the machinery by which the light reflected from the object was thrown on the prepared plate, and for all the improvements in this machinery, and in the materials, the remainder of the process is merely mechanical, with no place for novelty, invention, or originality. It is simply the manual operation, by the use of these instruments and preparations, of transferring to the plate the visible representation of some existing object, the accuracy of this representation being its highest merit. This may be true in regard to the ordinary production of a photograph, and that in such case a copyright is no protection. On the question as thus stated we decide nothing. ...

The third finding of facts says, in regard to the photograph in question, that it is a "useful, new, harmonious, characteristic, and graceful picture, and that plaintiff made the same ... entirely from his own original mental conception, to which he gave visible form by posing the said Oscar Wilde in front of the camera, selecting and arranging the costume, draperies, and other various accessories in said photograph, arranging the subject so as to present graceful outlines, arranging and disposing the light and shade, suggesting and evoking the desired expression, and from such disposition, arrangement, or representation, made entirely by plaintiff, he produced the picture in suit." These findings, we think, show this photograph to be an original work of art, the product of plaintiff's intellectual invention, of which plaintiff is the author, and of a class of inventions for which the constitution intended that congress should secure to him the exclusive right to use, publish, and sell, as it has done by section 4952 of the Revised Statutes. ...

The judgment of the circuit court is accordingly affirmed.

Oscar Wilde, No. 18,
Napoleon Sarony, photographer

Notes and Questions

1. *Burrow-Giles* is a good place to begin the study of copyrightable subject matter because the defendant claimed that Congress did not have the Constitutional authority to extend copyright protection to a photograph. This forced the Court to consider the outer limits of copyrightable subject matter. What limits did the Court identify?

2. The defendant made a simple argument against the copyrightability of photographs: Article 1, section 8 of the Constitution gives Congress the power to protect the "writings" of authors by copyright, and photographs are not "writings."[14] The Court could have followed this interpretation to establish a relatively "bright line" rule that would have been easy to understand and administer—namely that copyright was constitutionally disabled from protecting anything other than a written text. The Court chose instead to adopt a non-literal interpretation of "writings" that encompassed some items that were not written. Why did the Court reject the defendant's argument?

3. Does *Burrow-Giles* hold that all photographs are copyrightable? If not, how many photographs fall outside the constitutional limit of copyrightability? For example, could copyright protect a driver's license or college face book photograph?

Bleistein v. Donaldson Lithographing Co.
188 U.S. 239 (1903)

MR. JUSTICE HOLMES delivered the opinion of the court:

This case comes here from the United States circuit court of appeals for the sixth circuit by writ of error. ... It is an action brought by the plaintiffs in error to recover the penalties prescribed for infringements of copyrights. ... The alleged infringements consisted in the copying in reduced form of three chromolithographs prepared by employees of the plaintiffs for advertisements of a circus owned by one Wallace. Each of the three contained a portrait of Wallace in the corner, and lettering bearing some slight relation to the scheme of decoration, indicating the subject of the design and the fact that the reality was to be seen at the circus. One of the designs was of an ordinary ballet, one of a number of men and women, described as the Stirk family, performing on bicycles, and one of groups of men and women whitened to represent statues. The circuit court directed a verdict for the defendant on the ground that the

---

[14] The provision states that "Congress shall have the Power...[t]o promote the Progress of Science and useful Arts, by securing for limited Times to Authors and Inventors the exclusive Right to their respective Writings and Discoveries." U.S. CONST. Art. I, § 8, cl. 8.

chromolithographs were not within the protection of the copyright law, and this ruling was sustained by the circuit court of appeals. ...

We shall do no more than mention the suggestion that painting and engraving, unless for a mechanical end, are not among the useful arts, the progress of which Congress is empowered by the Constitution to promote. The Constitution does not limit the useful to that which satisfies immediate bodily needs. *Burrow-Giles Lithographing Co. v. Sarony*, 111 U.S. 53. It is obvious also that the plaintiff's case is not affected by the fact, if it be one, that the pictures represent actual groups—visible things. They seem from the testimony to have been composed from hints or description, not from sight of a performance. But even if they had been drawn from the life, that fact would not deprive them of protection. The opposite proposition would mean that a portrait by Velasquez or Whistler was common property because others might try their hand on the same face. Others are free to copy the original. They are not free to copy the copy. The copy is the personal reaction of an individual upon nature. Personality always contains something unique. It expresses its singularity even in handwriting, and a very modest grade of art has in it something irreducible, which is one man's alone. That something he may copyright unless there is a restriction in the words of the act.

If there is a restriction it is not to be found in the limited pretensions of these particular works. The least pretentious picture has more originality in it than directories and the like, which may be copyrighted. The amount of training required for humbler efforts than those before us is well indicated by Ruskin. "If any young person, after being taught what is, in polite circles, called 'drawing,' will try to copy the commonest piece of real work—suppose a lithograph on the title page of a new opera air, or a woodcut in the cheapest illustrated newspaper of the day—they will find themselves entirely beaten." Elements of Drawing, first ed. 3. There is no reason to doubt that these prints in their ensemble and in all their details, in their design and particular combinations of figures, lines, and colors, are the original work of the plaintiffs' designer. If it be necessary, there is express testimony to that effect. It would be pressing the defendant's right to the verge, if not beyond, to leave the question of originality to the jury upon the evidence in this case, as was done in *Hegeman v. Springer*, 110 F. 374.

We assume that the construction of Rev. Stat. 4952, allowing a copyright to the "author, designer, or proprietor . . . of any engraving, cut, print . . . [or] chromo" is affected by the act of 1874, 18 Stat. 78, 79, c. 301, § 3. That section provides that, "in the construction of this act, the words 'engraving,' 'cut,' and 'print' shall be applied only to pictorial illustrations or works connected with the fine arts." We see no reason for taking the words "connected with the fine arts" as qualifying anything except the word "works," but it would not change our decision if we should assume further that they also qualified "pictorial illustrations," as the defendant contends. These chromolithographs are "pictorial illustrations." The word "illustrations" does not mean that they must illustrate the text of a book, and that the etchings of Rembrandt or Muller's engraving of the Madonna di San Sisto could not be protected today if any man were able to produce them. Again, the act, however construed, does not mean that ordinary posters are not good enough to be considered within its scope. The antithesis to "illustrations or works connected with the fine arts" is not works of little merit or of humble degree, or illustrations addressed to the less educated classes; it is "prints or labels designed to be used for any other articles of manufacture." Certainly works are not the less connected with the fine arts because their pictorial quality attracts the crowd, and therefore gives them a real use—if use means to increase trade and to help to make money. A picture is none the less a picture, and none the less a subject of copyright, that it is used for an advertisement. And if pictures may be used to advertise soap, or the theatre, or monthly magazines, as they are, they may be used to advertise a circus. Of course, the ballet is as legitimate a subject for illustration as any other. A rule cannot be laid down that would excommunicate the paintings of Degas. ...

says judges aren't capable of making the decision of whether or its good or bad

[It would be a dangerous undertaking for persons trained only to the law to constitute themselves final judges of the worth of pictorial illustrations,] outside of the narrowest and most obvious limits. At the one extreme, some works of genius would be sure to miss appreciation. Their very novelty would make them repulsive until the public had learned the new language in which their author spoke. It may be more than doubted, for instance, whether the etchings of Goya or the paintings of Manet would have been sure of protection when seen for the first time. At the other end, copyright would be denied to pictures which appealed to a public less educated than the judge. Yet if they command the interest of any public, they have a commercial value—it would be bold to say that they have not an aesthetic and educational value—and the taste of any public is not to be treated with contempt. It is an ultimate fact for the moment, whatever may be our hopes for a change. That these pictures had their worth and their success is sufficiently shown by the desire to reproduce them without regard to the plaintiffs' rights. We are of opinion that there was evidence that the plaintiffs have rights entitled to the protection of the law.

The judgment of the Circuit Court of Appeals is reversed; the judgment of the Circuit Court is also reversed and the cause remanded to that court with directions to set aside the verdict and grant a new trial.

MR. JUSTICE HARLAN, dissenting:

Judges Lurton, Day, and Severens, of the circuit court of appeals, concurred in affirming the judgment of the district court. Their views were thus expressed in an opinion delivered by Judge Lurton:

"What we hold is this: That if a chromo, lithograph, or other print, engraving, or picture has no other use than that of a mere advertisement, and no value aside from this function, it would not be promotive of the useful arts, within the meaning of the constitutional provision, to protect the 'author' in the exclusive use thereof, and the copyright statute should not be construed as including such a publication, if any other construction is admissible. If a mere label simply designating or describing an article to which it is attached, and which has no value separated from the article, does not come within the constitutional clause upon the subject of copyright, it must follow that a pictorial illustration designed and useful only as an advertisement, and having no intrinsic value other than its function as an advertisement, must be equally without the obvious meaning of the Constitution. It must have some connection with the fine arts to give it intrinsic value, and that it shall have is the meaning which we attach to the act of June 18, 1874, amending the provisions of the copyright law. We are unable to discover anything useful or meritorious in the design copyrighted by the plaintiffs in error other than as an advertisement of acts to be done or exhibited to the public in Wallace's show. No evidence, aside from the deductions which are to be drawn from the prints themselves, was offered to show that these designs had any original artistic qualities. The jury could not reasonably have found merit or value aside from the purely business object of advertising a show, and the instruction to find for the defendant was not error. Many other points have been urged as justifying the result reached in the court below. We find it unnecessary to express any opinion upon them, in view of the conclusion already announced. The judgment must be affirmed." *Courier Lithographing Co. v. Donaldson Lithographing Co.*, 104 F. 993, 996.

I entirely concur in these views, and therefore dissent from the opinion and judgment of this court. The clause of the Constitution giving Congress power to promote the progress of science and useful arts, by securing for limited terms to authors and inventors the exclusive right to their respective works and discoveries, does not, as I think, embrace a mere advertisement of a circus.

Mr. Justice McKenna authorizes me to say that he also dissents.

————————

Notes and Questions

1.   *Bleistein* turned in large part on the Court's unwillingness to evaluate the artistic merit of the plaintiff's works. The circuit court below (and the dissent) thought that the works fell outside the scope of the copyright statute because the works were advertisements and lacked artistic merit. Extending copyright to the posters would therefore fail to promote the progress of art. Justice Holmes's majority opinion disagreed, and took the position that courts ought not evaluate the artistic merit of works, "outside of the narrowest and most obvious limits." This led to the adoption of a lenient standard of copyrightability that persists to this day. Why did Holmes interpret copyright in this manner? Did he do so for reasons related to promotion of art, or for reasons related to the limits of judicial competence?

2.   Is *Bleistein*'s interpretation of copyright consistent with the one expressed in *Burrow-Giles*? Regardless of your conclusion, is *Bleistein* correct about the proper construction of copyright law, and is it possible for judges to interpret copyright effectively without getting into the kind of judicial determinations that Holmes wanted to avoid?

3.   Consider the Court's statement that the plaintiff's works were copyrightable simply because the public valued them. Does this reasoning truly keep the courts from making subjective determinations about matters of artistic taste? If so, does it function as a workable definition of copyrightable subject matter, or does it abdicate any serious effort to limit the works protected by copyright?

Problem

Your client, the producer for a reality television show called "Sorry Home Videos," needs some advice about a videotape that she wants to include in her next episode. The tape shows a well-known public official fighting with and hitting a store owner after being caught shoplifting. Your client has a copy of the tape and wants to know if she needs to get permission from the store owner before broadcasting it.

The videotape exists because the store owner had suffered a rash of thefts involving expensive handbags. He purchased a security camera and placed it on the back wall of the store so that it had a clear view of the aisles and shelves containing the handbags. Once activated, the camera automatically recorded a 24 hour tape of the aisles and shelves. The store owner directed his employees to replace the tapes on a daily basis and keep the used tapes for a week before reusing them.

One day last week, the official came into the store. She began browsing the handbags, unaware that the security camera was recording her.

The store owner happened to notice the official behaving strangely and saw her take a handbag off the shelf and place it under her shirt. The official then began to walk quickly towards the exit, but the store owner stopped her. The official became distressed and tried to get away. When the store owner restrained her, she struggled and began hitting him with the handbag. The fight continued until the police arrived.

Your client received a copy of the tape from one of the store's employees, who made a copy of the original for his own amusement. He showed the tape to a friend who happens to be your client's production assistant. The assistant then brought the tape to your client, with the permission of the store's employee.

What advice do you have for your client?

* * *

Sarony and *Bleistein* are two seminal cases that established the basic contours of originality, yet they were decided over a century ago. Not surprisingly, courts have had many opportunities to interpret and elaborate upon originality, and the next cases introduce us to some of the challenges that *Sarony* and *Bleistein* left behind. Originality may be a low hurdle to copyrightability, but the hurdle still exists. What then separates copyrightable works from uncopyrightable ones? The answer depends on at least two things: the nature of originality and the amount of that quality necessary to support copyright. As you read the following cases, consider whether courts effectively grapple with these issues and whether their decisions are consistent with *Sarony* and *Bleistein*. If you perceive inconsistency, ask yourself why it has emerged and whether particular interpretations of originality are better than others.

* * *

Meshwerks v. Toyota Motor Sales U.S.A.
528 F.3d 1258 (10th Cir. 2008)

GORSUCH, Circuit Judge:

This case calls on us to apply copyright principles to a relatively new technology: digital modeling. Meshwerks insists that, contrary to the district court's summary judgment determination, its digital models of Toyota cars and trucks are sufficiently original to warrant copyright protection. Meshwerks' models, which form the base layers of computerized substitutes for product photographs in advertising, are unadorned, digital wire-frames of Toyota's vehicles. While fully appreciating that digital media present new frontiers for copyrightable creative expression, in this particular case the uncontested facts reveal that Meshwerks' models owe their designs and origins to Toyota and deliberately do not include anything original of their own; accordingly, we hold that Meshwerks' models are not protected by copyright and affirm.

I

A

In 2003, and in conjunction with Saatchi & Saatchi, its advertising agency, Toyota began work on its model-year 2004 advertising campaign. Saatchi and Toyota agreed that the campaign would involve, among other things, digital models of Toyota's vehicles for use on Toyota's website and in various other media. These digital models have substantial advantages over the product photographs for which they substitute. With a few clicks of a computer mouse, the advertiser can change the color of the car, its surroundings, and even edit its physical dimensions to portray changes in vehicle styling; before this innovation, advertisers had to conduct new photo shoots of whole fleets of vehicles each time the manufacturer made even a small design change to a car or truck.

To supply these digital models, Saatchi and Toyota hired Grace & Wild, Inc. ("G & W"). In turn, G & W subcontracted with Meshwerks to assist with two initial aspects of the project—digitization and modeling. Digitizing involves collecting physical data points from the object to be portrayed. In the case of Toyota's vehicles, Meshwerks took copious measurements of Toyota's vehicles by covering each car, truck, and van with a grid of tape and running an articulated arm tethered to a computer over the vehicle to measure all points of intersection in the grid. Based on these measurements, modeling software then generated a digital image resembling a wire-frame model. In other words, the vehicles' data points (measurements) were mapped onto a computerized grid and the modeling software connected the dots to create a "wire frame" of each vehicle.

At this point, however, the on-screen image remained far from perfect and manual "modeling" was necessary. Meshwerks personnel fine-tuned or, as the company prefers it, "sculpted," the lines on screen to resemble each vehicle as closely as possible. Approximately 90 percent of the data points contained in each final model, Meshwerks represents, were the result not of the first-step measurement process, but of the skill and effort its digital sculptors manually expended at the second step. For example, some areas of detail, such as wheels, headlights, door handles, and the Toyota emblem, could not be accurately measured using current technology; those features had to be added at the second "sculpting" stage, and Meshwerks had to recreate those features as realistically as possible by hand, based on photographs. Even for areas that were measured, Meshwerks faced the challenge of converting measurements taken of a three-dimensional car into a two-dimensional computer representation; to achieve this, its modelers had to sculpt, or move, data points to achieve a visually convincing result. The purpose and product of these processes, after nearly 80 to 100 hours of effort per vehicle, were two-dimensional wire-frame depictions of Toyota's vehicles that appeared three-dimensional on screen, but were utterly unadorned-lacking color, shading, and other details. Attached to this opinion as Appendix A are sample screen-prints of one of Meshwerks' digital wire-frame models.

With Meshwerks' wire-frame products in hand, G & W then manipulated the computerized models by, first, adding detail, the result of which appeared on screen as a "tightening" of the wire frames, as though significantly more wires had been added to the frames, or as though they were made of a finer mesh. Next, G & W digitally applied color, texture, lighting, and animation for use in Toyota's advertisements. An example of G & W's work product is attached as Appendix B to this opinion. G & W's digital models were then sent to Saatchi to be employed in a number of advertisements prepared by Saatchi and Toyota in various print, online, and television media.

B

This dispute arose because, according to Meshwerks, it contracted with G & W for only a single use of its models—as part of one Toyota television commercial—and neither Toyota nor any other defendant was allowed to use the digital models created from Meshwerks' wire-frames in other advertisements. Thus, Meshwerks contends defendants improperly—in violation of copyright laws as well as the parties' agreement—reused and redistributed the models created by Meshwerks in a host of other media. In support of the allegations that defendants misappropriated its intellectual property, Meshwerks points to the fact that it sought and received copyright registration on its wire-frame models.

In due course, defendants moved for summary judgment on the theory that Meshwerks' wire-frame models lacked sufficient originality to be protected by copyright. Specifically, defendants argued that any original expression found in Meshwerks' products was attributable to the Toyota designers who conceived of the vehicle designs in the first place; accordingly, defendants' use of the models could not give rise to a claim for copyright infringement.

The district court agreed. It found that the wire-frame models were merely copies of Toyota's products, not sufficiently original to warrant copyright protection, and stressed that Meshwerks' "intent was to replicate, as exactly as possible, the image of certain Toyota vehicles." Because there was no valid copyright, there could be no infringement, and, having granted summary judgment on the federal copyright claim, the district court declined to exercise supplemental jurisdiction over Meshwerks' state-law contract claim. Today, Meshwerks asks us to reverse and hold its digital, wire-frame models sufficiently original to warrant copyright protection.

II

...

A

... What exactly does it mean for a work to qualify as "original"? In *Feist,* the Supreme Court clarified that the work must be "independently created by the author (as opposed to copied from other works)." 499 U.S. at 345. In addition, the work must "possesses at least some minimal degree of creativity," *Id.,* though this is not to say that to count as containing a minimal degree of creativity a work must have aesthetic merit in the minds of judges (arguably not always the most artistically discerning lot). As the Court explained through Justice Holmes, even "a very modest grade of art has in it something irreducible, which is one man's alone. That something he may copyright...." *Bleistein,* 188. U.S. 239, 250 (1903) (all that's needed is some creative spark, "no matter how crude, humble, or obvious").

→ The parties focus most of their energy in this case on the question whether Meshwerks' models qualify as independent creations, as opposed to copies of Toyota's handiwork. ... While there is little authority explaining how our received principles of copyright law apply to the relatively new digital medium before us, some lessons may be discerned from how the law coped in an earlier time with a previous revolution in technology: photography.

As Judge Pauley admirably recounted in *SHL Imaging, Inc. v. Artisan House, Inc.,* photography was initially met by critics with a degree of skepticism: a photograph, some said, "copies everything and explains nothing," and it was debated whether a camera could do anything more than merely record the physical world. These largely aesthetic debates migrated into legal territory when Oscar Wilde toured the United States in the 1880s and sought out Napoleon Sarony for a series of publicity photographs to promote the event. Burrow-Giles, a lithography firm, quickly copied one of Sarony's photos and sold 85,000 prints without the photographer's permission. Burrow-Giles defended its conduct on the ground that the photograph was a "mere mechanical reproduction of the physical features" of Wilde and thus not copyrightable. Recognizing that Oscar Wilde's inimitable visage does not belong, or "owe its origins" to any photographer, the Supreme Court noted that photographs may well sometimes lack originality and are thus not *per se* copyrightable. ("the ordinary production of a photograph" may involve "no protection" in copyright). At the same time, the Court held, a copyright may be had to the extent a photograph involves "posing the said Oscar Wilde in front of the camera, selecting and arranging the costume, draperies, and other various accessories in said photograph, arranging the subject so as to present graceful outlines, arranging and disposing the light and shade, suggesting and evoking the desired expression...." Accordingly, the Court indicated, photographs are copyrightable, if only to the extent of their *original* depiction of the subject. Wilde's image is not copyrightable; but to the extent a photograph reflects the photographer's decisions regarding pose, positioning, background, lighting, shading, and the like, those elements can be said to "owe their origins" to the photographer, making the photograph copyrightable, at least to that extent. ...

B

Applying these principles, evolved in the realm of photography, to the new medium that has come to supplement and even in some ways to supplant it, we think Meshwerks' models are not so much independent creations as (very good) copies of Toyota's vehicles. In reaching this conclusion we rely on (1) an objective assessment of the particular models before us and (2) the parties' purpose in creating them. All the same, we do not doubt for an instant that the digital medium before us, like photography before it, can be employed to create vivid new expressions fully protectable in copyright.

1

Key to our evaluation of this case is the fact that Meshwerks' digital wire-frame computer models depict Toyota's vehicles without any individualizing features: they are untouched by a digital paintbrush; they are not depicted in front of a palm tree, whizzing down the open road, or climbing up a mountainside. Put another way, Meshwerks' models depict nothing more than unadorned Toyota vehicles—the car *as* car. *See* Appendix A. And the unequivocal lesson from *Feist* is that works are not copyrightable to the extent they do not involve any expression apart from the raw facts in the world. As Professor Nimmer has commented in connection with the predecessor technology of photography, "[a]s applied to a photograph of a pre-existing product, that bedrock principle [of originality] means that the photographer manifestly cannot claim to have originated the matter depicted therein. ... The upshot is that the photographer is entitled to copyright solely based on lighting, angle, perspective, and the other ingredients that traditionally apply to that art-form." Nimmer on Copyright § 3.03[C][3]. It seems to us that exactly the same holds true with the digital medium now before us: the facts in this case unambiguously show that Meshwerks did not make any decisions regarding lighting, shading, the background in front of which a vehicle would be posed, the angle at which to pose it, or the like—in short, its models reflect none of the decisions that can make depictions of things or facts in the world, whether Oscar Wilde or a Toyota Camry, new expressions subject to copyright protection. ...

Confirming this conclusion as well is the peculiar place where Meshwerks stood in the model-creation pecking order. On the one hand, Meshwerks had nothing to do with designing the appearance of Toyota's vehicles, distinguishing them from any other cars, trucks, or vans in the world. That expressive creation took place *before* Meshwerks happened along, and was the result of work done by Toyota and its designers. ... On the other hand, how the models Meshwerks created were to be deployed in advertising—including the backgrounds, lighting, angles, and colors—were all matters left to those (G & W, Saatchi, and 3D Recon) who came *after* Meshwerks left the scene. Meshwerks thus played a narrow, if pivotal, role in the process by simply, if effectively, copying Toyota's vehicles into a digital medium so they could be expressively manipulated by others.

Were we to afford copyright protection in this case, we would run aground on one of the bedrock principles of copyright law—namely, that originality, "as the term is used in copyright, means only that the work was independently created by the author (*as opposed to copied from other works*)." *Feist,* 499 U.S. at 345 (emphasis added). Because our copyright laws protect only "original" expression, the reason for refusing copyright protection to copies is clear, "since obviously a copier is not a creator, much less an 'independent' creator." Patry on Copyright § 3:28. ...

It is certainly true that what Meshwerks accomplished was a peculiar kind of copying. It did not seek to recreate Toyota vehicles outright-steel, rubber, and all; instead, it sought to depict Toyota's three-dimensional physical objects in a two-dimensional digital medium. But we hold, as many before us have already suggested, that, standing alone, "[t]he fact that a work in one medium has been copied from a work in another medium does not render it any the less a 'copy.'" Nimmer on Copyright § 8.01[B]. ...

In reaching this conclusion, we do not for a moment seek to downplay the considerable amount of time, effort, and skill that went into making Meshwerks' digital wire-frame models. But, in assessing the originality of a work for which copyright protection is sought, we look only at the final *product,* not the process, and the fact that intensive, skillful, and even creative labor is invested in the process of creating a product does not guarantee its copyrightability. ... In the case before us, there is no doubt that transposing the physical appearances of Toyota's vehicles from three dimensions to two, such that computer-screen images accurately reflect Toyota's products, was labor intensive and required a great amount of skill. But because the end-results were unadorned images of Toyota's vehicles, the appearances of which do not owe their origins to Meshwerks, we are unable to reward that skill, effort, and labor with copyright protection.

2

Meshwerks' intent in making its wire-frame models provides additional support for our conclusion. "In theory, the originality requirement tests the putative author's state of mind: Did he have an earlier work in mind when he created his own?" Paul Goldstein, Goldstein on Copyright § 2.2.1.1. If an artist affirmatively sets out to be unoriginal—to make a copy of someone else's creation, rather than to create an original work— it is far more likely that the resultant product will, in fact, be unoriginal. ... Of course, this is not to say that the accidental or spontaneous artist will be denied copyright protection for not intending to produce art; it is only to say that authorial intent sometimes can shed light on the question of whether a particular work qualifies as an independent creation or only a copy. ...

Other courts before us have examined and relied on a putative copyright holder's intent in holding that the resultant work was not original and thus subject to copyright protection. ... In *Bridgeman Art Library,* the court examined whether color transparencies of public domain works of art were sufficiently original for copyright protection, ultimately holding that, as "exact photographic copies of public domain works of art," they were not. In support of its holding, the court looked to the plaintiff's intent in creating the transparencies: where "the *point of the exercise* was to reproduce the underlying works with absolute fidelity," the "spark of originality" necessary for copyright protection was absent (emphasis added). Precisely the same holds true here, where, by design, all that was left in Meshwerks' digital wire-frame models were the designs of Toyota's vehicles.

C

… Digital modeling can be, surely is being, and no doubt increasingly will be used to create copyrightable expressions. Yet, just as photographs *can be,* but are not *per se,* copyrightable, the same holds true for digital models. There's little question that digital models *can* be devised of Toyota cars with copyrightable features, whether by virtue of unique shading, lighting, angle, background scene, or other choices. The problem for Meshwerks in this particular case is simply that the uncontested facts reveal that it wasn't involved in any such process, and indeed contracted to provide completely unadorned digital replicas of Toyota vehicles in a two-dimensional space. For this reason, we do not envision any "chilling effect" on creative expression based on our holding today, and instead see it as applying to digital modeling the same legal principles that have come, in the fullness of time and with an enlightened eye, to apply to photographs and other media.

* * *

Originality is the *sine qua non* of copyright. If the basic design reflected in a work of art does not owe its origin to the putative copyright holder, then that person must add something original to that design, and then only the original addition may be copyrighted. In this case, Meshwerks copied Toyota's designs in creating digital, wire-frame models of Toyota's vehicles. But the models reflect, that is, "express," no more than the depiction of the vehicles *as* vehicles. The designs of the vehicles, however, owe their origins to Toyota, not to Meshwerks, and so we are unable to reward Meshwerks' digital wire-frame models, no doubt the product of significant labor, skill, and judgment, with copyright protection. The judgment of the district court is affirmed, and defendants' request for attorneys' fees is denied.

APPENDIX A

06-4222, <u>Meshwerks v. Toyota</u>

APPENDIX B

06-4222, <u>Meshwerks v. Toyota</u>

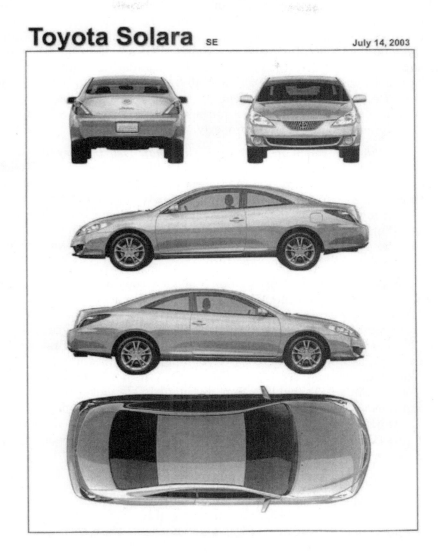

Toyota Solara SE   July 14, 2003

Notes and Questions

1. The *Meshwerks* court held that Meshwerks' drawings lacked originality because they were nothing more than "very good" copies of Toyota cars. Do you agree that Meshwerks' drawings were really copies? Perhaps the drawings were "copies" because they portrayed an existing object, but would this conclusion necessarily deprive the drawings of copyright? In *Bleistein*, the Supreme Court explained that copying alone does

not necessarily render a work uncopyrightable because "[t]he copy is the personal reaction of an individual upon nature. Personality always contains something unique. It expresses its singularity even in handwriting, and a very modest grade of art has in it something irreducible, which is one man's alone. That something he may copyright unless there is a restriction in the words of the act." This statement implies that the plaintiff's manual depiction of wheels, headlights, door handles and other detail supports originality. Do you agree? In formulating your response, look at the drawings found in Exhibit A above and consider whether they really look exactly like a Toyota car. If you conclude that they do not, should the differences matter for purposes of determining whether a work is original, or did the court properly overlook them?

2. *Meshwerks* relies in part on *Bridgeman Art Library v. Corel Corp.,* 36 F. Supp. 2d 191 (S.D.N.Y. 1991), in which the Southern District of New York held that photographic reproductions of public domain paintings lacked sufficient originality to support copyright. *Bridgeman* stated that attempting to make "slavish" copies of other works might require skill and effort, but it lacked any "spark" of originality because "the point of the exercise was to reproduce the underlying works with absolute fidelity."

What do you think of *Bridgeman*'s slavish copying argument, and how well does it support the *Meshwerks* result? Consider a plaintiff who tries to create an exact copy of another work, but fails. Should the law deny copyright because of the plaintiff's intent, or should it grant copyright because there is "distinguishable variation" from the first work? For an example of a case where copyright was granted despite the intent to make an exact copy, *see Alfred Bell & Co. v. Catalda Fine Arts,* 191 F.2d 99 (2d Cir. 1951) (holding that distinguishable variations support copyright, even when the objective is to mimic exactly the appearance of another work). If you believe that intent should control the existence of copyright, would you support a rule that any attempt to create something besides a slavish copy establishes a work's originality?

Gracen v. Bradford Exchange
698 F.2d 300 (7th Cir. 1983)

POSNER, Circuit Judge.

This appeal brings up to us questions of some novelty, at least in this circuit, regarding implied copyright licenses and the required originality for copyrighting a derivative work.

In 1939 MGM produced and copyrighted the movie "The Wizard of Oz." The central character in the movie, Dorothy, was played by Judy Garland. The copyright was renewed by MGM in 1966 and is conceded, at least for purposes of this case, to be valid and in effect today. In 1976 MGM licensed Bradford Exchange to use characters and scenes from the movie in a series of collectors' plates. Bradford invited several artists to submit paintings of Dorothy as played by Judy Garland, with the understanding that the artist who submitted the best painting would be offered a contract for the entire series. Bradford supplied each artist with photographs from the movie and with instructions for the painting that included the following: "We do want *your* interpretation of these images, but your interpretation must evoke all the warm feeling the people have for the film and its actors. So, *your* Judy/Dorothy must be very recognizable as everybody's Judy/Dorothy."

Jorie Gracen, an employee in Bradford's order-processing department, was permitted to join the competition. From photographs and her recollections of the movie (which she had seen several times) she made a painting of Dorothy as played by Judy Garland; Figure 1 at the end of this opinion is a reproduction of a photograph of Miss Gracen's painting (an inadequate one, because the original is in color). Bradford exhibited it along with the other contestants' paintings in a shopping center. The passersby liked Miss Gracen's the best, and Bradford pronounced her the winner of the competition and offered her a contract to do the series, as well as paying her, as apparently it paid each of the other contestants, $200. But she did not like the contract terms and refused to sign, and Bradford turned to another artist, James Auckland, who had not been one of the original contestants. He signed a contract to do the series and Bradford gave him Miss Gracen's painting to help him in doing his painting of Dorothy. The record does not indicate who has her painting now.

Gracen's counsel describes Auckland's painting of Dorothy as a "piratical copy" of her painting. Bradford could easily have refuted this charge, if it is false, by attaching to its motion for summary judgment a photograph of its Dorothy plate, but it did not, and for purposes of this appeal we must assume that the plate is a copy of Miss Gracen's painting. This is not an absurd supposition. Bradford, at least at first, was rapturous about Miss Gracen's painting of Dorothy. It called Miss Gracen "a true prodigy." It said that hers "was the one painting that conveyed the essence of Judy's character in the film ... the painting that left everybody saying, 'That's Judy in Oz.'" Auckland's deposition states that Bradford gave him her painting with directions to "clean it up," which he understood to mean: do the same thing but make it "a little more professional."

Miss Gracen also made five drawings of other characters in the movie, for example the Scarecrow as played by Ray Bolger. Auckland's affidavit states without contradiction that he had not seen any of the drawings when he made his paintings of those characters. Pictures of the plates that were made from his paintings are attached to the motion for summary judgment filed by MGM and Bradford, but there is no picture of his Dorothy plate, lending some support to the charge that it is a "piratical copy." But apparently the other plates are not copies at all.

Auckland completed the series, and the plates were manufactured and sold. But Miss Gracen meanwhile had obtained copyright registrations on her painting and drawings, and in 1978 she brought this action for copyright infringement against MGM, Bradford, Auckland, and the manufacturer of the plates. MGM and Bradford counterclaimed, alleging among other things that Miss Gracen had infringed the copyright on the movie by showing her drawings and a photograph of her painting to people whom she was soliciting for artistic commissions. ...

[W]e shall go on and consider [the proposed] ground for dismissal of the complaint—that Miss Gracen's painting and drawings are not original enough to be copyrightable.

Miss Gracen reminds us that judges can make fools of themselves pronouncing on aesthetic matters. But artistic originality is not the same thing as the legal concept of originality in the Copyright Act. Artistic originality indeed might inhere in a detail, a nuance, a shading too small to be apprehended by a judge. A contemporary school of art known as "Super Realism" attempts with some success to make paintings that are indistinguishable to the eye from color photographs. These paintings command high prices; buyers must find something original in them. Much Northern European painting of the Renaissance is meticulously representational and therefore in a sense—but not an aesthetic sense— less "original" than Cubism or Abstract Expressionism. A portrait is not unoriginal for being a good likeness.

But especially as applied to derivative works, the concept of originality in copyright law has as one would expect a legal rather than aesthetic function—to prevent overlapping claims. Suppose Artist A produces a reproduction of the Mona Lisa, a painting in the public domain, which differs slightly from the original. B also makes a reproduction of the Mona Lisa. A, who has copyrighted his derivative work, sues B for infringement. B's defense is that he was copying the original, not A's reproduction. But if the difference between the original and A's reproduction is slight, the difference between A's and B's reproductions will also be slight, so that if B had access to A's reproductions the trier of fact will be hard-pressed to decide whether B was copying A or copying the Mona Lisa itself. Miss Gracen's drawings illustrate the problem. They are very similar both to the photographs from the movie and to the plates designed by Auckland. Auckland's affidavit establishes that he did not copy or even see her drawings. But suppose he had seen them. Then it would be very hard to determine whether he had been copying the movie stills, as he was authorized to do, or copying her drawings.

The painting of Dorothy presents a harder question. A comparison of Figures 1 and 2 reveals perceptible differences. A painting (except, perhaps, one by a member of the Super Realist school mentioned earlier) is never identical to the subject painted, whether the subject is a photograph, a still life, a landscape, or a model, because most painters cannot and do not want to achieve a photographic likeness of their subject. Nevertheless, if the differences between Miss Gracen's painting of Dorothy and the photograph of Judy Garland as Dorothy were sufficient to make the painting original in the eyes of the law, then a painting by an Auckland also striving, as per his commission, to produce something "very recognizable as everybody's Judy/Dorothy" would look like the Gracen painting, to which he had access; and it would be difficult for the trier of fact to decide whether Auckland had copied her painting or the original movie stills. True, the background in Miss Gracen's painting differs from that in Figure 2, but it is drawn from the movie set. We do not consider a picture created by superimposing one copyrighted photographic image on another to be "original"—always bearing in mind that the purpose of the term in copyright law is not to guide aesthetic judgments but to assure a sufficiently gross difference between the underlying and the derivative work to avoid entangling subsequent artists depicting the underlying work in copyright problems.

We are speaking, however, only of the requirement of originality in derivative works. If a painter paints from life, no court is going to hold that his painting is not copyrightable because it is an exact photographic likeness. If that were the rule photographs could not be copyrighted—the photographs of Judy Garland in "The Wizard of Oz," for example—but of course they can be, 1 Nimmer on Copyright § 2.08[E] (1982). The requirement of originality is significant chiefly in connection with derivative works, where if interpreted too liberally it would paradoxically inhibit rather than promote the creation of such works by giving the first creator a considerable power to interfere with the creation of subsequent derivative works from the same underlying work.

Justice Holmes' famous opinion in *Bleistein v. Donaldson Lithographing Co.,* 188 U.S. 239 (1903), heavily relied on by Miss Gracen, is thus not in point. The issue was whether lithographs of a circus were copyrightable under a statute (no longer in force) that confined copyright to works "connected with the fine arts." Holmes' opinion is a warning against using aesthetic criteria to answer the question. If Miss Gracen had painted Judy Garland from life, her painting would be copyrightable even if we thought it *kitsch,* but a derivative work must be substantially different from the underlying work to be copyrightable. This is the test of *L. Batlin & Son, Inc. v. Snyder,* 536 F.2d at 491, a decision of the Second Circuit—the nation's premier copyright court—sitting *en banc.* Earlier Second Circuit cases discussed in *Batlin* that suggest a more liberal test must be considered superseded.

We agree with the district court that under the test of *Batlin* Miss Gracen's painting, whatever its artistic merit, is not an original derivative work within the meaning of the Copyright Act. Admittedly this is a harder case than *Durham Industries, Inc. v. Tomy Corp.,* 630 F.2d 905 (2d Cir. 1980), heavily relied on by the defendants. The underlying works in that case were Mickey Mouse and other Walt Disney cartoon characters, and the derivative works were plastic reproductions of them. Since the cartoon characters are extremely simple drawings, the reproductions were exact, differing only in the medium. The plastic Mickey and its cartoon original look more alike than Judy Garland's Dorothy and Miss Gracen's painting. But we do not think the difference is enough to allow her to copyright her painting even if, as we very much doubt, she was authorized by Bradford to do so.

The judgment dismissing the complaint is therefore affirmed.

Figure 1

Figure 2

Notes and Questions

1. Given Gracen's apparently successful attempt to create something other than a "slavish copy" of the Wizard of Oz, it seems that her painting would gain copyright protection under the rationale expressed in *Meshwerks*. If you agree, what explains the Seventh Circuit's denial of copyright? Did the *Gracen* court adopt a conception of originality that differs from those presented in the other cases you have read, and if so, was it wise to do so?

2. *Gracen* takes a controversial position on the quantum of originality necessary to support copyright. Ms. Gracen composed her painting after looking at images from the Wizard of Oz. As Judge Posner admitted, if Ms. Gracen had created an image of Judy Garland after looking at the live person, her painting would have been copyrightable. Why then should it matter that Ms. Gracen was looking at images of Judy Garland from a movie, and not Judy Garland herself? Posner's response to this question invokes a contested line of cases that apply a higher standard of originality to derivative works,[15] requiring substantial, as opposed to minimal, originality.[16] Is this higher standard of originality correct, especially in light of the lenient standard of copyrightability inherited from *Bleistein*? In formulating your response, consider *Schrock v. Learning Curve Int'l,* 586 F.3d 513 (7th Cir. 2009), in which the Seventh Circuit rejected the argument that promotional photographs of children's toys lacked sufficient originality under *Gracen*. In so ruling, the Seventh Circuit stated that "nothing in the Copyright Act suggests that derivative works are subject to a more exacting originality requirement than other works of authorship." Do you agree, or did *Gracen* articulate something important about the basic nature of originality?

3. Whatever one thinks about applying a different standard of originality to derivative works, one thing remains clear. The author of a derivative work can claim copyright only in new material she contributes.[17]

---

[15] The Copyright Act defines derivative works as follows:

> A "derivative work" is a work based upon one or more preexisting works, such as a translation, musical arrangement, dramatization, fictionalization, motion picture version, sound recording, art reproduction, abridgment, condensation, or any other form in which a work may be recast, transformed, or adapted.

17 U.S.C. § 101.

[16] For cases applying the higher standard, *see L. Batlin & Son, Inc. v. Snyder*, 536 F.2d 486 (2d Cir. 1976); *Sherry Mfg. Co. v. Towel King of Fla. Inc.*, 753 F.2d 1565 (11th Cir. 1985). For cases taking the opposite view, see *Alfred Bell & Co. v. Catalda Fine Arts*, 191 F.2d 99 (2d Cir. 1951); *Montogmery v. Noga*, 168 F.3d 1282 (11th Cir. 1999).

[17] Section 103 reads:

> *§ 103. Subject matter of copyright: Compilations and derivative works*
>
> (a) The subject matter of copyright as specified by section 102 includes compilations and derivative works, but protection for a work employing preexisting material in which copyright subsists does not extend to any part of the work in which such material has been used unlawfully.
>
> (b) The copyright in a compilation or derivative work extends only to the material contributed by the author of such work, as distinguished from the preexisting material employed in the work, and does not imply any exclusive right in the

This limitation makes sense. Material not contributed by the author could not be original to the author.

SECTION B. ORIGINALITY AND FACTS

Copyright's requirement of originality means that an author can claim copyright only in things she creates. Accordingly, it is a basic principle of copyright that a person who discovers a fact cannot own that fact. This section explores this principle and its consequences, including the extent to which copyright protects collections of facts. Our first case, *Feist Publications, Inc. v. Rural Telephone Service Company, Inc.*, contains the Supreme Court's most extensive modern explanation of originality.

Feist Publications v. Rural Telephone Service Co.
499 U.S. 340 (1991)

JUSTICE O'CONNOR delivered the opinion of the Court.

This case requires us to clarify the extent of copyright protection available to telephone directory white pages.

I

Rural Telephone Service Company, Inc., is a certified public utility that provides telephone service to several communities in northwest Kansas. It is subject to a state regulation that requires all telephone companies operating in Kansas to issue annually an updated telephone directory. Accordingly, as a condition of its monopoly franchise, Rural publishes a typical telephone directory, consisting of white pages and yellow pages. The white pages list in alphabetical order the names of Rural's subscribers, together with their towns and telephone numbers. The yellow pages list Rural's business subscribers alphabetically by category and feature classified advertisements of various sizes. Rural distributes its directory free of charge to its subscribers, but earns revenue by selling yellow pages advertisements.

Feist Publications, Inc., is a publishing company that specializes in area-wide telephone directories. Unlike a typical directory, which covers only a particular calling area, Feist's area-wide directories cover a much larger geographical range, reducing the need to call directory assistance or consult multiple directories. The Feist directory that is the subject of this litigation covers 11 different telephone service areas in 15 counties and contains 46,878 white pages listings—compared to Rural's approximately 7,700 listings. Like Rural's directory, Feist's is distributed free of charge and includes both white pages and yellow pages. Feist and Rural

---

preexisting material. The copyright in such work is independent of, and does not affect or enlarge the scope, duration, ownership, or subsistence of, any copyright protection in the preexisting material.

compete vigorously for yellow pages advertising.

As the sole provider of telephone service in its service area, Rural obtains subscriber information quite easily. Persons desiring telephone service must apply to Rural and provide their names and addresses; Rural then assigns them a telephone number. Feist is not a telephone company, let alone one with monopoly status, and therefore lacks independent access to any subscriber information. To obtain white pages listings for its area-wide directory, Feist approached each of the 11 telephone companies operating in northwest Kansas and offered to pay for the right to use its white pages listings.

Of the 11 telephone companies, only Rural refused to license its listings to Feist. Rural's refusal created a problem for Feist, as omitting these listings would have left a gaping hole in its area-wide directory, rendering it less attractive to potential yellow pages advertisers. In a decision subsequent to that which we review here, the District Court determined that this was precisely the reason Rural refused to license its listings. The refusal was motivated by an unlawful purpose "to extend its monopoly in telephone service to a monopoly in yellow pages advertising." *Rural Telephone Service Co. v. Feist Publications*, Inc., 737 F. Supp. 610, 622 (Kan. 1990).

Unable to license Rural's white pages listings, Feist used them without Rural's consent. Feist began by removing several thousand listings that fell outside the geographic range of its area-wide directory, then hired personnel to investigate the 4,935 that remained. These employees verified the data reported by Rural and sought to obtain additional information. As a result, a typical Feist listing includes the individual's street address; most of Rural's listings do not. Notwithstanding these additions, however, 1,309 of the 46,878 listings in Feist's 1983 directory were identical to listings in Rural's 1982-1983 white pages. Four of these were fictitious listings that Rural had inserted into its directory to detect copying.

Rural sued for copyright infringement in the District Court for the District of Kansas taking the position that Feist, in compiling its own directory, could not use the information contained in Rural's white pages. Rural asserted that Feist's employees were obliged to travel door-to-door or conduct a telephone survey to discover the same information for themselves. Feist responded that such efforts were economically impractical and, in any event, unnecessary because the information copied was beyond the scope of copyright protection. The District Court granted summary judgment to Rural, explaining that "[c]ourts have consistently held that telephone directories are copyrightable" and citing a string of lower court decisions. 663 F. Supp. 214, 218 (1987). In an unpublished opinion, the Court of Appeals for the Tenth Circuit affirmed. ... We granted certiorari to determine whether the copyright in Rural's directory protects the names, towns, and telephone numbers copied by Feist.

II

A

This case concerns the interaction of two well-established propositions. The first is that facts are not copyrightable; the other, that compilations of facts generally are. Each of these propositions possesses an impeccable pedigree. That there can be no valid copyright in facts is universally understood. The most fundamental axiom of copyright law is that "[n]o author may copyright his ideas or the facts he narrates." *Harper & Row, Publishers, Inc. v. Nation Enterprises,* 471 U.S. 539, 556 (1985). Rural wisely concedes this point, noting in its brief that "[f]acts and discoveries, of course, are not themselves subject to copyright protection." At the same time, however, it is beyond dispute that compilations of facts are within the subject matter of copyright. Compilations were expressly mentioned in the Copyright Act of 1909, and again in the Copyright Act of 1976.

There is an undeniable tension between these two propositions. Many compilations consist of nothing but raw data—i.e., wholly factual information not accompanied by any original written expression. On what basis may one claim a copyright in such a work? Common sense tells us that 100 uncopyrightable facts do not magically change their status when gathered together in one place. Yet copyright law seems to contemplate that compilations that consist exclusively of facts are potentially within its scope.

The key to resolving the tension lies in understanding why facts are not copyrightable. The *sine qua non* of copyright is originality. To qualify for copyright protection, a work must be original to the author. See *Harper & Row, supra,* at 547-549. Original, as the term is used in copyright, means only that the work was independently created by the author (as opposed to copied from other works), and that it possesses at least some minimal degree of creativity. 1 M. Nimmer & D. Nimmer, Copyright §§ 2.01[A], [B] (1990) (hereinafter Nimmer). To be sure, the requisite level of creativity is extremely low; even a slight amount will suffice. The vast majority of works make the grade quite easily, as they possess some creative spark, "no matter how crude, humble or obvious" it might be. *Id.,* § 1.08 [C] [1]. Originality does not signify novelty; a work may be original even though it closely resembles other works so long as the similarity is fortuitous, not the result of copying. To illustrate, assume that two poets, each ignorant of the other, compose identical poems. Neither work is novel, yet both are original and, hence, copyrightable.

Originality is a constitutional requirement. The source of Congress' power to enact copyright laws is Article I, § 8, cl. 8, of the Constitution, which authorizes Congress to "secur[e] for limited Times to Authors ... the exclusive Right to their respective Writings." In two decisions from the late 19th century—*The Trade-Mark Cases,* 100 U.S. 82 (1879); and *Burrow-Giles Lithographic Co. v. Sarony,* 111 U.S. 53 (1884)—this Court defined the crucial terms "authors" and "writings." In so doing, the Court made it unmistakably clear that these terms presuppose a degree of originality. ...

The originality requirement articulated in *The Trade-Mark Cases* and *Burrow-Giles* remains the touchstone of copyright protection today. Leading scholars agree on this point. As one pair of commentators succinctly puts it: "The originality requirement is *constitutionally mandated* for all works." Patterson & Joyce, *Monopolizing the Law: The Scope of Copyright Protection for Law Reports and Statutory Compilations*, 36 UCLA L. REV. 719, 763, n. 155 (1989) (emphasis in original) (hereinafter Patterson & Joyce).

It is this bedrock principle of copyright that mandates the law's seemingly disparate treatment of facts and factual compilations. "No one may claim originality as to facts." Nimmer, § 2.11[A], p. 2-157. This is because facts do not owe their origin to an act of authorship. The distinction is one between creation and discovery: The first person to find and report a particular fact has not created the fact; he or she has merely discovered its existence. To borrow from *Burrow-Giles,* one who discovers a fact is not its "maker" or "originator." 111 U.S., at 58. "The discoverer merely finds and records." Nimmer § 2.03[E]. Census takers, for example, do not "create" the population figures that emerge from their efforts; in a sense, they copy these figures from the world around them. Census data therefore do not trigger copyright because these data are not "original" in the constitutional sense. The same is true of all facts—scientific, historical, biographical, and news of the day. "[T]hey may not be copyrighted and are part of the public domain available to every person." *Miller, supra,* at 1369.

Factual compilations, on the other hand, may possess the requisite originality. The compilation author typically chooses which facts to include, in what order to place them, and how to arrange the collected data so that they may be used effectively by readers. These choices as to selection and arrangement, so long as they are made independently by the compiler and entail a minimal degree of creativity, are sufficiently original that Congress may protect such compilations through the copyright laws. Thus[even a directory that contains absolutely no protectible written expression, only facts, meets the constitutional minimum for copyright protection if it features an original selection or arrangement.]This protection is subject to an important limitation. The mere fact that a work is copyrighted does not mean that every element of the work may be protected. Originality remains the *sine qua non* of copyright; accordingly[copyright protection may extend only to those components of a work that are original to the author.]Thus, if the compilation author clothes facts with an original collocation of words, he or she may be able to claim a copyright in this written expression. Others may copy the underlying facts from the publication, but not the precise words used to present them. ... Where the compilation author adds no written expression but rather lets the facts speak for themselves, the expressive element is more elusive. The only conceivable expression is the manner in which the compiler has selected and arranged the facts. Thus, if the selection and arrangement are original, these elements of the work are eligible for copyright protection. No matter how original the format, however, the facts themselves do not become original through association.

This inevitably means that the copyright in a factual compilation is thin. Notwithstanding a valid copyright, a subsequent compiler remains free to use the facts contained in another's publication to aid in preparing a competing work, so long as the competing work does not feature the same selection and arrangement. As one commentator explains it: "[N]o matter how much original authorship the work displays, the facts and ideas it exposes are free for the taking. ... [T]he very same facts and ideas may be divorced from the context imposed by the author, and restated or reshuffled by second comers, even if the author was the first to discover the facts or to propose the ideas." Ginsburg, *Creation and Commercial Value: Copyright Protection of Works of Information*, 90 COLUM. L. REV. 1865, 1868 (1990).

It may seem unfair that much of the fruit of the compiler's labor may be used by others without compensation. As Justice Brennan has correctly observed, however, this is not "some unforeseen byproduct of a statutory scheme." *Harper & Row,* 471 U.S., at 589 (dissenting opinion). It is, rather, "the essence of copyright," *ibid.,* and a constitutional requirement. The primary objective of copyright is not to reward the labor of authors, but "[t]o promote the Progress of Science and useful Arts." Art. I, § 8, cl. 8. To this end, copyright assures authors the right to their original expression, but encourages others to build freely upon the ideas and information conveyed by a work. This principle, known as the idea/expression or fact/expression dichotomy, applies to all works of authorship. As applied to a factual compilation, assuming the absence of original written expression, only the compiler's selection and arrangement may be protected; the raw facts may be copied at will. This result is neither unfair nor unfortunate. It is the means by which copyright advances the progress of science and art.

This Court has long recognized that the fact/expression dichotomy limits severely the scope of protection in fact-based works. More than a century ago, the Court observed: "The very object of publishing a book on science or the useful arts is to communicate to the world the useful knowledge which it contains. But this object would be frustrated if the knowledge could not be used without incurring the guilt of piracy of the book." *Baker v. Selden,* 101 U.S. 99, 103 (1880). ...

This, then, resolves the doctrinal tension: Copyright treats facts and factual compilations in a wholly consistent manner. Facts, whether alone or as part of a compilation, are not original and therefore may not be copyrighted. A factual compilation is eligible for copyright if it features an original selection or arrangement of facts, but the copyright is limited to the particular selection or arrangement. In no event may copyright extend to the facts themselves.

B

As we have explained, originality is a constitutionally mandated pre-requisite for copyright protection. The Court's decisions announcing this rule predate the Copyright Act of 1909, but ambiguous language in the 1909 Act caused some lower courts temporarily to lose sight of this requirement.

The 1909 Act embodied the originality requirement, but not as clearly as it might have. ... Most courts construed the 1909 Act correctly, notwithstanding the less-than-perfect statutory language. They understood from this Court's decisions that there could be no copyright without originality. ...

But some courts misunderstood the statute. These courts developed a new theory to justify the protection of factual compilations. Known alternatively as "sweat of the brow" or "industrious collection," the underlying notion was that copyright was a reward for the hard work that went into compiling facts. The classic formulation of the doctrine appeared in *Jeweler's Circular Publishing Co.*, 281 F. at 88: "The right to copyright a book upon which one has expended labor in its preparation does not depend upon whether the materials which he has collected consist or not of matters which are *publici juris*, or whether such materials show literary skill *or originality,* either in thought or in language, or anything more than industrious collection. The man who goes through the streets of a town and puts down the names of each of the inhabitants, with their occupations and their street number, acquires material of which he is the author." (emphasis added).

[The "sweat of the brow" doctrine had numerous flaws,] the most glaring being that it extended copyright protection in a compilation beyond selection and arrangement—the compiler's original contributions—to the facts themselves. Under the doctrine, the only defense to infringement was independent creation. A subsequent compiler was "not entitled to take one word of information previously published," but rather had to "independently wor[k] out the matter for himself, so as to arrive at the same result from the same common sources of information." *Id.* at 88-89 (internal quotation marks omitted). "Sweat of the brow" courts thereby eschewed the most fundamental axiom of copyright law—that no one may copyright facts or ideas. ...

Without a doubt, the "sweat of the brow" doctrine flouted basic copyright principles. Throughout history, copyright law has "recognize[d] a greater need to disseminate factual works than works of fiction or fantasy." *Harper & Row,* 471 U.S., at 563. But "sweat of the brow" courts took a contrary view; they handed out proprietary interests in facts and declared that authors are absolutely precluded from saving time and effort by relying upon the facts contained in prior works. In truth, "[i]t is just such wasted effort that the proscription against the copyright of ideas and facts ... [is] designed to prevent." *Rosemont Enterprises, Inc. v. Random House, Inc.,* 366 F.2d 303, 310 (CA2 1966), *cert. denied* 385 U.S. 1009 (1967). "Protection for the fruits of such research ... may in certain circumstances be available under a theory of unfair competition. But to accord copyright protection on this basis alone distorts basic copyright principles in that it creates a monopoly in public domain materials without the necessary justification of protecting and encouraging the creation of 'writings' by 'authors.'" Nimmer § 3.04, p. 3-23 (footnote omitted).

C

"Sweat of the brow" decisions did not escape the attention of the Copyright Office. When Congress decided to overhaul the copyright statute and asked the Copyright Office to study existing problems, the Copyright Office promptly recommended that Congress clear up the confusion in the lower courts as to the basic standards of copyrightability. ...

Congress took the Register's advice. In enacting the Copyright Act of 1976, Congress dropped the reference to "all the writings of an author" and replaced it with the phrase "original works of authorship." 17 U.S.C. § 102(a). In making explicit the originality requirement, Congress announced that it was merely clarifying existing law: "The two fundamental criteria of copyright protection [are] originality and fixation in tangible form. ... The phrase 'original works of authorship,' which is purposely left undefined, is intended to incorporate without change *the standard of originality established by the courts under the present [1909] copyright statute.*" H.R. Rep. No. 94-1476, p. 51 (1976) (emphasis added) (hereinafter H.R. Rep.); S. Rep. No. 94-473, p. 50 (1975), U.S. Code Cong. & Admin. News 1976, pp. 5659, 5664 (emphasis added) (hereinafter S. Rep.). ...

Congress took another step to minimize confusion by deleting the specific mention of "directories ... and other compilations" in § 5 of the 1909 Act. ... [T]his section had led some courts to conclude that directories were copyrightable *per se* and that every element of a directory was protected. In its place, Congress enacted two new provisions. First, to make clear that compilations were not copyrightable *per se,* Congress provided a definition of the term "compilation." Second, to make clear that the copyright in a compilation did not extend to the facts themselves, Congress enacted § 103.

The definition of "compilation" is found in § 101 of the 1976 Act. It defines a "compilation" in the copyright sense as "a work formed by the collection and assembling of preexisting materials or of data *that* are selected, coordinated, or arranged *in such a way that* the resulting work as a whole constitutes an original work of authorship" (emphasis added).

The purpose of the statutory definition is to emphasize that collections of facts are not copyrightable *per se.* It conveys this message through its tripartite structure, as emphasized above by the italics. The statute identifies three distinct elements and requires each to be met for a work to qualify as a copyrightable compilation: (1) the collection and assembly of pre-existing material, facts, or data; (2) the selection, coordination, or arrangement of those materials; and (3) the creation, by virtue of the particular selection, coordination, or arrangement, of an "original" work of authorship. "[T]his tripartite conjunctive structure is self-evident, and should be assumed to 'accurately express the legislative purpose.'"

At first glance, the first requirement does not seem to tell us much. It merely describes what one normally thinks of as a compilation—a collection of pre-existing material, facts, or data. What makes it significant is that it is not the *sole* requirement. It is not enough for copyright purposes that an author collects and assembles facts. To satisfy the statutory definition, the work must get over two additional hurdles. In this way, the plain language indicates that not every collection of facts receives copyright protection. Otherwise, there would be a period after "data."

The third requirement is also illuminating. It emphasizes that a compilation, like any other work, is copyrightable only if it satisfies the originality requirement ("an *original* work of authorship"). Although § 102 states plainly that the originality requirement applies to all works, the point was emphasized with regard to compilations to ensure that courts would not repeat the mistake of the "sweat of the brow" courts by concluding that fact-based works are treated differently and measured by some other standard. As Congress explained it, the goal was to "make plain that the criteria of copyrightable subject matter stated in section 102 apply with full force to works ... containing preexisting material." H.R. Rep., at 57; S. Rep., at 55, U.S. Code Cong. & Admin. News 1976, p. 5670.

The key to the statutory definition is the second requirement. It instructs courts that, in determining whether a fact-based work is an original work of authorship, they should focus on the manner in which the collected facts have been selected, coordinated, and arranged. This is a straightforward application of the originality requirement. Facts are never original, so the compilation author can claim originality, if at all, only in the way the facts are presented. To that end, the statute dictates that the principal focus should be on whether the selection, coordination, and arrangement are sufficiently original to merit protection.

Not every selection, coordination, or arrangement will pass muster. This is plain from the statute. It states that, to merit protection, the facts must be selected, coordinated, or arranged "in such a way" as to render the work as a whole original. This implies that some "ways" will trigger copyright, but that others will not. ...

As discussed earlier, however, the originality requirement is not particularly stringent. A compiler may settle upon a selection or arrangement that others have used; novelty is not required. Originality requires only that the author make the selection or arrangement independently (i.e., without copying that selection or arrangement from another work), and that it display some minimal level of creativity. Presumably, the vast majority of compilations will pass this test, but not all will. There remains a narrow category of works in which the creative spark is utterly lacking or so trivial as to be virtually nonexistent. *See generally Bleistein v. Donaldson Lithographing Co.,* 188 U.S. 239, 251 (1903) (referring to "the narrowest and most obvious limits"). Such works are incapable of sustaining a valid copyright. Nimmer § 2.01[B].

Even if a work qualifies as a copyrightable compilation, it receives only limited protection. This is the point of § 103 of the Act. Section 103 explains that "[t]he subject matter of copyright ... includes compilations," but that copyright protects only the author's original contributions—not the facts or information conveyed: "The copyright in a compilation ... extends only to the material contributed by the author of such work, as distinguished from the preexisting material employed in the work, and does not imply any exclusive right in the preexisting material." § 103(b).

As § 103 makes clear, copyright is not a tool by which a compilation author may keep others from using the facts or data he or she has collected. "The most important point here is one that is commonly misunderstood today: copyright ... has no effect one way or the other on the copyright or public domain status of the preexisting material." H.R. Rep., at 57; S. Rep., at 55, U.S. Code Cong. & Admin. News 1976, p. 5670. The 1909 Act did not require, as "sweat of the brow" courts mistakenly assumed, that each subsequent compiler must start from scratch and is precluded from relying on research undertaken by another. Rather, the facts contained in existing works may be freely copied because copyright protects only the elements that owe their origin to the compiler—the selection, coordination, and arrangement of facts.

In summary, the 1976 revisions to the Copyright Act leave no doubt that originality, not "sweat of the brow," is the touchstone of copyright protection in directories and other fact-based works. Nor is there any doubt that the same was true under the 1909 Act. The 1976 revisions were a direct response to the Copyright Office's concern that many lower courts had misconstrued this basic principle, and Congress emphasized repeatedly that the purpose of the revisions was to clarify, not change, existing law. The revisions explain with painstaking clarity that copyright requires originality, that facts are never original, that the copyright in a compilation does not extend to the facts it contains, and that a compilation is copyrightable only to the extent that it features an original selection, coordination, or arrangement. ...

III

There is no doubt that Feist took from the white pages of Rural's directory a substantial amount of factual information. At a minimum, Feist copied the names, towns, and telephone numbers of 1,309 of Rural's subscribers. Not all copying, however, is copyright infringement. To establish infringement, two elements must be proven: (1) ownership of a valid copyright, and (2) copying of constituent elements of the work that are original. The first element is not at issue here; Feist appears to concede that Rural's directory, considered as a whole, is subject to a valid copyright because it contains some foreword text, as well as original material in its yellow pages advertisements.

The question is whether Rural has proved the second element. In other words, did Feist, by taking 1,309 names, towns, and telephone numbers from Rural's white pages, copy anything that was "original" to Rural? Certainly, the raw data does not satisfy the originality requirement. Rural may have been the first to discover and report the names, towns, and telephone numbers of its subscribers, but this data does not "'ow[e] its origin'" to Rural. *Burrow-Giles,* 111 U.S., at 58. Rather, these bits of information are uncopyrightable facts; they existed before Rural reported them and would have continued to exist if Rural had never published a telephone directory. The originality requirement "rule[s] out protecting ... names, addresses, and telephone numbers of which the plaintiff by no stretch of the imagination could be called the author." Patterson & Joyce 776.

Rural essentially concedes the point by referring to the names, towns, and telephone numbers as "preexisting material." Section 103(b) states explicitly that the copyright in a compilation does not extend to "the preexisting material employed in the work."

The question that remains is whether Rural selected, coordinated, or arranged these uncopyrightable facts in an original way. As mentioned, originality is not a stringent standard; it does not require that facts be presented in an innovative or surprising way. It is equally true, however, that the selection and arrangement of facts cannot be so mechanical or routine as to require no creativity whatsoever. The standard of originality is low, but it does exist. ...

[The selection, coordination, and arrangement of Rural's white pages do not satisfy the minimum constitutional standards for copyright protection.] As mentioned at the outset, Rural's white pages are entirely typical. Persons desiring telephone service in Rural's service area fill out an application and Rural issues them a telephone number. In preparing its white pages, Rural simply takes the data provided by its subscribers and lists it alphabetically by surname. The end product is a garden-variety white pages directory, devoid of even the slightest trace of creativity.

Rural's selection of listings could not be more obvious: It publishes the most basic information—name, town, and telephone number—about each person who applies to it for telephone service. This is "selection" of a sort, but it lacks the modicum of creativity necessary to transform mere selection into copyrightable expression. Rural expended sufficient effort to make the white pages directory useful, but insufficient creativity to make it original.

We note in passing that the selection featured in Rural's white pages may also fail the originality requirement for another reason. Feist points out that Rural did not truly "select" to publish the names and telephone numbers of its subscribers; rather, it was required to do so by the Kansas Corporation Commission as part of its monopoly franchise. Accordingly, one could plausibly conclude that this selection was dictated by state law, not by Rural.

Nor can Rural claim originality in its coordination and arrangement of facts. The white pages do nothing more than list Rural's subscribers in alphabetical order. This arrangement may, technically speaking, owe its origin to Rural; no one disputes that Rural undertook the task of alphabetizing the names itself. But there is nothing remotely creative about arranging names alphabetically in a white pages directory. It is an age-old practice, firmly rooted in tradition and so commonplace that it has come to be expected as a matter of course. It is not only unoriginal, it is practically inevitable. This time-honored tradition does not possess the minimal creative spark required by the Copyright Act and the Constitution.

We conclude that the names, towns, and telephone numbers copied by Feist were not original to Rural and therefore were not protected by the copyright in Rural's combined white and yellow pages directory. As a constitutional matter, copyright protects only those constituent elements of a work that possess more than a *de minimis* quantum of creativity. Rural's white pages, limited to basic subscriber information and arranged alphabetically, fall short of the mark. As a statutory matter, 17 U.S.C. § 101 does not afford protection from copying to a collection of facts that are selected, coordinated, and arranged in a way that utterly lacks originality. Given that some works must fail, we cannot imagine a more likely candidate. Indeed, were we to hold that Rural's white pages pass muster, it is hard to believe that any collection of facts could fail.

Because Rural's white pages lack the requisite originality, Feist's use of the listings cannot constitute infringement. This decision should not be construed as demeaning Rural's efforts in compiling its directory, but rather as making clear that copyright rewards originality, not effort. As this Court noted more than a century ago, "'great praise may be due to the plaintiffs for their industry and enterprise in publishing this paper, yet the law does not contemplate their being rewarded in this way.'" *Baker v. Selden,* 101 U.S. at 105.

The judgment of the Court of Appeals is

Reversed.

Notes and Questions

1.   *Feist* apparently stands on a few ostensibly simple and uncontroversial propositions. First, copyright is constitutionally reserved for original works that include minimal creativity. Second, copyright cannot protect facts because humans don't create facts; they simply report them. Accordingly, facts can never be original. Third, copyright must therefore protect compilations of fact only to the extent of any creative selection and arrangement of facts. Do you agree that these propositions are uncontroversial?

2. According to *Feist*, "Originality is a constitutional requirement." Was it necessary or desirable for the Court to invoke constitutional authority in deciding the case? For example, could the Court have decided *Feist* strictly on the basis of statutory interpretation? Consider the consequences of constitutionally limiting copyright to the creative selection and arrangement of factual compilations. Modern compilations, especially those designed for viewing by computer, often come as a database with no preconceived selection and arrangement. Indeed the purpose of the database is to be as inclusive as possible, thereby allowing the viewer to specify search criteria that extract and present information in the desired fashion. Does this mean that compilers of modern databases have no copyright protection at all, and that competitors can copy the databases at will? Would this be a desirable state of affairs? And, if Congress decided to extend copyright protection to modern databases, would it be able to do so in light of the *constitutional* requirement of originality expressed in *Feist*?

3. *Feist* rejected "sweat of the brow" as an acceptable basis for copyright protection. Leaving aside questions of constitutional or statutory interpretation, do you agree with the rejection of sweat as a policy matter? Remember, one of the principal explanations for copyright is that creators of new works need monopoly profits to recoup the costs of creation before free riding competitors enter the marketplace. Doesn't recognition of sweat allow copyright to protect the very thing that needs protection? Or, is there something undesirable about copyright based on sweat?

4. *Feist* elaborates the concept of originality by distinguishing the concepts of originality and novelty: "[T]he originality requirement is not particularly stringent. A compiler may settle upon a selection or arrangement that others have used; novelty is not required. Originality requires only that the author make the selection or arrangement independently (i.e., without copying that selection or arrangement from another work), and that it display some minimal level of creativity." This elaboration is important because students sometimes confuse originality and novelty (a concept found in patent law) in ways that lead to incorrect conclusions about a work's copyrightability.

In copyright, originality means that a work has a particular quality of the sort first encountered in *Burrow-Giles* and *Bleistein*. As *Feist* notes, courts often identify this quality by measuring the creativity of the selection and arrangement of a work's components. This analysis does not include comparing the work to other works that preceded it.

In patent, novelty means that an invention is not already known. If an invention lacks novelty, it cannot be patented. Courts generally assess an invention's novelty by comparing it to prior inventions. If an invention bears too many similarities to prior art, it will not receive patent protection.

Confusion begins when students analyze a work's originality by comparing it to earlier works. This sometimes leads to the mistaken conclusion that a work lacks originality because it resembles an earlier one. Such reasoning would represent an analysis of a work's novelty, not its originality. As *Feist* notes, originality does not encompass direct comparison with earlier works. A work is original as long as its author independently selects and arranges the work's components, even if the author's independent choices result in a work that resembles other works.

To illustrate the difference between novelty (which is irrelevant to copyrightability) and originality (necessary to support copyrightability), imagine that a poet writes a short poem that, by pure coincidence, is identical to a poem written 20 years earlier, by another poet. This poem is not novel because of its similarity to the earlier poem. However, if the later poet could prove that she created her poem independently, without copying from the earlier poet, then she would be able to satisfy the originality requirement and obtain a separate copyright.

5. *Feist* operates on the premise that facts are preexisting, actual truths. In many cases, these truths would be physical, such as the height of Mt. Everest or the weight of a particular rock. Humans cannot claim to have created these facts, so copyright cannot protect them. Problems arise quickly, however, when one realizes that human agency affects the creation and reporting of facts. Humans create many facts. For example, humans created the law school building in which you study, so they created its dimensions. Does this mean that the people who built your school have a copyright on those dimensions? And what about the fake telephone numbers in Rural Telephone's white pages, which it inserted to help detect copying?

CDN v. Kapes
197 F.3d 1256 (9th Cir. 1999)

O'SCANNLAIN, Circuit Judge:

We must decide whether prices listed in a wholesale coin price guide contain sufficient originality to merit the protection of the copyright laws.

Kenneth Kapes operates a coin business, Western Reserve Numismatics, in Ohio. In response to many inquiries he received regarding the price of coins, Kapes developed "The Fair Market Coin Pricer," which listed on his internet web page the retail prices of many coins. In order to generate the prices he listed, Kapes used a computer program he developed to create retail prices from wholesale prices. The exact process is unclear, but Kapes acknowledges using appellee CDN, Inc.'s wholesale price lists.

CDN publishes the Coin Dealer Newsletter, a weekly report of wholesale prices for collectible United States coins, as well as the Coin Dealer Newsletter Monthly Supplement and the CDN Quarterly. The

Newsletter, or "Greysheet" as it is known in the industry, includes prices for virtually all collectible coins and is used extensively by dealers. In December 1996, CDN discovered the existence of Kapes' internet site and list of current retail prices. CDN filed a complaint on February 21, 1997 in the U.S. District Court for the Central District of California, alleging that Kapes infringed CDN's copyrights by using CDN's wholesale prices as a baseline to arrive at retail prices. The complaint asked the court to determine that Kapes infringed its copyright and to enjoin Kapes from future infringement. ...

After reciting the parties' stipulation that the issue of copyrightability was dispositive of the case, the court ruled that CDN's "prices are original creations, not uncopyrightable facts." By order entered February 9, 1998, the court granted CDN's motion for summary judgment and denied that of Kapes. The court enjoined Kapes from infringing CDN's copyright.

Kapes timely appealed. ...

Appellant's attempt to equate the phone number listings in *Feist* with CDN's price lists does not withstand close scrutiny. First, Kapes conflates two separate arguments: (1) that the listing, selection, and inclusion of prices is not original enough to merit protection; and (2) that the prices themselves are not original creations. Whether CDN's selection and arrangement of the price lists is sufficiently original to merit protection is not at issue here. CDN does not allege that Kapes copied the entire lists, as the alleged infringer had in *Feist*. Rather, the issue in this case is whether the prices themselves are sufficiently original as compilations to sustain a copyright. Thus Kapes' argument that the selection is obvious or dictated by industry standards is irrelevant.

Although the requirement of originality is a constitutional one inherent in the grant to Congress of the power to promote science and the useful arts, the required level of originality is "minimal." *Feist,* 499 U.S. at 358. The telephone listings did not qualify because they fell into the "narrow category of works in which the creative spark is utterly lacking or so trivial as to be virtually nonexistent." *Id.* at 359. The numbers themselves were given by the phone company. Their selection (or rather universal inclusion) and arrangement in alphabetical order were too obvious to be original. Nevertheless, "the requisite level of creativity is extremely low; even a slight amount will suffice. The vast majority of works make the grade quite easily, as they possess some creative spark, 'no matter how crude, humble or obvious' it might be." *Feist,* 499 U.S. at 345 (quoting 1 M. Nimmer & D. Nimmer, *Copyright* § 1.08[C][1] (1990)). This spark glows in CDN's prices, which are compilations of data chosen and weighed with creativity and judgment.

Here, the district court, explicitly referencing *Feist,* held that the prices in CDN's guides are not facts, they are "wholly the product of [CDN's] creativity. The evidence indicates that the plaintiff uses its considerable expertise and judgment to determine how a multitude of variable factors impact upon available bid and ask price data. And it is this creative process which ultimately gives rise to the Plaintiff's 'best guess' as to what the current 'bid' and 'ask' prices should be. As such, the Court finds that these prices were created, not discovered." District Court Order Granting Summary Judgment, February 5, 1998.

We agree. CDN's process to arrive at wholesale prices begins with examining the major coin publications to find relevant retail price information. CDN then reviews this data to retain only that information it considers to be the most accurate and important. Prices for each grade of coin are determined with attention to whether the coin is graded by a professional service (and which one). CDN also reviews the online networks for the bid and ask prices posted by dealers. It extrapolates from the reported prices to arrive at estimates for prices for unreported coin types and grades. CDN also considers the impact of public auctions and private sales, and analyzes the effect of the economy and foreign policies on the price of coins. As the district court found, CDN does not republish data from another source or apply a set formula or rule to generate prices. The prices CDN creates are compilations of data that represent its best estimate of the value of the coins. ...

Our holding that the prices are copyrightable is consistent with that of the Second Circuit in *CCC Info. Servs., Inc. v. Maclean Hunter Mkt. Reports,* 44 F.3d 61 (2d Cir. 1994). Maclean Hunter published the Red Book, a list of car values for various regions of the United States. The Red Book listed the editors' projections of the value of different kinds of used cars for six weeks after publication. CCC Information Systems had used these values in compiling its computer databases. Maclean Hunter sued for infringement, and the district court found that the values were facts and as such were not copyrightable. The Second Circuit reversed. The court held that the valuations were not "pre-existing facts that had merely been discovered by the Red Book editors," but instead "represented predictions by the Red Book editors of future prices estimated to cover specified geographic regions." *CCC,* 44 F.3d at 67. Like CDN's prices, the prices in the Red Book granted copyright protection by the Second Circuit, are "based not only on a multitude of data sources, but also on professional judgment and expertise." *Id.*

Kapes attempts to distinguish *CCC* by arguing that the prices in the Red Book were projections of future values, while the prices in the Greysheet are estimates of present value. But the distinction between present and future values is not important to this case. What is important is the fact that both Maclean and CDN arrive at the prices they list through a process that involves using their judgment to distill and extrapolate from factual data. It is simply not a process through which they discover a preexisting historical fact, but rather a process by which they create a price which, in their best judgment, represents the value of an item as closely as possible. If CDN merely listed historical facts of actual transactions, the guides would be long, cumbersome, and of little use to anyone. Dealers looking through such data would have to use their own judgment and expertise to estimate the value of a coin. What CDN has done is use its own judgment and expertise in arriving at that

value for the dealers. This process imbues the prices listed with sufficient creativity and originality to make them copyrightable.

[The court's discussion of the so-called idea/expression dichotomy is
omitted.]

For the foregoing reasons, we affirm the district court's holding that
the prices in the guides contain sufficient originality to sustain copyright
protection.

Notes and Questions

1. CDN's coin prices amount to statements about the prices of certain coins. How do these statements differ for purposes of copyright from
the statement "Mt. Everest is 29,035 feet high"? Does *CDN* mean that
this statement is copyrightable?

2. Does *CDN* amount to implementation of the "sweat of the brow"
doctrine? If not, what could someone who wanted to compete in the coin
price market do besides start from scratch?

3. *CDN* is a controversial opinion because it arguably converts every day "facts" into copyrightable subject matter. Consider the annual
rankings of law schools published by U.S. News and World Report. The
magazine produces these rankings by using a specifically designed formula to convert selected information about each school into a score that
permits numerical ordering. If one takes seriously the conclusion that
individual estimated coin prices are copyrightable, it might follow that
an individual school's score and ranking are copyrightable, and that U.S.
News could prevent others from reporting or using an individual school's
score or ranking. Does *CDN* support such a result? Would the result
serve society's best interests?

Nash v. CBS
899 F.2d 1537 (7th Cir. 1990)

EASTERBROOK, Circuit Judge.

John Dillinger, Public Enemy No. 1, died on July 22, 1934, at the Biograph Theater in Chicago. He emerged from the air conditioned movie
palace into a sweltering evening accompanied by two women, one wearing a bright red dress. The "lady in red", Anna Sage, had agreed to be-
tray his presence for $10,000. Agents of the FBI were waiting. Alerted by
Polly Hamilton, the other woman, Dillinger wheeled to fire, but it was
too late. A hail of bullets cut him down, his .45 automatic unused. William C. Sullivan, *The Bureau* 30-33 (1979). Now a national historic site,
the Biograph bears a plaque commemorating the event. It still shows

movies, and the air conditioning is no better now than in 1934.

Jay Robert Nash believes that Dillinger did not die at the Biograph. In *Dillinger: Dead or Alive?* (1970), and *The Dillinger Dossier* (1983), Nash maintains that Dillinger learned about the trap and dispatched Jimmy Lawrence, a small-time hoodlum who looked like him, in his stead. The FBI, mortified that its set-up had no sting, kept the switch quiet. Nash points to discrepancies between Dillinger's physical characteristics and those of the corpse: Dillinger had a scar on his upper lip and the corpse did not; Dillinger lacked a tooth that the corpse possessed; Dillinger had blue eyes, the corpse brown eyes; Dillinger's eyebrows were thicker than those of the corpse. Although Dillinger's sister identified the dead man, Nash finds the circumstances suspicious, and he is struck by the decision of Dillinger's father to encase the corpse in concrete before burial. As part of the cover-up, according to Nash, the FBI planted Dillinger's fingerprints in the morgue. After interviewing many persons connected with Dillinger's gang and the FBI's pursuit of it, Nash tracked Dillinger to the west coast, where Dillinger married and lay low. Nash believes that he survived at least until 1979. *The Dillinger Dossier* contains pictures of a middle-aged couple and then an elderly man who, Nash believes, is Dillinger in dotage. Nash provides capsule versions of his conclusions in his *Bloodletters and Badmen: A Narrative Encyclopedia of American Criminals from the Pilgrims to the Present* (1973), and his exposé *Citizen Hoover* (1972).

Nash's reconstruction of the Dillinger story has not won adherents among historians—or the FBI. Someone in Hollywood must have read *The Dillinger Dossier,* however, because in 1984 CBS broadcast an episode of its *Simon and Simon* series entitled *The Dillinger Print. Simon and Simon* featured brothers Rick and A.J. Simon, private detectives in San Diego.

[The court then described the general plot of the *Simon and Simon* episode that involved the murder of a detective who believed that Dillinger did not die at the Biograph Theater. The plot used, among other things, the physical discrepancies between Dillinger's appearance and those of the corpse cited by Nash to make plausible the idea that Dillinger was still alive.]

Nash filed this suit seeking damages on the theory that *The Dillinger Print* violates his copyrights in the four books setting out his version of Dillinger's escape from death and new life on the west coast. The district court determined that the books' copyrighted material consists in Nash's presentation and exposition, not in any of the historical events. CBS then moved for summary judgment, conceding for this purpose both access to Nash's books and copying of the books' factual material. The court granted this motion, holding that *The Dillinger Print* did not appropriate any of the material protected by Nash's copyrights. ...

Nash does not portray *The Dillinger Dossier* and its companion works as fiction, however, which makes all the difference. The inventor of Sherlock Holmes controls that character's fate while the copyright lasts; the first person to conclude that Dillinger survived does not get dibs on history. If Dillinger survived, that fact is available to all. Nash's rights lie in his expression: in his words, in his arrangement of facts (his deployment of narration interspersed with interviews, for example), but not in the naked "truth". *The Dillinger Print* does not use any words from *The Dillinger Dossier* or Nash's other books; it does not take over any of Nash's presentation but instead employs a setting of its own invention with new exposition and development. Physical differences between Dillinger and the corpse, planted fingerprints, photographs of Dillinger and other gangsters in the 1930s, these and all the rest are facts as Nash depicts them. (Nash did not take the photographs and has no rights in them; *The Dillinger Print* used the photos but not Nash's arrangement of them.)

The cases closest to ours are not plays translated to the movie screen (as in *Sheldon*) but movies made from speculative works representing themselves as fact. For example, Universal made a motion picture based on the premise that an idealistic crewman planted a bomb that destroyed the dirigible *Hindenburg* on May 6, 1937. The theory came straight from A.A. Hoehling's *Who Destroyed the Hindenburg?* (1962), a monograph based on exhaustive research. The motion picture added subplots and development, but the thesis and the evidence adduced in support of it could be traced to Hoehling. Nonetheless, the Second Circuit concluded that this did not infringe Hoehling's rights, because the book placed the facts (as opposed to Hoehling's exposition) in the public domain. *Hoehling v. Universal City Studios, Inc.,* 618 F.2d 972 (1980).

Hoehling suggested that "[t]o avoid a chilling effect on authors who contemplate tackling an historical issue or event, broad latitude must be granted to subsequent authors who make use of historical subject matter, including theories or plots". As our opinion in *Toksvig v. Bruce Pub.,* 181 F.2d 664 (7th Cir. 1950), shows, we are not willing to say that "anything goes" as long as the first work is about history. *Toksvig* held that the author of a biography of Hans Christian Andersen infringed the copyright of the author of an earlier biography by using portions of Andersen's letters as well as some of the themes and structure. *Hoehling* rejected *Toksvig,* see 618 F.2d at 979, concluding that "[k]nowledge is expanded ... by granting new authors of historical works a relatively free hand to build upon the work of their predecessors." *Id.* at 980 (footnote omitted). With respect for our colleagues of the east, we think this goes to the extreme of looking at incentives only *ex post.* The authors in *Hoehling* and *Toksvig* spent years tracking down leads. If all of their work, right down to their words, may be used without compensation, there will be too few original investigations, and facts will not be available on which to build.

In *Toksvig* the first author, who knew Danish, spent three years learning about Andersen's life; the second author, who knew no Danish, wrote her biography in less than a year by copying out of the first book scenes and letters that the original author discovered or translated. Reducing the return on such effort, by allowing unhindered use, would make the initial leg-work less attractive and so less frequent. Copyright law does not protect hard work (divorced from expression), and hard work is not an essential ingredient of copyrightable expression (see *Rockford Map*); to the extent *Toksvig* confuses work or ideas with expression, it has been justly criticized. We need not revisit *Toksvig* on its own facts to know that it is a mistake to hitch up at *either* pole of the continuum between granting the first author a right to forbid all similar treatments of history and granting the second author a right to use anything he pleases of the first's work.

Authors of fiction do not (necessarily) need greater incentives than authors of non-fiction. Users of and elaborators on works of non-fiction are not (necessarily) more easily dissuaded than are those who use or elaborate on works of fiction. Decisions such as *Hoehling* do not come straight from first principles. They depend, rather, on the language of what is now 17 U.S.C. § 102(b): "In no case does copyright protection for an original work ... extend to any idea, ... or discovery, regardless of the form in which it is described, explained, illustrated, or embodied in such work." Long before the 1976 revision of the statute, courts had decided that historical facts are among the "ideas" and "discoveries" that the statute does not cover. This is not a natural law; Congress could have made copyright broader (as patent law is). But it is *law,* which will come as no surprise to Nash. His own books are largely fresh expositions of facts looked up in other people's books. ...

The producers of *Simon and Simon* used Nash's work as Nash has used others': as a source of facts and ideas, to which they added their distinctive overlay. As the district court found, CBS did no more than § 102(b)permits. Because *The Dillinger Print* uses Nash's analysis of history but none of his expression, the judgment is

Affirmed.

Notes and Questions

1.   *Nash* raises interesting questions about originality and the identification of facts. According to *Feist,* copyright does not protect facts because humans do not create facts. *CDN* adopted this reasoning in finding that copyright protected CDN's coin prices. In *Nash*, it is quite likely that the plaintiff's "facts" are not only created by a person, but also fiction. Since considerable judgment and creativity went into the creation of the plaintiff's theory about Dillinger, shouldn't the court have found the plaintiff's theory copyrightable because the plaintiff's originality exceeded the low threshold for copyrightability? Or, did the court correctly understand that something can still be a fact despite having been created by a person who employed minimal judgment and creativity? If so, what identifies a fact?

2. Do *CDN* and *Nash* adopt consistent interpretations of copyright? If not, what are the differences, and which interpretation better promotes the progress of science and art?

SECTION C. IDEAS

Section 102(b) of the Copyright Act denies copyright to, among other things, the ideas embodied in a copyrighted work. It reads: "In no case does copyright protection for an original work of authorship extend to any idea, procedure, process, system, method of operation, concept, principle, or discovery, regardless of the form in which it is described, explained, illustrated, or embodied in such work." As was the case with section 102(a), Congress clearly intended to codify case law made before the passage of the 1976 Act. This section therefore begins with two famous seminal cases.

Baker v. Selden
101 U.S. 99 (1879)

MR. JUSTICE BRADLEY delivered the opinion of the court.

Charles Selden, the testator of the complainant in this case, in the year 1859 took the requisite steps for obtaining the copyright of a book, entitled "Selden's Condensed Ledger, or Book-keeping Simplified," the object of which was to exhibit and explain a peculiar system of book-keeping. In 1860 and 1861, he took the copyright of several other books, containing additions to and improvements upon the said system. The bill of complaint was filed against the defendant, Baker, for an alleged infringement of these copyrights. The latter, in his answer, denied that Selden was the author or designer of the books, and denied the infringement charged, and contends on the argument that the matter alleged to be infringed is not a lawful subject of copyright. ...

A decree was rendered for the complainant, and the defendant appealed.

The book or series of books of which the complainant claims the copyright consists of an introductory essay explaining the system of book-keeping referred to, to which are annexed certain forms or banks, consisting of ruled lines, and headings, illustrating the system and showing how it is to be used and carried out in practice. This system effects the same results as book-keeping by double entry; but, by a peculiar arrangement of columns and headings, presents the entire operation, of a day, a week, or a month, on a single page, or on two pages facing each other, in an account-book. The defendant uses a similar plan so far as results are concerned; but makes a different arrangement of the columns, and uses different headings. If the complainant's testator had the exclusive right to the use of the system explained in his book, it would be difficult to contend that the defendant does not infringe it, notwithstanding the difference in his form of arrangement; but if it be assumed that the system is open to public use, it seems to be equally difficult to contend that the books made and sold by the defendant are a violation of the copyright of the complainant's book considered merely as a book explanatory of the system. Where the truths of a science or the methods of an art are the common property of the whole world, any author has the right to express the one, or explain and use the other, in his own way. As an author, Selden explained the system in a particular way. It may be conceded that Baker makes and uses account-books arranged on substantially the same system; but the proof fails to show that he has violated the copyright of Selden's book, regarding the latter merely as an explanatory work; or that he has infringed Selden's right in any way, unless the latter became entitled to an exclusive right in the system.

... It becomes important, therefore, to determine whether, in obtaining the copyright of his books, he secured the exclusive right to the use of the system or method of book-keeping which the said books are intended to illustrate and explain. It is contended that he has secured such exclusive right, because no one can use the system without using substantially the same ruled lines and headings which he was appended to his books in illustration of it. In other words, it is contended that the ruled lines and headings, given to illustrate the system, are a part of the book, and, as such, are secured by the copyright; and that no one can make or use similar ruled lines and headings, or ruled lines and headings made and arranged on substantially the same system, without violating the copyright. And this is really the question to be decided in this case. Stated in another form, the question is, whether the exclusive property in a system of book-keeping can be claimed, under the law or copyright, by means of a book in which that system is explained? The complainant's bill, and the case made under it, are based on the hypothesis that it can be. ...

There is no doubt that a work on the subject of book-keeping, though only explanatory of well-known systems, may be the subject of a copyright. ... But there is a clear distinction between the book, as such, and the art which it is intended to illustrate. The mere statement of the proposition is so evident, that it requires hardly any argument to support it. The same distinction may be predicated of every other art as well as that of book-keeping. A treatise on the composition and use of medicines, be they old or new; on the construction and use of ploughs, or watches, or churns; or on the mixture and application of colors for painting or dyeing; or on the mode of drawing lines to produce the effect of perspective, would be the subject of copyright; but no one would contend that the copyright of the treatise would give the exclusive right to the art or manufacture described therein. The copyright of the book, if not pirated from other works, would be valid without regard to the novelty, or want of novelty, of its subject-matter. The novelty of the art or thing described or explained has nothing to do with the validity of the copyright. To give to the author of the book an exclusive property in the art described therein, when no examination of its novelty has ever been officially made, would be a surprise and a fraud upon the public. That is the province of letters-patent, not of copyright. The claim to an invention or discovery of an art or manufacture must be subjected to the examination of the Patent Office before an exclusive right therein can be obtained; and it can only be secured by a patent from the government. ...

The copyright of a work on mathematical science cannot give to the author an exclusive right to the methods of operation which he propounds, or to the diagrams which he employs to explain them, so as to prevent an engineer from using them whenever occasion requires. The very object of publishing a book on science or the useful arts is to communicate to the world the useful knowledge which it contains. But this object would be frustrated if the knowledge could not be used without incurring the guilt of piracy of the book. And where the art it teaches cannot be used without employing the methods and diagrams used to illustrate the book, or such as are similar to them, such methods and diagrams are to be considered as necessary incidents to the art, and given therewith to the public; not given for the purpose of publication in other works explanatory of the art, but for the purpose of practical application. ...

Recurring to the case before us, we observe that Charles Selden, by his books, explained and described a peculiar system of book-keeping, and illustrated his method by means of ruled lines and blank columns, with proper headings on a page, or on successive pages. Now, whilst no one has a right to print or publish his book, or any material part thereof, as a book intended to convey instruction in the art, any person may practice and use the art itself which he has described and illustrated therein. The use of the art is a totally different thing from a publication of the book explaining it. The copyright of a book on book-keeping cannot secure the exclusive right to make, sell, and use account-books prepared upon the plan set forth in such book. Whether the art might or might not have been patented, is a question which is not before us. It was not patented, and is open and free to the use of the public. And, of course, in using the art, the ruled lines and headings of accounts must necessarily be used as incident to it.

The plausibility of the claim put forward by the complainant in this case arises from a confusion of ideas produced by the peculiar nature of the art described in the books which have been made the subject of copyright. In describing the art, the illustrations and diagrams employed happen to correspond more closely than usual with the actual work performed by the operator who uses the art. Those illustrations and diagrams consist of ruled lines and headings of accounts; and it is similar ruled lines and headings of accounts which, in the application of the art, the book-keeper makes with his pen, or the stationer with his press; whilst in most other cases the diagrams and illustrations can only be represented in concrete forms of wood, metal, stone, or some other physical embodiment. But the principle is the same in all. The description of the art in a book, though entitled to the benefit of copyright, lays no foundation for an exclusive claim to the art itself. The object of the one is explanation; the object of the other is use. The former may be secured by copyright. The latter can only be secured, if it can be secured at all, by letters-patent. ...

The conclusion to which we have come is, that blank account-books are not the subject of copyright; and that the mere copyright of Selden's book did not confer upon him the exclusive right to make and use account-books, ruled and arranged as designated by him and described and illustrated in said book.

The decree of the Circuit Court must be reversed, and the cause remanded with instructions to dismiss the complainant's bill; and it is

So ordered.

———

Notes and Questions

1. *Baker v. Selden* is among the most famous and widely cited of all copyright opinions. It introduces us to the proposition that copyright does not protect some apparently original creations such as the system of bookkeeping portrayed in Selden's work. Why doesn't copyright protect such things? What are the consequences of *Baker*'s restriction on copyrightable subject matter?

2. The *Baker* Court concluded that "blank account-books are not the subject of copyright." Was it correct in doing so? The Court could have decided for the defendant by finding that he simply did not copy anything copyrightable. This would have allowed Selden to sue others who made exact copies of the blank forms found in his book. Would that result have been better?

3. Regardless of how you interpret *Baker*, application of the idea/expression dichotomy depends on the identification of ideas. How do you know whether something is an idea or expression? The next case represents one of the most famous treatments of this question.

———

Problem

Your client is an exceptionally lazy cookbook author. He makes his living by publishing cookbooks that draw, as much as possible, from already-published cookbooks. Your client recently came across a very successful cookbook published by another author, which contains recipes from the region of Tuscany in Italy. The cookbook contains approximately 50 recipes. Each recipe includes a list of ingredients, step by step instructions, photographs illustrating specific techniques, photographs of the finished dishes, and descriptions of the history of each recipe. The cookbook clearly reflected a tremendous amount of work by the original author, testing and refining the recipes, and researching their histories. Your client would like to publish his own cookbook containing recipes from Tuscany, and he asks you how much he can take from the original cookbook. What advice do you give him?

Nichols v. Universal Pictures Corp.
45 F.2d 119 (2d Cir. 1930)

L. HAND, Circuit Judge.

The plaintiff is the author of a play, "Abie's Irish Rose," which it may be assumed was properly copyrighted. ... The defendant produced publicly a motion picture play, "The Cohens and The Kellys," which the plaintiff alleges was taken from it. As we think the defendant's play too unlike the plaintiff's to be an infringement, we may assume, arguendo, that in some details the defendant used the plaintiff's play, as will subsequently appear, though we do not so decide. It therefore becomes necessary to give an outline of the two plays.

"Abie's Irish Rose" presents a Jewish family living in prosperous circumstances in New York. The father, a widower, is in business as a merchant, in which his son and only child helps him. The boy has philandered with young women, who to his father's great disgust have always been Gentiles, for he is obsessed with a passion that his daughter-in-law shall be an orthodox Jewess. When the play opens the son, who has been courting a young Irish Catholic girl, has already married her secretly before a Protestant minister, and is concerned to soften the blow for his father, by securing a favorable impression of his bride, while concealing her faith and race. To accomplish this he introduces her to his father at his home as a Jewess, and lets it appear that he is interested in her, though he conceals the marriage. The girl somewhat reluctantly falls in with the plan; the father takes the bait, becomes infatuated with the girl, concludes that they must marry, and assumes that of course they will, if he so decides. He calls in a rabbi, and prepares for the wedding according to the Jewish rite.

Meanwhile the girl's father, also a widower, who lives in California, and is as intense in his own religious antagonism as the Jew, has been called to New York, supposing that his daughter is to marry an Irishman and a Catholic. Accompanied by a priest, he arrives at the house at the moment when the marriage is being celebrated, but too late to prevent it and the two fathers, each infuriated by the proposed union of his child to a heretic, fall into unseemly and grotesque antics. The priest and the rabbi become friendly, exchange trite sentiments about religion, and agree that the match is good. Apparently out of abundant caution, the priest celebrates the marriage for a third time, while the girl's father is inveigled away. The second act closes with each father, still outraged, seeking to find some way by which the union, thus trebly insured, may be dissolved.

The last act takes place about a year later, the young couple having meanwhile been abjured by each father, and left to their own resources. They have had twins, a boy and a girl, but their fathers know no more than that a child has been born. At Christmas each, led by his craving to see his grandchild, goes separately to the young folks' home, where they encounter each other, each laden with gifts, one for a boy, the other for a girl. After some slapstick comedy, depending upon the insistence of each that he is right about the sex of the grandchild, they become reconciled when they learn the truth, and that each child is to bear the given name of a grandparent. The curtain falls as the fathers are exchanging amenities, and the Jew giving evidence of an abatement in the strictness of his orthodoxy.

"The Cohens and The Kellys" presents two families, Jewish and Irish, living side by side in the poorer quarters of New York in a state of perpetual enmity. The wives in both cases are still living, and share in the mutual animosity, as do two small sons, and even the respective dogs. The Jews have a daughter, the Irish a son; the Jewish father is in the clothing business; the Irishman is a policeman. The children are in love with each other, and secretly marry, apparently after the play opens. The Jew, being in great financial straits, learns from a lawyer that he has fallen heir to a large fortune from a great-aunt, and moves into a great house, fitted luxuriously. Here he and his family live in vulgar ostentation, and here the Irish boy seeks out his Jewish bride, and is chased away by the angry father. The Jew then abuses the Irishman over the telephone, and both become hysterically excited. The extremity of his feelings make the Jew sick, so that he must go to Florida for a rest, just before which the daughter discloses her marriage to her mother.

On his return the Jew finds that his daughter has borne a child; at first he suspects the lawyer, but eventually learns the truth and is overcome with anger at such a low alliance. Meanwhile, the Irish family who have been forbidden to see the grandchild, go to the Jew's house, and after a violent scene between the two fathers in which the Jew disowns his daughter, who decides to go back with her husband, the Irishman takes her back with her baby to his own poor lodgings. The lawyer, who had hoped to marry the Jew's daughter, seeing his plan foiled, tells the Jew that his fortune really belongs to the Irishman, who was also related to the dead woman, but offers to conceal his knowledge, if the Jew will share the loot. This the Jew repudiates, and, leaving the astonished lawyer, walks through the rain to his enemy's house to surrender the property. He arrives in great defection, tells the truth, and abjectly turns to leave. A reconciliation ensues, the Irishman agreeing to share with him equally. The Jew shows some interest in his grandchild, though this is at most a minor motive in the reconciliation, and the curtain falls while the two are in their cups, the Jew insisting that in the firm name for the business, which they are to carry on jointly, his name shall stand first.

It is of course essential to any protection of literary property, whether at common-law or under the statute, that the right cannot be limited literally to the text, else a plagiarist would escape by immaterial variations. That has never been the law, but, as soon as literal appropriation ceases to be the test, the whole matter is necessarily at large, so that, as was recently well said by a distinguished judge, the decisions cannot help much in a new case. When plays are concerned, the plagiarist may excise a separate scene; or he may appropriate part of the dialogue. Then the question is whether the part so taken is "substantial," and therefore not a "fair use" of the copyrighted work; it is the same question as arises in the case of any other copyrighted work. But when the plagiarist does not take out a block in situ, but an abstract of the whole, decision is more troublesome. Upon any work, and especially upon a play, a great number of patterns of increasing generality will fit equally well, as more and more of the incident is left out. The last may perhaps be no more than the most general statement of what the play is about, and at times might consist only of its title; but there is a point in this series of abstractions where they are no longer protected, since otherwise the playwright could prevent the use of his "ideas," to which, apart from their expression, his property is never extended. Nobody has ever been able to fix that boundary, and nobody ever can. In some cases the question has been treated as though it were analogous to lifting a portion out of the copyrighted work; but the analogy is not a good one, because, though the skeleton is a part of the body, it pervades and supports the whole. In such cases we are rather concerned with the line between expression and what is expressed. As respects plays, the controversy chiefly centers upon the characters and sequence of incident, these being the substance.

... [W]e do not doubt that two plays may correspond in plot closely enough for infringement. How far that correspondence must go is another matter. Nor need we hold that the same may not be true as to the characters, quite independently of the "plot" proper, though, as far as we know such a case has never arisen. If Twelfth Night were copyrighted, it is quite possible that a second comer might so closely imitate Sir Toby Belch or Malvolio as to infringe, but it would not be enough that for one of his characters he cast a riotous knight who kept wassail to the discomfort of the household, or a vain and foppish steward who became amorous of his mistress. These would be no more than Shakespeare's "ideas" in the play, as little capable of monopoly as Einstein's Doctrine of Relativity, or Darwin's theory of the Origin of Species. It follows that the less developed the characters, the less they can be copyrighted; that is the penalty an author must bear for marking them too indistinctly.

In the two plays at bar we think both as to incident and character, the defendant took no more—assuming that it took anything at all— than the law allowed. The stories are quite different. One is of a religious zealot who insists upon his child's marrying no one outside his faith; opposed by another who is in this respect just like him, and is his foil. Their difference in race is merely an obbligato to the main theme, religion. They sink their differences through grandparental pride and affection. In the other, zealotry is wholly absent; religion does not even appear. It is true that the parents are hostile to each other in part because they differ in race; but the marriage of their son to a Jew does not apparently offend the Irish family at all, and it exacerbates the existing animosity of the Jew, principally because he has become rich, when he learns it. They are reconciled through the honesty of the Jew and the generosity of the Irishman; the grandchild has nothing whatever to do with it. The only matter common to the two is a quarrel between a Jewish and an Irish father, the marriage of their children, the birth of grandchildren and a reconciliation.

If the defendant took so much from the plaintiff, it may well have been because her amazing success seemed to prove that this was a subject of enduring popularity. Even so, granting that the plaintiff's play was wholly original, and assuming that novelty is not essential to a copyright, there is no monopoly in such a background. Though the plaintiff discovered the vein, she could not keep it to herself; so defined, the theme was too generalized an abstraction from what she wrote. It was only a part of her "ideas."

Nor does she fare better as to her characters. It is indeed scarcely credible that she should not have been aware of those stock figures, the low comedy Jew and Irishman. The defendant has not taken from her more than their prototypes have contained for many decades. If so, obviously so to generalize her copyright, would allow her to cover what was not original with her. But we need not hold this as matter of fact, much as we might be justified. Even though we take it that she devised her figures out of her brain de novo, still the defendant was within its rights.

There are but four characters common to both plays, the lovers and the fathers. The lovers are so faintly indicated as to be no more than stage properties. They are loving and fertile; that is really all that can be said of them, and anyone else is quite within his rights if he puts loving and fertile lovers in a play of his own, wherever he gets the cue. The Plaintiff's Jew is quite unlike the defendant's. His obsession in his religion, on which depends such racial animosity as he has. He is affectionate, warm and patriarchal. None of these fit the defendant's Jew, who shows affection for his daughter only once, and who has none but the most superficial interest in his grandchild. He is tricky, ostentatious and vulgar, only by misfortune redeemed into honesty. Both are grotesque, extravagant and quarrelsome; both are fond of display; but these common qualities make up only a small part of their simple pictures, no more than any one might lift if he chose. The Irish fathers are even more unlike; the plaintiff's a mere symbol for religious fanaticism and patriarchal pride, scarcely a character at all. Neither quality appears in the defendant's, for while he goes to get his grandchild, it is rather out of a truculent determination not to be forbidden, than from pride in his progeny. For the rest he is only a grotesque hobbledehoy, used for low comedy of the most conventional sort, which any one might borrow, if he chanced not to know the exemplar.

… We assume that the plaintiff's play is altogether original, even to an extent that in fact it is hard to believe. We assume further that, so far as it has been anticipated by earlier plays of which she knew nothing, that fact is immaterial. Still, as we have already said, her copyright did not cover everything that might be drawn from her play; its content went to some extent into the public domain. We have to decide how much, and while we are as aware as any one that the line, whereever it is drawn, will seem arbitrary, that is no excuse for not drawing it; it is a question such as courts must answer in nearly all cases. Whatever may be the difficulties a priori, we have no question on which side of the line this case falls. A comedy based upon conflicts between Irish and Jews, into which the marriage of their children enters, is no more susceptible of copyright than the outline of Romeo and Juliet.

The plaintiff has prepared an elaborate analysis of the two plays, showing a "quadrangle" of the common characters, in which each is represented by the emotions which he discovers. She presents the resulting parallelism as proof of infringement, but the adjectives employed are so general as to be quite useless. Take for example the attribute of "love" ascribed to both Jews. The plaintiff has depicted her father as deeply attached to his son, who is his hope and joy; not so, the defendant, whose father's conduct is throughout not actuated by any affection for his daughter, and who is merely once overcome for the moment by her distress when he has violently dismissed her lover. "Anger" covers emotions aroused by quite different occasions in each case; so do "anxiety," "despondency" and "disgust." It is unnecessary to go through the catalogue for emotions are too much colored by their causes to be a test when used so broadly. This is not the proper approach to a solution; it must be more ingenuous, more like that of a spectator, who would rely upon the complex of his impressions of each character.

We cannot approve the length of the record, which was due chiefly to the use of expert witnesses. Argument is argument whether in the box or at the bar, and its proper place is the last. The testimony of an expert upon such issues, especially his cross-examination, greatly extends the trial and contributes nothing which cannot be better heard after the evidence is all submitted. It ought not to be allowed at all; and while its admission is not a ground for reversal, it cumbers the case and tends to confusion, for the more the court is led into the intricacies of dramatic craftsmanship, the less likely it is to stand upon the firmer, if more naive, ground of its considered impressions upon its own perusal. We hope that in this class of cases such evidence may in the future be entirely excluded, and the case confined to the actual issues; that is, whether the defendant copied it, so far as the supposed infringement is identical. ...

Decree affirmed.

───────────

Notes and Questions

1. *Nichols* is the source of the famed abstractions test, which courts frequently use to separate a work's ideas from expressions. Interestingly, though, Judge Hand himself did not consider the test definitive. He candidly admitted that drawing the line between idea and expression will always seem arbitrary, but that courts must do it anyway. Why did Hand conclude that the defendant had borrowed only the plaintiff's ideas? If the determination made by Judge Hand seems arbitrary, how might future courts identify ideas in a less arbitrary way?

2. If ideas are generally more abstract than expressions, then copyright protection for abstract things presumably has undesirable consequences for copyright's promotion of creativity. Can you explain how those consequences might arise?

3. *Nichols* cites the earlier Supreme Court case of *Holmes v. Hurst*, 174 U.S. 82 (1898), which in turn cites the English case of *Jefferys v. Boosey*, 10 Eng. Rep. 681 (1854). *Jefferys* contains an interesting explanation for why copyright does not protect ideas:

> The subject of property is the order of words in the author's composition; not the words themselves, they being analogous to the elements of matter, which are not appropriated unless combined, nor the ideas expressed by those words, they existing the mind alone, which is [*sic*] not capable of appropriation.[18]

This statement apparently refers to the traditional notion that property derives from possession. Some things, however, cannot become property because they are physically incapable of being possessed as property. A person can possess air while it is in his lungs, but as soon as he exhales, the air is free for others to use. Moreover, human attempts to regulate the possession of air would likely fail. The state could pass a law prohibiting people from breathing air inhaled by others, but people would still inevitably violate the law unless they wanted to give up breathing.

Is the *Jefferys* court claiming that ideas are analogous to air, and if so, do you find that comparison convincing? After all, the point of copyright is to convert into property the intangible aspects of works that cannot be physically possessed. Why shouldn't ideas be made into property? Or, is there something about the inherent nature of ideas that makes them poor candidates for property?

––––––––––

––––––––––

[18] 10 Eng. Rep. at 702 (1854).

Problems

1. J. K. Rowling is the author of the extremely successful series of books based on the character Harry Potter. Imagine that another author would like to build upon the ideas in J. K. Rowling's *Harry Potter* books. How closely could this author mimic the basic plot and characters of the original books? At what point would the author cross over and begin taking, not just the ideas in the original books, but the protected expression? In answering this question, consider the following possible summaries of the "idea" in the Harry Potter books:

A boy wizard in a wizarding school.

A boy wizard, orphan, in a wizarding school.

A boy wizard orphaned by an evil wizard, in a wizarding school.

A boy wizard orphaned by an evil wizard, with eyeglasses and a scar, in a wizarding school

A boy wizard orphaned by an evil wizard, with eyeglasses and a scar, in a wizarding school, with a plucky group of friends....

At what point, in this series of abstractions (if at all), do we cross over from unprotectable idea to protectable expression? What are the practical implications, for subsequent authors, of defining the "idea" as the first sentence? The last?

Kregos v. Associated Press
937 F.2d 700 (2d Cir. 1991)

Jon O. Newman, Circuit Judge:

The primary issue on this appeal is whether the creator of a baseball pitching form is entitled to a copyright. The appeal requires us to consider the extent to which the copyright law protects a compiler of information. George L. Kregos appeals from the April 30, 1990, judgment of the District Court for the Southern District of New York (Gerard L. Goettel, Judge) dismissing on motion for summary judgment his copyright and trademark claims against the Associated Press ("AP") and Sports Features Syndicate, Inc. ("Sports Features"). We affirm dismissal of the trademark claims, but conclude that Kregos is entitled to a trial on his copyright claim, though the available relief may be extremely limited.

Facts

... Kregos distributes to newspapers a pitching form, discussed in detail below, that displays information concerning the past performances of the opposing pitchers scheduled to start each day's baseball games. The form at issue in this case, first distributed in 1983, is a redesign of an earlier form developed by Kregos in the 1970's. Kregos registered his form with the Copyright Office and obtained a copyright. Though the form, as distributed to subscribing newspapers, includes statistics, the controversy in this case concerns only Kregos' rights to the form without each day's data, in other words, his rights to the particular selection of categories of statistics appearing on his form.

In 1984, AP began publishing a pitching form provided by Sports Features. The AP's 1984 form was virtually identical to Kregos' 1983 form. AP and Sports Features changed their form in 1986 in certain respects, which are discussed in part I(d) below.

Kregos' 1983 form lists four items of information about each day's games—the teams, the starting pitchers, the game time, and the betting odds, and then lists nine items of information about each pitcher's past performance, grouped into three categories. Since there can be no claim of a protectable interest in the categories of information concerning each day's game, we confine our attention to the categories of information concerning the pitchers' past performances. For convenience, we will identify each performance item by a number from 1 to 9 and use that number whenever referring to the same item in someone else's form.

The first category in Kregos' 1983 form, performance during the entire season, comprises two items—won/lost record (1) and earned run average (2). The second category, performance during the entire season against the opposing team at the site of the game, comprises three items—won/lost record (3), innings pitched (4), and earned run average (5). The third category, performance in the last three starts, comprises four items—won/lost record (6), innings pitched (7), earned run average (8), and men on base average (9). This last item is the average total of hits and walks given up by a pitcher per nine innings of pitching.

It is undisputed that prior to Kregos' 1983 form, no form had listed the same nine items collected in his form. It is also undisputed that some but not all of the nine items of information had previously appeared in other forms. In the earlier forms, however, the few items common to Kregos' form were grouped with items different from those in Kregos' form. Siegel's 1978 form contained won/lost record (1) and earned run average for the season (2), but contained no "at site" information (3, 4, 5) and no information for recent starts (6, 7, 8, 9). It contained only two of Kregos' nine items (1, 2). Fratas' 1980 form contained "at site" information for the previous season (differing from Kregos' "at site" information for the current season (3, 4, 5)) and contained no information for recent starts (6, 7, 8, 9). It contained only two of Kregos' nine items (1, 2). Eckstein's 1981 form, the only prior form to contain information for recent starts (using two of the four items in Kregos' form (6, 7)) lacked the third and fourth "recent starts" items (earned run average and men on base average (8, 9)), contained "at site" information only for won/lost record and did not report that data for the current season against the opposing team and lacked earned run average for the season (2). It contained only three of Kregos' nine items (1, 6, 7).

Kregos' item (9), men on base average in recent starts, had not previously appeared anywhere. However, a supplier for the Associated Press Syndicate, Inc. had distributed on a weekly basis the men on base average for every pitcher for the entire season, rather than for the most recent three starts, as in Kregos' form.

District Court decision. The District Court granted summary judgment for the defendants on both Kregos' copyright and trademark claims. On the copyright side of the case, the Court ruled that Kregos lacked a copyrightable interest in his pitching form on three grounds. First, the Court concluded that Kregos' pitching form was insufficiently original in its selection of statistics to warrant a copyright as a compilation. Second, the Court concluded that, in view of the limited space available for displaying pitching forms in newspapers, the possible variations in selections of pitching statistics were so limited that the idea of a pitching form had merged into its expression. Third, the Court ruled that Kregos' pitching form was not entitled to a copyright because of the so-called "blank form" doctrine. On the trademark side of the case, the Court granted summary judgment for the defendants on the ground that Kregos' trademark claims encountered, as a matter of law, a functionality defense.

Discussion

I. Copyright Claim

A. *Copyright for a Compilation of Facts.* [The court's discussion about the originality of Kregos' selection of facts is omitted. The Court concluded that Kregos' selection of facts was original.]

B. *Idea/Expression Merger.* The fundamental copyright principle that only the expression of an idea and not the idea itself is protectable, has produced a corollary maxim that even expression is not protected in those instances where there is only one or so few ways of expressing an idea that protection of the expression would effectively accord protection to the idea itself. ...

Determining when the idea and its expression have merged is a task requiring considerable care: if the merger doctrine is applied too readily, arguably available alternative forms of expression will be precluded; if applied too sparingly, protection will be accorded to ideas. Recognizing this tension, courts have been cautious in applying the merger doctrine to selections of factual information.

In one sense, every compilation of facts can be considered to represent a merger of an idea with its expression. Every compiler of facts has the idea that his particular selection of facts is useful. If the compiler's idea is identified at that low level of abstraction, then the idea would always merge into the compiler's expression of it. Under that approach, there could never be a copyrightable compilation of facts. However, if the idea is formulated at a level of abstraction above the particular selection of facts the compiler has made, then merger of idea and expression is not automatic. Even with an idea formulated at a somewhat high level of abstraction, circumstances might occur where the realistic availability of differing expressions is so drastically limited that the idea can be said to have merged in its expression.

In this case, Judge Goettel understood Kregos' idea to be "to publish an outcome predictive pitching form." In dissent, Judge Sweet contends that Kregos' idea is that the nine statistics he has selected are the most significant ones to consider when attempting to predict the outcome of a baseball game. Unquestionably, if that is the idea for purposes of merger analysis, then merger of that idea and its expression has occurred—by definition.

Though there is room for fair debate as to the identification of the pertinent idea whenever merger analysis is applied to a compilation of facts, we think the "idea" in this case is the one as formulated by Judge Goettel. Kregos has not devised a system that he seeks to withdraw from the public domain by virtue of copyright. He does not present his selection of nine statistics as a method of predicting the outcome of baseball games. His idea is that of "an outcome predictive pitching form" in the general sense that it selects the facts that he thinks newspaper readers should consider in making their own predictions of outcomes. He does not purport to weight the nine statistics, much less provide a method for comparing the aggregate value of one pitcher's statistics against that of the opposing pitcher in order to predict an outcome or even its probability of occurring. He has not devised a system, as had the deviser of a bookkeeping system in *Baker v. Selden*. He has compiled facts, or at least categories of facts.

Though formulating the idea as "an outcome predictive pitching form," Judge Goettel applied the merger doctrine, concluding that the idea of selecting outcome predictive statistics to rate pitching performance was capable of expression in only a very limited number of ways. …

As the various pitching forms in the record indicate, the past performances of baseball pitchers can be measured by a variety of statistics, as can the past performances of race horses. Kregos' selection of categories includes three statistics for the pitcher's current season performance against the day's opponent at the site of the day's game; other charts select "at site" performance against the opponent during the prior season, and some select performance against the opponent over the pitcher's career, both home and away. Some charts include average men on base per nine innings; others do not. The data for most recent starts could include whatever number of games the compiler thought pertinent. These variations alone (and there are others) abundantly indicate that there are a sufficient number of ways of expressing the idea of rating pitchers' performances to preclude a ruling that the idea has merged into its expression.

In reaching this conclusion, we confess to some unease because of the risk that protection of selections of data, or, as in this case, categories of data, have the potential for according protection to ideas. Our concern may be illustrated by an example of a doctor who publishes a list of symptoms that he believes provides a helpful diagnosis of a disease. There might be many combinations of symptoms that others could select for the same purpose, but a substantial question would nonetheless arise as to whether that doctor could obtain a copyright in his list, based on the originality of his selection. If the idea that the doctor is deemed to be expressing is the general idea that the disease in question can be identified by observable symptoms, then the idea might not merge into the doctor's particular expression of that idea by his selection of symptoms. That general idea might remain capable of many other expressions. But it is arguable that the doctor has conceived a more precise idea—namely, the idea that his selection of symptoms is a useful identifier of the disease. That more limited idea can be expressed only by his selection of symptoms, and therefore might be said to have merged into his expression. Thus, as with the idea/expression dichotomy itself, *see Nichols v. Universal Pictures* (Judge Learned Hand's formulation of the "abstractions test"), application of the doctrine of an idea merging with its expression depends on the level of abstraction at which the idea is formulated.

As long as selections of facts involve matters of taste and personal opinion, there is no serious risk that withholding the merger doctrine will extend protection to an idea. ... However, where a selection of data is the first step in an analysis that yields a precise result or even a better-than-average probability of some result, protecting the "expression" of the selection would clearly risk protecting the idea of the analysis.

Kregos' pitching form is part way along the continuum spanning matters of pure taste to matters of predictive analysis. He is doing more than simply saying that he holds the opinion that his nine performance characteristics are the most pertinent. He implies that his selections have some utility in predicting outcomes. On the other hand, he has not gone so far as to provide a system for weighing the combined value of the nine characteristics for each of two opposing pitchers and determining a probability as to which is more likely to win. Like the compilers of horse racing statistics, Kregos has been content to select categories of data that he obviously believes have some predictive power, but has left it to all sports page readers to make their own judgments as to the likely outcomes from the sets of data he has selected. His "idea," for purposes of the merger doctrine, remains the general idea that statistics can be used to assess pitching performance rather than the precise idea that his selection yields a determinable probability of outcome. Since there are various ways of expressing that general idea, the merger doctrine need not be applied to assure that the idea will remain in the public domain.

C. *"Blank Form" Doctrine.* The District Court also ruled that Kregos could not obtain a valid copyright in his pitching form because of the so-called "blank form" doctrine. The doctrine derives from the Supreme Court's decision in *Baker v. Selden, supra.* The Court there denied copyright protection to blank forms contained in a book explaining a system of double-entry bookkeeping. The forms displayed an arrangement of columns and headings that permitted entries for a day, a week, or a month to be recorded on one page or two facing pages. The Court made clear that the author could not obtain copyright protection for an "art" that "might or might not have been patented" and reasoned that since the "art" was available to the public, "the ruled lines and headings of accounts must necessarily be used as incident to it." Then, in a concluding statement that is susceptible to overreading, the Court said that "blank account-books are not the subject of copyright." ...

The regulations of the Copyright Office are careful to preclude copyright registration to:

> Blank forms, such as ... account books, diaries, bank checks, scorecards, address books, report forms, order forms and the like, which are designed for recording information *and do not in themselves convey information;*

37 C.F.R. § 202.1(c) (1990) (emphasis added).

Of course, a form that conveys no information and serves only to provide blank space for recording information contains no expression or selection of information that could possibly warrant copyright protection. *See, e.g., John H. Harland Co. v. Clarke Checks, Inc.,* 711 F.2d 966, 971-72 (11th Cir. 1983) (check stubs). At the same time, it should be equally obvious that a writing that does contain a selection of categories of information worth recording, sufficiently original and creative to deserve a copyright as a compilation of facts, cannot lose that protection simply because the work also contains blank space for recording the information. When the Copyright Office denies a copyright to scorecards or diaries that "do not in themselves convey information," it must be contemplating works with headings so obvious that their selection cannot be said to satisfy even minimal creativity (a baseball scorecard with columns headed "innings" and lines headed "players"; a travel diary with headings for "cities" "hotels," and "restaurants"). Such a work conveys no information, not just because it contains blanks, but because its selection of headings is totally uninformative. On the other hand, if a scorecard or diary contained a group of headings whose selection (or possibly arrangement) displayed cognizable creativity, the author's choice of those headings would convey to users the information that this group of categories was something out of the ordinary. ...

In the pending case, once it is determined that Kregos' selection of categories of statistics displays sufficient creativity to preclude a ruling as a matter of law that it is not a copyrightable compilation of information, that same conclusion precludes rejecting his copyright as a "blank form."

D. *Extent of Protection.* Our ruling that Kregos' copyright claim survives defendants' motion for summary judgment does not, of course, mean that he will necessarily obtain much of a victory. "Even if a work qualifies as a copyrightable compilation, it receives only limited protection. ... [C]opyright protects only the elements that owe their origin to

the compiler—the selection, coordination, and arrangement of facts."
Feist, 111 S.Ct. at 1294. If Kregos prevails at trial on the factual issues
of originality and creativity, he will be entitled to protection only against
infringement of the protectable features of his form. Only the *selection* of
statistics might be entitled to protection. We agree entirely with Judge
Goettel that nothing in Kregos' *arrangement* of the selected statistics
displays the requisite creativity. As to the arrangement, Kregos' form is
surely a "garden-variety" pitching form. The statistics are organized into
the "obvious" arrangement of columns, and the form follows the pattern
of most other forms: the statistics are organized into three groups, first
the statistics about each pitcher's performance for the season, then the
statistics about the pitcher's performance against the day's opponent,
and finally the statistics concerning the pitcher's recent starts.

Even as to the *selection* of statistics, if Kregos establishes entitlement to protection, he will prevail only against other forms that can be
said to copy his selection. That would appear to be true of the AP's 1984
form, which, as Judge Goettel noted, is "identical in virtually every sense
to plaintiff's form." Whether it is also true of the AP's current form, revised in 1986, is far less certain. That form contains six of Kregos' nine
items (1, 2, 6, 7, 8, 9). It also includes four items that Kregos does not
have. Three of these items concern performance against the day's opposing team—won-lost record, innings pitched, and earned run average;
though these three statistics appear on Kregos' form, the AP's 1986 form
shows data for the current season both home and away, whereas Kregos'
form shows data for the pitcher's current season at the site of that day's
game. The fourth item on the AP's 1986 form and not on Kregos' form
shows the team's record in games started by that day's pitcher during
the season.

The reason for doubting that the AP's 1986 form infringes Kregos'
form arises from the same consideration that supports Kregos' claim to a
copyright. Kregos can obtain a copyright by displaying the requisite creativity in his selection of statistics. But if someone else displays the requisite creativity by making a selection that differs in more than a trivial
degree, Kregos cannot complain. Kregos contends that the AP's 1986
form makes insignificant changes from its 1984 form. But Kregos cannot
have it both ways. If his decision to select, in the category of performance
against the opposing team, statistics for the pitcher's current season at
the site of today's game displays, in combination with his other selections, enough creativity to merit copyright protection, then a competitor's decision to select in that same category performance statistics for
the pitcher's season performance both home and away may well insulate
the competitor from a claim of infringement. Thus, though issues remain
to be explored before any determination can be made, it may well be that
Kregos will have a valid claim only as to the AP's 1984 form.

[The Court's analysis of the trademark issues is omitted.]

Conclusion

The judgment of the District Court is reversed and remanded with respect to the copyright claim, and affirmed with respect to the trade-mark claims.

[The dissenting opinion of Judge Sweet is omitted.]

Notes and Questions

1.   Copyright gives copyright holders the power to stop others from making copies of copyrighted works. This does not mean, however, that all copying is prohibited. As *Nichols* and *Baker* showed, it is always per-missible to borrow a work's ideas, and ensuring this sometimes means denying copyright to entire works. The idea/expression dichotomy is one of the doctrines that determines whether borrowing from a copyrighted work constitutes infringement. If the defendant has copied expression, a finding of infringement will likely follow. But, if the defendant has cop-ied only the plaintiff's ideas, no liability exists. In short, the idea/expression dichotomy greatly influences the value of copyright. If most facets of a works are expression, then relatively little borrowing can take place without the copyright holder's permission. By contrast, if those facets are ideas, then borrowing will generally be permissible.

2.   It is important to think through the practical and normative con-sequences associated with different constructions of the idea/expression dichotomy. For example, where on Hand's levels of abstractions would a plaintiff draw the line between idea and expression, and how would a plaintiff respond to a defendant's use of the merger doctrine to defeat copyright? If you were a judge, how would you resolve disagreements between plaintiffs and defendants over the application of the idea/expression dichotomy?

3.   What do you think of the *Kregos* court's identification of the idea behind the pitching form? Was the court correct to identify a single idea, or could a work express multiple ideas? Even if we accept the court's identification of idea, what do you think about its merger analysis, par-ticularly its conclusion that there are sufficient alternate expressions of the idea?

4.   Let's take a closer look at *Kregos*' interpretation of the blank forms doctrine. The court understood the doctrine as another way of say-ing that copyright requires originality. Since Kregos' form exhibited orig-inality, it fell outside the blank forms doctrine. This explanation of the blank forms doctrine leads to interesting questions about *Baker v. Sel-den*. Remember, *Baker* reached the conclusion that copyright did not protect the bookkeeping forms in question because such protection would lead to copyright in the underlying system of bookkeeping itself. *Kregos* appears to be saying that *Baker*'s denial of copyright rested not on the idea/expression dichotomy, but on a lack of originality in Selden's bookkeeping forms. Is this a correct understanding of *Baker v. Selden*, and does it mean that the idea/expression dichotomy is simply another

manifestation of copyright's requirement of originality? Do you think it is important to have doctrines like the idea/expression dichotomy that limit the scope of copyright without regard to originality?

5. *Kregos* concludes by noting that the value of the plaintiff's copyright may be small because future competitors will be able to avoid infringement by making minor changes in their works. Is it socially beneficial to hand out copyrights of such small value?

Problem

Your client designs, prints, and sells various forms. One of her best sellers is this form, which she sells to lawn care companies for keeping track of labor and supplies:

Work Site Report

Employee Names: _____

Location Worked: _____

Date: _____ Day of Week: _____

Hours: _____ Wage: _____ Total Due: _____

Supplies used (enter amount, if any):   For Office Use Only:

    Fertilizer: _____ Cost: _____ Total: _____

    Weed Killer: _____ Cost: _____ Total: _____

    Moss Killer: _____ Cost: _____ Total: _____

    Grass Seed: _____ Cost: _____ Total: _____

    Insecticides: _____ Cost: _____ Total: _____

    Bark Mulch: _____ Cost: _____ Total: _____

Supervisor Signature: _____ Total Supplies: _____

Your client, who designed this form independently several years ago, ordinarily prints the form in pads of 100 sheets. Lawn care companies give these forms to crew supervisors, who fill them out at job sites. The supervisor returns completed forms to the main office, where they are used to generate bills to customers.

Recently, your client's sales have decreased because competitors have begun selling the following forms:

Work Site Report

Employee Names: _____

Location Worked: _____

Date: _____ Day of Week: _____

Hours: _____ Wage: _____ Total Due: _____

Supplies used (enter amount, if any):   For Office Use Only:

Fertilizer:	_____	Cost: ____ Total: ____
Weed Killer:	_____	Cost: ____ Total: ____
Moss Killer:	_____	Cost: ____ Total: ____
Grass Seed:	_____	Cost: ____ Total: ____
Insecticides:	_____	Cost: ____ Total: ____
Bark Mulch:	_____	Cost: ____ Total: ____

Supervisor Signature: _____   Total Supplies: _____

Lawn Care Work Site Report

Employee Names: _____

Location Worked: _____

Date: _____ Day of Week: _____

Hours: _____ Wage: _____ Total Due: _____

Supplies used (enter amount, if any):   *For Office Use Only*:

Weed Killer:	_____	Cost: _____ Total: ____
Crabgrass Killer:	_____	Cost: _____ Total: ____
Moss Killer:	_____	Cost: _____ Total: ____
Fertilizer:	_____	Cost: _____ Total: ____
Rye Seed:	_____	Cost: _____ Total: ____
Fescue Seed:	_____	Cost: _____ Total: ____
Other Seed (list type):	_____	Cost: _____ Total: ____
Insecticide (list types):	_____	Cost: _____ Total: ____
Bark Mulch:	_____	Cost: _____ Total: ____

Supervisor Signature: _____   Total Supplies: _____

Your client believes that her competitors created their forms by copying from hers. Assuming she is right, have they copied anything protected by copyright?

The next two cases provide examples of courts applying the idea/expression dichotomy in the modern, and very important, context of computer software. The first, *Apple Computer v. Franklin Computer Corporation*, is one of the leading cases that confirmed the broad inclusion of computer software within copyrightable subject matter. The second, *Lotus Development Corporation v. Borland International,* explores the limits of copyright protection for software. As you read these cases, think again about the challenges of identifying a work's ideas and the possibility of merger. Are these challenges meaningfully different when faced in the context of technology or other utilitarian works, or do they simply repeat the themes raised in the cases above?

Apple Computer v. Franklin Computer Corp.
714 F.2d 1240 (3d Cir. 1983)

SLOVITER, Circuit Judge.

I. INTRODUCTION

Apple Computer, Inc. appeals from the district court's denial of a motion to preliminarily enjoin Franklin Computer Corp. from infringing the copyrights Apple holds on fourteen computer programs. ...

In this case the district court denied the preliminary injunction, *inter alia,* because it had "some doubt as to the copyrightability of the programs." ... Because we conclude that the district court proceeded under an erroneous view of the applicable law, we reverse the denial of the preliminary injunction and remand.

II. FACTS AND PROCEDURAL HISTORY

Apple, one of the computer industry leaders, manufactures and markets personal computers (microcomputers), related peripheral equipment such as disk drives (peripherals), and computer programs (software). ...

Franklin, the defendant below, manufactures and sells the ACE 100 personal computer and at the time of the hearing employed about 75 people and had sold fewer than 1,000 computers. The ACE 100 was designed to be "Apple compatible," so that peripheral equipment and software developed for use with the Apple II computer could be used in conjunction with the ACE 100. Franklin's copying of Apple's operating system computer programs in an effort to achieve such compatibility precipitated this suit.

Like all computers both the Apple II and ACE 100 have a central processing unit (CPU) which is the integrated circuit that executes programs. In lay terms, the CPU does the work it is instructed to do. Those instructions are contained on computer programs.

There are three levels of computer language in which computer programs may be written. High level language, such as the commonly used

BASIC or FORTRAN, uses English words and symbols, and is relatively easy to learn and understand (e.g., "GO TO 40" tells the computer to skip intervening steps and go to the step at line 40). A somewhat lower level language is assembly language, which consists of alphanumeric labels (e.g., "ADC" means "add with carry"). Statements in high level language, and apparently also statements in assembly language, are referred to as written in "source code." The third, or lowest level computer language, is machine language, a binary language using two symbols, 0 and 1, to indicate an open or closed switch (e.g., "01101001" means, to the Apple, add two numbers and save the result). Statements in machine language are referred to as written in "object code."

The CPU can only follow instructions written in object code. However, programs are usually written in source code which is more intelligible to humans. Programs written in source code can be converted or translated by a "compiler" program into object code for use by the computer. Programs are generally distributed only in their object code version stored on a memory device.

A computer program can be stored or fixed on a variety of memory devices, two of which are of particular relevance for this case. The ROM (Read Only Memory) is an internal permanent memory device consisting of a semi-conductor "chip" which is incorporated into the circuitry of the computer. A program in object code is embedded on a ROM before it is incorporated in the computer. Information stored on a ROM can only be read, not erased or rewritten. The ACE 100 apparently contains EPROMS (Erasable Programmable Read Only Memory) on which the stored information can be erased and the chip reprogrammed, but the district court found that for purposes of this proceeding, the difference between ROMs and EPROMs is inconsequential. The other device used for storing the programs at issue is a diskette or "floppy disk," an auxiliary memory device consisting of a flexible magnetic disk resembling a phonograph record, which can be inserted into the computer and from which data or instructions can be read.

Computer programs can be categorized by function as either application programs or operating system programs. Application programs usually perform a specific task for the computer user, such as word processing, checkbook balancing, or playing a game. In contrast, operating system programs generally manage the internal functions of the computer or facilitate use of application programs. The parties agree that the fourteen computer programs at issue in this suit are operating system programs.

Apple filed suit in the United States District Court for the Eastern District of Pennsylvania ... alleging that Franklin was liable for copyright infringement of the fourteen computer programs, patent infringement, unfair competition, and misappropriation. Franklin's answer in respect to the copyright counts included the affirmative defense that the programs contained no copyrightable subject matter. ...

Franklin did not dispute that it copied the Apple programs. Its witness admitted copying each of the works in suit from the Apple programs. Its factual defense was directed to its contention that it was not feasible for Franklin to write its own operating system programs. David McWherter, now Franklin's vice-president of engineering, testified he spent 30-40 hours in November 1981 making a study to determine if it was feasible for Franklin to write its own Autostart ROM program and concluded it was not because "there were just too many entry points in relationship to the number of instructions in the program." Entry points at specific locations in the program can be used by programmers to mesh their application programs with the operating system program. McWherter concluded that use of the identical signals was necessary in order to ensure 100% compatibility with application programs created to run on the Apple computer. He admitted that he never attempted to rewrite Autostart ROM and conceded that some of the works in suit (i.e. Copy, Copy A, Master Create, and Hello) probably could have been rewritten by Franklin. Franklin made no attempt to rewrite any of the programs prior to the lawsuit except for Copy, although McWherter testified that Franklin was "in the process of redesigning" some of the Apple programs and that "[w]e had a fair degree of certainty that that would probably work." Apple introduced evidence that Franklin could have rewritten programs, including the Autostart ROM program, and that there are in existence operating programs written by third parties which are compatible with Apple II. ...

IV. DISCUSSION

A. Copyrightability of a Computer Program Expressed in Object Code

Certain statements by the district court suggest that programs expressed in object code, as distinguished from source code, may not be the proper subject of copyright. We find no basis in the statute for any such concern. ...

In 1976, after considerable study, Congress enacted a new copyright law to replace that which had governed since 1909. Under the law, two primary requirements must be satisfied in order for a work to constitute copyrightable subject matter—it must be an "original wor[k] of authorship" and must be "fixed in [a] tangible medium of expression."

Although section 102(a) does not expressly list computer programs as works of authorship, the legislative history suggests that programs were considered copyrightable as literary works. *See* H.R. Rep. No. 1476, 94th Cong., 2d Sess. 54, *reprinted in* 1976 U.S. Code Cong. & Ad. News 5659, 5667 ("'literary works' ... includes ... computer programs"). ...

We considered the issue of copyright protection for a computer program in *Williams Electronics, Inc. v. Artic International, Inc.,* and concluded that "the copyrightability of computer programs is firmly established after the 1980 amendment to the Copyright Act." At issue in *Williams* were not only two audiovisual copyrights to the "attract" and "play" modes of a video game, but also the computer program which was expressed in object code embodied in ROM and which controlled the sights and sounds of the game. Defendant there had argued "that when the issue is the copyright on a computer program, a distinction must be drawn between the 'source code' version of a computer program, which ... can be afforded copyright protection, and the 'object code' stage, which ... cannot be so protected," an argument we rejected.

Under the statute, copyright extends to works in any tangible means of expression "*from which they can be perceived,* reproduced, or otherwise communicated, either directly or *with the aid of a machine or device.*" 17 U.S.C. § 102(a). (emphasis added). Further, the definition of "computer program" adopted by Congress in the 1980 amendments is "sets of statements or instructions to be used *directly or indirectly* in a computer in order to bring about a certain result." 17 U.S.C. § 101 (emphasis added). As source code instructions must be translated into object code before the computer can act upon them, only instructions expressed in object code can be used "directly" by the computer. This definition was adopted following the CONTU Report in which the majority clearly took the position that object codes are proper subjects of copyright. *See* CONTU Report at 21. The majority's conclusion was reached although confronted by a dissent based upon the theory that the "machine-control phase" of a program is not directed at a human audience. *See* CONTU Report at 28-30 (dissent of Commissioner Hersey).[19]

The district court also expressed uncertainty as to whether a computer program in object code could be classified as a "literary work."[20] However, the category of "literary works", one of the seven copyrightable categories, is not confined to literature in the nature of Hemingway's *For Whom the Bell Tolls*. The definition of "literary works" in section 101 includes expression not only in words but also "numbers, or other ... numerical symbols or indicia," thereby expanding the common usage of "literary works." Thus a computer program, whether in object code or source code, is a "literary work" and is protected from unauthorized copying, whether from its object or source code version.

B. Copyrightability of a Computer Program Embedded on a ROM

Just as the district court's suggestion of a distinction between source code and object code was rejected by our opinion in *Williams* issued three days after the district court opinion, so also was its suggestion that embodiment of a computer program on a ROM, as distinguished from in a traditional writing, detracts from its copyrightability. In *Williams* we rejected the argument that "a computer program is not infringed when

---

[19] Editors' note: CONTU stands for National Commission on New Technological Uses of Copyrighted Works.

[20] [Footnote 7] The district court stated that a programmer working directly in object code appears to think more as a mathematician or engineer, that the process of constructing a chip is less a work of authorship than the product of engineering knowledge, and that it may be more apt to describe an encoded ROM as a pictorial three-dimensional object than as a literary work. The district court's remarks relied in part on a quotation about "microcode." Apple introduced testimony that none of the works in suit contain "microcode." Moreover, Apple does not seek to protect the ROM's architecture but only the program encoded upon it.

the program is loaded into electronic memory devices (ROMs) and used to control the activity of machines." Defendant there had argued that there can be no copyright protection for the ROMs because they are utilitarian objects or machine parts. We held that the statutory requirement of "fixation", the manner in which the issue arises, is satisfied through the embodiment of the expression in the ROM devices.

C. Copyrightability of Computer Operating System Programs

We turn to the heart of Franklin's position on appeal which is that computer operating system programs, as distinguished from application programs, are not the proper subject of copyright "regardless of the language or medium in which they are fixed." Brief of Appellee at 15 (emphasis deleted). Apple suggests that this issue too is foreclosed by our *Williams* decision because some portion of the program at issue there was in effect an operating system program. Franklin is correct that this was not an issue raised by the parties in *Williams* and it was not considered by the court. Thus we consider it as a matter of first impression.

Franklin contends that operating system programs are *per se* excluded from copyright protection under the express terms of section 102(b) of the Copyright Act, and under the precedent and underlying principles of *Baker v. Selden*. These separate grounds have substantial analytic overlap. ...

Franklin reads *Baker v. Selden* as "stand[ing] for several fundamental principles, each presenting ... an insuperable obstacle to the copyrightability of Apple's operating systems." It states:

> *First, Baker* teaches that use of a system itself does not infringe a copyright on the description of the system. *Second, Baker* enunciates the rule that copyright does not extend to purely utilitarian works. *Finally, Baker* emphasizes that the copyright laws may not be used to obtain and hold a monopoly over an idea. In so doing, *Baker* highlights the principal difference between the copyright and patent laws—a difference that is highly pertinent in this case.

Brief of Appellee at 22.

Section 102(b) of the Copyright Act, the other ground on which Franklin relies, appeared first in the 1976 version, long after the decision in *Baker v. Selden*. It provides:

> In no case does copyright protection for an original work of authorship extend to any idea, procedure, process, system, method of operation, concept, principle, or discovery, regardless of the form in which it is described, explained, illustrated, or embodied in such work.

It is apparent that section 102(b) codifies a substantial part of the holding and dictum of *Baker v. Selden*.

We turn to consider the two principal points of Franklin's argument.

1. *"Process", "System" or "Method of Operation"*

Franklin argues that an operating system program is either a "process", "system", or "method of operation" and hence uncopyrightable. Franklin correctly notes that underlying section 102(b) and many of the statements for which *Baker v. Selden* is cited is the distinction which must be made between property subject to the patent law, which protects discoveries, and that subject to copyright law, which protects the writings describing such discoveries. However, Franklin's argument misapplies that distinction in this case. Apple does not seek to copyright the method which instructs the computer to perform its operating functions but only the instructions themselves. The method would be protected, if at all, by the patent law, an issue as yet unresolved.

Franklin's attack on operating system programs as "methods" or "processes" seems inconsistent with its concession that application programs are an appropriate subject of copyright. Both types of programs instruct the computer to do something. Therefore, it should make no difference for purposes of section 102(b) whether these instructions tell the computer to help prepare an income tax return (the task of an application program) or to translate a high level language program from source code into its binary language object code form (the task of an operating system program such as "Applesoft"). Since it is only the instructions which are protected, a "process" is no more involved because the instructions in an operating system program may be used to activate the operation of the computer than it would be if instructions were written in ordinary English in a manual which described the necessary steps to activate an intricate complicated machine. There is, therefore, no reason to afford any less copyright protection to the instructions in an operating system program than to the instructions in an application program.

Franklin's argument, receptively treated by the district court, that an operating system program is part of a machine mistakenly focuses on the physical characteristics of the instructions. But the medium is not the message. We have already considered and rejected aspects of this contention in the discussion of object code and ROM. The mere fact that the operating system program may be etched on a ROM does not make the program either a machine, part of a machine or its equivalent. Furthermore, as one of Franklin's witnesses testified, an operating system does not have to be permanently in the machine in ROM, but it may be on some other medium, such as a diskette or magnetic tape, where it could be readily transferred into the temporary memory space of the computer. In fact, some of the operating systems at issue were on diskette. As the CONTU majority stated,

> Programs should no more be considered machine parts than videotapes should be considered parts of projectors or phonorecords parts of sound reproduction equipment.... That the words of a program are used ultimately in the implementation of a process should in no way affect their copyrightability.

CONTU Report at 21.

Franklin also argues that the operating systems cannot be copyrighted because they are "purely utilitarian works" and that Apple is seeking to block the use of the art embodied in its operating systems. This argument stems from the following dictum in *Baker v. Selden:*

> The very object of publishing a book on science or the useful arts is to communicate to the world the useful knowledge which it contains. But this object would be frustrated if the knowledge could not be used without incurring the guilt of piracy of the book. And where the art it teaches cannot be used without employing the methods and diagrams used to illustrate the book, or such as are similar to them, such methods and diagrams are to be considered as necessary incidents to the art, and given therewith to the public; not given for the purpose of publication in other works explanatory of the art, but for the purpose of practical application.

... Although a literal construction of this language could support Franklin's reading that precludes copyrightability if the copyright work is put to a utilitarian use, that interpretation has been rejected by a later Supreme Court decision. In *Mazer v. Stein,*[21] 347 U.S. 201 (1954), the Court stated: "We find nothing in the copyright statute to support the argument that the intended use or use in industry of an article eligible for copyright bars or invalidates its registration. We do not read such a limitation into the copyright law." The CONTU majority also rejected the expansive view some courts have given *Baker v. Selden,* and stated, "That the words of a program are used ultimately in the implementation of a process should in no way affect their copyrightability." It referred to "copyright practice past and present, which recognizes copyright protection for a work of authorship regardless of the uses to which it may be put." *Id.* The Commission continued: "The copyright status of the written rules for a game *or a system for the operation of a machine* is unaffected by the fact that those rules direct the actions of those who play the game or *carry out the process.*" *Id.* (emphasis added). As we previously noted, we can consider the CONTU Report as accepted by Congress since Congress wrote into the law the majority's recommendations almost verbatim.

Perhaps the most convincing item leading us to reject Franklin's argument is that the statutory definition of a computer program as a set of instructions to be used in a computer in order to bring about a certain result makes no distinction between application programs and operating programs. Franklin can point to no decision which adopts the distinction it seeks to make. In the one other reported case to have considered it, the court reached the same conclusion which we do, i.e. that an operating system program is not *per se* precluded from copyright. ...

---

[21] Editors' note: You will soon read *Mazer v. Stein* in the materials on the useful article doctrine.

2. *Idea/Expression Dichotomy*

Franklin's other challenge to copyright of operating system programs relies on the line which is drawn between ideas and their expression. *Baker v. Selden* remains a benchmark in the law of copyright for the reading given it in *Mazer v. Stein,* where the Court stated, "Unlike a patent, a copyright gives no exclusive right to the art disclosed; protection is given only to the expression of the idea—not the idea itself."

The expression/idea dichotomy is now expressly recognized in section 102(b) which precludes copyright for "any idea." This provision was not intended to enlarge or contract the scope of copyright protection but "to restate ... that the basic dichotomy between expression and idea remains unchanged." H.R. Rep. No. 1476, *supra,* at 57, *reprinted in* 1976 U.S. Code Cong. & Ad. News at 5670. The legislative history indicates that section 102(b) was intended "to make clear that the expression adopted by the programmer is the copyrightable element in a computer program, and that the actual processes or methods embodied in the program are not within the scope of the copyright law." *Id.*

Many of the courts which have sought to draw the line between an idea and expression have found difficulty in articulating where it falls. We believe that in the context before us, a program for an operating system, the line must be a pragmatic one, which also keeps in consideration "the preservation of the balance between competition and protection reflected in the patent and copyright laws." As we stated in *Franklin Mint Corp. v. National Wildlife Art Exchange, Inc.,* 575 F.2d 62, 64 (3d Cir.), *cert. denied,* 439 U.S. 880 (1978), "Unlike a patent, a copyright protects originality rather than novelty or invention." In that opinion, we quoted approvingly the following passage from *Dymow v. Bolton,* 11 F.2d 690, 691 (2d Cir. 1926):

> Just as a patent affords protection only to the means of reducing an inventive idea to practice, so the copyright law protects the means of expressing an idea; and it is as near the whole truth as generalization can usually reach that, *if the same idea can be expressed in a plurality of totally different manners, a plurality of copyrights may result,* and no infringement will exist.

(emphasis added).

We adopt the suggestion in the above language and thus focus on whether the idea is capable of various modes of expression. If other programs can be written or created which perform the same function as an Apple's operating system program, then that program is an expression of the idea and hence copyrightable. In essence, this inquiry is no different than that made to determine whether the expression and idea have merged, which has been stated to occur where there are no or few other ways of expressing a particular idea.

The district court made no findings as to whether some or all of Apple's operating programs represent the only means of expression of the idea underlying them. Although there seems to be a concession by

Franklin that at least some of the programs can be rewritten, we do not believe that the record on that issue is so clear that it can be decided at the appellate level. Therefore, if the issue is pressed on remand, the necessary finding can be made at that time.

Franklin claims that whether or not the programs can be rewritten, there are a limited "number of ways to arrange operating systems to enable a computer to run the vast body of Apple-compatible software," Brief of Appellee at 20. This claim has no pertinence to either the idea/expression dichotomy or merger. The idea which may merge with the expression, thus making the copyright unavailable, is the idea which is the subject of the expression. The idea of one of the operating system programs is, for example, how to translate source code into object code. If other methods of expressing that idea are not foreclosed as a practical matter, then there is no merger. Franklin may wish to achieve total compatibility with independently developed application programs written for the Apple II, but that is a commercial and competitive objective which does not enter into the somewhat metaphysical issue of whether particular ideas and expressions have merged.

In summary, Franklin's contentions that operating system programs are *per se* not copyrightable is unpersuasive. The other courts before whom this issue has been raised have rejected the distinction. Neither the CONTU majority nor Congress made a distinction between operating and application programs. We believe that the 1980 amendments reflect Congress' receptivity to new technology and its desire to encourage, through the copyright laws, continued imagination and creativity in computer programming. Since we believe that the district court's decision on the preliminary injunction was, to a large part, influenced by an erroneous view of the availability of copyright for operating system programs and unnecessary concerns about object code and ROMs, we must reverse the denial of the preliminary injunction and remand for reconsideration. ...

V.

For the reasons set forth in this opinion, we will reverse the denial of the preliminary injunction and remand to the district court for further proceedings in accordance herewith.

Notes and Questions

1. *Apple v. Franklin* explained that, according to the legislative history of the Copyright Act, Congress considered computer programs copyrightable, and that programs, whether in source or object code, are "literary works." Examination of the Copyright Act shows that literary works are one of many enumerated, but non-exhaustive, categories of original works of authorship. That having been said, the mere labeling of computer programs as literary works does not necessarily give computer

programs the originality that supports copyright. Did the *Apple v. Franklin* court satisfactorily explain why computer programs are original, and if not, can you?

2. It may be helpful to think about *Apple v. Franklin* as a case that accepted some dichotomies while rejecting others. For example, the court rejected distinctions between software in the form source code and object code, and software embodied as source code and on ROMs. By contrast, the court accepted distinctions between the method of operating Apple computers and the instructions that implemented that method, and between the ideas of the Apple programs and their expression. Is the court consistent in its acceptance and rejection of these dichotomies?

3. The defendant Franklin claimed that the idea expressed in the software at issue was the particular functioning of an Apple computer. The court disagreed, finding that the idea was "how to translate source code into object code." Was the court correct, and if so, why? Equally important, what was the practical significance of this definition of idea, particularly in terms of the kinds of competition that would exist in the computer industry?

Lotus Development Corp. v. Borland Int'l
49 F.3d 807 (1st Cir. 1995)

STAHL, Circuit Judge.

This appeal requires us to decide whether a computer menu command hierarchy is copyrightable subject matter. In particular, we must decide whether, as the district court held, plaintiff-appellee Lotus Development Corporation's copyright in Lotus 1-2-3, a computer spreadsheet program, was infringed by defendant-appellant Borland International, Inc., when Borland copied the Lotus 1-2-3 menu command hierarchy into its Quattro and Quattro Pro computer spreadsheet programs.

I. Background

Lotus 1-2-3 is a spreadsheet program that enables users to perform accounting functions electronically on a computer. Users manipulate and control the program via a series of menu commands, such as "Copy," "Print," and "Quit." Users choose commands either by highlighting them on the screen or by typing their first letter. In all, Lotus 1-2-3 has 469 commands arranged into more than 50 menus and submenus.

Lotus 1-2-3, like many computer programs, allows users to write what are called "macros." By writing a macro, a user can designate a series of command choices with a single macro keystroke. Then, to execute that series of commands in multiple parts of the spreadsheet, rather than typing the whole series each time, the user only needs to type the single pre-programmed macro keystroke, causing the program to recall and perform the designated series of commands automatically. Thus,

Lotus 1-2-3 macros shorten the time needed to set up and operate the program.

Borland released its first Quattro program to the public in 1987, after Borland's engineers had labored over its development for nearly three years. Borland's objective was to develop a spreadsheet program far superior to existing programs, including Lotus 1-2-3. In Borland's words, "[f]rom the time of its initial release ... Quattro included enormous innovations over competing spreadsheet products."

The district court found, and Borland does not now contest, that Borland included in its Quattro and Quattro Pro version 1.0 programs "a *virtually identical* copy of the entire 1-2-3 menu tree." In so doing, Borland did not copy any of Lotus's underlying computer code; it copied only the words and structure of Lotus's menu command hierarchy. Borland included the Lotus menu command hierarchy in its programs to make them compatible with Lotus 1-2-3 so that spreadsheet users who were already familiar with Lotus 1-2-3 would be able to switch to the Borland programs without having to learn new commands or rewrite their Lotus macros.

In its Quattro and Quattro Pro version 1.0 programs, Borland achieved compatibility with Lotus 1-2-3 by offering its users an alternate user interface, the "Lotus Emulation Interface." By activating the Emulation Interface, Borland users would see the Lotus menu commands on their screens and could interact with Quattro or Quattro Pro as if using Lotus 1-2-3, albeit with a slightly different looking screen and with many Borland options not available on Lotus 1-2-3. In effect, Borland allowed users to choose how they wanted to communicate with Borland's spreadsheet programs: either by using menu commands designed by Borland, or by using the commands and command structure used in Lotus 1-2-3 augmented by Borland-added commands. ...

II. Discussion

On appeal, Borland does not dispute that it factually copied the words and arrangement of the Lotus menu command hierarchy. Rather, Borland argues that it "lawfully copied the unprotectable menus of Lotus 1-2-3." Borland contends that the Lotus menu command hierarchy is not copyrightable because it is a system, method of operation, process, or procedure foreclosed from protection by 17 U.S.C. § 102(b). Borland also raises a number of affirmative defenses. ...

B.   *Matter of First Impression*

Whether a computer menu command hierarchy constitutes copyrightable subject matter is a matter of first impression in this court. While some other courts appear to have touched on it briefly in dicta, we know of no cases that deal with the copyrightability of a menu command hierarchy standing on its own (i.e., without other elements of the user interface, such as screen displays, in issue). Thus we are navigating in uncharted waters.

Borland vigorously argues, however, that the Supreme Court charted our course more than 100 years ago when it decided *Baker v. Selden.* In *Baker v. Selden,* the Court held that Selden's copyright over the textbook in which he explained his new way to do accounting did not grant him a monopoly on the use of his accounting system.

The facts of *Baker v. Selden,* and even the arguments advanced by the parties in that case, are identical to those in this case. The only difference is that the "user interface" of Selden's system was implemented by pen and paper rather than by computer. To demonstrate that *Baker v. Selden* and this appeal both involve accounting systems, Borland even supplied this court with a video that, with special effects, shows Selden's paper forms "melting" into a computer screen and transforming into Lotus 1-2-3.

We do not think that *Baker v. Selden* is nearly as analogous to this appeal as Borland claims. Of course, Lotus 1-2-3 is a computer spreadsheet, and as such its grid of horizontal rows and vertical columns certainly resembles an accounting ledger or any other paper spreadsheet. Those grids, however, are not at issue in this appeal for, unlike Selden, Lotus does not claim to have a monopoly over its accounting system. Rather, this appeal involves Lotus's monopoly over the commands it uses to operate the computer. Accordingly, this appeal is not, as Borland contends, "identical" to *Baker v. Selden.* ...

D. The Lotus Menu Command Hierarchy: A "Method of Operation"

Borland argues that the Lotus menu command hierarchy is uncopyrightable because it is a system, method of operation, process, or procedure foreclosed from copyright protection by 17 U.S.C. § 102(b). Section 102(b) states: "In no case does copyright protection for an original work of authorship extend to any idea, procedure, process, system, method of operation, concept, principle, or discovery, regardless of the form in which it is described, explained, illustrated, or embodied in such work." Because we conclude that the Lotus menu command hierarchy is a method of operation, we do not consider whether it could also be a system, process, or procedure.

We think that "method of operation," as that term is used in § 102(b) refers to the means by which a person operates something, whether it be a car, a food processor, or a computer. Thus a text describing how to operate something would not extend copyright protection to the method of operation itself; other people would be free to employ that method and to describe it in their own words. Similarly, if a new method of operation is used rather than described, other people would still be free to employ or describe that method.

We hold that the Lotus menu command hierarchy is an uncopyrightable "method of operation." The Lotus menu command hierarchy provides the means by which users control and operate Lotus 1-2-3. If users wish to copy material, for example, they use the "Copy" command. If users wish to print material, they use the "Print" command. Users must use the command terms to tell the computer what to do. Without the menu command hierarchy, users would not be able to access and control, or indeed make use of, Lotus 1-2-3's functional capabilities.

The Lotus menu command hierarchy does not merely explain and present Lotus 1-2-3's functional capabilities to the user; it also serves as the method by which the program is operated and controlled. The Lotus menu command hierarchy is different from the Lotus long prompts, for the long prompts are not necessary to the operation of the program; users could operate Lotus 1-2-3 even if there were no long prompts. The Lotus menu command hierarchy is also different from the Lotus screen displays, for users need not "use" any expressive aspects of the screen displays in order to operate Lotus 1-2-3; because the way the screens look has little bearing on how users control the program, the screen displays are not part of Lotus 1-2-3's "method of operation." The Lotus menu command hierarchy is also different from the underlying computer code, because while code is necessary for the program to work, its precise formulation is not. In other words, to offer the same capabilities as Lotus 1-2-3, Borland did not have to copy Lotus's underlying code (and indeed it did not); to allow users to operate its programs in substantially the same way, however, Borland had to copy the Lotus menu command hierarchy. Thus the Lotus 1-2-3 code is not a uncopyrightable "method of operation."

The district court held that the Lotus menu command hierarchy, with its specific choice and arrangement of command terms, constituted an "expression" of the "idea" of operating a computer program with commands arranged hierarchically into menus and submenus. Under the district court's reasoning, Lotus's decision to employ hierarchically arranged command terms to operate its program could not foreclose its competitors from also employing hierarchically arranged command terms to operate their programs, but it did foreclose them from employing the specific command terms and arrangement that Lotus had used. In effect, the district court limited Lotus 1-2-3's "method of operation" to an abstraction.

Accepting the district court's finding that the Lotus developers made some expressive choices in choosing and arranging the Lotus command terms, we nonetheless hold that that expression is not copyrightable because it is part of Lotus 1-2-3's "method of operation." We do not think that "methods of operation" are limited to abstractions; rather, they are the means by which a user operates something. If specific words are essential to operating something, then they are part of a "method of operation" and, as such, are unprotectable. This is so whether they must be highlighted, typed in, or even spoken, as computer programs no doubt will soon be controlled by spoken words.

The fact that Lotus developers could have designed the Lotus menu command hierarchy differently is immaterial to the question of whether it is a "method of operation." In other words, our initial inquiry is not whether the Lotus menu command hierarchy incorporates any expression. Rather, our initial inquiry is whether the Lotus menu command hierarchy is a "method of operation." Concluding, as we do, that users operate Lotus 1-2-3 by using the Lotus menu command hierarchy, and that the entire Lotus menu command hierarchy is essential to operating Lotus 1-2-3, we do not inquire further whether that method of operation could have been designed differently. The "expressive" choices of what to name the command terms and how to arrange them do not magically change the uncopyrightable menu command hierarchy into copyrightable subject matter.

Our holding that "methods of operation" are not limited to mere abstractions is bolstered by *Baker v. Selden.* In *Baker,* the Supreme Court explained that the teachings of science and the rules and methods of useful art have their final end in application and use; and this application and use are what the public derive from the publication of a book which teaches them.... Lotus wrote its menu command hierarchy so that people could learn it and use it. Accordingly, it falls squarely within the prohibition on copyright protection established in *Baker v. Selden* and codified by Congress in § 102(b).

In many ways, the Lotus menu command hierarchy is like the buttons used to control, say, a video cassette recorder ("VCR"). A VCR is a machine that enables one to watch and record video tapes. Users operate VCRs by pressing a series of buttons that are typically labeled "Record, Play, Reverse, Fast Forward, Pause, Stop/Eject." That the buttons are arranged and labeled does not make them a "literary work," nor does it make them an "expression" of the abstract "method of operating" a VCR via a set of labeled buttons. Instead, the buttons are themselves the "method of operating" the VCR.

When a Lotus 1-2-3 user chooses a command, either by highlighting it on the screen or by typing its first letter, he or she effectively pushes a button. Highlighting the "Print" command on the screen, or typing the letter "P," is analogous to pressing a VCR button labeled "Play."

Just as one could not operate a buttonless VCR, it would be impossible to operate Lotus 1-2-3 without employing its menu command hierarchy. Thus the Lotus command terms are not equivalent to the labels on the VCR's buttons, but are instead equivalent to the buttons themselves. Unlike the labels on a VCR's buttons, which merely make operating a VCR easier by indicating the buttons' functions, the Lotus menu commands are essential to operating Lotus 1-2-3. Without the menu commands, there would be no way to "push" the Lotus buttons, as one could push unlabeled VCR buttons. While Lotus could probably have designed a user interface for which the command terms were mere labels, it did not do so here. Lotus 1-2-3 depends for its operation on use of the precise command terms that make up the Lotus menu command hierarchy.

One might argue that the buttons for operating a VCR are not analogous to the commands for operating a computer program because VCRs are not copyrightable, whereas computer programs are. VCRs may not be copyrighted because they do not fit within any of the § 102(a) categories of copyrightable works; the closest they come is "sculptural work." Sculptural works, however, are subject to a "useful-article" exception whereby "the design of a useful article ... shall be considered a pictorial, graphic, or sculptural work only if, and only to the extent that, such design incorporates pictorial, graphic, or sculptural features that can be identified separately from, and are capable of existing independently of, the utilitarian aspects of the article." 17 U.S.C. § 101. A "useful article" is "an article having an intrinsic utilitarian function that is not merely to portray the appearance of the article or to convey information." *Id.* Whatever expression there may be in the arrangement of the parts of a VCR is not capable of existing separately from the VCR itself, so an ordinary VCR would not be copyrightable.

Computer programs, unlike VCRs, are copyrightable as "literary works." Accordingly, one might argue, the "buttons" used to operate a computer program are not like the buttons used to operate a VCR, for they are not subject to a useful-article exception. The response, of course, is that the arrangement of buttons on a VCR would not be copyrightable even without a useful-article exception, because the buttons are an uncopyrightable "method of operation." Similarly, the "buttons" of a computer program are also an uncopyrightable "method of operation."

That the Lotus menu command hierarchy is a "method of operation" becomes clearer when one considers program compatibility. Under Lotus's theory, if a user uses several different programs, he or she must learn how to perform the same operation in a different way for each program used. For example, if the user wanted the computer to print material, then the user would have to learn not just one method of operating the computer such that it prints, but many different methods. We find this absurd. The fact that there may be many different ways to operate a computer program, or even many different ways to operate a computer program using a set of hierarchically arranged command terms, does not make the actual method of operation chosen copyrightable; it still functions as a method for operating the computer and as such is uncopyrightable.

Consider also that users employ the Lotus menu command hierarchy in writing macros. Under the district court's holding, if the user wrote a macro to shorten the time needed to perform a certain operation in Lotus 1-2-3, the user would be unable to use that macro to shorten the time needed to perform that same operation in another program. Rather, the user would have to rewrite his or her macro using that other program's menu command hierarchy. This is despite the fact that the macro is clearly the user's own work product. We think that forcing the user to cause the computer to perform the same operation in a different way ignores Congress's direction in § 102(b) that "methods of operation" are not copyrightable. That programs can offer users the ability to write macros in many different ways does not change the fact that, once written, the macro allows the user to perform an operation automatically. As the Lotus menu command hierarchy serves as the basis for Lotus 1-2-3 macros, the Lotus menu command hierarchy is a "method of operation."

In holding that expression that is part of a "method of operation" cannot be copyrighted, we do not understand ourselves to go against the Supreme Court's holding in *Feist.* In *Feist,* the Court explained:

> The primary objective of copyright is not to reward the labor of authors, but to promote the Progress of Science and useful Arts. To this end, copyright assures authors the right to their original expression, but encourages others to build freely upon the ideas and information conveyed by a work.

We do not think that the Court's statement that "copyright assures authors the right to their original expression" indicates that all expression is necessarily copyrightable; while original expression is necessary for copyright protection, we do not think that it is alone sufficient. Courts must still inquire whether original expression falls within one of the categories foreclosed from copyright protection by § 102(b), such as being a "method of operation."

We also note that in most contexts, there is no need to "build" upon other people's expression, for the ideas conveyed by that expression can be conveyed by someone else without copying the first author's expression. In the context of methods of operation, however, "building" requires the use of the precise method of operation already employed; otherwise, "building" would require dismantling, too. Original developers are not the only people entitled to build on the methods of operation they create; anyone can. Thus, Borland may build on the method of operation that Lotus designed and may use the Lotus menu command hierarchy in doing so. ...

III. Conclusion

Because we hold that the Lotus menu command hierarchy is uncopyrightable subject matter, we further hold that Borland did not infringe Lotus's copyright by copying it. Accordingly, we need not consider any of Borland's affirmative defenses. The judgment of the district court is

Reversed.

BOUDIN, Circuit Judge, concurring.

The importance of this case, and a slightly different emphasis in my view of the underlying problem, prompt me to add a few words to the majority's tightly focused discussion.

I.

Most of the law of copyright and the "tools" of analysis have developed in the context of literary works such as novels, plays, and films. In this milieu, the principal problem—simply stated, if difficult to resolve—is to stimulate creative expression without unduly limiting access by others to the broader themes and concepts deployed by the author. The middle of the spectrum presents close cases; but a "mistake" in providing too much protection involves a small cost: subsequent authors treating the same themes must take a few more steps away from the original expression.

The problem presented by computer programs is fundamentally different in one respect. The computer program is a *means* for causing something to happen; it has a mechanical utility, an instrumental role, in accomplishing the world's work. Granting protection, in other words, can have some of the consequences of *patent* protection in limiting other people's ability to perform a task in the most efficient manner. Utility does not bar copyright (dictionaries may be copyrighted), but it alters the calculus.

Of course, the argument *for* protection is undiminished, perhaps even enhanced, by utility: if we want more of an intellectual product, a temporary monopoly for the creator provides incentives for others to create other, different items in this class. But the "cost" side of the equation may be different where one places a very high value on public access to a useful innovation that may be the most efficient means of performing a given task. Thus, the argument for extending protection may be the same; but the stakes on the other side are much higher.

It is no accident that patent protection has preconditions that copyright protection does not—notably, the requirements of novelty and non-obviousness—and that patents are granted for a shorter period than copyrights. This problem of utility has sometimes manifested itself in copyright cases, such as *Baker v. Selden*, and been dealt with through various formulations that limit copyright or create limited rights to copy. But the case law and doctrine addressed to utility in copyright have been brief detours in the general march of copyright law.

Requests for the protection of computer menus present the concern with fencing off access to the commons in an acute form. A new menu may be a creative work, but over time its importance may come to reside more in the investment that has been made by *users* in learning the menu and in building their own mini-programs-macros in reliance upon the menu. Better typewriter keyboard layouts may exist, but the familiar QWERTY keyboard dominates the market because that is what everyone has learned to use. *See* P. David, *CLIO and the Economics of QWERTY,* 75 AM. ECON. REV. 332 (1985). The QWERTY keyboard is nothing other than a menu of letters.

Thus, to assume that computer programs are just one more new means of expression, like a filmed play, may be quite wrong. The "form"—the written source code or the menu structure depicted on the screen—look hauntingly like the familiar stuff of copyright; but the "substance" probably has more to do with problems presented in patent law or, as already noted, in those rare cases where copyright law has confronted industrially useful expressions. Applying copyright law to computer programs is like assembling a jigsaw puzzle whose pieces do not quite fit.

All of this would make no difference if Congress had squarely confronted the issue, and given explicit directions as to what should be done.

The Copyright Act of 1976 took a different course. While Congress said that computer programs might be subject to copyright protection, it said this in very general terms; and, especially in § 102(b), Congress adopted a string of exclusions that if taken literally might easily seem to exclude most computer programs from protection. The only detailed prescriptions for computers involve narrow issues (like back-up copies) of no relevance here.

Of course, one could still read the statute as a congressional command that the familiar doctrines of copyright law be taken and applied to computer programs, in cookie cutter fashion, as if the programs were novels or play scripts. Some of the cases involving computer programs embody this approach. It seems to be mistaken on two different grounds: the tradition of copyright law, and the likely intent of Congress.

The broad-brush conception of copyright protection, the time limits, and the formalities have long been prescribed by statute. But the heart of copyright doctrine—what may be protected and with what limitations and exceptions—has been developed by the courts through experience with individual cases. B. Kaplan, *An Unhurried View of Copyright* 40 (1967). Occasionally Congress addresses a problem in detail. For the most part the interstitial development of copyright through the courts is our tradition.

Nothing in the language or legislative history of the 1976 Act, or at least nothing brought to our attention, suggests that Congress meant the courts to abandon this case-by-case approach. Indeed, by setting up § 102(b) as a counterpoint theme, Congress has arguably recognized the tension and left it for the courts to resolve through the development of case law. And case law development is *adaptive:* it allows new problems to be solved with help of earlier doctrine, but it does not preclude new doctrines to meet new situations.

II.

In this case, the raw facts are mostly, if not entirely, undisputed. Although the inferences to be drawn may be more debatable, it is very hard to see that Borland has shown any interest in the Lotus menu except as a fall-back option for those users already committed to it by prior experience or in order to run their own macros using 1-2-3 commands. At least for the amateur, accessing the Lotus menu in the Borland Quattro or Quattro Pro program takes some effort.

Put differently, it is unlikely that users who value the Lotus menu for its own sake—independent of any investment they have made themselves in learning Lotus' commands or creating macros dependent upon them—would choose the Borland program in order to secure access to the Lotus menu. Borland's success is due primarily to other features. Its rationale for deploying the Lotus menu bears the ring of truth.

Now, any use of the Lotus menu by Borland is a commercial use and deprives Lotus of a portion of its "reward," in the sense that an infringement claim if allowed would increase Lotus' profits. But this is circular reasoning: broadly speaking, every limitation on copyright or privileged use diminishes the reward of the original creator. Yet not every writing is copyrightable or every use an infringement. The provision of reward is one concern of copyright law, but it is not the only one. If it were, copyrights would be perpetual and there would be no exceptions.

The present case is an unattractive one for copyright protection of the menu. The menu commands (e.g., "print," "quit") are largely for standard procedures that Lotus did not invent and are common words that Lotus cannot monopolize. What is left is the particular combination and sub-grouping of commands in a pattern devised by Lotus. This arrangement may have a more appealing logic and ease of use than some other configurations; but there is a certain arbitrariness to many of the choices.

If Lotus is granted a monopoly on this pattern, users who have learned the command structure of Lotus 1-2-3 or devised their own macros are locked into Lotus, just as a typist who has learned the QWERTY keyboard would be the captive of anyone who had a monopoly on the production of such a keyboard. Apparently, for a period Lotus 1-2-3 has had such sway in the market that it has represented the *de facto* standard for electronic spreadsheet commands. So long as Lotus is the superior spreadsheet—either in quality or in price—there may be nothing wrong with this advantage.

But if a better spreadsheet comes along, it is hard to see why customers who have learned the Lotus menu and devised macros for it should remain captives of Lotus because of an investment in learning made by the users and not by Lotus. Lotus has already reaped a substantial reward for being first; assuming that the Borland program is now better, good reasons exist for freeing it to attract old Lotus customers: to enable the old customers to take advantage of a new advance, and to reward Borland in turn for making a better product. If Borland has not made a better product, then customers will remain with Lotus anyway.

Thus, for me the question is not whether Borland should prevail but on what basis. Various avenues might be traveled, but the main choices are between holding that the menu is not protectable by copyright and devising a new doctrine that Borland's use is privileged. No solution is perfect and no intermediate appellate court can make the final choice.

To call the menu a "method of operation" is, in the common use of those words, a defensible position. After all, the purpose of the menu is not to be admired as a work of literary or pictorial art. It is to transmit directions from the user to the computer, i.e., *to operate* the computer. The menu is also a "method" in the dictionary sense because it is a "planned way of doing something," an "order or system," and (aptly here) an "orderly or systematic arrangement, sequence or the like." *Random House Webster's College Dictionary* 853 (1991).

A different approach would be to say that Borland's use is privileged because, in the context already described, it is not seeking to appropriate the advances made by Lotus' menu; rather, having provided an arguably more attractive menu of its own, Borland is merely trying to give former Lotus users an option to exploit their own prior investment in learning or in macros. The difference is that such a privileged use approach would not automatically protect Borland if it had simply copied the Lotus menu (using different codes), contributed nothing of its own, and resold Lotus under the Borland label.

The closest analogue in conventional copyright is the fair use doctrine. Although invoked by Borland, it has largely been brushed aside in this case because the Supreme Court has said that it is "presumptively" unavailable where the use is a "commercial" one. In my view, this is something less than a definitive answer; "presumptively" does not mean "always" and, in any event, the doctrine of fair use was created by the courts and can be adapted to new purposes.

But a privileged use doctrine would certainly involve problems of its own. It might more closely tailor the limits on copyright protection to the reasons for limiting that protection; but it would entail a host of administrative problems that would cause cost and delay, and would also reduce the ability of the industry to predict outcomes. Indeed, to the extent that Lotus' menu is an important standard in the industry, it might be argued that any use ought to be deemed privileged.

In sum, the majority's result persuades me and its formulation is as good, if not better, than any other that occurs to me now as within the reach of courts. Some solutions (e.g., a very short copyright period for menus) are not options at all for courts but might be for Congress. In all events, the choices are important ones of policy, not linguistics, and they should be made with the underlying considerations in view.

Notes and Questions

1.   How broadly do you understand the term "method of operation"? Consider a computer program used by a person to control a piece of machinery such as a nuclear reactor. Is such a program a method of operation, and if so, does it fall outside the scope of copyright protection? Or consider the "home screen" for the Apple iPhone, with its layout of icons for the varius "apps." If a competing cellphone maker wanted to install an "iPhone Emulation Interface" on its cellphone which would make it appear exactly like the Apple iPhone home page (copying everything exactly, including the icons), could it do so? Could it successfully argue that the iPhone home page is an unprotectible "method of operation"?

2.   Is *Lotus* consistent with *Apple*, particularly in its approach to the definition of "method of operation"? Both cases concern efforts by a copyright holder to eliminate competition. In *Apple*, the plaintiff wanted to stop a competitor from making computers that were fully compatible

with software written for Apple computers. In *Lotus*, the plaintiff wanted to stop a competitor from making software that was "fully compatible" with command structures already familiar to users of Lotus 1-2-3. In either case, a decision for the plaintiff would make it difficult for users to switch to products made by competitors without incurring some kind of retooling cost. In *Apple*, those switching would have to incur the cost of new software that would run on non-Apple machines, while in *Lotus*, switchers would have to incur the cost of learning to use non-Lotus commands. Why then did the cases come out differently? Did one decision do more to promote the progress of science and art, or the public interest?

3. Judge Boudin's concurrence is included here because it offers thoughtful reflection on the nature of software and the consequences of copyrighting it. What do you think of his ideas, and how far do you think Judge Boudin is prepared to push them? For example, he notes that Lotus has already reaped substantial rewards for being the first to offer a spreadsheet program. If others can now produce better competing products, society has reason to facilitate the public's migration to the new product. Would he have reached the same conclusion if he had decided *Apple*, and would you agree with such a decision? Or, are Judge Boudin's ideas problematic because they threaten the incentives offered by copyright?

SECTION D. USEFUL ARTICLE DOCTRINE

The useful article doctrine limits the extent to which copyright protects utilitarian objects. Like the idea/expression dichotomy, this doctrine entered the present Copyright Act when Congress accepted the results of earlier case law.[22] This section begins with the leading Supreme Court case of *Mazer v. Stein* and follows with three cases from the Second Circuit. As you read these cases, ask yourself whether the courts have developed a coherent interpretation of the useful article doctrine and whether courts can decide useful article doctrine cases (or any copyrightable subject matter cases, for that matter) without getting into pre-

---

[22] The location of the useful article doctrine in the Copyright Act is a bit elusive. Section 102(a) of the Code includes "pictorial, graphic, and sculptural works" as examples of original works of authorship. Section 101 in turn defines "pictorial, graphic, and sculptural works" as follows:

"Pictorial, graphic, and sculptural works" include two-dimensional and three-dimensional works of fine, graphic, and applied art, photographs, prints and art reproductions, maps, globes, charts, diagrams, models, and technical drawings, including architectural plans. Such works shall include works of artistic craftsmanship insofar as their form but not their mechanical or utilitarian aspects are concerned; the design of a useful article, as defined in this section, shall be considered a pictorial, graphic, or sculptural work only if, and only to the extent that, such design incorporates pictorial, graphic, or sculptural features that can be identified separately from, and are capable of existing independently of, the utilitarian aspects of the article.

cisely the kind of trouble that Justice Holmes warned against in *Bleistein*.

Mazer v. Stein
347 U.S. 201 (1954)

MR. JUSTICE REED delivered the opinion of the Court.

This case involves the validity of copyrights obtained by respondents for statuettes of male and female dancing figures made of semivitreous china. The controversy centers around the fact that although copyrighted as "works of art," the statuettes were intended for use and used as bases for table lamps, with electric wiring, sockets and lamp shades attached.

Respondents are partners in the manufacture and sale of electric lamps. One of the respondents created original works of sculpture in the form of human figures by traditional clay-model technique. From this model, a production mold for casting copies was made. The resulting statuettes, without any lamp components added, were submitted by the respondents to the Copyright Office for registration as "works of art" or reproductions thereof under s 5(g) or s 5(h) of the copyright law, and certificates of registration issued. ...

Petitioners are partners and, like respondents, make and sell lamps. Without authorization, they copied the statuettes, embodied them in lamps and sold them.

Petitioners, charged by the present complaint with infringement of respondents' copyrights of reproductions of their works of art, seek here a reversal of the Court of Appeals decree upholding the copyrights. Petitioners in their petition for certiorari present a single question:

> "Can statuettes be protected in the United States by copyright when the copyright applicant intended primarily to use the statuettes in the form of lamp bases to be made and sold in quantity and carried the intentions into effect?"

> "Stripped down to its essentials, the question presented is: Can a lamp manufacturer copyright his lamp bases?"

The first paragraph accurately summarizes the issue. The last gives it a quirk that unjustifiably, we think, broadens the controversy. The case requires an answer, not as to a manufacturer's right to register a lamp base but as to an artist's right to copyright a work of art intended to be reproduced for lamp bases. As petitioners say in their brief, their contention "questions the validity of the copyright based upon the actions of respondents." Petitioners question the validity of a copyright of a work of art for "mass" production. "Reproduction of a work of art" does not mean to them unlimited reproduction. Their position is that a copyright does not cover industrial reproduction of the protected article. Thus their reply brief states: "When an artist becomes a manufacturer or a designer for a manufacturer he is subject to the limitations of design patents and deserves no more consideration than any other manufacturer or designer."...

The successive acts, the legislative history of the 1909 Act and the practice of the Copyright Office unite to show that "works of art" and "reproductions of works of art" are terms that were intended by Congress to include the authority to copyright these statuettes. Individual perception of the beautiful is too varied a power to permit a narrow or rigid concept of art. [Copyrightable works] must be original, that is, the author's tangible expression of his ideas. Such expression, whether meticulously delineating the model or mental image or conveying the meaning by modernistic form or color, is copyrightable. ...

The conclusion that the statues here in issue may be copyrighted goes far to solve the question whether their intended reproduction as lamp stands bars or invalidates their registration. ... [P]etitioners assert that congressional enactment of the design patent laws should be interpreted as denying protection to artistic articles embodied or reproduced in manufactured articles. ... Their argument is that design patents require the critical examination given patents to protect the public against monopoly. ...

As we have held the statuettes here involved copyrightable, we need not decide the question of their patentability. Though other courts have passed upon the issue as to whether allowance by the election of the author or patentee of one bars a grant of the other, we do not. We do hold that the patentability of the statuettes, fitted as lamps or unfitted, does not bar copyright as works of art. Neither the Copyright Statute nor any other says that because a thing is patentable it may not be copyrighted. We should not so hold. ...

The economic philosophy behind the clause empowering Congress to grant patents and copyrights is the conviction that encouragement of individual effort by personal gain is the best way to advance public welfare through the talents of authors and inventors in "Science and useful Arts." Sacrificial days devoted to such creative activities deserve rewards commensurate with the services rendered.

Affirmed.

Notes and Questions

1. Exactly how does the *Mazer* Court reach the conclusion that the objects in question are copyrightable? Did the Court emphasize the objects' physical characteristics, the intention of the creator, or the perceptions of people who saw the objects?

2. The *Mazer* Court goes to considerable lengths to frame the issue of the case carefully. The Court was happy to answer the question "Can statuettes be protected in the United States by copyright when the copy-

right applicant intended primarily to use the statuettes in the form of lamp bases to be made and sold in quantity and carried the intentions into effect?" However, the Court did not want to answer the question "Can a lamp manufacturer copyright his lamp bases?" Why was this so? What would be wrong with allowing a lamp manufacturer to copyright his lamp bases?

3. *Mazer* ends with the statement, "[t]he economic philosophy behind the clause empowering Congress to grant patents and copyrights is the conviction that encouragement of individual effort by personal gain is the best way to advance public welfare through the talents of authors and inventors in 'Science and useful Arts.' Sacrificial days devoted to such creative activities deserve rewards commensurate with the services rendered." What do you think of this statement? Did *Mazer* advance the public welfare? Did it give authors and inventors "rewards commensurate with the services rendered"?

4. As a Supreme Court case, *Mazer* presumably dictates how lower courts should decide the copyrightability of utilitarian objects. With this in mind, consider whether the following cases are faithful to analytical methods of *Mazer* and consistent with each other.

Kieselstein-Cord v. Accessories By Pearl
632 F.2d 989 (2d Cir. 1980)

OAKES, Circuit Judge:

This case is on a razor's edge of copyright law. It involves belt buckles, utilitarian objects which as such are not copyrightable. But these are not ordinary buckles; they are sculptured designs cast in precious metals—decorative in nature and used as jewelry is, principally for ornamentation. We say "on a razor's edge" because the case requires us to draw a fine line under applicable copyright law and regulations. Drawing the line in favor of the appellant designer, we uphold the copyrights granted to him by the Copyright Office and reverse the district court's grant of summary judgment in favor of the appellee, the copier of appellant's designs.

FACTS

Appellant Barry Kieselstein-Cord designs, manufactures exclusively by hand craftsmanship, and sells fashion accessories. To produce the two buckles in issue here, the "Winchester" and the "Vaquero," he worked from original renderings which he had conceived and sketched. He then carved by hand a waxen prototype of each of the works from which molds were made for casting the objects in gold and silver. Difficult to describe, the buckles are solid sculptured designs, in the words of district court Judge Goettel, "with rounded corners, a sculpted surface, a rectangular cut-out at one end for the belt attachment," and "several surface levels."

The Vaquero gives the appearance of two curved grooves running diagonally across one corner of a modified rectangle and a third groove running across the opposite corner. On the Winchester buckle two parallel grooves cut horizontally across the center of a more tapered form, making a curving ridge which is completed by the tongue of the buckle. A smaller single curved groove flows diagonally across the corner above the tongue.

The Vaquero buckle, created in 1978, was part of a series of works that the designer testified was inspired by a book on design of the art nouveau school and the subsequent viewing of related architecture on a trip to Spain. The buckle was registered with the Copyright Office by appellant's counsel on March 3, 1980, with a publication date of June 1, 1978, as "jewelry," although the appellant's contribution was listed on the certificate as "original sculpture and design." Explaining why he named the earlier buckle design "Winchester," the designer said that he saw "in (his) mind's eye a correlation between the art nouveau period and the butt of an antique Winchester rifle" and then "pulled these elements together graphically." The registration, which is recorded on a form used for works of art, or models or designs for works of art, specifically describes the nature of the work as "sculpture."

The Winchester buckle in particular has had great success in the marketplace: more than 4,000 belts with Winchester buckles were sold from 1976 to early 1980, and in 1979 sales of the belts amounted to 95% of appellant's more than $300,000 in jewelry sales. A small women's size in silver with "double truncated triangle belt loops" sold, at the time this lawsuit commenced, at wholesale for $147.50 and a larger silver version for men sold at wholesale with loops for $662 and without loops for $465. Lighter-weight men's versions in silver wholesaled for $450 and $295, with and without loops respectively. The gold versions sold at wholesale from $1,200 to $6,000. A shortened version of the belt with the small Winchester buckle is sometimes worn around the neck or elsewhere on the body rather than around the waist. Sales of both buckles were made primarily in high fashion stores and jewelry stores, bringing recognition to appellant as a "designer." This recognition included a 1979 Coty American Fashion Critics' Award for his work in jewelry design as well as election in 1978 to the Council of Fashion Designers of America. Both the Winchester and the Vaquero buckles, donated by appellant after this lawsuit was commenced, have been accepted by the Metropolitan Museum of Art for its permanent collection.

As the court below found, appellee's buckles "appear to be line-for-line copies but are made of common metal rather than" precious metal. Appellee admitted to copying the Vaquero and selling its imitations, and to selling copies of the Winchester. Indeed some of the order blanks of appellee's customers specifically referred to "Barry K Copy," "BK copy," and even "Barry Kieselstein Knock-off." ...

DISCUSSION

We commence our discussion by noting that no claim has been made that the appellant's work here in question lacks originality or creativity, elements necessary for copyrighting works of art. The thrust of appellee's argument, as well as of the court's decision below, is that appellant's buckles are not copyrightable because they are "useful articles" with no "pictorial, graphic, or sculptural features that can be identified separately from, and are capable of existing independently of, the utilitarian aspects" of the buckles. The 1976 copyright statute does not provide for the copyrighting of useful articles except to the extent that their designs incorporate artistic features that can be identified separately from the functional elements of the articles. ...

[N]one of the authorities—the *Mazer* opinion, the old regulations, or the statute—offer any "ready answer to the line-drawing problem inherent in delineating the extent of copyright protection available for works of applied art." ...

We see in appellant's belt buckles conceptually separable sculptural elements, as apparently have the buckles' wearers who have used them as ornamentation for parts of the body other than the waist. The primary ornamental aspect of the Vaquero and Winchester buckles is conceptually separable from their subsidiary utilitarian function. ...

Appellant's designs are not, as the appellee suggests in an affidavit, mere variations of "the well-known western buckle." As both the expert witnesses for appellant testified and the Copyright Office's action implied, the buckles rise to the level of creative art. Indeed, body ornamentation has been an art form since the earliest days, as anyone who has seen the Tutankhamen or Scythian gold exhibits at the Metropolitan Museum will readily attest. The basic requirements of originality and creativity, which the two buckles satisfy and which all works of art must meet to be copyrighted, would take the vast majority of belt buckles wholly out of copyrightability. The Copyright Office continually engages in the drawing of lines between that which may be and that which may not be copyrighted. It will, so long as the statute remains in its present form, always be necessary to determine whether in a given case there is a physically or conceptually separable artistic sculpture or carving capable of existing independently as a work of art.

We reverse the grant of summary judgment to the appellees. ...

[The dissenting opinion of Judge Weinstein is omitted.]

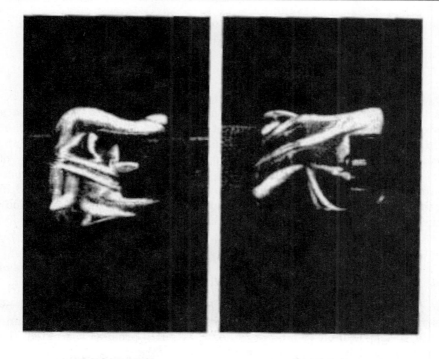

Winchester   Vaquero

Notes and Questions

1. *Kieselstein-Cord* states the conventional test for the copyrightability of useful articles, namely whether the useful article contains artistic features that can be identified separately from the article's function. How does the court go about applying this test? Do you agree with the court's conclusion that there is something artistic about these buckles (but not others), or could the same thing be said about any belt buckle?

2. If you are unsure about whether *Kieselstein-Cord* is consistent with *Mazer*, it may be helpful to consider the different ways in which such consistency might exist. First, do you think the *Mazer* Court would have reached the same result? Second, did the *Kieselstein-Cord* court follow the analytical methods used in *Mazer*? What mattered most to the court—the particular physical shape of the buckles, the intentions of Mr. Kieselstein-Cord, or the reactions of others—and were these the same things that mattered to the *Mazer* court?

Carol Barnhart v. Economy Cover Corp.
773 F.2d. 411 (2d Cir. 1985)

MANSFIELD, Circuit Judge:

Carol Barnhart Inc. ("Barnhart"), which sells display forms to department stores, distributors, and small retail stores, appeals from a judgment of the Eastern District of New York, Leonard D. Wexler, *Judge,* granting a motion for summary judgment made by defendant Economy Cover Corporation ("Economy"), which sells a wide variety of display products primarily to jobbers and distributors. Barnhart's complaint alleges that Economy has infringed its copyright and engaged in unfair competition by offering for sale display forms copied from four original "sculptural forms" to which Barnhart holds the copyright. Judge Wexler granted Economy's motion for summary judgment on the ground that plaintiff's mannequins of partial human torsos used to display articles of clothing are utilitarian articles not containing separable works of art, and thus are not copyrightable. We affirm.

The bones of contention are four human torso forms designed by Barnhart, each of which is life-size, without neck, arms, or a back, and made of expandable white styrene. Plaintiff's president created the forms in 1982 by using clay, buttons, and fabric to develop an initial mold, which she then used to build an aluminum mold into which the poly-styrene is poured to manufacture the sculptural display form. There are two male and two female upper torsos. One each of the male and female torsos is unclad for the purpose of displaying shirts and sweaters, while the other two are sculpted with shirts for displaying sweaters and jackets. All the forms, which are otherwise life-like and anatomically accurate, have hollow backs designed to hold excess fabric when the garment is fitted onto the form. Barnhart's advertising stresses the forms' uses to display items such as sweaters, blouses, and dress shirts, and states that they come "[p]ackaged in UPS-size boxes for easy shipping and [are] sold in multiples of twelve."

Plaintiff created the first of the forms, Men's Shirt, shortly after its founding in March, 1982, and by the end of July it had attracted $18,000 worth of orders. By December 1982, plaintiff had designed all four forms, and during the first morning of the twice-yearly trade show sponsored by the National Association of the Display Industry ("NADI"), customers had placed $35,000 in orders for the forms. Plaintiff's president maintains that the favorable response from visual merchandisers, Barnhart's primary customers, "convinced me that my forms were being purchased not only for their function but for their artistically sculptured features."

Economy, which sells its wide range of products primarily to jobbers, distributors, and national chain stores, not to retail stores, first learned in early 1983 that Barnhart was selling its display forms directly to retailers. After observing that no copyright notice appeared either on Barnhart's forms or in its promotional literature, Economy contracted to have produced for it four forms which it has conceded, for purposes of its summary judgment motion, were "copied from Barnhart's display forms" and are "substantially similar to Barnhart's display forms."...

DISCUSSION

... Since the four Barnhart forms are concededly useful articles, the crucial issue in determining their copyrightability is whether they possess artistic or aesthetic features that are physically or conceptually separable from their utilitarian dimension. ...

[The court's review of the statute, legislative history and prior case law, including *Burrow-Giles, Bleistein,* and *Mazer v. Stein*, is omitted.]

The legislative history thus confirms that, while copyright protection has increasingly been extended to cover articles having a utilitarian dimension, Congress has explicitly refused copyright protection for works of applied art or industrial design which have aesthetic or artistic features that cannot be identified separately from the useful article. Such works are not copyrightable regardless of the fact that they may be "aesthetically satisfying and valuable." H.R. Rep. No. 1476, *supra,* at 55, 1976 U.S. Code Cong. & Ad. News at 5668.

Applying these principles, we are persuaded that since the aesthetic and artistic features of the Barnhart forms are inseparable from the forms' use as utilitarian articles the forms are not copyrightable. Appellant emphasizes that clay sculpting, often used in traditional sculpture, was used in making the molds for the forms. It also stresses that the forms have been responded to as sculptural forms, and have been used for purposes other than modeling clothes, e.g., as decorating props and signs without any clothing or accessories. While this may indicate that the forms are "aesthetically satisfying and valuable," it is insufficient to show that the forms possess aesthetic or artistic features that are physically or conceptually separable from the forms' use as utilitarian objects to display clothes. On the contrary, to the extent the forms possess aesthetically pleasing features, even when these features are considered in the aggregate, they cannot be conceptualized as existing independently of their utilitarian function.

Appellant seeks to rebut this conclusion by arguing that the four forms represent a concrete expression of a particular idea, e.g., the idea of a woman's blouse, and that the form involved, a human torso, is traditionally copyrightable. Appellant suggests that since the Barnhart forms fall within the traditional category of sculpture of the human body, they should be subjected to a lower level of scrutiny in determining its copyrightability. We disagree. We find no support in the statutory language or legislative history for the claim that merely because a utilitarian article falls within a traditional art form it is entitled to a lower level of scrutiny in determining its copyrightability. Recognition of such a claim would in any event conflict with the anti-discrimination principle Justice Holmes enunciated in *Bleistein v. Donaldson Lithographing Co., supra,* 188 U.S. at 251-52.

Nor do we agree that copyrightability here is dictated by our decision in *Kieselstein-Cord v. Accessories by Pearl, Inc.,* 632 F.2d 989 (2d Cir. 1980), a case we described as being "on a razor's edge of copyright law." There we were called on to determine whether two belt buckles bearing sculptured designs cast in precious metals and principally used for decoration were copyrightable. Various versions of these buckles in silver and gold sold wholesale at prices ranging from $147.50 to $6,000 and were offered by high fashion and jewelry stores. Some had also been accepted by the Metropolitan Museum of Art for its permanent collection.

In concluding that the two buckles were copyrightable we relied on the fact that "[t]he primary ornamental aspect of the Vaquero and Winchester buckles is conceptually separable from their subsidiary utilitarian function." *Id.* at 993. A glance at the pictures of the two buckles, reproduced at *id.* 995, coupled with the description in the text, confirms their highly ornamental dimensions and separability. What distinguishes those buckles from the Barnhart forms is that the ornamented surfaces of the buckles were not in any respect required by their utilitarian functions; the artistic and aesthetic features could thus be conceived of as having been added to, or superimposed upon, an otherwise utilitarian article. The unique artistic design was wholly unnecessary to performance of the utilitarian function. In the case of the Barnhart forms, on the other hand, the features claimed to be aesthetic or artistic, e.g., the life-size configuration of the breasts and the width of the shoulders, are inextricably intertwined with the utilitarian feature, the display of clothes. Whereas a model of a human torso, in order to serve its utilitarian function, must have some configuration of the chest and some width of shoulders, a belt buckle can serve its function satisfactorily without any ornamentation of the type that renders the *Kieselstein-Cord* buckles distinctive.

The judgment of the district court is affirmed.

[The dissenting opinion of Judge Newman is omitted.]

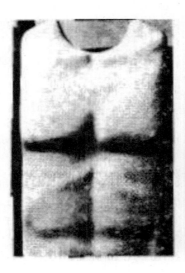

Notes and Questions

1. *Carol Barnhart* explains that the articles in question have no aesthetic features separable from their function. Do you agree? You probably have seen many mannequins in various stores. Do they all have the same features as the plaintiff's forms? If not, how could the court have decided the case in favor of the defendants?

2. The Second Circuit decided *Kieselstein-Cord* in 1980 and *Carol Barnhart* in 1985. If *Kieselstein-Cord* was a well-reasoned, correctly decided case, one would expect the *Carol Barnhart* court to adopt *Kieselstein-Cord* as guiding precedent. Did this happen?

3. What if the exact same mannequins in *Carol Barnhart* had been displayed in a museum as a sculpture? Would they have been copyrightable, under the reasoning of the court's decision?

Brandir Int'l v. Cascade Pacific Lumber Co.
834 F.2d 1142 (2d Cir. 1987)

OAKES, Circuit Judge:

In passing the Copyright Act of 1976 Congress attempted to distinguish between protectable "works of applied art" and "industrial designs not subject to copyright protection." The courts, however, have had difficulty framing tests by which the fine line establishing what is and what is not copyrightable can be drawn. Once again we are called upon to draw such a line, this time in a case involving the "RIBBON Rack," a bicycle rack made of bent tubing that is said to have originated from a wire sculpture. (A photograph of the rack is contained in the appendix to this opinion.) ... [T]he district court granted summary judgment on both the copyright and trademark claims to defendant Cascade Pacific Lumber Co., d/b/a Columbia Cascade Co., manufacturer of a similar bicycle rack. We affirm as to the copyright claim, but reverse and remand as to the trademark claim.

[The court reviewed prior case law, including *Mazer v. Stein, Kieselstein-Cord v. Accessories by Pearl*, and *Carol Barnhart v. Economy Cover*.]

Perhaps the differences between the majority and the dissent in *Carol Barnhart* might have been resolved had they had before them the Denicola article on *Applied Art and Industrial Design: A Suggested Approach to Copyright in Useful Articles,* 67 MINN. L. REV. 707 (1983). There, Professor Denicola points out that although the Copyright Act of 1976 was an effort "'to draw as clear a line as possible,'" in truth "there is no line, but merely a spectrum of forms and shapes responsive in varying degrees to utilitarian concerns." 67 MINN. L. REV. at 741. Denicola argues that "the statutory directive requires a distinction between works of industrial design and works whose origins lie outside the design process, despite the utilitarian environment in which they appear." He views the statutory limitation of copyrightability as "an attempt to identify elements whose form and appearance reflect the unconstrained perspective of the artist," such features not being the product of industrial design. *Id.* at 742. "Copyrightability, therefore, should turn on the relationship between the proffered work and the process of industrial design." *Id.* at 741. He suggests that "the dominant characteristic of industrial design is the influence of nonaesthetic, utilitarian concerns" and hence concludes that copyrightability "ultimately should depend on the extent to which the work reflects artistic expression uninhibited by functional considerations." *Id.* To state the Denicola test in the language of conceptual separability, if design elements reflect a merger of aesthetic and functional considerations, the artistic aspects of a work cannot be said to be conceptually separable from the utilitarian elements. Conversely, where design elements can be identified as reflecting the designer's artistic judgment exercised independently of functional influences, conceptual separability exists.

We believe that Professor Denicola's approach provides the best test for conceptual separability and, accordingly, adopt it here for several reasons. First, the approach is consistent with the holdings of our previous cases. In *Kieselstein-Cord,* for example, the artistic aspects of the belt buckles reflected purely aesthetic choices, independent of the buckles' function, while in *Carol Barnhart* the distinctive features of the torsos—the accurate anatomical design and the sculpted shirts and collars—showed clearly the influence of functional concerns. Though the torsos bore artistic features, it was evident that the designer incorporated those features to further the usefulness of the torsos as mannequins. Second, the test's emphasis on the influence of utilitarian concerns in the design process may help, as Denicola notes, to "alleviate the de facto discrimination against nonrepresentational art that has regrettably accompanied much of the current analysis." *Id.* at 745. Finally, and perhaps most importantly, we think Denicola's test will not be too difficult to administer in practice. The work itself will continue to give "mute testimony" of its origins. In addition, the parties will be required to present evidence relating to the design process and the nature of the work, with the trier of fact making the determination whether the aesthetic design elements are significantly influenced by functional considerations.

Turning now to the facts of this case, we note first that Brandir contends, and its chief owner David Levine testified, that the original design of the RIBBON Rack stemmed from wire sculptures that Levine had created, each formed from one continuous undulating piece of wire. These sculptures were, he said, created and displayed in his home as a means of personal expression, but apparently were never sold or displayed elsewhere. He also created a wire sculpture in the shape of a bicycle and states that he did not give any thought to the utilitarian application of any of his sculptures until he accidentally juxtaposed the bicycle sculpture with one of the self-standing wire sculptures. It was not until November 1978 that Levine seriously began pursuing the utilitarian application of his sculptures, when a friend, G. Duff Bailey, a bicycle buff and author of numerous articles about urban cycling, was at Levine's home and informed him that the sculptures would make excellent bicycle racks, permitting bicycles to be parked under the overloops as well as on top of the underloops. Following this meeting, Levine met several times with Bailey and others, completing the designs for the RIBBON Rack by the use of a vacuum cleaner hose, and submitting his drawings to a fabricator complete with dimensions. The Brandir RIBBON Rack began being nationally advertised and promoted for sale in September 1979. ...

Applying Professor Denicola's test to the RIBBON Rack, we find that the rack is not copyrightable. It seems clear that the form of the rack is influenced in significant measure by utilitarian concerns and thus any aesthetic elements cannot be said to be conceptually separable from the utilitarian elements. This is true even though the sculptures which inspired the RIBBON Rack may well have been—the issue of originality aside—copyrightable.

Brandir argues correctly that a copyrighted work of art does not lose its protected status merely because it subsequently is put to a functional use. The Supreme Court so held in *Mazer v. Stein*, and Congress specifically intended to accept and codify *Mazer* in section 101 of the Copyright Act of 1976. *See* H.R. Rep. No. 1476 at 54-55. The district court thus erred in ruling that, whatever the RIBBON Rack's origins, Brandir's commercialization of the rack disposed of the issue of its copyrightability.

Had Brandir merely adopted one of the existing sculptures as a bicycle rack, neither the application to a utilitarian end nor commercialization of that use would have caused the object to forfeit its copyrighted status. Comparison of the RIBBON Rack with the earlier sculptures, however, reveals that while the rack may have been derived in part from one of more "works of art," it is in its final form essentially a product of industrial design. In creating the RIBBON Rack, the designer has clearly adapted the original aesthetic elements to accommodate and further a utilitarian purpose. These altered design features of the RIBBON Rack, including the spacesaving, open design achieved by widening the upper loops to permit parking under as well as over the rack's curves, the straightened vertical elements that allow in- and above-ground installation of the rack, the ability to fit all types of bicycles and mopeds, and the heavy-gauged tubular construction of rustproof galvanized steel, are all features that combine to make for a safe, secure, and maintenance-free system of parking bicycles and mopeds. Its undulating shape is said in *Progressive Architecture,* January 1982, to permit double the storage of conventional bicycle racks. Moreover, the rack is manufactured from 2 3/8-inch standard steam pipe that is bent into form, the six-inch radius of the bends evidently resulting from bending the pipe according to a standard formula that yields bends having a radius equal to three times the nominal internal diameter of the pipe.

Brandir argues that its RIBBON Rack can and should be characterized as a sculptural work of art within the minimalist art movement. Minimalist sculpture's most outstanding feature is said to be its clarity and simplicity, in that it often takes the form of geometric shapes, lines, and forms that are pure and free of ornamentation and void of association. As Brandir's expert put it, "The meaning is to be found in, within, around and outside the work of art, allowing the artistic sensation to be experienced as well as intellectualized." People who use Foley Square in New York City see in the form of minimalist art the "Tilted Arc," which is on the plaza at 26 Federal Plaza. Numerous museums have had exhibitions of such art, and the school of minimalist art has many admirers.

It is unnecessary to determine whether to the art world the RIBBON Rack properly would be considered an example of minimalist sculpture. The result under the copyright statute is not changed. Using the test we have adopted, it is not enough that, to paraphrase Judge Newman, the rack may stimulate in the mind of the reasonable observer a concept separate from the bicycle rack concept. While the RIBBON Rack may be worthy of admiration for its aesthetic qualities alone, it remains nonetheless the product of industrial design. Form and function are inextricably intertwined in the rack, its ultimate design being as much the result of utilitarian pressures as aesthetic choices. Indeed, the visually pleasing proportions and symmetricality of the rack represent design changes made in response to functional concerns. Judging from the awards the rack has received, it would seem in fact that Brandir has achieved with the RIBBON Rack the highest goal of modern industrial design, that is, the harmonious fusion of function and aesthetics. Thus there remains no artistic element of the RIBBON Rack that can be identified as separate and "capable of existing independently, of, the utilitarian aspects of the article." Accordingly, we must affirm on the copyright claim.

[The dissenting opinion of Judge Winter is omitted.]

APPENDIX

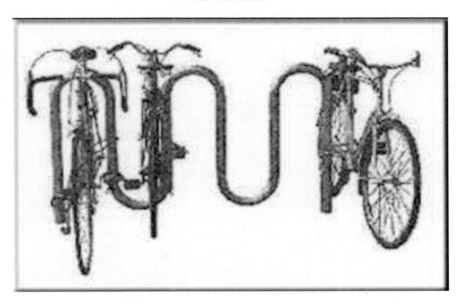

Notes and Questions

1.   Under *Brandir*, courts should decide useful article cases by examining the plaintiff's thought process when creating the object in question. How should a court go about doing this? Is such a test more or less subject to manipulation than the tests suggested in *Mazer, Kieselstein-Cord,* and *Barnhart*? How would the bike rack in *Brandir* have fared under these other tests?

What if the author in *Brandir* had created the final product as an actual, full-sized sculpture, and then later realized that it made a terrific bike rack, selling it to the public without any alteration? Under these facts, would the exact same bike rack in *Brandir* now be protected by copyright? Does this result make sense?

2.   *Brandir* follows *Carol Barnhart* by a mere two years, yet the Second Circuit has adopted a new test for conceptual separability that is supposedly consistent with prior precedent and devoid of the aesthetic discrimination that courts want to avoid. Do you agree? Before answering this question, you may find it helpful to consider the following definitions of art:

First, there are definitions focused on the physical properties of works. Clive Bell asserted that certain physical configurations provoke aesthetic responses from humans, but not others. He labeled the formal properties of these configurations "significant form," claiming that significant form "is the one quality common to all works of visual art."[23]

Second, there are definitions that emphasize the intentions of putative artists. For example, Monroe Beardsley argued that "An artwork is something produced with the intention of giving it the capacity to satisfy the aesthetic interest."[24]

Third, there are definitions that study the reactions of those who perceive an object. George Dickie offered a seminal statement of this view, concluding that art is: (1) an artifact (2) a set of the aspects of which as had conferred upon it the status of candidate for appreciation by some person or persons acting on behalf of a certain social institution (the artworld).[25]

Do these definitions of art correspond to the different analytical methods used to decide useful article doctrine cases? Do they correspond to analytical methods used elsewhere in copyright? If so, can courts decide cases and resolve inconsistencies in the law without making aesthetic determinations?

3. As some of the opinions above have noted, there are alternatives to copyright for the protection of useful articles. Patent law allows companies to apply for design patents (distinct from the more common utility patents) to protect novel and inventive product designs. However, such patents are time-consuming and costly to obtain. Trademark law also provides some protection for product designs that are distinctive and indicate the source of the product. However, trademark law excludes from protection elements of a product design that are functional in nature.

4. How much protection is necessary to provide incentives for good product design? Are incentives necessary? Or are competitive pressures sufficient to induce companies to invest in good design? What costs need to be balanced against the need for protection? Which of the above opinions does the best job of balancing these competing concerns?

---

[23] Clive Bell, ART 17-18 (1958).
[24] Monroe C. Beardsley, *An Aesthetic Definition of Art*, in WHAT IS ART? 15-29 (Hugh Cutler, ed. 1983), at 21.
[25] George Dickie, ART AND THE AESTHETIC: AN INSTITUTIONAL ANALYSIS 34 (1974).

SECTION E. FIXATION

We have already learned that copyright does not protect a work unless the work is original. As noted earlier, the Copyright Act further limits copyright to original works of authorship "fixed in any tangible medium of expression." Section 101 of the Code goes on to define fixation as follows:

> A work is "fixed" in a tangible medium of expression when its embodiment in a copy or phonorecord, by or under the authority of the author, is sufficiently permanent or stable to permit it to be perceived, reproduced, or otherwise communicated for a period of more than transitory duration.

The requirement of fixation means that some otherwise copyrightable works (i.e. original works) will not receive federal copyright protection because they have not been fixed. For example, copyright does not protect an extemporaneous speech unless the speaker writes down or otherwise records her words. Protection for such work exists, if at all, only under state law.

The uncertainty of state law protection gives fixation considerable importance in copyright. Authors who fix their works gain the relative certainty of uniform federal protection, while authors who fail to do so face the possibility that their works are in the public domain, at least until they fix the work. Congress recognized this and tried to make fixation a clear and easily met requirement. The legislative history clearly indicates that authors can fix their works in almost any conceivable fashion, including writing, photographs, magnetic tape, compact discs, DVDs, punch cards, or "any other stable form."[26] However, as the next case shows, Congress did not foresee the impact that computers would have on the creation and preservation of works.

Williams Electronics v. Artic Int'l
685 F.2d 870 (3d Cir. 1982)

SLOVITER, Circuit Judge.

Defendant Artic International, Inc. appeals from the district court's entry of a final injunction order permanently restraining and enjoining it from infringing plaintiff's copyrights on audiovisual works and a computer program relating to the electronic video game DEFENDER. ...

Plaintiff-appellee Williams Electronics, Inc. manufactures and sells coin-operated electronic video games. A video game machine consists of a cabinet containing, inter alia, a cathode ray tube (CRT), a sound system, hand controls for the player, and electronic circuit boards. The electronic

---

[26] H.R. Rep. No. 94-1476, 94th Cong., 2d Sess. 52 (1976).

circuitry includes a microprocessor and memory devices, called ROMs (*R*ead *O*nly *M*emory), which are tiny computer "chips" containing thousands of data locations which store the instructions and data of a computer program. The microprocessor executes the computer program to cause the game to operate. Judge Newman of the Second Circuit described a similar type of memory device as follows: "The (ROM) stores the instructions and data from a computer program in such a way that when electric current passes through the circuitry, the interaction of the program stored in the (ROM) with the other components of the game produces the sights and sounds of the audiovisual display that the player sees and hears. The memory devices determine not only the appearance and movement of the (game) images but also the variations in movement in response to the player's operation of the hand controls." *Stern Electronics, Inc. v. Kaufman,* 669 F.2d 852, 854 (2d Cir. 1982).

In approximately October 1979 Williams began to design a new video game, ultimately called DEFENDER, which incorporated various original and unique audiovisual features. The DEFENDER game was introduced to the industry at a trade show in 1980 and has since achieved great success in the marketplace. One of the attractions of video games contributing to their phenomenal popularity is apparently their use of unrealistic fantasy creatures, a fad also observed in the popularity of certain current films. In the DEFENDER game, there are symbols of a spaceship and aliens who do battle with symbols of human figures. The player operates the flight of and weapons on the spaceship, and has the mission of preventing invading aliens from kidnapping the humans from a ground plane. ...

Defendant-appellant Artic International, Inc. is a seller of electronic components for video games in competition with Williams. The district court made the following relevant findings which are not disputed on this appeal. Artic has sold circuit boards, manufactured by others, which contain electronic circuits including a microprocessor and memory devices (ROMs). These memory devices incorporate a computer program which is virtually identical to Williams' program for its DEFENDER game. The result is a circuit board "kit" which is sold by Artic to others and which, when connected to a cathode ray tube, produces audiovisual effects and a game almost identical to the Williams DEFENDER game including both the attract mode and the play mode. The play mode and actual play of Artic's game, entitled "DEFENSE COMMAND," is virtually identical to that of the Williams game, *i.e.,* the characters displayed on the cathode ray tube including the player's spaceship are identical in shape, size, color, manner of movement and interaction with other symbols. Also, the attract mode of the Artic game is substantially identical to that of Williams' game, with minor exceptions such as the absence of the Williams name and the substitution of the terms "DEFENSE" and/or "DEFENSE COMMAND" for the term "DEFENDER" in its display. Based on the evidence before it, the district court found that the defendant Artic had infringed the plaintiff's computer program copyright for the DEFENDER game by selling kits which contain a computer program which is a copy of plaintiff's computer program, and that the defendant had infringed both of the plaintiff's audiovisual copyrights for the DEFENDER game by selling copies of those audiovisual works.

In the appeal before us, defendant does not dispute the findings with respect to copying but instead challenges the conclusions of the district court with respect to copyright infringement and the validity and scope of plaintiff's copyrights. ...

[D]efendant contends that there can be no copyright protection for the DEFENDER game's attract mode and play mode because these works fail to meet the statutory requirement of "fixation." ... The fixation requirement is defined in section 101 in relevant part as follows: A work is "fixed" in a tangible medium of expression when its embodiment in a copy or phonorecord, by or under the authority of the author, is sufficiently permanent or stable to permit it to be perceived, reproduced, or otherwise communicated for a period of more than transitory duration.

Defendant claims that the images in the plaintiff's audiovisual game are transient, and cannot be "fixed." Specifically, it contends that there is a lack of "fixation" because the video game generates or creates "new" images each time the attract mode or play mode is displayed, notwithstanding the fact that the new images are identical or substantially identical to the earlier ones.

We reject this contention. The fixation requirement is met whenever the work is "sufficiently permanent or stable to permit it to be ... reproduced, or otherwise communicated" for more than a transitory period. Here the original audiovisual features of the DEFENDER game repeat themselves over and over. The identical contention was previously made by this defendant and rejected by the court in *Midway Manufacturing Co. v. Artic International, Inc., supra*, slip op. at 16-18. Moreover, the rejection of a similar contention by the Second Circuit is also applicable here. The court stated:

> The (video game's) display satisfies the statutory definition of an original "audiovisual work," and the memory devices of the game satisfy the statutory requirement of a "copy" in which the work is "fixed." The Act defines "copies" as "material objects ... in which a work is fixed by any method now known or later developed, and from which the work can be perceived, reproduced, or otherwise communicated, either directly or with the aid of a machine or device" and specifies that a work is "fixed" when "its embodiment in a copy ... is sufficiently permanent or stable to permit it to be perceived, reproduced, or otherwise communicated for a period of more than transitory duration." 17 U.S.C. § 101 (1976). The audiovisual work is permanently embodied in a material object, the memory devices, from which it can be perceived with the aid of the other components of the game.

Stern Electronics, Inc. v. Kaufman, 669 F.2d at 855-56.

Defendant also apparently contends that the player's participation withdraws the game's audiovisual work from copyright eligibility because there is no set or fixed performance and the player becomes a co-author of what appears on the screen. Although there is player interaction with the machine during the play mode which causes the audiovisual presentation to change in some respects from one game to the next in response to the player's varying participation,(there is always a repetitive sequence of a substantial portion of the sights and sounds of the game, and many aspects of the display remain constant from game to game regardless of how the player operates the controls.)Furthermore, there is no player participation in the attract mode which is displayed repetitively without change. ...

For the above reasons, the district court's order granting the injunction will be affirmed. ... The case will be remanded for further proceedings consistent with this opinion.

Notes and Questions

1.   As noted earlier, the requirement of fixation means that clearly original works will not gain protection and may fall into the public domain. What purpose does this potential forfeiture of rights serve? At least two possibilities come to mind. Perhaps it increases the likelihood that society will enjoy benefits of the author's creativity by forcing the author to preserve the work in a reasonably permanent form. Or, perhaps fixation helps define the boundaries of a particular copyright claim by committing authors to specific embodiments of their works. This allows courts to be certain that they know the identity and characteristics of any works in litigation. Does either of these purposes convince you that copyright should depend on fixation?

2.   Does *Williams* take the law of fixation in an undesirable direction? Writings on paper, images captured on film, and sounds on tape satisfy fixation because they create a permanent record that reproduces the author's work exactly upon each viewing. By contrast, the fixation accepted in *Williams* allows variation of the supposedly copyrightable images and sounds by the person playing the video game. How then do we know what the author created? The court finessed this in part by noting that the attract mode and certain other images always appeared in a particular fashion, but what would happen if the video game in question had no original images or sounds that always appeared in the same way? Would fixation become impossible?

Recently, the Seventh Circuit denied copyright in a case raising these issues. In *Kelley v. Chicago Park Dist.*, 635 F.3d 290 (7th Cir.), *cert. denied*, 132 S. Ct. 380 (2011), the court held that the Copyright Act did not protect an outdoor garden designed and installed by artist Richard Kelley because the garden was not fixed. The court stated that a garden's elements, though conceivably artistic, are "alive and inherently changeable, not fixed." The court further wrote that a garden's "appearance is too inherently variable to supply a baseline for determining questions of copyright creation and infringement. If a garden can qualify as a "work of authorship" sufficiently "embodied in a copy," at what point has fixation occurred? When the garden is newly planted? When its first blossoms appear? When it is in full bloom? How—and at what point in time—is a court to determine whether infringing copying has occurred?" *Id.* at 304-05. Do you agree with the court's analysis?

3.　An even trickier problem arises with the possibility of fixation in a computer's random access memory, or "RAM." RAM differs from the ROM at issue in *Williams.* Whereas ROM holds its contents permanently (hence the name "read only memory"), RAM holds its contents only as long as the computer's user directs it to, or until the user or a loss of power turns the computer off. For example, a user who creates a new word processing document stores that document in her computer's RAM until she saves it to her hard disk. If the computer is turned off or the document is closed without saving, it disappears. Obviously, our hypothetical user fixes her document by saving it to her hard disk. But what if she chooses not to save the document, but leaves it in RAM? Does this constitute fixation?

A quick reading of the Copyright Act suggests that fixation has not occurred, because RAM does not store the work for more than a "transitory" duration. However, authority exists for the proposition that fixation in RAM is possible. *See MAI Systems Corp. v. Peak Computer,* 991 F.2d 511 (9th Cir. 1993) (holding that a person who loads a computer program into RAM has created a fixed copy for purposes of potential copyright infringement).

Do you think that allowing fixation in RAM is desirable, and why?

SECTION F. GOVERNMENT WORKS

It is important to note that § 105 of the Copyright Act denies protection to works authored by the United States government, even if those works otherwise meet basic requirements of originality and fixation. Section 105 does not, however, prevent the federal government from holding copyrights it acquires from others, nor does it prohibit copyright in works authored by state governments.

The section 105 denial of copyright can be justified on the ground that the federal government does not author works in hopes of financial gain. Indeed, one could argue that society has already paid for the development of government-authored work through taxes. Do you accept this reasoning? If so, what about works authored by state (as opposed to federal) governments? Shouldn't they also be in the public domain?

Chapter Three

INITIAL OWNERSHIP AND TRANSFER

Initial ownership of copyright is straightforward when an individual creates a copyrightable work of her own accord. For cases like that, section 201(a) of the Copyright Act assigns the copyright to the work's author.[27] Complications arise quickly, however, for authors do not always work alone or of their own accord. What happens when a person commissions an author to create a work, when people work collaboratively, or when one person helps another? This chapter investigates how Congress and the courts have resolved this question.

As you read the materials that follow, you may find it helpful to consider various perspectives from which to evaluate the law. The Copyright Act defines terms like "work made for hire" and "joint work," but does this mean that a court can determine the correct outcome of a case by studying the statute and its legislative history? If not, how should courts understand the statute? Courts could think about directing copyright incentives to spur the creation of new works. Alternatively, they could assign copyrights on the basis of fairness or equity. Perhaps courts should consider the operation of markets for the copyrighted works and assign rights in a way that facilitates economic transactions. Finally, courts may want to assign rights to the person who will best preserve the artistic vision behind the original work. In some cases, these considerations will all point courts in the same direction. In others, however, they will imply different outcomes. What should happen then?

---

[27] Section 201(a) provides:
> Initial Ownership. — Copyright in a work protected under this title vests initially in the author or authors of the work. The authors of a joint work are coowners of copyright in the work.

SECTION A. WORKS MADE FOR HIRE

People commonly hire others to create copyrightable works. Newlyweds hire photographers, newspapers hire reporters, moviemakers hire composers, and software companies hire programmers. Who owns the copyright in the resulting works? As you will soon see, the answer to this question is rather complicated. Section 201(b) gives copyright to the hiring party of a "work made for hire."[28] Section 101 defines a work made for hire as:

(1) a work prepared by an employee within the scope of his or her employment; or

(2) a work specially ordered or commissioned for use as a contribution to a collective work, as a part of a motion picture or other audiovisual work, as a translation, as a supplementary work, as a compilation, as an instructional text, as a test, as answer material for a test, or as an atlas, if the parties expressly agree in a written instrument signed by them that the work shall be considered a work made for hire. For the purpose of the foregoing sentence, a "supplementary work" is a work prepared for publication as a secondary adjunct to a work by another author for the purpose of introducing, concluding, illustrating, explaining, revising, commenting upon, or assisting in the use of the other work, such as forewords, afterwords, pictorial illustrations, maps, charts, tables, editorial notes, musical arrangements, answer material for tests, bibliographies, appendixes, and indexes, and an "instructional text" is a literary, pictorial, or graphic work prepared for publication and with the purpose of use in systematic instructional activities.

Our first case presents the Supreme Court's first and only interpretation of this language.

Community For Creative Non-Violence v. Reid
490 U.S. 730 (1989)

JUSTICE MARSHALL delivered the opinion of the Court.

In this case, an artist and the organization that hired him to produce a sculpture contest the ownership of the copyright in that work. To resolve this dispute, we must construe the "work made for hire" provisions of the Copyright Act of 1976 (Act or 1976 Act), 17 U.S.C. §§ 101 and

---

[28] Section 201(b) provides:

Works Made for Hire. — In the case of a work made for hire, the employer or other person for whom the work was prepared is considered the author for purposes of this title, and, unless the parties have expressly agreed otherwise in a written instrument signed by them, owns all of the rights comprised in the copyright.

201(b), and in particular, the provision in § 101, which defines as a "work made for hire" a "work prepared by an employee within the scope of his or her employment" (hereinafter § 101(1)).

I

Petitioners are the Community for Creative Non-Violence (CCNV), a nonprofit unincorporated association dedicated to eliminating homelessness in America, and Mitch Snyder, a member and trustee of CCNV. In the fall of 1985, CCNV decided to participate in the annual Christmastime Pageant of Peace in Washington, D.C., by sponsoring a display to dramatize the plight of the homeless. As the District Court recounted:

> Snyder and fellow CCNV members conceived the idea for the nature of the display: a sculpture of a modern Nativity scene in which, in lieu of the traditional Holy Family, the two adult figures and the infant would appear as contemporary homeless people huddled on a streetside steam grate. The family was to be black (most of the homeless in Washington being black); the figures were to be life-sized, and the steam grate would be positioned atop a platform "pedestal," or base, within which special-effects equipment would be enclosed to emit simulated "steam" through the grid to swirl about the figures. They also settled upon a title for the work—"Third World America"—and a legend for the pedestal: "and still there is no room at the inn."

Snyder made inquiries to locate an artist to produce the sculpture. He was referred to respondent James Earl Reid, a Baltimore, Maryland, sculptor. In the course of two telephone calls, Reid agreed to sculpt the three human figures. CCNV agreed to make the steam grate and pedestal for the statue. Reid proposed that the work be cast in bronze, at a total cost of approximately $100,000 and taking six to eight months to complete. Snyder rejected that proposal because CCNV did not have sufficient funds, and because the statue had to be completed by December 12 to be included in the pageant. Reid then suggested, and Snyder agreed, that the sculpture would be made of a material known as "Design Cast 62," a synthetic substance that could meet CCNV's monetary and time constraints, could be tinted to resemble bronze, and could withstand the elements. The parties agreed that the project would cost no more than $15,000, not including Reid's services, which he offered to donate. The parties did not sign a written agreement. Neither party mentioned copyright.

After Reid received an advance of $3,000, he made several sketches of figures in various poses. At Snyder's request, Reid sent CCNV a sketch of a proposed sculpture showing the family in a crèche like setting: the mother seated, cradling a baby in her lap; the father standing behind her, bending over her shoulder to touch the baby's foot. Reid testified that Snyder asked for the sketch to use in raising funds for the sculpture. Snyder testified that it was also for his approval. Reid sought a black family to serve as a model for the sculpture. Upon Snyder's suggestion, Reid visited a family living at CCNV's Washington shelter but decided that only their newly born child was a suitable model. While Reid was in Washington, Snyder took him to see homeless people living on the streets. Snyder pointed out that they tended to recline on steam grates, rather than sit or stand, in order to warm their bodies. From that time on, Reid's sketches contained only reclining figures.

Throughout November and the first two weeks of December 1985, Reid worked exclusively on the statue, assisted at various times by a dozen different people who were paid with funds provided in installments by CCNV. On a number of occasions, CCNV members visited Reid to check on his progress and to coordinate CCNV's construction of the base. CCNV rejected Reid's proposal to use suitcases or shopping bags to hold the family's personal belongings, insisting instead on a shopping cart. Reid and CCNV members did not discuss copyright ownership on any of these visits.

On December 24, 1985, 12 days after the agreed-upon date, Reid delivered the completed statue to Washington. There it was joined to the steam grate and pedestal prepared by CCNV and placed on display near the site of the pageant. Snyder paid Reid the final installment of the $15,000. The statue remained on display for a month. In late January 1986, CCNV members returned it to Reid's studio in Baltimore for minor repairs. Several weeks later, Snyder began making plans to take the statue on a tour of several cities to raise money for the homeless. Reid objected, contending that the Design Cast 62 material was not strong enough to withstand the ambitious itinerary. He urged CCNV to cast the statue in bronze at a cost of $35,000, or to create a master mold at a cost of $5,000. Snyder declined to spend more of CCNV's money on the project.

In March 1986, Snyder asked Reid to return the sculpture. Reid refused. He then filed a certificate of copyright registration for "Third World America" in his name and announced plans to take the sculpture on a more modest tour than the one CCNV had proposed. Snyder, acting in his capacity as CCNV's trustee, immediately filed a competing certificate of copyright registration.

Snyder and CCNV then commenced this action against Reid and his photographer, Ronald Purtee, seeking return of the sculpture and a determination of copyright ownership. The District Court granted a preliminary injunction, ordering the sculpture's return. After a 2-day bench trial, the District Court declared that "Third World America" was a "work made for hire" under § 101 of the Copyright Act and that Snyder, as trustee for CCNV, was the exclusive owner of the copyright in the sculpture. ...

The Court of Appeals for the District of Columbia Circuit reversed and remanded, holding that Reid owned the copyright because "Third World America" was not a work for hire. ...

We granted certiorari to resolve a conflict among the Courts of Appeals over the proper construction of the "work made for hire" provisions of the Act. We now affirm.

II

A

The Copyright Act of 1976 provides that copyright ownership "vests initially in the author or authors of the work." 17 U.S.C. § 201(a). As a general rule, the author is the party who actually creates the work, that is, the person who translates an idea into a fixed, tangible expression entitled to copyright protection. The Act carves out an important exception, however, for "works made for hire." If the work is for hire, "the employer or other person for whom the work was prepared is considered the author" and owns the copyright, unless there is a written agreement to the contrary. § 201(b). ...

Section 101 of the 1976 Act provides that a work is "for hire" under two sets of circumstances:

(1) a work prepared by an employee within the scope of his or her employment; or

(2) a work specially ordered or commissioned for use as a contribution to a collective work, as a part of a motion picture or other audiovisual work, as a translation, as a supplementary work, as a compilation, as an instructional text, as a test, as answer material for a test, or as an atlas, if the parties expressly agree in a written instrument signed by them that the work shall be considered a work made for hire.

Petitioners do not claim that the statue satisfies the terms of § 101(2). Quite clearly, it does not. Sculpture does not fit within any of the nine categories of "specially ordered or commissioned" works enumerated in that subsection, and no written agreement between the parties establishes "Third World America" as a work for hire.

The dispositive inquiry in this case therefore is whether "Third World America" is "a work prepared by an employee within the scope of his or her employment" under § 101(1). The Act does not define these terms. In the absence of such guidance, four interpretations have emerged. The first holds that a work is prepared by an employee whenever the hiring party retains the right to control the product. Petitioners take this view. A second, and closely related, view is that a work is prepared by an employee under § 101(1) when the hiring party has actually wielded control with respect to the creation of a particular work. This approach was formulated by the Court of Appeals for the Second Circuit and adopted by the Fourth Circuit, ... and, at times, by petitioners. A third view is that the term "employee" within § 101(1) carries its common-law agency law meaning. This view was endorsed by the Fifth Circuit and by the Court of Appeals below. Finally, respondent and numerous *amici curiae* contend that the term "employee" only refers to "formal, salaried" employees. *See, e.g.*, Brief for Respondent 23-24; Brief for Register of Copyrights as *Amicus Curiae* 7. The Court of Appeals for the Ninth Circuit recently adopted this view.

The starting point for our interpretation of a statute is always its language. The Act nowhere defines the terms "employee" or "scope of employment." It is, however, well established that "[w]here Congress uses terms that have accumulated settled meaning under ... the common law, a court must infer, unless the statute otherwise dictates, that Congress means to incorporate the established meaning of these terms." *NLRB v Amax Coal Co.* 453 U.S. 322, 329 (1981) ... In the past, when Congress has used the term "employee" without defining it, we have concluded that Congress intended to describe the conventional master-servant relationship as understood by common-law agency doctrine. ... Nothing in the text of the work for hire provisions indicates that Congress used the words "employee" and "employment" to describe anything other than "'the conventional relation of employer and employee.'" *Kelley*, *supra*, at 323. On the contrary, Congress' intent to incorporate the agency law definition is suggested by § 101(1)'s use of the term, "scope of employment," a widely used term of art in agency law.

In past cases of statutory interpretation, when we have concluded that Congress intended terms such as "employee," "employer," and "scope of employment" to be understood in light of agency law, we have relied on the general common law of agency, rather than on the law of any particular State, to give meaning to these terms. This practice reflects the fact that "federal statutes are generally intended to have uniform nationwide application." *Mississippi Band of Choctaw Indians v. Holyfield*, 490 U.S. 30, 43 (1989). Establishment of a federal rule of agency, rather than reliance on state agency law, is particularly appropriate here given the Act's express objective of creating national, uniform copyright law by broadly pre-empting state statutory and common-law copyright regulation. We thus agree with the Court of Appeals that the term "employee" should be understood in light of the general common law of agency.

In contrast, neither test proposed by petitioners is consistent with the text of the Act. The exclusive focus of the right to control the product test on the relationship between the hiring party and the product clashes with the language of § 101(1), which focuses on the relationship between the hired and hiring parties. The right to control the product test also would distort the meaning of the ensuing subsection, § 101(2). Section 101 plainly creates two distinct ways in which a work can be deemed for hire: one for works prepared by employees, the other for those specially ordered or commissioned works which fall within one of the nine enumerated categories and are the subject of a written agreement. The right to control the product test ignores this dichotomy by transforming into a work for hire under § 101(1) any "specially ordered or commissioned" work that is subject to the supervision and control of the hiring party. Because a party who hires a "specially ordered or commissioned" work by definition has a right to specify the characteristics of the product desired, at the time the commission is accepted, and frequently until it is completed, the right to control the product test would mean that many works that could satisfy § 101(2) would already have been deemed works for hire under § 101(1). Petitioners' interpretation is particularly hard to square with § 101(2)'s enumeration of the nine specific categories of specially ordered or commissioned works eligible to be works for hire, e.g., "a contribution to a collective work," "a part of a motion picture," and "answer material for a test." The unifying feature of these works is that they are usually prepared at the instance, direction, and risk of a publisher or producer. By their very nature, therefore, these types of works would be works by an employee under petitioners' right to control the product test.

The actual control test, articulated by the Second Circuit in *Aldon Accessories*, fares only marginally better when measured against the language and structure of § 101. Under this test independent contractors who are so controlled and supervised in the creation of a particular work are deemed "employees" under § 101(1). Thus work for hire status under § 101(1) depends on a hiring party's actual control of, rather than right to control, the product. Under the actual control test, a work for hire could arise under § 101(2), but not under § 101(1), where a party commissions, but does not actually control, a product which falls into one of the nine enumerated categories. Nonetheless, we agree with the Court of Appeals for the Fifth Circuit that "[t]here is simply no way to milk the 'actual control' test of *Aldon Accessories* from the language of the statute." *Easter Seal Society*, 815 F.2d, at 334. Section 101 clearly delineates between works prepared by an employee and commissioned works. Sound though other distinctions might be as a matter of copyright policy, there is no statutory support for an additional dichotomy between commissioned works that are actually controlled and supervised by the hiring party and those that are not.

We therefore conclude that the language and structure of § 101 of the Act do not support either the right to control the product or the actual control approaches.[29] The structure of § 101 indicates that a work for hire can arise through one of two mutually exclusive means, one for employees and one for independent contractors, and ordinary canons of

---

[29] [Footnote 8] We also reject the suggestion of respondent and *amici* that the § 101(1) term "employee" refers only to formal, salaried employees. While there is some support for such a definition in the legislative history, *see* Varmer, Works Made for Hire 130; n. 11, *infra,* the language of § 101(1) cannot support it. The Act does not say "formal" or "salaried" employee, but simply "employee." Moreover, respondent and those *amici* who endorse a formal, salaried employee test do not agree upon the content of this test. *Compare, e.g.,* Brief for Respondent 37 (hired party who is on payroll is an employee within § 101(1)) *with* Tr. of Oral Arg. 31 (hired party who receives a salary or commissions regularly is an employee within § 101(1)); *and* Brief for Volunteer Lawyers for the Arts Inc. *et al.* as *Amici Curiae* 4 (hired party who receives a salary and is treated as an employee for Social Security and tax purposes is an employee within § 101(1)). Even the one Court of Appeals to adopt what it termed a formal, salaried employee test in fact embraced an approach incorporating numerous factors drawn from the agency law definition of employee which we endorse. *See Dumas,* 865 F.2d at 1104.

statutory interpretation indicate that the classification of a particular hired party should be made with reference to agency law.

This reading of the undefined statutory terms finds considerable support in the Act's legislative history. The Act, which almost completely revised existing copyright law, was the product of two decades of negotiation by representatives of creators and copyright-using industries, supervised by the Copyright Office and, to a lesser extent, by Congress. Despite the lengthy history of negotiation and compromise which ultimately produced the Act, two things remained constant. First, interested parties and Congress at all times viewed works by employees and commissioned works by independent contractors as separate entities. Second, in using the term "employee," the parties and Congress meant to refer to a hired party in a conventional employment relationship. These factors militate in favor of the reading we have found appropriate.

In 1955, when Congress decided to overhaul copyright law, the existing work for hire provision was § 62 of the 1909 Copyright Act. It provided that "the word 'author' shall include an employer in the case of works made for hire." Because the 1909 Act did not define "employer" or "works made for hire," the task of shaping these terms fell to the courts. They concluded that the work for hire doctrine codified in § 62 referred only to works made by employees in the regular course of their employment. As for commissioned works, the courts generally presumed that the commissioned party had impliedly agreed to convey the copyright, along with the work itself, to the hiring party.

In 1961, the Copyright Office's first legislative proposal retained the distinction between works by employees and works by independent contractors. After numerous meetings with representatives of the affected parties, the Copyright Office issued a preliminary draft bill in 1963. Adopting the Register's recommendation, it defined "work made for hire" as "a work prepared by an employee within the scope of the duties of his employment, but not including a work made on special order or commission." Preliminary Draft for Revised U.S. Copyright Law and Discussions and Comments on the Draft, 88th Cong., 2d Sess., Copyright Law Revision, Part 3, p. 15, n. 11 (H. Judiciary Comm. Print 1964) (hereinafter Preliminary Draft).

In response to objections by book publishers that the preliminary draft bill limited the work for hire doctrine to "employees," the 1964 revision bill expanded the scope of the work for hire classification to reach, for the first time, commissioned works. The bill's language, proposed initially by representatives of the publishing industry, retained the definition of work for hire insofar as it referred to "employees," but added a separate clause covering commissioned works, without regard to the subject matter, "if the parties so agree in writing." S. 3008, H.R. 11947, H.R. 12354, 88th Cong., 2d Sess., 54 (1964). Those representing authors objected that the added provision would allow publishers to use their superior bargaining position to force authors to sign work for hire agreements, thereby relinquishing all copyright rights as a condition of getting their books published.

In 1965, the competing interests reached a historic compromise, which was embodied in a joint memorandum submitted to Congress and the Copyright Office, incorporated into the 1965 revision bill, and ultimately enacted in the same form and nearly the same terms 11 years later, as § 101 of the 1976 Act. The compromise retained as subsection (1) the language referring to "a work prepared by an employee within the scope of his employment." However, in exchange for concessions from publishers on provisions relating to the termination of transfer rights, the authors consented to a second subsection which classified four categories of commissioned works as works for hire if the parties expressly so agreed in writing: works for use "as a contribution to a collective work, as a part of a motion picture, as a translation, or as supplementary work." S. 1006, H.R. 4347, H.R. 5680, H.R. 6835, 89th Cong., 1st Sess., § 101 (1965). The interested parties selected these categories because they concluded that these commissioned works, although not prepared by employees and thus not covered by the first subsection, nevertheless should be treated as works for hire because they were ordinarily prepared "at the instance, direction, and risk of a publisher or producer." Supplementary Report, at 67. The Supplementary Report emphasized that only the "four special cases specifically mentioned" could qualify as works made for hire; "[o]ther works made on special order or commission would not come within the definition." *Id.*, at 67-68.

In 1966, the House Committee on the Judiciary endorsed this compromise in the first legislative Report on the revision bills. See H.R. Rep. No. 2237, 89th Cong., 2d Sess., 114, 116 (1966). Retaining the distinction between works by employees and commissioned works, the House Committee focused instead on "how to draw a statutory line between those works written on special order or commission that should be considered as works made for hire, and those that should not." *Id.*, at 115. The House Committee added four other enumerated categories of commissioned works that could be treated as works for hire: compilations, instructional texts, tests, and atlases. *Id.*, at 116. With the single addition of "answer material for a test," the 1976 Act, as enacted, contained the same definition of works made for hire as did the 1966 revision bill, and had the same structure and nearly the same terms as the 1966 bill. Indeed, much of the language of the 1976 House and Senate Reports was borrowed from the Reports accompanying the earlier drafts.

Thus, the legislative history of the Act is significant for several reasons. First, the enactment of the 1965 compromise with only minor modifications demonstrates that Congress intended to provide two mutually exclusive ways for works to acquire work for hire status: one for employees and the other for independent contractors. Second, the legislative history underscores the clear import of the statutory language: only enumerated categories of commissioned works may be accorded work for hire status. The hiring party's right to control the product simply is not determinative. Indeed, importing a test based on a hiring party's right to control, or actual control of, a product would unravel the "'carefully worked out compromise aimed at balancing legitimate interests on both sides.'" H.R. Rep. No. 2237, *supra*, at 114, quoting Supplemental Report, at 66.

We do not find convincing petitioners' contrary interpretation of the history of the Act. They contend that Congress, in enacting the Act, meant to incorporate a line of cases decided under the 1909 Act holding that an employment relationship exists sufficient to give the hiring party copyright ownership whenever that party has the right to control or supervise the artist's work. ...

We are unpersuaded. Ordinarily, "Congress' silence is just that— silence." *Alaska Airlines, Inc. v. Brock*, 480 U.S. 678, 686 (1987). Petitioners' reliance on legislative silence is particularly misplaced here because the text and structure of § 101 counsel otherwise. Furthermore, the structure of the work for hire provisions was fully developed in 1965, and the text was agreed upon in essentially final form by 1966. At that time, however, the courts had applied the work for hire doctrine under the 1909 Act exclusively to traditional employees. Indeed, it was not until after the 1965 compromise was forged and adopted by Congress that a federal court for the first time applied the work for hire doctrine to commissioned works. Congress certainly could not have "jettisoned" a line of cases that had not yet been decided.

Finally, petitioners' construction of the work for hire provisions would impede Congress' paramount goal in revising the 1976 Act of enhancing predictability and certainty of copyright ownership. In a "copyright marketplace," the parties negotiate with an expectation that one of them will own the copyright in the completed work. With that expectation, the parties at the outset can settle on relevant contractual terms, such as the price for the work and the ownership of reproduction rights.

To the extent that petitioners endorse an actual control test, CCNV's construction of the work for hire provisions prevents such planning. Because that test turns on whether the hiring party has closely monitored the production process, the parties would not know until late in the process, if not until the work is completed, whether a work will ultimately fall within § 101(1). Under petitioners' approach, therefore, parties would have to predict in advance whether the hiring party will sufficiently control a given work to make it the author. "If they guess incorrectly, their reliance on 'work for hire' or an assignment may give them a copyright interest that they did not bargain for." *Easter Seal Society*, 815 F.2d, at 333. This understanding of the work for hire provisions clearly thwarts Congress' goal of ensuring predictability through advance planning. Moreover, petitioners' interpretation "leaves the door open for hiring parties, who have failed to get a full assignment of copyright rights from independent contractors falling outside the subdivision (2) guidelines, to unilaterally obtain work-made-for-hire rights years after the work has been completed as long as they directed or supervised the work, a standard that is hard not to meet when one is a hiring party."

Hamilton, Commissioned Works as Works Made for Hire Under the 1976 Copyright Act: Misinterpretation and Injustice, 135 U. PA. L. REV. 1281, 1304 (1987).

In sum, we must reject petitioners' argument. Transforming a commissioned work into a work by an employee on the basis of the hiring party's right to control, or actual control of, the work is inconsistent with the language, structure, and legislative history of the work for hire provisions. To determine whether a work is for hire under the Act, a court first should ascertain, using principles of general common law of agency, whether the work was prepared by an employee or an independent contractor. After making this determination, the court can apply the appropriate subsection of § 101.

B

We turn, finally, to an application of § 101 to Reid's production of "Third World America." In determining whether a hired party is an employee under the general common law of agency, we consider the hiring party's right to control the manner and means by which the product is accomplished. Among the other factors relevant to this inquiry are the skill required; the source of the instrumentalities and tools; the location of the work; the duration of the relationship between the parties; whether the hiring party has the right to assign additional projects to the hired party; the extent of the hired party's discretion over when and how long to work; the method of payment; the hired party's role in hiring and paying assistants; whether the work is part of the regular business of the hiring party; whether the hiring party is in business; the provision of employee benefits; and the tax treatment of the hired party. See Restatement 220(2) (setting forth a nonexhaustive list of factors relevant to determining whether a hired party is an employee). No one of these factors is determinative.

Examining the circumstances of this case in light of these factors, we agree with the Court of Appeals that Reid was not an employee of CCNV but an independent contractor. True, CCNV members directed enough of Reid's work to ensure that he produced a sculpture that met their specifications. But the extent of control the hiring party exercises over the details of the product is not dispositive. Indeed, all the other circumstances weigh heavily against finding an employment relationship. Reid is a sculptor, a skilled occupation. Reid supplied his own tools. He worked in his own studio in Baltimore, making daily supervision of his activities from Washington practicably impossible. Reid was retained for less than two months, a relatively short period of time. During and after this time, CCNV had no right to assign additional projects to Reid. Apart from the deadline for completing the sculpture, Reid had absolute freedom to decide when and how long to work. CCNV paid Reid $15,000, a sum dependent on "completion of a specific job, a method by which independent contractors are often compensated." *Holt v. Winpisinger*, 811 F.2d 1532, 1540 (1987). Reid had total discretion in hiring and paying assistants. "Creating sculptures was hardly 'regular business' for

CCNV." 846 F.2d, at 1494, n. 11. Indeed, CCNV is not a business at all. Finally, CCNV did not pay payroll or Social Security taxes, provide any employee benefits, or contribute to unemployment insurance or workers' compensation funds.

Because Reid was an independent contractor, whether "Third World America" is a work for hire depends on whether it satisfies the terms of § 101(2). This petitioners concede it cannot do. Thus, CCNV is not the author of "Third World America" by virtue of the work for hire provisions of the Act. However, as the Court of Appeals made clear, CCNV nevertheless may be a joint author of the sculpture if, on remand, the District Court determines that CCNV and Reid prepared the work "with the intention that their contributions be merged into inseparable or interdependent parts of a unitary whole." 17 U.S.C. § 101. In that case, CCNV and Reid would be co-owners of the copyright in the work.

For the aforestated reasons, we affirm the judgment of the Court of Appeals for the District of Columbia Circuit.

Notes and Questions

1. The *CCNV v. Reid* Court had to choose between 4 different interpretations of the word "employee": 1) the physical control test, where copyright goes to a hiring party who retains the right to control the product, 2) the creative control test, where copyright goes to a hiring party who has actually wielded control with respect to the creation of a work, 3) the common law agency test, and 4) the "formal, salaried" employee test. The Court chose option 3 because, according to the Court, the other possibilities were inconsistent with the language and legislative history of the Copyright Act. How convincing do you find the Court's reasoning? Do the language and legislative history of the Copyright Act conclusively dictate the Court's choice of option 3 over option 4?

2. *CCNV* arose because Congress abandoned the pre-1976 Act rule by which the hiring party always gained the copyright from an independent contractor in the absence of a writing to the contrary. By changing the law, Congress apparently thought it desirable to force employers to acquire copyright rights from at least some of the people they hire.

Would it be desirable for Congress to go even further by granting copyright to the creator in all cases, without regard to employee status? Under such a regime, employers wanting copyright rights would always have to obtain an assignment or license from the employee. Such a rule would have the benefit of clarity, and it would place the burden of action upon what is usually the more legally-sophisticated party.

On the other hand, if nearly every employer under this rule would, in practice, require an employee to sign over his or her copyrights, then perhaps the pre-1976 Act rule always favoring employers would be better because it would reflect commercial reality and save the costs of documenting routine copyright assignments from hired parties to employers. Of course, this would force employees and independent contractors alike to negotiate if they want to retain copyright in works they create.

Do either of these options strike you as superior to the agency test adopted in *CCNV* or the formal, salaried employee test supported by the Register of Copyrights? In thinking through your response, you might find it helpful to consider whether it is better to decide work made for hire cases with a bright-line, relatively inflexible test or a more ambiguous, flexible one. *CCNV*'s endorsement of the agency test means that copyright prefers flexibility over certainty. Do you agree with that choice?

3.   If a work is deemed to be a work made for hire, the employer is considered the author of the work. As a consequence, the employee who actually created the work, and whose creative labor is embodied in the work, has no legal entitlement to the work at all. Indeed, if the employee subsequently tried to copy or distribute the copyrighted work, he or she could be sued by the employer for copyright infringement. Does such an arrangement seem consistent with all of the theories underlying copyright more generally?

Hi-Tech Video Productions v. Capital Cities/ABC
58 F.3d 1093 (6th Cir. 1995)

BATCHELDER, Circuit Judge.

Hi-Tech Video Productions, Inc. ("Hi-Tech"), filed suit against Capital Cities/ABC, Inc. (ABC), alleging a single count of copyright infringement. At the close of a two-day bench trial, the district court denied from the bench ABC's motion to dismiss the complaint due to [Hi-Tech's failure to properly acquire copyright in relevant portions of the work it purports to own]. ...

ABC filed this appeal contesting the district court's rulings. ... Because we find Hi-Tech's copyright invalid, we reverse the judgment below. ...

I.

Hi-Tech is a production company in Traverse City, Michigan. In addition to contractual work, such as the creation of commercials and other promotional tapes for companies, Hi-Tech independently produces and distributes "video postcards" of northern Michigan vacation spots.

In May 1990, Hi-Tech released a travel video entitled "Mackinac Island: The Mackinac Video." Stan Akey, sole owner of Hi-Tech, produced and directed the video. He enlisted the help of freelance subcontractors: Ted Cline as aerial videographer, Steve Cook as scriptwriter/narrator, and Michael Mueller as principal videographer. As one of Hi-Tech's independent productions, the Mackinac video received its funding from Hi-Tech itself, not from a commercial client. Effective August 3, 1990, Hi-Tech registered a copyright in the Mackinac video as a "work made for hire."

Also in early 1990, the producers of "Good Morning America" (GMA), a news and information program on ABC, decided to feature Mackinac Island's annual Lilac Festival in GMA's June 8, 1990, broadcast. Donna Vislocky, then an associate producer of GMA, was charged with preparing a one-minute videotape on Mackinac Island and its history. Twice, Vislocky obtained footage of the island from an ABC affiliate in Traverse City. Two days before the air date, Vislocky determined the scenes to be insufficient.

Vislocky telephoned Sarah Bolger, Executive Director of the Mackinac Island Chamber of Commerce. Bolger sent Vislocky two videos, including the Mackinac video, via overnight mail. Upon receiving the videos, Vislocky identified scenes from Hi-Tech's video that were appropriate for use in GMA's background piece on Mackinac Island. Vislocky rearranged those scenes for use in the background piece but did not use Hi-Tech's narration or music.

The next morning, Spencer Christian of GMA reported the weather from Mackinac Island and conducted an interview of Bolger regarding the annual Lilac Festival. Introducing Christian's segment was the background piece that Vislocky had edited to include scenes from the visual portion of Hi-Tech's video.

II.

... Hi-Tech's certificate of copyright registration labels the Mackinac video a "work made for hire." In the case of a "work made for hire," the Copyright Act of 1976 ("the Act") considers the employer or person for whom the work was prepared to be the "author" for purposes of copyright registration and ownership. Section 101 of the Act defines a "work made for hire" [as "a work prepared by an employee within the scope of his or her employment"]. ...

The district court found Akey's assistants in the production of the video to be employees within the meaning of § 101(1). This Court conducts a de novo review of the district court's application of § 101(1) to the facts of the case.

III.

The United States Supreme Court construed the "work made for hire" provision in *Community for Creative Non-Violence v. Reid*, 490 U.S. 730 (1989) (hereinafter *CCNV*), and concluded that the term "employee" in § 101 must be understood through application of the general common law of agency. The Court then set forth a nonexclusive list of factors relevant to the determination of "employee" status:

(1)   the hiring party's right to control the manner and means by which the product is accomplished;

(2)   the skill required;

(3)   the source of the instrumentalities and tools;

(4)   the location of the work;

(5)   the duration of the relationship between the parties;

(6)   whether the hiring party has the right to assign additional projects to the hired party;

(7)   the extent of the hired party's discretion over when and how long to work;

(8)   the method of payment;

(9)   the hired party's role in hiring and paying assistants;

(10)   whether the work is part of the regular business of the hiring party;

(11)   whether the hiring party is in business;

(12)   the provision of employee benefits; and

(13)   the tax treatment of the hired party.

No single factor is determinative.

In finding "employee" status in this case, the district court relied on six of the above factors: Hi-Tech's right to control and actual control, the source of the instrumentalities, Hi-Tech's right to assign additional projects, the assistants' role in hiring and paying their own assistants, the scope of Hi-Tech's regular business, and Hi-Tech's status as a business. The court mentioned several factors that weigh in favor of independent contractor status, but summarily found them insufficient to affect its conclusion that an employer-employee relationship existed between Akey and his assistants.

The district court clearly erred in two of its factual findings. First, the district court found that Akey supplied the production equipment to his assistants. To the contrary, the record shows that Cline, the aerial videographer, supplied his own plane, which was specially equipped to accommodate aerial photography. Also, Akey provided the camera for principal photographer Mueller, but not the computer with which Mueller developed the video's graphics.

Second, the district court found that Akey retained the right to assign additional projects to his assistants. The record does not support this finding. While Akey may have previously engaged one or more of his Mackinac video assistants for other projects, there is no suggestion that Cline, Cook, and Mueller were bound to accept assignments unrelated to the Mackinac video. Rather, the record indicates that Akey hired Cline, Cook, and Mueller to make specific contributions to the Mackinac video only. For example, Akey testified that when a "particular job ... comes out," he hires "freelance people" to assist with "that project." Akey also testified that Mueller's primary occupation is in the computer field, but that Mueller takes on "contractual jobs" in the photography field as well. Indeed, Akey testified that Cline, too, has his own business of flying his Cessna for aerial photography.

More importantly, the district court erred as a matter of law in its application of the common law of agency to the facts of this case. The district court misapprehended the Supreme Court's statement that no single factor is conclusive in the agency analysis and improperly used this principle to dismiss the relative importance of several factors. As one court has said of CCNV,

> It does not necessarily follow that because no one factor is dispositive all factors are equally important, or indeed that all factors will have relevance in every case. The factors should not merely be tallied but should be weighed according to their significance in the case.

Aymes v. Bonelli, 980 F.2d 857, 861 (2d Cir. 1992). We agree with the Second Circuit's approach to applying the factors in the agency analysis. The factors that warrant significant weight in this case are discussed below.

A. The Right to Control, Actual Control, and Skill Required

In CCNV, the Supreme Court adopted the agency principles test and rejected the tests that made the right to exercise control over production, or the actual exercise of control, dispositive in the "work made for hire" analysis. Nevertheless, the Supreme Court retained the "control" factor as simply one of the many relevant factors.

In this case, Hi-Tech, through its sole proprietor Stan Akey, had the right to control the manner and means by which the video was completed. Akey exercised this right through his involvement in almost every step of the creative and administrative processes required to produce "Mackinac Island: The Video."

Nevertheless, while Akey may have had control of the artistic objectives of the project, it is also true that Akey relied on the skill of the artists he solicited to accomplish those objectives. In Akey's own words, he "coordinate[d] the entire project from its inception to completion, the creative input into the tape, and coordinate[d] the efforts of all the freelance people who worked with [him]." Akey further testified that he considered himself the producer and director of the Mackinac video and that he depended on each assistant's "creative, artistic ability" in his particular field.

Akey's control of the video production thus weighs in favor of finding an employer-employee relationship, but not significantly, in light of the skill required of the assistants, as well as the assistants' artistic contributions to the product.

B. Method of Payment, Employee Benefits, and Tax Treatment

In virtually every case, a strong indication of a worker's employment status can be garnered through examining how the employer compensates the worker (including benefits provided) and how the employer treats the worker for tax purposes. For example, in *Aymes*, 980 F.2d 857, the hiring party provided a computer programmer no benefits and withheld neither social security nor federal or state income taxes. The Second Circuit reasoned that the choice to treat a skilled worker as an independent contractor for compensation and tax purposes was entirely inconsistent with an employer-employee relationship.

The record reveals that Akey paid Mueller on a per diem basis. Regular wages, as opposed to payment by the job, suggest employee status, but the fact that Mueller worked on the Mackinac video for only five days suggests otherwise. The record does not specify the method of payment for Cline and Cook. Overall, the evidence on the method of payment is indeterminate.

However, the same cannot be said of the other relevant economic factors. Akey neither withheld payroll taxes from his assistants' compensation nor provided the assistants employment benefits such as medical or life insurance. Contrary to the district court's analysis, these factors weigh very heavily in favor of finding independent contractor status.

C.   Perceptions of the Parties

In applying the common law of agency to copyright cases, the Supreme Court typically refers to the Restatement of Agency for guidance. In addition to the factors listed above, the Restatement cites the parties' perceptions or understanding as relevant to a worker's employment status. Restatement (Second) of Agency 220(2)(i) (1957).

Akey is the only full-time employee of Hi-Tech. He testified that when the need arises for a production team, he hires "freelance people," including photographers, scriptwriters, musicians, and narrators. In his testimony, Akey referred to his assistants on the Mackinac video as "freelancers," "independent contractors," "subcontractors," or the like no fewer than eight times. Akey also specifically stated that the assistants were not his employees.

The district court did not accord any weight to Akey's understanding of his employment relationship with the assistants. This Court considers Akey's perceptions highly indicative of his assistants' independent contractor status.

D.   The Scope of the Business

If the work at issue is not a part of the hiring party's regular business, the hiring party is more likely to enlist the services of an independent contractor on a periodic basis (that is, when and if the need arises), rather than hire a full-time employee. In *CCNV*, for instance, the hiring party was a charity, and the hired party was an artist. The Supreme Court found this suggestive of independent contractor status. Although the district court does not emphasize this factor, Hi-Tech relies heavily on it in its appellate brief.

Hi-Tech is in the business of producing videos. Accordingly, it would be perfectly understandable for Hi-Tech to maintain employees skilled in the various aspects of video production. Nevertheless, similarity between the hiring party's regular business and the hired party's work does not necessarily weigh significantly in favor of finding an employer-employee relationship. In *Marco v. Accent Publishing Co.*, 969 F.2d 1547 (3d Cir. 1992), Accent, a publisher of a trade journal, regularly published photographs of its own conception. The Third Circuit noted, however, that a hiring party in Accent's situation "might easily accomplish its regular business by using independent contractors rather than employees" to produce the required photographs. Accordingly, the regular business factor did not undermine the court's conclusion that the plaintiff photographer was an independent contractor.

By Akey's own admission, Hi-Tech uses independent contractors to accomplish its regular business. Akey testified that he is the only full-time employee and then explained, "And when we have a particular job that comes out, then, yes, we do hire freelance people to get involved in that project." As in *Marco*, the fact that the assistants' work was part of Hi-Tech's regular business is not particularly probative evidence of employment status.

E.   The Remaining Factors

Of the remaining factors, several find little foundation in the record at all. The live photography was obviously completed on site at Mackinac Island. It is, however, unclear whether Mueller and Cook completed their work (such as developing the graphics and writing the script, respectively) in their own studios or at Hi-Tech. Similarly, the record does not indicate the extent of Hi-Tech's discretion over when and how long to work.

Akey testified that Mueller worked on the Mackinac video for five days. The duration of Cline's and Cook's assistance on the Mackinac video is unknown. Furthermore, any assistance Cline, Mueller, and Cook rendered on earlier projects would be relevant to, though not dispositive of, employment status. This information is also unknown.

The district court found, however, that two of the remaining factors weigh in favor of finding an employer-employee relationship: (1) the fact that Akey's assistants did not have a role in hiring and paying additional assistants and (2) the fact that Hi-Tech is in business. Neither of these considerations is significant in the context of this case. The fact that Akey's assistants did not hire their own assistants is not surprising. In light of the scope of the project and the nature of the work, it is appropriate that Akey's assistants would work without assistants of their own. Indeed, it would seem that a hired party's failure to hire her own assistants is rarely, if ever, significant in determining whether a party is an independent contractor. On the other hand, however, the exercise of authority to hire assistants tends to show independent contractor status. Thus, we accord no weight to this factor.

As discussed above, the fact that Hi-Tech is in business does not make it more likely that it would hire employees, because Hi-Tech could effectively accomplish its regular work through independent contractors instead of employees. Contrary to the district court, then, this factor does not approach proof of the actual employment status of Mueller, Cline, and Cook. Therefore, we decline to give weight to this factor either.

IV.

In sum, Akey's right to control and actual control of the video's production suggests, at first blush, that his assistants were employees. However, neither the right to control nor actual control alone can turn an otherwise independent contractor into an employee. The economic treatment of the assistants, the skill required of the assistants, and Akey's own perceptions of the assistants' status compel the conclusion that Cline, Mueller, and Cook were independent contractors.

Because the video was produced in part by independent contractors, Hi-Tech's Mackinac video is not a "work made for hire," and the copyright in the video as a "work made for hire" is invalid. Therefore, we reverse and remand the case with instruction to enter judgment in ABC's favor.

JONES, Circuit Judge, dissenting.

I disagree with the majority's conclusion that Akey's production assistants were not "employees." ...

It is undisputed that Akey was clearly an employee of Hi-Tech. He hired others to do some of the camera work. He, himself, however, shot the scene of the island from an aircraft, which was used on "Good Morning America", and he, himself, edited and composed the film from the footage that others shot. He also designed the packaging of the work. Thus, he was an employee who "prepared" the work under § 101(1). I believe that this is, in itself, enough to establish that Hi-Tech could copyright the work as the "work for hire" of an employee.

Akey did delegate some of the creative work to others. Mike Mueller, whom Akey referred to as a non-employee, shot most of the film. Akey, however, maintained control over the work. Akey was obviously skilled and experienced at video production work. This seems quite different from the situation in *CCNV*, where non-artists in an anti-homelessness agency hired a sculptor to create a sculpture. The *CCNV* factors that support a work for hire in the instant case include: (1) the hiring party's right to control the manner and means by which the product is accomplished (Akey maintained full control over the final product—what shots would be included, what order, the transitions, etc.); (2) the source of the instrumentalities (Akey supplied the cameras and other equipment); (3) the hired party's role in hiring and paying assistants (Akey completely controlled all aspects of hiring and paying assistants); (4) whether the work is part of the regular business of the hiring party (making videos was Akey's business, unlike the association in *CCNV*); and (5) whether the hiring party is in business (same).

Finally, I note that the district court found that "the vast majority of the creativity that was encompassed in this work was the work that Mr. Akey did by putting it all together, sequencing it, and packaging it as it was done." This is a finding of fact that should not be disturbed, and lends support to the conclusion that the video was a product of Akey, as a Hi-Tech employee. Moreover, the cases from other circuits applying *CCNV* are not especially relevant here, as each includes different circumstances than those now at issue. Therefore, I would affirm the district court's determination that this was a work for hire.

I respectfully dissent.

Notes and Questions

1. Did the *Hi-Tech* court correctly conclude that the people Akey hired were not employees? Consider the various perspectives from which you might answer this question. Did the logic of *CCNV*'s agency test dictate the *Hi-Tech* result? Did *Hi-Tech* direct copyright incentives in a way that would encourage the creation of new works? Did *Hi-Tech* give copyright ownership to the person who most deserved it? Which of these perspectives is the correct way to evaluate *Hi-Tech*?

2. *Hi-Tech* raises some potentially interesting questions about *CCNV*. Like Akey, Reid used a number of assistants to complete the sculpture. Under *Hi-Tech,* did these assistants act as Reid's employees, or as independent contractors? If Reid's assistants were independent contractors (i.e. not employees), what becomes of Reid's case against CCNV and the final ownership of the sculpture? Alternatively, if Reid's assistants were employees, does it follow that *CCNV* implicitly stands for the proposition that assistants are actually employees? If so, would it then follow that *Hi-Tech* reached the wrong result?

3. Hi-Tech, the company, did something quite common. It hired people to help with a project creating copyrightable subject matter. Given the decision in this case, what should Hi-Tech have done to acquire the copyrights in question? Two possibilities come to mind. First, Hi-Tech could have gotten Akey to assign his copyright to Hi-Tech. Second, Hi-Tech could have gotten Akey to sign a writing acknowledging that his work was (to quote from § 101's definition of work made for hire) "specially ordered or commissioned for use as a contribution to a collective work, as a part of a motion picture or other audiovisual work" and that he agreed to work made for hire treatment.

As a general rule, entities like Hi-Tech prefer work made for hire treatment when they can get it. The reasons for this require knowledge of topics not yet presented in this book. First, work made for hire treatment would give all components of Hi-Tech's video the same duration of copyright.[30] Second, such treatment would remove the ability of the

----

[30] The duration of copyright for works authored by individuals varies because copyright lasts for the life of the author plus 70 years. By contrast copyright in a work made for hire lasts 95 years from the date of publication. *See* 17 U.S.C. § 302; Chapter 4, *infra.*

commissioned party to terminate the assignment under § 203 of the Copyright Act.[31] Unfortunately, entities like Hi-Tech cannot always get work made for hire treatment, even if the hired party will agree to it. Remember that a work made for hire can exist only when the hired party is an employee of the hiring party or when the hired party creates one of the works specified in part 2 of the work made for hire definition and further agrees in writing to treat the work as one made for hire.

The foregoing suggests that a person in Hi-Tech's position would probably not know what to do without consulting fairly specialized (and potentially expensive) legal counsel. Most people do not familiarize themselves with copyright law, let alone the complications of the work made for hire doctrine. Does this mean that the work made for hire doctrine helps primarily those wealthy enough to hire legal counsel, and if so, should the law be changed to avoid this problem?

4. It worth repeating that there are two kinds of work made for hire. The first arises when a hired party is the employee of the hiring party and produces a work within the scope of employment. In these cases, the hiring party acquires the copyright even in the absence of a writing. The second arises when the hiring party is not the employee of the hiring party and produces "a work specially ordered or commissioned for use as a contribution to a collective work, as a part of a motion picture or other audiovisual work, as a translation, as a supplementary work, as a compilation, as an instructional text, as a test, as answer material for a test, or as an atlas." In those cases, the resulting work is a work made for hire if the parties expressly so agree in writing.

Note that, under the second type of work made for hire, works not expressly listed in the statute cannot be works made for hire, even if the parties sign a writing to that effect. Thus, for example, if a party commissions an independent contractor to write a book, the resulting work cannot be a work made for hire, even if the contract states that it is one. Instead, at most, the commissioning party can only get an assignment of the copyright. Why did Congress limit the types of works that can be made into works made for hire by contract? As the court in *CCNV* noted, Congress was concerned that, if it allowed all works to be turned into works made for hire by contract, unequal bargaining power would soon force many authors to contract into such arrangements. Congress thus limited the works to certain industries as part of a legislative compromise.

––––––––––

Cases like *CCNV* and *Hi-Tech* illuminate whether the creator of a work is an employee. However, a determination that the creator of a work is an employee does not necessarily mean that copyright in the work belongs to the creator's employer. For that to happen, the work

––––––––––

[31] Section 203 of the Copyright Act allows authors to terminate assignments of copyright rights 35-40 years after making the assignment. *See* 17 U.S.C. § 203; Chapter 4, *infra.*

must also have been created within the scope of the creator's employment. As you might imagine, it has not always been easy for courts to determine exactly how far the scope of a creator's employment extends.

Miller v. CP Chemicals
808 F. Supp. 1238 (D. S.C. 1992)

ANDERSON, JR., District Judge.

This is an action by David Miller, Sr., a former employee of the defendant, CP Chemicals, Inc. ("CP") arising out of a dispute over the ownership to certain rights in computer programs. In his complaint, Miller alleges that he owns the copyrights to computer programs he developed while he was employed by CP. He further alleges that the defendant has continued to use these programs without authorization and that such use constitutes copyright infringement, breach of an employment contract, wrongful conversion, breach of contract accompanied by fraudulent act, and a violation of the South Carolina Unfair Trade Practices Act. For the reasons set forth below, the court concludes that the plaintiff's claim for copyright infringement should be dismissed ...

The facts viewed in the light most favorable to the plaintiff are as follows: Miller was initially employed by CP as a technician in the quality control laboratory. His job entailed analyzing finished products to assure their conformance to customer specifications. After about three months, Miller was promoted to the position of senior laboratory chemist. In that capacity, he first began working with a computer in connection with his job by utilizing a Lotus 1-2-3 software package, which he had requested that CP purchase, for the purpose of keying in the company's computer analytical data regarding customer product specifications. In February, 1989 Miller was promoted to laboratory supervisor and, in that capacity, assumed overall responsibility for the operation of the quality control laboratory. At this time, CP began renovating the quality control lab, and Miller organized the laboratory's records to meet EPA and OSHA regulations. Miller also completed the computerization of all analytical data generated in the lab. During this process, Miller became concerned about the efficiency of performing manual calculations in the quality control lab for in-process adjustments to one of CP's commercial products. As a result, Miller wrote a computer program that computed complex mathematical calculations, eliminating manual calculations previously used to make the required adjustments to this product. This computer program simplified his duties with CP and reduced the chance of error in calculation.

At this time, Miller's supervisors, Jerry Poe and Wilson Oldhouser, approached him regarding computerizing the calculations for other product adjustments. Oldhouser then told Miller to continue writing the programs, and Miller did develop more computer programs.

Miller performed most of the work on the computer programs at his home and on his own time. Miller, who was an employee paid by the hour, never requested or received additional or overtime pay for his work on the computer programs.

According to Miller, Poe and Oldhouser orally agreed with him that Miller would retain the copyrights in the computer programs that he developed and that CP could use them only so long as he remained employed with CP.

Miller was terminated from his employment in June, 1991, immediately following his arrest in a drug related charge. Subsequent to his termination, Miller demanded that CP either return the computer programs that he had written or pay him a license fee for continued use of the programs. CP refused these demands. ...

Section 101 of the Copyright Act defines "work for hire" two different ways. Subsection (1) provides that a "work prepared by an employee within the scope of his or her employment" is a work for hire. Subsection (2) deals with works specially ordered or commissioned. ...

In this case, Miller was a full-time employee of CP. Clearly, the relationship between Miller and CP was that of master and servant as opposed to employer and independent contractor. Thus, subsection (1) of section 101 is the correct definition to apply in this case. ...

Miller contends that the computer programs were a result of his own initiative and that they were written and tested at his home on his personal computer. Miller also asserts that he is an hourly employee and was never paid for the work that he did in developing the computer programs.

On the other hand, CP asserts that the computer programs were created during the course of Miller's employment with CP and solely for the purpose of simplifying his duties at CP. CP also asserts that the programs are product specific in that they relate directly with the calculations done for specific products manufactured by CP. CP also claims that Miller, as supervisor, had broad responsibilities for organizing and updating the quality control lab, and that writing the computer programs, although not required, was in connection with and incidental to his job. Finally, CP argues that Miller's position that the computer programs were not created within the scope of his employment is inconsistent with his other claim that those same programs were developed pursuant to an alleged employment contract.

In *Commission [sic] For Creative Non-violence v. Reid*, 490 U.S. 730, 741 (1989), the Court held that "the term 'employee' should be understood in light of the general common law of agency." Thus, this court finds that the general common law of agency would also be relevant to the analysis of the term "within the scope of employment."

The Restatement (Second) of Agency 228 (1958) provides:

(1) Conduct of a servant is within the scope of employment if, but only if: (a) it is of the kind he is employed to perform; (b) it occurs substantially within the authorized time and space limits; [and] (c) it is actuated, at least in part, by a purpose to serve the master.

The comments to section 229 state that acts incidental to authorized acts may be within the scope of the employment:

Acts incidental to authorized acts. An act may be incidental to an authorized act, although considered separately it is an entirely different kind of an act. To be incidental, however, it must be one which is subordinate to or pertinent to an act which the servant is employed to perform. It must be within the ultimate objective of the principal and an act which it is not unlikely that such a servant might do. The fact that a particular employer has no reason to expect the particular servant to perform the act is not conclusive.

Restatement (Second) of Agency 229 comment b (1958).

In this case, Miller was not hired primarily for the development of computer programs. However, as supervisor of the quality control laboratory, he was responsible for the organization and updating of the laboratory. Thus, the development of the computer programs was at least incidental to his job responsibilities because it was "within the ultimate objective of the principal and an act which it is not unlikely that such a servant might do."

With regard to the second element, Miller worked primarily, if not entirely, on the computer programs at his home on his own time and for no additional pay. On the other hand, the work was performed during the time period in which he was employed by CP.

With regard to the third element, there is no question but that the development of the computer programs was actuated, at least in part, by a purpose to serve the master. The initial program was created to simplify Miller's job and to eliminate errors, which was for the benefit of both Miller and CP. Officials at CP expressly asked Miller to continue to develop computer programs that dealt with other products of CP. Finally, each computer program dealt specifically with a product manufactured by CP. The ultimate purpose of the development of the computer programs was to benefit CP by maximizing the efficiency of the operation of the quality control lab. ...

After considering the factual circumstances in this case in light of the Restatement factors ..., the court concludes that the development of the computer programs by Miller was within the scope of his employment. ...

Although [the work made for hire doctrine] may sometimes create harsh results, it clearly places the burden on the employee to obtain a written agreement, and not merely an oral understanding, that the employee will retain the copyright interests in the works he creates while within the scope of his employment. Miller has not met that burden in this case, and the programs must therefore be considered "work for hire."

[The court's discussion of state law claims is omitted.]

For all of the reasons set out above, the defendant's motion for summary judgment is granted.

Notes and Questions

1.   *Miller* gives you a rough idea of the reasoning courts use to determine whether an employee has created a work within the scope of his employment. What do you think of the court's reasoning? The court quoted the Restatement 2d of Agency, which provides that:

> Conduct of a servant is within the scope of employment if, but only if: (a) it is of the kind he is employed to perform; (b) it occurs substantially within the authorized time and space limits; [and] (c) it is actuated, at least in part, by a purpose to serve the master.

Did the court interpret these requirements correctly? Remember, the plaintiff Miller lost at summary judgment, so the court had to find that no reasonable jury could find in Miller's favor. Among other things, the court said that the second requirement was satisfied because, although Miller developed the program on his own time away from the office, "the work was performed during the time period in which he was employed by CP." If you find the court's reasoning questionable, why do you think the court ruled against Miller? Did it simply misunderstand the law?

2.   The *Miller* court stated that the work made for hire doctrine "clearly places the burden on the employee to obtain a written agreement, and not merely an oral understanding, that the employee will retain copyright interests in the works he creates while within the scope of employment." Is this statement accurate? If so, is it desirable for copyright to place the burden on employees to get written agreements about copyright ownership from their employers?

Roeslin v. District of Columbia
921 F. Supp. 793 (D.D.C. 1995)

GREENE, District Judge.

In this action, plaintiff, an employee of the Department of Employment Services ("D.O.E.S.") of the District of Columbia, claims copyright infringement against the District for its use and copying of a computer software program (the "DC-790" system) that plaintiff developed. The matter was tried, and it is now ripe for these findings of fact and conclusions of law.

Findings of Fact

D.O.E.S. is responsible for collecting and tabulating employment statistics for the District of Columbia and the D.C. metropolitan area. It collects the statistics by mailing the Current Employment Service ("CES") survey to area employers, and tabulating their responses. D.O.E.S. transmits these statistics and estimates based thereon to the Federal Bureau of Labor Statistics ("BLS") for its use in computing national labor statistics.

Plaintiff was hired by D.O.E.S. in November, 1986 for the position of a Labor Economist for a four year term, and began work in the Labor Management Information Section of D.O.E.S. He received a salary from the District and full benefits. At the time plaintiff was hired, he had no computer programming skills, nor was his supervisor, Mr. Groner, aware of whether plaintiff had any computer programming skills.

As a Labor Economist, plaintiff was charged with three tasks: (1) to improve employer response rate to the CES survey; (2) to expand the CES sample size; and (3) to develop industry and occupational employment projections. ... He had discretion in determining how to carry out these duties.

When plaintiff began working at D.O.E.S., employees manually collected the information from returned CES surveys and recorded the information on office record cards. A data processing staff would enter this data into the mainframe system. The estimates derived from this data were computed manually with the aid of a computer. The District anticipated the future development of the Automated Current Employment Statistics ("ACES") mainframe system.

Prior to developing the DC-790 system, plaintiff did use a computer to assist in the carrying out of his duties, although he did not do any computer programming. Plaintiff also assisted in the "automation" of the office, that is, in transferring some of the work that was done manually to already existing computer software applications. This task also did not involve any computer programming.

Plaintiff was motivated to create the DC-790 system in June 1988 when he attended a CES conference. Upon returning from the conference, plaintiff informed his supervisor, Mr. Groner, that he believed a personal computer ("PC") based system could be created for the District's CES surveys. Plaintiff testified that after checking with BLS, Mr. Groner informed plaintiff that creation of a PC-based program was neither feasible nor desirable, and told plaintiff not to pursue the idea because he would be too busy with his other job duties, and because D.O.E.S. had already decided to eventually implement ACES, the mainframe system. Nonetheless, plaintiff informed Mr. Groner that he would create a PC-based system on his own time. Plaintiff testified that his motivation in creating the program was to prove that it could be done and to develop job opportunities for himself. Mr. Groner told the plaintiff that the program would be "in the public domain," which plaintiff took to mean that the system would not be owned by anybody. Mr. Groner actually believed that the District would own the program; he testified that he thought that the phrase "in the public domain" meant that the District would own the program.

In August 1988, plaintiff purchased a personal computer with his own funds. In October 1988, he purchased software using his own funds. Plaintiff taught himself how to program computers using books that he purchased with his own funds. He spent approximately 3,000 hours creating the various modules necessary to complete the DC-790 program, and creating enhancements to the system. He completed the final module in January, 1991, although most of the modules were completed by 1990. Plaintiff did all of this work at home. He also tested each module at home, using hypothetical data. Nobody at D.O.E.S. directed plaintiff to create the DC-790 system, supervised his doing so, or assisted him in doing so. He was not offered compensation for the creation of the system.

After testing each module at home, plaintiff brought each module into work to test with actual data. Some of the testing and debugging of various modules was done during office hours. Once each module worked properly, plaintiff incorporated the modules into the PC system operating at D.O.E.S. Shortly after the DC-790 system became operational, D.O.E.S. personnel ceased using office record cards. Plaintiff also created an operating manual for the DC-790 system in May 1990 in response to a request by an employee of the BLS Regional Office. Plaintiff received positive performance appraisals based, in part, on his development of the DC-790 system. Prior to April 1991, plaintiff attempted to promote the DC-790 system to BLS, and demonstrated the system to some of its personnel during office hours.

Throughout this period, according to plaintiff's testimony, he relied on Mr. Groner's statement to him that nobody would own the DC-790 system and that it would be in the public domain. Plaintiff stated that he first learned that the District asserted a proprietary interest in the program in April of 1991. At that time, he was provided with a copy of a letter from the District to the State of Maine, in which the District stated that it had a proprietary interest in the program. Defendant does not dispute that this is when plaintiff first learned that defendant asserted a proprietary interest. ...

Conclusions of Law

I

The central issue in this case is whether plaintiff, as the author of the DC-790 system, or defendant, as plaintiff's employer, is the owner of the copyright on the DC-790 system. Generally, the author of a work is the owner of a copyright. However, in the case of a "work made for hire," the owner of the copyright is the entity for whom the work was prepared. The copyright statute defines a work made for hire as "a work prepared by an employee within the scope of his or her employment." 17 U.S.C. § 101. ...

The Supreme Court has held that to determine whether an individual was an employee, and whether he created a work within the scope of his employment, courts should look to the general common law of agency. *Community for Creative Non-Violence v. Reid*, 490 U.S. 730, 740 (1989). There is no dispute in this case that plaintiff was an employee of defendant. The question is whether he created the DC-790 system within the scope of his employment.

The Restatement (Second) of Agency, which the Supreme Court cited in *Reid*, states that:

> (1) Conduct of a servant is within the scope of employment if, but only if:
>   (a) it is within the kind he is employed to perform;
>   (b) it occurs substantially within the authorized time and space limits; [and]
>   (c) it is actuated, at least in part, by a purpose to serve the master.

Restatement at § 228. The employer must demonstrate that these three of these factors exist to prove that the work is a work made for hire.

A. With regard to the first prong, the Court finds that developing computer software is not the kind of work plaintiff was employed to perform. Plaintiff was hired as a labor economist, not as a computer programmer. There is no reference in his job description to computer programming; nor was his supervisor aware of whether plaintiff had any programming skills when he was hired. Plaintiff was hired to improve certain aspects of the CES survey and develop projections based on that survey. He was not hired to create a computer program that would assist the entire office and receive, process, and transmit the survey results.

Defendant makes much of the fact that plaintiff used computers at work, and that defendant allowed plaintiff, during work hours, to learn how to use computers. This, however, does not prove that computer programming was part of plaintiff's job duties or necessary to performing his job duties. Many people use computers in the work place, including plaintiff's coworkers, but do not program computers. The two skills are quite different—while many people operate computers, few have the technical ability or training necessary to program them.

To be sure, work that is incidental to the conduct authorized by the employer, even if it is not central to the employee's job duties, also falls within the scope of employment. Restatement at § 229. To determine whether computer programming was incidental to plaintiff's employment, a court may consider such factors as whether this was the type of activity commonly done by labor economists, and whether it was likely that plaintiff would engage in such an activity. *Id*. The Court finds that while developing the DC-790 system did help the functioning of the work place, it was not the type of activity in which plaintiff would be reasonable [sic] expected to engage.

Moreover, it is disingenuous for the District now to claim that developing the DC-790 system was within the scope of plaintiff's job duties. Plaintiff originally approached Mr. Groner about writing a computer program that would perform the functions of the system. Plaintiff testifies, very credibly, that Mr. Groner discouraged him from doing so, stating that it would detract from his ability to perform his other job duties and that D.O.E.S. had already decided to implement the ACES system. It is unfair for the District to now claim that an activity it discouraged— developing the system—was within the scope of plaintiff's employment.

B. Second, the Court must determine whether the development of the system "occurred substantially within the authorized time and space limits." The Court finds that it did not. Plaintiff credibly testified that he spent 3,000 hours outside of normal working hours creating the modules of the DC-790 system. He did this at home using a computer he purchased with his own funds. It is true that plaintiff tested each module at work. It is also true that once each module was operational, it was used in the work place. Nonetheless, the substantial amount of time plaintiff spent creating the DC-790 system, which is what is at issue in this case, was done on his own time outside of the office. Accordingly, the system was not developed within the authorized time and space limits.

C. Finally, the Court will address whether plaintiff was motivated to create the system, at least in part, by a purpose to serve the master. Plaintiff testified that he created the program for two reasons: (1) to create job opportunities for himself; and (2) to prove it could be done. The Court finds that plaintiff was motivated by each of these purposes. To be sure, the DC-790 system benefited [sic] his employer, and the Court could fairly infer that part of plaintiff's motivation was to achieve this result. However, the Court finds that plaintiff was primarily motivated by self-fulfilling purposes. Additionally, it finds, as stated above, that it is disingenuous for the District to initially have stated that the plaintiff could not create the system, and now assert that plaintiff did so for the District's benefit.

On the whole, then, the Court finds that defendant has not established that the DC-790 system was a work made for hire. The program was not the type of work plaintiff was employed to perform, nor was it incidental to his job duties. Moreover, the substantial proportion of the creating of the program took place outside the office during non-office hours. Finally, the plaintiff was primarily motivated to create the system for his own benefit.

[The court's discussion of infringement, defenses and damages is omitted.]

For the reasons stated, the Court finds for the plaintiff. An Order is being issued contemporaneously herewith.

Notes and Questions

1. Is *Roeslin* consistent with *Miller*? If not, which case takes the correct approach towards defining the scope of employment?

2. *Roeslin* places considerable emphasis on the plaintiff's creation of the DC-790 to further his own personal goals. What about the manual the plaintiff wrote "in response to a request by an employee of the BLS Regional Office"? Was this a work made for hire?

3. Universities provide an interesting context in which to test the scope of employment. For example, professors are clearly employees of universities. Does this mean that universities own the copyright to all works written by their faculty? The argument in the universities' favor would note that professors get paid to write. Indeed, it is a job expectation and requirement for tenure. That having been said, many believe that there is a "professor exception" to the work made for hire doctrine. Do you think that this exception ought to exist, and if so, for what works? Remember, professors create a wide variety of copyrightable works. They write academic scholarship, class handouts, and teaching notes. If you conclude that universities own professors' works, what would the consequences be? For example, if the university owns copyright in a professor's course syllabus and teaching notes, could he use them at another university without committing infringement?

SECTION B. JOINT AUTHORSHIP

Just as people frequently engage others to create works on their behalf, people also work together to create copyrightable subject matter. Sometimes they do so with an explicit understanding about the contributions of each party, as when a composer and lyricist combine to write a song. Cases like these fit comfortably under the Copyright Act's definition of "joint work," and the two authors share an undivided interest in their work. At other times, however, people work together with a far murkier understanding of their roles and the outcome. This section examines how the Copyright Act resolves disputes that arise when two parties who have worked together do not agree on copyright ownership.

Erickson v. Trinity Theatre
13 F.3d 1061 (7th Cir. 1994)

RIPPLE, Circuit Judge.

The plaintiff Karen Erickson brought this action seeking a preliminary and permanent injunction to prevent the defendant Trinity Theatre d/b/a/ Trinity Square Ensemble ("Trinity") from performing three plays and using two videotapes to which she owned the copyrights. The magistrate judge recommended enjoining the performance of the plays but not the use of the videotapes. Both parties filed objections. The district court sustained Ms. Erickson's objections to the portions of the recommendation addressing the videotapes but denied Trinity's objections to the portion of the recommendation addressing performance of the plays. Accordingly, the district court enjoined Trinity from using either the plays or the videotapes. Trinity now appeals. We now affirm.

I. BACKGROUND

A. Facts

Ms. Erickson was one of the founders of a theatre company in Evanston, Illinois, that ultimately became known as Trinity Theatre. Between 1981 and January 1991, Ms. Erickson served Trinity in various capacities: as playwright, artistic director, actress, play director, business manager, and member of the board of directors. This suit revolves around Ms. Erickson's role as playwright.

At issue here are the rights to three plays: *Much Ado About Shakespeare ("Much Ado"); The Theatre Time Machine ("Time Machine"); and Prairie Voices: Tales from Illinois ("Prairie Voices")*. *Much Ado* is a compilation of scenes and sonnets from William Shakespeare and other writers of his time. Ms. Erickson revised this work from an earlier script entitled *Sounds and Sweet Aires*. Michael Osborne, a Trinity actor, testified that Ms. Erickson compiled *Much Ado* in 1988 and that many decisions about what was to be included were made during rehearsals. Osborne identified two portions of the copyrighted script that resulted from his suggestions: a passage to *Macbeth* and the introduction to the play. The editing of the text, Osborne continued, was accomplished largely by consensus; however, when a consensus could not be had, Ms. Erickson made the final decisions. Osborne further testified that he understood at the time that the play was being created for Trinity and not for Ms. Erickson. Ms. Erickson does not dispute the process described by Osborne, but characterizes it differently. She perceived the process only as actors making suggestions for her script.

Time Machine is a play of five scenes based on a public domain Native American folk tale. Each scene depicts dramatic styles from different historical periods. Ms. Erickson received a copyright registration for *Time Machine* on September 12, 1988. She described the development of the play as beginning in 1977 when she was in school. At that time, she wrote the Greek-style drama scene. Later, while teaching high school drama, she wrote the second scene based on *commedia dell'arte*. She also began work on the melodrama and improvisational scenes of the play at that time. Ms. Erickson started producing the play independently of Trinity in 1984 with two other actors, Paddy Lynn and Will Clinger. Ms. Erickson claimed that she worked to develop the scenes alone; however, the evidence shows that the actors were involved in the development of the melodrama and improvisational scenes. The improvisational process, as described by Ms. Lynn, is a form of theatre in which there is no script.

Rather, actors work with an idea and a loose structure to create a play. Ms. Lynn described the development of the improvisational scene in *Time Machine* as a collaborative effort. However, she conceded that Ms. Erickson took all of the notes from rehearsals and compiled them into the script; furthermore, nothing was included in the script without Ms. Erickson's approval. Initially, Ms. Erickson attributed the script to both herself and to Ms. Lynn. Ms. Lynn also received royalties for performances of the play. Ms. Erickson denied that she ever intended to include Ms. Lynn as joint author. She conceded that Ms. Lynn was credited on publicity materials as an author but denied that she approved such credit. The later change in attribution, Ms. Erickson claims, merely corrected the initial error.

In 1990, Ms. Erickson developed *Prairie Voices*, a play based on tales from Illinois history. She had the idea to develop the play as a Trinity production. Her original intent was to launch a collaborative effort in which each of the actors would contribute a story to the play. However, none of the actors initiated writing a script and the play, as it resulted, was based entirely on tales provided by Ms. Erickson. As with *Time Machine*, Ms. Erickson worked with the actors in the improvisational format. Although testifying that she alone wrote the play, Ms. Erickson admitted that the actors provided ideas for the dialogue. Another actor, Ruth Ann Weyna, testified that the writing of the play was a creative process involving a number of actors. However, she conceded that Ms. Erickson controlled what eventually was put in the script.

In 1987, Trinity began paying Ms. Erickson royalties for its performances of her plays. On July 5, 1988, Ms. Erickson entered into a two-year licensing agreement with Trinity that designated her as a "playwright" entitling her to royalties for performances of two of her plays, *Much Ado* and *Time Machine*. Trinity stipulated that it also paid Erickson royalties for its performances of *Prairie Voices*, although that play was not expressly covered by the licensing agreement. Trinity continued to pay Ms. Erickson royalties after the expiration of the licensing agreement. Trinity discontinued making royalty payments on November 15, 1990.

Ms. Erickson was also subject to an actors' agreement with Trinity. In July 1988, Ms. Erickson signed the agreement which stated: "The actor expressly agrees that Trinity reserves the rights to any recording, audio, video or both of the Production...." The contract covered the tour which was forecast to run through June 30, 1989.

Ms. Erickson left Trinity Theatre in January 1991. Shortly thereafter, she applied for and was issued copyright registration for *Much Ado* and *Prairie Voices*. Concurrently, she received registration for the video productions of *Time Machine*, taped in October 1989, and *Prairie Voices*, taped in November 1990. She had previously obtained a copyright certificate for *Time Machine* on September 12, 1988. On January 21, 1991, Ms. Erickson's attorneys wrote Trinity a letter demanding that the theatre discontinue performing the plaintiff's plays. Trinity refused to comply with the request.

On April 3, 1991, Ms. Erickson filed a seventeen-count complaint against Trinity Theatre, members of Trinity's management, and individual Trinity actors seeking injunctive and legal relief in which she alleged copyright infringement, unfair competition, and other related tortious activity. In October 1992, Ms. Erickson filed a motion for a preliminary injunction to prevent the defendant from producing or performing five plays for which Ms. Erickson claimed exclusive copyright ownership, from displaying videotapes, photographs, and brochures regarding these plays, and from reproducing any materials from a copyrighted work entitled "Drama/Learning Process." After a partial settlement agreement, the parties stipulated that the district court did not need to resolve the plaintiff's request for injunctive relief as to two of the five plays. As a result, the only plays at issue for purposes of the plaintiff's motion for preliminary injunction were *Time Machine, Much Ado, and Prairie Voices*, as well as videotapes of *Time Machine* and *Prairie Voices*. ...

II. ANALYSIS

... We now turn to the issue of whether any of the material in question is a "joint work." In a joint work, the joint authors hold undivided interests in a work, despite any differences in each author's contribution. 17 U.S.C. § 201. Each author as co-owner has the right to use or to license the use of the work, subject to an accounting to the other co-owners for any profits. Thus, even a person whose contribution is relatively minor, if accorded joint authorship status, enjoys a significant benefit.

In determining whether any of the works at issue in this case may be classified as a "joint work," our starting point must be the language of the statute. Section 101 of the Copyright Act defines a "joint work" as a work prepared by two or more authors with the intention that their contributions be merged into inseparable or interdependent parts of a unitary whole. 17 U.S.C. § 101.

1.

Neither the Act nor its legislative history defines "inseparable" or "interdependent." The legislative history states that examples of inseparable parts are the joint contributions of two authors to a single novel or the contributions of two painters to a single work; an example of interdependent parts are the lyrics and music for a song. Apart from these examples, the reports do little to clarify the criteria for determining joint authorship. Indeed, they increase the ambiguity. The committee reports state:

> [A] work is "joint" if the authors collaborated with each other, *or* if *each* of the authors prepared his or her contribution with the knowledge and *intention* that it would be merged with the contributions of other authors as "inseparable or interdependent parts of a unitary whole." The touchstone here is *the intention, at*

the time the writing is done, that the parts be absorbed or combined into an integrated unit....

House Report at 120; Senate Report at 103, U.S. Code Cong. & Admin. News 1976, pp. 5736 (emphasis added). The statute clearly requires a focus on the intention to collaborate. However, the disjunctive first sentence in the legislative reports, set out directly above, seemingly contradicts that statutory language by focusing on collaboration and not mentioning intent to create a joint work.

This ambiguity presents analytical problems in cases such as this one, in which the parties have collaborated in some sense but dispute whether there was a mutual intent to create a joint work. In resolving this ambiguity, we believe that it is important to note, at the outset, that the statute itself requires that there be an intent to create a joint work. Therefore, reliance on collaboration alone, as Trinity suggests, would be incompatible with the clear statutory mandate. On this point, we find ourselves in agreement with the analysis of Judge Newman writing for the Second Circuit in *Childress v. Taylor,* 945 F.2d 500, (2d Cir. 1991). He pointed out that a disjunctive standard based solely on the legislative history would not square with the plain meaning of the statute:

> This passage appears to state two alternative criteria—one focusing on the act of collaboration and the other on the parties' intent. However, it is hard to imagine activity that would constitute meaningful "collaboration" unaccompanied by the requisite intent on the part of both participants that their contributions be merged into a unitary whole, and the case law has read the statutory language literally so that the intent requirement applies to all works of joint authorship.

Childress, 945 F.2d at 505-06. Like the Second Circuit in *Childress,* we believe that the statutory language clearly requires that each author intend that their respective contributions be merged into a unitary whole. Focusing solely upon the fact of contemporaneous input by several parties does not satisfy the statutory requirement that the parties intend to merge their contributions into a unified work. In addition, the "collaboration alone" standard would frustrate the goal of the Act "[t]o promote the Progress of Science and the useful Arts." U.S. Const. art. I, § 8, cl. 8. Seldom would an author subject his work to pre-registration peer review if this were the applicable test. Those seeking copyrights would not seek further refinement that colleagues may offer if they risked losing their sole authorship. Thus, we cannot accept Trinity's proposed "collaboration alone" test as compatible with the language and purpose of the Act.

2.

Even if two or more persons collaborate with the intent to create a unitary work, the product will be considered a "joint work" only if the collaborators can be considered "authors." Courts have applied two tests to evaluate the contributions of authors claiming joint authorship status:

Professor Nimmer's de minimis test and Professor Goldstein's copyrightable subject matter ("copyrightability") test. The de minimis and copyrightability tests differ in one fundamental respect. The de minimis test requires that only the combined product of joint efforts must be copyrightable. By contrast, Professor Goldstein's copyrightability test requires that each author's contribution be copyrightable. We evaluate each of these tests in turn.

In undertaking this task, we focus on how well the test promotes the primary objective of the Act. This objective is not to reward an author for her labors, but "[t]o promote the Progress of Science and useful Arts." U.S. Const. art. I, § 8, cl. 8; *see also Feist Publications, Inc. v. Rural Tel. Serv. Co., Inc.*, 499 U.S. 340, 350 (1991). This objective is accomplished by "assur[ing] authors the right to their original expression," but also by "encourag[ing] others to build freely upon the ideas and information conveyed by a work." *Feist Publications*, 499 U.S. at 349-50 (citing *Harper & Row, Publishers, Inc. v. Nation Enters.*, 471 U.S. 539, 556-57 (1984)). It is in light of this goal that § 102(b) exempts ideas from protection under the Copyright Act.

In addition to promoting the Act's primary objective, we must consider how well the test will further goals of administrative and judicial efficiency. In this inquiry, we must adopt a standard that is sufficiently clear to enable parties to predict whether their contributions to a work will receive copyright protection. A standard satisfying these aims will allow contributors to avoid post-contribution disputes concerning authorship, and to protect themselves by contract if it appears that they would not enjoy protections of the Act itself.

a. Professor Nimmer's de minimis standard

Professor Nimmer, the late scholar on copyright, took the position that all that should be required to achieve joint author status is more than a de minimis contribution by each author. "De minimis" requires that "more than a word or line must be added by one who claims to be a joint author." *Nimmer* 6.07, at 6-21. Professor Nimmer distinguishes his de minimis standard from the standard for copyrightability. *Id*. As an example, Professor Nimmer asserts that if two authors collaborate, with one contributing only uncopyrightable plot ideas and another incorporating those ideas into a completed literary expression, the two authors should be regarded as joint authors of the resulting work. *Id*.

This position has not found support in the courts. The lack of support in all likelihood stems from one of several weaknesses in Professor Nimmer's approach. First, Professor Nimmer's test is not consistent with one of the Act's premises: ideas and concepts standing alone should not receive protection. Because the creative process necessarily involves the development of existing concepts into new forms, any restriction on the free exchange of ideas stifles creativity to some extent. Restrictions on an author's use of existing ideas in a work, such as the threat that accepting suggestions from another party might jeopardize the author's sole entitlement to a copyright, would hinder creativity. Second, contribution of an idea is an exceedingly ambiguous concept. Professor Nimmer provides little guidance to courts or parties regarding when a contribution rises to the level of joint authorship except to state that the contribution must be "more than a word or a line." *Nimmer*, § 6.07, at 6-20.

Professor Nimmer's approach is of little pragmatic use in resolving actual cases. Rarely will minor contributors have the presumption to claim authorship status. In such easy cases, the parties' intent as to authorship status likely will be apparent without resort to any formal test evaluating the parties' respective contributions to discern intent. In the more complex situations, such as the case before us, in which the improvisational process undoubtedly yielded valuable insights to the primary author, the test gives no guidance on how we are to assess the respective contributions of the parties to distinguish the author from the critic or advisor. For these reasons, we, as the majority of the other courts, cannot accept Professor Nimmer's test as an adequate judicial tool to ascertain joint authorship.

b.   Professor Goldstein's copyrightability test

The copyrightable subject matter test was formulated by Professor Paul Goldstein and has been adopted, in some form, by a majority of courts that have considered the issue. According to Professor Goldstein, "[a] collaborative contribution will not produce a joint work, and a contributor will not obtain a co-ownership interest, unless the contribution represents original expression that could stand on its own as the subject matter of copyright." Paul Goldstein, *Copyright: Principles, Law, and Practice* § 4.2.1.2, at 379 (1989). Furthermore, the parties must have intended to be joint authors at the time the work was created. *Id.* Professor Goldstein and the courts adopting his test justify this position by noting that § 101's and 302(b)'s use of the word "authors" suggests that each collaborator's contribution must be a copyrightable "work of authorship" within the meaning of § 102(a).

We agree that the language of the Act supports the adoption of a copyrightability requirement. Section 101 of the Act defines a "joint work" as a "work prepared by two or more *authors*" (emphasis added). To qualify as an author, one must supply more than mere direction or ideas. An author is "the party who actually creates the work, that is, the person who translates an idea into a fixed, tangible expression entitled to copyright protection." *Community for Creative Non-Violence v. Reid*, 490 U.S. 730, 737 (1989). As to the requirement of fixation, § 101 states:

> A work is "fixed" in a tangible medium of expression when its embodiment in a copy or phonorecord, by or under the authority of the author, is sufficiently permanent or stable to permit it to be perceived, reproduced, or otherwise communicated for a period of more than transitory duration.

17 U.S.C. § 101.

The copyrightable subject matter test does not suffer from the same infirmities as Professor Nimmer's de minimis test. The copyrightability test advances creativity in science and art by allowing for the unhindered exchange of ideas, and protects authorship rights in a consistent and predictable manner. It excludes contributions such as ideas which are not protected under the Copyright Act. This test also enables parties to predict whether their contributions to a work will entitle them to copyright protection as a joint author. Compared to the uncertain exercise of divining whether a contribution is more than de minimis, reliance on the copyrightability of an author's proposed contribution yields relatively certain answers. The copyrightability standard allows contributors to avoid post-contribution disputes concerning authorship, and to protect themselves by contract if it appears that they would not enjoy the benefits accorded to authors of joint works under the Act.

We agree with the *Childress* court's observation that the copyrightability test "strikes an appropriate balance in the domains of both copyright and contract law." 945 F.2d at 507. Section 201(b) of the Act allows any person to contract with another to create a work and endow the employer with authorship status under the Act. A contributor of uncopyrightable ideas may also protect her rights to compensation under the Act by contract. Section 201(d) of the Act provides in part that any of the exclusive ownership rights comprised in a copyright may be transferred from the person who satisfied the requirements for obtaining the copyright to one who contracts for such rights. Thus, anyone who contributes to the creation of a work, either as patron, employer, or contributor of ideas, has the opportunity to share in the profits produced by the work through an appropriate contractual arrangement.

C. Application

We now address Trinity's claims of joint authorship under the copyrightability test. As stated above, Trinity must clear two hurdles in order to establish that the plays at issue are joint works. First, it must show the parties intended to be joint authors at the time the work was created. Second, Trinity must show that its contributions to the works were independently copyrightable.

It is clear that, with regard to at least two works, *Much Ado* and *Prairie Voices*, Trinity cannot clear the first hurdle. *Much Ado* is based on a work that Ms. Erickson had largely completed before Trinity actors improvised based on Ms. Erickson's creation. The fact that one actor, Michael Osborne, suggested that Ms. Erickson include a passage from Macbeth and an introduction to the play does not make him a joint author. He conceded that whether his contributions were included and where they went into the compilation were entirely Ms. Erickson's decisions. Furthermore, neither Ms. Erickson nor Trinity considered any of the actors to be co-authors with her in *Much Ado*, as is evidenced by the licensing agreement. Similarly with *Prairie Voices*, Ms. Erickson provided the stories on which the play was based, and she decided which of the actors' suggestions were incorporated into the script. The actors did not consider themselves to be joint authors with Ms. Erickson, and there is no evidence that Ms. Erickson considered the actors as co-authors of the script. Because Trinity cannot establish the requisite intent for *Much Ado* or *Prairie Voices*, the actors cannot be considered joint authors for the purposes of copyright protection.

Time Machine, as both the magistrate judge and the district court noted, is more problematic. Paddy Lynn testified that at least two scenes from *Time Machine* were developed through a collaborative process. Ms. Lynn considered the created dialogue to be hers as well as Ms. Erickson's. Furthermore, there is evidence that Ms. Erickson, too, intended at the time to create a joint work because she initially attributed the script to both Ms. Lynn and herself. Consequently, Trinity has produced some evidence that there was the requisite intent for joint authorship with regard to *Time Machine*. In *Childress*, the Second Circuit specifically acknowledged that "'billing' or 'credit'" may be evidence of intent to create a joint work. Here there is evidence that Ms. Lynn was credited with authorship of *Time Machine*.

In order for the plays to be joint works under the Act, Trinity also must show that actors' contributions to Ms. Erickson's work could have been independently copyrighted. Trinity cannot establish this requirement for any of the above works. The actors, on the whole, could not identify specific contributions that they had made to Ms. Erickson's works. Even when Michael Osborne was able to do so, the contributions that he identified were not independently copyrightable. Ideas, refinements, and suggestions, standing alone, are not the subjects of copyrights. Consequently, Trinity cannot establish the two necessary elements of the copyrightability test and its claims must fail.

Trinity cannot establish joint authorship to the plays at issue. As a result, Trinity cannot overcome the presumption in favor of the validity of Ms. Erickson's copyrights. Consequently, Ms. Erickson is very likely to succeed on the merits of her claims for copyright infringement.

Conclusion

For the foregoing reasons, the judgment of the district court is affirmed.

Gaiman v. McFarlane
360 F.3d 644 (7th Cir. 2004)

POSNER, Circuit Judge.

Neil Gaiman brought suit under the Copyright Act against Todd McFarlane and corporations controlled by him that we can ignore, seeking a declaration that he (Gaiman) owns copyrights jointly with McFarlane in certain comic-book characters. He sought additional relief under the Act, other provisions of federal law, and state law, as well. The case was tried to a jury, which brought in a verdict for Gaiman. ...

We need to do some stage setting. Gaiman and McFarlane are both celebrated figures in the world of comic books, but they play different though overlapping roles. Gaiman just writes scripts; McFarlane writes scripts too, but he also illustrates and publishes the comic books. In 1992, shortly after forming his own publishing house, McFarlane began publishing a series of comic books entitled *Spawn*, which at first he wrote and illustrated himself. "Spawn," more precisely "Hellspawn," are officers in an army of the damned commanded by a devil named Malebolgia, who hopes one day to launch his army against Heaven. The leading character in the series is a man named Al Simmons, who is dead but has returned to the world of the living as a Hellspawn.

Al's story is an affecting one. Born in a quiet neighborhood outside of Pittsburgh, he was recruited by the CIA and eventually became a member of an elite military unit that guards the President. He saved the President from an assassin's bullet and was rewarded with a promotion to lieutenant colonel. He was placed under the command of Jason Wynn, who became his mentor and inducted him into the sinister inner recesses of the intelligence community. When Al began to question Wynn's motives, Wynn sent two agents, significantly named Chapel and Priest, to kill Al with laser weapons, and they did, burning him beyond recognition. Al was buried with great fanfare in Arlington National Cemetery.

Now Al had always had an Achilles' heel, namely that he loved his wife beyond bearing and so, dying, he vowed that he would do anything to see her again. Malebolgia took him at his word ("would do anything") and returned Al to Earth. But a deal with the devil is always a Faustian pact. Al discovered that he was now one of Malebolgia's handpicked Hellspawn and had been remade (a full makeover, as we'll see) and infused with Hell-born energy.

Returned to Earth in his new persona, Al discovers that his wife has remarried his best friend, who was able to give her the child he never could. He absorbs the blow but thirsts for revenge against Jason Wynn. He bides his time, living with homeless people and pondering the unhappy fact that once he exhausts his Hell-born energy he will be returned to Malebolgia's domain and become a slave in an army of the damned with no hope of redemption. He must try somehow to break his pact with the devil.

The early issues in the series were criticized for bad writing, so McFarlane decided to invite four top writers each to write the script for one issue of *Spawn*. One of those invited was Gaiman. He accepted the invitation and wrote the script for *Spawn* issue No. 9. Their contract, made in 1992, was oral. There was no mention of copyright, nor, for that matter, of how Gaiman would be compensated for his work, beyond McFarlane's assuring Gaiman that he would treat him "better than the big guys" did. The reference was to the two leading comic book publishers, Marvel Comics (not to be confused with Gaiman's company, Marvels and Miracles) and DC Comics, for which Gaiman and other writers write on a "work made for hire" basis. This means that the publishers own the copyrights on their work.

It might seem that when McFarlane told Gaiman that he would treat Gaiman "better than the big guys" did, he just meant he'd compensate him more generously for work made for hire. But McFarlane rightly does not argue this. Gaiman's work for him was not work made for hire. It was neither (1) work created by an employee within the scope of his employment nor (2) "a work specially ordered or commissioned for use as a contribution to a collective work, as a part of a motion picture or other audiovisual work, as a translation, as a supplementary work, as a compilation, as an instructional text, as a test, as answer material for a test, or as an atlas, if the parties expressly agree in a written instrument signed by them that the work shall be considered a work made for hire." 17 U.S.C. § 101. There was no written agreement between Gaiman and McFarlane, and Gaiman was not an employee of McFarlane. ...

In his script for *Spawn* No. 9, Gaiman introduced three new characters—Medieval Spawn (as he was later called by McFarlane—Gaiman had not named it and in the issue he is just referred to as a Spawn, with no further identifier), Angela (no last name), and Count Nicholas Cogliostro. Gaiman described, named, and wrote the dialogue for them, but McFarlane drew them. Gaiman contends that he and McFarlane are joint owners of the copyrights on the three characters by reason of their respective contributions to joint (indivisible) work. McFarlane concedes Gaiman's joint ownership of Angela, but not of the other two. ...

Spawn No. 9 was a huge success, selling more than a million copies. McFarlane paid Gaiman $100,000 for his work on it. ... Because Angela was a big hit with *Spawn*'s readers, McFarlane asked Gaiman to do a "mini-series" of three issues starring her, which he did. He also wrote several pages for *Spawn* No. 26 to form a bridge to the Angela series, [which] was first published in 1994. The following year, having created a toy company to manufacture statuettes ("action figures") of *Spawn* characters, one a statuette of Medieval Spawn, McFarlane mailed Gaiman a check for $20,000 designated as royalties, presumably on sales of the statuette, though the record is unclear. ...

[Unfortunately, relations between Gaiman and McFarlane eventually broke down, with McFarlane claiming sole ownership of copyright in, among other things, Medieval Spawn and Count Nicholas Cogliostro. Gaiman responded by filing suit. Despite the litigation, the commercial success of the *Spawn* series continued.] ... By the time of trial, *Spawn* was up to issue No. 120 and had spawned a large number of derivative works, including posters, trading cards, clothing, the statuettes, an animated series on HBO, video games, and a motion picture. Many of these derivative works include all three characters to which Gaiman contributed, so that the financial stakes in the case are considerable. ...

McFarlane makes two arguments for why Gaiman does not have copyright in Medieval Spawn (the name that McFarlane settled on for

Olden Days Spawn) or Cogliostro. The first is that all that Gaiman contributed was the idea for the characters, and ideas are not copyrightable, only expression is and the expression was due to McFarlane's drawing of the characters. It is true that people who contribute merely nonexpressive elements to a work are not copyright owners. As we said in *Seshadri v. Kasraian*, 130 F.3d at 803, "the assistance that a research assistant or secretary or draftsman or helpfully commenting colleague provides in the preparation of a scholarly paper does not entitle the helper to claim the status of a joint author." There has to be some original expression contributed by anyone who claims to be a co-author, and the rule (we'll consider an exception momentarily) is that his contribution must be independently copyrightable. Had someone merely remarked to McFarlane one day, "you need a medieval Spawn" or "you need an old guy to move the story forward," and McFarlane had carried it from there, and if later a copyeditor had made some helpful editorial changes, neither the suggester nor the editor would be a joint owner. Otherwise almost every expressive work would be a jointly authored work, and copyright would explode.

But where two or more people set out to create a character jointly in such mixed media as comic books and motion pictures and succeed in creating a copyrightable character, it would be paradoxical if though the result of their joint labors had more than enough originality and creativity to be copyrightable, no one could claim copyright. That would be peeling the onion until it disappeared. The decisions that say, rightly in the generality of cases, that each contributor to a joint work must make a contribution that if it stood alone would be copyrightable weren't thinking of the case in which it couldn't stand alone because of the nature of the particular creative process that had produced it.

Here is a typical case from academe. One professor has brilliant ideas but can't write; another is an excellent writer, but his ideas are commonplace. So they collaborate on an academic article, one contributing the ideas, which are not copyrightable, and the other the prose envelope, and unlike the situation in the superficially similar case of *Balkin v. Wilson*, 863 F. Supp. 523 (W.D. Mich. 1994), they sign as coauthors. Their intent to be the joint owners of the copyright in the article would be plain, and that should be enough to constitute them joint authors within the meaning of 17 U.S.C. § 201(a). This is the valid core of the Nimmers' heretical suggestion that "if authors A and B work in collaboration, but A's contribution is limited to plot ideas that standing alone would not be copyrightable, and B weaves the ideas into a completed literary expression, it would seem that A and B are joint authors of the resulting work." 1 Nimmer & Nimmer, *Nimmer on Copyright* 6.07, p. 6-23.

The contents of a comic book are typically the joint work of four artists—the writer, the penciler who creates the art work (McFarlane), the inker (also McFarlane, in the case of *Spawn* No. 9, but it would often be a different person from the penciler) who makes a black and white plate of the art work, and the colorist who colors it. The finished product is copyrightable, yet one can imagine cases in which none of the separate contributions of the four collaborating artists would be. The writer might have contributed merely a stock character (not copyrightable, as we're about to see) that achieved the distinctiveness required for copyrightability only by the combined contributions of the penciler, the inker, and the colorist, with each contributing too little to have by his contribution alone carried the stock character over the line into copyright land. ...

McFarlane argues that even as dolled up by the penciler, the inker, and the colorist, Cogliostro is too commonplace to be copyrightable. Gaiman could not copyright a character described merely as an unexpectedly knowledgeable old wino, that is true; but that is not his claim. He claims to be the joint owner of the copyright on a character that has a specific name and a specific appearance. Cogliostro's age, obviously phony title ("Count"), what he knows and says, his name, and his faintly Mosaic facial features combine to create a distinctive character. No more is required for a character copyright. ...

Although Gaiman's verbal description of Cogliostro may well have been of a stock character, once he was drawn and named and given speech he became sufficiently distinctive to be copyrightable. Gaiman's contribution may not have been copyrightable by itself, but his contribution had expressive content without which Cogliostro wouldn't have been a character at all, but merely a drawing. The expressive work that is the comic-book character Count Nicholas Cogliostro was the joint work of Gaiman and McFarlane—their contributions strike us as quite equal—and both are entitled to ownership of the copyright. ...

[The court used similar reasoning to conclude that the Medieval Spawn characters were also copyrightable.]

To summarize, we find no error in the district court's decision, and since the decision gave Gaiman all the relief he sought, there is no need to consider the cross-appeal.

AFFIRMED.

———————

Notes and Questions

1. *Erickson* follows the conventional view that a would-be joint author must contribute copyrightable subject matter to the work in question. Is this interpretation of the law correct? *Erickson* rejected Melville Nimmer's contrary position that a minimal contribution could support a claim of join authorship. What policies would support this contrary position?

2. According to *Gaiman*, at least one situation requires an exception to the copyrightable subject matter requirement for joint authorship—the case where several authors contribute non-copyrightable material which, when combined, result in a copyrightable work. Let us take a moment to consider the implications of *Gaiman's* reasoning.

Under *Gaiman,* if four people make otherwise uncopyrightable contributions to a work, but their resulting collaboration is copyrightable, then each of those four becomes a joint author of the finished work. This implies that, if three of those four made identical contributions, but worked instead with a fourth person who did make a copyrightable contribution, those making the uncopyrightable contributions would lose their status as joint authors. Is this the correct way to handle questions of joint authorship?

3. The Copyright Act's definition of joint work says that joint authors must have "the intention that their contributions be merged into inseparable or interdependent parts of a unitary whole." How easy is it to meet this requirement? Is it enough that two people understand that their contributions will be part of an integrated new work, or must they specifically recognize each other as joint authors? *Erickson* cites with approval the case of *Childress v. Taylor,* 945 F.2d 500 (2d. Cir. 1991), in which the Second Circuit considered a claim of joint authorship by an actress who had engaged a playwright to write a script about the comedienne Jackie "Moms" Mabley. The actress wound up assisting the playwright by researching Mabley's life and suggesting scenes that were included in the final play. In deciding for the defendant, the Second Circuit took the position that a simple intent to merge contributions into a work did not support joint authorship. At the very least, in situations that involve a "dominant author," evidence that the parties "regarded themselves as joint authors is especially important." Why would this be so? Also, what does it mean for two parties to "regard themselves as joint authors" when the statute defines a joint work simply as one "prepared by two or more authors with the intention that their contributions be merged into inseparable or interdependent parts of a unitary whole"? Does this definition encompass anything more than a simple intent to merge contributions?

4. Joint authors hold undivided interests in a work. This means that each author can exploit the work as she sees fit so long as she shares any profits equally with her co-authors. What effect on the efficient exploitation of works does joint authorship have? Is it better to have a single owner of a copyright, or to have multiple owners, if society wants a work to be allocated to its highest and best use?

5. Let us turn once again to the world of academic authorship. Scientific writing often requires the collaboration of many people. For example, a principal investigator may design a study and get grant money to support research, another person may conduct experiments and collect data, and still another may write the text of the paper. Academic convention often results in listing all of these people (and sometimes many others) as co-authors of the resulting scholarship. Which of these people owns copyright in the work? In answering this question, consider the intentions of each party and copyrightability of each contribution. Does the law as you understand it reach the correct result?

Aalmuhammed v. Lee
202 F.3d 1227 (9th Cir. 2000)

KLEINFELD, Circuit Judge:

I. FACTS

In 1991, Warner Brothers contracted with Spike Lee and his production companies to make the movie *Malcolm X*, to be based on the book, *The Autobiography of Malcolm X*. Lee co-wrote the screenplay, directed, and co-produced the movie, which starred Denzel Washington as Malcolm X. Washington asked Jefri Aalmuhammed to assist him in his preparation for the starring role because Aalmuhammed knew a great deal about Malcolm X and Islam. Aalmuhammed, a devout Muslim, was particularly knowledgeable about the life of Malcolm X, having previously written, directed, and produced a documentary film about Malcolm X.

Aalmuhammed joined Washington on the movie set. The movie was filmed in the New York metropolitan area and Egypt. Aalmuhammed presented evidence that his involvement in making the movie was very extensive. He reviewed the shooting script for Spike Lee and Denzel Washington and suggested extensive script revisions. Some of his script revisions were included in the released version of the film; others were filmed but not included in the released version. Most of the revisions Aalmuhammed made were to ensure the religious and historical accuracy and authenticity of scenes depicting Malcolm X's religious conversion and pilgrimage to Mecca.

Aalmuhammed submitted evidence that he directed Denzel Washington and other actors while on the set, created at least two entire scenes with new characters, translated Arabic into English for subtitles, supplied his own voice for voice-overs, selected the proper prayers and religious practices for the characters, and edited parts of the movie during post production. Washington testified in his deposition that Aalmuhammed's contribution to the movie was "great" because he "helped to rewrite, to make more authentic." Once production ended, Aalmuhammed met with numerous Islamic organizations to persuade them that the movie was an accurate depiction of Malcolm X's life.

Aalmuhammed never had a written contract with Warner Brothers, Lee, or Lee's production companies, but he expected Lee to compensate him for his work. He did not intend to work and bear his expenses in New York and Egypt gratuitously. Aalmuhammed ultimately received a check for $25,000 from Lee, which he cashed, and a check for $100,000 from Washington, which he did not cash.

During the summer before *Malcolm X*'s November 1992 release, Aalmuhammed asked for a writing credit as a co-writer of the film, but was turned down. When the film was released, it credited Aalmuhammed only as an "Islamic Technical Consultant," far down the list. In November 1995, Aalmuhammed applied for a copyright with the U.S.

Copyright Office, claiming he was a co-creator, co-writer, and co-director of the movie. The Copyright Office issued him a "Certificate of Registration," but advised him in a letter that his "claims conflict with previous registrations" of the film.

II. ANALYSIS

A. Copyright claim

Aalmuhammed claimed that the movie *Malcolm X* was a "joint work" of which he was an author, thus making him a co-owner of the copyright. He sought a declaratory judgment to that effect, and an accounting for profits. He is not claiming copyright merely in what he wrote or contributed, but rather in the whole work, as a co-author of a "joint work." The district court granted defendants summary judgment against Mr. Aalmuhammed's copyright claims. We review de novo....

Aalmuhammed argues that he established a genuine issue of fact as to whether he was an author of a "joint work," *Malcolm X*. The Copyright Act does not define "author," but it does define "joint work":

A "joint work" is a work prepared by two or more authors with the intention that their contributions be merged into inseparable or interdependent parts of a unitary whole.

... The statutory language establishes that for a work to be a "joint work" there must be (1) a copyrightable work, (2) two or more "authors," and (3) the authors must intend their contributions be merged into inseparable or interdependent parts of a unitary whole. A "joint work" in this circuit "requires each author to make an independently copyrightable contribution" to the disputed work. *Malcolm X* is a copyrightable work, and it is undisputed that the movie was intended by everyone involved with it to be a unitary whole. It is also undisputed that Aalmuhammed made substantial and valuable contributions to the movie, including technical help, such as speaking Arabic to the persons in charge of the mosque in Egypt, scholarly and creative help, such as teaching the actors how to pray properly as Muslims, and script changes to add verisimilitude to the religious aspects of the movie. Speaking Arabic to persons in charge of the mosque, however, does not result in a copyrightable contribution to the motion picture. Coaching of actors, to be copyrightable, must be turned into an expression in a form subject to copyright. The same may be said for many of Aalmuhammed's other activities. Aalmuhammed has, however, submitted evidence that he rewrote several specific passages of dialogue that appeared in Malcolm X, and that he wrote scenes relating to Malcolm X's Hajj pilgrimage that were enacted in the movie. If Aalmuhammed's evidence is accepted, as it must be on summary judgment, these items would have been independently copyrightable. Aalmuhammed, therefore, has presented a genuine issue of fact as to whether he made a copyrightable contribution. All persons involved intended that Aalmuhammed's contributions would be merged into interdependent parts of the movie as a unitary whole. Aalmuhammed maintains that he has shown a genuine issue of fact for each element of a "joint work."

But there is another element to a "joint work." A "joint work" includes "two or more authors." Aalmuhammed established that he contributed substantially to the film, but not that he was one of its "authors." We hold that authorship is required under the statutory definition of a joint work, and that authorship is not the same thing as making a valuable and copyrightable contribution. We recognize that a contributor of an expression may be deemed to be the "author" of that expression for purposes of determining whether it is independently copyrightable. The issue we deal with is a different and larger one: is the contributor an author of the joint work within the meaning of 17 U.S.C. § 101.

By statutory definition, a "joint work" requires "two or more authors." The word "author" is taken from the traditional activity of one person sitting at a desk with a pen and writing something for publication. It is relatively easy to apply the word "author" to a novel. It is also easy to apply the word to two people who work together in a fairly traditional pen-and-ink way, like, perhaps, Gilbert and Sullivan. In the song, "I Am the Very Model of a Modern Major General," Gilbert's words and Sullivan's tune are inseparable, and anyone who has heard the song knows that it owes its existence to both men, Sir William Gilbert and Sir Arthur Sullivan, as its creative originator. But as the number of contributors grows and the work itself becomes less the product of one or two individuals who create it without much help, the word is harder to apply.

Who, in the absence of contract, can be considered an author of a movie? The word is traditionally used to mean the originator or the person who causes something to come into being, or even the first cause, as when Chaucer refers to the "Author of Nature." For a movie, that might be the producer who raises the money. Eisenstein thought the author of a movie was the editor. The "auteur" theory suggests that it might be the director, at least if the director is able to impose his artistic judgments on the film. Traditionally, by analogy to books, the author was regarded as the person who writes the screenplay, but often a movie reflects the work of many screenwriters. Grenier suggests that the person with creative control tends to be the person in whose name the money is raised, perhaps a star, perhaps the director, perhaps the producer, with control gravitating to the star as the financial investment in scenes already shot grows. Where the visual aspect of the movie is especially important, the chief cinematographer might be regarded as the author. And for, say, a Disney animated movie like "The Jungle Book," it might perhaps be the animators and the composers of the music.

The Supreme Court dealt with the problem of defining "author" in new media in *Burrow–Giles Lithographic Co. v. Sarony*. The question there was, who is the author of a photograph: the person who sets it up and snaps the shutter, or the person who makes the lithograph from it. Oscar Wilde, the person whose picture was at issue, doubtless offered some creative advice as well. The Court decided that the photographer was the author, quoting various English authorities: "the person who has superintended the arrangement, who has actually formed the picture by putting the persons in position, and arranging the place where the people are to be—the man who is the effective cause of that"; "'author' involves originating, making, producing, as the inventive or master mind, the thing which is to be protected"; "the man who really represents, creates, or gives effect to the idea, fancy, or imagination." The Court said that an "author," in the sense that the Founding Fathers used the term in the Constitution, was "'he to whom anything owes its origin; originator; maker; one who completes a work of science or literature.'"

Answering a different question, what is a copyrightable "work," as opposed to who is the "author," the Supreme Court held in *Feist Publications* that "some minimal level of creativity" or "originality" suffices. But that measure of a "work" would be too broad and indeterminate to be useful if applied to determine who are "authors" of a movie. So many people might qualify as an "author" if the question were limited to whether they made a substantial creative contribution that that test would not distinguish one from another. Everyone from the producer and director to casting director, costumer, hairstylist, and "best boy" gets listed in the movie credits because all of their creative contributions really do matter. It is striking in *Malcolm X* how much the person who controlled the hue of the lighting contributed, yet no one would use the word "author" to denote that individual's relationship to the movie. A creative contribution does not suffice to establish authorship of the movie.

.... *Burrow–Giles* defines author as the person to whom the work owes its origin and who superintended the whole work, the "master mind." In a movie this definition, in the absence of a contract to the contrary, would generally limit authorship to someone at the top of the screen credits, sometimes the producer, sometimes the director, possibly the star, or the screenwriter—someone who has artistic control. After all, in *Burrow–Giles* the lithographer made a substantial copyrightable creative contribution, and so did the person who posed, Oscar Wilde, but the Court held that the photographer was the author....

[S]everal factors suggest themselves as among the criteria for joint authorship, in the absence of contract. First, an author "superintend[s]" the work by exercising control. This will likely be a person "who has actually formed the picture by putting the persons in position, and arranging the place where the people are to be—the man who is the effective cause of that," or "the inventive or master mind" who "creates, or gives effect to the idea." Second, putative coauthors make objective manifestations of a shared intent to be coauthors, as by denoting the authorship of *The Pirates of Penzance* as "Gilbert and Sullivan." We say objective manifestations because, were the mutual intent to be determined by subjective intent, it could become an instrument of fraud, were one coauthor to hide from the other an intention to take sole credit for the work. Third, the audience appeal of the work turns on both contributions and "the share of each in its success cannot be appraised." Control in many cases will be the most important factor.

The best objective manifestation of a shared intent, of course, is a contract saying that the parties intend to be or not to be co-authors. In the absence of a contract, the inquiry must of necessity focus on the facts. The factors articulated in this decision ... cannot be reduced to a rigid formula, because the creative relationships to which they apply vary too much. Different people do creative work together in different ways, and even among the same people working together the relationship may change over time as the work proceeds.

Aalmuhammed did not at any time have superintendence of the work. Warner Brothers and Spike Lee controlled it. Aalmuhammed was not the person "who has actually formed the picture by putting the persons in position, and arranging the place...." Spike Lee was, so far as we can tell from the record. Aalmuhammed, like Larson's dramaturg, could make extremely helpful recommendations, but Spike Lee was not bound to accept any of them, and the work would not benefit in the slightest unless Spike Lee chose to accept them. Aalmuhammed lacked control over the work, and absence of control is strong evidence of the absence of co-authorship.

Also, neither Aalmuhammed, nor Spike Lee, nor Warner Brothers, made any objective manifestations of an intent to be coauthors. Warner Brothers required Spike Lee to sign a "work for hire" agreement, so that even Lee would not be a co-author and co-owner with Warner Brothers. It would be illogical to conclude that Warner Brothers, while not wanting to permit Lee to own the copyright, intended to share ownership with individuals like Aalmuhammed who worked under Lee's control, especially ones who at the time had made known no claim to the role of co-author. No one, including Aalmuhammed, made any indication to anyone prior to litigation that Aalmuhammed was intended to be a co-author and co-owner.

Aalmuhammed offered no evidence that he was the "inventive or master mind" of the movie. He was the author of another less widely known documentary about Malcolm X, but was not the master of this one. What Aalmuhammed's evidence showed, and all it showed, was that, subject to Spike Lee's authority to accept them, he made very valuable contributions to the movie. That is not enough for co-authorship of a joint work.

The Constitution establishes the social policy that our construction of the statutory term "authors" carries out. The Founding Fathers gave Congress the power to give authors copyrights in order "[t]o promote the progress of Science and useful arts." Progress would be retarded rather than promoted, if an author could not consult with others and adopt their useful suggestions without sacrificing sole ownership of the work. Too open a definition of author would compel authors to insulate themselves and maintain ignorance of the contributions others might make. Spike Lee could not consult a scholarly Muslim to make a movie about a religious conversion to Islam, and the arts would be the poorer for that.

The broader construction that Aalmuhammed proposes would extend joint authorship to many "overreaching contributors,"... and deny sole authors "exclusive authorship status simply because another person render[ed] some form of assistance." Claimjumping by research assistants, editors, and former spouses, lovers and friends would endanger authors who talked with people about what they were doing, if creative copyrightable contribution were all that authorship required....

Because the record before the district court established no genuine issue of fact as to Aalmuhammed's co-authorship of *Malcolm X* as a joint work, the district court correctly granted summary judgment dismissing his claims for declaratory judgment and an accounting resting on co-authorship.

Notes and Questions

1.   Under *Aalmuhammed*, how do we determine who is the author of a movie, in the absence of a contract that spells this out? Does the decision provide clear guidance? The court expressly rejected a hard and fast rule, noting that creative arrangements are too varied. Do you think this was wise? How would you apply the standard in *Aalmuhammed* to other works involving collaboration by many parties? What about, for example, a complicated software program created by a team of dozens of computer programmers, graphic artists, etc.? Or what about a sound recording, created by a band, several independent session-musicians, and the sound engineer? Who should be the "author" or authors of such works?

2.   The decision in *Aalmuhammed* provides an extreme example of the strong drive in copyright law to find "an author" or only a few authors, rather than awarding rights to everyone who made contributions to a collaborative work. What reasons did the court provide for limiting authorship in this fashion? Do you find those reasons persuasive? Are there any downsides?

3.   Note once again the importance of contracting. Like many of the other cases in this section, the dispute in this case could have been avoided with some foresight. However, as these cases indicate, individuals (and even sophisticated corporations, as in this case) do not always exercise foresight, and copyright law must determine ownership in the absence of a writing.

4.   Compare the result in *Gaiman* with the result in *Aalmuhammed*. In the former, one of the parties did not contribute anything copyrightable, but was found to be a joint author. In the latter, one of the parties contributed copyrightable material, but was found not be a joint author. Are these results consistent? What explains the difference?

5.   It is possible to view the application of the work made for hire and joint work doctrines as a search for the "true" author of a work. Our

culture often constructs authorship as the solitary endeavor of an inspired individual who produces something new that would not have existed but for the author's creative spirit. In its purest form, this romantic author labors alone and deserves sole credit for the works she creates. The vision of the romantic author supports copyright's search for a work's true author. The creative individual who genuinely deserves credit for a work may interact with others who fancy themselves as authors, but they have neither the creativity nor the sweat of true authors. Accordingly, the work made for hire and joint work doctrines separate the "true" authors from those who pretend to be authors.

What do you think about copyright's search for "true" authors? Cases like *CCNV*, *Hi-Tech*, *Erickson*, and *Aalmuhammed* show us that the creation of works is often highly collaborative. Should the law continue to identify a work's "true" authors, or should it frankly recognize that works always owe their existence to multiple individuals and find another method of assigning copyright ownership that does not depend on authorship?

Problem

Imagine that you have a client who is a website designer. One year ago, your client was approached by a local retail store and asked to design a website for that store. Over the course of several months, your client worked on the website, collecting information about what the store wanted, creating and presenting mock-ups of the web pages, revising the webpages in response to input from the store, and coding the html for the webpages. In coming up with the design of the website, your client incorporated a number of helpful suggestions from the retail store. During the creation of the website, your client asked a friend of his, who was a graphic designer, to design various graphics that appear throughout the website. Your client paid his friend a fixed fee for his work, but did not enter into any written contract. Your client did, however, enter into a contract with the retail store. A key provision of the contract stated:

> Web Designer acknowledges that the Web Site is being created by Web Designer as a "work made for hire" under the United States Copyright Act and the Web Site shall be and remain the sole and exclusive property of the Retail Store.

Your client presented the finished website to the retail store, and the retail store paid your client his fee.

Several months later, your client was approached by another local retail store and asked to design a very similar website for this retail store. Rather than reinventing the wheel, your client intends to take the design and graphics from his earlier project and make minor changes to adapt it for use by the new client. What potential copyright issues do you see? What advice would you give your client?

SECTION C. TRANSFER OF COPYRIGHT

Having studied the initial ownership of copyrighted works, we examine next some issues related to the transfer of such ownership. The ability to transfer an ownership interest in a copyright is important because it greatly enhances the ability of the original owner to economically exploit that work. In many cases, the individual who created the work, i.e. the author, may not be best placed to commercialize that work through, for example, printing copies, distributing them to the public, advertising and promotion, etc. Thus, the ability to transfer an interest in a copyright allows the author to take advantage of entities that specialize in these activities. An important part of the work of many copyright lawyers involves drafting and negotiating these kinds of transfers.

Under the 1909 Act, copyrights were considered indivisible. This meant that authors could transfer their entire interest in the copyright, or not at all. They were not generally able to transfer only a limited portion of the copyright (for example, only the right to make copies, but not the right to publicly perform). Although this made it easier to identify who owned the copyright at any given time, it limited the ability of the author to exploit the work, since he or she could only transfer it once.

Congress changed this rule in the 1976 Act and made copyright interests fully divisible. Thus authors can now choose to transfer the entire copyright or choose instead to transfer only a more limited set of rights in the copyright. A transfer of the entire copyright is generally referred to as an "assignment." With an assignment, the original owner no longer retains any rights in the copyrighted work. A transfer of less than the full interest in the copyright is generally referred to as a "license." A license can be limited along many different dimensions, for example by duration (e.g. for only one year), exclusive right (e.g. only the right to reproduce), geographic scope (e.g. only within the U.S.), etc. Licenses can also be exclusive (such that the original owner cannot license the same right to anyone else or exercise that right him or herself) or nonexclusive (such that the original owner remains free to license the same right to any third party).

1. WRITING REQUIREMENT

The Copyright Act requires that certain transfers of an interest in copyright be in writing in order to be enforceable. Specifically, section 204(a) of the Copyright Act provides:

> A transfer of copyright ownership, other than by operation of law, is not valid unless an instrument of conveyance, or a note or memorandum of the transfer, is in writing and signed by the owner of the rights conveyed or such owner's duly authorized agent.

What happens, then, when a purported transfer of a copyright is not in writing?

Effects Associates v. Cohen
908 F.2d 555 (9th Cir. 1990)

KOZINSKI, Circuit Judge:

What we have here is a failure to compensate. Larry Cohen, a low-budget horror movie mogul, paid less than the agreed price for special effects footage he had commissioned from Effects Associates. Cohen then used this footage without first obtaining a written license or assignment of the copyright; Effects sued for copyright infringement. We consider whether a transfer of copyright without a written agreement, an arrangement apparently not uncommon in the motion picture industry, conforms with the requirements of the Copyright Act.

Facts

This started out as a run-of-the-mill Hollywood squabble. Defendant Larry Cohen wrote, directed and executive produced "The Stuff," a horror movie with a dash of social satire: Earth is invaded by an alien life form that looks (and tastes) like frozen yogurt but, alas, has some unfortunate side effects—it's addictive and takes over the mind of anyone who eats it. Marketed by an unscrupulous entrepreneur, the Stuff becomes a big hit. An industrial spy hired by ice cream manufacturers eventually uncovers the terrible truth; he alerts the American people and blows up the yogurt factory, making the world safe once again for lovers of frozen confections.

In cooking up this gustatory melodrama, Cohen asked Effects Associates, a small special effects company, to create footage to enhance certain action sequences in the film. In a short letter dated October 29, 1984, Effects offered to prepare seven shots, the most dramatic of which would depict the climactic explosion of the Stuff factory. Cohen agreed to the deal orally, but no one said anything about who would own the copyright in the footage.

Cohen was unhappy with the factory explosion Effects created, and he expressed his dissatisfaction by paying Effects only half the promised amount for that shot. Effects made several demands for the rest of the money (a little over $8,000), but Cohen refused. Nevertheless, Cohen incorporated Effects's footage into the film and turned it over to New World Entertainment for distribution. Effects then brought this copyright infringement action, claiming that Cohen (along with his production company and New World) had no right to use the special effects footage unless he paid Effects the full contract price. ...

[T]he district court granted summary judgment to Cohen ..., holding that Effects had granted Cohen an implied license to use the shots. ... We review the district court's grant of summary judgment de novo.

Discussion

A.   Transfer of Copyright Ownership

The law couldn't be clearer: The copyright owner of "a motion picture or other audiovisual work" has the exclusive rights to copy, distribute or display the copyrighted work publicly. 17 U.S.C. § 106. While the copyright owner can sell or license his rights to someone else, section 204 of the Copyright Act invalidates a purported transfer of ownership unless it is in writing. Here, no one disputes that Effects is the copyright owner of the special effects footage used in "The Stuff," and that defendants copied, distributed and publicly displayed this footage without written authorization.

Cohen suggests that section 204's writing requirement does not apply to this situation, advancing an argument that might be summarized, tongue in cheek, as: Moviemakers do lunch, not contracts. Cohen concedes that "[i]n the best of all possible legal worlds" parties would obey the writing requirement, but contends that moviemakers are too absorbed in developing "joint creative endeavors" to "focus upon the legal niceties of copyright licenses." Thus, Cohen suggests that we hold section 204's writing requirement inapplicable here because "it [i]s customary in the motion picture industry ... not to have written licenses." To the extent that Cohen's argument amounts to a plea to exempt moviemakers from the normal operation of section 204 by making implied transfers of copyrights "the rule, not the exception," we reject his argument.

Common sense tells us that agreements should routinely be put in writing. This simple practice prevents misunderstandings by spelling out the terms of a deal in black and white, forces parties to clarify their thinking and consider problems that could potentially arise, and encourages them to take their promises seriously because it's harder to backtrack on a written contract than on an oral one. Copyright law dovetails nicely with common sense by requiring that a transfer of copyright ownership be in writing. Section 204 ensures that the creator of a work will not give away his copyright inadvertently and forces a party who wants to use the copyrighted work to negotiate with the creator to determine precisely what rights are being transferred and at what price. Most importantly, section 204 enhances predictability and certainty of copyright ownership—"Congress' paramount goal" when it revised the Act in 1976. Rather than look to the courts every time they disagree as to whether a particular use of the work violates their mutual understanding, parties need only look to the writing that sets out their respective rights.

Section 204's writing requirement is not unduly burdensome; it necessitates neither protracted negotiations nor substantial expense. The rule is really quite simple: If the copyright holder agrees to transfer ownership to another party, that party must get the copyright holder to sign a piece of paper saying so. It doesn't have to be the Magna Charta; a one-line pro forma statement will do.

Cohen's attempt to exempt moviemakers from the requirements of the Copyright Act is largely precluded by recent Supreme Court and circuit authority construing the work-for-hire doctrine. Section 101 of the Act defines, in relevant part, a work made for hire as "a work prepared by an employee within the scope of his or her employment." 17 U.S.C. § 101 (1988). Section 201(b) provides that the copyright in such a work is presumed to vest in the employer, not the employee. Prior to the Supreme Court's decision in *Community for Creative Non-Violence*, some circuits had broadly construed section 101's use of the term employee, holding a work to have been prepared by an employee whenever the hiring party controlled, or had the right to control, the product. *See Community for Creative Non-Violence*, 109 S.Ct. at 2172. This broad definition encompassed virtually all contributions to books and movies because, as the Court recognized, such contributions are "usually prepared at the instance, direction, and risk of a publisher or producer." *Id.* at 2173. The Court rejected this rule as inconsistent with both the language and purpose of the Copyright Act. It held instead that the term employee was to be defined according to general agency principles; where a non-employee contributes to a book or movie, as Effects did here, the exclusive rights of copyright ownership vest in the creator of the contribution, unless there is a written transfer to the contrary. ...

Thus, section 101 specifically addresses the movie and book publishing industries, affording moviemakers a simple, straightforward way of obtaining ownership of the copyright in a creative contribution-namely, a written agreement. The Supreme Court and this circuit, while recognizing the custom and practice in the industry, have refused to permit moviemakers to sidestep section 204's writing requirement. Accordingly, we find unpersuasive Cohen's contention that section 204's writing requirement, which singles out no particular group, somehow doesn't apply to him. As section 204 makes no special allowances for the movie industry, neither do we.

B.   Nonexclusive Licenses

Although we reject any suggestion that moviemakers are immune to section 204, we note that there is a narrow exception to the writing requirement that may apply here. Section 204 provides that all transfers of copyright ownership must be in writing; section 101 defines transfers of ownership broadly, but expressly removes from the scope of section 204 a "nonexclusive license." The sole issue that remains, then, is whether Cohen had a nonexclusive license to use plaintiff's special effects footage.

The leading treatise on copyright law states that "[a] nonexclusive license may be granted orally, or may even be implied from conduct." 3 M. Nimmer & D. Nimmer, *Nimmer on Copyright* § 10.03[A], at 10-36 (1989). Cohen relies on the latter proposition; he insists that, although Effects never gave him a written or oral license, Effects's conduct created an implied license to use the footage in "The Stuff."

Cohen relies largely on our decision in *Oddo v. Ries*, 743 F.2d 630 (9th Cir. 1984). There, we held that Oddo, the author of a series of articles on how to restore Ford F-100 pickup trucks, had impliedly granted a limited non-exclusive license to Ries, a publisher, to use plaintiff's articles in a book on the same topic. We relied on the fact that Oddo and Ries had formed a partnership to create and publish the book, with Oddo writing and Ries providing capital. Oddo prepared a manuscript consisting partly of material taken from his prior articles and submitted it to Ries. Because the manuscript incorporated pre-existing material, it was a derivative work; by publishing it, Ries would have necessarily infringed the copyright in Oddo's articles, unless Oddo had granted him a license. We concluded that, in preparing and handing over to Ries a manuscript intended for publication that, if published, would infringe Oddo's copyright, Oddo "impliedly gave the partnership a license to use the articles insofar as they were incorporated in the manuscript, for without such a license, Oddo's contribution to the partnership venture would have been of minimal value."

The district court agreed with Cohen, and we agree with the district court: *Oddo* controls here. Like the plaintiff in *Oddo*, Effects created a work at defendant's request and handed it over, intending that defendant copy and distribute it. To hold that Effects did not at the same time convey a license to use the footage in "The Stuff" would mean that plaintiff's contribution to the film was "of minimal value," a conclusion that can't be squared with the fact that Cohen paid Effects almost $56,000 for this footage. Accordingly, we conclude that Effects impliedly granted nonexclusive licenses to Cohen and his production company to incorporate the special effects footage into "The Stuff" and to New World Entertainment to distribute the film.

Conclusion

We affirm the district court's grant of summary judgment in favor of Cohen and the other defendants. We note, however, that plaintiff doesn't leave this court empty-handed. Copyright ownership is comprised of a bundle of rights; in granting a nonexclusive license to Cohen, Effects has given up only one stick from that bundle-the right to sue Cohen for copyright infringement. It retains the right to sue him in state court on a variety of other grounds, including breach of contract. Additionally, Effects may license, sell or give away for nothing its remaining rights in the special effects footage. Those rights may not be particularly valuable, of course: "The Stuff" was something less than a blockbuster, and it remains to be seen whether there's a market for shots featuring great gobs of alien yogurt oozing out of a defunct factory. On the other hand, the shots may have much potential for use in music videos. In any event, whatever Effects chooses to do with the footage, Cohen will have no basis for complaining. And that's an important lesson that licensees of more versatile film properties may want to take to heart.

Notes and Questions

1. As *Effects Associates* indicates, assignments and exclusive licesnes are considered "transfer[s] of copyright ownership" within the meaning of § 204(a), and thus will not be enforceable unless they are in writing. However, nonexclusive licenses are not "transfer[s] of copyright ownership," and can thus be oral or even, as in the case of *Effects Associates*, implied through a course of conduct.

2. *Effects Associates* illustrates the distinction between possession of the material object embodying a work and ownership of the work's copyright. Section 202 of the Copyright Act states:

> Ownership of a copyright, or of any of the exclusive rights under a copyright, is distinct from ownership of any material object in which the work is embodied. Transfer of ownership of any material object, including the copy or phonorecord in which the work is first fixed, does not of itself convey any rights in the copyrighted work embodied in the object; nor, in the absence of an agreement, does transfer of ownership of a copyright or of any exclusive rights under a copyright convey property rights in any material object.

A court could read sections 201(d) and 202 to deny defendants like Cohen any rights to use works that they commission. After all, Cohen paid for creation of a work, took possession of a copy of the work, and did nothing to get a written assignment of the rights he needed. Decisions like *Effects Associates* soften the potentially hard edges of sections 201(d) and 202 by giving limited non-exclusive licenses to defendants like Cohen who have failed to properly document their deals.

3. *Effects Associates* affirmed a grant of summary judgment in favor of the defendant Cohen. The Ninth Circuit found that the pattern of conduct between the plaintiff and defendant implied the grant of nonexclusive license in Cohen's favor. Such a conclusion seems plausible, but was it the only conclusion a jury could reasonably have reached? For example, might the plaintiff have intended that Cohen get permission to use the work only upon payment in full, and not before? If you conclude that a jury could have reasonably reached alternate conclusions like this, then summary judgment in Cohen's favor becomes questionable. Does this mean that *Effects Associates* was wrongly decided? Or, are there good reasons for finding summarily in the defendant's favor?

4. Courts frequently grant preliminary and permanent injunctive relief to plaintiffs in copyright cases. These injunctions give plaintiffs an effective veto over the economic exploitation of an infringing work, and they often lead to quick settlements favorable to plaintiffs. Of course, *Effects Associates* did not get such an injunction. Instead, all it had was a breach of contract action for money damages against Cohen.

The contrast between injunctive relief and money damages raises interesting questions about cases like *Effects Associates*. Cohen did not pay

Effects Associates the agreed upon price for the work Cohen commissioned, yet he went ahead and used the work in *The Stuff*, taking the full benefit of the plaintiff's work. If there had been no agreement between Cohen and Effects Associates, a court would probably have found against Cohen on infringement and granted an injunction in favor of Effects Associates. Does the existence of a breached oral contract justify depriving plaintiffs like Effects Associates the benefits of injunctive relief? Or, does the logic behind implied licenses suggest that courts should not grant injunctive relief in copyright cases, and that money damages alone sufficiently compensate victorious plaintiffs?

2. INTERPRETATION AND DRAFTING

Even when parties enter into a written contract, ambiguities can arise in the interpretation of that contract. This is a particularly tricky issue when the ambiguities arise from the creation of new technologies. For example, in *Random House v. Rosetta Books*, 150 F. Supp. 2d 613 (S.D.N.Y. 2001), *aff'd*, 283 F.3d 490 (2d Cir. 2002), the court had to determine whether a clause in a 1960s contract that granted to the publishing house the exclusive right to "print, publish and sell the work in book form" included the right to distribute and sell the work as a digital "eBook." Interpreting this clause under New York law, the court ultimately concluded that it did not.

Although such ambiguities are typically resolved based upon principles of contract law, sometimes specific provisions of the Copyright Act may affect the result. For example, in *New York Times v. Tasini*, 533 U.S. 483 (2001), the U.S. Supreme Court faced an interesting question regarding whether a new technological use belonged to the New York Times or its freelance reporters. The reporters, as independent contractors, retained the copyrights in their articles, but granted the New York Times a license to publish their articles in a particular issue of the newspaper, which was a "collective work" within the meaning of the Copyright Act (insofar as the newspaper issue consisted of many separate underlying copyrighted works). The dispute arose when the New York Times gave permission to Lexis/Nexis and other database companies to reproduce back issues of the New York Times in its searchable databases. The freelance reporters objected, arguing that this use exceeded the scope of the licenses they granted to the New York Times.

The resolution of this issue turned, not on the language of the licenses, but on interpretation of a particular provision of the CopyrightAct governing rights in collective works. Section 201(c) provides:

> In the absence of an express transfer of the copyright or of any rights under it, the owner of copyright in the collective work is presumed to have acquired only the privilege of reproducing and distributing the contribution as part of that particular collective work, any revision of that collective work, and any later collective work in the same series

The New York Times argued that the licensing of back issues to the database companies consistuted a "revision" of the original collective work, and thus they had the right to use the articles in this fashion. The freelance reporters argued that this was a new use, and could not be understood as a "revision" of the original work.

The Supreme Court agreed with the reporters and held that this was not a "revision." The Court noted that the articles appeared in the databases as freestanding articles, in response to searches conducted by the database user, and without any of the surrounding context in the original print issue. The Court thus rejected the argument that the databases were functional equivalents to the original print issues or other archival versions, such as microfiche. The Court also rejected concerns that this result might lead to gaps in the historical record, stating that the New York Times (and other similarly-situated companies) would need to secure licenses for such uses, or that the district court could award damages rather than order that the articles be removed from the databases.

As noted above, copyright lawyers are often asked to draft, negotiate, and/or review copyright licensing agreements. The range and variety of such agreements is extremely broad, encompassing everything from a book publishing agreement, to a music-industry contract, to a license for use of a photograph, to an option for movie rights in a book, to a software end-user license. A full consideration of all of the issues raised by such licenses is beyond the scope of an introductory course. However, it is at least worth taking a preliminary look at a simple sample copyright license clause, to illustrate some of the issues and considerations that commonly arise.

Problem

Imagine that you represent a client who is a chemistry professor at a local university. She has agreed to write a new introductory chemistry textbook and has found a national textbook publisher, who has agreed to publish, market, and distribute the textbook. The publisher sent your client a copy of its "Standard Publishing Agreement," and she has asked you to review it. In particular, she has asked you to pay attention to the following provision:

> 2. Grant of Rights. Author hereby exclusively grants, assigns, and transfers to Publisher, its successors, representatives, and assigns, the entire copyright and all right, title, and interest in the Work and any part thereof, for the full term of such rights, throughout the world and in all languages, and in all media and

forms of expression now known or later devised.

Your client has expressed a number of concerns about this provision. First, she expects to incorporate into her textbook a number of problems that she has assigned to her students in the past. If she does not use her own textbook for a particular chemistry course, may she still use those problems in class? Second, she will likely include in her textbook a number of charts and graphics that she often uses in her academic presentations. Will she be able to continue to use those charts and graphics in future academic presentations? Third, although she is happy to have her textbook published in print form, she is planning to create a website in the future, which would help teach basic chemistry concepts to students in under-developed countries. Will she be able to use any of the materials from her casebook in such a website?

How might you propose redrafting the agreement to accommodate your client's concerns? Consider, for example, the following alternative provision:

> 2. Grant of Rights. Author hereby grants, assigns, and transfers to Publisher, its successors, representatives, and assigns, the sole and exclusive rights to print, publish, distribute, sell, and license the Work in the English language in book form in the United States of America, its territories and dependencies, and Canada, during the full term of copyright and any renewals and extensions thereof, except as provided herein.

How does this clause differ from the prior clause? Would such a clause address all of your client's concerns? If not, how might you redraft the license to accommodate her concerns? If the publisher objects to this clause, can you imagine other provisions that might address both your client's and the publisher's concerns?

Chapter Four

FORMALITIES, DURATION, RENEWAL

So far, we have covered what types of works can be copyrighted and who owns the resulting copyright. In this chapter, we turn to a set of technical issues that affect whether otherwise copyrightable subject matter actually receives protection. We will look first at the formal requirements for copyright protection, such as publication, notice, registration and deposit. Although these formal requirements have largely been eliminated as a condition of copyright today, they are still relevant insofar as they apply to works created before 1989. We will then turn to the issue of copyright duration, i.e. how long copyrights last. We will also take a look at the related issues of copyright renewal and termination of transfers.

By way of warning, the materials covered in this chapter represent some of the more technical aspects of copyright practice and require careful attention to some complex statutory rules. At the same time, we will find embedded in these technical issues some very basic policy concerns regarding the proper balance struck by our copyright laws. In particular, how long should copyright last? And what, if any, obligations should be imposed on copyright owners to establish and maintain their copyrights?

SECTION A. FORMALITIES

Copyright formalities are technical requirements, above and beyond the subject matter requirements covered in the previous chapters, that copyright owners must comply with in order to receive protection for their works under the Copyright Act. Historically, these formalities included publication of the work, notice of copyright date and ownership, registration of the work with the Copyright Office, and deposit of copies with the Library of Congress. Under the 1909 Act, failure to comply with some of these formalities could (and often did) lead to the forfeiture of federal copyright protection and cast works into the public domain. Thus, formalities played a significant role in determining whether a work was subject to copyright.

Today, copyright formalities have largely been abolished as a condition of copyright protection. The Berne Convention, the major international copyright treaty, requires signatory countries to protect works of authorship without regard to compliance with formalities. Accordingly, the formalities requirements found in previous versions of the Copyright Act effectively prevented the U.S. from joining the Berne Convention. In 1988, the U.S. decided to join the Berne Convention and, in order to satisfy its obligations under Berne, amended the Copyright Act to do away with formalities as a condition of copyright protection. Thus today, once a work is original and fixed, it is automatically protected under copyright law without any further action by the copyright owner.

Copyright formalities remain important, however, for two reasons. First, the abolition of formalities was not retroactive. Older works published or created before the change in the law could fall into the public domain if their copyright holders failed to comply with certain formalities. Thus, any case involving such a work today raises at least the possibility that the work may have lost its copyright protection. Second, although formalities today are not a condition for copyright protection, there are still a number of significant benefits that accrue from compliance with such formalities.

In order to understand the impact of formalities, it is important to note the timing of the changes in the law. As mentioned above, formalities played a significant role under the 1909 Act. In the major 1976 revision to the Copyright Act, Congress kept formalities largely intact, but somewhat weakened their impact. Then in 1988, Congress effectively did away with formalities entirely as a condition of copyright protection when it passed the Berne Convention Implementation Act ("BCIA").

Accordingly, the time during which a work was created or published generally governs the extent to which formalities affect the work's copyright. The table below briefly summarizes the varying requirements under these time periods.

	1909 Act *Published before 1/1/78*	**1976 Act** *Created on or after 1/1/78 but before 3/1/89*	**1988 BCIA** *Created on or after 3/1/89*
Publication	Required for protection of works reproduced for sale.	Not required for protection, but triggers notice requirement.	Not required for protection.
Notice	Required for protection.	Required for protection. But limited opportunity to cure if publication without notice occurs.	Not required for protection. But significant benefits.
Deposit	Required for filing suit. Sanctions (including forfeiture) for failure to deposit. Deposit with claim of copyright also secured protection for works not reproduced for sale (i.e. unpublished works).	Required for filing suit. Sanctions (not including forfeiture) for failure to deposit.	
Registration	Required for renewal and for filing suit.	Required for filing suit.	Required for filing suit. Exception for Berne Convention works.

The following subsections develop each of these formalities in more detail. As you read through these sections, keep in mind the broader policy questions. What purpose did formalities serve under older versions of the Copyright Act? Why were formalities subsequently eliminated? What impact did this have on copyright markets? Should formalities play a continuing role in copyright law? More broadly, what conditions, if any, should copyright owners have to satisfy before they are entitled to copyright?

1. PUBLICATION

Section 10 of the 1909 Act allowed an eligible party to secure copyright by publishing her work with a statutorily prescribed notice.[32] With the exception of works not reproduced for sale, unpublished works received no federal copyright protection.[33] Instead, those works were protected, if at all, by an uneven and unreliable patchwork of state common law copyright doctrines. Publication thus played a critical role in determining whether a work was subject to federal copyright protection. The rationale for this requirement was straightforward. Publication marked the point at which the benefit of the author's work was conveyed to the public, thus warranting a corresponding benefit granted to the author.

As noted in previous chapters, the 1976 Act shifted the trigger of federal copyright protection from publication to fixation. Creative works were thus protected under federal copyright law as soon as they were created, without regard to publication. The Act effectively eliminated the dual system (and the correspondingly complex case law) under which published works were subject to federal copyright and unpublished works were subject to state common law copyright. Under the Act, both published and unpublished works are protected under federal law as soon as they are created.

Although publication is no longer a condition of federal copyright protection for newly-created works, it remains relevant for works created and published before March 1, 1989, the effective date of the Berne Convention Implementation Act. As we will see below, works published without notice prior to this date potentially lost copyright protection. Thus, publication still governs whether certain works have been inadvertently cast into the public domain.

The key question, then, is when a work has been published. As we will see, "publication" does not refer simply to the act of making a work available or accessible to the public. Instead, courts have developed a complex case law identifying the kinds of acts that constitute publication. As you review the materials below, ask yourselves why the courts adopted the particular rules they did.

Estate of Martin Luther King, Jr. v. CBS
194 F.3d 1211 (11th Cir. 1999)

ANDERSON, Chief Judge.

... The facts underlying this case form part of our national heritage and are well-known to many Americans. On the afternoon of August 28,

---

[32] Section 10 provided: "Any person entitled thereto by this title may secure copyright for his work by publication thereof with the notice of copyright required by this title; and such notice shall be affixed to each copy thereof published or offered for sale in the United States by authority of the copyright proprietor, except in the case of books seeking ad interim protection under section 22 of this title."

[33] Section 12 of the 1909 Act allowed the author of a work not reproduced for sale to gain copyright by depositing with the Register of Copyrights a copy or copies of the work, along with a claim of copyright.

1963, the Southern Christian Leadership Conference ("SCLC") held the March on Washington ("March") to promote the growing civil rights movement. The events of the day were seen and heard by some 200,000 people gathered at the March, and were broadcast live via radio and television to a nationwide audience of millions of viewers. The highlight of the March was a rousing speech that Dr. Martin Luther King, Jr., the SCLC's founder and president, gave in front of the Lincoln Memorial ("Speech"). The Speech contained the famous utterance, "I have a dream ...," which became symbolic of the civil rights movement. The SCLC had sought out wide press coverage of the March and the Speech, and these efforts were successful; the Speech was reported in daily newspapers across the country, was broadcast live on radio and television, and was extensively covered on television and radio subsequent to the live broadcast.

On September 30, 1963, approximately one month after the delivery of the Speech, Dr. King took steps to secure federal copyright protection for the Speech under the Copyright Act of 1909, and a certificate of registration of his claim to copyright was issued by the Copyright Office on October 2, 1963. Almost immediately thereafter, Dr. King filed suit in the Southern District of New York to enjoin the unauthorized sale of recordings of the Speech and won a preliminary injunction on December 13, 1963.

For the next twenty years, Dr. King and the Estate enjoyed copyright protection in the Speech and licensed it for a variety of uses, and renewed the copyright when necessary. In 1994, CBS entered into a contract with the Arts & Entertainment Network to produce a historical documentary series entitled "The 20th Century with Mike Wallace." One segment was devoted to "Martin Luther King, Jr. and The March on Washington." That episode contained material filmed by CBS during the March and extensive footage of the Speech (amounting to about 60% of its total content). CBS, however, did not seek the Estate's permission to use the Speech in this manner and refused to pay royalties to the Estate. The instant litigation ensued.

On summary judgment, the district court framed the issue as "whether the public delivery of Dr. King's speech ... constituted a general publication of the speech so as to place it in the public domain." After discussing the relevant case law, the district court held that Dr. King's "performance coupled with such wide and unlimited reproduction and dissemination as occurred concomitant to Dr. King's speech during the March on Washington can be seen only as a general publication which thrust the speech into the public domain." Thus, the district court granted CBS's motion for summary judgment. The Estate now appeals to this Court. ...

Because of the dates of the critical events, the determinative issues in this case are properly analyzed under the Copyright Act of 1909 ("1909 Act"), rather than the Copyright Act of 1976 ("1976 Act") that is currently in effect. The question is whether Dr. King's attempt to obtain statutory copyright protection on September 30, 1963 was effective, or whether it was a nullity because the Speech had already been forfeited to the public domain via a general publication.

Under the regime created by the 1909 Act, an author received state common law protection automatically at the time of creation of a work. This state common law protection persisted until the moment of a general publication. When a general publication occurred, the author either forfeited his work to the public domain, or, if he had therebefore complied with federal statutory requirements, converted his common law copyright into a federal statutory copyright.

In order to soften the hardship of the rule that publication destroys common law rights, courts developed a distinction between a "general publication" and a "limited publication." Only a general publication divested a common law copyright. A general publication occurred "when a work was made available to members of the public at large without regard to their identity or what they intended to do with the work." Conversely, a non-divesting limited publication was one that communicated the contents of a work to a select group and for a limited purpose, and without the right of diffusion, reproduction, distribution or sale. The issue before us is whether Dr. King's delivery of the Speech was a general publication.

Numerous cases stand for the proposition that the performance of a work is not a general publication.

It appears from the case law that a general publication occurs only in two situations. First, a general publication occurs if tangible copies of the work are distributed to the general public in such a manner as allows the public to exercise dominion and control over the work. Second, a general publication may occur if the work is exhibited or displayed in such a manner as to permit unrestricted copying by the general public. However, the case law indicates that restrictions on copying may be implied, and that express limitations in that regard are deemed unnecessary.

The case law indicates that distribution to the news media, as opposed to the general public, for the purpose of enabling the reporting of a contemporary newsworthy event, is only a limited publication. For example, in *Public Affairs Assoc., Inc. v. Rickover*, 284 F.2d 262 (D.C. Cir. 1960), *vacated on other grounds*, 369 U.S. 111 (1962), the court said that general publication occurs only when there is "a studied effort not only to secure publicity for the contents of the addresses through the channels of information, but to go beyond customary sources of press or broadcasting in distributing the addresses to any interested individual." Although the *Rickover* court ultimately held that a general publication had occurred, it contrasted the "limited use of the addresses by the press for fair comment," i.e., limited publication, with "the unlimited distribution to anyone who was interested," i.e., general publication. This rule comports with common sense; it does not force an author whose message happens to be newsworthy to choose between obtaining news coverage for his work and preserving his common-law copyright. As the dissenting judge in the *Rickover* case remarked (which remark was entirely consistent with the majority opinion in the case), "[t]here is nothing in the law which would compel this court to deprive the creator of the right to reap financial benefits from these efforts because, at the time of their creation, they had the added virtue of being newsworthy events of immediate public concern."

With the above principles in mind, in the summary judgment posture of this case and on the current state of this record, we are unable to conclude that CBS has demonstrated beyond any genuine issue of material fact that Dr. King, simply through his oral delivery of the Speech, engaged in a general publication making the Speech "available to members of the public at large without regard to their identity or what they intended to do with the work." A performance, no matter how broad the audience, is not a publication; to hold otherwise would be to upset a long line of precedent. This conclusion is not altered by the fact that the Speech was broadcast live to a broad radio and television audience and was the subject of extensive contemporaneous news coverage. We follow the above cited case law indicating that release to the news media for contemporary coverage of a newsworthy event is only a limited publication. ...

The district court held that "the circumstances in this case take the work in question outside the parameters of the 'performance is not a publication' doctrine." These circumstances included "the overwhelmingly public nature of the speech and the fervent intentions of the March organizers to draw press attention." Certainly, the Speech was one of a kind—a unique event in history. However, the features that make the Speech unique—e.g., the huge audience and the Speech's significance in terms of newsworthiness and history—are features that, according to the case law, are not significant in the general versus limited publication analysis. With respect to the huge audience, the case law indicates that the general publication issue depends, not on the number of people involved, but rather on the fact that the work is made available to the public without regard to who they are or what they propose to do with it. ...

Because there exist genuine issues of material fact as to whether a general publication occurred, we must reverse the district court's grant of summary judgment for CBS. It would be inappropriate for us to address CBS's other arguments, e.g., fair use and the First Amendment, because the district court did not address them, and because the relevant facts may not yet be fully developed. ...

Notes and Questions

1. As the opinion above demonstrates, "publication" is very much a term of art, with a meaning quite distinct from the common, lay under-

standing. Even though the speech had been heard by potentially millions of people and quoted in many news reports, the court found that the broadcast of the speech did not amount to a general publication.

In reaching its result, the court relied upon the well-established rule that a mere performance does not, without more, amount to a publication. Does this rule make sense? For example, Dr. King's speech could be broadcast every day for an entire year and yet remain unpublished.

As a doctrinal matter, the rule against publication via performance was based on the idea that it would be difficult to place a notice on the performance of a work. Thus, if performance constituted publication, it would lead inevitably to the work being cast into the public domain. Do you find this rationale persuasive?

2.   The opinion also indicates that distribution of a limited number of copies of the work might, under some circumstances, not amount to a general publication. More specifically, if copies were distributed in a limited fashion for a specific purpose, and not generally to the public, such a "limited publication" might not trigger the notice requirement. Courts have, in some cases, found implied limitations from the circumstances in order to avoid forfeiture. *See, e.g., Academy of Motion Pictures Arts & Sciences v. Creative House Promotions*, 944 F.2d 1446 (9th Cir. 1991) (Oscar statuettes not published because distribution to award winners was for a limited purpose). In *King*, the court expressly did not address whether the distribution of certain copies of the speech amounted to a general publication because there were genuine issues of disputed fact surrounding those allegations.

3.   Some courts interpreting the 1909 Act made a distinction between "divestive" and "investive" publication. *See, e.g., American Visuals Corp. v. Holland*, 239 F.2d 740 (2d Cir. 1956). Divestive publication was publication sufficient to divest the copyright owner of state common law copyright protection. Investive publication was publication with notice, sufficient to invest the copyright owner with federal copyright protection. In order to avoid the harsh effects of inadvertent forfeiture, some courts required more widespread distribution of copies before finding a divestive publication. The 1976 Act's elimination of the publication requirement was, in part, motivated by a desire to move away from these technical distinctions.

4.   As noted above, the 1976 Act for the first time extended copyright protection to unpublished works, which had previously been protected only under state common law copyright. Why should copyright be extended to unpublished works, such as private letters, notes, etc.? When a work is published, the public derives a benefit, which might justify protection of the underlying work. But when a work is completely private, why should copyright extend to such a work absent some public benefit?

2. NOTICE

Copyright owners often place a copyright notice on copies of their works that are distributed to the public. The notice often consists of the copyright symbol © and/or the word "Copyright" along with the year of creation or publication and the name of the copyright owner. Providing such notice serves a number of purposes. It gives notice to readers that the work is subject to the protections of copyright, and thus that they must take care in what uses they make of the work. It provides the date of publication, which may be relevant for determining whether a work is still subject to copyright. It also provides a name that the reader may contact in order to secure permission or a license to use the work in a certain way.

Before adoption of the 1976 Act, courts consistently held that the publication of a work without adequate notice automatically cast the work into the public domain. Thus, the public distribution of a limited number of copies without notice often destroyed a work's copyright protection, even if the author had no intention of donating the work to the public. The harsh effects of this rule created a strong incentive for copyright owners to scrupulously abide by the notice requirements. However, those unfamiliar with the technical requirements of copyright often inadvertently failed to do so and lost their copyrights.

The 1976 Act kept notice as a condition of copyright protection, but took a number of steps to soften the consequences of publishing without notice. Such publication could still cast a work into the public domain, but only if there were "more than a relatively small number of copies" distributed. Moreover, a copyright owner could cure this defect by taking certain steps within five years of publication without notice. These steps included registering the work with the Copyright Office and taking reasonable steps, upon discovering the omission of notice, to attach notice to copies that had been already distributed. Thus, failure to attach notice to some copies was not necessarily fatal.

After the 1989 Berne Convention Implementation Act, notice is now no longer required as a condition of copyright. Thus, for any works created on or after March 1, 1989, publication without notice has no impact on the copyright status of the work. At the same time, publication with notice comes with a number of significant benefits. Most notably, notice prevents potential defendants from claiming that they innocently infringed upon the copyrighted work, thus exposing them to actual and statutory damages. For this reason, many copyright owners still put copyright notices on their copyrighted works.

As mentioned above, and as illustrated by the *King* case, notice remains important for works created under the prior regimes, as the changes in the law were not retroactive. Works published or created under those prior regimes and distributed without notice may well have been cast into the public domain, and the subsequent changes in the law had no effect on such works. Thus any case involving a work created before March 1, 1989 raises the possibility that the work might have been cast into the public domain as a result of failure to place notice.[34]

The gradual elimination of notice as a requirement of copyright protection was driven primarily by two factors. First, many perceived that the forfeiture rules under the 1909 Act were overly harsh. Second, the elimination of formalities was required if the U.S. was to join the Berne Convention. Thus, in the end, the decision to eliminate formalities such as notice was driven largely by a perception that the benefits of joining Berne outweighed any costs.

Notes and Questions

1. Although eliminating formalities may have been required as a political matter, we can still ask what policy purpose formalities once served and what impact their elimination has had on copyright law in the U.S. Although the notice requirement did sometimes serve as a trap to the unwary, it also played an important role in notifying others about the copyright status of a certain work. Under the old regime, if a copy of the work did not contain a copyright notice, one could generally assume that the work was not copyrighted. Under the new regime, by contrast, all works are presumptively protected by copyright, whether or not notice is attached.

The old notice requirement also had the important practical effect of casting a significant number of works into the public domain, works that were not important enough for their authors to affix copyright notice to. If the author could not be bothered to place a copyright notice on the work, this suggests that copyright must not have played a significant role in the decision to create the work in the first place. Eliminating notice thus had the practical effect of expanding the number of works protected by copyright law.

Were the effects of the old formalities system worth trying to preserve in some other form? Or was the abolition of notice as a formality an unalloyed good? More generally, what should we require of potential copyright owners before we confer copyright protection on their works?

---

[34] A notable exception to the rule that changes in formalities are not retroactive has to do with certain foreign works. In two instances, Congress revived copyrights in certain foreign works that had passed into the public domain due to failure to comply with formalities under prior law. In 1993, in implementing the U.S.'s obligations under the North American Free Trade Agreement ("NAFTA"), Congress restored copyrights in Mexican and Canadian motion pictures that had previously fallen into the public domain due to failure to comply with formalities. Then in 1996, in implementing the U.S.'s obligations under the GATT-TRIPS, Congress restored copyrights in an even broader range of foreign works that had passed into the public domain as a result of failure to comply with formalities. The constitutionality of these restorations was upheld by the U.S. Supreme Court in *Golan v. Holder*, 132 S. Ct. 873 (2011), discussed *infra* Chapter Six.

3. DEPOSIT

The Copyright Act requires a copyright owner to deposit with the Library of Congress copies of any work published in the U.S. with notice of copyright. Unpublished works or works published without notice are exempted from this requirement. In addition, the Copyright Office exempts from the deposit requirement certain categories of works for which deposit would be burdensome or inappropriate (e.g., three-dimensional sculptural works).

The deposit requirement serves two purposes. First, as described in more detail below, it is required in order to register a copyright. In this capacity, the deposit requirement serves to document the extent of the claimed copyrighted work. Second, deposit was designed to help the U.S. build up its collection via the Library of Congress, which serves as a repository of knowledge.

Failure to deposit, unlike publication without notice, does not lead to loss of the copyright. 17 U.S.C. § 407(a). Instead, the deposit requirement today is enforced via a system of fines. Thus, failure to deposit within three months of publication can lead to a fine of up to $250. In practice, such fines are generally not leveled until an author has refused to comply with a demand to deposit from the Library of Congress. A willful failure to comply with a demand for deposit can lead to substantially greater fines. Moreover, under the 1909 Act, failure to comply with such a demand could lead to forfeiture.

4. REGISTRATION

Copyright owners may register their claims of copyright with the Copyright Office, a department of the Library of Congress. To register a copyright, a copyright owner must submit an application, pay a modest fee, and send in a number of copies of the copyrighted work. The Copyright Office will then examine the application to check that the work is copyrightable subject matter and that "other legal and formal requirements ... have been met." This examination is far less rigorous than the examination for patents or trademarks. If the work passes examination, the Office will approve the registration.

Registration is not, and has never been, required as a condition of copyright. Under the 1909 Act, works were copyrighted once published with notice, and under the 1976 Act, works are copyrighted once fixed. In neither case is registration required.

However, registration of a copyright confers substantial benefits, so many copyright owners register their copyrighted works. First, if a work is registered within five years of initial publication, this constitutes *prima facie* evidence of copyright ownership and validity. 17 U.S.C. § 410(c).

Thus, in any subsequent litigation involving the work, the burden of disputing copyrightability or ownership will rest on the defendant. Second, registration enables copyright owners to receive statutory damages and attorneys fees for infringements occurring after registration. 17 U.S.C. § 412. Because, as we will see, actual damages are sometimes difficult to prove, the entitlement to statutory damages and attorneys fees is a significant benefit. Third, registration is a jurisdictional requirement before a copyright owner can file suit to enforce the copyright in federal court. 17 U.S.C. § 411. Thus, for example, if an unregistered work is infringed upon, the copyright owner would first have to register the work before filing suit. Note that, as part of the U.S.'s accession to the Berne Convention, Congress in 1989 exempted certain foreign works from this jurisdictional requirement.

The ostensible purpose of copyright registration is similar to the purpose behind the registration of other property claims, such as real estate. Registration allows the Copyright Office to maintain a central repository of copyright claims. Third parties may then search the registry to find out whether a work is copyrighted, when the term is expected to expire, who owns the copyright, etc. This helps provide notice regarding copyrights and facilitate market transactions such as licensing.

Note, however, that the registration requirement serves these purposes imperfectly. Most seriously, the optional nature of registration means that the registry is not comprehensive. Thus, a particular work's absence from the registry does not mean that there is no copyright claim. Moreover, because transfers of copyrights often go unrecorded, the registry may not accurately identify the current owner of a work.

Because of concerns that this uncertainty may hinder attempts to build upon or license existing copyrighted works, the Copyright Office has recently considered the issue of so-called "orphan works," copyrighted works whose owners cannot be easily identified due to the passage of time or multiple transfers. More specifically, the Copyright Office has considered proposals for providing a kind of limited safe harbor for uses of works whose owners are difficult to identify after a reasonable search. The issue of orphan works will be discussed in more detail in Chapter Six.

SECTION B. DURATION AND RENEWAL

Copyrights last for a limited time, although that time period is currently quite long. For works created today by an individual author, copyright will last the lifetime of the author plus 70 years.[35] For works made for hire, anonymous works, and pseudonymous works, the copyright will last for 95 years from publication or 120 years from creation, which ever

---

[35] 17 U.S.C. § 302(a). In General.— Copyright in a work created on or after January 1, 1978, subsists from its creation and, except as provided by the following subsections, endures for a term consisting of the life of the author and 70 years after the author's death.

expires first. Once the copyright has expired, the work passes into the public domain and is free for others to copy, distribute, or build upon as they wish. So, for example, the works of Shakespeare, music composed by many great classical composers, and countless other works created long ago are now free for others to copy, use, and adapt.

In this section, we will first explore the policy issues raised by copyright duration. Specifically, why is copyright limited in time, and how long should copyrights ideally last? We will then cover the basics of duration, specifically how to determine whether a copyright has expired. As part of this consideration, we will look at the process of copyright renewal, which was a feature of the 1909 Act and is still relevant today for some works published under that Act. In particular, we will ask why a renewal term was such an important feature of all of the copyright acts prior to the 1976 Act, and why the 1976 Act eventually eliminated the renewal requirement.

1. DURATION POLICY

Why is copyright limited in time? In other words, why shouldn't copyrights last forever? The descriptive answer to this is that the U.S. Constitution mandates that copyrights expire. The copyright clause expressly gives Congress the power to protect copyrights for "limited times." Thus, any attempt to confer unlimited copyright terms would exceed the authority granted to Congress under the Constitution.

But this answer merely pushes the question back one step: why does the Constitution limit copyright terms? One possible explanation reflects the basic policy balance we have seen in other areas of copyright law. On the one hand, we want sufficient protection to induce authors to engage in creative activity and to reward them for their labor. On the other hand, we want widespread public access to works once they have been created, and we want others to be able to build upon preexisting copyrighted works. There is also a sense that, once an author has been sufficiently rewarded for his or her efforts, the work should pass into the public domain and take its place in the cultural repository from which all authors (like the copyright owner) draw for inspiration.

Limited copyright terms offer one method for effectuating this balance. Thus, if a 50-year term were sufficient to induce an author to create a work and to reward the author for his or her labor, any protection beyond that term would generally hinder access, dissemination, and future creativity without any corresponding benefit.

If we accept that the copyright term should be limited, the next question is, how long should copyrights last? The original copyright act of 1790 established a very short term of 14 years with an additional renewal term of 14 years, for a total of 28 years. Since that time, Congress has consistently expanded the copyright term. In 1831, the renewal term was extended to 28 years, leaving a total potential term of 42 years. In 1909, both the initial and renewal terms were set at 28 years, leaving a total potential term of 56 years. In 1976, Congress changed the term to the life of the author plus 50 years. And most recently, in 1998 Congress added another 20 years, making the maximum term now life of the author plus 70 years.

The expansion of the copyright term has thus been consistent and rather dramatic. But has it been justified? And who should ultimately determine how long the copyright term should be? The following U.S. Supreme Court case addresses these issues in the context of the most recent copyright term extension.

Eldred v. Ashcroft
537 U.S. 186 (2003)

JUSTICE GINSBURG delivered the opinion of the Court.

This case concerns the authority the Constitution assigns to Congress to prescribe the duration of copyrights. The Copyright and Patent Clause of the Constitution provides as to copyrights: "Congress shall have Power ... [t]o promote the Progress of Science ... by securing [to Authors] for limited Times ... the exclusive Right to their ... Writings." In 1998 ... Congress enlarged the duration of copyrights by 20 years. ...

Petitioners are individuals and businesses whose products or services build on copyrighted works that have gone into the public domain. They seek a determination that the CTEA fails constitutional review under both the Copyright Clause's "limited Times" prescription and the First Amendment's free speech guarantee. ...

I

A

We evaluate petitioners' challenge to the constitutionality of the CTEA against the backdrop of Congress' previous exercises of its authority under the Copyright Clause. The Nation's first copyright statute, enacted in 1790, provided a federal copyright term of 14 years from the date of publication, renewable for an additional 14 years if the author survived the first term. The 1790 Act's renewable 14-year term applied to existing works (i.e., works already published and works created but not yet published) and future works alike. Congress expanded the federal copyright term to 42 years in 1831 (28 years from publication, renewable for an additional 14 years), and to 56 years in 1909 (28 years from publication, renewable for an additional 28 years). Both times, Congress applied the new copyright term to existing and future works; to qualify for the 1831 extension, an existing work had to be in its initial copyright term at the time the Act became effective.

In 1976, Congress altered the method for computing federal copyright terms. For works created by identified natural persons, the 1976

Act provided that federal copyright protection would run from the work's creation, not—as in the 1790, 1831, and 1909 Acts—its publication; protection would last until 50 years after the author's death. ... For anonymous works, pseudonymous works, and works made for hire, the 1976 Act provided a term of 75 years from publication or 100 years from creation, whichever expired first. ...

The measure at issue here, the CTEA, installed the fourth major duration extension of federal copyrights. Retaining the general structure of the 1976 Act, the CTEA enlarges the terms of all existing and future copyrights by 20 years. For works created by identified natural persons, the term now lasts from creation until 70 years after the author's death. This standard harmonizes the baseline United States copyright term with the term adopted by the European Union in 1993. For anonymous works, pseudonymous works, and works made for hire, the term is 95 years from publication or 120 years from creation, whichever expires first.

Paralleling the 1976 Act, the CTEA applies these new terms to all works not published by January 1, 1978. For works published before 1978 with existing copyrights as of the CTEA's effective date, the CTEA extends the term to 95 years from publication. Thus, in common with the 1831, 1909, and 1976 Acts, the CTEA's new terms apply to both future and existing copyrights. ...

II

A

... We address first the determination of the courts below that Congress has authority under the Copyright Clause to extend the terms of existing copyrights. Text, history, and precedent, we conclude, confirm that the Copyright Clause empowers Congress to prescribe "limited Times" for copyright protection and to secure the same level and duration of protection for all copyright holders, present and future.

The CTEA's baseline term of life plus 70 years, petitioners concede, qualifies as a "limited Tim[e]" as applied to future copyrights. Petitioners contend, however, that existing copyrights extended to endure for that same term are not "limited." Petitioners' argument essentially reads into the text of the Copyright Clause the command that a time prescription, once set, becomes forever "fixed" or "inalterable." The word "limited," however, does not convey a meaning so constricted. At the time of the Framing, that word meant what it means today: "confine[d] within certain bounds," "restrain[ed]," or "circumscribe[d]." S. Johnson, A Dictionary of the English Language (7th ed. 1785). Thus understood, a timespan appropriately "limited" as applied to future copyrights does not automatically cease to be "limited" when applied to existing copyrights. And as we observe, *infra*, there is no cause to suspect that a purpose to evade the "limited Times" prescription prompted Congress to adopt the CTEA.

To comprehend the scope of Congress' power under the Copyright Clause, "a page of history is worth a volume of logic." *New York Trust Co. v. Eisner*, 256 U.S. 345, 349 (1921) (Holmes, J.). History reveals an unbroken congressional practice of granting to authors of works with existing copyrights the benefit of term extensions so that all under copyright protection will be governed evenhandedly under the same regime. As earlier recounted, the First Congress accorded the protections of the Nation's first federal copyright statute to existing and future works alike. Since then, Congress has regularly applied duration extensions to both existing and future copyrights. ...

Congress' consistent historical practice of applying newly enacted copyright terms to future and existing copyrights reflects a judgment stated concisely by Representative Huntington at the time of the 1831 Act: "[J]ustice, policy, and equity alike forb[id]" that an "author who had sold his [work] a week ago, be placed in a worse situation than the author who should sell his work the day after the passing of [the] act." The CTEA follows this historical practice by keeping the duration provisions of the 1976 Act largely in place and simply adding 20 years to each of them. Guided by text, history, and precedent, we cannot agree with petitioners' submission that extending the duration of existing copyrights is categorically beyond Congress' authority under the Copyright Clause.

Satisfied that the CTEA complies with the "limited Times" prescription, we turn now to whether it is a rational exercise of the legislative authority conferred by the Copyright Clause. On that point, we defer substantially to Congress.

The CTEA reflects judgments of a kind Congress typically makes, judgments we cannot dismiss as outside the Legislature's domain. As respondent describes, a key factor in the CTEA's passage was a 1993 European Union (EU) directive instructing EU members to establish a copyright term of life plus 70 years. Consistent with the Berne Convention, the EU directed its members to deny this longer term to the works of any non-EU country whose laws did not secure the same extended term. By extending the baseline United States copyright term to life plus 70 years, Congress sought to ensure that American authors would receive the same copyright protection in Europe as their European counterparts. The CTEA may also provide greater incentive for American and other authors to create and disseminate their work in the United States.

In addition to international concerns, Congress passed the CTEA in light of demographic, economic, and technological changes, and rationally credited projections that longer terms would encourage copyright holders to invest in the restoration and public distribution of their works.

In sum, we find that the CTEA is a rational enactment; we are not at liberty to second-guess congressional determinations and policy judgments of this order, however debatable or arguably unwise they may be. Accordingly, we cannot conclude that the CTEA—which continues the unbroken congressional practice of treating future and existing copyrights in parity for term extension purposes—is an impermissible exercise of Congress' power under the Copyright Clause.

B

Petitioners' Copyright Clause arguments rely on several novel readings of the Clause. We next address these arguments and explain why we find them unpersuasive. ...

2

[P]etitioners contend that the CTEA's extension of existing copyrights does not "promote the Progress of Science" as contemplated by the preambular language of the Copyright Clause. To sustain this objection, petitioners do not argue that the Clause's preamble is an independently enforceable limit on Congress' power. Rather, they maintain that the preambular language identifies the sole end to which Congress may legislate; accordingly, they conclude, the meaning of "limited Times" must be "determined in light of that specified end." The CTEA's extension of existing copyrights categorically fails to "promote the Progress of Science," petitioners argue, because it does not stimulate the creation of new works but merely adds value to works already created.

As petitioners point out, we have described the Copyright Clause as "both a grant of power and a limitation," *Graham v. John Deere Co. of Kansas City*, 383 U.S. 1, 5 (1966), and have said that "[t]he primary objective of copyright" is "[t]o promote the Progress of Science," *Feist*, 499 U.S., at 349. The "constitutional command," we have recognized, is that Congress, to the extent it enacts copyright laws at all, create a "system" that "promote[s] the Progress of Science." *Graham*, 393 U.S., at 6.

We have also stressed, however, that it is generally for Congress, not the courts, to decide how best to pursue the Copyright Clause's objectives. The justifications we earlier set out for Congress' enactment of the CTEA provide a rational basis for the conclusion that the CTEA "promote[s] the Progress of Science."

On the issue of copyright duration, Congress, from the start, has routinely applied new definitions or adjustments of the copyright term to both future works and existing works not yet in the public domain. Such consistent congressional practice is entitled to "very great weight, and when it is remembered that the rights thus established have not been disputed during a period of [over two] centur[ies], it is almost conclusive." *Burrow-Giles Lithographic Co. v. Sarony*, 111 U.S., at 57. Indeed, "[t]his Court has repeatedly laid down the principle that a contemporaneous legislative exposition of the Constitution when the founders of our Government and framers of our Constitution were actively participating in public affairs, acquiesced in for a long term of years, fixes the construction to be given [the Constitution's] provisions." *Myers v. United States*, 272 U.S. 52, 175 (1926). Congress' unbroken practice since the founding generation thus overwhelms petitioners' argument that the

CTEA's extension of existing copyrights fails per se to "promote the Progress of Science." ...

III

[See *infra*, chapter 6 for the portion of the opinion addressing the First Amendment challenge to the CTEA].

[The dissenting opinion of Justice Stevens is omitted.]

JUSTICE BREYER, dissenting.

The Constitution's Copyright Clause grants Congress the power to "*promote* the *Progress* of Science ... by securing for *limited* Times to *Authors* ... the exclusive Right to their respective Writings." (emphasis added). The statute before us, the 1998 Sonny Bono Copyright Term Extension Act, extends the term of most existing copyrights to 95 years and that of many new copyrights to 70 years after the author's death. The economic effect of this 20-year extension—the longest blanket extension since the Nation's founding—is to make the copyright term not limited, but virtually perpetual. Its primary legal effect is to grant the extended term not to authors, but to their heirs, estates, or corporate successors. And most importantly, its practical effect is not to promote, but to inhibit, the progress of "Science"—by which word the Framers meant learning or knowledge.

The majority believes these conclusions rest upon practical judgments that at most suggest the statute is unwise, not that it is unconstitutional. Legal distinctions, however, are often matters of degree. And in this case the failings of degree are so serious that they amount to failings of constitutional kind. Although the Copyright Clause grants broad legislative power to Congress, that grant has limits. And in my view this statute falls outside them.

I

The "monopoly privileges" that the Copyright Clause confers "are neither unlimited nor primarily designed to provide a special private benefit." This Court has made clear that the Clause's limitations are judicially enforceable. And, in assessing this statute for that purpose, I would take into account the fact that the Constitution is a single document, that it contains both a Copyright Clause and a First Amendment, and that the two are related. ...

Thus, I would find that the statute lacks the constitutionally necessary rational support (1) if the significant benefits that it bestows are private, not public; (2) if it threatens seriously to undermine the expressive values that the Copyright Clause embodies; and (3) if it cannot find justification in any significant Clause-related objective. ...

II

B

... This statute, like virtually every copyright statute, imposes upon the public certain expression-related costs in the form of (1) royalties that may be higher than necessary to evoke creation of the relevant work, and (2) a requirement that one seeking to reproduce a copyrighted work must obtain the copyright holder's permission. The first of these costs translates into higher prices that will potentially restrict a work's dissemination. The second means search costs that themselves may prevent reproduction even where the author has no objection. Although these costs are, in a sense, inevitable concomitants of copyright protection, there are special reasons for thinking them especially serious here.

First, the present statute primarily benefits the holders of existing copyrights, i.e., copyrights on works already created. And a Congressional Research Service (CRS) study prepared for Congress indicates that the added royalty-related sum that the law will transfer to existing copyright holders is large. In conjunction with official figures on copyright renewals, the CRS Report indicates that only about 2% of copyrights between 55 and 75 years old retain commercial value—i.e., still generate royalties after that time. But books, songs, and movies of that vintage still earn about $400 million per year in royalties. Hence, (despite declining consumer interest in any given work over time) one might conservatively estimate that 20 extra years of copyright protection will mean the transfer of several billion extra royalty dollars to holders of existing copyrights—copyrights that, together, already will have earned many billions of dollars in royalty "reward."

The extra royalty payments will not come from thin air. Rather, they ultimately come from those who wish to read or see or hear those classic books or films or recordings that have survived. Even the $500,000 that United Airlines has had to pay for the right to play George Gershwin's 1924 classic *Rhapsody in Blue* represents a cost of doing business, potentially reflected in the ticket prices of those who fly. Further, the likely amounts of extra royalty payments are large enough to suggest that unnecessarily high prices will unnecessarily restrict distribution of classic works (or lead to disobedience of the law)—not just in theory but in practice.

A second, equally important, cause for concern arises out of the fact that copyright extension imposes a "permissions" requirement—not only upon potential users of "classic" works that still retain commercial value, but also upon potential users of any other work still in copyright. Again using CRS estimates, one can estimate that, by 2018, the number of such works 75 years of age or older will be about 350,000. Because the Copyright Act of 1976 abolished the requirement that an owner must renew a copyright, such still-in-copyright works (of little or no commercial value) will eventually number in the millions.

The potential users of such works include not only movie buffs and aging jazz fans, but also historians, scholars, teachers, writers, artists, database operators, and researchers of all kinds—those who want to make the past accessible for their own use or for that of others. The permissions requirement can inhibit their ability to accomplish that task. Indeed, in an age where computer-accessible databases promise to facilitate research and learning, the permissions requirement can stand as a significant obstacle to realization of that technological hope.

The reason is that the permissions requirement can inhibit or prevent the use of old works (particularly those without commercial value): (1) because it may prove expensive to track down or to contract with the copyright holder, (2) because the holder may prove impossible to find, or (3) because the holder when found may deny permission either outright or through misinformed efforts to bargain. The CRS, for example, has found that the cost of seeking permission "can be prohibitive." And *amici*, along with petitioners, provide examples of the kinds of significant harm at issue. ...

As I have said, to some extent costs of this kind accompany any copyright law, regardless of the length of the copyright term. But to extend that term, preventing works from the 1920's and 1930's from falling into the public domain, will dramatically increase the size of the costs just as—perversely—the likely benefits from protection diminish. The older the work, the less likely it retains commercial value, and the harder it will likely prove to find the current copyright holder. The older the work, the more likely it will prove useful to the historian, artist, or teacher. The older the work, the less likely it is that a sense of authors' rights can justify a copyright holder's decision not to permit reproduction, for the more likely it is that the copyright holder making the decision is not the work's creator, but, say, a corporation or a great-grandchild whom the work's creator never knew. Similarly, the costs of obtaining permission, now perhaps ranging in the millions of dollars, will multiply as the number of holders of affected copyrights increases from several hundred thousand to several million. The costs to the users of nonprofit databases, now numbering in the low millions, will multiply as the use of those computer-assisted databases becomes more prevalent. And the qualitative costs to education, learning, and research will multiply as our children become ever more dependent for the content of their knowledge upon computer-accessible databases—thereby condemning that which is not so accessible, say, the cultural content of early 20th-century history, to a kind of intellectual purgatory from which it will not easily emerge. ...

C

What copyright-related benefits might justify the statute's extension of copyright protection? First, no one could reasonably conclude that copyright's traditional economic rationale applies here. The extension will not act as an economic spur encouraging authors to create new works. No potential author can reasonably believe that he has more than a tiny chance of writing a classic that will survive commercially long enough for the copyright extension to matter. After all, if, after 55 to 75 years, only 2% of all copyrights retain commercial value, the percentage surviving after 75 years or more (a typical pre-extension copyright term) must be far smaller. And any remaining monetary incentive is diminished dramatically by the fact that the relevant royalties will not arrive until 75 years or more into the future, when, not the author, but distant heirs, or shareholders in a successor corporation, will receive them. Using assumptions about the time value of money provided us by a group of economists (including five Nobel prize winners), it seems fair to say that, for example, a 1% likelihood of earning $100 annually for 20 years, starting 75 years into the future, is worth less than seven cents today.

What potential Shakespeare, Wharton, or Hemingway would be moved by such a sum? What monetarily motivated Melville would not realize that he could do better for his grandchildren by putting a few dollars into an interest-bearing bank account? ...

[T]he incentive-related numbers are far too small for Congress to have concluded rationally, even with respect to new works, that the extension's economic-incentive effect could justify the serious expression-related harms earlier described. And, of course, in respect to works already created—the source of many of the harms previously described — *the statute creates no economic incentive at all.*

Second, the Court relies heavily for justification upon international uniformity of terms. Although it can be helpful to look to international norms and legal experience in understanding American law, in this case the justification based upon foreign rules is surprisingly weak. Those who claim that significant copyright-related benefits flow from greater international uniformity of terms point to the fact that the nations of the European Union have adopted a system of copyright terms uniform among themselves. And the extension before this Court implements a term of life plus 70 years that appears to conform with the European standard. But how does "uniformity" help to justify this statute?

Despite appearances, the statute does not create a uniform American-European term with respect to the lion's share of the economically significant works that it affects—all works made "for hire" and all existing works created prior to 1978. With respect to those works the American statute produces an extended term of 95 years while comparable European rights in "for hire" works last for periods that vary from 50 years to 70 years to life plus 70 years. Neither does the statute create uniformity with respect to anonymous or pseudonymous works. ...

Third, several publishers and filmmakers argue that the statute provides incentives to those who act as publishers to republish and to redistribute older copyrighted works. This claim cannot justify this statute, however, because the rationale is inconsistent with the basic purpose of the Copyright Clause—as understood by the Framers and by this Court. The Clause assumes an initial grant of monopoly, designed primarily to encourage creation, followed by termination of the monopoly grant in order to promote dissemination of already-created works. It assumes that it is the *disappearance* of the monopoly grant, not its *perpetuation*, that will, on balance, promote the dissemination of works already in existence. This view of the Clause does not deny the empirical possibility that grant of a copyright monopoly to the heirs or successors of a long-dead author could on occasion help publishers resurrect the work, say, of a long-lost Shakespeare. But it does deny Congress the Copyright Clause power to base its actions primarily upon that empirical possibility—lest copyright grants become perpetual, lest on balance they restrict dissemination, lest too often they seek to bestow benefits that are solely retroactive. ...

Fourth, the statute's legislative history suggests another possible justification. That history refers frequently to the financial assistance the statute will bring the entertainment industry, particularly through the promotion of exports. I recognize that Congress has sometimes found that suppression of competition will help Americans sell abroad—though it has simultaneously taken care to protect American buyers from higher domestic prices. In doing so, however, Congress has exercised its commerce, not its copyright, power. I can find nothing in the Copyright Clause that would authorize Congress to enhance the copyright grant's monopoly power, likely leading to higher prices both at home and abroad, solely in order to produce higher foreign earnings. That objective is not a copyright objective. Nor, standing alone, is it related to any other objective more closely tied to the Clause itself. Neither can higher corporate profits alone justify the grant's enhancement. The Clause seeks public, not private, benefits.

Finally, the Court mentions as possible justifications "demographic, economic, and technological changes"—by which the Court apparently means the facts that today people communicate with the help of modern technology, live longer, and have children at a later age. The first fact seems to argue not for, but instead against, extension. The second fact seems already corrected for by the 1976 Act's life-plus-50 term, which automatically grows with lifespans. And the third fact—that adults are having children later in life—is a makeweight at best, providing no explanation of why the 1976 Act's term of 50 years after an author's death—a longer term than was available to authors themselves for most of our Nation's history—is an insufficient potential bequest. The weakness of these final rationales simply underscores the conclusion that emerges from consideration of earlier attempts at justification: There is no legitimate, serious copyright-related justification for this statute. ...

Notes and Questions

1. Do you think the most recent extension of the copyright term was warranted as a matter of copyright policy? Were you persuaded by the arguments in favor of copyright term extension, as summarized in the majority, or the arguments against, as summarized in the dissent? Do you make a distinction between prospective and retroactive extension?

2. What role should the courts play in determining the optimal duration of copyright? The Constitution clearly gives Congress the responsibility for setting the copyright term. But at what point, if any, does Congress exceed its powers such that the courts could and should step in? Put another way, how much deference should the courts give to Congress's determinations? For example, what if Congress made the copyright term 1,000 years? Would this exceed the "limited times" injunction? What about the clause "to promote progress of science and the useful arts"?

3. The best descriptive explanation for the dramatic copyright term extension can be found in the political economy of copyright legislation. Copyright owners represent a small, focused, and highly motivated class that has the ability and resources to lobby Congress for expansion of the copyright term, as they will benefit most directly from such an expansion. Indeed, the CEO of Disney, Michael Eisner, personally lobbied Congress for the extension, motivated by the fact that Mickey Mouse and other Disney copyrights were scheduled to expire absent extension. At the same time, the public at large and other future authors, who would be hurt from such an expansion, are too diffuse and ill-organized to mount much resistance. Thus, public choice theory would predict exactly the kind of systematic expansion of the copyright term. Should judicial interpretation of the Copyright Clause take account of the peculiar structure of copyright's political economy, particularly if that structure gives disproportionate influence over copyright legislation?

4. Why is the copyright term the same for all kinds of different works? For example, a classic novel like *Gone With the Wind*, which still has significant sales nearly 100 years later, is given the same long term as a piece of computer software, whose commercial shelf-life will probably not exceed 10 years. What justifies protecting these very different kinds of works with the same term? Would the additional costs of administering a more finely-tailored copyright term be worth the compensating benefits?

2. DURATION BASICS

How do you tell if a work is still copyrighted? And how do you determine when a copyright will expire? Unfortunately, there is no simple way to answer these questions. Complications arise because multiple versions of the Copyright Act often affect the duration of a work's copyright. For example, a copyright gained under the 1909 Act could easily have lasted until the 1976 Act took effect and extended copyright duration. The copyright might then have survived until 1998, when Congress extended copyrights yet again. An attorney calculating such a copyright's duration would therefore have to understand 3 different legislative schemes and analyze whether the copyright lasted long enough under each scheme to take advantage of various term extensions.

In the end, starting with the date of a work's publication or creation offers the most effective way to calculate the duration of copyright. The rules vary based on the following categories:

Works Created On Or After January 1, 1978

For works created on or after January 1, 1978 (the effective date of the 1976 Act), the duration rules are straightforward. For works created by individual authors, the term is the life of the author plus 70 years. For works made for hire, anonymous works, and pseudonymous works, the term is 95 years from publication or 120 years from creation, whichever is shorter. For joint works, the term is measured by the life of the longest-surviving joint author.[36]

For all of these works, § 305 of the Copyright Act extends the term of copyright to the end of the calendar year in which the term would otherwise have expired. Thus, for example, if an author died on April 2, 2000, the copyright in all of his or her works created after January 1, 1978 would expire, not on April 2, 2070, but on December 31, 2070. This rule is designed to make it easier to track the expiration of copyrights.

Note that the rules effectively mean that any works created after January 1, 1978 are still under copyright as of today. The earliest possible date for a work created after January 1, 1978 to enter the public domain would thus be December 31, 2048. (Can you see why?)

Works Created But Unpublished Before January 1, 1978

Recall that prior to the 1976 Act, federal copyright protection generally applied only to published works; most unpublished works were subject to state common law copyright. When the 1976 Act moved the locus of copyright from publication to fixation, it eliminated the distinction between unpublished and published works and brought all of the unpublished works out of state common law copyright and into the federal copyright system.

The 1976 Act contained specific provisions to deal with the term of works that were created, but not published, before January 1, 1978. For such works, the term would generally be equal to the term for works created under the 1976 Act as summarized in the preceding section, i.e. life

---

[36] 17 U.S.C. § 302. (b) Joint Works.— In the case of a joint work prepared by two or more authors who did not work for hire, the copyright endures for a term consisting of the life of the last surviving author and 70 years after such last surviving author's death.

of the author plus 50 years for individual authors (now life of the author plus 70 years, after the most recent term extension), etc. However, Congress was concerned that a simple life plus 50 term would cast certain unpublished works into the public domain, as some of authors of unpublished works had died more than 50 years before January 1, 1978. Rather than completely divest these works of any protection, Congress provided that copyright protection for such works would last at least until December 31, 2002. Additionally, if a work created before January 1, 1978 was published after that date but before December 31, 2002, it would be protected until December 31, 2047. This encouraged the authors of unpublished works to publish, thereby making their works more broadly available to the public.

Putting these rules all together, imagine that an author wrote an unpublished letter in 1909 and then died in 1910. Imagine that this letter remained unpublished as of January 1, 1978. Prior to that date, the work would have been the subject of state copyright protection, which is generally perpetual. As of January 1, 1978, the work would have been placed under federal protection, but the term would have expired, i.e. the term would have lasted until 1960 (under the life plus 50 term as of the 1976 Act). However, the work would have remained protected until the minimum date of December 31, 2002. Imagine, however, that the letter was subsequently published in 2000. Under this scenario, the copyright would extend until December 31, 2047.

Works Published Before January 1, 1978

For works published before January 1, 1978, the analysis is a bit more complicated. Recall that such works were subject to the term set forth in the 1909 Act, which meant that the term was initially 28 years, with a renewal period of 28 years, for a potential total of 56 years. In order to obtain the benefit of the renewal term, the author or her statutorily specified successors had to apply for and register a claim for renewal during the 28th year of the initial copyright term. Failure to comply with this requirement cast the work into the public domain, and many copyright owners lost their rights in just this fashion.

On January 1, 1978, the 1976 Act extended the renewal terms of works published before January 1, 1978 from 28 years to 47 years, for a total potential term of 75 years from publication. The 1976 Act provided that works whose copyright survived to December 31, 1976 automatically received 19 additional years of protection.[37] Thus, to take an example,

---

[37] Note that the statute specifically made December 31, 1976 the effective date for works benefitting from the term extension (whereas the effective date for the rest of the 1976 Act was set at January 1, 1978). It is also worth noting that the class of works receiving this extra protection included more than works copyrighted within 56 years of December 31, 1976. The 56 year term granted by the 1909 Act implied that works gaining copyright more than 56 years before December 31, 1976 would ordinarily have fallen into the public domain before gaining the benefits of term extension. However, in Public Laws 87-668, 89-142, 90-141, 90-416, 91-147, 91-555, 92-170, 92-566, and 93-573, Congress passed a number of interim extensions to copyrights that otherwise would have expired during the drafting of the 1976 Act. Accordingly, works copyrighted as early as 1906 actually survived to take

a work originally copyrighted in 1922 would ordinarily have fallen into the public domain in 1978. However, since the copyright survived until December 31, 1976, the new expiration date became December 31, 1997. All works published prior to 1922 expired in earlier years, under a similar calculation.

In 1998, Congress passed the Sonny Bono Copyright Term Extension Act, adding yet another 20 years to the renewal term of works copyrighted before January 1, 1978, for a maximum potential term of 95 years from publication. This new term did not have the effect of resurrecting works that had already passed into the public domain. Thus works published in 1922 and earlier remained in the public domain. However, copyright for works published in 1923 would now not expire in 1998 (as would have been the case under the previous term), but instead in the year 2018. The net effect of the most recent term extension was thus to temporarily freeze the public domain at works created prior to 1923. Works will once again begin passing into the public domain on December 31, 2018, starting with works published in 1923.

A further complication involves renewal. The above analysis assumes that the work was properly renewed and therefore entitled to the maximum possible term. However, many copyrights were lost under the 1909 Act due to a failure to renew. If this happened, then the works would be in the public domain, regardless of the additional years added to the renewal term. Thus, for example, if a work was published in 1963, the initial 28-year term would have expired on December 31, 1991. If the author renewed the copyright, the term would last for an additional 67 years until December 31, 2058. However, if the copyright owner failed to renew, the work would have passed into the public domain on December 31, 1991. Thus for works published between 1923 and 1963, there is the possibility that a work is in the public domain for failure to renew.

This possibility does not exist for works published between 1964 and 1977, because in 1992, Congress passed a law making the renewal of copyrights in works published prior to January 1, 1978 automatic. Copyright owners no longer had to renew their copyrights. Instead, they were automatically entitled to the additional 67 year renewal term. The automatic renewal applied to works published from 1964 through 1977,[38] since such works were still in their initial term as of 1992, when the legislation was passed. The change had no effect on works that had already passed into the public domain for failure to renew, i.e. works published prior to 1964.

Although it is difficult to follow the above reasoning, the net effect of these rules is easy to keep in mind. For works published between 1964 and 1977, the term of copyright is an initial 28 years from publication

---

advantage of the 1976 Act's extended renewal terms. These copyrights began expiring in 1981.

[38] Note that works published in 1978 or later have no renewal issues because they are subject to a single term of copyright under the 1976 Act.

plus an automatic 67 years, for a total of 95 years from publication. For works published between 1923 and 1963, the term is an initial 28 years from publication plus a potential 67 years if the copyright was properly renewed, for a total potential term of 95 years from publication. Works published prior to 1923 are in the public domain.

The table below summarizes the rules regarding duration. Take a look at these rules and see if you can apply them to the problems following them.

	Start	**Term**	
Works created on or after Jan. 1, 1978	Fixation	Individuals	Life of author plus 70 years
		Works made for hire, anonymous works, pseudonymous works	95 years from publication or 120 years from fixation, whichever is shorter
Works created but not published before Jan. 1, 1978	Jan. 1, 1978	Life of author plus 70 years, but copyright lasts at least until December 31, 2002. If published before December 31, 2002, then until December 31, 2047.	
Works published between 1964 and 1977	Publication	28 year initial term	67 year renewal term, automatic
Works published between 1923 and 1963	Publication	28 year initial term	67 year renewal term, but only if properly renewed
Works published before 1923		No copyright protection	

Problems

1. An author writes a book on July 1, 1979 and publishes it on August 1, 1979. She dies on February 1, 1986. When will/did the copyright on the book expire?

2. An employee of Acme Corp. writes an internal memo to his files, as part of his employment at Acme Corp. on April 1, 1992. Acme later publishes the memo in a handbook on employee procedures on June 1, 2007. When will/did the copyright in the memo expire?

3. A famous individual writes a diary entry on January 1, 1912 and dies on July 1, 1918. The diary is unpublished as of January 1, 1978. When will/did the copyright in the diary entry expire? What if the individual's daughter published the diary on March 1, 2001?

4. An author publishes an article on May 1, 1945. She dies on September 1, 1970. When will/did the copyright in the article expire?

5. An author publishes an article on May 1, 1970. She dies on September 1, 2001. When will/did the copyright in the article expire?

6. An author publishes a song on October 1, 1921. He dies on November 1, 1971. When will/did the copyright in the song expire?

3. RENEWAL

Renewal of copyright was an essential feature of every copyright act prior to the 1976 Act. Under all of these previous acts, an author enjoyed an initial term of copyright protection. At the end of that initial term, the author had to take certain steps to renew the copyright and obtain an additional term of protection. If he or she failed to do so, the work fell into the public domain. So, as we have already seen, under the 1909 Act, copyright owners received an initial term of 28 years and a renewal term of an additional 28 years.

In 1976, Congress did away with the renewal term. Instead of an initial 28-year term, followed by a renewal term of 28 years, Congress set forth a single, unitary term of life of the author plus 50 years (later extended to 70 years). It did so in part because there were many examples of authors inadvertently failing to renew their copyrights and accidentally letting their valuable works pass into the public domain. In addition, Congress wanted to eliminate some of the confusing case law that had developed surrounding renewal. Thus for works created today, renewal is no longer an issue.

Renewal remains relevant today, however, because many works created under the 1909 Act are still potentially subject to copyright today. Accordingly, the copyright status today of a work published under the prior Act might well depend on whether the work was properly renewed, as we saw in the previous section. In addition, the renewal system furthered a number of policies that were retained in different form in the 1976 Act. Renewal thus presents a good introduction to the policies underlying termination of transfers, which we will cover in the following section.

A key feature of the renewal system was that the renewal term automatically reverted to the original author, even if that author had transferred rights in the copyright initially. Thus, for example, if an author published a work in 1930 and transferred the copyright to a publishing house, the author could renew the copyright in 1958 and thereby recapture the copyright for the renewal term. The author would then be free to make and sell copies himself or retransfer the copyright to another publishing house (or even the same publishing house).

The purpose of the renewal term was to benefit authors. It allowed authors to recapture copyrights in works that later became successful. The assumption was that many authors would be in a poor bargaining position when they first assigned away their rights, and if a work later became successful, many authors might not be able to share as fully in the subsequent success of their works. The renewal term thus gave authors a "second bite at the apple," a chance to recapture and profit from their successful works.

As we will soon see, however, a number of judicial opinions later undercut the efficacy of the renewal term in this capacity.

Fred Fisher Music Co. v. M. Witmark & Sons
318 U.S. 643 (1943)

MR. JUSTICE FRANKFURTER delivered the opinion of the Court,

This case presents a question never settled before, even though it concerns legislation having a history of more than two hundred years. The question itself can be stated very simply. Under § 23 of the Copyright Act of 1909, a copyright in a musical composition lasts for twenty-eight years from the date of its first publication, and the author can renew the copyright, if he is still living, for a further term of twenty-eight years by filing an application for renewal within a year before the expiration of the first twenty-eight year period. Section 42 of the Act provides that a copyright "may be assigned ... by an instrument in writing signed by the proprietor of the copyright ...." Concededly, the author can assign the original copyright and, after he has secured it, the renewal copyright as well. The question is—does the Act prevent the author from assigning his interest in the renewal copyright before he has secured it?

This litigation arises from a controversy over the renewal rights in the popular song "When Irish Eyes Are Smiling". It was written in 1912 by Ernest R. Ball, Chauncey Olcott, and George Graff, Jr., each of whom was under contract to a firm of music publishers, M. Witmark & Sons. Pursuant to the contracts Witmark on August 12, 1912, applied for and obtained the copyright in the song. On May 19, 1917, Graff and Witmark made a further agreement under which, for the sum of $1600, Graff assigned to Witmark "all rights, title and interest" in a number of songs, including "When Irish Eyes Are Smiling." The contract provided for the conveyance of "all copyrights and renewals of copyrights and the right to secure all copyrights and renewals of copyrights in the (songs), and any and all rights therein that I (Graff) or my heirs, executors, administrators or next of kin may at any time be entitled to." To that end Witmark was given an irrevocable power of attorney to execute in Graff's name all documents "necessary to secure to (Witmark) the renewals and extensions of the copyrights in said compositions and all rights therein for the terms of such renewals and extensions." In addition, Graff agreed that, "upon the expiration of the first term of any copyright," he would execute and deliver to Witmark "all papers necessary in order to secure to it the renewals and extensions of all copyrights in said compositions and all rights therein for the terms of such renewals and extensions." This agreement was duly recorded in the Copyright Office.

On August 12, 1939, the first day of the twenty-eighth year of the copyright in "When Irish Eyes Are Smiling," Witmark applied for and registered the renewal copyright in Graff's name. On the same day, exercising its power of attorney under the agreement of May 19, 1917, Witmark also assigned to itself Graff's interest in the renewal. Eleven days later Graff himself applied for and registered the renewal copyright in his own name, and on October 24, 1939, he assigned his renewal interest to another music publishing firm, Fred Fisher Music Co., Inc. Both Graff and Fisher knew of the prior registration of the renewal by Witmark and of the latter's assignment to itself. Relying upon the validity of the assignment made to it on October 24, 1939, and without obtaining permission from Witmark, Fisher published and sold copies of "When Irish Eyes Are Smiling," representing to the trade that it owned the renewal rights in the song. Witmark thereupon brought this suit to enjoin these activities. ...

Plainly, there is only one question before us—does the Copyright Act nullify an agreement by an author, made during the original copyright term, to assign his renewal? The explicit words of the statute give the author an unqualified right to renew the copyright. No limitations are placed upon the assignability of his interest in the renewal. If we look only to what the Act says, there can be no doubt as to the answer. But each of the parties finds support for its conclusion in the historical background of copyright legislation, and to that we must turn to discover whether Congress meant more than it said. ...

In December, 1905, President Theodore Roosevelt urged the Congress to undertake a revision of the copyright laws. In response to this message the Librarian of Congress, under whose authority the Copyright Office functions, invited persons interested in copyright legislation to attend a conference for the purpose of devising a satisfactory measure. Several conferences were held in 1905 and 1906, resulting in a bill which was introduced in the House and Senate by the chairman of the Committee on Patents in each body. This bill provided, in the case of books and musical compositions, for a single copyright term lasting for the life of the author and for fifty years thereafter. Joint hearings by the House and Senate Committees were held on this bill, but no action was taken by the Fifty-ninth Congress. At the next session of Congress this and other bills to revise the copyright laws were again introduced. Extensive public hearings were held. The result of this elaborate legislative consideration of the problem of copyright was a bill which became the Copyright Act of 1909. As stated in the report of the House committee, this bill "differs in many respects from any of the bills previously introduced.

Your committee believes that in all its essential features it fairly meets
and solves the difficult problems with which the committee had to deal
....” Under the bill copyright was given for twenty-eight years, with a
renewal period of the same duration. The report of the House committee
indicates the reasons for this provision. This section of the report, to
which much importance has been attached by the judges of the court below and by the parties, must be read in the light of the specific problem
with which the Congress was presented: should there be one long term,
as was provided for in the bill resulting from the conferences held by the
Librarian of Congress, or should there be two shorter terms? The House
and Senate committees chose the latter alternative. They were aware
that an assignment by the author of his “copyright” in general terms did
not include conveyance of his renewal interest. During the hearings of
the Joint Committee, Representative Currier, the chairman of the House
committee, referred to the difficulties encountered by Mark Twain:

> Mr. Clemens told me that he sold the copyright for Innocents
> Abroad for a very small sum, and he got very little out of the In-
> nocents Abroad until the twenty-eight year period expired, and
> then his contract did not cover the renewal period, and in the
> fourteen years of the renewal period he was able to get out of it
> all of the profits.

By providing for two copyright terms, each of relatively short duration, Congress enabled the author to sell his “copyright” without losing
his renewal interest. If the author’s copyright extended over a single,
longer term, his sale of the “copyright” would terminate his entire interest. That this is the basic consideration of policy underlying the renewal
provision of the Copyright Act of 1909 clearly appears from the report of
the House committee which submitted the legislation:

> Section 23 deals with the term of the copyright. Under exist-
> ing law the copyright term is twenty-eight years, with the right
> of renewal by the author, or by the author’s widow or children if
> he be dead, for a further term of fourteen years. The act of 1790
> provided for an original term of fourteen years, with the right of
> renewal for fourteen years. The act of 1831 extended the term to
> its present length. It was urged before the committee that it
> would be better to have a single term without any right of re-
> newal, and a term of life and fifty years was suggested. Your
> committee, after full consideration, decided that it was distinctly
> to the advantage of the author to preserve the renewal period. It
> not infrequently happens that the author sells his copyright out-
> right to a publisher for a comparatively small sum. If the work
> proves to be a great success and lives beyond the term of twenty-
> eight years, your committee felt that it should be the exclusive
> right of the author to take the renewal term, and the law should
> be framed as is the existing law (italics ours), so that he could
> not be deprived of that right.

The present term of twenty-eight years, with the right of renewal for fourteen years, in many cases is insufficient. The
terms, taken together, ought to be long enough to give the author
the exclusive right to his work for such a period that there would
be no probability of its being taken away from him in his old age,
when, perhaps, he needs it the most. A very small percentage of
the copyrights are ever renewed. All use of them ceases in most
cases long before the expiration of twenty-eight years. In the
comparatively few cases where the work survives the original
term the author ought to be given an adequate renewal term. In
the exceptional case of a brilliant work of literature, art, or musical composition it continues to have a value for a long period,
but this value is dependent upon the merit of the composition.
Just in proportion as the composition is meritorious and deserving will it continue to be profitable, provided the copyright is extended so long; and it is believed that in all such cases where the
merit is very high this term is certainly not too long.

Your committee do not favor and the bill does not provide for
any extension of the original term of twenty-eight years, but it
does provide for an extension of the renewal term from fourteen
years to twenty-eight years; and it makes some change in existing law as to those who may apply for the renewal. Instead of
confining the right of renewal to the author, if still living, or to
the widow or children of the author, if he be dead, we provide
that the author of such work, if still living, may apply for the renewal, or the widow, widower, or children of the author, if the
author be not living, or if such author, widow, widower, or children be not living, then the author's executors, or, in the absence
of a will, his next of kin. It was not the intention to permit the
administrator to apply for the renewal, but to permit the author
who had no wife or children to bequeath by will the right to apply for the renewal.

The report cannot be tortured, by reading it without regard to the
circumstances in which it was written, into an expression of a legislative
purpose to nullify agreements by authors to assign their renewal interests. If Congress, speaking through its responsible members, had any
intention of altering what theretofore had not been questioned, namely,
that there were no statutory restraints upon the assignment by authors
of their renewal rights, it is almost certain that such purpose would have
been manifested. The legislative materials reveal no such intention.

We agree with the court below, therefore, that neither the language
nor the history of the Copyright Act of 1909 lend support to the conclusion that the "existing law" prior to 1909, under which authors were free
to assign their renewal interests if they were so disposed, was intended
to be altered. We agree, also, that there are no compelling considerations
of policy which could justify reading into the Act a construction so at variance with its history. The policy of the copyright law, we are told, is to

protect the author—if need be, from himself—and a construction under which the author is powerless to assign his renewal interest furthers this policy. We are asked to recognize that authors are congenitally irresponsible, that frequently they are so sorely pressed for funds that they are willing to sell their work for a mere pittance, and therefore assignments made by them should not be upheld. ...

It is not for courts to judge whether the interests of authors clearly lie upon one side of this question rather than the other. If an author cannot make an effective assignment of his renewal, it may be worthless to him when he is most in need. Nobody would pay an author for something he cannot sell. We cannot draw a principle of law from the familiar stories of garret-poverty of some men of literary genius. Even if we could do so, we cannot say that such men would regard with favor a rule of law preventing them from realizing on their assets when they are most in need of funds. Nor can we be unmindful of the fact that authors have themselves devised means of safeguarding their interests. We do not have such assured knowledge about authorship, and particularly about song writing, or the psychology of gifted writers and composers, as to justify us as judges in importing into Congressional legislation a denial to authors of the freedom to dispose of their property possessed by others. While authors may have habits making for intermittent want, they may have no less a spirit of independence which would resent treatment of them as wards under guardianship of the law.

We conclude, therefore, that the Copyright Act of 1909 does not nullify agreements by authors to assign their renewal interests. ...

Affirmed.

MR. JUSTICE BLACK, MR. JUSTICE DOUGLAS, AND MR. JUSTICE MURPHY conclude that the analysis of the language and history of the copyright law in the dissenting opinion of Judge Frank in the court below, demonstrates a Congressional purpose to reserve the renewal privilege for the personal benefit of authors and their families. They believe the judgment below should be reversed.

Notes and Questions

1. Is Justice Frankfurter's reasoning consistent with the underlying purpose and legislative history behind the renewal provisions? After all, if Congress wanted to give authors a second bite at the apple, why would they permit authors to easily contract away their rights? If such contracts are enforceable, what is to prevent publishers from always insisting that authors convey their renewal rights at the same time they convey the rights to the initial term? How is this different from a single unitary term?

2.   Do you agree with the policy rationale underlying renewal? Does renewal adequately further its intended policy? In other words, would the existence of a non-assignable renewal term ultimately help or hurt authors? Justice Frankfurter writes: "If an author cannot make an effective assignment of his renewal, it may be worthless to him when he is most in need. Nobody would pay an author for something he cannot sell." Is he right?

3.   After *Fred Fisher*, publishers routinely required authors to assign away their renewal rights at the same time they assigned away their initial copyrights. This had the effect of greatly reducing the efficacy of renewal as a means of giving authors a "second bite at the apple."

At the same time, assignment of the renewal term was not a perfect solution for the publishers, because courts interpreted this to require that an author still be alive at the time of renewal. If an author died before the renewal option vested (i.e. before the last year of the initial term), the right to renew would pass by statute to the author's surviving spouse and children, if any. Moreover, the author could not assign these future, unvested rights away. Thus, publishers had to hope that the author stayed healthy until renewal.

In part because of the limitations placed by the *Fred Fisher* case, Congress in 1976 did away with renewal and instead substituted termination of transfers as the mechanism for protecting author interests. We cover termination in the following section.

4.   Say a work is transferred to another party, who then makes a derivative work based on the original. What happens to the derivative work when the original author renews the copyright in the original work? This question was addressed by the Supreme Court in *Stewart v. Abend*, 495 U.S. 207 (1990), which involved the short story "It Had to Be Murder." The director Alfred Hitchcock and actor Jimmy Stewart obtained the rights to the story and made the movie "Rear Window." The author of the story died before the renewal right vested, and the author's estate renewed the copyright. When the movie was re-released after the renewal date, the author's estate sued for copyright infringement.

The Supreme Court held that, once an author or his/her heirs renews a copyright, the owner of a derivative work based on the original copyrighted work can no longer exploit that work without permission of the copyright owner of the underlying work. Thus, the owners of the movie "Rear Window" could no longer exploit the movie without first obtaining permission from the owners of the short story. The Court's ruling thus dramatically favored the rights of the original authors, at the expense of the authors of derivative works.

Is this result fair to the owners of the derivative work? After all, the derivative work may include substantial additional original expression, which is owned by the derivative work author. If the underlying copyrighted work is so intermingled with the derivative expression, the effect of the ruling is to prevent the author of the derivative work from distributing his or her own creative expression. Moreover, the author of the derivative work may not be able to adequately protect him or herself through contracting, since the author of the original work could die before the renewal term vests. How might this have affected a movie studio's decision to acquire the rights to a pre-existing copyrighted work?

On the other hand, the owner of the derivative work could always renegotiate with the copyright owner in the renewal term. Thus, perhaps this in fact serves the policies underlying renewal by providing the original author's heirs with a strong bargaining chip to recapture some of the economic value of the derivative work.

5. Although the purpose of the renewal term was to protect authors, it also had a broader public policy effect of channeling certain works into the public domain. In some cases, failure to renew was inadvertent. In other cases, however, failure to renew indicated that an author did not believe the work was important enough to be worth the minor costs of renewal. A Copyright Office study noted that less than 15% of copyrighted works were renewed. *See* Barbara Ringer, "Study No. 31: Renewal of Copyright" (1960), *reprinted in* Library of Congress Copyright Office, *Copyright Law Revision: Studies,* prepared for the Subcomm. on Patents, Trademarks, and Copyrights of Sen. Comm. on the Judiciary, 86th Cong., 1st Sess. (Washington: U. S. Govt. Print. Off. 1961). When the 1976 Act did away with the renewal term, it removed this source of works entering the public domain. Should authors be required to take steps to renew their copyrights?

SECTION C. TERMINATION

Although the 1976 Act eliminated copyright renewal, it preserved the pro-author policies underlying renewal by allowing authors to terminate transfers of copyright interests. As we saw in the prior chapter, copyright owners may, and quite frequently do, transfer their copyright interests in many different ways, e.g. through assignment or licensing. The 1976 Act permits authors to terminate these transfers under certain circumstances, thereby recapturing the copyright interests previously granted to third parties. Termination thus serves broadly the same purpose as renewal, giving authors a chance to recapture rights in works that later become economically successful. It is important to note, however, that there are significant differences in the way termination accomplishes this result.

Perhaps most importantly, termination rights cannot be transferred. In passing the termination provisions, Congress was aware of the effect of the *Fred Fisher* case discussed in the preceding section, which effectively undercut the ability of authors to recapture their renewal rights. Congress apparently disapproved of this result, and declared that termination rights could not be alienated. Thus, section 203(a)(5) of the Copyright Act provides, "Termination of the grant may be effected notwithstanding any agreement to the contrary, including an agreement to make a will or to make any future grant." Accordingly, if an author licenses away rights in a novel that is later made into a movie, there is no way for the movie studio to prevent the author from potentially terminating the assignment.

At the same time, Congress was also aware of the effect of the *Stewart* case on derivative works owners. Congress therefore included a provision that permitted the owners of derivative works to continue to exploit those works even after the original transfer had been terminated.[39] Thus, in the example above, even after the author terminates the assignment, the movie studio may still economically exploit the movie. However, the movie studio may not exercise any rights beyond merely exploiting already-created derivative work.

Note that the termination provisions do not apply to works made for hire. This explains why those who commission works would much prefer the works to be works made for hire rather than assignments of copyrights.

The mechanics of termination are complicated, and we will only cover them briefly in the materials below. The statute draws a distinction between transfers made after January 1, 1978 and transfers made before January 1, 1978.

Transfers Made On or After January 1, 1978

For transfers made after January 1, 1978, authors have the right to terminate 35 years after those transfers were made. 17 U.S.C. § 203. The statute gives authors a 5-year window, starting in the 35th year, within which to terminate the transfer. In order to effectuate the termination, the author must serve notice to the transferee between two and 10 years of the effective date of the termination. In addition, the author must satisfy certain procedural requirements. If an author fails to terminate the transfer, then the transferee will continue to exercise the rights under the original transfer.

So, for example, say that an author of a book licenses the movie rights in the book to a movie studio on January 2, 1978. The author would have the right to terminate the license as early as January 2, 2013 (35 years from the date of transfer) and as late as January 2, 2018. Assuming that she wanted to terminate on the earliest possible date, the author would have to serve notice as early as January 2, 2003 (10 years before the effective date), but in no case later than January 2, 2011 (2 years before the effective date). As the above example shows, termination of post-January 1, 1978 transfers have just recently started to occur, beginning in 2013, and we can expect a good deal of litigation in upcom-

---

[39] For example, section 203(b)(1) provides, "(1) A derivative work prepared under authority of the grant before its termination may continue to be utilized under the terms of the grant after its termination, but this privilege does not extend to the preparation after the termination of other derivative works based upon the copyrighted work covered by the terminated grant."

ing years interpreting the key terms of § 203 for the first time. *See, e.g.,,* Larry Rohter, "A Copyright Victory 35 Years Later," N.Y. TIMES (Sep. 10, 2013) (describing the successful termination of the assignment of copyright in the song "YMCA" by Victor Willis, one of the original members of the Village People).

In order to effectuate termination, the author must comply with certain statutory formalities. Any attempt to effectuate termination or provide notice outside these statutory windows would be deemed ineffective. In addition, the notice must contain the signatures of those necessary to effectuate termination. There are particular requirements for service of the notice. In addition, notice of the intent to terminate the transfer must be recorded with the Copyright Office.

Termination can be effectuated with respect to any transfer of any interest in copyright made by the author during his or her lifetime. It thus applies equally to assignments as well as exclusive and nonexclusive licenses. It does not apply, however, to transfers made by third parties. Thus, for example, if an author assigned her right to a movie studio, the movie studio's subsequent assignment to another party would not be subject to a termination right by the movie studio. Similarly, transfers made by an author's heirs or estate are not subject to termination. This reflects the fact that the termination provisions were designed specifically to benefit the authors.

Who can effectuate the termination? Under sections 203(a)(1)-(2), if the author is alive at the time, then the author may exercise the termination right. For a joint work, a majority of the authors who exercised the transfer may do so. If an author is dead, then the termination right rests 50% with the author's spouse (if any) and 50% with the author's children (if any). If an author's child is deceased but has surviving children, those children take the child's share proportionally. If the spouse is not living, then the children get 100%; if there are no surviving children (or descendants of the children), then the spouse gets 100%. If there are neither living spouses nor children, then the right goes to the author's estate. So, for example, if an author died and had a surviving wife, one surviving child, and one deceased child who had two surviving children, the termination right would be allocated as follows: 50% to the wife, 25% to the surviving child, 12.5% to each of the surviving grandchildren.

In order to exercise the termination right, a majority of those with an interest in the termination must sign the termination. In the case of surviving grandchildren, a majority of the grandchildren would be needed to exercise the deceased child's right. Thus, in the example above, the wife and one of the surviving children could exercise the termination right. Alternatively, the wife and both of the surviving grandchildren could exercise the termination right. (But the wife and only one of the surviving grandchildren would not be sufficient, even though their total share would be more than 50%, since a majority of the grandchildren would be needed to exercise the deceased child's right). Moreover, the rights vest upon service of the termination notice. Thus, if the surviving spouse were to die after serving notice, her interest would pass to her estate.

Termination means that the transferred right reverts back to those who own the termination right, relative to their proportional ownership of the termination right. This happens whether or not a particular owner of the right signed the termination. Thus, in the example above, if the wife and a surviving child exercised the termination right, all of the owners of the termination right would share in the subsequent terminated right. In order to re-grant the right, any transfer must be signed by a majority of those who owned the termination right. This differs from the situation of joint ownership of copyright, where any of the joint owners may transfer his or her interest without approval by the other joint owner. Any re-grant can only be exercised after the effective date of the termination.

Transfers Made Before January 1, 1978

For transfers made before January 1, 1978, the rules are slightly different. 17 U.S.C. § 304(c)-(d). Recall that under the 1909 Act, authors had an initial 28-year term and a renewal 28-year term, for a total of 56 years. The 1976 Act extended the renewal term by 19 years and the 1998 extension added another 20 years. The 1976 Act and later 1998 term extension essentially allow the author (or in some cases, the author's heirs), under certain circumstances, to terminate pre-1978 transfers to recapture the benefits of these two term extensions. The result is to mitigate some of the effects of the *Fred Fisher* decision by ensuring that the benefits of term extension accrue to the authors rather than the transferees.

Thus, an author may terminate any pre-1978 transfer 56 years after the work was first published. This allows the author to receive the benefit of the term extensions under both the 1976 Act and the 1998 term extension. If the opportunity to terminate at the 56 year mark had already expired unexercised as of the effective date of the 1998 term extension, then the author may terminate the transfer 75 years after the work was first published. This enables the author at least to capture the additional 19 years from the 1998 term extension.

So for example, imagine that an author publishes a work in 1936 and transfers the copyright and renewal right. The initial and renewal terms under the 1909 Act would have ended in 1992, 56 years after publication. At that point, the author could have terminated the transfer and recaptured the remaining term (at that time, the additional 19 years added by the 1976 Act). If the author missed this window, the author could again terminate 19 years later in 2011 to capture the additional 20 years added by the 1998 term extension.

The mechanics of termination are similar (though not completely identical) to the post-1978 transfers. Termination may be effectuated within a five-year period after the relevant date. Similarly, notice must be provided between two and 10 years of the effective date of termination. Similar procedural requirements—e.g. notice, service and registration—apply. Ownership of the termination right is also the same, in that the surviving spouse takes 50% and the surviving children (or their children) take 50%, *per stirpes*.

One difference from post-1978 transfers is that the termination right for pre-1978 transfers applies not only to transfers by the original author but also transfers of the renewal term by third parties. Recall that under the 1909 Act, if an author died before the renewal right vested, the right would pass to the author's spouse and children, if any. If these parties renewed the copyright, they could then subsequently transfer the renewal term. Such transfers are also subject to the termination right. For such transfers, termination must be effectuated by unanimous consent of those surviving who exercised the transfer.

Notes and Questions

1. Although the mechanics of termination are complicated, the policy underlying termination is the same straightforward policy that underlay renewal, namely a desire to permit authors to benefit from the subsequent success of their works and to shield them from the effects of unequal bargaining power earlier in their careers. The termination provisions arguably do a better job of furthering these policies, insofar as they do not permit authors to alienate their termination rights and do not pose the risk to authors of loss of copyright.

But do the termination provisions in fact benefit authors? The termination provisions restrict the freedom of authors by disabling them from contracting away more than 35 years (for post-1978 transfers) of their copyright terms. Even if an author wanted to contract away the entire term, the Copyright Act effectively prevents him or her from doing so. One would expect this to affect how much a potential purchaser would be willing to pay for the rights. Thus, it could be argued that the termination provisions harm rather than help authors. Do you agree? Can you come up with any responses?

2. The problem of derivative works is handled very differently under termination as compared to renewal. Recall that, once a copyright was renewed, the owner of a derivative work was barred from continuing to exploit that work without permission from the copyright owner in the underlying work. When a transfer is terminated, however, the 1976 Act expressly provides that the owner of the derivative work can continue to exploit the work, but can no longer create any new works based on the original. Which rule better balances the interests of initial authors and derivative work owners?

3. A peculiar feature of both the termination and renewal provisions is the statutory definition of those who can exercise rights of termination or renewal should the author pass away. *See* 17 U.S.C. §§

203(a)(2) and 304(a). Notice that these provisions override any attempt by an author to pass her termination or renewal rights to someone other than this list of potential beneficiaries. Thus, an author could not leave her renewal rights to a non-profit foundation. Why would Congress want to restrict an author in such a way?

4. As noted above, although pre-1978 transfer terminations have been taking place for some time, post-1978 transfer terminations are just now starting to occur, as the window for such terminations first opened in 2013 (35 years after 1978). These terminations will likely generate a good deal of new caselaw. For example, sound recordings were first brought within the scope of federal copyright protection in 1972, and many popular sound recordings were made in the years after 1978. The current owners of the copyrights in these sound recordings (i.e. record labels) are beginning to receive termination notices for post-1978 transfers. This raises a number of tricky legal questions. For example, are the sound recordings "works made for hire," and therefore not subject to termination? Are the musicians and band members who performed the music for the sound recordings "employees" or "independent contractors"? These and other issues are likely to generate a good deal of litigation in coming years.

Termination rights create some peculiar challenges for those practicing copyright, challenges many will overlook because the earliest effective date for a §203 termination is 2013 (35 years after 1978). Unless attorneys carefully review how their clients have exploited their copyrights and calendar the relevant deadlines for exercising termination rights, it will be extremely easy to lose termination rights through inaction. Even if attorneys remember those dates, they must also comply with the statutory requirements for how termination rights may be exercised. Care must be taken to ensure that the right party exercises the relevant rights in the correct fashion. For example, an author's surviving spouse and children will generally have to terminate copyright conveyances even if the author left all of his copyright rights to a trust. In situations like this, termination by the trustee would be technically invalid.

Termination rights also challenge those who would like to avoid losing rights. As noted earlier, the 1976 Act gives authors and their heirs the right to terminate "notwithstanding any agreement to the contrary, including an agreement to make a will or to make any future grant."[40] Nevertheless, those who face losing rights through termination will argue that authors or their heirs have somehow managed to waive that right. Our next case introduces some of the issues in the context of section 304(c) terminations.

----

[40] 17 U.S.C. § 203(a)(5), 304(c)(5).

Classic Media v. Mewborn
532 F.3d 978 (9th Cir. 2008)

WARDLAW, Circuit Judge:

Winifred Knight Mewborn ("Mewborn"), daughter of Eric Knight, the author of the world-famous children's story and novel, *Lassie Come Home* (collectively, the "Lassie Works"), appeals the district court's grant of summary judgment in favor of Classic Media, Inc. ("Classic") and denial of Mewborn's partial summary judgment motion. Each party sought declaratory relief as to their respective copyright interests in the Lassie Works, works that were in their renewal copyright terms on January 1, 1978 when the Copyright Act of 1976 (the "Act" or the "1976 Act") took effect. This appeal requires us to determine whether the Act's termination of transfer right, 17 U.S.C. § 304(c), can be extinguished by a post-1978 re-grant of the very rights previously assigned before 1978. Because we conclude that such a result would circumvent the plain statutory language of the 1976 Act, as well as the congressional intent to give the benefit of the additional renewal term to the author and his heirs, we hold that the post-1978 assignment did not extinguish Mewborn's statutory termination rights.

I. Factual and Procedural Background

Eric Knight authored the beloved children's story, "Lassie Come Home," about a boy and his dog who, when sold to a rich duke by the boy's poverty-stricken family, makes an arduous journey to return home to her original owner. Inspired by the harsh realities of life during the Great Depression, the story of the fearless collie, Lassie, and the boy who loved her was first published in the December 17, 1938 issue of *The Saturday Evening Post,* and was registered in the U.S. Copyright Office that year. Knight later developed the story into a novel, which was published and registered in the U.S. Copyright Office in 1940. Knight granted the rights to make the popular *Lassie* television series to Classic's predecessors-in-interest, but died in 1943, before the renewal rights had vested. Under section 24 of the 1909 Copyright Act, the interest in the renewal term of the copyrights reverted to Knight's wife, Ruth, and their three daughters, Jennie Knight Moore, Betty Knight Myers and Winifred Knight Mewborn. Each heir timely filed a renewal of copyright with the U.S. Copyright Office in each of the works between 1965 and 1967. Because Classic's predecessors-in-interest had an agreement only with Knight's widow as to the television series, it became necessary to secure agreements from the three daughters for the renewal term of motion picture, television and radio rights. Thus, Lassie Television, Inc. ("LTI") approached Mewborn and her sisters, Moore and Myers, to obtain the necessary rights.

In a written agreement dated July 14, 1976, Mewborn assigned her 25 percent share of the motion picture, television and radio rights in the Lassie Works to LTI for $11,000 ("1976 Assignment"). The contract states, in relevant part:

I, Winifred Knight Mewborn, ... hereby sell, grant, and assign to [LTI] all of the following rights in and to the story entitled LASSIE COME-HOME written by Eric Knight and published in the Saturday Evening Post on December 17, 1938 and the novel or book based thereon also written by Eric Knight and published by John C. Winston Co. in 1940 ...:

All motion picture (including musical motion picture), television and radio rights in and to the said literary work[s] ... throughout the world for the full period of the renewal copyrights in the work[s] and any further renewals or extensions thereof.

It was not until March 1978 that LTI was able to obtain similar assignments from Mewborn's two sisters. On March 17, 1978 and March 22, 1978, Myers and Moore, respectively, assigned their motion picture, television and radio rights to LTI, as well as ancillary rights such as merchandising, dramatic, recording and certain publishing rights. They each received $3,000 in exchange. To conform the grant of rights among the sisters, on March 16, 1978, Mewborn signed a second agreement, furnished by LTI ("1978 Assignment"). The assignment reads:

I, Winifred Knight Mewborn, ... hereby grant, assign and set over unto [LTI] and its successors and assigns forever, all the following rights in and to the literary work entitled "LASSIE COME-HOME" ... (a) [a]ll motion picture (including musical motion picture) rights, television rights, radio rights, recording rights, and dramatic rights on the legitimate stage ... and all merchandising, commercial tie-up and related rights, and certain publication rights....

The 1978 Assignment contained the identical transfer of motion picture, television and radio rights as the 1976 Assignment, but added language assigning ancillary rights to LTI, including recording and dramatic rights, all merchandising, commercial tie-up and related rights and certain publication rights, as well as language stating:

[a]ll of the foregoing rights are granted to [LTI] throughout the world in perpetuity, *to the extent such rights are owned by me,* as hereinafter provided .... The rights granted herein to [LTI] are *in addition to* the rights granted by me to [LTI] under and pursuant to an assignment dated July 14, 1976, recorded with the United States Copyright Office on July 12, 1976 in Volume 1589 at Pages 258-259....

(emphasis added). In exchange, LTI also paid Mewborn $3,000. Apart from references to the 1976 Assignment, which only Mewborn had entered into, the three sisters' 1978 assignments were identical.

On April 12, 1996, Mewborn served a notice of termination ("Termination Notice") within the five-year period required by § 304(c) on Palladium Limited Partnership ("Palladium"), LTI's then successor-in-interest in the Lassie Works. Mewborn sought to recapture her motion picture, television and radio rights by terminating the 1976 Assignment effective May 1, 1998. This began the Lassie Works' difficult journey home, as counsel on behalf of the parties—but predominantly Classic— spewed acrimonious charges, threats and demands over the rights to the works in a series of correspondence of not much relevance, but nonetheless included in the record before us. ...

As a result, on May 27, 2005, Classic filed a declaratory relief action in the Central District of California against Mewborn seeking a declaration that Mewborn has no interest in the Lassie film or in any of the rights she previously assigned to LTI in the 1978 Assignment, and that Mewborn's Termination Notice was ineffective. On June 29, 2005, Mewborn counterclaimed seeking a declaration that, in fact, Mewborn had recaptured some of her previously assigned rights, and requesting an accounting of Classic's profits as of May 1, 1998, the effective termination date under the Termination Notice.

The parties filed cross-motions for summary judgment. On February 9, 2006, the district court granted Classic's motion for summary judgment and denied Mewborn's motion as moot. Interpreting the § 304(c) termination right to be inalienable but subject to waiver or relinquishment, the district court found that the parties intended that the 1978 Assignment "give away" all of Mewborn's additional rights not transferred in 1976, which included her newly acquired § 304(c) right to terminate the 1976 Assignment. Accordingly, Mewborn had relinquished her termination right, and the 1996 Notice of Termination was ineffective because Mewborn no longer had any interest in the rights transferred in 1976 and 1978. The district court also found that the 1978 Assignment did not substitute for or revoke the 1976 Assignment and that the 1976 Assignment remained intact. ...

III. Discussion

Despite (1) the express statutory language that termination of a pre-1978 transfer "may be effected notwithstanding any agreement to the contrary," 17 U.S.C. § 304(c)(5); (2) Congress's clear intent to benefit authors and their heirs with additional years of copyright protection in the 1976 Act, as recognized by the Supreme Court; and (3) the omission of any language transferring termination rights in the 1978 Assignment or even a mention of the right of termination, the district court concluded that Mewborn intended to relinquish and impliedly waived her "newly acquired right of termination" when she executed the 1978 Assignment. The district court reasoned that by virtue of the 1976 Assignment, "Mewborn had already transferred her interest in all motion picture, television and radio rights" and that "the only reasonable interpretation of the 1978 contract language is that she intended to give away any additional motion picture, television and radio rights not given away in 1976, thus relinquishing her newly acquired right of termination." We disagree.

On October 19, 1976–between the dates that Mewborn executed the two assignments–Congress enacted the 1976 Copyright Act, which took effect on January 1, 1978. The Act extended the length of copyright protection for copyrights in existence on January 1, 1978 by 19 years, from 56 years to 75 years (the "Extended Renewal Term"). *See* 17 U.S.C. § 304(a). The Act also created a right of termination, under § 304(c), which allows an author, if he is living, or his widow and children, if he is not, to recapture, for the Extended Renewal Term, the rights that had previously been transferred to third parties. The rights thus revert to the author or his statutory heirs. The termination of transfer right, as applied to the widow and children, is limited to transfers executed before January 1, 1978. The termination of transfer may be effected only during a five year window beginning at the end of what would have been the copyright's original and renewal terms (the end of 56 years from the date the copyright was originally secured), or beginning on January 1, 1978, whichever is later. Thus, the five-year termination window for the Lassie copyrights opened in 1994 for the 1938 story, and 1996 for the 1940 novel.

Under § 304(c)(4)(A), advance notice of termination must be served not less than two or more than ten years before the effective termination date. Most significantly, under § 304(c)(5), "[t]ermination of the grant may be effected *notwithstanding any agreement to the contrary,* including an agreement to make a will or to make any future grant." (emphasis added). Under 17 U.S.C. § 101, the term "including" is "illustrative" not "limitative" and thus we must interpret the term "agreement[s] to the contrary" under § 304(c)(5) as inclusive of agreements other than the two examples Congress explicitly mentioned.

Congress enacted the inalienability of termination rights provision in § 304(c)(5) to resurrect the fundamental purpose underlying the two-tiered structure of the duration of copyrights it originally adopted: to award to the author, and not to the assignee of the right to exploit the copyright during its initial term, the monetary rewards of a work that may have been initially undervalued, but which later becomes a commercial success. ...

The 1976 Act, and in particular its twin termination of transfer provisions, were in large measure designed to assure that its new benefits would be for the authors and their heirs. Thus, with the termination of transfer provisions, authors or their heirs are able to negotiate additional compensation for previously granted rights. Without such a right of termination, the Extended Renewal Term would constitute a windfall to grantees. As stated in the 1976 Act House Report: "[T]he extended term represents a completely new property right, and there are strong reasons for giving the author, who is the fundamental beneficiary of copyright under the Constitution, an opportunity to share in it." H.R.Rep. No. 94-1476, at 140 (1976), *reprinted in* 1976 U.S.C.C.A.N. 5659, 5756. ...

[*Marvel Characters Inc. v. Simon,* 310 F.3d 280, 284 (2d Cir. 2002)] inform[s] our analysis. In 1999, Joe Simon, author of the *Captain America Comics,* served a termination notice on Marvel pursuant to § 304(c). The notice sought to terminate a 1969 settlement agreement whereby Simon assigned his rights in *Captain America Comics* and the Captain America character to Marvel's predecessor. Marvel argued that the termination notice was ineffective because Simon had unambiguously acknowledged in the 1969 agreement that the works, many years after their creation, were "work[s] made for hire" thus making them ineligible for termination under § 304(c). The Second Circuit found that to the extent that the retroactive recharacterization of the works in the 1969 agreement was construed to extinguish the termination right long before vesting, it was void as an "agreement to the contrary" under § 304(c)(5).

In finding for Simon, the Second Circuit affirmed that "the clear Congressional purpose behind § 304(c) was to prevent authors from waiving their termination right by contract." The court reasoned that ruling otherwise would allow "litigation-savvy publishers" to use their superior bargaining power to compel authors to similarly recharacterize their works, thus rendering § 304(c) a "nullity." According to the court, the "notwithstanding any agreement to the contrary" language was intended to protect against attempted contractual circumvention of the termination right. ...

We conclude that insofar as Classic urges us to hold that the 1978 Assignment transferred the motion picture, television and radio rights subject to Mewborn's termination rights, we cannot so hold because such an assignment would be void as an "agreement to the contrary" pursuant to § 304(c)(5). Moreover, all that Mewborn had at the time of the 1978 Assignment was future rights that would revert upon termination of the grant and the 1978 Assignment does not purport to grant those rights.

The 1976 Assignment transferred all of Mewborn's motion picture, television and radio rights to the Lassie Works in exchange for $11,000 and, as the district court correctly concluded, was not substituted or revoked by the 1978 Assignment but remained intact. Because LTI owned the motion picture, television and radio rights to the Lassie Works in 1978, Mewborn had nothing to transfer by virtue of the 1978 Assignment other than the additional ancillary rights she transferred for $3,000. Therefore, the language in the 1978 Assignment purporting to assign the motion picture, television and radio rights is a nullity.

Under § 304(c)(4)(A), a termination notice "shall be served not less than two or more than ten years before [the effective date of the termination]." The "effective date of the termination" must "fall within the five-year period" "beginning at the end of fifty-six years from the date copyright was originally secured, or beginning on January 1, 1978, which-ever is later." In Mewborn's case, the fifty-six year term of copyright was set to expire in the story in 1994 and in the novel in 1996. Mewborn could not have filed a notice of termination of the assignment of rights to exploit the story any earlier than 1984 or any later than 1997; she could not have done so for the novel any earlier than 1986 or any later than 1999. Therefore the future rights that would revert upon termination of the grant could not have vested any earlier than 1984 for the story and 1986 for the novel.

Mewborn was entitled to effect the termination of the 1976 grant during the five year window commencing in 1994 for the story rights and

1996 for the novel rights. She was required to serve advance notice no less than two and no more than ten years before the effective date of the termination. She chose as the effective date May 1, 1998, a date that was within the termination window for both of the works—1994 to 1999 for the story rights and 1996 to 2001 for the rights in the novel. As of May 1, 1998, she validly terminated the rights she granted to LTI in the 1976 Assignment.

The district court misrelied upon *Milne v. Stephen Slesinger, Inc.,* 430 F.3d 1036 (9th Cir.2005), *cert. denied,* 548 U.S. 904. *Milne* presented quite a distinct factual scenario with very different statutory implications. Whereas Mewborn in 1978 did not even have the right to serve an advance notice of termination so as to vest her termination rights as to the Lassie Works, and could not have served advance notice for another six years as to the story and eight for the novel, the heir in *Milne* had the present right to serve an advance notice of termination, and could exercise it at any moment. Thus when the Milne heir chose to use the leverage of imminent vesting to revoke the pre-1978 grant and enter into a highly remunerative new grant of the same rights, it was tantamount to following the statutory formalities, and achieved the exact policy objectives for which § 304(c) was enacted.

Milne involved the copyright interests in four Winnie-the-Pooh works, most significantly the book *House at Pooh Corner,* authored by A.A. Milne, for which he secured United States statutory copyright protection between 1924 and 1928. Copyrights in the works were duly renewed between 1952 and 1956. Two pre-1978 grants of rights to exploit the copyrighted works were executed. Congress then enacted the termination of transfer provision set forth in 17 U.S.C. § 304(c).

Under § 304(c), the heirs, specifically Christopher Milne, received the right to terminate the 1930 and 1961 grants, upon serving a notice of an effective date of termination within five year windows following the expiration of the first and renewal terms of copyright. But, under the Copyright Act, the advance notice of termination was required to be served "not less than two or more than ten years" before the effective date. Thus, although the five year window for setting an effective date of termination for the work copyrighted in 1924 extended to 1985, for the "future rights that [would] revert upon termination of the grant [to] become vested" in Christopher, he was required to serve the advance notice no later than 1983 for that work. If he failed to serve advance notice by that date, he would lose his right to terminate the grant for the original works, from which the later works derived. As to the latest of the copyrighted works, Christopher similarly was required to serve advance notice no later than 1987 or lose his right of termination. In 1983, the studio, recognizing Christopher's existing right to terminate the grant of rights to exploit the original work, chose to renegotiate the pre-1978 agreements. Christopher, in turn, chose to avoid the statutory formalities whereby the rights would actually vest in him and then he would have to renegotiate with the studio. The new agreement revoked those earlier transfers and re-granted to the studio the very same rights. In return for Christopher's agreement not to exercise his termination rights, which would have invested in him the copyright interests in all the works at issue, the deal resulted in a net gain of hundreds of millions of dollars to Christopher and the remaining heirs, landing the studio and Christopher in the same place had he followed the formalities.

In concluding that the renegotiated deal was not an "agreement to the contrary," the court relied on the facts that the new grant was more lucrative for the author's heirs, that it was freely and intelligently entered into by the parties and that "[t]he beneficiaries of the Pooh Properties Trust were able to obtain considerably more money as a result of the bargaining power wielded by the author's son, Christopher, who was believed to own a statutory right to terminate the 1930 grant under section 304(c) of the 1976 Copyright Act."

Our court in *Milne* did not find waiver or relinquishment of any right. What it did conclude was that the particular negotiated deal before it was not "any agreement to the *contrary,*" it was an agreement consistent with, and which fully honored Christopher's right of termination which could vest immediately if he served notice. As we noted, "[a]lthough Christopher presumably could have served a termination notice, he elected instead to use his leverage to obtain a better deal." The avenue chosen by Christopher and the studio secured the exact equivalent result for him and his fellow heirs, and in no way subverted the termination rights and the congressional purpose underlying them.

Mewborn's predicament is a far cry from Christopher Milne's. Milne had—and knew that he had—the right to vest copyright in himself at the very time he revoked the prior grants and leveraged his termination rights to secure the benefits of the copyrighted works for A.A. Milne's heirs. Mewborn, on the other hand, would not have the right to serve the advance notice that would vest her rights under § 304(c)(6)(B) until at the very earliest six years later. Thus, unlike Milne, Mewborn had nothing in hand with which to bargain.

Examining the language of Milne's 1983 revocation and regrant of rights in comparison to Mewborn's 1978 Assignment further underscores the different nature of the intended agreements. Unlike Christopher Milne's 1983 assignment, which expressly revoked the earlier 1930 and 1961 assignments and simultaneously re-granted the same rights, Mewborn's 1978 Assignment explicitly stated that it granted rights "in addition to" the rights granted in the 1976 Assignment and confirmed that the 1976 Assignment had been recorded in the U.S. Copyright Office. And while Mewborn's 1978 assignment was silent on the issue, the post-1978 assignment in *Milne* expressly stated that it was made in exchange for non-exercise of the immediately investative termination right.

Nor is there any evidence in the record to support a finding that Mewborn or LTI, when entering into the 1978 Agreement, considered Mewborn's termination rights under § 304(c), or that Mewborn intended to waive or relinquish them. Rather, the evidence suggests that Mewborn did not intend to waive her termination rights. There is no evidence in the record that Mewborn was even aware of her termination rights in March 1978, just two months after § 304(c) became effective. And if LTI had entered into the 1978 Assignment intending that the termination right was on the bargaining table, the contract language fails to reflect this intention or provide any consideration for that right. There is also no evidence that either party intended to revoke and replace (or even modify) the 1976 Assignment. Rather, the 1978 Assignment explicitly affirms the 1976 Assignment. Finally, Mewborn's deposition testimony suggests that she had no conversations with LTI regarding the 1978 Assignment, and that she signed the contract "as is" without the advice of counsel and without negotiating any of its terms.

Mewborn did not intend to relinquish a known termination right. Because we conclude that the 1978 Assignment did not expressly or impliedly transfer Mewborn's termination right as to the 1976 Assignment, and that the circumstances here are not even close to those in *Milne,* the district court improperly concluded that the 1978 Assignment included a grant of Mewborn's termination right. The 1978 Assignment simply assigned to Classic's predecessor-in-interest the additional enumerated rights that Mewborn had not assigned in 1976. The 1996 Termination Notice was properly served not less than two years and not more than ten years before the effective termination date of May 1, 1998, which itself fell within the five year window of termination for both the story and the novel. We thus find the Termination Notice to have been valid and effective. ...

IV. Conclusion

For the reasons stated, we reverse the district court's order granting Classic's motion for summary judgment and direct the district court to enter partial summary judgment in favor of Mewborn on her declaratory relief claim. ...

Notes and Questions

1.   Under what circumstances could an author or heir successfully relinquish termination rights? *Classic Media* considered three approaches that you may want to think through. First, the court discussed *Milne v. Stephen Slesinger,* in which the Ninth Circuit held a waiver valid because of the particular timing and circumstances of the purported waiver. Second, the *Classic Media* court carefully studied the specific language of the 1978 agreement. Third, the court found that Mewborn did not intend to waive her termination rights when signing the 1978 agreement. How do these approaches affect the validity of any possible waiver? If you were an attorney drafting a document to divest an author or heir of termination rights, how would you do it, and how confident are you of success?

2. People exploiting copyrights sometimes voluntarily agree to re-scind existing deals in favor of new ones. For example, an author might assign his copyright in a first novel to a publisher for a given royalty rate. In the future, that author might sign a new agreement to cover his first and second novels at a higher royalty rate. Such an agreement could take various forms. The parties could "tear up" the original agree-ment, with the author re-conveying rights in the first novel as part of the new agreement. Alternatively, the parties could sign an amendment to the original agreement, leaving the original conveyance in place while changing the royalty rate. Finally, the publisher could formally convey the copyright back to the author, and the author could immediately con-vey the rights back to the publisher at the new royalty rate. If the par-ties executed the initial agreement in 1976, and the new agreement in 1979, would there be any effect on § 304(c) or (d) termination rights?

In answering this question, remember that §304(c) and (d) termina-tion rights apply only to copyright assignments made before 1978. Agreements of the sort outlined above arguably result in a new, post-1978 conveyance that cannot be terminated under §304(c) or (d) (alt-hough it would be terminable under §203 if the assignment is made by an author, as opposed to an heir). In *Penguin Group (USA) Inc. v. Stein-beck*, 537 F.3d 193 (2d Cir. 2008), the Second Circuit considered this is-sue in a case involving conveyances and purported terminations by heirs of John Steinbeck. The court held that the post-1978 conveyance de-stroyed all termination rights associated with the pre-1978 conveyance. Was this the right decision?

Chapter Five

EXCLUSIVE RIGHTS AND INFRINGEMENT

What does it mean for a person to commit copyright infringement? Section 106 of the Copyright Act identifies six exclusive rights that belong to a copyright owner:

> Subject to sections 107 through 122, the owner of copyright under this title has the exclusive rights to do and to authorize any of the following:
>
> (1) to reproduce the copyrighted work in copies or phonorecords;
>
> (2) to prepare derivative works based upon the copyrighted work;
>
> (3) to distribute copies or phonorecords of the copyrighted work to the public by sale or other transfer of ownership, or by rental, lease, or lending;
>
> (4) in the case of literary, musical, dramatic, and choreographic works, pantomimes, and motion pictures and other audiovisual works, to perform the copyrighted work publicly;
>
> (5) in the case of literary, musical, dramatic, and choreographic works, pantomimes, and pictorial, graphic, or sculptural works, including the individual images of a motion picture or other audiovisual work, to display the copyrighted work publicly; and
>
> (6) in the case of sound recordings, to perform the copyrighted work publicly by means of a digital audio transmission.

Section 501(a) of the Act defines a copyright infringer as anyone who violates one of these exclusive rights.

The definition of copyright infringement raises fundamental questions about the nature of copyright and the kind of behavior that society should prohibit. As you will see, courts have not always thought about these issues clearly or consistently. Moreover, Congress has chosen to vary the rights of copyright holders in different situations. For example, the owner of copyright in a book can decide for herself whether to license certain uses of the book, and she can set the price she charges for those uses. By contrast, the owner of copyright in a song must sometimes license his work to others at statutorily prescribed rates.

The complications referred to above take up many pages of the Copyright Act and its associated case law. This chapter presents materials chosen to reflect the basic doctrinal and policy themes that characterize this area of law.

SECTION A. BASIC INFRINGEMENT: COPYING AND IMPROPER APPROPRIATION

Section 106(1) of the Copyright Act gives a copyright holder the exclusive right to make copies of her work. Accordingly, a person who duplicates an entire copyrighted work without permission commits infringement and will face liability absent a defense like fair use. The law of copyright infringement gets complicated because a defendant need not copy an entire work in order to commit infringement. Courts must therefore undertake the difficult task of defining the type of copying that constitutes infringement.

Infringement cases often arise when the plaintiff discovers that the defendant has produced a work that resembles one created by the plaintiff. Our first case, *Arnstein v. Porter*, offers a clear and influential explanation of the elements that govern the outcome of such disputes. As you read this case and the ones that follow it, pay attention to the logical relationship between the elements of copying and improper appropriation, as well as the different ways in which these elements evaluate the similarity between two works.

Arnstein v. Porter
154 F.2d 464 (2d Cir. 1946)

FRANK, Circuit Judge

[The plaintiff Ira Arnstein filed suit against Cole Porter alleging that various Porter songs infringed a number of Arnstein's works. The Southern District of New York granted Porter's motion for summary judgment, and Arnstein appealed.]

... The principal question on this appeal is whether the lower court, under Rule 56, properly deprived plaintiff of a trial of his copyright infringement action. The answer depends on whether "there is the slightest doubt as to the facts." In applying that standard here, it is important to avoid confusing two separate elements essential to a plaintiff's case in such a suit: (a) that defendant copied from plaintiff's copyrighted work and (b) that the copying (assuming it to be proved) went too far as to constitute improper appropriation.

As to the first—copying—the evidence may consist (a) of defendant's admission that he copied or (b) of circumstantial evidence—usually evidence of access—from which the trier of the facts may reasonably infer copying. Of course, if there are no similarities, no amount of evidence of access will suffice to prove copying. If there is evidence of access and similarities exist, then the trier of the facts must determine whether the similarities are sufficient to prove copying. On this issue, analysis ("dissection") is relevant, and the testimony of experts may be received to aid the trier of the facts. If evidence of access is absent, the similarities must be so striking as to preclude the possibility that plaintiff and defendant independently arrived at the same result.

If copying is established, then only does there arise the second issue, that of illicit copying (unlawful appropriation). On that issue (as noted more in detail below) the test is the response of the ordinary lay hearer; accordingly, on that issue, 'dissection' and expert testimony are irrelevant.

In some cases, the similarities between the plaintiff's and defendant's work are so extensive and striking as, without more, both to justify an inference of copying and to prove improper appropriation. But such double-purpose evidence is not required; that is, if copying is otherwise shown, proof of improper appropriation need not consist of similarities which, standing alone, would support an inference of copying.

Each of these two issues—copying and improper appropriation—is an issue of fact. If there is a trial, the conclusions on those issues of the trier of the facts—of the judge if he sat without a jury, or of the jury if there was a jury trial—bind this court on appeal, provided the evidence supports those findings, regardless of whether we would ourselves have reached the same conclusions. But a case could occur in which the similarities were so striking that we would reverse a finding of no access, despite weak evidence of access (or no evidence thereof other than the similarities); and similarly as to a finding of no illicit appropriation.

We turn first to the issue of copying. After listening to the compositions as played in the phonograph recordings submitted by defendant, we find similarities; but we hold that unquestionably, standing alone, they do not compel the conclusion, or permit the inference, that defendant copied. The similarities, however, are sufficient so that, if there is enough evidence of access to permit the case to go to the jury, the jury may properly infer that the similarities did not result from coincidence.

Summary judgment was, then, proper if indubitably defendant did not have access to plaintiff's compositions. Plainly that presents an issue of fact. ... On the record now before us, more than a million copies of one of his compositions were sold; copies of others were sold in smaller quantities or distributed to radio stations or band leaders or publishers, or the pieces were publicly performed. If, after hearing both parties testify, the jury disbelieves defendant's denials, it can, from such facts, reasonably infer access. It follows that, as credibility is unavoidably involved, a genuine issue of material fact presents itself. With credibility a vital factor, plaintiff is entitled to a trial where the jury can observe the witnesses while testifying. Plaintiff must not be deprived of the invaluable privilege of cross-examining the defendant—the "crucial test of credibility"—in the presence of the jury. Plaintiff, or a lawyer on his behalf, on such examination may elicit damaging admissions from defendant; more important, plaintiff may persuade the jury, observing defendant's manner when testifying, that defendant is unworthy of belief. ...

Assuming that adequate proof is made of copying, that is not enough; for there can be "permissible copying," copying which is not illicit. Whether (if he copied) defendant unlawfully appropriated presents, too, an issue of fact. The proper criterion on that issue is not an analytic or other comparison of the respective musical compositions as they appear on paper or in the judgment of trained musicians. The plaintiff's legally protected interest is not, as such, his reputation as a musician but his interest in the potential financial returns from his compositions which derive from the lay public's approbation of his efforts. The question, therefore, is whether defendant took from plaintiff's works so much of what is pleasing to the ears of lay listeners, who comprise the audience for whom such popular music is composed, that defendant wrongfully appropriated something which belongs to the plaintiff.

Surely, then, we have an issue of fact which a jury is peculiarly fitted to determine. Indeed, even if there were to be a trial before a judge, it would be desirable (although not necessary) for him to summon an advisory jury on this question.

We should not be taken as saying that a plagiarism case can never arise in which absence of similarities is so patent that a summary judgment for defendant would be correct. Thus suppose that Ravel's "Bolero" or Shostakovitch's "Fifth Symphony" were alleged to infringe "When Irish Eyes Are Smiling." But this is not such a case. For, after listening to the playing of the respective compositions, we are, at this time, unable to conclude that the likenesses are so trifling that, on the issue of misappropriation, a trial judge could legitimately direct a verdict for defendant.

At the trial, plaintiff may play, or cause to be played, the pieces in such manner that they may seem to a jury to be inexcusably alike, in terms of the way in which lay listeners of such music would be likely to react. The plaintiff may call witnesses whose testimony may aid the jury in reaching its conclusion as to the responses of such audiences. Expert testimony of musicians may also be received, but it will in no way be controlling on the issue of illicit copying, and should be utilized only to assist in determining the reactions of lay auditors. The impression made on the refined ears of musical experts or their views as to the musical excellence of plaintiff's or defendant's works are utterly immaterial on the issue of misappropriation; for the views of such persons are caviar to

the general—and plaintiff's and defendant's compositions are not caviar.
...

Modified in part; otherwise reversed and remanded.

[The dissenting opinion of Judge Clark is omitted.]

Notes and Questions

1. *Arnstein* differentiates between proof of copying and proof of improper appropriation. This is an important distinction that lawyers and judges frequently misunderstand or overlook. Let us take a moment to make sure that you understand what separates the two. For both copying and improper appropriation, the plaintiff argues that the defendant's work is too similar to the plaintiff's work. What distinguishes similarity in copying from similarity in improper appropriation, and why are both necessary to a finding of infringement? To ask the questions somewhat differently, can a plaintiff win an infringement case simply by arguing that the two works share too many similarities?

2. *Arnstein* says that copying and improper appropriation differ in the appropriate use of what the opinion calls "dissection" and expert testimony. What is dissection, and why is it helpful when considering copying? Why would the court object to its use when analyzing improper appropriation? And what about expert testimony? Do you agree that expert testimony should not be used when analyzing improper appropriation?

3. You can listen to excerpts of some of both Arnstein and Porter's compositions at this URL:

http://mcir.usc.edu/cases/1940-1949/Pages/arnsteinporter.html

Do you think that the court correctly sent this case on for trial, and why?

1. COPYING

Arnstein v. Porter describes two distinct methods for proving copying. The first is direct proof such as an admission from the defendant of copying or testimony from a witness who observed the defendant copying the plaintiff's work. The second is circumstantial proof, in which evidence such as similarity between two works creates an inference of copying. With respect to circumstantial proof, courts often state that access and substantial similarity establish copying. Logically, copying cannot exist unless the defendant had access to the plaintiff's work, and substantial similarity refers to the degree of similarity required to prove copying by circumstantial evidence.

Do access and substantial similarity represent two independent and separate objects of proof, or does the strength of evidence about one influence the amount of proof necessary on the other? For example, if evidence of access is weak, will strong evidence of similarity between the defendant's work and the plaintiff's work overcome this problem and establish infringement? The *Arnstein* court wrote, "If evidence of access is absent, the similarities must be so striking as to preclude the possibility that plaintiff and defendant independently arrived at the same result." Was the court right to imply that strong evidence of access overcome weak or nonexistent evidence of similarity? Our next case, *Selle v. Gibb*, critically examines *Arnstein v. Porter*'s suggestion that similarity alone sometimes establishes copying.

Selle v. Gibb
741 F.2d 896 (7th Cir. 1984)

CUDAHY, Circuit Judge.

The plaintiff, Ronald H. Selle, brought a suit against three brothers, Maurice, Robin and Barry Gibb, known collectively as the popular singing group, the Bee Gees, alleging that the Bee Gees, in their hit tune, "How Deep Is Your Love," had infringed the copyright of his song, "Let It End." The jury returned a verdict in plaintiff's favor on the issue of liability in a bifurcated trial. The district court, Judge George N. Leighton, granted the defendants' motion for judgment notwithstanding the verdict and, in the alternative, for a new trial. We affirm the grant of the motion for judgment notwithstanding the verdict.

I

Selle composed his song, "Let It End," in one day in the fall of 1975 and obtained a copyright for it on November 17, 1975. He played his song with his small band two or three times in the Chicago area and sent a tape and lead sheet of the music to eleven music recording and publishing companies. Eight of the companies returned the materials to Selle; three did not respond. This was the extent of the public dissemination of Selle's song. Selle first became aware of the Bee Gees' song, "How Deep Is Your Love," in May 1978 and thought that he recognized the music as his own, although the lyrics were different. He also saw the movie, "Saturday Night Fever," the sound track of which features the song "How Deep Is Your Love," and again recognized the music. He subsequently sued the three Gibb brothers; Paramount Pictures Corporation, which made and distributed the movie; and Phonodisc, Inc., now known as Polygram Distribution, Inc., which made and distributed the cassette tape of "How Deep Is Your Love."

The Bee Gees are internationally known performers and creators of popular music. They have composed more than 160 songs; their sheet music, records and tapes have been distributed worldwide, some of the albums selling more than 30 million copies. The Bee Gees, however, do not themselves read or write music. In composing a song, their practice was to tape a tune, which members of their staff would later transcribe and reduce to a form suitable for copyrighting, sale and performance by both the Bee Gees and others.

In addition to their own testimony at trial, the Bee Gees presented testimony by their manager, Dick Ashby, and two musicians, Albhy Galuten and Blue Weaver, who were on the Bee Gees' staff at the time "How Deep Is Your Love" was composed. These witnesses described in detail how, in January 1977, the Bee Gees and several members of their staff went to a recording studio in the Chateau d'Herouville about 25 miles northwest of Paris. There the group composed at least six new songs and mixed a live album. Barry Gibb's testimony included a detailed explanation of a work tape which was introduced into evidence and played in court. This tape preserves the actual process of creation during which the brothers, and particularly Barry, created the tune of the accused song while Weaver, a keyboard player, played the tune which was hummed or sung by the brothers. Although the tape does not seem to preserve the very beginning of the process of creation, it does depict the process by which ideas, notes, lyrics and bits of the tune were gradually put together. ...

The only expert witness to testify at trial was Arrand Parsons, a professor of music at Northwestern University who has had extensive professional experience primarily in classical music. He has been a program annotator for the Chicago Symphony Orchestra and the New Orleans Symphony Orchestra and has authored works about musical theory. Prior to this case, however, he had never made a comparative analysis of two popular songs. Dr. Parsons testified on the basis of several charts comparing the musical notes of each song and a comparative recording prepared under his direction.

According to Dr. Parsons' testimony, the first eight bars of each song (Theme A) have twenty-four of thirty-four notes in plaintiff's composition and twenty-four of forty notes in defendants' composition which are identical in pitch and symmetrical position. Of thirty-five rhythmic impulses in plaintiff's composition and forty in defendants', thirty are identical. In the last four bars of both songs (Theme B), fourteen notes in each are identical in pitch, and eleven of the fourteen rhythmic impulses are identical. Both Theme A and Theme B appear in the same position in each song but with different intervening material.

Dr. Parsons testified that, in his opinion, "the two songs had such striking similarities that they could not have been written independent of one another." He also testified that he did not know of two songs by different composers "that contain as many striking similarities" as do the two songs at issue here. However, on several occasions, he declined to say that the similarities could only have resulted from copying.

Following presentation of the case, the jury returned a verdict for the plaintiff on the issue of liability, the only question presented to the jury.

Judge Leighton, however, granted the defendants' motion for judgment notwithstanding the verdict and, in the alternative, for a new trial. He relied primarily on the plaintiff's inability to demonstrate that the defendants had access to the plaintiff's song, without which a claim of copyright infringement could not prevail regardless how similar the two compositions are. Further, the plaintiff failed to contradict or refute the testimony of the defendants and their witnesses describing the independent creation process of "How Deep Is Your Love." Finally, Judge Leighton concluded that "the inferences on which plaintiff relies is not a logical, permissible deduction from proof of 'striking similarity' or substantial similarity; it is 'at war with the undisputed facts,' and it is inconsistent with the proof of nonaccess to plaintiff's song by the Bee Gees at the time in question." ...

III

Selle's primary contention on this appeal is that the district court misunderstood the theory of proof of copyright infringement on which he based his claim. Under this theory, copyright infringement can be demonstrated when, even in the absence of any direct evidence of access, the two pieces in question are so strikingly similar that access can be inferred from such similarity alone. Selle argues that the testimony of his expert witness, Dr. Parsons, was sufficient evidence of such striking similarity that it was permissible for the jury, even in the absence of any other evidence concerning access, to infer that the Bee Gees had access to plaintiff's song and indeed copied it. ...

Proof of copying is crucial to any claim of copyright infringement because no matter how similar the two works may be (even to the point of identity), if the defendant did not copy the accused work, there is no infringement. However, because direct evidence of copying is rarely available, the plaintiff can rely upon circumstantial evidence to prove this essential element, and the most important component of this sort of circumstantial evidence is proof of access. The plaintiff may be able to introduce direct evidence of access when, for example, the work was sent directly to the defendant (whether a musician or a publishing company) or a close associate of the defendant. On the other hand, the plaintiff may be able to establish a reasonable possibility of access when, for example, the complaining work has been widely disseminated to the public.

If, however, the plaintiff does not have direct evidence of access, then an inference of access may still be established circumstantially by proof of similarity which is so striking that the possibilities of independent creation, coincidence and prior common source are, as a practical matter, precluded. If the plaintiff presents evidence of striking similarity sufficient to raise an inference of access, then copying is presumably proved simultaneously, although the fourth element (substantial similarity) still requires proof that the defendant copied a substantial amount of the complaining work. The theory which Selle attempts to apply to this case is based on proof of copying by circumstantial proof of access established by striking similarity between the two works.

One difficulty with plaintiff's theory is that no matter how great the similarity between the two works, it is not their similarity *per se* which establishes access; rather, their similarity tends to prove access in light of the nature of the works, the particular musical genre involved and other circumstantial evidence of access. In other words, striking similarity is just one piece of circumstantial evidence tending to show access and must not be considered in isolation; it must be considered together with other types of circumstantial evidence relating to access.

As a threshold matter, therefore, it would appear that there must be at least some other evidence which would establish a reasonable possibility that the complaining work was available to the alleged infringer. As noted, two works may be identical in every detail, but, if the alleged infringer created the accused work independently or both works were copied from a common source in the public domain, then there is no infringement. Therefore, if the plaintiff admits to having kept his or her creation under lock and key, it would seem logically impossible to infer access through striking similarity. Thus, although it has frequently been written that striking similarity alone can establish access, the decided cases suggest that this circumstance would be most unusual. The plaintiff must always present sufficient evidence to support a reasonable possibility of access because the jury cannot draw an inference of access based upon speculation and conjecture alone. ...

In granting the defendants' motion for judgment notwithstanding the verdict, Judge Leighton relied primarily on the plaintiff's failure to adduce any evidence of access and stated that an inference of access may not be based on mere conjecture, speculation or a bare possibility of access. Thus, in *Testa v. Janssen*, 492 F. Supp. 198, 202-03 (W.D. Pa. 1980), the court stated that "[T]o support a finding of access, plaintiffs' evidence must extend beyond mere speculation or conjecture. And, while circumstantial evidence is sufficient to establish access, a defendant's opportunity to view the copyrighted work must exist by a reasonable possibility—not a bare possibility" (citation omitted).

Judge Leighton thus based his decision on what he characterized as the plaintiff's inability to raise more than speculation that the Bee Gees had access to his song. The extensive testimony of the defendants and their witnesses describing the creation process went essentially uncontradicted, and there was no attempt even to impeach their credibility. Judge Leighton further relied on the principle that the testimony of credible witnesses concerning a matter within their knowledge cannot be rejected without some impeachment, contradiction or inconsistency with other evidence on the particular point at issue. Judge Leighton's conclusions that there was no more than a bare possibility that the defendants could have had access to Selle's song and that this was an insufficient basis from which the jury could have reasonably inferred the existence of access seem correct. The plaintiff has failed to meet even the minimum threshold of proof of the possibility of access and, as Judge Leighton has stated, an inference of access would thus seem to be "at war with the undisputed facts." ...

Therefore, because the plaintiff failed both to establish a basis from which the jury could reasonably infer that the Bee Gees had access to his song ..., the grant by the district court of the defendants' motion for judgment notwithstanding the verdict is affirmed. ...

Notes and Questions

1. In *Selle*, two works shared practically identical melodies. Ordinarily, such similarity would give the plaintiff a strong case on the issue of copying if there was proof that the defendant had access to the two works. However, the Bee Gees had reasonably persuasive evidence showing that they did not have access to the plaintiff's work. The plaintiff responded by litigating his case under an alternate formulation of copying that allows unusually strong similarity to make up for weak evidence of access. Many courts, including *Arnstein*, adopt this position and state that plaintiffs can prove copying by "striking similarity" alone when there is no evidence of access. How literally should we take these statements? Can striking similarity establish copying as long as there is a theoretical possibility of access, however remote? When neither the plaintiff nor the defendant introduces evidence concerning access? When a defendant successfully refutes the possibility of access? Is striking similarity itself evidence of access?

2. Is the striking similarity method for proving copying truly distinct from the usual "access plus substantial similarity" formulation? Can you think of a case where there truly is no evidence of access?

3. Why did the court reject the understanding of copying adopted by Selle, and was it correct in doing so?

4. The works from *Selle* can be heard at:

http://mcir.usc.edu/cases/1980-1989/Pages/sellegibb.html .

Having listened to the two works, do you believe that the court was right in excusing the Bee Gees?

Bright Tunes Music v. Harrisongs Music
420 F. Supp. 177 (S.D.N.Y. 1976)

OWEN, District Judge.

This is an action in which it is claimed that a successful song, My Sweet Lord, listing George Harrison as the composer, is plagiarized from an earlier successful song, He's So Fine, composed by Ronald Mack, recorded by a singing group called the "Chiffons," the copyright of which is owned by plaintiff, Bright Tunes Music Corp.

He's So Fine, recorded in 1962, is a catchy tune consisting essentially of four repetitions of a very short basic musical phrase, "sol-mi-re," (hereinafter motif A),[41] altered as necessary to fit the words, followed by four repetitions of another short basic musical phrase, "sol-la-do-la-do," (hereinafter motif B).[42] While neither motif is novel, the four repetitions of A, followed by four repetitions of B, is a highly unique pattern. In addition, in the second use of the motif B series, there is a grace note inserted making the phrase go "sol-la-do-la-re-do."[43]

My Sweet Lord, recorded first in 1970, also uses the same motif A (modified to suit the words) four times, followed by motif B, repeated three times, not four. In place of He's So Fine's fourth repetition of motif B, My Sweet Lord has a transitional passage of musical attractiveness of the same approximate length, with the identical grace note in the identical second repetition. The harmonies of both songs are identical.

George Harrison, a former member of The Beatles, was aware of He's So Fine. In the United States, it was No. 1 on the billboard charts for five weeks; in England, Harrison's home country, it was No. 12 on the charts on June 1, 1963, a date upon which one of the Beatle songs was, in fact, in first position. For seven weeks in 1963, He's So Fine was one of the top hits in England.

According to Harrison, the circumstances of the composition of My Sweet Lord were as follows. Harrison and his group, which include an American black gospel singer named Billy Preston, were in Copenhagen, Denmark, on a singing engagement. There was a press conference involving the group going on backstage. Harrison slipped away from the press conference and went to a room upstairs and began "vamping" some guitar chords, fitting on to the chords he was playing the words, "Hallelujah" and "Hare Krishna" in various ways. During the course of this vamping, he was alternating between what musicians call a Minor II chord and a Major V chord.

At some point, germinating started and he went down to meet with others of the group, asking them to listen, which they did, and everyone began to join in, taking first "Hallelujah" and then "Hare Krishna" and putting them into four part harmony. Harrison obviously started using the "Hallelujah," etc., as repeated sounds, and from there developed the

lyrics, to wit, "My Sweet Lord," "Dear, Dear Lord," etc. In any event, from this very free-flowing exchange of ideas, with Harrison playing his two chords and everybody singing "Hallelujah" and "Hare Krishna," there began to emerge the My Sweet Lord text idea, which Harrison sought to develop a little bit further during the following week as he was playing it on his guitar. Thus developed motif A and its words interspersed with "Hallelujah" and "Hare Krishna."

Approximately one week after the idea first began to germinate, the entire group flew back to London because they had earlier booked time to go to a recording studio with Billy Preston to make an album. In the studio, Preston was the principal musician. Harrison did not play in the session. He had given Preston his basic motif A with the idea that it be turned into a song, and was back and forth from the studio to the engineer's recording booth, supervising the recording "takes." Under circumstances that Harrison was utterly unable to recall, while everybody was working toward a finished song, in the recording studio, somehow or other the essential three notes of motif A reached polished form.

> "Q. (By the Court): . . . you feel that those three notes . . . the motif A in the record, those three notes developed somewhere in that recording session?
> "Mr. Harrison: I'd say those three there were finalized as beginning there."
> "Q. (By the Court): Is it possible that Billy Preston hit on those (notes comprising motif A)?
> "Mr. Harrison: Yes, but it's possible also that I hit on that, too, as far back as the dressing room, just scat singing."

Similarly, it appears that motif B emerged in some fashion at the recording session as did motif A. This is also true of the unique grace note in the second repetition of motif B.

> "Q. (By the Court): All I am trying to get at, Mr. Harrison, is if you have a recollection when that (grace) note popped into existence as it ends up in the Billy Preston recording.
> "Mr. Harrison: . . . (Billy Preston) might have put that there on every take, but it just might have been on one take, or he might have varied it on different takes at different places."

The Billy Preston recording, listing George Harrison as the composer, was thereafter issued by Apple Records. The music was then reduced to paper by someone who prepared a "lead sheet" containing the melody, the words and the harmony for the United States copyright application.

Seeking the wellsprings of musical composition why a composer chooses the succession of notes and the harmonies he does whether it be George Harrison or Richard Wagner is a fascinating inquiry. It is apparent from the extensive colloquy between the Court and Harrison covering forty pages in the transcript that neither Harrison nor Preston were conscious of the fact that they were utilizing the He's So Fine theme. However, they in fact were, for it is perfectly obvious to the listener that in musical terms, the two songs are virtually identical except for one phrase. There is motif A used four times, followed by motif B, four times in one case, and three times in the other, with the same grace note in the second repetition of motif B.

What happened? I conclude that the composer, in seeking musical materials to clothe his thoughts, was working with various possibilities. As he tried this possibility and that, there came to the surface of his mind a particular combination that pleased him as being one he felt would be appealing to a prospective listener; in other words, that this combination of sounds would work. Why? Because his subconscious knew it already had worked in a song his conscious mind did not remember. Having arrived at this pleasing combination of sounds, the recording was made, the lead sheet prepared for copyright and the song became an enormous success. Did Harrison deliberately use the music of He's So Fine? I do not believe he did so deliberately. Nevertheless, it is clear that My Sweet Lord is the very same song as He's So Fine with different words, and Harrison had access to He's So Fine. This is, under the law, infringement of copyright, and is no less so even though subconsciously accomplished.

Given the foregoing, I find for the plaintiff on the issue of plagiarism, and set the action down for trial on November 8, 1976 on the issue of damages and other relief as to which the plaintiff may be entitled. The foregoing constitutes the Court's findings of fact and conclusions of law.

Notes and Questions

1. The previous case, *Selle v. Gibb*, accepts the proposition that a few authors independently create songs that coincidentally bear great similarity to other existing works. Accordingly, some cases that initially look like strong infringement cases actually involve no copying at all. In *Harrisongs*, George Harrison essentially claimed that he was one of these innocent authors, but he lost because "He's So Fine" achieved wide distribution. If *Harrisongs* differs from *Selle* primarily in the fame of the plaintiff's work, what would have happened to the Bee Gees if Selle's song had been famous? If the Bee Gees would have lost, does this mean that any author who independently creates a work very similar to a famous work will lose an infringement case? Is this desirable or fair?

2. *Harrisongs* raises an interesting question about what it means to copy. Copying could refer only to knowing, deliberate acts taken for the express purpose of imitating the plaintiff's work. Alternatively, it could refer to unconscious acts in which an author has been influenced by prior work and inadvertently replicates part or all of the prior work. According to *Harrisongs*, this latter form of inadvertent replication is copying. Do you agree? Other courts considering the issue have generally concurred, largely on the ground that copyright infringement is a strict liability of-

fense. From a fault point of view, Harrison's behavior seems reasonable. He worked with his fellow musicians, trying out melodies and harmonies, and chose the ones he thought were most pleasing. He had no idea he was copying "He's So Fine," so there was nothing he could reasonably have done to avoid infringing. He therefore did not deserve liability. From a strict liability point of view, the characterization of Harrison's behavior means nothing. Copyright rights are property, so violation of those rights demands compensation. Which of these positions is better?

3.   You can hear "He's So Fine" and "My Sweet Lord" at:

http://mcir.usc.edu/cases/1970-1979/Pages/brightharrisongs.html.

2.   IMPROPER APPROPRIATION

Having explored the issue of copying, we now turn to the question of improper appropriation. If a defendant has copied from the plaintiff's work, how do courts decide whether the defendant has copied too much? The answer to this question depends, at its most basic level, on how similar the defendant's work is to the plaintiff's. Thus, in *Arnstein v. Porter*, if Porter had copied from Arnstein, and if Porter's work were identical to Arnstein's, a finding of infringement would likely have followed. By contrast, if Porter had copied, but the works merely resembled one another, the likelihood of infringement would be lower. Of course, this observation does not identify the amount of similarity necessary to establish improper appropriation.

In short, the existence of improper appropriation depends on how sensitive courts are to the similarities and differences between two works. If courts easily notice similarity, but overlook difference, they will tend to conclude that a defendant has borrowed too much from the plaintiff because the works appear too similar. Conversely, if courts see difference, but ignore similarity, they will lean towards thinking that a defendant has not borrowed enough to become an infringer because the works lack sufficient similarity.

As you will soon see, courts do not agree about how to make this determination. However, the materials presented here accomplish two things that are crucial to making sense of this area. First, they provide examples of various approaches to improper appropriation. Second, they illustrate two major themes in the law: 1) the choice between impression-oriented and detail-oriented analysis and 2) the use of the ordinary observer to guide the thinking of judges and juries.

a.   Impression-Oriented and Detail-Oriented Analysis

In the vast majority of cases, the defendant's work contains some material not found in the plaintiff's work. This allows the defendant to argue that her work embodies the independent, meaningfully different expression of ideas found in the plaintiff's work. Any copying attributable to the defendant does not amount to infringement because she has borrowed only facts, ideas, and other uncopyrightable material.

A plaintiff generally responds to arguments like this by urging courts to ignore the differences between his work and the defendant's. It cannot possibly be true that any difference between two works defeats a claim of infringement. Moreover, copyrightable expression exists in the combination of uncopyrightable material. The defendant's copying therefore constitutes infringement because she has borrowed the plaintiff's copyrightable combination of ideas and has failed to alter that expression in any legally meaningful way.

Our first two cases, *Roth Greeting Cards v. United Card Company* and *Satava v. Lowry*, illustrate two very different ways of choosing between these arguments. We call the *Roth Greeting Cards* approach impression-oriented because it evaluates whether the overall impression of the two works in question is the same. We call the *Satava* approach detail-oriented because it looks beyond overall impression to analyze whether the specific points of similarity are copyrightable subject matter. If they are not, the test ignores those similarities.

Roth Greeting Cards v. United Card Co.
429 F.2d 1106 (9th Cir. 1970)

HAMLEY, Circuit Judge:

Roth Greeting Cards (Roth) and United Card Company (United), both corporations, are engaged in the greeting card business. Roth brought this suit against United to recover damages and obtain injunctive relief for copyright infringement of seven studio greeting cards. After a trial to the court without a jury, judgment was entered for defendant. Plaintiff appeals.

Roth's claim involves the production and distribution by United of seven greeting cards which bear a remarkable resemblance to seven of Roth's cards on which copyrights had been granted. Roth employed a writer to develop the textual material for its cards. When Roth's president determined that a textual idea was acceptable, he would integrate that text into a rough layout of a greeting card with his suggested design for the art work. He would then call in the company artist who would make a comprehensive layout of the card. If the card was approved, the artist would do a finished layout and the card would go into production.

During the period just prior to the alleged infringements, United did not have any writers on its payroll. Most of its greeting cards came into fruition primarily through the activities of United's president, Mr. Koenig, and its vice-president, Edward Letwenko.

The source of the art and text of the cards of United, here in question, is unclear. Letwenko was unable to recall the origin of the ideas for most of United's cards. He speculated that the gags used may have come from plant personnel, persons in bars, friends at a party, Koenig, or someone else. He contended that the art work was his own. But he also stated that he visited greeting card stores and gift shows in order to observe what was going on in the greeting card business. Letwenko admitted that he may have seen the Roth cards during these visits or that the Roth cards may have been in his office prior to the time that he did his art work on the United cards.

On these facts, the trial court held for defendant on alternative grounds, lack of jurisdiction and lack of infringement of any copyrightable material. ...

Turning to the merits, the trial court found that the art work in plaintiff's greeting cards was copyrightable, but not infringed by defendant. The trial court also found that, although copied by defendant, the wording or textual matter of each of the plaintiff's cards in question consist of common and ordinary English words and phrases which are not original with Roth and were in the public domain prior to first use by plaintiff.

Arguing that the trial court erred in ruling against it on merits, Roth agrees that the textual material involved in their greeting cards may have been in the public domain, but argues that this alone did not end the inquiry into the copyrightability of the entire card. Roth argued that "It is the arrangement of the words, their combination and plan, together with the appropriate art work. ..." which is original, the creation of Roth, and entitled to copyright protection. ...

United argues, and we agree, that there was substantial evidence to support the district court's finding that the textual matter of each card, considered apart from its arrangement on the cards and its association with artistic representations, was not original to Roth and therefore not copyrightable. However, proper analysis of the problem requires that all elements of each card, including text, arrangement of text, art work, and association between art work and text, be considered as a whole.

Considering all of these elements together, the Roth cards are, in our opinion, both original and copyrightable. In reaching this conclusion we recognize that copyright protection is not available for ideas, but only for the tangible expression of ideas. We conclude that each of Roth's cards, considered as a whole, represents a tangible expression of an idea and that such expression was, in totality, created by Roth.

This brings us to the question of infringement. ...

To constitute an infringement under the Act there must be substantial similarity between the infringing work and the work copyrighted; and that similarity must have been caused by the defendant's having copied the copyright holder's creation. The protection is thus against copying—not against any possible infringement caused when an independently created work coincidentally duplicates copyrighted material.

It appears to us that in total concept and feel the cards of United are the same as the copyrighted cards of Roth. With the possible exception of one United card (exhibit 6), the characters depicted in the art work, the mood they portrayed, the combination of art work conveying a particular mood with a particular message, and the arrangement of the words on the greeting card are substantially the same as in Roth's cards. In several instances the lettering is also very similar.

It is true, as the trial court found, that each of United's cards employed art work somewhat different from that used in the corresponding Roth cards. However, "The test of infringement is whether the work is recognizable by an ordinary observer as having been taken from the copyrighted source." *White-Smith Music Pub. Co. v. Apollo Company,* 209 U.S. 1 (1907), *Bradbury v. Columbia Broadcasting System, Inc.,* 287 F.2d 478, 485 (9th Cir. 1961).

The remarkable similarity between the Roth and United cards in issue (with the possible exception of exhibits 5 and 6) is apparent to even a casual observer. For example, one Roth card (exhibit 9) has, on its front, a colored drawing of a cute moppet suppressing a smile and, on the inside, the words "i wuv you." With the exception of minor variations in color and style, defendant's card (exhibit 10) is identical. Likewise, Roth's card entitled "I miss you already," depicts a forlorn boy sitting on a curb weeping, with an inside message reading "... and You Haven't even Left ..." (exhibit 7), is closely paralleled by United's card with the same caption, showing a forlorn and weeping man, and with the identical inside message (exhibit 8).

The question remains whether United did in fact copy the Roth cards. Since direct evidence of copying is rarely available, copying may be established by proof of access and substantial similarity. Although in some circumstances the mere proof of access and substantial similarity will not demand that the trier automatically find copying, the absence of any countervailing evidence of creation independent of the copyrighted source may well render clearly erroneous a finding that there was not copying.

In the present case there was clear and uncontradicted testimony establishing United's access to the Roth cards. United brought Roth cards to its offices. It sent its employees out to gift shows and retail stores where the Roth cards were on display to observe "what the competition was doing." In addition, there was testimony almost compelling the inference that it was United's practice to look at the cards produced by other companies and make similar cards for sale under the United label. These circumstances, together with the marked similarity between the cards on which this suit was brought, with the possible exception of one card, convince us that each of United's cards in question, considered as combined compositions of art and text, were in fact copied from the Roth cards. It follows that there was infringement.

The judgment is therefore reversed and the cause is remanded for further proceedings consistent with this opinion.

KILKENNY, Circuit Judge (dissenting).

The majority agrees with a specific finding of the lower court that the words on the cards are not the subject of copyright. By strong implication, it likewise accepts the finding of the trial court that the art work on the cards, although subject to copyright, was not infringed. Thus far, I agree.

I cannot, however, follow the logic of the majority in holding that the uncopyrightable words and the imitated, but not copied art work, constitutes such total composition as to be subject to protection under the copyright laws. The majority concludes that in the overall arrangement of the text, the art work and the association of the art work to the text, the cards were copyrightable and the copyright infringed. This conclusion, as I view it, results in the whole becoming substantially greater than the sum total of its parts. With this conclusion, of course, I cannot agree. ...

I call attention to the fact that a number of experts appeared in the lower court and testified that the phrases on the cards were in common use and that Roth's writer often obtained his ideas from others. In these circumstances, we should not set aside the findings of the lower court. Beyond that, ordinary phraseology within the public domain is not copyrightable.

Feeling, as I do, that the copyright act is a grant of limited monopoly to the authors of creative literature and art, I do not think that we should extend a 56-year monopoly in a situation where neither infringement of text, nor infringement of art work can be found. On these facts, we should adhere to our historic philosophy requiring freedom of competition. I would affirm.

EXHIBITS:

Exhibit 7 (Card by Roth Greeting Cards)

Exhibit 8 (Card by United Card Cò.)

Notes and Questions

1. Two of the cards under litigation, Exhibits 7 and 8, are reproduced above. Having seen them, do you agree that they share, to use the court's words, "remarkable similarity" that supports a finding of improper appropriation?

2. *Roth* reaches the unremarkable conclusion that Roth's cards were copyrightable, and it follows copyright orthodoxy by identifying copyrightable subject matter as the combination of uncopyrightable items. However, *Roth*'s emphasis on a work's "total concept and feel" represents a relatively generous approach to the copyrightable aggregation of uncopyrightable items. What do you think about basing copyright claims on this aspect of a work? Whatever you think about total concept and feel, how far do you think courts should go in combining ideas into copyrightable expression?

3. *Roth* is one of many important cases whose language obscures the distinction between copying and improper appropriation. For example, the court wrote:

> To constitute an infringement under the Act there must be substantial similarity between the infringing work and the work copyrighted; and that similarity must have been caused by the defendant's having copied the copyright holder's creation. The protection is thus against copying—not against any possible infringement caused when an independently created work coincidentally duplicates copyrighted material.

Statements like this suggest that infringement occurs when the defendant simply copies from the plaintiff's work. However, consideration of the entire opinion shows that the court did consider copying and improper appropriation separately, if not clearly. Two of the final paragraphs clearly discuss access and substantial similarity for purposes of copying, while the discussion of total concept and feel corresponds to the lay listener test espoused in *Arnstein*'s explanation of improper appropriation. As students of copyright, it is important to read cases carefully in order to avoid confusion of the sort found in *Roth*.

Satava v. Lowry
323 F.3d 805 (9th Cir. 2003)

GOULD, Circuit Judge.

...

I

Plaintiff Richard Satava is a glass artist from California. In the late 1980s, Satava was inspired by the jellyfish display at an aquarium. He began experimenting with jellyfish sculptures in the glass-in-glass medium and, in 1990, began selling glass-in-glass jellyfish sculptures. The sculptures sold well, and Satava made more of them. By 2002, Satava was designing and creating about three hundred jellyfish sculptures each month. Satava's sculptures are sold in galleries and gift shops in forty states, and they sell for hundreds or thousands of dollars, depending on size. Satava has registered several of his works with the Register of Copyrights.

Satava describes his sculptures as "vertically oriented, colorful, fanciful jellyfish with tendril-like tentacles and a rounded bell encased in an outer layer of rounded clear glass that is bulbous at the top and tapering toward the bottom to form roughly a bullet shape, with the jellyfish portion of the sculpture filling almost the entire volume of the outer, clear-glass shroud." Satava's jellyfish appear lifelike. They resemble the pelagia colorata that live in the Pacific Ocean: [44]

During the 1990s, defendant Christopher Lowry, a glass artist from Hawaii, also began making glass-in-glass jellyfish sculptures. Lowry's sculptures look like Satava's, and many people confuse them:[45]

---

[44] Editors' note: The photograph depicted here appeared in the court's opinion. Satava still makes jellyfish in glass. One can view color photographs of his work at: https://satava.com/moon-jellyfish.

[45] Editors' note: The photograph depicted here appeared in the court's opinion. Lowry still makes jellyfish in glass as well, in collaboration with Chris Richards. One can view color photographs of their work at: http://www.glass-art.com/ArtistPages/Lowry_Richards.htm.

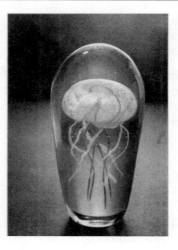

In Hawaii, Satava's sculptures have appeared in tourist brochures and art magazines. The sculptures are sold in sixteen galleries and gift shops, and they appear in many store windows. Lowry admits he saw a picture of Satava's jellyfish sculptures in American Craft magazine in 1996. And he admits he examined a Satava jellyfish sculpture that a customer brought him for repair in 1997.

Glass-in-glass sculpture is a centuries-old art form that consists of a glass sculpture inside a second glass layer, commonly called the shroud. The artist creates an inner glass sculpture and then dips it into molten glass, encasing it in a solid outer glass shroud. The shroud is malleable before it cools, and the artist can manipulate it into any shape he or she desires.

Satava filed suit against Lowry accusing him of copyright infringement. Satava requested, and the district court granted, a preliminary injunction, enjoining Lowry from making sculptures that resemble Satava's. Lowry appealed to us.

II

A preliminary injunction must be affirmed on appeal unless the district court (1) abused its discretion or (2) based its decision on an erroneous legal standard or on clearly erroneous findings of fact. We hold that the district court based its decision on an erroneous legal standard, so we reverse.

Copyright protection is available for "original works of authorship fixed in any tangible medium of expression, now known or later developed, from which they can be perceived, reproduced, or otherwise communicated, either directly or with the aid of a machine or device." 17 U.S.C. § 102(a). Copyright protection does not, however, "extend to any idea, procedure, process, system, method of operation, concept, principle, or discovery...." 17 U.S.C. § 102(b).

Any copyrighted expression must be "original." Although the amount of creative input by the author required to meet the originality standard is low, it is not negligible. There must be something more than a "merely trivial" variation, something recognizably the artist's own.

The originality requirement mandates that objective "facts" and ideas are not copyrightable. Similarly, expressions that are standard, stock, or common to a particular subject matter or medium are not protectable under copyright law.

It follows from these principles that no copyright protection may be afforded to the idea of producing a glass-in-glass jellyfish sculpture or to elements of expression that naturally follow from the idea of such a sculpture. Satava may not prevent others from copying aspects of his sculptures resulting from either jellyfish physiology or from their depiction in the glass-in-glass medium.

Satava may not prevent others from depicting jellyfish with tendril-like tentacles or rounded bells, because many jellyfish possess those body parts. He may not prevent others from depicting jellyfish in bright colors, because many jellyfish are brightly colored. He may not prevent others from depicting jellyfish swimming vertically, because jellyfish swim vertically in nature and often are depicted swimming vertically.

Satava may not prevent others from depicting jellyfish within a clear outer layer of glass, because clear glass is the most appropriate setting for an aquatic animal. He may not prevent others from depicting jellyfish "almost filling the entire volume" of the outer glass shroud, because such proportion is standard in glass-in-glass sculpture. And he may not prevent others from tapering the shape of their shrouds, because that shape is standard in glass-in-glass sculpture.

Satava's glass-in-glass jellyfish sculptures, though beautiful, combine several unprotectable ideas and standard elements. These elements are part of the public domain. They are the common property of all, and Satava may not use copyright law to seize them for his exclusive use.

It is true, of course, that a combination of unprotectable elements may qualify for copyright protection. But it is not true that any combination of unprotectable elements automatically qualifies for copyright protection. Our case law suggests, and we hold today, that a combination of unprotectable elements is eligible for copyright protection only if those elements are numerous enough and their selection and arrangement original enough that their combination constitutes an original work of authorship.

The combination of unprotectable elements in Satava's sculpture falls short of this standard. The selection of the clear glass, oblong shroud, bright colors, proportion, vertical orientation, and stereotyped jellyfish form, considered together, lacks the quantum of originality needed to merit copyright protection. These elements are so commonplace in glass-in-glass sculpture and so typical of jellyfish physiology that to recognize copyright protection in their combination effectively would give Satava a monopoly on lifelike glass-in-glass sculptures of single jellyfish with vertical tentacles. Because the quantum of originality Satava added in combining these standard and stereotyped elements must be considered "trivial" under our case law, Satava cannot prevent other artists from combining them.

We do not mean to suggest that Satava has added nothing copyrightable to his jellyfish sculptures. He has made some copyrightable contributions: the distinctive curls of particular tendrils; the arrangement of certain hues; the unique shape of jellyfishes' bells. To the extent that these and other artistic choices were not governed by jellyfish physiology or the glass-in-glass medium, they are original elements that Satava theoretically may protect through copyright law. Satava's copyright on these original elements (or their combination) is "thin," however, comprising no more than his original contribution to ideas already in the public domain. Stated another way, Satava may prevent others from copying the original features he contributed, but he may not prevent others from copying elements of expression that nature displays for all observers, or that the glass-in-glass medium suggests to all sculptors. Satava possesses a thin copyright that protects against only virtually identical copying.

We do not hold that realistic depictions of live animals cannot be protected by copyright. In fact, we have held to the contrary. We recognize, however, that the scope of copyright protection in such works is narrow. Nature gives us ideas of animals in their natural surroundings: an eagle with talons extended to snatch a mouse; a grizzly bear clutching a salmon between its teeth; a butterfly emerging from its cocoon; a wolf howling at the full moon; a jellyfish swimming through tropical waters. These ideas, first expressed by nature, are the common heritage of humankind, and no artist may use copyright law to prevent others from depicting them.

An artist may, however, protect the original expression he or she contributes to these ideas. An artist may vary the pose, attitude, gesture, muscle structure, facial expression, coat, or texture of animal. An artist may vary the background, lighting, or perspective. Such variations, if original, may earn copyright protection. Because Satava's jellyfish sculptures contain few variations of this type, the scope of his copyright is narrow.

We do not mean to short-change the legitimate need of creative artists to protect their original works. After all, copyright law achieves its high purpose of enriching our culture by giving artists a financial incentive to create. But we must be careful in copyright cases not to cheat the public domain. Only by vigorously policing the line between idea and expression can we ensure both that artists receive due reward for their original creations and that proper latitude is granted other artists to make use of ideas that properly belong to us all.

Notes and Questions

1. Take a moment to follow the logic of *Satava*. The plaintiff Satava had pretty good evidence of copying. Satava's jellyfish sculptures achieved fairly wide notoriety, and the defendant Lowry admitted seeing them. The works depicted in the opinion look a great deal alike. Given the abuse of discretion standard applied in the case, it seems unlikely that the Ninth Circuit could have reversed the district court on the issue of copying. This means that Satava fell short on the issue of improper appropriation. Do you agree with the Ninth Circuit's conclusion that the similarities between Satava's work and Lowry's could not establish improper appropriation because they were ideas or other uncopyrightable subject matter, or did the Ninth Circuit mistakenly ignore the total concept and feel that forms the heart of Satava's artistic expression?

2. How do the analytical methods of *Roth* and *Satava* affect judicial sensitivity to the similarities and differences between two works? Which case's analysis would you urge a court to adopt if you were a copyright plaintiff or defendant, and why? If you are unsure, consider how these analyses affect a court's responsiveness to arguments that a defendant borrowed only ideas from the plaintiff's work.

3. *Roth* and *Satava* demonstrate the significance of a decision to use either impression-oriented or detail-oriented analysis. Both opinions agree that copyright does not protect an author's ideas, and that courts should interpret copyright to ensure that ideas do not gain copyright protection. With such clear agreement about a fundamental proposition, how did the two courts manage to interpret the law so differently? If the *Satava* court had employed the impression-oriented analysis of *Roth*, it seems likely that *Satava* would have come out the other way. After all, the works of Satava and Lowry looked alike to the point that people sometimes confused the work of one man for the other's. Surely this established similarity of impression greater than the similarity between Roth's and United's greeting cards. By contrast, if *Roth* had used the detail-oriented approach of *Satava*, it seems likely that Roth's claim would have failed because many important points of similarity like the words and general appearance of the various cards would have been ignored as similarities of idea. With all of this in mind, which method of analysis do you consider correct, and why? Does your answer mean that either *Roth* or *Satava* was wrongly decided, or can you reconcile the two cases?

4. Some of the frustration that lawyers encounter when analyzing improper appropriation comes from the judiciary's inability to state a clear preference for impression-oriented or detail-oriented analysis. Ample precedent supports the vitality of either approach. For cases adopting an impression-oriented analysis, *see Sid & Marty Krofft Television Prods, Inc. v. McDonald's Corp.*, 562 F.2d 1157 (9th Cir. 1977); *Sturdza v. United Arab Emirates*, 281 F.3d 1287 (D.C. Cir. 2002); *Steinberg v.*

Columbia Pictures Industries, 663 F. Supp. 706 (S.D.N.Y. 1987). For cases adopting a detail-oriented analysis, see *Cooling Systems and Flexibles v. Stuart Radiator,* 777 F.2d 485 (9th Cir. 1985);. *Laureyssens v. Idea Group,* 964 F.2d 131 (2d Cir. 1992); *Ideal Toy Corp. v. Kenner Prods. Div. of Gen'l Mills Fun Group,* 443 F. Supp. 291 (S.D.N.Y. 1977).

b. The Ordinary Observer Test and Alternatives

Impression-oriented or detail-oriented tests influence judicial sensitivity to the similarities and differences between two works. This section studies a related, but distinct, method for accomplishing the same task. As you saw in *Arnstein v. Porter*, judges sometimes decide questions of improper appropriation not by applying their personal analysis to the works in question, but by adopting the perspective of the ordinary observer. Our first case contains a brief, but candid, discussion about the reasons for the use of the ordinary observer.

Peter Pan Fabrics v. Martin Weiner Corp.
274 F.2d 487 (2d Cir. 1960)

HAND, Circuit Judge

This is an appeal from a preliminary injunction, granted by Judge Herlands, forbidding the defendant to copy an ornamental design, printed upon cloth. The plaintiffs—which for the purposes of this appeal are to be regarded as one—and the defendant are both "converters" of textiles, used in the manufacture of women's dresses. A "converter" buys uncolored cloth upon which he prints ornamental designs, and which he then sells to dressmakers. The plaintiffs bought from a Parisian designer a design, known as "Byzantium," which it registered as a "reproduction of a work of art," (§ 5(h) of Title 17 U.S. Code) and for which the Copyright Office issued Certificate No. H.7290. This design they print upon uncolored cloth, sold in bolts to dressmakers. ... The appeal raises two questions: (1) whether the defendant has in fact copied so much of the registered design as to infringe the copyright; and (2) whether the design was dedicated to the public, because it was sold without adequate notice of copyright as required by § 10 of the statute.

The test for infringement of a copyright is of necessity vague. In the case of verbal "works" it is well settled that although the "proprietor's" monopoly extends beyond an exact reproduction of the words, there can be no copyright in the "ideas" disclosed but only in their "expression." Obviously, no principle can be stated as to when an imitator has gone beyond copying the "idea," and has borrowed its "expression." Decisions must therefore inevitably be ad hoc. In the case of designs, which are addressed to the aesthetic sensibilities of an observer, the test is, if possible, even more intangible. No one disputes that the copyright extends beyond a photographic reproduction of the design, but one cannot say how far an imitator must depart from an undeviating reproduction to escape infringement. In deciding that question one should consider the uses for which the design is intended, especially the scrutiny that observers will give to it as used. In the case at bar we must try to estimate how far its overall appearance will determine its aesthetic appeal when the cloth is made into a garment. Both designs have the same general color, and the arches, scrolls, rows of symbols, etc. on one resemble those on the other though they are not identical. Moreover, the patterns in which these figures are distributed to make up the design as a whole are not identical. However, the ordinary observer, unless he set out to detect the disparities, would be disposed to overlook them, and regard their aesthetic appeal as the same. That is enough; and indeed, it is all that can be said, unless protection against infringement is to be denied because of variants irrelevant to the purpose for which the design is intended.

[The court's discussion of dedication of the copyright to the public is omitted.]

Order affirmed.

Notes and Questions

1. Judge Hand begins with the premise that the question of copyright infringement "is of necessity vague." He deals with this problem by adopting the sensibilities of the "ordinary observer." How does the ordinary observer test ostensibly deal with the problem of vagueness in copyright infringement? Why would a judge find the ordinary observer test superior to authoritative pronouncements about the existence of infringement from appellate judges?

2. *Peter Pan* clearly demonstrates the importance of judicial sensitivity to similarities and differences between two works. The designs are similar in overall appearance, but scrutiny reveals many disparities. It is therefore understandable that Hand wants an authoritative pronouncement about the appropriate level of sensitivity. Hand's opinion states that the ordinary observer would generally overlook the differences between the two works in question, and "regard their aesthetic appeal as the same." What is the basis for Hand's assertion that an ordinary observer would actually evaluate the two works this way? Consider again the works at issue in *Roth* and *Satava*. Presumably your class contains a number of "ordinary observers" of these works. Do they agree on the existence of infringing similarity between the two works? If not, how can Hand pronounce the ordinary observer's views with such confidence? Of course, a court could require copyright litigants to present evidence of what "ordinary people" think about two works. Would you consider this desirable? If not, what might this say about the normative merits of the ordinary observer test? For whatever it is worth, courts do not generally want copyright litigants to provide evidence of what ordinary people think about any works in question. Instead, they prefer judges or juries

to use their own experience (perhaps as ordinary observers themselves?) to conclude what the ordinary observer thinks.

3.   One virtue of the ordinary observer test is its relationship to copyright's incentive rationale. Recall *Arnstein's* explanation of the improper appropriation test:

> The plaintiff's legally protected interest is not, as such, his reputation as a musician but his interest in the potential financial returns from his compositions which derive from the lay public's approbation of his efforts. The question, therefore, is whether defendant took from plaintiff's works so much of what is pleasing to the ears of lay listeners, who comprise the audience for whom such popular music is composed, that defendant wrongfully appropriated something which belongs to the plaintiff.

This statement implies that a defendant's copying becomes infringement when the defendant has reproduced the commercial appeal of the plaintiff's work. The ordinary observer test captures this view of improper appropriation because it is the ordinary observer's taste that drives the market for the plaintiff's work. Does this explanation convince you that courts should adopt the ordinary observer's perspective in all improper appropriation cases? Or might there be reasons to abandon the test? Consider the following case.

Dawson v. Hinshaw
905 F.2d 731 (4th Cir. 1990)

MURNAGHAN, Circuit Judge

I

William L. Dawson possesses a valid copyright of an arrangement of the spiritual "Ezekiel Saw De Wheel." Dawson, over the years, has sold many copies of his arrangement. In 1980, Gilbert M. Martin composed an arrangement of the spiritual. That same year, Martin granted Hinshaw Music, Inc. ("Hinshaw"), the exclusive rights to publish, distribute, and sell his arrangement. Martin agreed to indemnify Hinshaw for any loss resulting from infringement of copyright. Dawson brought suit against Hinshaw and Martin, alleging copyright infringement under 17 U.S.C. § 501 *et seq.* After a bench trial, the district court held for the defendants. ...

[T]he district court ruled against Dawson on the second prong of the substantial similarity inquiry, holding that Dawson had not shown that the expression of ideas in Martin's work was substantially similar to the expression of ideas in Dawson's work. The court applied what has come to be known as the ordinary observer test, sometimes referred to as an "intrinsic" or "subjective" test, inquiring into the "total concept and feel" of the works without the aid of expert testimony. More specifically, the court interpreted the ordinary observer test to be an ordinary lay observer test, which imposed upon Dawson the obligation to prove to a lay observer that the expression of ideas in the works was substantially similar. Other than the expert testimony used in evaluating the extrinsic similarity of the two works, the only evidence on substantial similarity was the sheet music of the two arrangements. Dawson had not presented recordings of performances of the two arrangements. The district court found that, as an ordinary lay observer, with nothing before him other than the sheet music, he could not determine that the two works were substantially similar. It is the district court's holding as to the second prong of the substantial similarity test that we now examine.

II

We direct our attention to the district court's characterization of the ordinary observer test as an ordinary lay observer test. We are well aware of the existence of that characterization in the case law. However, as demonstrated below, obedience to the undisputed principles of copyright law and the policy underlying the ordinary observer test requires a recognition of the limits of the ordinary lay observer characterization of the ordinary observer test. Those principles require orientation of the ordinary observer test to the works' intended audience, permitting an ordinary lay observer characterization of the test only where the lay public fairly represents the works' intended audience.

A

Arnstein v. Porter provides the source of modern theory regarding the ordinary observer test. *Arnstein* involved the alleged infringement of a popular musical composition. Writing for the panel, Judge Jerome Frank first explained that "the plaintiff's legally protected interest is not, as such, his reputation as a musician but his interest in the potential financial returns from his compositions which derive from the lay public's approbation." This initial observation gave force to the recognized purpose of the copyright laws of providing creators with a financial incentive to create for the ultimate benefit of the public.

Consistent with its economic incentive view of copyright law, the *Arnstein* court concluded that "the question, therefore, is whether defendant took from plaintiff's works so much of what is pleasing to the ears of lay listeners, *who comprise the audience for whom such popular music is composed*, that defendant wrongfully appropriated something which belongs to plaintiff." (emphasis added). Thus, under *Arnstein*, a court should look to the reaction of "lay listeners," because they comprise the audience of the plaintiff's work. The lay listener's reaction is relevant because it gauges the effect of the defendant's work on the plaintiff's market.

Although *Arnstein* established a sound foundation for the appeal to audience reaction, its reference to "lay listeners" may have fostered the development of a rule that has come to be stated too broadly. Under the facts before it, with a popular composition at issue, the *Arnstein* court appropriately perceived "lay listeners" and the works' "audience" to be the same. However, under *Arnstein*'s sound logic, the lay listeners are relevant only because they comprise the relevant audience. Although *Arnstein* does not address the question directly, we read the case's logic to require that [where the intended audience is significantly more specialized than the pool of lay listeners, the reaction of the intended audience would be the relevant inquiry.] In light of the copyright law's purpose of protecting a creator's market, we think it sensible to embrace *Arnstein*'s command that the ultimate comparison of the works at issue be oriented towards the works' intended audience. ...

We suspect that courts have been slow to recognize explicitly the need for refining the ordinary observer test in such a way that it would adopt the perspective of the intended audience because, in most fact scenarios, the general lay public fairly represents the works' intended audience. As a result, "a considerable degree of ambiguity exists in this area; courts have not always made it apparent whether they were using a member of a specific audience, or simply an average lay observer as their spectator." Note, *Copyright Infringement Actions: The Proper Role for Audience Reactions in Determining Substantial Similarity*, 54 S. CAL. L. REV. 385, 386 (1981) [hereinafter *Role for Audience Reaction*]. Fortunately, the advent of computer programming infringement actions has forced [courts to recognize that sometimes the non-interested or uninformed lay observer simply lacks the necessary expertise to determine similarities] or differences between products. In *Whelan Associates v. Jaslow Dental Laboratory*, 797 F.2d 1222 (3d Cir. 1986) the Third Circuit concluded that the ordinary observer arm of the substantial similarity test was not appropriate for the complex computer program copyright case before it. Writing for a unanimous panel, Judge Becker reasoned that the complexity of computer programs, combined with the general public's unfamiliarity with such programs, rendered the ordinary observer test senseless. ...

We believe the *Whelan* analysis further supports our view. As *Whelan* reveals, only a reckless indifference to common sense would lead a court to embrace a doctrine that requires a copyright case to turn on the opinion of someone who is ignorant of the relevant differences and similarities between two works. Instead, the judgment should be informed by people who are familiar with the media at issue. ...

B

Under the foregoing logic, we state the law to be as follows. [When conducting the second prong of the substantial similarity inquiry, a district court must consider the nature of the intended audience of the plaintiff's work.] If, as will most often be the case, the lay public fairly represents the intended audience, the court should apply the lay observer formulation of the ordinary observer test. However, if the intended audience is more narrow in that it possesses specialized expertise, relevant to the purchasing decision, that lay people would lack, the court's inquiry should focus on whether a member of the intended audience would find the two works to be substantially similar. Such an inquiry may include, and no doubt in many cases will require, admission of testimony from members of the intended audience or, possibly, from those who possess expertise with reference to the tastes and perceptions of the intended audience.

We recognize the appeal of blind adherence to the lay observer characterization of the ordinary observer test even where the intended audience possesses specialized knowledge and such adherence is therefore theoretically inappropriate. The lay observer test spares a court the burden of inquiring into, and drawing conclusions regarding, the nature of the works' intended audience. That burden would be a substantial one if our holding were read as an invitation to every litigant in every copyright case to put before the court the seemingly unanswerable question of whether a product's audience is sufficiently specialized to justify departure from the lay characterization of the ordinary observer test. Although the existence of difficulties attendant to application of a test that a doctrine compels is an insufficient reason not to use the test, concerns about copyright actions becoming unwieldy are legitimate.

We therefore believe that, in any given case, a court should be hesitant to find that the lay public does not fairly represent a work's intended audience. In our opinion, departure from the lay characterization is warranted only where the intended audience possesses "specialized expertise." We thereby pay heed to the need for hesitancy when departing from the indiscriminately selected lay public in applying the test. To warrant departure from the lay characterization of the ordinary observer test, "specialized expertise" must go beyond mere differences in taste and instead must rise to the level of the possession of knowledge that the lay public lacks.

We believe that, especially given the explicitness of our holding, "intended audience" should supplant "ordinary observer" as the label for the appropriate test. The new label is appropriate not because we have changed the test, but because the imprecision of the old label leads to application of an ordinary lay observer test even where such a test is inappropriate. However, mindful of the harm that has resulted from reliance upon labels in this doctrinal area, we emphasize that our clarification of the doctrine is motivated by the policies underlying the doctrine, namely, the theoretical propriety of looking to the effect of the defendant's work on the plaintiff's market and the practical evil of having an unaided uninformed finder of fact deciding the crucial issue in a case. We intend to make the rule more precise, not to change it.

III

In light of our statement of the law in Section II, we think remand is necessary because the district court did not inquire into whether the audience of Dawson's work possessed specialized expertise that the lay public lacks and, therefore, whether the general, undifferentiated lay public fairly represents the intended audience of Dawson's arrangement.

It is true that the case with which we contend involves music and courts routinely, and properly, apply the ordinary lay observer test to music cases. However, Dawson alleged infringement of a spiritual arrangement, not a popular recording. We suspect that the distinction may have implications for the determination of the intended audience of Dawson's work. It may be that a popular recording of a love ditty pitched at the broadest of audiences is marketed to the general public far more so than is a spiritual arrangement. It is quite possible that spiritual arrangements are purchased primarily by choral directors who possess specialized expertise relevant to their selection of one arrangement instead of another. Whereas a lay person's reaction may be an accurate indicator of the extent to which those in the market for a popular recording will perceive another recording to be substantially similar, a lay person's reaction might not be an accurate indicator of how expert choral directors would compare two spiritual arrangements.

Given the need to measure substantial similarity by the reaction of the ordinary observer within the intended audience, Dawson's failure to enter into evidence recordings of performances of the two arrangements is not fatal to his case. Use of a recording is obviously appropriate where a plaintiff sells recordings for the public to buy. However, Dawson does not sell recordings. He apparently sells sheet music arrangements to those who may make a purchasing decision on the basis of the sheet music. Although the district court's heavy reliance upon Dawson's failure to present a recording of the arrangements made sense in light of its application of the ordinary lay observer test, the conclusion would not make sense if it were the case that the audience for Dawson's spiritual arrangement had specialized expertise relevant to its purchasing decision. There is no reason for Dawson to submit recordings to persuade a lay listener that the arrangements are substantially similar if the lay listener's conclusion would not reflect the response of the choral directors who would purchase one arrangement over another on the basis of the arrangement's sheet music.

Furthermore, it may be that recordings of performances of the arrangements would not only be irrelevant but could indeed hinder the relevant inquiry. It may be that the sound of the performance of an arrangement is a function of not only the arrangement itself, but of the choral director's interpretation of the arrangement. Thus, differences and similarities in the sound of performances of two arrangements may represent something other than differences and similarities in the arrangements themselves. In addition, comparison of two recordings of performances of the arrangements would fail to take account of the different interpretations to the arrangements that purchasers intended to inject, rendering such a comparison even more misleading. These problems, of course, are not presented when actual recordings are at issue and therefore further distinguish the problems posed by spiritual arrangements as compared to popular recordings.

The district court did not make explicit factual findings on the issues of what the intended audience was and whether members of that audience have specialized expertise relevant to their purchasing decision. We offer our suspicions merely as explanations for why remand is necessary, not as predictions of the outcome of factual inquiry. Therefore, we decline to remand with instructions that the district court define an audience distinct from the ordinary lay observer. Instead, we remand with instructions that the district court determine whether definition of a distinct audience is appropriate in this case. Assuming such a definition is appropriate, the district court should then take additional evidence to determine whether members of the intended audience would find the arrangements to be substantially similar.

The facts of this case present a particularly inviting context in which to refine the ordinary observer test by requiring that the ordinary observer be the intended audience. To say the least, Dawson's claim is not bogus. The district court found extensive similarities between Dawson's and Martin's works. The logic of traditional copyright doctrine, as reflected in the case law and the consensus of the commentaries that have addressed the matter, compels our result. To hold otherwise would be to allow the imprecise "ordinary lay observer" label to effect a betrayal of the fundamental purposes of copyright doctrine and the substantial similarity test.

Notes and Questions

1.   Does the intended observer truly serve the purposes of copyright as the *Dawson* court claims? Suppose that an author creates a cartoon strip aimed at an intended audience of 10-12 year old boys. To the author's surprise, the cartoon does not sell well to that audience. It does, however, sell very well to adults. If our hypothetical author winds up litigating a question of improper appropriation, would the intended observer test be the correct one to use? And what if a work appeals to more than one audience with vastly different tastes? What should be done then?

2.   Courts often identify children as the intended observers of works such as toys. What effect does this have on a court's sensitivity to similarities and differences between works? Are children more or less discerning than adults when it comes to similarities and differences between items like toys?

3.   *Dawson* explains that the intended observer test is necessary to fix problems with the ordinary observer test. Has *Dawson* convinced you that the intended observer test fixes these problems, and that it is the best way to handle improper appropriation? Should it be applied to all copyright disputes?

Computer Associates Int'l v. Altai
982 F.2d 693 (2d. Cir. 1992)

WALKER, Circuit Judge:

... [T]his case deals with the challenging question of whether and to what extent the "non-literal" aspects of a computer program, that is, those aspects that are not reduced to written code, are protected by copyright. While a few other courts have already grappled with this issue, this case is one of first impression in this circuit. As we shall discuss, we find the results reached by other courts to be less than satisfactory. Drawing upon long-standing doctrines of copyright law, we take an approach that we think better addresses the practical difficulties embedded in these types of cases. In so doing, we have kept in mind the necessary balance between creative incentive and industrial competition.

This appeal comes to us from the United States District Court for the Eastern District of New York, the Honorable George C. Pratt, Circuit Judge, sitting by designation. By Memorandum and Order entered August 12, 1991, Judge Pratt found that defendant Altai, Inc.'s ("Altai"), OSCAR 3.4 computer program had infringed plaintiff Computer Associates' ("CA"), copyrighted computer program entitled CA-SCHEDULER. Accordingly, the district court awarded CA $364,444 in actual damages and apportioned profits. Altai has abandoned its appeal from this award. With respect to CA's second claim for copyright infringement, Judge Pratt found that Altai's OSCAR 3.5 program was not substantially similar to a portion of CA-SCHEDULER called ADAPTER, and thus denied relief. ... CA appealed from these findings.

Because we are in full agreement with Judge Pratt's decision and in substantial agreement with his careful reasoning regarding CA's copyright infringement claim, we affirm the district court's judgment on that issue. ...

BACKGROUND

...

I.   COMPUTER PROGRAM DESIGN

Certain elementary facts concerning the nature of computer programs are vital to the following discussion. The Copyright Act defines a computer program as "a set of statements or instructions to be used directly or indirectly in a computer in order to bring about a certain result." 17 U.S.C. § 101(b). In writing these directions, the programmer works "from the general to the specific." *Whelan Assocs., Inc. v. Jaslow Dental Lab., Inc.*, 797 F.2d 1222, 1229 (3d Cir. 1986).

The first step in this procedure is to identify a program's ultimate function or purpose. An example of such an ultimate purpose might be the creation and maintenance of a business ledger. Once this goal has been achieved, a programmer breaks down or "decomposes" the program's ultimate function into "simpler constituent problems or 'subtasks,'" [citation omitted] which are also known as subroutines or modules. In the context of a business ledger program, a module or subroutine might be responsible for the task of updating a list of outstanding accounts receivable. Sometimes, depending upon the complexity of its task, a subroutine may be broken down further into sub-subroutines.

Having sufficiently decomposed the program's ultimate function into its component elements, a programmer will then arrange the subroutines or modules into what are known as organizational or flow charts. Flow charts map the interactions between modules that achieve the program's end goal. ...

"The functions of the modules in a program together with each module's relationships to other modules constitute the 'structure' of the program." ...

In fashioning the structure, a programmer will normally attempt to maximize the program's speed, efficiency, as well as simplicity for user operation, while taking into consideration certain externalities such as the memory constraints of the computer upon which the program will be run. ...

Once each necessary module has been identified, designed, and its relationship to the other modules has been laid out conceptually, the resulting program structure must be embodied in a written language that the computer can read. This process is called "coding," and requires two steps. First, the programmer must transpose the program's structural blue-print into a source code. This step has been described as "comparable to the novelist fleshing out the broad outline of his plot by crafting from words and sentences the paragraphs that convey the ideas." The source code may be written in any one of several computer languages, such as COBAL, FORTRAN, BASIC, EDL, etc., depending upon the type of computer for which the program is intended. Once the source code has been completed, the second step is to translate or "compile" it into object code. Object code is the binary language comprised of zeros and ones through which the computer directly receives its instructions.

After the coding is finished, the programmer will run the program on the computer in order to find and correct any logical and syntactical errors. This is known as "debugging" and, once done, the program is complete.

II. FACTS

... The subject of this litigation originates with one of CA's marketed programs entitled CA-SCHEDULER. CA-SCHEDULER is a job scheduling program designed for IBM mainframe computers. Its primary functions are straightforward: to create a schedule specifying when the computer should run various tasks, and then to control the computer as it executes the schedule. CA-SCHEDULER contains a sub-program entitled ADAPTER, also developed by CA. ADAPTER is not an independently marketed product of CA; it is a wholly integrated component of CA-SCHEDULER and has no capacity for independent use.

Nevertheless, ADAPTER plays an extremely important role. It is an "operating system compatibility component," which means, roughly speaking, it serves as a translator. An "operating system" is itself a program that manages the resources of the computer, allocating those resources to other programs as needed. The IBM System 370 family of computers, for which CA-SCHEDULER was created, is, depending upon the computer's size, designed to contain one of three operating systems: DOS/VSE, MVS, or CMS. As the district court noted, the general rule is that "a program written for one operating system, e.g., DOS/VSE, will not, without modification, run under another operating system such as MVS." ADAPTER's function is to translate the language of a given program into the particular language that the computer's own operating system can understand. ...

A program like ADAPTER, which allows a computer user to change or use multiple operating systems while maintaining the same software, is highly desirable. It saves the user the costs, both in time and money, that otherwise would be expended in purchasing new programs, modifying existing systems to run them, and gaining familiarity with their operation. The benefits run both ways. The increased compatibility afforded by an ADAPTER-like component, and its resulting popularity among consumers, makes whatever software in which it is incorporated significantly more marketable.

Starting in 1982, Altai began marketing its own job scheduling program entitled ZEKE. The original version of ZEKE was designed for use in conjunction with a VSE operating system. By late 1983, in response to customer demand, Altai decided to rewrite ZEKE so that it could be run in conjunction with an MVS operating system.

At that time, James P. Williams ("Williams"), then an employee of Altai and now its President, approached Claude F. Arney, III ("Arney"), a computer programmer who worked for CA. Williams and Arney were longstanding friends, and had in fact been co-workers at CA for some time before Williams left CA to work for Altai's predecessor. Williams wanted to recruit Arney to assist Altai in designing an MVS version of ZEKE.

At the time he first spoke with Arney, Williams was aware of both the CA-SCHEDULER and ADAPTER programs. However, Williams was not involved in their development and had never seen the codes of either program. When he asked Arney to come work for Altai, Williams did not know that ADAPTER was a component of CA-SCHEDULER.

Arney, on the other hand, was intimately familiar with various aspects of ADAPTER. While working for CA, he helped improve the VSE version of ADAPTER, and was permitted to take home a copy of

ADAPTER'S source code. This apparently developed into an irresistible habit, for when Arney left CA to work for Altai in January, 1984, he took with him copies of the source code for both the VSE and MVS versions of ADAPTER. He did this in knowing violation of the CA employee agreements that he had signed.

Once at Altai, Arney and Williams discussed design possibilities for adapting ZEKE to run on MVS operating systems. Williams, who had created the VSE version of ZEKE, thought that approximately 30% of his original program would have to be modified in order to accommodate MVS. Arney persuaded Williams that the best way to make the needed modifications was to introduce a "common system interface" component into ZEKE. He did not tell Williams that his idea stemmed from his familiarity with ADAPTER. They decided to name this new component-program OSCAR.

Arney went to work creating OSCAR at Altai's offices using the ADAPTER source code. The district court accepted Williams' testimony that no one at Altai, with the exception of Arney, affirmatively knew that Arney had the ADAPTER code, or that he was using it to create OSCAR/VSE. However, during this time period, Williams' office was adjacent to Arney's. Williams testified that he and Arney "conversed quite frequently" while Arney was "investigating the source code of ZEKE" and that Arney was in his office "a number of times daily, asking questions." In three months, Arney successfully completed the OSCAR/VSE project. In an additional month he developed an OSCAR/MVS version. When the dust finally settled, Arney had copied approximately 30% of OSCAR's code from CA's ADAPTER program.

The first generation of OSCAR programs was known as OSCAR 3.4. From 1985 to August 1988, Altai used OSCAR 3.4 in its ZEKE product, as well as in programs entitled ZACK and ZEBB. In late July 1988, CA first learned that Altai may have appropriated parts of ADAPTER. After confirming its suspicions, CA secured copyrights on its 2.1 and 7.0 versions of CA-SCHEDULER. CA then brought this copyright and trade secret misappropriation action against Altai.

Apparently, it was upon receipt of the summons and complaint that Altai first learned that Arney had copied much of the OSCAR code from ADAPTER. After Arney confirmed to Williams that CA's accusations of copying were true, Williams immediately set out to survey the damage. Without ever looking at the ADAPTER code himself, Williams learned from Arney exactly which sections of code Arney had taken from ADAPTER.

Upon advice of counsel, Williams initiated OSCAR's rewrite. The project's goal was to save as much of OSCAR 3.4 as legitimately could be used, and to excise those portions which had been copied from ADAPTER. Arney was entirely excluded from the process, and his copy of the ADAPTER code was locked away. Williams put eight other programmers on the project, none of whom had been involved in any way in the development of OSCAR 3.4. Williams provided the programmers with a description of the ZEKE operating system services so that they could rewrite the appropriate code. The rewrite project took about six months to complete and was finished in mid-November 1989. The resulting program was entitled OSCAR 3.5.

From that point on, Altai shipped only OSCAR 3.5 to its new customers. Altai also shipped OSCAR 3.5 as a "free upgrade" to all customers that had previously purchased OSCAR 3.4. ...

DISCUSSION

... CA makes two arguments. First, CA contends that the district court applied an erroneous method for determining whether there exists substantial similarity between computer programs, and thus, erred in determining that OSCAR 3.5 did not infringe the copyrights held on the different versions of its CA-SCHEDULER program. CA asserts that the test applied by the district court failed to account sufficiently for a computer program's non-literal elements. Second, CA maintains that the district court erroneously concluded that its state law trade secret claims had been preempted by the federal Copyright Act. We shall address each argument in turn.

I.   COPYRIGHT INFRINGEMENT

...

A.   Copyright Protection for the Non-literal Elements of Computer Programs

It is now well settled that the literal elements of computer programs, i.e., their source and object codes, are the subject of copyright protection. Here, as noted earlier, Altai admits having copied approximately 30% of the OSCAR 3.4 program from CA's ADAPTER source code, and does not challenge the district court's related finding of infringement.

In this case, the hotly contested issues surround OSCAR 3.5. As recounted above, OSCAR 3.5 is the product of Altai's carefully orchestrated rewrite of OSCAR 3.4. After the purge, none of the ADAPTER source code remained in the 3.5 version; thus, Altai made sure that the literal elements of its revamped OSCAR program were no longer substantially similar to the literal elements of CA's ADAPTER.

According to CA, the district court erroneously concluded that Altai's OSCAR 3.5 was not substantially similar to its own ADAPTER program. CA argues that this occurred because the district court "committed legal error in analyzing [its] claims of copyright infringement by failing to find that copyright protects expression contained in the non-literal elements of computer software." We disagree.

CA argues that, despite Altai's rewrite of the OSCAR code, the resulting program remained substantially similar to the structure of its ADAPTER program. As discussed above, a program's structure includes its non-literal components such as general flow charts as well as the more specific organization of inter-modular relationships, parameter lists, and macros. In addition to these aspects, CA contends that OSCAR 3.5 is also substantially similar to ADAPTER with respect to the list of services that both ADAPTER and OSCAR obtain from their respective operating systems. We must decide whether and to what extent these elements of computer programs are protected by copyright law.

The statutory terrain in this area has been well explored. The Copyright Act affords protection to "original works of authorship fixed in any tangible medium of expression...." This broad category of protected "works" includes "literary works," which are defined by the Act as

> works, other than audiovisual works, expressed in words, numbers, or other verbal or numerical symbols or indicia, regardless of the nature of the material objects, such as books, periodicals, manuscripts, phonorecords, film tapes, disks, or cards, in which they are embodied.

17 U.S.C. § 101. While computer programs are not specifically listed as part of the above statutory definition, the legislative history leaves no doubt that Congress intended them to be considered literary works.

The syllogism that follows from the foregoing premises is a powerful one: if the non-literal structures of literary works are protected by copyright; and if computer programs are literary works, as we are told by the legislature; then the non-literal structures of computer programs are protected by copyright. We have no reservation in joining the company of those courts that have already ascribed to this logic. However, that conclusion does not end our analysis. We must determine the scope of copyright protection that extends to a computer program's non-literal structure. ...

1) Idea vs. Expression Dichotomy

It is a fundamental principle of copyright law that a copyright does not protect an idea, but only the expression of the idea. ...

Drawing the line between idea and expression is a tricky business. Judge Learned Hand noted that "[n]obody has ever been able to fix that boundary, and nobody ever can." *Nichols*, 45 F.2d at 121. Thirty years later his convictions remained firm. "Obviously, no principle can be stated as to when an imitator has gone beyond copying the 'idea,' and has borrowed its 'expression,'" Judge Hand concluded. "Decisions must therefore inevitably be *ad hoc*." *Peter Pan Fabrics, Inc. v. Martin Weiner Corp.*, 274 F.2d 487, 489 (2d Cir.1960). ...

The doctrinal starting point in analyses of utilitarian works, is the seminal case of *Baker v. Selden*, 101 U.S. 99 (1879). ... To the extent that an accounting text and a computer program are both "a set of statements or instructions ... to bring about a certain result," 17 U.S.C. § 101, they are roughly analogous. In the former case, the processes are ultimately conducted by human agency; in the latter, by electronic means. In either case, as already stated, the processes themselves are not protectable.

But the holding in *Baker* goes farther. The Court concluded that those aspects of a work, which "must necessarily be used as incident to" the idea, system or process that the work describes, are also not copyrightable. Selden's ledger sheets, therefore, enjoyed no copyright protection because they were "necessary incidents to" the system of accounting that he described. From this reasoning, we conclude that those elements of a computer program that are necessarily incidental to its function are similarly unprotectable.

While *Baker v. Selden* provides a sound analytical foundation, it offers scant guidance on how to separate idea or process from expression, and moreover, on how to further distinguish protectable expression from that expression which "must necessarily be used as incident to" the work's underlying concept. In the context of computer programs, the Third Circuit's noted decision in Whelan has, thus far, been the most thoughtful attempt to accomplish these ends.

The court in *Whelan* faced substantially the same problem as is presented by this case. There, the defendant was accused of making off with the non-literal structure of the plaintiff's copyrighted dental lab management program, and employing it to create its own competitive version. In assessing whether there had been an infringement, the court had to determine which aspects of the programs involved were ideas, and which were expression. In separating the two, the court settled upon the following conceptual approach:

> [T]he line between idea and expression may be drawn with reference to the end sought to be achieved by the work in question. In other words, *the purpose or function of a utilitarian work would be the work's idea, and everything that is not necessary to that purpose or function would be part of the expression of the idea*.... Where there are various means of achieving the desired purpose, then the particular means chosen is not necessary to the purpose; hence, there is expression, not idea.

797 F.2d at 1236 (citations omitted). The "idea" of the program at issue in *Whelan* was identified by the court as simply "the efficient management of a dental laboratory." *Id*. at n. 28.

So far, in the courts, the *Whelan* rule has received a mixed reception. While some decisions have adopted its reasoning, others have rejected it.

Whelan has fared even more poorly in the academic community, where its standard for distinguishing idea from expression has been widely criticized for being conceptually overbroad. The leading commentator in the field has stated that "[t]he crucial flaw in [*Whelan* 's] reasoning is that it assumes that only one 'idea,' in copyright law terms, underlies any computer program, and that once a separable idea can be identified, everything else must be expression." 3 Nimmer § 13.03(F), at 13-62.34. This criticism focuses not upon the program's ultimate purpose but upon the reality of its structural design. As we have already noted, a computer program's ultimate function or purpose is the composite result of interacting subroutines. Since each subroutine is itself a program, and thus, may be said to have its own "idea," Whelan's general formulation that a program's overall purpose equates with the program's idea is descriptively inadequate.

Accordingly, we think that Judge Pratt wisely declined to follow *Whelan*. In addition to noting the weakness in the *Whelan* definition of "program-idea," mentioned above, Judge Pratt found that *Whelan*'s synonymous use of the terms "structure, sequence, and organization," demonstrated a flawed understanding of a computer program's method of operation. Rightly, the district court found *Whelan*'s rationale suspect because it is so closely tied to what can now be seen—with the passage of time—as the opinion's somewhat outdated appreciation of computer science.

2) Substantial Similarity Test for Computer Program Structure: Abstraction-Filtration-Comparison

We think that *Whelan*'s approach to separating idea from expression in computer programs relies too heavily on metaphysical distinctions and does not place enough emphasis on practical considerations. As the cases that we shall discuss demonstrate, a satisfactory answer to this problem cannot be reached by resorting, a priori, to philosophical first principals [sic].

As discussed herein, we think that district courts would be well-advised to undertake a three-step procedure, based on the abstractions test utilized by the district court, in order to determine whether the non-literal elements of two or more computer programs are substantially similar. This approach breaks no new ground; rather, it draws on such familiar copyright doctrines as merger, *scenes a faire*, and public domain. In taking this approach, however, we are cognizant that computer technology is a dynamic field which can quickly outpace judicial decisionmaking. Thus, in cases where the technology in question does not allow for a literal application of the procedure we outline below, our opinion should not be read to foreclose the district courts of our circuit from utilizing a modified version.

In ascertaining substantial similarity under this approach, a court would first break down the allegedly infringed program into its constituent structural parts. Then, by examining each of these parts for such things as incorporated ideas, expression that is necessarily incidental to those ideas, and elements that are taken from the public domain, a court would then be able to sift out all non-protectable material. Left with a kernel, or possible kernels, of creative expression after following this process of elimination, the court's last step would be to compare this material with the structure of an allegedly infringing program. The result of this comparison will determine whether the protectable elements of the programs at issue are substantially similar so as to warrant a finding of infringement. It will be helpful to elaborate a bit further.

Step One: Abstraction

As the district court appreciated, the theoretic framework for analyzing substantial similarity expounded by Learned Hand in the *Nichols* case is helpful in the present context. In *Nichols*, we enunciated what has now become known as the "abstractions" test for separating idea from expression:

> Upon any work ... a great number of patterns of increasing generality will fit equally well, as more and more of the incident is left out. The last may perhaps be no more than the most general statement of what the [work] is about, and at times might consist only of its title; but there is a point in this series of abstractions where they are no longer protected, since otherwise the [author] could prevent the use of his "ideas," to which, apart from their expression, his property is never extended.

Nichols, 45 F.2d at 121.

While the abstractions test was originally applied in relation to literary works such as novels and plays, it is adaptable to computer programs. In contrast to the Whelan approach, the abstractions test "implicitly recognizes that any given work may consist of a mixture of numerous ideas and expressions." 3 Nimmer § 13.03[F], at 13-62.34-63.

As applied to computer programs, the abstractions test will comprise the first step in the examination for substantial similarity. Initially, in a manner that resembles reverse engineering on a theoretical plane, a court should dissect the allegedly copied program's structure and isolate each level of abstraction contained within it. This process begins with the code and ends with an articulation of the program's ultimate function. Along the way, it is necessary essentially to retrace and map each of the designer's steps—in the opposite order in which they were taken during the program's creation. ...

Step Two: Filtration

Once the program's abstraction levels have been discovered, the substantial similarity inquiry moves from the conceptual to the concrete. Professor Nimmer suggests, and we endorse, a "successive filtering method" for separating protectable expression from non-protectable material. *See generally* 3 Nimmer § 13.03[F]. This process entails examining the structural components at each level of abstraction to determine whether their particular inclusion at that level was "idea" or was dictated by considerations of efficiency, so as to be necessarily incidental to that idea; required by factors external to the program itself; or taken from the public domain and hence is nonprotectable expression. The structure of any given program may reflect some, all, or none of these considerations. Each case requires its own fact specific investigation.

Strictly speaking, this filtration serves "the purpose of defining the scope of plaintiff's copyright." By applying well developed doctrines of copyright law, it may ultimately leave behind a "core of protectable material." 3 Nimmer § 13.03[F][5], at 13-72. Further explication of this second step may be helpful.

(a) Elements Dictated by Efficiency

The portion of *Baker v. Selden*, discussed earlier, which denies copyright protection to expression necessarily incidental to the idea being expressed, appears to be the cornerstone for what has developed into the doctrine of merger. ...

[W]hen one considers the fact that programmers generally strive to create programs "that meet the user's needs in the most efficient manner," Peter S. Menell, *An Analysis of the Scope of Copyright Protection for Application Programs*, 41 STAN. L. REV. 1045, 1052 (1989), the applicability of the merger doctrine to computer programs becomes compelling. In the context of computer program design, the concept of efficiency is akin to deriving the most concise logical proof or formulating the most succinct mathematical computation. Thus, the more efficient a set of modules are, the more closely they approximate the idea or process embodied in that particular aspect of the program's structure.

While, hypothetically, there might be a myriad of ways in which a programmer may effectuate certain functions within a program,—i.e., express the idea embodied in a given subroutine—efficiency concerns may so narrow the practical range of choice as to make only one or two forms of expression workable options. See 3 Nimmer § 13.03[F][2], at 13-63. Of course, not all program structure is informed by efficiency concerns. It follows that in order to determine whether the merger doctrine precludes copyright protection to an aspect of a program's structure that is so oriented, a court must inquire "whether the use of this particular set of modules is necessary efficiently to implement that part of the program's process" being implemented. Steven R. Englund, *Note, Idea, Process, or Protected Expression?: Determining the Scope of Copyright Protection of the Structure of Computer Programs*, 88 MICH. L. REV. 866, 902 (1990). If the answer is yes, then the expression represented by the programmer's choice of a specific module or group of modules has merged with their underlying idea and is unprotected.

Another justification for linking structural economy with the application of the merger doctrine stems from a program's essentially utilitarian nature and the competitive forces that exist in the software marketplace. Working in tandem, these factors give rise to a problem of proof which merger helps to eliminate.

Efficiency is an industry-wide goal. Since, as we have already noted, there may be only a limited number of efficient implementations for any given program task, it is quite possible that multiple programmers, working independently, will design the identical method employed in the allegedly infringed work. Of course, if this is the case, there is no copyright infringement.

Under these circumstances, the fact that two programs contain the same efficient structure may as likely lead to an inference of independent creation as it does to one of copying. Thus, since evidence of similarly efficient structure is not particularly probative of copying, it should be disregarded in the overall substantial similarity analysis. ...

(b) Elements Dictated By External Factors

We have stated that where "it is virtually impossible to write about a particular historical era or fictional theme without employing certain 'stock' or standard literary devices," such expression is not copyrightable. *Hoehling v. Universal City Studios, Inc.*, 618 F.2d 972, 979 (2d Cir. 1980). For example, the *Hoehling* case was an infringement suit stemming from several works on the Hindenberg disaster. There we concluded that similarities in representations of German beer halls, scenes depicting German greetings such as "Heil Hitler," or the singing of certain German songs would not lead to a finding of infringement because they were " 'indispensable, or at least standard, in the treatment of' " life in Nazi Germany. This is known as the *scenes a faire* doctrine, and like "merger," it has its analogous application to computer programs.

Professor Nimmer points out that "in many instances it is virtually impossible to write a program to perform particular functions in a specific computing environment without employing standard techniques." 3 Nimmer § 13.03[F][3], at 13-65. This is a result of the fact that a programmer's freedom of design choice is often circumscribed by extrinsic considerations such as (1) the mechanical specifications of the computer on which a particular program is intended to run; (2) compatibility requirements of other programs with which a program is designed to operate in conjunction; (3) computer manufacturers' design standards; (4) demands of the industry being serviced; and (5) widely accepted programming practices within the computer industry. *Id.* at 13-66-71. ...

[W]e conclude that a court must also examine the structural content of an allegedly infringed program for elements that might have been dictated by external factors.

(c) Elements taken From the Public Domain

Closely related to the non-protectability of *scenes a faire*, is material found in the public domain. Such material is free for the taking and cannot be appropriated by a single author even though it is included in a copyrighted work. We see no reason to make an exception to this rule for elements of a computer program that have entered the public domain by virtue of freely accessible program exchanges and the like. *See* 3 Nimmer § 13.03[F][4]. Thus, a court must also filter out this material from the allegedly infringed program before it makes the final inquiry in its substantial similarity analysis.

Step Three: Comparison

The third and final step of the test for substantial similarity that we believe appropriate for non-literal program components entails a comparison. Once a court has sifted out all elements of the allegedly infringed program which are "ideas" or are dictated by efficiency or external factors, or taken from the public domain, there may remain a core of protectable expression. In terms of a work's copyright value, this is the golden nugget. At this point, the court's substantial similarity inquiry focuses on whether the defendant copied any aspect of this protected expression, as well as an assessment of the copied portion's relative importance with respect to the plaintiff's overall program.

3) Policy Considerations

We are satisfied that the three step approach we have just outlined not only comports with, but advances the constitutional policies underlying the Copyright Act. Since any method that tries to distinguish idea from expression ultimately impacts on the scope of copyright protection afforded to a particular type of work, "the line [it draws] must be a pragmatic one, which also keeps in consideration 'the preservation of the balance between competition and protection....'" *Apple Computer, Inc. v. Franklin Computer Corp.*, 714 F.2d 1240, 1253 (3d Cir. 1983) (citation omitted).

CA and some *amici* argue against the type of approach that we have set forth on the grounds that it will be a disincentive for future computer program research and development. At bottom, they claim that if programmers are not guaranteed broad copyright protection for their work, they will not invest the extensive time, energy and funds required to design and improve program structures. While they have a point, their argument cannot carry the day. The interest of the copyright law is not in simply conferring a monopoly on industrious persons, but in advancing the public welfare through rewarding artistic creativity, in a manner that permits the free use and development of non-protectable ideas and processes. ...

B. The District Court Decision

We turn now to our review of the district court's decision in this particular case. ...

The district court had to determine whether Altai's OSCAR 3.5 program was substantially similar to CA's ADAPTER. ... [W]e agree with Judge Pratt's systematic exclusion of non-protectable expression. With respect to code, the district court observed that after the rewrite of OSCAR 3.4 to OSCAR 3.5, "there remained virtually no lines of code that were identical to ADAPTER." Accordingly, the court found that the code "present[ed] no similarity at all."

Next, Judge Pratt addressed the issue of similarity between the two programs' parameter lists and macros. He concluded that, viewing the conflicting evidence most favorably to CA, it demonstrated that "only a few of the lists and macros were similar to protected elements in ADAPTER; the others were either in the public domain or dictated by the functional demands of the program." As discussed above, functional elements and elements taken from the public domain do not qualify for copyright protection. With respect to the few remaining parameter lists and macros, the district court could reasonably conclude that they did not warrant a finding of infringement given their relative contribution to the overall program. In any event, the district court reasonably found that, for lack of persuasive evidence, CA failed to meet its burden of proof on whether the macros and parameter lists at issue were substantially similar.

The district court also found that the overlap exhibited between the list of services required for both ADAPTER and OSCAR 3.5 was "determined by the demands of the operating system and of the applications program to which it [was] to be linked through ADAPTER or OSCAR...." In other words, this aspect of the program's structure was dictated by the nature of other programs with which it was designed to interact and, thus, is not protected by copyright.

Finally, in his infringement analysis, Judge Pratt accorded no weight to the similarities between the two programs' organizational charts, "because [the charts were] so simple and obvious to anyone exposed to the operation of the program[s]." CA argues that the district court's action in this regard "is not consistent with copyright law"—that "obvious" expression is protected, and that the district court erroneously failed to realize this. However, to say that elements of a work are "obvious," in the manner in which the district court used the word, is to say that they "follow naturally from the work's theme rather than from the author's creativity." 3 Nimmer § 13.03 [F][3], at 13-65. This is but one formulation of the *scenes a faire* doctrine, which we have already endorsed as a means of weeding out unprotectable expression. ...

Since we accept Judge Pratt's factual conclusions and the results of his legal analysis[we affirm his denial of CA's copyright infringement claim based upon OSCAR 3.5.] We emphasize that, like all copyright infringement cases, those that involve computer programs are highly fact specific. The amount of protection due structural elements, in any given case, will vary according to the protectable expression found to exist within the program at issue.

[The court's discussion of trade secrets is omitted.]

CONCLUSION

In adopting the above three step analysis for substantial similarity between the non-literal elements of computer programs, we seek to insure two things: (1) that programmers may receive appropriate copyright protection for innovative utilitarian works containing expression; and (2) that non-protectable technical expression remains in the public domain for others to use freely as building blocks in their own work. At first blush, it may seem counter-intuitive that someone who has benefitted to some degree from illicitly obtained material can emerge from an infringement suit relatively unscathed. However, so long as the appropriated material consists of non-protectable expression, "[t]his result is neither unfair nor unfortunate. It is the means by which copyright advances the progress of science and art." *Feist*, 499 U.S. at 350. ...

Accordingly, we affirm the judgment of the district court in part; vacate in part; and remand for further proceedings. The parties shall bear their own costs of appeal, including the petition for rehearing.

[The opinion of Altimari, Circuit Judge, concurring in part and dissenting in part, is omitted.]

Notes and Questions

1.   Given all of the theoretical support placed behind the ordinary and intended observer tests in cases like *Arnstein* and *Dawson*, why didn't the *Altai* court apply one of those tests? A possible virtue of the ordinary observer test is its potential solution to the problem of how sensitive courts should be to similarities and differences between two works. Judges need not struggle to define a universal definition of infringing similarity that brings consistent and appropriate results to all cases. Instead, they can consult the values of the ordinary observer, whose sensitivities are not defined by law but by whatever ordinary people happen to think in the "real world." If ordinary people wind up having inconsistent or unexplainable tastes, then so be it. If, in at least some cases, a detailed, formal analysis of the type used in *Altai* is superior to the ordinary observer test, would it be a good idea to use the *Altai* test in all infringement cases? Have you read other improper appropriation cases that employ an approach similar to *Altai*'s?

2.   Do you think the court reached the correct result? Remember that a rationale behind ordinary observer test was the desire to protect the market for the plaintiff's work created by the taste of the buying public (i.e. the ordinary observer). If people buy software because it performs a particular function, shouldn't copyright protect the appeal of the software—namely its function? If so, how would that rationale have affected *Altai*?

3.   *Altai* discusses another case, *Whelan v. Jaslow Dental Labs*, that had similar facts but reached a different, relatively pro-plaintiff result in large part because the Third Circuit did not apply the idea/expression dichotomy as aggressively as the *Altai* court did. Although *Whelan* was for a time the leading case in copyright infringement of computer code, *Altai*'s approach has now gained the upper hand.

Much of *Altai* rests on the court's understanding of computer software, namely that the chosen function of software practically dictates various aspects of the computer code. This limits the range of expression from which a programmer may choose, making merger applicable. Do you agree with this conclusion? You may not be a computer programmer, but consider even simple sets of instructions, such as baking recipes, with which you may be more familiar. If you were writing out such a rec-ipe, how many different ways of effectively expressing the underlying idea (such as a chocolate cake) would there be? Would there be enough to avoid application of the merger doctrine, and if so, to what extent? Now consider what happens as sets of instructions get more and more elabo-rate. What if the instructions were for building a house? A skyscraper? At some point these instructions would become similarly complicated to those found in a piece of software. Imagine the choices available to a per-son writing a word processing program. Should merger limit the scope of copyright in these instructions, and if so, how much?

4. In both *Altai* and *Lotus v. Borland* in Chapter Two, *supra*, the courts noted that software does not fit neatly into existing copyright cat-egories, in light of its strong functional nature. When Congress decided to bring software within the scope of copyright as a literary work, it an-ticipated that the courts would adapt existing copyright doctrines to the special case of software, and the *Altai* case is an example of this kind of judicial adaptation. In particular, the court in *Altai* was careful to make sure that copyright did not lock up important functional aspects of com-puter software.

As a result of the *Altai* test, copyright law appears to provide rela-tively thin protection for non-literal elements of software. Is this prob-lematic? After all, useful and functional aspects of computer software design may require significant investment, and without some protection against copying, there may be insufficient incentives to engage in this kind of effort. The *Altai* court acknowledges this possibility, but never-theless suggests that such concerns are outside the scope of copyright law.

If you think that it is important to protect the useful and functional aspects of software, remember that these things may be entitled to pro-tection under patent law, which is expressly designed to provide protec-tion for useful inventions. In theory, the scope of patent protection re-flects some kind of judgment about the amount of intellectual property protection given to useful inventions. If this is true, is it socially benefi-cial for copyright to protect software in ways that patent does not?

3. COPYING AND SOUND RECORDINGS

Our examination of infringement has shown that a copyright hold-er's § 106(1) right of reproduction includes the ability to recover from some defendants whose work resembles, but does not duplicate, the cop-yrighted work of the plaintiff. While this is true for most copyrighted works, it is not true for one specific subset of works: sound recordings. Sound recordings are defined as "works that result from the fixation of a series of musical, spoken, or other sounds." 17 U.S.C. § 101. Sound re-cordings are often made of musical works (i.e. the tune and lyrics of a song), but are separately copyrightable, based on the particular performance fixed in that particular recording.

So, for example, a digital MP3 file of a particular piece of recorded music is protected by multiple underlying copyrights. First, there is a copyright in the underlying musical work, i.e. the melody and lyrics, which may be owned by a particular songwriter. Second, there is a copyright in the sound recording, i.e. the particular performance of the musical work fixed in the digital file, which may be owned by the performer or the record company.

Congress added sound recordings to the list of works protected under federal copyright in 1972, and in doing so, limited the scope of the copyright in several ways.[46] Section 114(b) of the Copyright Act limits copyright in a sound recording to "the right to duplicate the sound recording in the form of phonorecords or copies that directly or indirectly recapture the actual sounds fixed in the recording." This means that a recording artist cannot stop others from recording the same music and imitating his performances. Infringement occurs only when a defendant mechanically reproduces the actual sounds found in a recording. It is perfectly legal to imitate slavishly the recordings of others, as long as one has permission to record the underlying musical composition.[47]

If infringement of sound recordings occurs only when the defendant duplicates the actual sounds fixed in the recording, how should courts analyze cases in which the defendant duplicates only a portion of a recording? Should courts consider whether the defendant's borrowing rises to the level of improper appropriation, or does any reproduction of a sound recording constitute infringement? These issues are most clearly raised in the context of digital sampling.

In *Bridgeport Music v. Dimension Films*, 410 F.3d 792 (6th Cir. 2005), the U.S. Court of Appeals for the Sixth Circuit held that the use of a two-second sample from existing sound recording infringed on the copyright in the underlying sound recording. In *Bridgeport*, the hip hop group NWA recorded a rap song "100 Miles and Runnin," which took a two-second sample of a three-note guitar riff from a sound recording of the song "Get Off Your Ass and Jam," by George Clinton, Jr. and the Funkadelics. NWA lowered the pitch of the sample, "looped" (i.e. repeated) the sample to increase its length to seven seconds, and used the sample in five different places in its own sound recording. The trial court, after listening to the two songs, found that no reasonable juror, even one familiar with the works of George Clinton, would have recognized that the sample came from the original sound recording, and therefore held that the use was *de minimis* and noninfringing.

On appeal, the Sixth Circuit reversed, holding that the *de minimis* doctrine did not apply to digital sampling of sound recordings. In reach-

---

[46] Prior to 1972, sound recordings were protected, if at all, under state common law copyright.

[47] As we shall see *infra*, sound recordings also lack a general public performance right.

ing this result, the court contrasted prior caselaw, which had found that a short sample of a *musical work* (as opposed to a *sound recording*) could be *de minimis*. For example, in *Newton v. Diamond*, 388 F.3d. 1189 (9th Cir. 2004), the Ninth Circuit held that a three note digital sample of a sound recording did not infringe the copyright in the underlying *musical composition* because the taking was *de minimis*. In that case, the defendants had secured a license from the owner of the copyright in the sound recording, so the only issue was whether the sample infringed upon the underlying musical work. The court in that case held that it did not.

The court of appeals in *Bridgeport* held that sound recordings, unlike musical works, were not subject to the *de minimis* doctrine because the sound recording copyright was limited to the actual fixed sounds in the recording itself. The court read this limited right to imply a greater ability to prevent any literal uses of the fixed sounds. The court rejected concerns about the affect of its decision on subsequent creativity, since those who wished to use the sample could either seek a license or re-record the underlying musical work sample, and thus avoid liability. Finally, the court believed that the virtues of a bright line rule outweighed any potential downsides. (Note that the court did not address whether the use could have been subject to the fair use defense, as that issue was not before it).

Notes and Questions

1. You can hear clips of the original sound recording and the sample at issue in *Bridgeport* at:

http://mcir.usc.edu/cases/2000-2009/Pages/bridgeportdimension.html

Upon listening to the clips, do you agree with the district court that no reasonable juror, even one familiar with the work of George Clinton, would recognize the sample? If the sample is unrecognizable, what is the justification for calling it infringement, particularly on a bright line basis? You may recall that courts supported the audience test for infringing similarity because it prevented erosion of the market for a copyrighted work. If the *Bridgeport* sample is unrecognizable, its effect on the market for the plaintiff's work must be small to nonexistent. Can you articulate an understanding of infringement unrelated to the market for the plaintiff's work?

2. As noted above, copyright in sound recordings extends only to "the right to duplicate the sound recording in the form of phonorecords or copies that directly or indirectly recapture the actual sounds fixed in the recording." Are there good reasons to give those who create sound recordings fewer rights than most other copyright holders?

3. The caselaw currently appears to treat digital sampling of sound recordings differently from digital sampling of the underlying musical work. Does this different treatment make sense from a policy perspective? Are you persuaded by the rationale in *Bridgeport*? How do the above rules affect the behavior of artists who are interested in sampling a pre-existing work? If you represented an artist who wanted to sample, how would you advise her to proceed?

4. More broadly, to what extent should artists be permitted to sample pre-existing copyrighted works (whether sound recordings or musical works) without permission in creating their own works? Many genres of music rely heavily upon such sampling. The cases above involve short three-second samples, which may or many not be *de minimis*. What about more extensive sampling? For example, what about a longer 6-second sample that is clearly recognizable as deriving from a pre-existing work? Should the new artist have to get permission from the prior artist?

SECTION B. DERIVATIVE WORKS

Section 106(2) of the Copyright Act grants the copyright holder the exclusive right "to prepare derivative works based upon the copyrighted work." Section 101 of the Act in turn defines "derivative work" as:

> a work based upon one or more preexisting works, such as a translation, musical arrangement, dramatization, fictionalization, motion picture version, sound recording, art reproduction, abridgment, condensation, or any other form in which a work may be recast, transformed, or adapted. A work consisting of editorial revisions, annotations, elaborations, or other modifications which, as a whole, represent an original work of authorship, is a "derivative work".

The core of this right is familiar. If someone wants to make a movie from a copyrighted book or adapt a copyrighted song, he will need the copyright holder's permission to do so.

Although the derivative work right is quite familiar, it is important to note that it is not an inevitable part of the Copyright Act. Indeed, earlier versions of the Copyright Act did not give authors an exclusive right to prepare derivative works. For example, in *Stowe v. Thomas*, 23 F. Cas. 201 (C.C.E.D. Pa. 1853) a court held that a German translation of Harriet Beecher Stowe's *Uncle Tom's Cabin* did not infringe upon Stowe's copyright.

Later Copyright Acts, however, expanded the scope of copyright to include derivative works. Thus, the author of a book, for example the first *Harry Potter* book, receives not only the right to prevent unauthorized reproductions of that particular book, but also the right to control sequels, movies based on the book, action figures, board games, and other licensing opportunities. Indeed, for some works, the derivative work right may be worth far more than the initial right to control reproductions of the original work.

Why does copyright law grant authors the right to control derivative works? On the one hand, the right to control derivative works may provide additional incentive to create the work in the first place (for example, when an author writes a novel with the hope that it may be turned into a movie). The derivative work right may also represent recognition of the author's labor in creating the initial work. A derivative work right may also permit the author to create and/or authorize later works in an orderly fashion, rather than rushing to create such works in the absence of an exclusive right. Thus there are many reasons why copyright law might grant such a right to the author.

At the same time, the derivative work right does have the effect of limiting the ability of third parties who might want to build upon existing works to create their own new works (for example, their own version of the *Harry Potter* story). In addition, the derivative work right may give the original author the ability to control subsequent uses of the work that may be critical of that work, or involve interpretations with which the author disagrees. Thus, the derivative work right may have the effect of reducing the incentives of others to engage in creative work.

Although the concept of a derivative work right is relatively straightforward, difficulties arise because the definition of derivative work is extremely broad, arguably including any work that builds upon, improves, or refers to an existing copyrighted work. Magazine articles about popular movies, books containing answers to problems in high school math textbooks, and software written for particular operating systems are all "based upon one or more preexisting works." This Section explores the extent to which those who create these works should worry about copyright infringement.

Lewis Galoob Toys v. Nintendo of America
964 F.2d 965 (9th Cir. 1992)

FARRIS, Circuit Judge:

Nintendo of America appeals the district court's judgment following a bench trial (1) declaring that Lewis Galoob Toys' Game Genie does not violate any Nintendo copyrights and dissolving a temporary injunction and (2) denying Nintendo's request for a permanent injunction enjoining Galoob from marketing the Game Genie. ... We affirm.

FACTS

The Nintendo Entertainment System is a home video game system marketed by Nintendo. To use the system, the player inserts a cartridge containing a video game that Nintendo produces or licenses others to produce. By pressing buttons and manipulating a control pad, the player controls one of the game's characters and progresses through the game. The games are protected as audiovisual works under 17 U.S.C. § 102(a)(6).

The Game Genie is a device manufactured by Galoob that allows the player to alter up to three features of a Nintendo game. For example, the Game Genie can increase the number of lives of the player's character, increase the speed at which the character moves, and allow the character to float above obstacles. The player controls the changes made by the Game Genie by entering codes provided by the Game Genie Programming Manual and Code Book. The player also can experiment with variations of these codes.

The Game Genie functions by blocking the value for a single data byte sent by the game cartridge to the central processing unit in the Nintendo Entertainment System and replacing it with a new value. If that value controls the character's strength, for example, then the character can be made invincible by increasing the value sufficiently. The Game Genie is inserted between a game cartridge and the Nintendo Entertainment System. The Game Genie does not alter the data that is stored in the game cartridge. Its effects are temporary.

DISCUSSION

1. Derivative work

The Copyright Act of 1976 confers upon copyright holders the exclusive right to prepare and authorize others to prepare derivative works based on their copyrighted works. Nintendo argues that the district court erred in concluding that the audiovisual displays created by the Game Genie are not derivative works. The court's conclusions of law are reviewed *de novo*. Its findings of fact are reviewed for clear error.

A derivative work must incorporate a protected work in some concrete or permanent "form." The Copyright Act defines a derivative work as follows:

> A "derivative work" is a work based upon one or more preexisting works, such as a translation, musical arrangement, dramatization, fictionalization, motion picture version, sound recording, art reproduction, abridgment, condensation, *or any other form in which a work may be recast, transformed, or adapted.* A work consisting of editorial revisions, annotations, elaborations, or other modifications which, as a whole, represent an original work of authorship, is a "derivative work."

17 U.S.C. § 101 (emphasis added). The examples of derivative works provided by the Act all physically incorporate the underlying work or works. The Act's legislative history similarly indicates that "the infringing work must incorporate a portion of the copyrighted work in some form." 1976 U.S. Code Cong. & Admin. News 5659, 5675.

Our analysis is not controlled by the Copyright Act's definition of "fixed." The Act defines copies as "material objects, other than phonorecords, in which a work is *fixed* by any method." 17 U.S.C. § 101 (emphasis added). The Act's definition of "derivative work," in contrast, lacks any such reference to fixation. Further, we have held in a copyright infringement action that "[I]t makes no difference that the derivation may not satisfy certain requirements for statutory copyright registration itself." *Lone Ranger Television v. Program Radio Corp.*, 740 F.2d 718, 722 (9th Cir. 1984). A derivative work must be fixed to be *protected* under the Act, *see* 17 U.S.C. § 102(a), but not to *infringe*.

The argument that a derivative work must be fixed because "[a] 'derivative work' is a work," 17 U.S.C. § 101, and "[a] work is 'created' when it is fixed in a copy or phonorecord for the first time," *id.*, relies on a misapplication of the Copyright Act's definition of "created":

A work is "created" when it is fixed in a copy or phonorecord for the first time; where a work is prepared over a period of time, the portion of it that has been fixed at any particular time constitutes the work as of that time, and where the work has been prepared in different versions, each version constitutes a separate work.

Id. The definition clarifies the time at which a work is created. If the provision were a definition of "work," it would not use that term in such a casual manner. The Act does not contain a definition of "work." Rather, it contains specific definitions: "audiovisual works," "literary works," and "pictorial, graphic and sculptural works," for example. The definition of "derivative work" does not require fixation.

The district court's finding that no independent work is created is supported by the record. The Game Genie merely enhances the audiovisual displays (or underlying data bytes) that originate in Nintendo game cartridges. The altered displays do not incorporate a portion of a copyrighted work in some concrete or permanent form. Nintendo argues that the Game Genie's displays are as fixed in the hardware and software used to create them as Nintendo's original displays. Nintendo's argument ignores the fact that the Game Genie cannot produce an audiovisual display; the underlying display must be produced by a Nintendo Entertainment System and game cartridge. Even if we were to rely on the Copyright Act's definition of "fixed," we would similarly conclude that the resulting display is not "embodied," in the Game Genie. It cannot be a derivative work. ...

Nintendo asserted at oral argument that the existence of a $150 million market for the Game Genie indicates that its audiovisual display must be fixed. We understand Nintendo's argument; consumers clearly would not purchase the Game Genie if its display was not "sufficiently permanent or stable to permit it to be perceived ... for a period of more than transitory duration." 17 U.S.C. § 101. But, Nintendo's reliance on the Act's definition of "fixed" is misplaced. Nintendo's argument also proves too much; the existence of a market does not, and cannot, determine conclusively whether a work is an infringing derivative work. For example, although there is a market for kaleidoscopes, it does not necessarily follow that kaleidoscopes create unlawful derivative works when pointed at protected artwork. The same can be said of countless other products that enhance, but do not replace, copyrighted works.

Nintendo also argues that our analysis should focus exclusively on the audiovisual displays created by the Game Genie, i.e., that we should compare the altered displays to Nintendo's original displays. Nintendo emphasizes that " '[a]udiovisual works' are works that consist of a series of related images ... *regardless of the nature of the material objects ... in which the works are embodied.*" 17 U.S.C. § 101 (emphasis added). The Copyright Act's definition of "audiovisual works" is inapposite; the only question before us is whether the audiovisual displays created by the Game Genie are "derivative works." The Act does not similarly provide that a work can be a derivative work regardless of the nature of the material objects in which the work is embodied. A derivative work must incorporate a protected work in some concrete or permanent form. We cannot ignore the actual source of the Game Genie's display.

Nintendo relies heavily on *Midway Mfg. Co. v. Artic Int'l, Inc.*, 704 F.2d 1009 (7th Cir. 1983). *Midway* can be distinguished. The defendant in *Midway*, Artic International, marketed a computer chip that could be inserted in Galaxian video games to speed up the rate of play. The Seventh Circuit held that the speeded-up version of Galaxian was a derivative work. Artic's chip substantially copied and replaced the chip that was originally distributed by Midway. Purchasers of Artic's chip also benefited economically by offering the altered game for use by the general public. The Game Genie does not physically incorporate a portion of a copyrighted work, nor does it supplant demand for a component of that work. The court in *Midway* acknowledged that the Copyright Act's definition of "derivative work" "must be stretched to accommodate speeded-up video games." *Id.* at 1014. Stretching that definition further would chill innovation and fail to protect "society's competing interest in the free flow of ideas, information, and commerce." *Sony Corp. of America v. Universal Studios, Inc.*, 464 U.S. 417, 429 (1984).

In holding that the audiovisual displays created by the Game Genie are not derivative works, we recognize that technology often advances by improvement rather than replacement. Some time ago, for example, computer companies began marketing spell-checkers that operate within existing word processors by signalling [sic] the writer when a word is misspelled. These applications, as well as countless others, could not be produced and marketed if courts were to conclude that the word processor and spell-checker combination is a derivative work based on the word processor alone. The Game Genie is useless by itself, it can only enhance, and cannot duplicate or recast, a Nintendo game's output. It does not contain or produce a Nintendo game's output in some concrete or permanent form, nor does it supplant demand for Nintendo game cartridges.

Such innovations rarely will constitute infringing derivative works under the Copyright Act.⌋

[The court's discussion of fair use is omitted.]

3. Temporary and permanent injunction

Galoob has not violated the Copyright Act. Nintendo therefore is not entitled to a temporary or permanent injunction.

AFFIRMED.

Micro Star v. Formgen
154 F.3d 1107 (9th Cir. 1998)

KOZINSKI, Circuit Judge.

Duke Nukem routinely vanquishes Octabrain and the Protozoid Slimer. But what about the dreaded Micro Star?

I

FormGen Inc., GT Interactive Software Corp. and Apogee Software, Ltd. (collectively FormGen) made, distributed and own the rights to Duke Nukem 3D (D/N-3D), an immensely popular (and very cool) computer game. D/N-3D is played from the first-person perspective; the player assumes the personality and point of view of the title character, who is seen on the screen only as a pair of hands and an occasional boot, much as one might see oneself in real life without the aid of a mirror. Players explore a futuristic city infested with evil aliens and other hazards. The goal is to zap them before they zap you, while searching for the hidden passage to the next level. The basic game comes with twenty-nine levels, each with a different combination of scenery, aliens, and other challenges. The game also includes a "Build Editor," a utility that enables players to create their own levels. With FormGen's encouragement, players frequently post levels they have created on the Internet where others can download them. Micro Star, a computer software distributor, did just that: It downloaded 300 user-created levels and stamped them onto a CD, which it then sold commercially as Nuke It (N/I). N/I is packaged in a box decorated with numerous "screen shots," pictures of what the new levels look like when played.

Micro Star filed suit in district court, seeking a declaratory judgment that N/I did not infringe on any of FormGen's copyrights. FormGen counterclaimed, seeking a preliminary injunction barring further production and distribution of N/I. Relying on *Lewis Galoob Toys, Inc. v. Nintendo of Am., Inc.*, 964 F.2d 965 (9th Cir. 1992), the district court held that N/I was not a derivative work and therefore did not infringe FormGen's copyright. The district court did, however, grant a preliminary injunction as to the screen shots, finding that N/I's packaging violated FormGen's copyright by reproducing pictures of D/N-3D characters without a license. The court rejected Micro Star's fair use claims. Both sides appeal their losses.

II

[Discussion of the standard for preliminary injunctive relief is omitted.]

III

... FormGen alleges that its copyright is infringed by Micro Star's unauthorized commercial exploitation of user-created game levels. In order to understand FormGen's claims, one must first understand the way D/N-3D works. The game consists of three separate components: the game engine, the source art library and the MAP files. The game engine is the heart of the computer program; in some sense, it is the program. It tells the computer when to read data, save and load games, play sounds and project images onto the screen. In order to create the audiovisual display for a particular level, the game engine invokes the MAP file that corresponds to that level. Each MAP file contains a series of instructions that tell the game engine (and, through it, the computer) what to put where. For instance, the MAP file might say scuba gear goes at the bottom of the screen. The game engine then goes to the source art library, finds the image of the scuba gear, and puts it in just the right place on the screen. The MAP file describes the level in painstaking detail, but it does not actually contain any of the copyrighted art itself; everything that appears on the screen actually comes from the art library. Think of the game's audiovisual display as a paint-by-numbers kit. The MAP file might tell you to put blue paint in section number 565, but it doesn't contain any blue paint itself; the blue paint comes from your palette, which is the low-tech analog of the art library, while you play the role of the game engine. When the player selects one of the N/I levels, the game engine references the N/I MAP files, but still uses the D/N-3D art library to generate the images that make up that level.

FormGen points out that a copyright holder enjoys the exclusive right to prepare derivative works based on D/N-3D. According to FormGen, the audiovisual displays generated when D/N-3D is run in conjunction with the N/I CD MAP files are derivative works that infringe this exclusivity. Is FormGen right? The answer is not obvious.

The Copyright Act defines a derivative work as

> a work based upon one or more preexisting works, such as a translation, musical arrangement, dramatization, fictionalization, motion picture version, sound recording, art reproduction, abridgment, condensation, or any other form in which a work may be recast, transformed, or adapted. A work consisting of editorial revisions, annotations, elaborations, or other modifications which, as a whole, represent an original work of authorship, is a "derivative work."

The statutory language is hopelessly overbroad, however, for "[e]very book in literature, science and art, borrows and must necessarily borrow, and use much which was well known and used before." *Emerson v. Davies*, 8 F. Cas. 615, 619 (C.C.D. Mass. 1845) (No. 4436), quoted in 1 Nimmer on Copyright, § 3.01, at 3-2 (1997). To narrow the statute to a manageable level, we have developed certain criteria a work must satisfy in order to qualify as a derivative work. One of these is that a derivative work must exist in a "concrete or permanent form," *Galoob*, 964 F.2d at 967 (internal quotation marks omitted), and must substantially incorporate protected material from the preexisting work. Micro Star argues that N/I is not a derivative work because the audiovisual displays generated when D/N-3D is run with N/I's MAP files are not incorporated in any concrete or permanent form, and the MAP files do not copy any of D/N-3D's protected expression. It is mistaken on both counts.

[The requirement that a derivative work must assume a concrete or permanent form was recognized without much discussion in *Galoob*.] There, we noted that all the Copyright Act's examples of derivative works took some definite, physical form and concluded that this was a requirement of the Act. ... But what about the audiovisual displays generated when D/N-3D runs the N/I MAP files—i.e., the actual game level as displayed on the screen? Micro Star argues that, because the audiovisual displays in *Galoob* didn't meet the "concrete or permanent form" requirement, neither do N/I's.

In *Galoob*, we considered audiovisual displays created using a device called the Game Genie, which was sold for use with the Nintendo Entertainment System. The Game Genie allowed players to alter individual features of a game, such as a character's strength or speed, by selectively "blocking the value for a single data byte sent by the game cartridge to the [Nintendo console] and replacing it with a new value." *Galoob*, 964 F.2d at 967. Players chose which data value to replace by entering a code; over a billion different codes were possible. The Game Genie was dumb; it functioned only as a window into the computer program, allowing players to temporarily modify individual aspects of the game.

Nintendo sued, claiming that when the Game Genie modified the game system's audiovisual display, it created an infringing derivative work. We rejected this claim because "[a] derivative work must incorporate a protected work in some concrete or permanent form." *Galoob*, 964 F.2d at 967 (internal quotation marks omitted). The audiovisual displays generated by combining the Nintendo System with the Game Genie were not incorporated in any permanent form; when the game was over, they were gone. Of course, they could be reconstructed, but only if the next player chose to reenter the same codes.

Micro Star argues that the MAP files on N/I are a more advanced version of the Game Genie, replacing old values (the MAP files in the original game) with new values (N/I's MAP files). But, whereas the audiovisual displays created by Game Genie were never recorded in any permanent form, the audiovisual displays generated by D/N-3D from the

N/I MAP files are in the MAP files themselves. In *Galoob*, the audiovisual display was defined by the original game cartridge, not by the Game Genie; no one could possibly say that the data values inserted by the Game Genie described the audiovisual display. In the present case the audiovisual display that appears on the computer monitor when a N/I level is played is described-in exact detail-by a N/I MAP file.

This raises the interesting question whether an exact, down to the last detail, description of an audiovisual display (and—by definition—we know that MAP files do describe audiovisual displays down to the last detail) counts as a permanent or concrete form for purposes of *Galoob*. We see no reason it shouldn't. What, after all, does sheet music do but describe in precise detail the way a copyrighted melody sounds? To be copyrighted, pantomimes and dances may be "described in sufficient detail to enable the work to be performed from that description." *Id.* at 243 (citing Compendium II of Copyright Office Practices § 463); *see also Horgan v. Macmillan, Inc.*, 789 F.2d 157, 160 (2d Cir. 1986). Similarly, the N/I MAP files describe the audiovisual display that is to be generated when the player chooses to play D/N-3D using the N/I levels. Because the audiovisual displays assume a concrete or permanent form in the MAP files, *Galoob* stands as no bar to finding that they are derivative works.

In addition, "[a] work will be considered a derivative work only if it would be considered an infringing work if the material which it has derived from a preexisting work had been taken without the consent of a copyright proprietor of such preexisting work." *Mirage Editions v. Albuquerque A.R.T. Co.*, 856 F.2d 1341, 1343 (quoting 1 Nimmer on Copyright § 3.01 (1986)) (internal quotation marks omitted). "To prove infringement, [FormGen] must show that [D/N-3D's and N/I's audiovisual displays] are substantially similar in both ideas and expression." *Litchfield v. Spielberg*, 736 F.2d 1352, 1356 (9th Cir. 1984) (emphasis omitted). Similarity of ideas may be shown by comparing the objective details of the works: plot, theme, dialogue, mood, setting, characters, etc. Similarity of expression focuses on the response of the ordinary reasonable person, and considers the total concept and feel of the works. FormGen will doubtless succeed in making these showings since the audiovisual displays generated when the player chooses the N/I levels come entirely out of D/N-3D's source art library.

Micro Star further argues that the MAP files are not derivative works because they do not, in fact, incorporate any of D/N-3D's protected expression. In particular, Micro Star makes much of the fact that the N/I MAP files reference the source art library, but do not actually contain any art files themselves. Therefore, it claims, nothing of D/N-3D's is reproduced in the MAP files. In making this argument, Micro Star misconstrues the protected work. The work that Micro Star infringes is the D/N-3D story itself—a beefy commando type named Duke who wanders around post-Apocalypse Los Angeles, shooting Pig Cops with a gun, lobbing hand grenades, searching for medkits and steroids, using a jetpack to leap over obstacles, blowing up gas tanks, avoiding radioactive slime. A copyright owner holds the right to create sequels, and the stories told in the N/I MAP files are surely sequels, telling new (though somewhat repetitive) tales of Duke's fabulous adventures. A book about Duke Nukem would infringe for the same reason, even if it contained no pictures.

[The court's discussion of fair use is omitted.]

IV

Because FormGen will likely succeed at trial in proving that Micro Star has infringed its copyright, we reverse the district court's order denying a preliminary injunction and remand for entry of such an injunction. Of course, we affirm the grant of the preliminary injunction barring Micro Star from selling N/I in boxes covered with screen shots of the game.

AFFIRMED in part, REVERSED in part, and REMANDED. Micro Star to bear costs of both appeals.

Notes and Questions

1. *Micro Star*'s facts bear considerable resemblance to *Galoob*'s, and Judge Kozinski spends a lot of time distinguishing the two cases. Did he convince you, or do you find *Micro Star* and *Galoob* fundamentally inconsistent?

2. *Micro Star* candidly admits that the language of the Copyright Act permits an overly-broad construction of infringing derivative works, and it identifies two limits that prevent this from happening, the requirement that a derivative work must incorporate a protected work in some concrete or permanent form, and the requirement that the material so incorporated be taken without permission of the copyright holder. Do those limits work?

3. FormGen apparently encouraged users of Duke Nukem to create their own MAP files and post them on the Internet for others to enjoy. Did these users commit infringement? If not, how did FormGen become liable simply for selling MAP files created with FormGen's consent?

4. *Galoob* expresses concern about the consequences of finding against the defendant:

> In holding that the audiovisual displays created by the Game Genie are not derivative works, we recognize that technology often advances by improvement rather than replacement. Some time ago, for example, computer companies began marketing spell-checkers that operate within existing word processors by signalling [sic] the writer when a word is misspelled. These ap-

plications, as well as countless others, could not be produced and marketed if courts were to conclude that the word processor and spell-checker combination is a derivative work based on the word processor alone.

Is this concern important, and if so, did *Micro Star* give it sufficient attention?

5.   To help you think this through, consider the following defendants: the creator of software to run on a particular operating system, the author of a book entitled "The Musical Theater of Andrew Lloyd Webber," and the author of a study guide based on a particular law school casebook. Have any of them created an infringing derivative work? As a descriptive matter, a number of cases suggest that such works would infringe.

For example, in *Twin Peaks Prods. Inc. v. Publications Int'l Ltd.*, 996 F.2d 1366 (2d Cir. 1993), the Second Circuit held that the book *Welcome to Twin Peaks: A Complete Guide to Who's Who and What's What* infringed the popular television series. In *Horgan v. Macmillan*, 789 F.2d 157 (2d Cir. 1986), same court suggested that a book with photographs of the New York City Ballet's performance of George Balanchine's *The Nutcracker* constituted an infringing derivative work. And, in *Addison–Wesley Publishing Co. v. Brown*, 223 F. Supp. 219 (E.D.N.Y. 1963), the Eastern District of New York held that the authors of pamphlet containing answers to questions from famous physics textbooks committed infringement.

What do you think of cases like this? If you think that these cases "go too far," how would you rectify the problem? Or, are there strong policy reasons to support these outcomes?

6.   Must a subsequent work reproduce an initial copyrighted work to constitute a derivative work? Consider, for example, a case where the defendant validly purchases a book containing reproductions of famous art work, cuts out the pages with the reproductions, and glues them onto ceramic tiles for sale to the public. Has the defendant violated the derivative work right? *Contrast Mirage Editions v. Albuquerque A.R.T.*, 856 F.2d 1341 (9th Cir. 1988) (yes), *with Lee v. A.R.T.*, 125 F.3d 580 (7th Cir. 1997) (no).

SECTION C. PUBLIC DISPLAY

Section 106(5) of the Copyright Act gives copyright holders the exclusive right to publicly display copyrighted literary, musical, dramatic, choreographic, pictorial, graphic, and sculptural works. Section 101 provides that:

> To "display" a work means to show a copy of it, either directly or by means of a film, slide, television image, or any other device or

process or, in the case of a motion picture or other audiovisual work, to show individual images nonsequentially.

The section further provides that:

To perform or display a work "publicly" means—

(1) to perform or display it at a place open to the public or at any place where a substantial number of persons outside of a normal circle of a family and its social acquaintances is gathered; or

(2) to transmit or otherwise communicate a performance or display of the work to a place specified by clause (1) or to the public, by means of any device or process, whether the members of the public capable of receiving the performance or display receive it in the same place or in separate places and at the same time or at different times.

Taken literally, the reservation of public display rights prohibits many ordinary uses of copyrighted works. For example, a museum that owned a copyrighted painting would commit infringement by putting the work on display. Congress, however, has significantly limited the display right by enacting Section 109(c) of the Copyright Act, which provides:

Notwithstanding the provisions of section 106(5), the owner of a particular copy lawfully made under this title, or any person authorized by such owner, is entitled, without the authority of the copyright owner, to display that copy publicly, either directly or by the projection of no more than one image at a time, to viewers present at the place where the copy is located.

The legislative history of § 109(c) clearly indicates that Congress had adopted "the general principle that the lawful owner of a copy of a work should be able to put his copy on public display without the consent of the copyright owner." Note, however, that the limitations found in 109(c) do not protect those who gain possession of, but not ownership of, copyrighted works. Accordingly, renters or licensees do not gain the right to publicly display a work unless they specifically negotiate for such rights.

Section 109(c) has largely eliminated litigation about the "live" exhibition of copyrighted works. This does not mean, however, that the display right has faded into obscurity. Copyright holders occasionally use the public display right to sue those who incidentally capture and use images of copyrighted works. For example, the holder of a copyrighted billboard might claim infringement when a filmmaker includes the billboard in the background of a scene. Resolution of these cases depends on the clarity, prominence, and importance of the allegedly infringing display. *See Sandoval v. New Line Cinema Corp.*, 147 F.3d 215 (2d. Cir. 1998) (no infringing display because plaintiff's work was shown for a relatively brief time and out of focus in defendant's film); *Davis v. The Gap*, 246 F.3d 152 (2d Cir. 2001) (defendant Gap committed infringement by photographing a model wearing a pair of plaintiff's copyrighted eyewear in a manner drawing attention to the eyewear).

SECTION D. PUBLIC DISTRIBUTION

Section 106 of the Copyright Act reserves to the copyright holder the right "to distribute copies or phonorecords of the copyrighted work to the public by sale or other transfer of ownership, or by rental, lease, or lending." Reservation of this right makes sense to support the right of reproduction.

Typical copyright defendants make unauthorized copies of the plaintiff's work and sell those infringing copies to the public. Plaintiffs can easily sue these defendants for violating the reproduction right of § 106(1). In some cases, however, defendants distribute infringing copies of work without having made the copies in question. For example, a defendant might purchase infringing copies of movies for resale or rental. A plaintiff could not sue such a defendant for violating the reproduction right, but the distribution right permits recovery. The right therefore closes a loophole that unscrupulous distributors of infringing material might otherwise exploit.

1. FIRST SALE DOCTRINE

Taken literally, the right of public distribution could encompass every distribution of a copyrighted work to the public. While this makes sense for initial distributions of works (i.e. the sale or other transfer of title from a copyright holder or her authorized representative to others), allowing copyright holders to control subsequent distribution of works becomes more problematic. For example, private individuals sometimes sell compact discs they no longer want, or libraries lend books to their patrons. If the right of public distribution applied to these scenarios, copyright would strongly limit the free alienation of physical property.

Congress responded to this possibility by codifying the so-called "first sale doctrine" in Section 109 of the Copyright Act. It provides in part:

> Notwithstanding the provisions of section 106(3), the owner of a particular copy or phonorecord lawfully made under this title, or any person authorized by such owner, is entitled, without the authority of the copyright owner, to sell or otherwise dispose of the possession of that copy or phonorecord.

Our next case illustrates how this provision limits the distribution right.

Walt Disney Productions v. Basmajian
600 F. Supp. 439 (S.D.N.Y. 1984)

ROBERT L. CARTER, District Judge.

Plaintiff Walt Disney Productions ("Disney") seeks a preliminary injunction to restrain Christie, Manson & Woods International, Inc. ("Christie's") from proceeding with an auction scheduled for Saturday, December 8, 1984, of various Disney celluloids ("cels"), background, pre-production and production sketches on consignment from John Basmajian, Sr. This is a collection of original Disney artwork, including animated cels and background drawings used in the production of Disney motion pictures which are all under copyright. Disney asserts that Basmajian took the art work from Disney studios without permission and that sale of the artwork now would infringe Disney's copyright.

Basmajian worked at Disney's in the animation department in 1943-46. There is no dispute about that. According to John Hench, who has worked at Disney's since 1939 and is now a senior vice president of WED Enterprises, a Disney affiliate, during the period of Basmajian's employment, cels and sketches were not supposed to be taken off the premises of the studio without permission. The cels were kept near the cameras until after completion of any retakes. Then they were stored in the morgue. Background sketches, exposure and model sheets were stored in the morgue, as well.

During the period when Basmajian was employed, the estimate is that some 20 million pieces of artwork (cels and sketches) were completed in connection with the Disney short subjects and feature films. Hench testified that roughly 10% of this material was considered important. Some of this material was used again, some was sold to the public through an authorized vendor, Courvoisier Galleries. David R. Smith, who came on as Disney's archivist in June, 1970, testified that Disney has only some 50 cels and sketches from this 1943-46 period in its possession at present.

According to Basmajian Disney systematically destroyed the cels and sketches kept in the morgue. Basmajian states that he secured the permission of Disney employees John Bond and Ben Mosley to take from the morgue the material which now comprise his Disney collection (and part of which he proposes to sell through Christie's). It is undisputed that Bond worked at Disney in the animation department during the period of Basmajian's employment and until Bond's retirement in 1973. According to Basmajian, Bond was head of the animation department. It is also undisputed that Mosley worked in the morgue during the period Basmajian was at Disney.

According to Basmajian's son, John Basmajian, Jr., the collection was kept at the Basmajian home and was shown to anyone who came to visit. Much of it was stored in the garage but pieces were on display throughout the house all during Basmajian, Jr.'s years at home. (The son is now 43 years old and was born in 1941.) Some 20 years ago Basmajian, Sr. and his wife began to make mats and place these pieces in frames. ...

In December, 1983, Christie's entered the picture. Through Basmajian's lawyer or agent, Christie's representatives met Basmajian, saw the collection and entered into an agreement to auction it off. In July, 1984, when the date for the December auction had been set, Hilary Holland, a Christie's employee working in Los Angeles, concluded that it would be a good idea to have a charity benefit co-sponsored by Disney and Christie's given close to the date of the auction. She voiced this idea to Disney personnel in August, 1984. During the course of these discussions, Holland told Disney representatives about the Basmajian collection, what Christie's had been told about how Basmajian came into possession of the material—that the material was being destroyed and thrown out and that he had been given permission to take cels and sketches home—and Christie's plan to auction the materials off in the first week of December. The benefit proposal was turned down. In September, Holland talked to Disney's general counsel. Again she was forthright about revealing all she had been told about how the Basmajian collection came into being. The general counsel told her he would look into it. ...

In order to secure a preliminary injunction in this circuit, a plaintiff must show irreparable injury and either the likelihood of success on the merits or serious questions going to the merits making them a fair ground for litigation with the balance of hardships tipping in favor of the plaintiff. The absence of a showing of irreparable injury is fatal.

One of the affidavits presented in this case is that of Peter F. Nolan, Disney Vice President, Rights and Business Affairs, Consumer Products. He requests return of the artwork and cancellation of the auction because "this unique property belongs to [Disney], because Disney must maintain its policy of prohibiting its employees from obtaining property belonging to Disney and because Disney needs to protect its own program of selling this material, which currently produces revenue of about $270,000 per year." Disney wants to protect its monetary interest in materials which comprise the Basmajian collection and/or it wants to make a market for the material itself. In either case the damage it seeks to avert is one that can be calculated in dollars and cents. Those are not damages requiring equitable relief but mere legal damages capable of evaluation by a jury.

Moreover, Basmajian has established a prima facie case of lawful possession of the collection. The story of how he came into possession of the material is more plausible and more consistent with the objective facts than plaintiff's testimony seeking to establish wrongful conversion. Whatever Bond's and Mosley's position, they clearly had access to the cels and sketches. Mosley worked in the morgue where the sketches, and eventually the cels, were stored. Bond was supervisor of cleanup and breakdown. That meant putting finishing touches on the cels and sketches, and it also meant breaking down the sets when shooting was completed. Thus both Bond and Mosley had control of material that was ready to be discarded or destroyed and had authority to give to Basmajian material the studio was prepared to get rid of as waste. Hench testifies that the studio placed great value on these cels and sketches. But on what is a conservative estimate of some 20 million cels, sketches, etc. created during the period in question, with 2 million of them being of value, and with Disney now in possession of only 50 of these materials, it is clear enough that the studio did not place great value on most of this kind of material. Some were considered of sufficient value to sell to the public through a vendor. No estimate is in the record of numbers in this regard, but it is safe to estimate that the numbers were in the hundreds and no more than several thousand. That leaves millions of pieces of cels, sketches, etc. unaccounted for. The purported careful policy of preservation on this evidence was simply non-existent. ...

The record establishes lawful possession by Basmajian and notice to Disney. The first sale doctrine, 17 U.S.C. § 109(a), states that where the copyright owner sells or transfer a particular copy of his copyrighted work, he divests himself of the exclusive right in that copy and the right to sell passes to the transferee. To trigger the first sale doctrine, the copyright owner must "part [ ] with title to [the] particular copy." *United States v. Atherton*, 561 F.2d 747, 750 (9th Cir. 1977). "In each case the court must analyze the arrangement at issue and decide whether it should be considered a first sale." *United States v. Bily*, 406 F. Supp. 726, 731 (E.D. Pa. 1975). Title may be transferred by gift. M. Nimmer, The Law of Copyright § 8.12[B] (1984 ed.). Here the defendant Basmajian has established that the collection now in his possession was a gift from Disney. His claim that he was given this material by persons at Disney authorized in 1943-46 to give him the material has not been rebutted by any credible evidence produced by plaintiff. As lawful possessor of this material Basmajian has the right to consign it to Christie's for auction. ...

Notes and Questions

1. *Basmajian* illustrates the basic operation of the first sale doctrine. Once the copyright holder transfers title to a lawfully made copy of a work, he can no longer control its distribution or other disposition. The first sale doctrine is thus responsible for the existence of lending libraries, used book stores, and DVD rental companies. In the past, some copyright owners (for example, textbook publishers) have argued for a selective repeal of the first sale doctrine, arguing that the re-sale and rental markets deprive them of valuable revenues. Would you be in favor of such legislation? Why or why not?

2. Can copyright owners contract around the first sale doctrine? Copyright holders often dislike the first sale doctrine because the sale of second-hand copies of works undercuts the market for new copies. Not surprisingly, copyright holders sometimes try to evade the first sale doctrine by characterizing the distribution of copies as licenses, not sales. The vast majority of software is distributed with licenses that grant only specific rights to the user, and the practice may spread to the distribution of books, music, or movies.

Would you consider these transactions bona fide licenses, or sales subject to the first sale doctrine? Recent decisions reflect potential disagreement. In *UMG Recordings, v. Augusto*, 628 F.3d 1175 (9th Cir. 2011), the Ninth Circuit found that a purported license accompanying promotional music CDs did not render the first sale doctrine inapplicable. By contrast, in *Vernor v. Autodesk*, 621 F.3d 1102 (9th Cir. 2010), the same court decided that a purported license accompanying software rendered the first sale doctrine inapplicable.

How easy should it be for a copyright holder to draft a license that avoids the first sale doctrine, and what provisions would be necessary? For example, say that casebook publishers routinely distributed casebooks subject to a license that barred the law student from re-selling the book. Under what circumstances, if any, would such a license be enforceable?

3. How, if at all, should the first sale doctrine apply to digital works? For example, a person who clips a newspaper article and sends it to a friend does not commit infringement under the first sale doctrine. What happens to a person who cuts and pastes the same newspaper article from a website and emails it to a friend?

At least one company has tried, unsuccessfully, to apply the first sale doctrine to the transfer of digital works. In *Capitol Records v. ReDigi*, 934 F. Supp.2d 640 (S.D.N.Y. 2014), a company called ReDigi created an online service that allowed users to sell their digital music files to third parties. Users could upload digital music files onto ReDigi's servers, and ReDigi's software would verify that the same digital music files had been deleted from the user's computer. The user could then sell the uploaded files to a third party, who would then be able to access and download the file from ReDigi's servers.

Capitol Records sued ReDigi for copyright infringement, alleging that the copies on the servers were unauthorized reproductions of its copyrighted sound recordings. ReDigi defended, arguing that users were simply exercising their rights to first sale. The district court rejected ReDigi's first sale defense, holding that the first sale doctrine was only a limitation on the public distribution right, and not a limit on the reproduction right. And although ReDigi's technology attempted to create the equivalent of a public distribution, by deleting the original file after making a copy, the court held that this nevertheless resulted in the creation of an infringing copy of the original work.

The *ReDigi* opinion suggests that the first sale doctrine may have far more limited application with respect to digital copies of copyrighted works. Should this raise any concerns?

4. A significant exception to the first sale doctrine exists with respect to the lending or rental of sound recordings and software. In response to concerns that renters would make multiple free personal copies, Congress amended section 109 of the Copyright Act to prohibit the "rental, lease, or lending" of such items without the copyright holder's permission.

5. Sometimes copyright holders claim that the physical disposition of a work violates the derivative work right. For example, what would happen if a manufacturer of paperweights purchased hundreds of copyrighted postcards, encased them in clear resin, and sold them as paperweights? Would the manufacturer have violated the derivative work right because the paperweights were new works based on the copyrighted postcards? Or would the first sale doctrine shield this behavior? Case law on this issue appears inconsistent. *See Mirage Editions v. Albuquerque A.R.T. Co.,* 856 F.2d 1341 (9th Cir. 1988) (holding such behavior is infringement); *Lee v. A.R.T. Co.,* 125 F.3d 580 (7th Cir. 1997) (holding that such behavior is not infringement).

2. IMPORTATION RIGHTS

The right of distribution is also supported and augmented by Section 602(a) of the Copyright Act, which provides in part:

(1) Importation into the United States, without the authority of the owner of copyright under this title, of copies or phonorecords of a work that have been acquired outside the United States is an infringement of the exclusive right to distribute copies or phonorecords under section 106, actionable under section 501.

Section 602(a)(1) thus gives copyright owners the right to prevent unauthorized importation of copies acquired outside of the U.S., as any such act of importation amounts to a violation of the public distribution right. (Note that this section includes an exception for limited copies acquired abroad and imported for personal use).

A tricky question is how the importation restriction in section 602(a) interacts with the first sale doctrine. Specifically, does the first sale doctrine apply to works acquired in other countries? The first sale doctrine would not, of course, apply to importation of infringing works acquired in other countries (e.g. pirated DVDs), since the doctrine does not apply to unlawfully created works. But what about works that are not infringing, but legitimately sold in another country under authorization by the copyright owner? For example, could someone purchase 1,000 licensed copies of Microsoft Word in China, import them into the U.S., and re-sell them in the U.S.?

This raises the so-called parallel imports or gray market problem. Why might someone seek to import and resell copyrighted works from another country? Because copyright owners often sell the same exact product at different prices in different countries, engaging in so-called price discrimination. Because the market in, say, China cannot support the same price for a particular product as the market in the U.S., a copyright owner may seek to maximize its profits by selling the same work at a lower price in China. The resulting price difference, however, creates an opportunity for arbitrage, as individuals can then purchase the cheaper version from China and resell it in the U.S.

The question is whether section 602(a) bars this activity. The Supreme Court recently addressed this issue in the following case.

Kirtsaeng v. John Wiley & Sons
133 S. Ct. 1351 (2013)

JUSTICE BREYER delivered the opinion of the Court.

Section 106 of the Copyright Act grants "the owner of copyright under this title" certain "exclusive rights," including the right "to distribute copies ... of the copyrighted work to the public by sale or other transfer of ownership." These rights are qualified, however, by the application of various limitations set forth in the next several sections of the Act, §§ 107 through 122. Those sections, typically entitled "Limitations on exclusive rights," include, for example, the principle of "fair use" (§ 107), permission for limited library archival reproduction, (§ 108), and the doctrine at issue here, the "first sale" doctrine (§ 109).

Section 109(a) sets forth the "first sale" doctrine as follows:

"Notwithstanding the provisions of section 106(3) [the section that grants the owner exclusive distribution rights], the owner of a particular copy or phonorecord lawfully made under this title ... is entitled, without the authority of the copyright owner, to sell or otherwise dispose of the possession of that copy or phonorecord."

Thus, even though § 106(3) forbids distribution of a copy of, say, the copyrighted novel *Herzog* without the copyright owner's permission, § 109(a) adds that, once a copy of *Herzog* has been lawfully sold (or its ownership otherwise lawfully transferred), the buyer of that copy and subsequent owners are free to dispose of it as they wish. In copyright jargon, the "first sale" has "exhausted" the copyright owner's § 106(3) exclusive distribution right.

What, however, if the copy of *Herzog* was printed abroad and then initially sold with the copyright owner's permission? Does the "first sale" doctrine still apply? Is the buyer, like the buyer of a domestically manufactured copy, free to bring the copy into the United States and dispose of it as he or she wishes?

To put the matter technically, an "importation" provision, §
602(a)(1), says that

> "[i]mportation into the United States, without the authority of
> the owner of copyright under this title, of copies ... of a work that
> have been acquired outside the United States is an infringement
> of the exclusive right to distribute copies ... under section 106...."

Thus § 602(a)(1) makes clear that importing a copy without permission violates the owner's exclusive distribution right. But in doing so, §
602(a)(1) refers explicitly to the § 106(3) exclusive distribution right. As
we have just said, § 106 is by its terms "[s]ubject to" the various doctrines and principles contained in §§ 107 through 122, including §
109(a)'s "first sale" limitation. Do those same modifications apply—in
particular, does the "first sale" modification apply—when considering
whether § 602(a)(1) prohibits importing a copy?

In *Quality King Distributors, Inc. v. L'anza Research Int'l, Inc.,* 523
U.S. 135, 145 (1998), we held that § 602(a)(1)'s reference to § 106(3)'s
exclusive distribution right incorporates the later subsections' limitations, including, in particular, the "first sale" doctrine of § 109. Thus, it
might seem that, § 602(a)(1) notwithstanding, one who buys a copy
abroad can freely import that copy into the United States and dispose of
it, just as he could had he bought the copy in the United States.

But *Quality King* considered an instance in which the copy, though
purchased abroad, was initially manufactured in the United States (and
then sent abroad and sold). This case is like *Quality King* but for one important fact. The copies at issue here were manufactured abroad. That
fact is important because § 109(a) says that the "first sale" doctrine applies to "a particular copy or phonorecord lawfully made under this title."
And we must decide here whether the five words, "lawfully made under
this title," make a critical legal difference.

Putting section numbers to the side, we ask whether the "first sale"
doctrine applies to protect a buyer or other lawful owner of a copy (of a
copyrighted work) lawfully manufactured abroad. Can that buyer bring
that copy into the United States (and sell it or give it away) without obtaining permission to do so from the copyright owner? Can, for example,
someone who purchases, say at a used bookstore, a book printed abroad
subsequently resell it without the copyright owner's permission?

In our view, the answers to these questions are, yes. We hold that
the "first sale" doctrine applies to copies of a copyrighted work lawfully
made abroad.

I

A

Respondent, John Wiley & Sons, Inc., publishes academic textbooks.
Wiley obtains from its authors various foreign and domestic copyright
assignments, licenses and permissions—to the point that we can, for

present purposes, refer to Wiley as the relevant American copyright owner. Wiley often assigns to its wholly owned foreign subsidiary, John Wiley & Sons (Asia) Pte Ltd., rights to publish, print, and sell Wiley's English language textbooks abroad. Each copy of a Wiley Asia foreign edition will likely contain language making clear that the copy is to be sold only in a particular country or geographical region outside the United States....

The upshot is that there are two essentially equivalent versions of a Wiley textbook, each version manufactured and sold with Wiley's permission: (1) an American version printed and sold in the United States, and (2) a foreign version manufactured and sold abroad. And Wiley makes certain that copies of the second version state that they are not to be taken (without permission) into the United States.

Petitioner, Supap Kirtsaeng, a citizen of Thailand, moved to the United States in 1997 to study mathematics at Cornell University. He paid for his education with the help of a Thai Government scholarship which required him to teach in Thailand for 10 years on his return. Kirtsaeng successfully completed his undergraduate courses at Cornell, successfully completed a Ph.D. program in mathematics at the University of Southern California, and then, as promised, returned to Thailand to teach. While he was studying in the United States, Kirtsaeng asked his friends and family in Thailand to buy copies of foreign edition English-language textbooks at Thai book shops, where they sold at low prices, and mail them to him in the United States. Kirtsaeng would then sell them, reimburse his family and friends, and keep the profit.

B

In 2008 Wiley brought this federal lawsuit against Kirtsaeng for copyright infringement. Wiley claimed that Kirtsaeng's unauthorized importation of its books and his later resale of those books amounted to an infringement of Wiley's § 106(3) exclusive right to distribute as well as § 602's related import prohibition. Kirtsaeng replied that the books he had acquired were "'lawfully made'" and that he had acquired them legitimately. Thus, in his view, § 109(a)'s "first sale" doctrine permitted him to resell or otherwise dispose of the books without the copyright owner's further permission....

II

We must decide whether the words "lawfully made under this title" restrict the scope of § 109(a)'s "first sale" doctrine geographically. The Second Circuit, the Ninth Circuit, Wiley, and the Solicitor General (as amicus) all read those words as imposing a form of geographical limitation. The Second Circuit held that they limit the "first sale" doctrine to particular copies "made in territories in which the Copyright Act is law," which (the Circuit says) are copies "manufactured domestically," not "outside of the United States." Wiley agrees that those five words limit the "first sale" doctrine "to copies made in conformance with the [United States] Copyright Act where the Copyright Act is applicable," which

(Wiley says) means it does not apply to copies made "outside the United States" and at least not to "foreign production of a copy for distribution exclusively abroad."...

Under any of these geographical interpretations, § 109(a)'s "first sale" doctrine would not apply to the Wiley Asia books at issue here. And, despite an American copyright owner's permission to make copies abroad, one who buys a copy of any such book or other copyrighted work—whether at a retail store, over the Internet, or at a library sale— could not resell (or otherwise dispose of) that particular copy without further permission.

Kirtsaeng, however, reads the words "lawfully made under this title" as imposing a non-geographical limitation. He says that they mean made "in accordance with" or "in compliance with" the Copyright Act. In that case, § 109(a)'s "first sale" doctrine would apply to copyrighted works as long as their manufacture met the requirements of American copyright law. In particular, the doctrine would apply where, as here, copies are manufactured abroad with the permission of the copyright owner.

In our view, § 109(a)'s language, its context, and the common-law history of the "first sale" doctrine, taken together, favor a non-geographical interpretation. We also doubt that Congress would have intended to create the practical copyright-related harms with which a geographical interpretation would threaten ordinary scholarly, artistic, commercial, and consumer activities. We consequently conclude that Kirtsaeng's nongeographical reading is the better reading of the Act.

A

The language of § 109(a) read literally favors Kirtsaeng's nongeographical interpretation, namely, that "lawfully made under this title" means made "in accordance with" or "in compliance with" the Copyright Act. The language of § 109(a) says nothing about geography. The word "under" can mean "[i]n accordance with." 18 OXFORD ENGLISH DICTIONARY 950 (2d ed.1989). And a nongeographical interpretation provides each word of the five-word phrase with a distinct purpose. The first two words of the phrase, "lawfully made," suggest an effort to distinguish those copies that were made lawfully from those that were not, and the last three words, "under this title," set forth the standard of "lawful[ness]." Thus, the nongeographical reading is simple, it promotes a traditional copyright objective (combatting piracy), and it makes word-by-word linguistic sense.

The geographical interpretation, however, bristles with linguistic difficulties. It gives the word "lawfully" little, if any, linguistic work to do. (How could a book be unlawfully "made under this title"?) It imports geography into a statutory provision that says nothing explicitly about it. And it is far more complex than may at first appear.

To read the clause geographically, Wiley, like the Second Circuit and the Solicitor General, must first emphasize the word "under." Indeed,

Wiley reads "under this title" to mean "in conformance with the Copyright Act where the Copyright Act is applicable." Wiley must then take a second step, arguing that the Act "is applicable" only in the United States....

One difficulty is that neither "under" nor any other word in the phrase means "where." See, e.g., 18 OXFORD ENGLISH DICTIONARY, *supra*, at 947–952 (definition of "under"). It might mean "subject to," but as this Court has repeatedly acknowledged, the word evades a uniform, consistent meaning.

A far more serious difficulty arises out of the uncertainty and complexity surrounding the second step's effort to read the necessary geographical limitation into the word "applicable" (or the equivalent). Where, precisely, is the Copyright Act "applicable"? The Act does not instantly protect an American copyright holder from unauthorized piracy taking place abroad. But that fact does not mean the Act is inapplicable to copies made abroad. As a matter of ordinary English, one can say that a statute imposing, say, a tariff upon "any rhododendron grown in Nepal" applies to all Nepalese rhododendrons. And, similarly, one can say that the American Copyright Act is applicable to all pirated copies, including those printed overseas. Indeed, the Act itself makes clear that (in the Solicitor General's language) foreign-printed pirated copies are "subject to" the Act. § 602(a)(2) (2006 ed., Supp. V) (referring to importation of copies "the making of which either constituted an infringement of copyright, or which would have constituted an infringement of copyright if this title had been applicable")....

In sum, we believe that geographical interpretations create more linguistic problems than they resolve. And considerations of simplicity and coherence tip the purely linguistic balance in Kirtsaeng's, nongeographical, favor....

D

Associations of libraries, used-book dealers, technology companies, consumer-goods retailers, and museums point to various ways in which a geographical interpretation would fail to further basic constitutional copyright objectives, in particular "promot[ing] the Progress of Science and useful Arts."

The American Library Association tells us that library collections contain at least 200 million books published abroad...; that many others were first published in the United States but printed abroad because of lower costs; and that a geographical interpretation will likely require the libraries to obtain permission (or at least create significant uncertainty) before circulating or otherwise distributing these books.

How, the American Library Association asks, are the libraries to obtain permission to distribute these millions of books? How can they find, say, the copyright owner of a foreign book, perhaps written decades ago? They may not know the copyright holder's present address. And, even

where addresses can be found, the costs of finding them, contacting owners, and negotiating may be high indeed. Are the libraries to stop circulating or distributing or displaying the millions of books in their collections that were printed abroad?

Used-book dealers tell us that, from the time when Benjamin Franklin and Thomas Jefferson built commercial and personal libraries of foreign books, American readers have bought used books published and
printed abroad. The dealers say that they have "operat[ed] ... for centu-
ries" under the assumption that the "first sale" doctrine applies. But under a geographical interpretation a contemporary tourist who buys, say,
at Shakespeare and Co. (in Paris), a dozen copies of a foreign book for
American friends might find that she had violated the copyright law.
The used-book dealers cannot easily predict what the foreign copyright
holder may think about a reader's effort to sell a used copy of a novel.
And they believe that a geographical interpretation will injure a large
portion of the used-book business.

Technology companies tell us that "automobiles, microwaves, calculators, mobile phones, tablets, and personal computers" contain copyrightable software programs or packaging. Many of these items are made
abroad with the American copyright holder's permission and then sold
and imported (with that permission) to the United States. A geographical interpretation would prevent the resale of, say, a car, without the
permission of the holder of each copyright on each piece of copyrighted
automobile software. Yet there is no reason to believe that foreign auto
manufacturers regularly obtain this kind of permission from their software component suppliers, and Wiley did not indicate to the contrary
when asked. Without that permission a foreign car owner could not sell
his or her used car....

These examples, and others previously mentioned, help explain why
Lord Coke considered the "first sale" doctrine necessary to protect "Trade
and Traffi[c], and bargaining and contracting," and they help explain
why American copyright law has long applied that doctrine.

Neither Wiley nor any of its many amici deny that a geographical interpretation could bring about these "horribles"—at least in principle.
Rather, Wiley essentially says that the list is artificially invented. It
points out that a federal court first adopted a geographical interpretation
more than 30 years ago. Yet, it adds, these problems have not occurred.
Why not? Because, says Wiley, the problems and threats are purely theoretical; they are unlikely to reflect reality.

We are less sanguine. For one thing, the law has not been settled for
long in Wiley's favor. The Second Circuit, in its decision below, is the
first Court of Appeals to adopt a purely geographical interpretation. The
Third Circuit has favored a nongeographical interpretation. The Ninth
Circuit has favored a modified geographical interpretation with a nongeographical (but textually unsustainable) corollary designed to diminish

the problem. And other courts have hesitated to adopt, and have cast doubt upon, the validity of the geographical interpretation.

For another thing, reliance upon the "first sale" doctrine is deeply embedded in the practices of those, such as booksellers, libraries, museums, and retailers, who have long relied upon its protection.... That inertia means a dramatic change is likely necessary before these institutions, instructed by their counsel, would begin to engage in the complex permission-verifying process that a geographical interpretation would demand. And this Court's adoption of the geographical interpretation could provide that dramatic change....

Finally, the fact that harm has proved limited so far may simply reflect the reluctance of copyright holders so far to assert geographically based resale rights. They may decide differently if the law is clarified in their favor. Regardless, a copyright law that can work in practice only if unenforced is not a sound copyright law. It is a law that would create uncertainty, would bring about selective enforcement, and, if widely unenforced, would breed disrespect for copyright law itself.

Thus, we believe that the practical problems that petitioner and his amici have described are too serious, too extensive, and too likely to come about for us to dismiss them as insignificant—particularly in light of the ever-growing importance of foreign trade to America. The upshot is that copyright-related consequences along with language, context, and interpretive canons argue strongly against a geographical interpretation of § 109(a).

III

Wiley and the dissent make several additional important arguments in favor of the geographical interpretation....

....Wiley and the dissent claim that a nongeographical interpretation will make it difficult, perhaps impossible, for publishers (and other copyright holders) to divide foreign and domestic markets. We concede that is so. A publisher may find it more difficult to charge different prices for the same book in different geographic markets. But we do not see how these facts help Wiley, for we can find no basic principle of copyright law that suggests that publishers are especially entitled to such rights.

The Constitution describes the nature of American copyright law by providing Congress with the power to "secur[e]" to "[a]uthors" "for limited [t]imes" the "exclusive [r]ight to their ... [w]ritings." Art. I, § 8, cl. 8. The Founders, too, discussed the need to grant an author a limited right to exclude competition. But the Constitution's language nowhere suggests that its limited exclusive right should include a right to divide markets or a concomitant right to charge different purchasers different prices for the same book, say to increase or to maximize gain. Neither, to our knowledge, did any Founder make any such suggestion. We have found no precedent suggesting a legal preference for interpretations of copyright statutes that would provide for market divisions.

To the contrary, Congress enacted a copyright law that (through the "first sale" doctrine) limits copyright holders' ability to divide domestic markets. And that limitation is consistent with antitrust laws that ordinarily forbid market divisions. Whether copyright owners should, or should not, have more than ordinary commercial power to divide international markets is a matter for Congress to decide. We do no more here than try to determine what decision Congress has taken.

IV

For these reasons we conclude that the considerations supporting Kirtsaeng's nongeographical interpretation of the words "lawfully made under this title" are the more persuasive. The judgment of the Court of Appeals is reversed, and the case is remanded for further proceedings consistent with this opinion.

It is so ordered.

JUSTICE KAGAN, with whom JUSTICE ALITO joins, concurring.

I concur fully in the Court's opinion. Neither the text nor the history of 17 U.S.C. § 109(a) supports removing first-sale protection from every copy of a protected work manufactured abroad. I recognize, however, that the combination of today's decision and *Quality King Distributors, Inc. v. L'anza Research Int'l, Inc.*, 523 U.S. 135 (1998), constricts the scope of § 602(a)(1)'s ban on unauthorized importation. I write to suggest that any problems associated with that limitation come not from our reading of § 109(a) here, but from *Quality King's* holding that § 109(a) limits § 602(a)(1).

As the Court explains, the first-sale doctrine has played an integral part in American copyright law for over a century. No codification of the doctrine prior to 1976 even arguably limited its application to copies made in the United States. And nothing in the text or history of § 109(a)—the Copyright Act of 1976's first-sale provision—suggests that Congress meant to enact the new, geographical restriction John Wiley proposes, which at once would deprive American consumers of important rights and encourage copyright holders to manufacture abroad.

That said, John Wiley is right that the Court's decision, when combined with *Quality King*, substantially narrows § 602(a)(1)'s ban on unauthorized importation. *Quality King* held that the importation ban does not reach any copies receiving first-sale protection under § 109(a). So notwithstanding § 602(a)(1), an "owner of a particular copy ... lawfully made under this title" can import that copy without the copyright owner's permission. § 109(a). In now holding that copies "lawfully made under this title" include copies manufactured abroad, we unavoidably diminish § 602(a)(1)'s scope—indeed, limit it to a fairly esoteric set of applications.

But if Congress views the shrinking of § 602(a)(1) as a problem, it should recognize *Quality King*—not our decision today—as the culprit. Here, after all, we merely construe § 109(a); *Quality King* is the decision holding that § 109(a) limits § 602(a)(1). Had we come out the opposite way in that case, § 602(a)(1) would allow a copyright owner to restrict the importation of copies irrespective of the first-sale doctrine. That result would enable the copyright owner to divide international markets in the way John Wiley claims Congress intended when enacting § 602(a)(1). But it would do so without imposing downstream liability on those who purchase and resell in the United States copies that happen to have been manufactured abroad. In other words, that outcome would target unauthorized importers alone, and not the "libraries, used-book dealers, technology companies, consumer-goods retailers, and museums" with whom the Court today is rightly concerned. Assuming Congress adopted § 602(a)(1) to permit market segmentation, I suspect that is how Congress thought the provision would work—not by removing first-sale protection from every copy manufactured abroad (as John Wiley urges us to do here), but by enabling the copyright holder to control imports even when the first-sale doctrine applies (as *Quality King* now prevents)...

JUSTICE GINSBURG, with whom JUSTICE KENNEDY joins, and with whom JUSTICE SCALIA joins except as to Parts III and V–B–1, dissenting.

... Instead of adhering to the Legislature's design, the Court today adopts an interpretation of the Copyright Act at odds with Congress' aim to protect copyright owners against the unauthorized importation of low-priced, foreign-made copies of their copyrighted works...

To justify a holding that shrinks to insignificance copyright protection against the unauthorized importation of foreign-made copies, the Court identifies several "practical problems." The Court's parade of horribles, however, is largely imaginary. Congress' objective in enacting 17 U.S.C. § 602(a)(1)'s importation prohibition can be honored without generating the absurd consequences hypothesized in the Court's opinion....

II

... Section 109(a), properly read, affords Kirtsaeng no defense against Wiley's claim of copyright infringement. The Copyright Act, it has been observed time and again, does not apply extraterritorially. The printing of Wiley's foreign-manufactured textbooks therefore was not governed by Title 17. The textbooks thus were not "lawfully made under [Title 17]," the crucial precondition for application of § 109(a). And if § 109(a) does not apply, there is no dispute that Kirtsaeng's conduct constituted copyright infringement under § 602(a)(1)....

The logical implication of the Court's definition of the word "under" is that any copy manufactured abroad—even a piratical one made without the copyright owner's authorization and in violation of the law of the country where it was created—would fall within the scope of § 109(a). Any such copy would have been made "in accordance with" or "in compliance with" the U.S. Copyright Act, in the sense that manufacturing the copy did not violate the Act (because the Act does not apply extraterritorially).

The Court rightly refuses to accept such an absurd conclusion. Instead, it interprets § 109(a) as applying only to copies whose making actually complied with Title 17, or would have complied with Title 17 had Title 17 been applicable (i.e., had the copies been made in the United States). Congress, however, used express language when it called for such a counterfactual inquiry in 17 U.S.C. §§ 602(a)(2) and (b)....

Not only does the Court adopt an unnatural construction of the § 109(a) phrase "lawfully made under this title." Concomitantly, the Court reduces § 602(a)(1) to insignificance. As the Court appears to acknowledge, the only independent effect § 602(a)(1) has under today's decision is to prohibit unauthorized importations carried out by persons who merely have possession of, but do not own, the imported copies. If this is enough to avoid rendering § 602(a)(1) entirely "superfluous," it hardly suffices to give the owner's importation right the scope Congress intended it to have. Congress used broad language in § 602(a)(1); it did so to achieve a broad objective. Had Congress intended simply to provide a copyright remedy against larcenous lessees, licensees, consignees, and bailees of films and other copyright-protected goods, it likely would have used language tailored to that narrow purpose....

The far more plausible reading of §§ 109(a) and 602(a), then, is that Congress intended § 109(a) to apply to copies made in the United States, not to copies manufactured and sold abroad....

V

...

B

The Court sees many "horribles" following from a holding that the § 109(a) phrase "lawfully made under this title" does not encompass foreign-made copies. If § 109(a) excluded foreign-made copies, the Court fears, then copyright owners could exercise perpetual control over the downstream distribution or public display of such copies. A ruling in Wiley's favor, the Court asserts, would shutter libraries, put used-book dealers out of business, cripple art museums, and prevent the resale of a wide range of consumer goods, from cars to calculators. Copyright law and precedent, however, erect barriers to the anticipated horribles.

1

... Under the logic of *Bobbs–Merrill* [the case that first recognized copyright exhaustion, the precursor to the first-sale doctrine], the sale of a foreign-manufactured copy in the United States carried out with the copyright owner's authorization would exhaust the copyright owner's right to "vend" that copy. The copy could thenceforth be resold, lent out, or otherwise redistributed without further authorization from the copyright owner.... Thus, in accord with *Bobbs–Merrill*, the first authorized distribution of a foreign-made copy in the United States exhausts the copyright owner's distribution right under § 106(3). After such an authorized distribution, a library may lend, or a used-book dealer may resell, the foreign-made copy without seeking the copyright owner's permission.

For example, if Wiley, rather than Kirtsaeng, had imported into the United States and then sold the foreign-made textbooks at issue in this case, Wiley's § 106(3) distribution right would have been exhausted under the rationale of *Bobbs–Merrill*. Purchasers of the textbooks would thus be free to dispose of the books as they wished without first gaining a license from Wiley....

2

Other statutory prescriptions provide further protection against the absurd consequences imagined by the Court. For example, § 602(a)(3)(C) permits "an organization operated for scholarly, educational, or religious purposes" to import, without the copyright owner's authorization, up to five foreign-made copies of a non-audiovisual work—notably, a book—for "library lending or archival purposes."

The Court also notes that amici representing art museums fear that a ruling in Wiley's favor would prevent museums from displaying works of art created abroad. These amici observe that a museum's right to display works of art often depends on 17 U.S.C. § 109(c). That provision addresses exhaustion of a copyright owner's exclusive right under § 106(5) to publicly display the owner's work. Because § 109(c), like § 109(a), applies only to copies "lawfully made under this title," amici contend that a ruling in Wiley's favor would prevent museums from invoking § 109(c) with respect to foreign-made works of art.

Limiting § 109(c) to U.S.-made works, however, does not bar art museums from lawfully displaying works made in other countries. Museums can, of course, seek the copyright owner's permission to display a work. Furthermore, the sale of a work of art to a U.S. museum may carry with it an implied license to publicly display the work. Displaying a work of art as part of a museum exhibition might also qualify as a "fair use" under 17 U.S.C. § 107.

The Court worries about the resale of foreign-made consumer goods "contain [ing] copyrightable software programs or packaging." For example, the Court observes that a car might be programmed with diverse forms of software, the copyrights to which might be owned by individuals or entities other than the manufacturer of the car. Must a car owner, the Court asks, obtain permission from all of these various copyright owners before reselling her car? Although this question strays far from the one presented in this case and briefed by the parties, principles of fair use and implied license (to the extent that express licenses do not exist) would likely permit the car to be resold without the copyright owners' authorization.

Most telling in this regard, no court, it appears, has been called upon to answer any of the Court's "horribles" in an actual case. Three decades have passed since a federal court first published an opinion reading §

109(a) as applicable exclusively to copies made in the United States. Yet Kirtsaeng and his supporting amici cite not a single case in which the owner of a consumer good authorized for sale in the United States has been sued for copyright infringement after reselling the item or giving it away as a gift or to charity. The absence of such lawsuits is unsurprising. Routinely suing one's customers is hardly a best business practice. Manufacturers, moreover, may be hesitant to do business with software programmers taken to suing consumers. Manufacturers may also insist that software programmers agree to contract terms barring such lawsuits....

Notes and Questions

1. The majority and dissent differ drastically in their interpretation of the term "lawfully made," in §109(a), and in their assessment of the "parade of horribles" that could follow from a geographic interpretation of the term. Which opinion had the better argument as a matter of statutory interpretation? Which did a better job of addressing the potential "parade of horribles"?

2. The Court's decision in *Kirtsaeng* effectively limits the ability of copyright owners to engage in price discrimination, i.e. to sell the same work for different prices in different countries. The majority acknowledges this, but notes that nothing in the Copyright Act suggests copyright owners are entitled to engage in price discrimination, and that if Congress wishes to give copyright owners this ability, they can do so. The dissent argues, however, that this is precisely what Congress intended in enacting §601(a)(1). Which interpretation of Congress's intent do you find more persuasive?

3. Justice Kagan's concurrence suggests that some of the tricky questions raised in *Kirtsaeng* result from the Court's prior decision in *Quality King Distributors, Inc. v. L'anza Research Int'l, Inc.*, 523 U.S. 135 (1998), which held that the first sale doctrine acts as a limitation on the importation right. If the first sale did not apply to the importation right, then publishers would be able to prevent unauthorized importation, but purchasers in the U.S. would still be able to exercise their first sale rights domestically.

4. Note that in the wake of *Kirtsaeng*, Congress has considered amendments to the Copyright Act that would restore the ability of copyright owners to prevent importation of authorized copies of works created abroad, while at the same time preserving the operation of the first sale doctrine domestically, to avoid the "parade of horribles" listed by the majority in *Kirtsaeng*. Would you support such legislation? As a policy matter, should the Copyright Act support the efforts of copyright owners to engage in differential pricing in different countries?

SECTION E. PUBLIC PERFORMANCE

The law reserving rights of public performance to copyright holders has changed over the years. The Copyright Act of 1856 recognized such rights for "dramatic compositions," and similar rights for musical compositions did not arise until 1897. The 1909 Act granted exclusive rights of public performance for dramatic works, while granting exclusive rights of public "for profit" performance for musical works.

Section 106(4) of the 1976 Act defines the current right of public performance, extending such rights to "literary, musical, dramatic, and choreographic works, pantomimes, and motion pictures and other audiovisual works." Note that § 106(4) conspicuously omits any requirement that an infringing performance be "for profit." Instead, the scope of the right depends entirely on the term "public performance" and a number of separate statutory provisions that add a number of complications.

Let us begin with the Copyright Act's definition of "public performance." Section 101 defines both "perform" and "perform publicly":

To "perform" a work means to recite, render, play, dance, or act it, either directly or by means of any device or process or, in the case of a motion picture or other audiovisual work, to show its images in any sequence or to make the sounds accompanying it audible.

To perform or display a work "publicly" means—

(1) to perform or display it at a place open to the public or at any place where a substantial number of persons outside of a normal circle of a family and its social acquaintances is gathered; or

(2) to transmit or otherwise communicate a performance or display of the work to a place specified by clause (1) or to the public, by means of any device or process, whether the members of the public capable of receiving the performance or display receive it in the same place or in separate places and at the same time or at different times.

These definitions show that "perform" encompasses a fairly broad range of conduct beyond the act of playing music on a piano before an audience. Playing a CD or DVD also constitutes performance, and its legality generally depends on who had access to the location of the performance or who has gathered there. Thus, playing a CD in one's home would not infringe unless more than family and social acquaintances attended. By contrast, playing the same CD at a dance club would constitute infringement, regardless of how small the audience happened to be. Of course, as the following cases will show, there are many locations whose status as "place open to the public" is unclear.

Columbia Pictures Industries v. Aveco
800 F.2d 59 (3d Cir. 1986)

STAPLETON, Circuit Judge.

Plaintiffs, appellees in this action, are producers of motion pictures ("Producers") and bring this copyright infringement action against the defendant, Aveco, Inc. Producers claim that Aveco's business, which includes renting video cassettes of motion pictures in conjunction with rooms in which they may be viewed, violates their exclusive rights under the Copyright Act of 1976, 17 U.S.C. § 101 et seq. The district court agreed and we affirm. ...

I

Among their other operations, Producers distribute video cassette copies of motion pictures in which they own registered copyrights. They do so knowing that many retail purchasers of these video cassettes, including Aveco, rent them to others for profit. Aveco also makes available private rooms of various sizes in which its customers may view the video cassettes that they have chosen from Aveco's offerings. For example, at one location, Lock Haven, Aveco has thirty viewing rooms, each containing seating, a video cassette player, and television monitor. Aveco charges a rental fee for the viewing room that is separate from the charge for the video cassette rental.

Customers of Aveco may (1) rent a room and also rent a video cassette for viewing in that room, (2) rent a room and bring a video cassette obtained elsewhere to play in the room, or (3) rent a video cassette for out-of-store viewing.

Aveco has placed its video cassette players inside the individual viewing rooms and, subject to a time limitation, allows the customer complete control over the playing of the video cassettes. Customers operate the video cassette players in each viewing room and Aveco's employees assist only upon request. Each video cassette may be viewed only from inside the viewing room, and is not transmitted beyond the particular room in which it is being played. Aveco asserts that it rents its viewing rooms to individual customers who may be joined in the room only by members of their families and social acquaintances. Furthermore, Aveco's stated practice is not to permit unrelated groups of customers to share a viewing room while a video cassette is being played. For purposes of this appeal we assume the veracity of these assertions.

II

... Producers' claim in this litigation is based on the alleged infringement of their "exclusive right ... to perform the copyrighted work publicly" and to "authorize" such performances. Producers assert that Aveco, by renting its viewing rooms to the public for the purpose of watching Producers' video cassettes, is authorizing the public performance of copyrighted motion pictures.

Our analysis begins with the language of the Act. We first observe that there is no question that "performances" of copyrighted materials take place at Aveco's stores. "To perform" a work is defined in the Act as, "in the case of a motion picture or other audiovisual work, to show its images in any sequence or to make the sounds accompanying it audible." Section 101. As the House Report notes, this definition means that an individual is performing a work whenever he does anything by which the work is transmitted, repeated, or made to recur. H.R. Rep. No. 1476, 94th Cong., 2d Sess. 63, *reprinted in* 1976 U.S. Code Cong. & Ad. News 5659, 5676-77.

Producers do not argue that Aveco itself performs the video cassettes. They acknowledge that under the Act Aveco's customers are the ones performing the works, for it is they who actually place the video cassette in the video cassette player and operate the controls. As we said in *Columbia Pictures Industries v. Redd Horne*, 749 F.2d 154, 158 (3d Cir. 1984), "[p]laying a video cassette ... constitute[s] a performance under Section 101." However, if there is a public performance, Aveco may still be responsible as an infringer even though it does not actually operate the video cassette players. In granting copyright owners the exclusive rights to "authorize" public performances, Congress intended "to avoid any questions as to the liability of contributory infringers. For example, a person who lawfully acquires an authorized copy of a motion picture would be an infringer if he or she engages in the business of renting it to others for purposes of an unauthorized public performance." H.R. Rep. No. 1476, 94th Cong., 2d Sess. 61, *reprinted in* 1976 U.S. Code Cong. & Ad. News at 5674; see S. Rep. No. 473, 94th Cong., 1st Sess. 57 (1975). In our opinion, this rationale applies equally to the person who knowingly makes available other requisites of a public performance. Accordingly, we agree with the district court that Aveco, by enabling its customers to perform the video cassettes in the viewing rooms, authorizes the performances.

The performances of Producers' motion pictures at Aveco's stores infringe their copyrights, however, only if they are "public." The copyright owners' rights do not extend to control over private performances. The Act defines a public performance.

To perform ... a work "publicly" means-

(1) to perform or display it at a place open to the public or at any place where a substantial number of persons outside of a normal circle of a family and its social acquaintances are gathered; or

(2) to transmit or otherwise communicate a performance or display of the work to a place specified by clause (1) or to the public, by means of any device or process, whether the members of the public capable of receiving the performance or display receive it in the same place or in separate places and at the same or at different times.

17 U.S.C. § 101.

We recently parsed this definition in *Redd Horne*, a case similar to the one at bar. The principal factual distinction is that in Redd Horne's operation, known as Maxwell's Video Showcase, Ltd. ("Maxwell's"), the video cassette players were located in the stores' central areas, not in each individual screening room. Maxwell's customers would select a video cassette from Maxwell's stock and rent a room which they entered to watch the motion picture on a television monitor. A Maxwell's employee would play the video cassette for the customers in one of the centrally-located video cassette players and transmit the performance to the monitor located in the room. Thus, unlike Aveco's customers, Maxwell's clientele had no control over the video cassette players.

The *Redd Horne* court began its analysis with the observation that the two components of clause (1) of the definition of a public performance are disjunctive. 749 F.2d at 159. "The first category is self-evident; it is 'a place open to the public.' The second category, commonly referred to as a semi-public place, is determined by the size and composition of the audience." *Id.*

The court then concluded that the performances were occurring at a place open to the public, which it found to be the entire store, including the viewing rooms.

> Any member of the public can view a motion picture by paying the appropriate fee. The services provided by Maxwell's are essentially the same as a movie theatre, with the additional feature of privacy. The relevant "place" within the meaning of Section 101 is each of Maxwell's two stores, not each individual booth within each store. Simply because the cassettes can be viewed in private does not mitigate the essential fact that Maxwell's is unquestionably open to the public.

749 F.2d at 159.

The *Redd Horne* court reached this conclusion despite the fact that when a customer watched a movie at Maxwell's, the viewing room was closed to other members of the public. Nevertheless, Aveco asserts that factual differences between Maxwell's stores and its own require a different result in this case.

Aveco first observes that when Maxwell's employees "performed" the video cassettes, they did so in a central location, the store's main area. This lobby was undeniably "open to the public." Aveco suggests that, in *Redd Horne*, the location of the customers in the private rooms was simply irrelevant, for the performers were in a public place, the lobby. In the case at bar, Aveco continues, its employees do not perform anything, the customers do. Unlike Maxwell's employees located in the public lobby, Aveco's customers are in private screening rooms. Aveco argues that while these viewing rooms are available to anyone for rent, they are private during each rental period, and therefore, not "open to the public." The performance-the playing of the video cassette-thus occurs not in the public lobby, but in the private viewing rooms.

We disagree. The necessary implication of Aveco's analysis is that Redd Horne would have been decided differently had Maxwell's located its video cassette players in a locked closet in the back of the stores. We do not read Redd Horne to adopt such an analysis. The Copyright Act speaks of performances at a place open to the public. It does not require that the public place be actually crowded with people. A telephone booth, a taxi cab, and even a pay toilet are commonly regarded as "open to the public," even though they are usually occupied only by one party at a time. Our opinion in *Redd Horne* turned not on the precise whereabouts of the video cassette players, but on the nature of Maxwell's stores. Maxwell's, like Aveco, was willing to make a viewing room and video cassette available to any member of the public with the inclination to avail himself of this service. It is this availability that made Maxwell's stores public places, not the coincidence that the video cassette players were situated in the lobby. Because we find Redd Horne indistinguishable from the case at bar, we find that Aveco's operations constituted an authorization of public performances of Producers' copyrighted works. ...

III

We therefore conclude that Aveco, by renting its rooms to members of the general public in which they may view performances of Producers' copyrighted video cassettes, obtained from any source, has authorized public performances of those cassettes. This is a violation of Producers' Section 106 rights and is appropriately enjoined. We therefore will affirm the order of the district court.

Columbia Pictures Indus. v. Professional Real Estate Investors
866 F.2d 278 (9th Cir. 1989)

O'SCANNLAIN, Circuit Judge:

Columbia Pictures, Inc. and other appellants, all of which are motion picture producers, appeal the district court's grant of summary judgment in favor of Professional Real Estate Investors, Inc. and Kenneth Irwin, operators of La Mancha, a hotel resort in Palm Springs, California. The district court (William P. Gray, Senior United States District Judge, presiding) concluded that a hotel did not violate the Copyright Act by renting videodiscs for viewing on hotel-provided video equipment in guests' rooms. We affirm Judge Gray's decision.

FACTS AND PROCEEDINGS

La Mancha hotel guests may rent movie videodiscs from the lobby gift shop for a $5 to $7.50 daily fee per disc, which can be charged on the hotel bill. Each guest room is equipped with a large screen projection television and videodisc player. Hotel employees are available upon request to answer questions by guests about operating the in-room equipment. Guests view the videodisc movies projected on the television screens in their rooms.

After learning of these activities at La Mancha, Columbia Pictures, Inc. and six other motion picture studios ("Columbia") filed suit to prevent La Mancha from renting videodiscs to its guests, alleging copyright infringement. La Mancha counterclaimed, alleging unfair competition and violation of antitrust laws. Cross-motions for summary judgment concerning the copyright infringement claim were thereafter filed.

The district court granted La Mancha's motion for summary judgment, concluding as a matter of law that the movies were not performed "publicly" within the meaning of the Copyright Act when hotel guests viewed them in their own hotel rooms. Columbia timely appealed. ...

DISCUSSION

... Because it is uncontroverted that the motion pictures have been "performed" within the meaning of the Act, the narrow issue before us is whether La Mancha performed copyrighted works "publicly" within the meaning of 17 U.S.C. § 106(4). ... Columbia argues that when La Mancha permits hotel guests to rent videodiscs for in-room viewing on hotel provided equipment, such actions constitute a public performance....

A. Does the Public Place Clause Apply?

... Applying the public place clause of Section 101, Columbia argues that because La Mancha's hotel rooms can be rented by members of the public, they are "open to the public," and therefore, movies viewed in a guest's room at La Mancha are "performed ... publicly." The plain language and the legislative history together lead us to conclude that hotel guest rooms are not "public" for purposes of the Act.

Columbia largely relies upon two Third Circuit cases for its position. In *Columbia Pictures Industries v. Redd Horne*, 749 F.2d 154 (3d Cir. 1984), the Third Circuit held that private viewing rooms would not escape the "public place" clause because the pertinent place was the entire store—which was public. That court drew its conclusion after determining that "[t]he services provided by Maxwells [the video stores] are essentially the same as movie theaters."

In *Columbia Pictures Industries, Inc. v. Aveco, Inc.* 800 F.2d 59 (3d Cir. 1986), the court noted that "[o]ur opinion in Redd Horne turned not on the precise whereabouts of the video cassette players, but on the *nature* of Maxwell's stores. Maxwell's, like Aveco, was willing to make a viewing room and video cassette available to any member of the public with the inclination to avail himself of this service." *Id.* at 63 (emphasis added).

La Mancha's operation differs from those in Aveco and Redd Horne because its "nature" is the providing of living accommodations and general hotel services, which may incidentally include the rental of videodiscs to interested guests for viewing in guest rooms.

While the hotel may indeed be "open to the public," a guest's hotel room, once rented, is not. This conclusion is further supported by common experience. La Mancha guests do not view the videodiscs in hotel meeting rooms used for large gatherings. The movies are viewed exclusively in guest rooms, places where individuals enjoy a substantial degree of privacy, not unlike their own homes.

Consideration of pertinent legislative history also compels our rejection of appellant's claim. The House Commentary on the 1976 version of the Act attempted to clarify the meaning of "perform the copyrighted work publicly":

> Under Clause (1) of the definition of "publicly" in § 101, a performance ... is "public" if it takes place "at a place open to the public or at any place where a substantial number of persons outside of a normal circle of a family and its social acquaintances is gathered." One of the principal purposes of the definition was to make clear that, contrary to the decision in *Metro-Goldwyn-Mayer Dist. Corp. v. Wyatt*, 21 C.O. Bull. 203 (D. Md. 1932), performances in "semi-public" places such as clubs, lodges, factories, summer camps and schools are "public performances" subject to copyright control. The term "a family" in this context would include an individual living alone, so that a gathering confined to the individual's social acquaintances would normally be regarded as private. Routine meetings of businesses and governmental personnel would be excluded because they do not represent the gathering of a "substantial number of persons."

H.R. Rep. No. 1476, 64, 94th Cong., 2d Sess., *reprinted in* 1976 U.S. Code Cong. & Admin. News 5659, 5677-78. This passage from the legislative history reveals that Congress intended neither the number of persons at a performance nor the location of the performance to be determinative of the public character of a performance. Nevertheless, to the extent that a gathering of one's social acquaintances is normally regarded as private, we conclude that in-room videodisc movie showings do not occur at a "place open to the public." ...

CONCLUSION

We conclude that La Mancha does not violate section 106(4) by providing in-room videodisc players and renting videodiscs to its guests. In drawing this conclusion, we are aware that technology has often leapfrogged statutory schemes. Nevertheless, it is for Congress, not for the courts, to update the Copyright Act if it wishes to protect viewing of videodisc movies in guest rooms at La Mancha.

Notes and Questions

1. Is *Professional Real Estate* consistent with *Aveco*? A key intellectual maneuver in *Aveco* was the evaluation of the defendant's entire store, and not simply the rented booths, as public places. On that rationale, aren't hotels equally "open to the public"?

2. The decision in *Aveco* seems far from obvious. If a "member of the public" had tried to enter one of Aveco's rooms while it was occupied, presumably the intruder would have been told that the room "was not open" until the occupant left. It therefore would have been easy to conclude that the rooms were not a place open to the public. And what about the court's conclusion that Aveco authorized the performances in question? True, Aveco facilitated the performances, but is facilitation the same thing as authorization? If you believe the court was "stretching" doctrine to find infringement, do you think that the court hoped to advance an unstated policy by doing so?

3. The litigation over the alleged public performance of movies in hotel rooms took one more turn in *On Command Video Corp. v. Columbia Pictures Industries*, 777 F. Supp. 787 (N.D. Cal. 1991). In that case, the plaintiff On Command sued for declaratory relief, claiming that its electronic delivery of on demand video tape signals to hotel rooms did not constitute public performance of the defendant's movies. The court ruled against On Command, finding that although hotel rooms were not open to the public, the guests requesting the movie signals were "members of the public." Was this conclusion correct in light of *Professional Real Estate*?

1. PERFORMANCE RIGHTS IN SOUND RECORDINGS

Section 106(4) of the Copyright Act conspicuously omits sound recordings from the list of works whose copyright holders have a right of public performance. Thus, whenever a piece of recorded music is played in public—for example over the radio, at a ballpark, in a department store, or by a DJ at a club—the owners of the sound recording copyright are not entitled to any licensing fees. Instead, only the owners of the copyright in the underlying musical work are entitled to receive licensing fees. This is the case even though the performers of the sound recording may be far more famous than individual who wrote the song.

This omission exists because of the peculiar history of copyright protection for sound recordings. Before 1972, state law provided the only protection for sound recordings, and the spottiness of those rights created an environment in which piracy flourished. The recording industry understandably wanted federal copyright protection and lobbied for change, but it faced a significant obstacle. The absence of federal protection for sound recordings meant that those who publicly performed recorded music, particularly radio stations, owed royalties only to composers of music or their successors in interest. They owed nothing to the performers and predictably resisted the recording industry's entreaties for change. Eventually, the two sides compromised. In 1972, The Sound Recording Amendment Act changed federal copyright law to prohibit only the unauthorized mechanical reproduction of sound recordings. The recording industry could now bring federal copyright actions against record pirates, but radio stations remained free to perform recorded music without paying royalties to performers.

The limited protection of sound recordings carried over into the 1976 Act. This did not mean that the recording industry was satisfied. Performers contribute a great deal when they record music written by others, so why shouldn't they share in the profits from public performances of recorded music? The recording industry regularly advanced this argument to Congress in an attempt to add full performance rights to the Copyright Act, but to no avail. However, Congress did eventually enact additional limited performance rights.

In the late 20th Century, the advent of digital technology raised the possibility that consumers might stop purchasing traditional recorded music like CDs and listen instead to music transmitted over the Internet. This possibility would, if fully realized, damage the revenue stream traditionally relied upon by the recording industry. Congress responded in 1995 by enacting § 106(6) of the Copyright Act, which gives copyright holders the exclusive right to publicly perform sound recordings by means of "digital audio transmission."

The precise contours of digital music performance rights are quite complicated, and full consideration is beyond the scope of a basic course in copyright. It is, however, worth noting the rough contours of those rights as expressed in § 114(d) of the Copyright Act. In particular, the Copyright Act sets up a three-tiered system for digital sound recording performance rights:

1. *Performances requiring a license from the sound recording owner.* Digital performances that are "interactive," i.e. that allow a consumer to choose which songs are performed and to significantly control the playback of the song, require an express license from the sound recording owner. These kinds of performances are mostly likely to substitute for purchases of copies of sound recordings, and sound recording owners therefore have the strongest rights in this area. 17 U.S.C. § 114(d)(2)(A)(i).

2. *Performances subject to a compulsory license.* Digital performances that are "non-interactive," i.e. that transmit sound recordings in a manner that is largely not controlled by the consumer, are subject to a statutory license. 17 U.S.C. § 114(d)(2). The Copyright Act sets forth detailed requirements for this license, including limitations on preannouncing upcoming songs, the number of songs by a given artist or from a certain album that can be played in a given time period, etc. Royalty levels are set through voluntary industry negotiation, subject to

administrative determination if the parties cannot reach agreement. Many music webcasting services are designed to fall within this category.

3. *Performances exempt from any license.* Digital over-the-air broadcasts provided without subscription are completely exempt from either negotiated or compulsory licenses, and therefore not subject to the digital public performance right. 17 U.S.C. § 144(d)(1). Thus, for example, FCC-licensed digital radio broadcasts would be exempt from any licensing requirement. Note that this exemption applies only to over-the-air digital broadcasts, so does not apply to traditional analog radio stations who wish to re-broadcast their content over the Internet. *See Bonneville Int'l Corp. v. Peters*, 347 F.3d 485 (3d Cir. 2003). Such re-broadcasts would require either an express or compulsory license.

As noted above, the provisions dealing with digital sound recording licenses are extremely complicated, reflecting detailed bargaining between numerous industry participants. To some extent, the complexity of these provisions can make it difficult to engage with these aspects of the copyright system. However, it is important to note that these provisions directly govern a significant part of the music industry and are responseble for its current shape and structure.

As more sound recording performances are delivered in digital form, we can expect these complicated provisions to gain increasing importance and have a greater effect on the shape and structure of the music industry.

Notes and Questions

1. Note that the complicated digital public performance provisions above cover only the copyrights in the *sound recordings*. Any company wishing to provide digital public performances would, in addition to complying with the complicated provisions above, also have to secure licenses for publicly performing all of the *musical works* that are embodied in the sound recordings. Thus, such companies would be required to secure licenses at least twice over. Licensing of the public performance rights in musical works is typically handled by collective rights organizations, described in the next section, *infra*.

2. The detailed statutory structure surrounding musical works, sound recordings, and public performance rights represents a relatively extreme example of the Copyright Act tailoring its rights and limitations to the peculiarities of a specific industry. Much of this structure can be explained as a response to historical happenstance as well as interest group pressure and bargaining. But does it make sense from a policy perspective? If you could start from scratch, would you design a statutory structure that resembles the one we have? If not, how would you change it?

3. In 2015, the Copyright Office issued a comprehensive report on music licensing, in which it noted:

> There is a widespread perception that our licensing system is broken. Songwriters and recording artists are concerned that they cannot make a living under the existing structure, which raises serious and systemic concerns for the future. Music publishers and performance rights organizations are frustrated that so much of their licensing activity is subject to government control, so they are constrained in the marketplace. Record labels and digital services complain that the licensing process is burdensome and inefficient, making it difficult to innovate.

U.S. Copyright Office, *Copyright and the Music Marketplace: A Report of the Register of Copyrights*, at 1 (Feb. 2015). The Copyright Office noted that, although there was a general consensus that some reform is needed, there was far less agreement about precisely what should be done. In the end, the Office proposed a number of changes that would seek to simplify the regulatory structure, treat musical works and sound recordings more consistently, make the music licensing process simpler and more transparent, and reduce the scope of government involvement in the details of the music industry. To date, Congress has not passed any legislation in response to the Office's report.

2. SECTION 110 LIMITATIONS ON PUBLIC PERFORMANCE RIGHTS

The decision to give copyright holders control over all public performances creates the possibility of unintuitive results in at least some cases. For example, what happens if a group of friends turns on a portable radio in a public park? Or what about a teacher who shows a film to her class? Such acts constitute public performances under the definition provided in § 101. Do people really owe royalties for such ordinary, everyday behavior? Congress has responded to this problem by enacting a series of limitations on the right of public performance in § 110 of the Copyright Act. These limitations permit public performances, under certain limited circumstances, for:

(1) Face-to-face teaching activities
(2) Instructional broadcasting and distance learning
(3) Religious services
(4) Live performances of musical and literary works with no commercial advantage
(5) Reception of broadcasts in a public place
(6) Performance of music by agricultural fairs
(7) Performance of music in connection with sale of phonorecords or sheet music
(8) and (9) Noncomercial performances for the deaf and blind
(10) Charitable performances by veterans and fraternal organizations

Each of these limitations is subject to specific requirements and conditions. *See* 17 U.S.C. § 110 for detailed provisions.

These limitations reflect a mix of pragmatic policy and political compromise, making their coverage spotty and sometimes difficult to understand. For example, it is easy to explain § 110(1) and (2), which exempt from the § 106 performance right the performance or display of works in the course of face-to-face teaching and instructional activities transmitted over digital networks. It is also fairly easy to make sense of § 110(4), which exempts the non-profit performance of nondramatic literary and musical works, although you might wonder why the same exemption does not exist for the non-profit performance of other works. By contrast, it seems a harder to explain why § 106(6) exempts the "performance of a nondramatic musical work by a governmental body or a nonprofit agricultural or horticultural organization, in the course of an annual agricultural or horticultural fair or exhibition conducted by such body or organization," but not other fairs conducted by similar organizations.

Perhaps the most complex of these provisions is § 110(5). At root, its basic provision, § 110(5)(A), exempts from the public performance right those performances accomplished by turning on a radio or other device "of a kind commonly used in private homes," as long as there is no charge. Thus, the friends who turn on a portable radio in a public park do not commit infringement. However, complications quickly follow in § 110(5)(B), which contains more detailed provisions that govern the use of equipment in retail stores, depending on their square footage. Why would Congress choose to regulate the public performance of music in this way? The answer lies once again in the peculiar history of the Copyright Act.

From 1931 until the enactment of the 1976 Act, the Supreme Court struggled to define coherently infringing public performances of copyrighted works. Many of these cases involved the retransmission of radio or television signals, a subject now regulated by sections 110(5), 111, 119 and 122 of the Copyright Act. Then, in 1975, the Court decided *Twentieth Century Music Corp. v. Aiken*, 422 U.S. 151 (1975). In *Aiken*, the plaintiff claimed that the defendant committed infringement by playing a conventional radio through a system of four in-ceiling speakers that could be heard by customers and employees at the defendant's fast food restaurant. The intuition behind the plaintiff's claim was simple. The defendant would need a license if he wanted a live band to play the plaintiff's music in the restaurant. Why should the result be any different if the defendant accomplished that result by using a radio? The defendant's response was equally simple. The plaintiff had already received compensation for the performance via payment from the radio stations whose broadcasts were heard in the restaurant. The Court decided against the plaintiff on the ground that Aiken did not perform the plaintiff's music. The Court considered a contrary result inequitable for two reasons:

First, a person in Aiken's position would have no sure way of protecting himself from liability for copyright infringement except by keeping his radio set turned off. For even if he secured a license from ASCAP,[48] he would have no way of either foreseeing or controlling the broadcast of compositions whose copyright was held by someone else. Secondly, to hold that all in Aiken's position "performed" these musical compositions would be to authorize the sale of an untold number of licenses for what is basically a single public rendition of a copyrighted work. The exaction of such multiple tribute would go far beyond what is required for the economic protection of copyright owners, and would be wholly at odds with the balanced congressional purpose behind [the Copyright Act].[49]

Congress responded to the *Aiken* decision in the 1976 Act. The legislative history clearly takes the position that the § 106(4) public performance right included multiple transmissions of a single origin performance:

[A] singer is performing when he or she sings a song; a broadcasting network is performing when it transmits his or her performance (whether simultaneously or from records); a local broadcaster is performing when it transmits the network broadcast; a cable television system is performing when it retransmits the broadcast to its subscribers, and any individual is performing whenever he or she plays a phonorecord embodying the performance or communicates the performance by turning on a receiving set.

This position obviously reflected some sympathy for the position taken by the plaintiff in *Aiken*, but it also created problems because, as noted in the quotation above, a person turning the radio on performs the works heard. Limitations therefore became necessary in order to avoid making ordinary radio listeners into infringers. Congress accomplished this through a series of statutory limitations on the general public performance right that included § 110(5).

When originally enacted, § 110(5) had only a single provision that is now § 110(5)(A). That provision exempted those performers who received transmission "on a single receiving apparatus of a kind commonly used in private homes," a clear nod to the facts and result of *Aiken*. Predictably, this led to litigation over the kind of equipment that qualified as "commonly used in private homes" as larger, better funded commercial establishments used higher quality, more powerful sound systems to avoid paying license fees for having the radio on. The resulting patchwork of confusing decisions, along with aggressive claims made by the owners of music copyrights, led Congress to amend § 110(5) by adding §

---

[48] Editor's Note: ASCAP is a collective rights organization that provides blanket licenses for public performance of musical works. *See* the next section, *infra*.

[49] *Aiken*, 422 U.S. 151, 163 (1975).

110(5)(B). That section adopted a bright-line, square foot limit approach to the kinds of establishments that would owe a license fee for having the radio or television on.

3. PERFORMING RIGHTS ORGANIZATIONS

If copyright holders get to collect royalties for public performances of their work, how do they enforce their rights? It would be extremely burdensome, if not impossible, for a single individual to detect unauthorized public performances (for example, in restaurants, retail stores, or other establishments across the country) or to handle all the license requests that would come in daily for a popular piece of music. It would also be extremely difficult for a commercial establishment like a nightclub, restaurant, or retail store to get licenses for every individual musical work that might be performed there.

Performing rights organizations offer a solution to this problem by collecting the rights to perform numerous works and licensing those rights on a collective basis. This enables radio stations, restaurants, and other public places to buy licenses (so-called "blanket licenses") for thousands of works at one time for a single fee. The performing rights organizations then distribute the collected money to the various copyright holders according to some predetermined formula. Performing rights organizations also watch for and bring enforcement actions against those who perform works in the organization's library without consent. For ordinary public performance of music, the primary such organizations are the American Society of Composers, Authors and Publishers (ASCAP), Broadcast Music, Inc. (BMI), and the Society of European Stage Authors and Composers (SESAC). Other, smaller organizations exist to collect royalties for digital performances of music.

The convenience of a blanket license from organizations like ASCAP comes at a price. It may work well for a business that wants to perform a significant part of ASCAP's library (perhaps true of some radio stations), but what about someone who wants to perform only a small portion of that library, or someone who wants to perform works only infrequently? In theory, ASCAP could offer licenses to fit every conceivable purchaser, but it has not. Those unhappy with the choices offered by performing rights organizations have brought antitrust suits. These suits have not generally succeeded, but they have led the Justice Department to scrutinize the behavior of ASCAP and BMI, who now operate under consent decrees that submit disputes about to blanket license fees to federal district court.

SECTION F. COMPULSORY LICENSING

Copyright holders generally have complete control over the rights they hold. For example, the owner of the copyright in a book sets the terms and conditions for adapting a book into a movie, or he can decide to prohibit the use. Such exclusivity parallels the general operation of property rights in our society. However, the Copyright Act imposes a number of statutory or "compulsory" licenses that disrupt this system of exclusivity. Although the details of various compulsory licenses differ, they all force copyright holders to permit certain otherwise infringing uses of their works at statutorily prescribed rates.

The best-known compulsory license gives record producers the right to make and distribute phonorecords of musical works as long as they pay the fee set by a panel of administrative Copyright Royalty Judges. To appreciate how this license works, keep in mind that in its absence, the copyright holder in a musical work decides whether to exploit the work through recording, and if so, by whom and at what price. This means that the copyright holder could decide to allow only himself to make such records, or he could permit only those whose performances he liked to do so.

Section 115 of the Copyright Act changes this by allowing any person to make recordings of a musical work if the copyright holder has authorized the manufacture and distribution of at least one recording of the work. Once this condition has been satisfied, a person wanting to make and sell a recording of the work need only give notice of such recording, comply with various statutory formalities, and arrange to pay the prescribed fee. The copyright holder therefore controls only the decision about whether the work will be recorded at all. Once such a recording gets made and distributed, anyone can do so without the copyright holder's permission. Indeed, the recording artist can even arrange the work to suit his or her recording style, even if the copyright holder dislikes the resulting performance (although the recording artist may not go so far as to "change the basic melody or fundamental character of the work"). All the copyright holder gets to do is collect royalties.

Congress enacted an early version of the § 115 compulsory license because it worried about the potential concentration of market power in the production of recorded music. Without the compulsory license, powerful companies could have collected exclusive rights to create recorded music, thereby reducing competition in the market for recorded music. The compulsory license prevented this from happening by forcing copyright holders to accept competition in the market for recorded music.

The compulsory license has apparently had the desired effect. The music industry has flourished since 1909. Indeed, the music industry seems to have grown accustomed to the limited rights introduced the compulsory license scheme. Although some copyright holders complained about compulsory licensing in 1909, no one seriously tried to get rid of it when Congress drafted the 1976 Act. Accordingly, the compulsory license seems here to stay.

Although the compulsory license in § 115 was the first example of a compulsory license in U.S. copyright law, Congress has since created compulsory licenses in other areas as well. These include compulsory licenses for secondary transmissions by cable television companies, § 111(c), public performances of music by jukeboxes, § 116, public television companies, § 118, and secondary transmission of "superstation" programs, § 119. As already discussed in the preceding sections, Congress most recently created a compulsory license for certain non-interactive digital public performances of sound recordings. § 114(d).

Notes and Questions

1.   What do you think of compulsory licensing? Do you consider it a fair or efficient solution to imperfections in markets for copyrighted works? Alternatively, does compulsory licensing harm the operation of those markets by robbing copyright holders of the ability to control the use of their works? These are not idle questions, for people have proposed compulsory licensing in many areas affected by copyright, including the online swapping of music files. Do you favor widespread use of compulsory licensing?

2.   Today, relatively few recording artists actually use the compulsory licensing process outlined in § 115. Instead, the Harry Fox Agency has emerged as the private commercial entity that grants mechanical reproduction licenses, collects and distributes royalties, and enforces copyright infringement claims. Obviously, the § 115 royalty rates act as a ceiling on rates set through Harry Fox, whose operations are outlined at their website, www.harryfox.com.

SECTION G. DIGITAL TECHNOLOGY AND EXCLUSIVE RIGHTS

Congress wrote the 1976 Act before the widespread use of computers and digital networks. Not surprisingly, these technologies complicate the interpretation of exclusive rights like reproduction, distribution, and public performance. This section studies how courts have responded to some of these challenges. We begin with two cases that highlight some of the immediate challenges raised by digital technology.

Playboy Enterprises v. Frena
839 F. Supp. 1552 (M.D. Fla. 1993)

SCHLESINGER, District Judge.

This cause is before the Court on Plaintiff's First Motion for Partial Summary Judgment (Copyright Infringement) as to Defendant Frena ...

Defendant George Frena operates a subscription computer bulletin board service, Techs Warehouse BBS ("BBS"), that distributed unauthorized copies of Plaintiff Playboy Enterprises, Inc.'s ("PEI") copyrighted photographs. BBS is accessible via telephone modem to customers. For a fee, or to those who purchase certain products from Defendant Frena, anyone with an appropriately equipped computer can log onto BBS. Once logged on subscribers may browse through different BBS directories to look at the pictures and customers may also download the high quality computerized copies of the photographs and then store the copied image from Frena's computer onto their home computer. Many of the images found on BBS include adult subject matter. One hundred and seventy of the images that were available on BBS were copies of photographs taken from PEI's copyrighted materials. ...

Subscribers can upload material onto the bulletin board so that any other subscriber, by accessing their computer, can see that material. Defendant Frena states in his Affidavit filed August 4, 1993, that he never uploaded any of PEI's photographs onto BBS and that subscribers to BBS uploaded the photographs. Defendant Frena states that as soon as he was served with a summons and made aware of this matter, he removed the photographs from BBS and has since that time monitored BBS to prevent additional photographs of PEI from being uploaded. ...

Public distribution of a copyrighted work is a right reserved to the copyright owner, and usurpation of that right constitutes infringement. PEI's right under 17 U.S.C. § 106(3) to distribute copies to the public has been implicated by Defendant Frena. Section 106(3) grants the copyright owner "the exclusive right to sell, give away, rent or lend any material embodiment of his work." 2 Melville B. Nimmer, Nimmer on Copyright § 8.11[A], at 8-124.1 (1993). There is no dispute that Defendant Frena supplied a product containing unauthorized copies of a copyrighted work. It does not matter that Defendant Frena claims he did not make the copies itself. ...

There is irrefutable evidence of direct copyright infringement in this case. It does not matter that Defendant Frena may have been unaware of the copyright infringement. Intent to infringe is not needed to find copyright infringement. Intent or knowledge is not an element of infringement, and thus even an innocent infringer is liable for infringement; rather, innocence is significant to a trial court when it fixes statutory damages, which is a remedy equitable in nature.

... The Court finds that the undisputed facts mandate partial summary judgment that Defendant Frena's unauthorized display and distribution of PEI's copyrighted material is copyright infringement under 17 U.S.C. § 501. ...

[The court's discussion of other causes of action is omitted.]

Religious Technology Center v. Netcom
907 F. Supp. 1361 (N.D. Cal. 1995)

WHYTE, District Judge.

This case concerns an issue of first impression regarding intellectual property rights in cyberspace. Specifically, this order addresses whether the operator of a computer bulletin board service ("BBS"), and the large Internet access provider that allows that BBS to reach the Internet, should be liable for copyright infringement committed by a subscriber of the BBS.

Plaintiffs Religious Technology Center ("RTC") and Bridge Publications, Inc. ("BPI") hold copyrights in the unpublished and published works of L. Ron Hubbard, the late founder of the Church of Scientology ("the Church"). Defendant Dennis Erlich ("Erlich") is a former minister of Scientology turned vocal critic of the Church, whose pulpit is now the Usenet newsgroup alt.religion.scientology ("a.r.s."), an on-line forum for discussion and criticism of Scientology. Plaintiffs maintain that Erlich infringed their copyrights when he posted portions of their works on a.r.s. Erlich gained his access to the Internet through defendant Thomas Klemesrud's ("Klemesrud's") BBS "support.com." Klemesrud is the operator of the BBS, which is run out of his home and has approximately 500 paying users. Klemesrud's BBS is not directly linked to the Internet, but gains its connection through the facilities of defendant Netcom On-Line Communications, Inc. ("Netcom"), one of the largest providers of Internet access in the United States.

After failing to convince Erlich to stop his postings, plaintiffs contacted defendants Klemesrud and Netcom. Klemesrud responded to plaintiffs' demands that Erlich be kept off his system by asking plaintiffs to prove that they owned the copyrights to the works posted by Erlich. However, plaintiffs refused Klemesrud's request as unreasonable. Netcom similarly refused plaintiffs' request that Erlich not be allowed to gain access to the Internet through its system. Netcom contended that it would be impossible to prescreen Erlich's postings and that to kick Erlich off the Internet meant kicking off the hundreds of users of Klemesrud's BBS. Consequently, plaintiffs named Klemesrud and Netcom in their suit against Erlich. ...

Plaintiffs argue that, although Netcom was not itself the source of any of the infringing materials on its system, it nonetheless should be

→liable for infringement, either directly, contributorily, or vicariously. ... Netcom disputes these theories of infringement. ...

The parties do not dispute the basic processes that occur when Erlich posts his allegedly infringing messages to a.r.s. Erlich connects to Klemesrud's BBS using a telephone and a modem. Erlich then transmits his messages to Klemesrud's computer, where they are automatically briefly stored. According to a prearranged pattern established by Netcom's software, Erlich's initial act of posting a message to the Usenet results in the automatic copying of Erlich's message from Klemesrud's computer onto Netcom's computer and onto other computers on the Usenet. In order to ease transmission and for the convenience of Usenet users, Usenet servers maintain postings from newsgroups for a short period of time-eleven days for Netcom's system and three days for Klemesrud's system. Once on Netcom's computers, messages are available to Netcom's customers and Usenet neighbors, who may then download the messages to their own computers. Netcom's local server makes available its postings to a group of Usenet servers, which do the same for other servers until all Usenet sites worldwide have obtained access to the postings, which takes a matter of hours. ...

The court believes that Netcom's act of designing or implementing a system that automatically and uniformly creates temporary copies of all data sent through it is not unlike that of the owner of a copying machine who lets the public make copies with it. Although some of the people using the machine may directly infringe copyrights, courts analyze the machine owner's liability under the rubric of contributory infringement, not direct infringement. Plaintiffs' theory would create many separate acts of infringement and, carried to its natural extreme, would lead to unreasonable liability. It is not difficult to conclude that Erlich infringes by copying a protected work onto his computer and by posting a message to a newsgroup. However, plaintiffs' theory further implicates a Usenet server that carries Erlich's message to other servers regardless of whether that server acts without any human intervention beyond the initial setting up of the system. It would also result in liability for every single Usenet server in the worldwide link of computers transmitting Erlich's message to every other computer. These parties, who are liable under plaintiffs' theory, do no more than operate or implement a system that is essential if Usenet messages are to be widely distributed. There is no need to construe the Act to make all of these parties infringers. Although copyright is a strict liability statute, there should still be some element of volition or causation which is lacking where a defendant's system is merely used to create a copy by a third party. ...

[*Playboy Enterprises, Inc. v. Frena*] concluded that the defendant infringed the plaintiff's exclusive rights to publicly distribute and display copies of its works. The court is not entirely convinced that the mere possession of a digital copy on a BBS that is accessible to some members of the public constitutes direct infringement by the BBS operator. ... Only the subscriber should be liable for causing the distribution of plaintiffs' work, as the contributing actions of the BBS provider are automatic and indiscriminate. Erlich could have posted his messages through countless access providers and the outcome would be the same: anyone with access to Usenet newsgroups would be able to read his messages. There is no logical reason to draw a line around Netcom and Klemesrud and say that they are uniquely responsible for distributing Erlich's messages. Netcom is not even the first link in the chain of distribution-Erlich had no direct relationship with Netcom but dealt solely with Klemesrud's BBS, which used Netcom to gain its Internet access. Every Usenet server has a role in the distribution, so plaintiffs' argument would create unreasonable liability. Where the BBS merely stores and passes along all messages sent by its subscribers and others, the BBS should not be seen as causing these works to be publicly distributed or displayed.

... Although the Internet consists of many different computers networked together, some of which may contain infringing files, it does not make sense to hold the operator of each computer liable as an infringer merely because his or her computer is linked to a computer with an infringing file. It would be especially inappropriate to hold liable a service that acts more like a conduit, in other words, one that does not itself keep an archive of files for more than a short duration. Finding such a service liable would involve an unreasonably broad construction of public distribution and display rights. No purpose would be served by holding liable those who have no ability to control the information to which their subscribers have access, even though they might be in some sense helping to achieve the Internet's automatic "public distribution" and the users' "public" display of files. ...

The court is not persuaded by plaintiffs' argument that Netcom is directly liable for the copies that are made and stored on its computer. Where the infringing subscriber is clearly directly liable for the same act, it does not make sense to adopt a rule that could lead to the liability of countless parties whose role in the infringement is nothing more than setting up and operating a system that is necessary for the functioning of the Internet. Such a result is unnecessary as there is already a party directly liable for causing the copies to be made. Plaintiffs occasionally claim that they only seek to hold liable a party that refuses to delete infringing files after they have been warned. However, such liability cannot be based on a theory of direct infringement, where knowledge is irrelevant. The court does not find workable a theory of infringement that would hold the entire Internet liable for activities that cannot reasonably be deterred. Billions of bits of data flow through the Internet and are necessarily stored on servers throughout the network and it is thus practically impossible to screen out infringing bits from noninfringing bits. Because the court cannot see any meaningful distinction (without regard to knowledge) between what Netcom did and what every other Usenet server does, the court finds that Netcom cannot be held liable for direct infringement.

[The court's discussion of third party copyright liability, fair use, and the case against Klemesrud is omitted.]

Notes and Questions

1. *Frena* and *Netcom* illustrate how the ubiquity of copying in the digital world could allow copyright holders to hold a broad range of actors liable for infringement. Those who operate computer networks effectively provide equipment that users can direct to make and distribute copies of copyrighted works. Does this mean that network operators themselves make and distribute copies of works, and if so, do they commit copyright infringement?

Frena and *Netcom* answer this question differently. Which one of them is correct, and why? Does one position or the other imply consequences that you think are unwarranted? As a descriptive matter, the position taken by *Netcom* has generally prevailed. Courts have instead preferred to analyze questions of service provider liability under the rubric of third party copyright liability, and not direct liability.

2. The Digital Millennium Copyright Act, passed in 1998 and now codified at 17 U.S.C. § 512, addressed some of the issues raised in *Frena* and *Netcom* by limiting the liability of Internet "service providers" in certain situations. We will study this later in Chapter Seven along with the problem of third party copyright liability.

3. *Frena* invokes the strict liability of copyright infringement to justify its decision. *Netcom* apparently disagrees, stating that "some element of volition or causation" must exist for liability when the defendant's system passively duplicates and transmits copyrighted works at the direction of others. What does the *Netcom* court mean by "some element of volition or causation"? Service providers like Netcom construct their systems to obey user commands with full knowledge that some users will commit infringement. Does acting in the face of such knowledge provide the necessary volition, or must a service provider affirmatively want its users to commit infringement?

Cartoon Network v. CSC Holdings
536 F.3d 121 (2d Cir. 2008)

WALKER, Circuit Judge:

Defendant-Appellant Cablevision Systems Corporation ("Cablevision") wants to market a new "Remote Storage" Digital Video Recorder system ("RS-DVR"), using a technology akin to both traditional, set-top digital video recorders, like TiVo ("DVRs"), and the video-on-demand

("VOD") services provided by many cable companies. Plaintiffs-Appellees produce copyrighted movies and television programs that they provide to Cablevision pursuant to numerous licensing agreements. They contend that Cablevision, through the operation of its RS-DVR system as proposed, would directly infringe their copyrights both by making unauthorized reproductions, and by engaging in public performances, of their copyrighted works. The material facts are not in dispute. Because we conclude that Cablevision would not directly infringe plaintiffs' rights under the Copyright Act by offering its RS-DVR system to consumers, we reverse the district court's award of summary judgment to plaintiffs, and we vacate its injunction against Cablevision.

BACKGROUND

Today's television viewers increasingly use digital video recorders ("DVRs") instead of video cassette recorders ("VCRs") to record television programs and play them back later at their convenience. DVRs generally store recorded programming on an internal hard drive rather than a cassette. But, as this case demonstrates, the generic term "DVR" actually refers to a growing number of different devices and systems. Companies like TiVo sell a stand-alone DVR device that is typically connected to a user's cable box and television much like a VCR. Many cable companies also lease to their subscribers "set-top storage DVRs," which combine many of the functions of a standard cable box and a stand-alone DVR in a single device.

In March 2006, Cablevision, an operator of cable television systems, announced the advent of its new "Remote Storage DVR System." As designed, the RS-DVR allows Cablevision customers who do not have a stand-alone DVR to record cable programming on central hard drives housed and maintained by Cablevision at a "remote" location. RS-DVR customers may then receive playback of those programs through their home television sets, using only a remote control and a standard cable box equipped with the RS-DVR software. Cablevision notified its content providers, including plaintiffs, of its plans to offer RS-DVR, but it did not seek any license from them to operate or sell the RS-DVR.

Plaintiffs, which hold the copyrights to numerous movies and television programs, sued Cablevision for declaratory and injunctive relief. They alleged that Cablevision's proposed operation of the RS-DVR would directly infringe their exclusive rights to both reproduce and publicly perform their copyrighted works. Critically for our analysis here, plaintiffs alleged theories only of direct infringement, not contributory infringement, and defendants waived any defense based on fair use.

Ultimately, the United States District Court for the Southern District of New York (Denny Chin, *Judge*), awarded summary judgment to the plaintiffs and enjoined Cablevision from operating the RS-DVR system without licenses from its content providers. At the outset, we think it helpful to an understanding of our decision to describe, in greater detail, both the RS-DVR and the district court's opinion.

I.   Operation of the RS-DVR System

Cable companies like Cablevision aggregate television programming from a wide variety of "content providers"—the various broadcast and cable channels that produce or provide individual programs—and transmit those programs into the homes of their subscribers via coaxial cable. At the outset of the transmission process, Cablevision gathers the content of the various television channels into a single stream of data. Generally, this stream is processed and transmitted to Cablevision's customers in real time. Thus, if a Cartoon Network program is scheduled to air Monday night at 8pm, Cartoon Network transmits that program's data to Cablevision and other cable companies nationwide at that time, and the cable companies immediately re-transmit the data to customers who subscribe to that channel.

Under the new RS-DVR, this single stream of data is split into two streams. The first is routed immediately to customers as before. The second stream flows into a device called the Broadband Media Router ("BMR"), which buffers the data stream, reformats it, and sends it to the "Arroyo Server," which consists, in relevant part, of two data buffers and a number of high-capacity hard disks. The entire stream of data moves to the first buffer (the "primary ingest buffer"), at which point the server automatically inquires as to whether any customers want to record any of that programming. If a customer has requested a particular program, the data for that program move from the primary buffer into a secondary buffer, and then onto a portion of one of the hard disks allocated to that customer. As new data flow into the primary buffer, they overwrite a corresponding quantity of data already on the buffer. The primary ingest buffer holds no more than 0.1 seconds of each channel's programming at any moment. Thus, every tenth of a second, the data residing on this buffer are automatically erased and replaced. The data buffer in the BMR holds no more than 1.2 seconds of programming at any time. While buffering occurs at other points in the operation of the RS-DVR, only the BMR buffer and the primary ingest buffer are utilized absent any request from an individual subscriber.

As the district court observed, "the RS-DVR is not a single piece of equipment," but rather "a complex system requiring numerous computers, processes, networks of cables, and facilities staffed by personnel twenty-four hours a day and seven days a week." To the customer, however, the processes of recording and playback on the RS-DVR are similar to that of a standard set-top DVR. Using a remote control, the customer can record programming by selecting a program in advance from an on-screen guide, or by pressing the record button while viewing a given program. A customer cannot, however, record the earlier portion of a program once it has begun. To begin playback, the customer selects the show from an on-screen list of previously recorded programs. The principal difference in operation is that, instead of sending signals from the remote to an on-set box, the viewer sends signals from the remote, through the cable, to the Arroyo Server at Cablevision's central facility.

In this respect, RS-DVR more closely resembles a VOD service, whereby a cable subscriber uses his remote and cable box to request transmission of content, such as a movie, stored on computers at the cable company's facility. But unlike a VOD service, RS-DVR users can only play content that they previously requested to be recorded.

Cablevision has some control over the content available for recording: a customer can only record programs on the channels offered by Cablevision (assuming he subscribes to them). Cablevision can also modify the system to limit the number of channels available and considered doing so during development of the RS-DVR. ...

DISCUSSION

... "Section 106 of the Copyright Act grants copyright holders a bundle of exclusive rights...." This case implicates two of those rights: the right "to reproduce the copyrighted work in copies," and the right "to perform the copyrighted work publicly." 17 U.S.C. § 106(1), (4). As discussed above, the district court found that Cablevision infringed the first right by 1) buffering the data from its programming stream and 2) copying content onto the Arroyo Server hard disks to enable playback of a program requested by an RS-DVR customer. In addition, the district court found that Cablevision would infringe the public performance right by transmitting a program to an RS-DVR customer in response to that customer's playback request. We address each of these three allegedly infringing acts in turn.

I. The Buffer Data

It is undisputed that Cablevision, not any customer or other entity, takes the content from one stream of programming, after the split, and stores it, one small piece at a time, in the BMR buffer and the primary ingest buffer. As a result, the information is buffered before any customer requests a recording, and would be buffered even if no such request were made. The question is whether, by buffering the data that make up a given work, Cablevision "reproduce[s]" that work "in copies," and thereby infringes the copyright holder's reproduction right.

"Copies," as defined in the Copyright Act, "are material objects ... in which a work is fixed by any method ... and from which the work can be ... reproduced." The Act also provides that a work is "'fixed' in a tangible medium of expression when its embodiment ... is sufficiently permanent or stable to permit it to be ... reproduced ... *for a period of more than transitory duration*." (emphasis added). We believe that this language plainly imposes two distinct but related requirements: the work must be embodied in a medium, i.e., placed in a medium such that it can be perceived, reproduced, etc., from that medium (the "embodiment requirement"), and it must remain thus embodied "for a period of more than transitory duration" (the "duration requirement"). Unless both requirements are met, the work is not "fixed" in the buffer, and, as a result, the buffer data is not a "copy" of the original work whose data is buffered.

The district court mistakenly limited its analysis primarily to the embodiment requirement. As a result of this error, once it determined that the buffer data was "[c]learly ... capable of being reproduced," i.e., that the work was embodied in the buffer, the district court concluded that the work was therefore "fixed" in the buffer, and that a copy had thus been made. In doing so, it relied on a line of cases beginning with *MAI Systems Corp. v. Peak Computer Inc.*, 991 F.2d 511 (9th Cir.1993). It also relied on the United States Copyright Office's 2001 report on the Digital Millennium Copyright Act, which states, in essence, that an embodiment is fixed "[u]nless a reproduction manifests itself so fleetingly that *it cannot be copied.*" U.S. Copyright Office, *DMCA Section 104 Report* 111 (Aug.2001) ("*DMCA Report* ") (emphasis added), *available at* http://www. copyright.gov/reports/studies/dmca/sec-104-report-vol-1.pdf.

The district court's reliance on cases like *MAI Systems* is misplaced. In general, those cases conclude that an alleged copy is fixed without addressing the duration requirement; it does not follow, however, that those cases assume, much less establish, that such a requirement does not exist. Indeed, the duration requirement, by itself, was not at issue in *MAI Systems* and its progeny. As a result, they do not speak to the issues squarely before us here: If a work is only "embodied" in a medium for a period of transitory duration, can it be "fixed" in that medium, and thus a copy? And what constitutes a period "of more than transitory duration"? ...

The *MAI Systems* court referenced the "transitory duration" language but did not discuss or analyze it. The opinion notes that the defendants "vigorously" argued that the program's embodiment in the RAM was not a copy, but it does not specify the arguments defendants made. This omission suggests that the parties did not litigate the significance of the "transitory duration" language, and the court therefore had no occasion to address it. This is unsurprising, because it seems fair to assume that in these cases the program was embodied in the RAM for at least several minutes.

Accordingly, we construe *MAI Systems* and its progeny as holding that loading a program into a computer's RAM *can* result in copying that program. We do not read *MAI Systems* as holding that, as a matter of law, loading a program into a form of RAM *always* results in copying. Such a holding would read the "transitory duration" language out of the definition, and we do not believe our sister circuit would dismiss this statutory language without even discussing it. It appears the parties in *MAI Systems* simply did not dispute that the duration requirement was satisfied; this line of cases simply concludes that when a program is loaded into RAM, the embodiment requirement is satisfied—an important holding in itself, and one we see no reason to quibble with here. ...

In sum, no case law or other authority dissuades us from concluding that the definition of "fixed" imposes both an embodiment requirement and a duration requirement. We now turn to whether, in this case, those requirements are met by the buffer data.

Cablevision does not seriously dispute that copyrighted works are "embodied" in the buffer. Data in the BMR buffer can be reformatted and transmitted to the other components of the RS-DVR system. Data in the primary ingest buffer can be copied onto the Arroyo hard disks if a user has requested a recording of that data. Thus, a work's "embodiment" in either buffer "is sufficiently permanent or stable to permit it to be perceived, reproduced," (as in the case of the ingest buffer) "or otherwise communicated" (as in the BMR buffer). The result might be different if only a single second of a much longer work was placed in the buffer in isolation. In such a situation, it might be reasonable to conclude that only a minuscule portion of a work, rather than "a work" was embodied in the buffer. Here, however, where every second of an entire work is placed, one second at a time, in the buffer, we conclude that the work is embodied in the buffer.

Does any such embodiment last "for a period of more than transitory duration"? No bit of data remains in any buffer for more than a fleeting 1.2 seconds. And unlike the data in cases like *MAI Systems,* which remained embodied in the computer's RAM memory until the user turned the computer off, each bit of data here is rapidly and automatically overwritten as soon as it is processed. While our inquiry is necessarily fact-specific, and other factors not present here may alter the duration analysis significantly, these facts strongly suggest that the works in this case are embodied in the buffer for only a "transitory" period, thus failing the duration requirement.

Against this evidence, plaintiffs argue only that the duration is not transitory because the data persist "long enough for Cablevision to make reproductions from them." As we have explained above, however, this reasoning impermissibly reads the duration language out of the statute, and we reject it. Given that the data reside in no buffer for more than 1.2 seconds before being automatically overwritten, and in the absence of compelling arguments to the contrary, we believe that the copyrighted works here are not "embodied" in the buffers for a period of more than transitory duration, and are therefore not "fixed" in the buffers. Accordingly, the acts of buffering in the operation of the RS-DVR do not create copies, as the Copyright Act defines that term. Our resolution of this issue renders it unnecessary for us to determine whether any copies produced by buffering data would be de minimis, and we express no opinion on that question.

II. Direct Liability for Creating the Playback Copies

In most copyright disputes, the allegedly infringing act and the identity of the infringer are never in doubt. These cases turn on whether the conduct in question does, in fact, infringe the plaintiff's copyright. In this case, however, the core of the dispute is over the authorship of the infringing conduct. After an RS-DVR subscriber selects a program to record, and that program airs, a copy of the program—a copyrighted work—

resides on the hard disks of Cablevision's Arroyo Server, its creation un-authorized by the copyright holder. The question is *who* made this copy. If it is Cablevision, plaintiffs' theory of direct infringement succeeds; if it is the customer, plaintiffs' theory fails because Cablevision would then face, at most, secondary liability, a theory of liability expressly disa-vowed by plaintiffs.

Few cases examine the line between direct and contributory liability. Both parties cite a line of cases beginning with *Religious Technology Center v. Netcom On-Line Communication Services,* 907 F.Supp. 1361 (N.D Cal. 1995). In *Netcom,* a third-party customer of the defendant Internet service provider ("ISP") posted a copyrighted work that was auto-matically reproduced by the defendant's computer. The district court re-fused to impose direct liability on the ISP, reasoning that "[a]lthough copyright is a strict liability statute, there should still be some element of volition or causation which is lacking where a defendant's system is merely used to create a copy by a third party." Recently, the Fourth Cir-cuit endorsed the *Netcom* decision, noting that

> to establish *direct* liability under ... the Act, something more must be shown than mere ownership of a machine used by oth-ers to make illegal copies. There must be actual infringing con-duct with a nexus sufficiently close and causal to the illegal copy-ing that one could conclude that the machine owner himself trespassed on the exclusive domain of the copyright owner."

CoStar Group, Inc. v. LoopNet, Inc., 373 F.3d 544, 550 (4th Cir.2004).

Here, the district court pigeon-holed the conclusions reached in *Net-com* and its progeny as "premised on the unique attributes of the Inter-net." While the *Netcom* court was plainly concerned with a theory of di-rect liability that would effectively "hold the entire Internet liable" for the conduct of a single user, its reasoning and conclusions, consistent with precedents of this court and the Supreme Court, and with the text of the Copyright Act, transcend the Internet. Like the Fourth Circuit, we reject the contention that "the *Netcom* decision was driven by expedience and that its holding is inconsistent with the established law of copy-right," and we find it "a particularly rational interpretation of § 106," rather than a special-purpose rule applicable only to ISPs.

When there is a dispute as to the author of an allegedly infringing instance of reproduction, *Netcom* and its progeny direct our attention to the volitional conduct that causes the copy to be made. There are only two instances of volitional conduct in this case: Cablevision's conduct in designing, housing, and maintaining a system that exists only to produce a copy, and a customer's conduct in ordering that system to produce a copy of a specific program. In the case of a VCR, it seems clear—and we know of no case holding otherwise—that the operator of the VCR, the person who actually presses the button to make the recording, supplies the necessary element of volition, not the person who manufactures, maintains, or, if distinct from the operator, owns the machine. We do not believe that an RS-DVR customer is sufficiently distinguishable from a VCR user to impose liability as a direct infringer on a different party for copies that are made automatically upon that customer's command.

The district court emphasized the fact that copying is "instrumental" rather than "incidental" to the function of the RS-DVR system. While that may distinguish the RS-DVR from the ISPs in *Netcom* and *CoStar,* it does not distinguish the RS-DVR from a VCR, a photocopier, or even a typical copy shop. And the parties do not seem to contest that a company that merely makes photocopiers available to the public on its premises, without more, is not subject to liability for direct infringement for reproductions made by customers using those copiers. They only dispute whether Cablevision is similarly situated to such a proprietor.

The district court found Cablevision analogous to a copy shop that makes course packs for college professors. In the leading case involving such a shop, for example, "[t]he professor [gave] the copyshop the materials of which the coursepack [was] to be made up, and the copyshop [did] the rest." *Princeton Univ. Press v. Mich. Document Servs.,* 99 F.3d 1381, 1384 (6th Cir. 1996) (en banc). There did not appear to be any serious dispute in that case that the shop itself was directly liable for reproducing copyrighted works. The district court here found that Cablevision, like this copy shop, would be "doing" the copying, albeit "at the customer's behest."

But because volitional conduct is an important element of direct liability, the district court's analogy is flawed. In determining who actually "makes" a copy, a significant difference exists between making a request to a human employee, who then volitionally operates the copying system to make the copy, and issuing a command directly to a system, which automatically obeys commands and engages in no volitional conduct. In cases like *Princeton University Press,* the defendants operated a copying device and sold the product they made using that device. Here, by selling access to a system that automatically produces copies on command, Cablevision more closely resembles a store proprietor who charges customers to use a photocopier on his premises, and it seems incorrect to say, without more, that such a proprietor "makes" any copies when his machines are actually operated by his customers.

The district court also emphasized Cablevision's "unfettered discretion in selecting the programming that it would make available for recording." This conduct is indeed more proximate to the creation of illegal copying than, say, operating an ISP or opening a copy shop, where all copied content was supplied by the customers themselves or other third parties. Nonetheless, we do not think it sufficiently proximate to the copying to displace the customer as the person who "makes" the copies when determining liability under the Copyright Act. Cablevision, we note, also has subscribers who use home VCRs or DVRs (like TiVo), and has significant control over the content recorded by these customers. But this control is limited to the channels of programming available to a customer and not to the programs themselves. Cablevision has no control over what programs are made available on individual channels or when those programs will air, if at all. In this respect, Cablevision possesses far less control over recordable content than it does in the VOD context, where it actively selects and makes available beforehand the individual programs available for viewing. For these reasons, we are not inclined to say that Cablevision, rather than the user, "does" the copying produced by the RS-DVR system. As a result, we find that the district court erred in concluding that Cablevision, rather than its RS-DVR customers, makes the copies carried out by the RS-DVR system. ...

We conclude only that on the facts of this case, copies produced by the RS-DVR system are "made" by the RS-DVR customer. ... Therefore, Cablevision is entitled to summary judgment on this point, and the district court erred in awarding summary judgment to plaintiffs.

III. Transmission of RS-DVR Playback

Plaintiffs' final theory is that Cablevision will violate the Copyright Act by engaging in unauthorized public performances of their works through the playback of the RS-DVR copies. The Act grants a copyright owner the exclusive right, "in the case of ... motion pictures and other audiovisual works, to perform the copyrighted work publicly." 17 U.S.C. § 106(4). Section 101, the definitional section of the Act, explains that

> [t]o perform or display a work "publicly" means (1) to perform or display it at a place open to the public or at any place where a substantial number of persons outside of a normal circle of a family and its social acquaintances is gathered; or (2) to transmit or otherwise communicate a performance or display of the work to a place specified by clause (1) or to the public, by means of any device or process, whether the members of the public capable of receiving the performance or display receive it in the same place or in separate places and at the same time or at different times.

Id. § 101.

The parties agree that this case does not implicate clause (1). Accordingly, we ask whether these facts satisfy the second, "transmit clause" of the public performance definition: Does Cablevision "transmit ... a performance ... of the work ... to the public"? No one disputes that the RS-DVR playback results in the transmission of a performance of a work— the transmission from the Arroyo Server to the customer's television set. Cablevision contends that (1) the RS-DVR customer, rather than Cablevision, does the transmitting and thus the performing and (2) the transmission is not "to the public" under the transmit clause. ...

The statute itself does not expressly define the term "performance" or the phrase "to the public." It does explain that a transmission may be "to the public ... whether the members of the public capable of receiving the performance ... receive it in the same place or in separate places and at the same time or at different times." This plain language instructs us that, in determining whether a transmission is "to the public," it is of no moment that the potential recipients of the transmission are in different places, or that they may receive the transmission at different times. The implication from this same language, however, is that it is relevant, in determining whether a transmission is made to the public, to discern who is "capable of receiving" the performance being transmitted. The fact that the statute says "capable of receiving the performance," instead of "capable of receiving the transmission," underscores the fact that a transmission of a performance is itself a performance. ...

From the foregoing, it is evident that the transmit clause directs us to examine who precisely is "capable of receiving" a particular transmission of a performance. Cablevision argues that, because each RS-DVR transmission is made using a single unique copy of a work, made by an individual subscriber, one that can be decoded exclusively by that subscriber's cable box, only one subscriber is capable of receiving any given RS-DVR transmission. This argument accords with the language of the transmit clause, which, as described above, directs us to consider the potential audience of a given transmission. We are unpersuaded by the district court's reasoning and the plaintiffs' arguments that we should consider a larger potential audience in determining whether a transmission is "to the public."

The district court, in deciding whether the RS-DVR playback of a program to a particular customer is "to the public," apparently considered all of Cablevision's customers who subscribe to the channel airing that program and all of Cablevision's RS-DVR subscribers who request a copy of that program. Thus, it concluded that the RS-DVR playbacks constituted public performances because "Cablevision would transmit the *same program* to members of the public, who may receive the performance at different times, depending on whether they view the program in real time or at a later time as an RS-DVR playback." *Cablevision I,* 478 F.Supp.2d at 623 (emphasis added). In essence, the district court suggested that, in considering whether a transmission is "to the public," we consider not the potential audience of a particular transmission, but the potential audience of the underlying work (i.e., "the program") whose content is being transmitted.

We cannot reconcile the district court's approach with the language of the transmit clause. That clause speaks of people capable of receiving a particular "transmission" or "performance," and not of the potential audience of a particular "work." Indeed, such an approach would render the "to the public" language surplusage. Doubtless the *potential* audience for every copyrighted audiovisual work is the general public. As a result, any transmission of the content of a copyrighted work would constitute a public performance under the district court's interpretation. But the transmit clause obviously contemplates the existence of non-public transmissions; if it did not, Congress would have stopped drafting that clause after "performance." ...

In sum, none of the arguments advanced by plaintiffs or the district court alters our conclusion that, under the transmit clause, we must ex-

amine the potential audience of a given transmission by an alleged infringer to determine whether that transmission is "to the public." And
because the RS-DVR system, as designed, only makes transmissions to
one subscriber using a copy made by that subscriber, we believe that the
universe of people capable of receiving an RS-DVR transmission is the
single subscriber whose self-made copy is used to create that transmission.

Plaintiffs contend that it is "wholly irrelevant, in determining the existence of a public performance, whether 'unique' *copies* of the same work
are used to make the transmissions." But plaintiffs cite no authority for
this contention. And our analysis of the transmit clause suggests that, in
general, any factor that limits the *potential* audience of a transmission is
relevant.

Furthermore, no transmission of an audiovisual work can be made,
we assume, without using a copy of that work: to transmit a performance
of a movie, for example, the transmitter generally must obtain a copy of
that movie. As a result, in the context of movies, television programs,
and other audiovisual works, the right of reproduction can reinforce and
protect the right of public performance. If the owner of a copyright believes he is injured by a particular transmission of a performance of his
work, he may be able to seek redress not only for the infringing transmission, but also for the underlying copying that facilitated the transmission. Given this interplay between the various rights in this context,
it seems quite consistent with the Act to treat a transmission made using Copy A as distinct from one made using Copy B, just as we would
treat a transmission made by Cablevision as distinct from an otherwise
identical transmission made by Comcast. Both factors—the identity of
the transmitter and the source material of the transmission—limit the
potential audience of a transmission in this case and are therefore germane in determining whether that transmission is made "to the public."
...

In sum, we find that the transmit clause directs us to identify the potential audience of a given transmission, i.e., the persons "capable of receiving" it, to determine whether that transmission is made "to the public." Because each RS-DVR playback transmission is made to a single
subscriber using a single unique copy produced by that subscriber, we
conclude that such transmissions are not performances "to the public,"
and therefore do not infringe any exclusive right of public performance.
We base this decision on the application of undisputed facts; thus, Cablevision is entitled to summary judgment on this point. ...

[B]ecause we find, on undisputed facts, that Cablevision's proposed
RS-DVR system would not directly infringe plaintiffs' exclusive rights to
reproduce and publicly perform their copyrighted works, we grant summary judgment in favor of Cablevision with respect to both rights.

CONCLUSION

For the foregoing reasons, the district court's award of summary judgment to the plaintiffs is REVERSED and the district court's injunction against Cablevision is VACATED. The case is REMANDED for further proceedings consistent with this opinion.

Notes and Questions

1.   *Cartoon Network* illustrates yet another way in which digital technology's reliance on copying challenges copyright. In 1978, cases involving the public performance right generally did not implicate the reproduction and distribution rights. For example, the performances in *Columbia Pictures* and *Aveco* were created by playing legitimately purchased copies of the works in question. Today, digital performances frequently involve some kind of unauthorized copying or distribution because copies are made by one computer (if only in a computer's random access memory) and sent to another. For example, in *Cartoon Network*, the unauthorized performance of the plaintiff's work required an unauthorized copy on Cablevision's Arroyo server. This challenges copyright because the copying arguably increases the control that copyright holders have over digital performances.

Subject to defenses like fair use, copyright holders have exclusive rights to reproduce their works, but they only have exclusive rights over public performances. Others may privately perform a work without permission. However, if private performances now involve making unauthorized copies of works, then copyright holders can arguably control those private performances by asserting their reproduction rights. This is what the plaintiff attempted to do in *Cartoon Network*. Did the court correctly reject this attempt?

2.   The court in *Cartoon Network*, in evaluating the claim that Cablevision's temporary buffering of the copyrighted works constituted infringement, discussed at length the Ninth Circuit's opinion in *MAI Systems Corp. v. Peak Computer Inc.,* 991 F.2d 511 (9th Cir.1993). In that case, the Ninth Circuit held that running a software program on a computer resulted in an unauthorized reproduction of the program, since this necessarily required the computer to copy portions of the software into the computer's random access memory (RAM) chips and those copies could remain fixed for more than a "transitory period of duration."

The holding in *MAI* has been criticized, as it potentially expands copyright liability dramatically for digital works by sweeping in any use of a computer to run a software program or view any copyrighted material without the permission of the copyright owner. For example, merely viewing an infringing photograph with your web browser creates an unauthorized reproduction of that photograph in the RAM of your computer. In some cases, an individual may have an express or implied license to create such RAM copies (for example, if he is the owner or licensor of the software program), or may have a fair use defense. But in cases where there is no such license (e.g. an infringing photograph on a website), there would be a prima facie case of infringement under *MAI* for simply viewing the work.

The court in *Cartoon Network* distinguishes *MAI* by noting that *MAI* contained no discussion of the duration of the copy fixed in RAM. The court in *Cartoon Network* held that the very brief fixation of the work in the buffer (1.2 seconds) was not enough to be more than for a period of "transitory duration." How long would have been enough to constitute an infringing reproduction? Five seconds? Ten seconds? More generally, do you agree with the broader holding that copies fixed in RAM are "reproductions" within the meaning of the Copyright Act? From a policy perspective, what harm is caused by RAM copying?

3. *Cartoon Network* held that users, not Cablevision, made unauthorized copies on the Arroyo server. In so ruling, the court cited *Netcom*. You may recall *Netcom*'s statement that "[a]lthough copyright is a strict liability statute, there should still be some element of volition or causation which is lacking where a defendant's system is merely used to create a copy by a third party." Does *Netcom*'s rationale govern *Cartoon Network*, or does *Cartoon Network* extend *Netcom*?

4. *Cartoon Network* proceeds on the premise that a video on demand service constitutes public performance, but that the remote DVR does not. Do you find this distinction convincing? In answering this question, you may find it helpful to think about whether the existence of a public performance turns on the people who can receive a particular transmission, the technical mechanics of how a performance is generated, or a combination of the two. For example, consider the following ways in which a cable provider might enable viewing of a particular work. First, the provider could use one copy of the work to generate multiple streams that go to multiple customers at the same time. Second, it could use the copy to generate multiple streams to customers at different times. Third, it could use multiple copies to generate multiple streams to customers at the same time. Fourth, it could use multiple copies to generate multiple streams to customers at different times. Is there a principled basis on which to treat these situations differently?

Cartoon Network's interpretation of the public performance right was subsequently addressed by the U.S. Supreme Court in the following case.

———

American Broadcasting Companies v. Aereo
134 S. Ct. 2498 (2014)

JUSTICE BREYER delivered the opinion of the Court:

The Copyright Act of 1976 gives a copyright owner the "exclusive righ[t]" to "perform the copyrighted work publicly." 17 U.S.C. § 106(4).

The Act's Transmit Clause defines that exclusive right as including the right to

> "transmit or otherwise communicate a performance ... of the [copyrighted] work ... to the public, by means of any device or process, whether the members of the public capable of receiving the performance ... receive it in the same place or in separate places and at the same time or at different times." § 101.

We must decide whether respondent Aereo, Inc., infringes this exclusive right by selling its subscribers a technologically complex service that allows them to watch television programs over the Internet at about the same time as the programs are broadcast over the air. We conclude that it does.

I

A

For a monthly fee, Aereo offers subscribers broadcast television programming over the Internet, virtually as the programming is being broadcast. Much of this programming is made up of copyrighted works. Aereo neither owns the copyright in those works nor holds a license from the copyright owners to perform those works publicly.

Aereo's system is made up of servers, transcoders, and thousands of dime-sized antennas housed in a central warehouse. It works roughly as follows: First, when a subscriber wants to watch a show that is currently being broadcast, he visits Aereo's website and selects, from a list of the local programming, the show he wishes to see.

Second, one of Aereo's servers selects an antenna, which it dedicates to the use of that subscriber (and that subscriber alone) for the duration of the selected show. A server then tunes the antenna to the over-the-air broadcast carrying the show. The antenna begins to receive the broadcast, and an Aereo transcoder translates the signals received into data that can be transmitted over the Internet.

Third, rather than directly send the data to the subscriber, a server saves the data in a subscriber-specific folder on Aereo's hard drive. In other words, Aereo's system creates a subscriber-specific copy—that is, a "personal" copy—of the subscriber's program of choice.

Fourth, once several seconds of programming have been saved, Aereo's server begins to stream the saved copy of the show to the subscriber over the Internet. (The subscriber may instead direct Aereo to stream the program at a later time, but that aspect of Aereo's service is not before us.) The subscriber can watch the streamed program on the screen of his personal computer, tablet, smart phone, Internet-connected television, or other Internet-connected device. The streaming continues, a mere few seconds behind the over-the-air broadcast, until the subscriber has received the entire show.

Aereo emphasizes that the data that its system streams to each subscriber are the data from his own personal copy, made from the broadcast signals received by the particular antenna allotted to him. Its system does not transmit data saved in one subscriber's folder to any other subscriber. When two subscribers wish to watch the same program, Aereo's system activates two separate antennas and saves two separate copies of the program in two separate folders. It then streams the show to the subscribers through two separate transmissions—each from the subscriber's personal copy.

B

Petitioners are television producers, marketers, distributors, and broadcasters who own the copyrights in many of the programs that Aereo's system streams to its subscribers. They brought suit against Aereo for copyright infringement in Federal District Court. They sought a preliminary injunction, arguing that Aereo was infringing their right to "perform" their works "publicly," as the Transmit Clause defines those terms....

II

This case requires us to answer two questions: First, in operating in the manner described above, does Aereo "perform" at all? And second, if so, does Aereo do so "publicly"? We address these distinct questions in turn.

Does Aereo "perform"? Phrased another way, does Aereo "transmit ... a performance" when a subscriber watches a show using Aereo's system, or is it only the subscriber who transmits? In Aereo's view, it does not perform. It does no more than supply equipment that "emulate[s] the operation of a home antenna and [digital video recorder (DVR)]." Like a home antenna and DVR, Aereo's equipment simply responds to its subscribers' directives. So it is only the subscribers who "perform" when they use Aereo's equipment to stream television programs to themselves.

Considered alone, the language of the Act does not clearly indicate when an entity "perform[s]" (or "transmit[s]") and when it merely supplies equipment that allows others to do so. But when read in light of its purpose, the Act is unmistakable: An entity that engages in activities like Aereo's performs.

A

History makes plain that one of Congress' primary purposes in amending the Copyright Act in 1976 was to overturn this Court's determination that community antenna television (CATV) systems (the precursors of modern cable systems) fell outside the Act's scope. In *Fortnightly Corp. v. United Artists Television, Inc.*, 392 U.S. 390 (1968), the Court considered a CATV system that carried local television broadcasting, much of which was copyrighted, to its subscribers in two cities. The CATV provider placed antennas on hills above the cities and used coaxial cables to carry the signals received by the antennas to the home television sets of its subscribers. The system amplified and modulated the signals in order to improve their strength and efficiently transmit them to subscribers. A subscriber "could choose any of the ... programs he wished to view by simply turning the knob on his own television set." The CATV provider "neither edited the programs received nor originated any programs of its own."

Asked to decide whether the CATV provider infringed copyright holders' exclusive right to perform their works publicly, the Court held that the provider did not "perform" at all. The Court drew a line: "Broadcasters perform. Viewers do not perform." And a CATV provider "falls on the viewer's side of the line."

The Court reasoned that CATV providers were unlike broadcasters:

> "Broadcasters select the programs to be viewed; CATV systems simply carry, without editing, whatever programs they receive. Broadcasters procure programs and propagate them to the public; CATV systems receive programs that have been released to the public and carry them by private channels to additional viewers."

Instead, CATV providers were more like viewers, for "the basic function [their] equipment serves is little different from that served by the equipment generally furnished by" viewers. "Essentially," the Court said, "a CATV system no more than enhances the viewer's capacity to receive the broadcaster's signals [by] provid[ing] a well-located antenna with an efficient connection to the viewer's television set." Viewers do not become performers by using "amplifying equipment," and a CATV provider should not be treated differently for providing viewers the same equipment.

In *Teleprompter Corp. v. Columbia Broadcasting System, Inc.*, 415 U.S. 394 (1974), the Court considered the copyright liability of a CATV provider that carried broadcast television programming into subscribers' homes from hundreds of miles away. Although the Court recognized that a viewer might not be able to afford amplifying equipment that would provide access to those distant signals, it nonetheless found that the CATV provider was more like a viewer than a broadcaster. It explained: "The reception and rechanneling of [broadcast television signals] for simultaneous viewing is essentially a viewer function, irrespective of the distance between the broadcasting station and the ultimate viewer."...

B

In 1976 Congress amended the Copyright Act in large part to reject the Court's holdings in *Fortnightly* and *Teleprompter*. Congress enacted new language that erased the Court's line between broadcaster and viewer, in respect to "perform[ing]" a work. The amended statute clarifies that to "perform" an audiovisual work means "to show its images in any sequence or to make the sounds accompanying it audible." § 101. Under this new language, both the broadcaster and the viewer of a television program "perform," because they both show the program's images and make audible the program's sounds.

Congress also enacted the Transmit Clause, which specifies that an entity performs publicly when it "transmit[s] ... a performance ... to the public." § 101. Cable system activities, like those of the CATV systems in *Fortnightly* and *Teleprompter*, lie at the heart of the activities that Congress intended this language to cover. The Clause thus makes clear that an entity that acts like a CATV system itself performs, even if when doing so, it simply enhances viewers' ability to receive broadcast television signals.

Congress further created a new section of the Act to regulate cable companies' public performances of copyrighted works. Section 111 creates a complex, highly detailed compulsory licensing scheme that sets out the conditions, including the payment of compulsory fees, under which cable systems may retransmit broadcasts.

Congress made these three changes to achieve a similar end: to bring the activities of cable systems within the scope of the Copyright Act.

C

This history makes clear that Aereo is not simply an equipment provider. Rather, Aereo, and not just its subscribers, "perform[s]" (or "transmit[s]"). Aereo's activities are substantially similar to those of the CATV companies that Congress amended the Act to reach. Aereo sells a service that allows subscribers to watch television programs, many of which are copyrighted, almost as they are being broadcast. In providing this service, Aereo uses its own equipment, housed in a centralized warehouse, outside of its users' homes....

Aereo's equipment may serve a "viewer function"; it may enhance the viewer's ability to receive a broadcaster's programs. It may even emulate equipment a viewer could use at home. But the same was true of the equipment that was before the Court, and ultimately before Congress, in *Fortnightly* and *Teleprompter*.

We recognize, and Aereo and the dissent emphasize, one particular difference between Aereo's system and the cable systems at issue in *Fortnightly* and *Teleprompter*. The systems in those cases transmitted constantly; they sent continuous programming to each subscriber's television set. In contrast, Aereo's system remains inert until a subscriber indicates that she wants to watch a program. Only at that moment, in automatic response to the subscriber's request, does Aereo's system activate an antenna and begin to transmit the requested program.

This is a critical difference, says the dissent. It means that Aereo's subscribers, not Aereo, "selec[t] the copyrighted content" that is "perform[ed]," and for that reason they, not Aereo, "transmit" the performance. Aereo is thus like "a copy shop that provides its patrons with a library card." A copy shop is not directly liable whenever a patron uses the shop's machines to "reproduce" copyrighted materials found in that library. And by the same token, Aereo should not be directly liable whenever its patrons use its equipment to "transmit" copyrighted television programs to their screens.

In our view, however, the dissent's copy shop argument, in whatever form, makes too much out of too little. Given Aereo's overwhelming likeness to the cable companies targeted by the 1976 amendments, this sole technological difference between Aereo and traditional cable companies does not make a critical difference here. The subscribers of the *Fortnightly* and *Teleprompter* cable systems also selected what programs to display on their receiving sets. Indeed, as we explained in *Fortnightly*, such a subscriber "could choose any of the ... programs he wished to view by simply turning the knob on his own television set." The same is true of an Aereo subscriber. Of course, in *Fortnightly* the television signals, in a sense, lurked behind the screen, ready to emerge when the subscriber turned the knob. Here the signals pursue their ordinary course of travel through the universe until today's "turn of the knob"—a click on a website—activates machinery that intercepts and reroutes them to Aereo's subscribers over the Internet. But this difference means nothing to the subscriber. It means nothing to the broadcaster. We do not see how this single difference, invisible to subscriber and broadcaster alike, could transform a system that is for all practical purposes a traditional cable system into "a copy shop that provides its patrons with a library card."

In other cases involving different kinds of service or technology providers, a user's involvement in the operation of the provider's equipment and selection of the content transmitted may well bear on whether the provider performs within the meaning of the Act. But the many similarities between Aereo and cable companies, considered in light of Congress' basic purposes in amending the Copyright Act, convince us that this difference is not critical here. We conclude that Aereo is not just an equipment supplier and that Aereo "perform[s].

III

Next, we must consider whether Aereo performs petitioners' works "publicly," within the meaning of the Transmit Clause....

... As we have said, an Aereo subscriber receives broadcast television signals with an antenna dedicated to him alone. Aereo's system makes from those signals a personal copy of the selected program. It streams the content of the copy to the same subscriber and to no one else. One and only one subscriber has the ability to see and hear each Aereo transmission. The fact that each transmission is to only one subscriber, in Aereo's view, means that it does not transmit a performance "to the public."

In terms of the Act's purposes, these differences do not distinguish Aereo's system from cable systems, which do perform "publicly." Viewed in terms of Congress' regulatory objectives, why should any of these technological differences matter? They concern the behind-the-scenes way in which Aereo delivers television programming to its viewers' screens. They do not render Aereo's commercial objective any different from that of cable companies. Nor do they significantly alter the viewing experience of Aereo's subscribers. Why would a subscriber who wishes to watch a television show care much whether images and sounds are delivered to his screen via a large multisubscriber antenna or one small dedicated antenna, whether they arrive instantaneously or after a few seconds' delay, or whether they are transmitted directly or after a personal copy is made? And why, if Aereo is right, could not modern CATV systems simply continue the same commercial and consumer-oriented activities, free of copyright restrictions, provided they substitute such new technologies for old? Congress would as much have intended to protect a copyright holder from the unlicensed activities of Aereo as from those of cable companies.

The text of the Clause effectuates Congress' intent. Aereo's argument to the contrary relies on the premise that "to transmit ... a performance" means to make a single transmission. But the Clause suggests that an entity may transmit a performance through multiple, discrete transmissions. That is because one can "transmit" or "communicate" something through a set of actions. Thus one can transmit a message to one's friends, irrespective of whether one sends separate identical e-mails to each friend or a single e-mail to all at once. So can an elected official communicate an idea, slogan, or speech to her constituents, regardless of whether she communicates that idea, slogan, or speech during individual phone calls to each constituent or in a public square.

The fact that a singular noun ("a performance") follows the words "to transmit" does not suggest the contrary. One can sing a song to his family, whether he sings the same song one-on-one or in front of all together. Similarly, one's colleagues may watch a performance of a particular play—say, this season's modern-dress version of "Measure for Measure"—whether they do so at separate or at the same showings. By the same principle, an entity may transmit a performance through one or several transmissions, where the performance is of the same work.

The Transmit Clause must permit this interpretation, for it provides that one may transmit a performance to the public "whether the members of the public capable of receiving the performance ... receive it ... at the same time or at different times." § 101. Were the words "to transmit ... a performance" limited to a single act of communication, members of the public could not receive the performance communicated "at different times." Therefore, in light of the purpose and text of the Clause, we conclude that when an entity communicates the same contemporaneously perceptible images and sounds to multiple people, it transmits a performance to them regardless of the number of discrete communications it makes.

We do not see how the fact that Aereo transmits via personal copies of programs could make a difference. The Act applies to transmissions "by means of any device or process." And retransmitting a television program using user-specific copies is a "process" of transmitting a performance. A "cop[y]" of a work is simply a "material objec[t] ... in which a work is fixed ... and from which the work can be perceived, reproduced, or otherwise communicated." So whether Aereo transmits from the same or separate copies, it performs the same work; it shows the same images and makes audible the same sounds. Therefore, when Aereo streams the same television program to multiple subscribers, it "transmit[s] ... a performance" to all of them.

Moreover, the subscribers to whom Aereo transmits television programs constitute "the public." Aereo communicates the same contemporaneously perceptible images and sounds to a large number of people who are unrelated and unknown to each other. This matters because, although the Act does not define "the public," it specifies that an entity performs publicly when it performs at "any place where a substantial number of persons outside of a normal circle of a family and its social acquaintances is gathered." The Act thereby suggests that "the public" consists of a large group of people outside of a family and friends.

Neither the record nor Aereo suggests that Aereo's subscribers receive performances in their capacities as owners or possessors of the underlying works. This is relevant because when an entity performs to a set of people, whether they constitute "the public" often depends upon their relationship to the underlying work. When, for example, a valet parking attendant returns cars to their drivers, we would not say that the parking service provides cars "to the public." We would say that it provides the cars to their owners. We would say that a car dealership, on the other hand, does provide cars to the public, for it sells cars to individuals who lack a pre-existing relationship to the cars. Similarly, an entity that transmits a performance to individuals in their capacities as owners or possessors does not perform to "the public," whereas an entity like Aereo that transmits to large numbers of paying subscribers who lack any prior relationship to the works does so perform....

IV

Aereo and many of its supporting amici argue that to apply the Transmit Clause to Aereo's conduct will impose copyright liability on other technologies, including new technologies, that Congress could not possibly have wanted to reach. We agree that Congress, while intending the Transmit Clause to apply broadly to cable companies and their equivalents, did not intend to discourage or to control the emergence or use of different kinds of technologies. But we do not believe that our limited holding today will have that effect.

For one thing, the history of cable broadcast transmissions that led to the enactment of the Transmit Clause informs our conclusion that Aereo "perform[s]," but it does not determine whether different kinds of providers in different contexts also "perform." For another, an entity only transmits a performance when it communicates contemporaneously perceptible images and sounds of a work.

Further, we have interpreted the term "the public" to apply to a group of individuals acting as ordinary members of the public who pay primarily to watch broadcast television programs, many of which are copyrighted. We have said that it does not extend to those who act as owners or possessors of the relevant product. And we have not considered whether the public performance right is infringed when the user of a service pays primarily for something other than the transmission of copyrighted works, such as the remote storage of content. In addition, an entity does not transmit to the public if it does not transmit to a substantial number of people outside of a family and its social circle....]

We cannot now answer more precisely how the Transmit Clause or other provisions of the Copyright Act will apply to technologies not before us. We agree with the Solicitor General that "[q]uestions involving cloud computing, [remote storage] DVRs, and other novel issues not before the Court, as to which 'Congress has not plainly marked [the] course,' should await a case in which they are squarely presented." And we note that, to the extent commercial actors or other interested entities may be concerned with the relationship between the development and use of such technologies and the Copyright Act, they are of course free to seek action from Congress....

JUSTICE SCALIA, with whom JUSTICE THOMAS and JUSTICE ALITO join, dissenting.

... The Networks sued Aereo for several forms of copyright infringement, but we are here concerned with a single claim: that Aereo violates the Networks' "exclusive righ[t]" to "perform" their programs "publicly." That claim fails at the very outset because Aereo does not "perform" at all....

I. Legal Standard

... The Networks' claim is governed by a simple but profoundly important rule: A defendant may be held directly liable only if it has engaged in volitional conduct that violates the Act. This requirement is firmly grounded in the Act's text, which defines "perform" in active, affirmative terms: One "perform[s]" a copyrighted "audiovisual work," such as a movie or news broadcast, by "show[ing] its images in any sequence" or "mak[ing] the sounds accompanying it audible." And since the Act makes it unlawful to copy or perform copyrighted works, not to copy or perform in general, the volitional-act requirement demands conduct directed to the plaintiff's copyrighted material....

The volitional-conduct requirement is not at issue in most direct-infringement cases; the usual point of dispute is whether the defendant's conduct is infringing (e.g., Does the defendant's design copy the plaintiff's?), rather than whether the defendant has acted at all (e.g., Did this defendant create the infringing design?). But it comes right to the fore when a direct-infringement claim is lodged against a defendant who does nothing more than operate an automated, user-controlled system. Internet-service providers are a prime example. When one user sends data to another, the provider's equipment facilitates the transfer automatically. Does that mean that the provider is directly liable when the transmission happens to result in the "reproduc[tion]" of a copyrighted work? It does not. The provider's system is "totally indifferent to the material's content," whereas courts require "some aspect of volition" directed at the copyrighted material before direct liability may be imposed. The defendant may be held directly liable only if the defendant itself "trespassed on the exclusive domain of the copyright owner." Most of the time that issue will come down to who selects the copyrighted content: the defendant or its customers.

A comparison between copy shops and video-on-demand services illustrates the point. A copy shop rents out photocopiers on a per-use basis. One customer might copy his 10–year–old's drawings—a perfectly lawful thing to do—while another might duplicate a famous artist's copyrighted photographs—a use clearly prohibited by § 106(1). Either way, the customer chooses the content and activates the copying function; the photocopier does nothing except in response to the customer's commands. Because the shop plays no role in selecting the content, it cannot be held directly liable when a customer makes an infringing

Video-on-demand services, like photocopiers, respond automatically to user input, but they differ in one crucial respect: They choose the content. When a user signs in to Netflix, for example, "thousands of ... movies [and] TV episodes" carefully curated by Netflix are "available to watch instantly." That selection and arrangement by the service provider constitutes a volitional act directed to specific copyrighted works and thus serves as a basis for direct liability....

II. Application to Aereo

So which is Aereo: the copy shop or the video-on-demand service? In truth, it is neither. Rather, it is akin to a copy shop that provides its patrons with a library card. Aereo offers access to an automated system consisting of routers, servers, transcoders, and dime-sized antennae. Like a photocopier or VCR, that system lies dormant until a subscriber activates it. When a subscriber selects a program, Aereo's system picks up the relevant broadcast signal, translates its audio and video components into digital data, stores the data in a user-specific file, and transmits that file's contents to the subscriber via the Internet—at which point the subscriber's laptop, tablet, or other device displays the broadcast just as an ordinary television would. The result of that process fits the statutory definition of a performance to a tee: The subscriber's device "show[s]" the broadcast's "images" and "make[s] the sounds accompanying" the broadcast "audible." The only question is whether those performances are the product of Aereo's volitional conduct.

They are not. Unlike video-on-demand services, Aereo does not provide a prearranged assortment of movies and television shows. Rather, it assigns each subscriber an antenna that—like a library card—can be used to obtain whatever broadcasts are freely available. Some of those broadcasts are copyrighted; others are in the public domain. The key point is that subscribers call all the shots: Aereo's automated system does not relay any program, copyrighted or not, until a subscriber selects the program and tells Aereo to relay it. Aereo's operation of that system is a volitional act and a but-for cause of the resulting performances, but, as in the case of the copy shop, that degree of involvement is not enough for direct liability.

In sum, Aereo does not "perform" for the sole and simple reason that it does not make the choice of content. And because Aereo does not perform, it cannot be held directly liable for infringing the Networks' public-performance right. That conclusion does not necessarily mean that Aereo's service complies with the Copyright Act. Quite the contrary. The Networks' complaint alleges that Aereo is directly and secondarily liable for infringing their public-performance rights. Their request for a preliminary injunction—the only issue before this Court—is based exclusively on the direct-liability portion of the public-performance claim (and further limited to Aereo's "watch" function, as opposed to its "record" function). Affirming the judgment below would merely return this case to the lower courts for consideration of the Networks' remaining claims.

III. Guilt By Resemblance

The Court's conclusion that Aereo performs boils down to the following syllogism: (1) Congress amended the Act to overrule our decisions holding that cable systems do not perform when they retransmit over-the-air broadcasts; (2) Aereo looks a lot like a cable system; therefore (3) Aereo performs. That reasoning suffers from a trio of defects.

First, it is built on the shakiest of foundations. Perceiving the text to be ambiguous, the Court reaches out to decide the case based on a few isolated snippets of legislative history....

Second, the Court's reasoning fails on its own terms because there are material differences between the cable systems at issue in *Teleprompter Corp. v. Columbia Broadcasting System, Inc.*, and *Fortnightly Corp. v. United Artists Television, Inc.*, on the one hand and Aereo on the other. The former (which were then known as community-antenna television systems) captured the full range of broadcast signals and forwarded them to all subscribers at all times, whereas Aereo transmits only specific programs selected by the user, at specific times selected by the user....

Third, and most importantly, even accepting that the 1976 amendments had as their purpose the overruling of our cable-TV cases, what they were meant to do and how they did it are two different questions—and it is the latter that governs the case before us here. The injury claimed is not violation of a law that says operations similar to cable TV are subject to copyright liability, but violation of § 106(4) of the Copyright Act. And whatever soothing reasoning the Court uses to reach its result ("this looks like cable TV"), the consequence of its holding is that someone who implements this technology "perform[s]" under that provision. That greatly disrupts settled jurisprudence which, before today, applied the straightforward, bright-line test of volitional conduct directed at the copyrighted work....

Making matters worse, the Court provides no criteria for determining when its cable-TV-lookalike rule applies. Must a defendant offer access to live television to qualify? If similarity to cable-television service is the measure, then the answer must be yes. But consider the implications of that answer: Aereo would be free to do exactly what it is doing right now so long as it built mandatory time shifting into its "watch" function. Aereo would not be providing live television if it made subscribers wait to tune in until after a show's live broadcast ended. A subscriber could watch the 7 p.m. airing of a 1–hour program any time after 8 p.m.

.... The Court vows that its ruling will not affect cloud-storage providers and cable-television systems, but it cannot deliver on that promise given the imprecision of its result-driven rule....

* * *

I share the Court's evident feeling that what Aereo is doing (or enabling to be done) to the Networks' copyrighted programming ought not to be allowed. But perhaps we need not distort the Copyright Act to forbid it. As discussed at the outset, Aereo's secondary liability for performance infringement is yet to be determined, as is its primary and secondary liability for reproduction infringement. If that does not suffice, then (assuming one shares the majority's estimation of right and wrong) what we have before us must be considered a "loophole" in the law. It is not the role of this Court to identify and plug loopholes. It is the role of good lawyers to identify and exploit them, and the role of Congress to eliminate them if it wishes. Congress can do that, I may add, in a much more targeted, better informed, and less disruptive fashion than the crude "looks-like-cable-TV" solution the Court invents today.

Notes and Questions

1. The Court in *Aereo* concluded that Aereo engaged in the act of performance by streaming the copyrighted works to subscribers. The dissent, by contrast, would have held that the *subscribers* performed the works by selecting which channel to view, and that Aereo merely provided the equipment (i.e. the individual antenna and storage space). Which view do you find more persuasive? If Aereo had simply rented subscribers an antenna and a hard drive, both located at the subscriber's home, would the majority have reached a different conclusion? Should the physical location of the equipment make a difference?

Recall that in *Cartoon Network, supra,* the Second Circuit held that Cablevision was not directly liable for providing its remote DVR service because the subscribers were the ones who engaged in the act of reproduction when they chose which shows to record. Is this holding still good law after *Aereo*? Is there any way to distinguish the facts in *Cartoon Network* from the facts in *Aereo*?

2. In concluding that Aereo performed the copyrighted works, the Court was heavily influenced by the legislative history of the Transmit Clause and Congress's intent to bring CATV companies within the ambit of the public performance right. The Court held that Aereo's service more closely resembled the CATV companies' services rather than the provision of equipment to the subscriber. Did you find this analogy persuasive? If so, does this mean that Aereo could take advantage of the compulsory license for CATV systems in § 111? Alternatively, did you find the distinctions identified by the dissent more persuasive?

3. In concluding that Aereo performed the works "publicly," the Court rejected Aereo's argument that the performances were not public because each subscriber received a streamed video from a separate copy of the work residing on a portion of the hard drive dedicated to that particular subscriber. The Court reached this conclusion by noting that, from the subscriber's point of view, it would not make a difference whether the video was being streamed from a particular copy or from a copy commonly shared by many other subscribers, and that the underlying Congressional policy applied to both.

Recall that in *Cartoon Network*, *supra*, the Second Circuit held that the one-to-one relationship between streamed copies and subscribers meant that the streaming performance was not "public." Is this still good law after *Aereo*? Which of these two views do you find more persuasive?

4. Aereo's system was clearly designed in an attempt to avoid liability under the Copyright Act. Having thousands of tiny antennas and thousands of individual hard drive folders storing thousands of copies of the same show is clearly a very inefficient way to design a technological system. It would have been far more efficient to have had a single antenna and a single copy of every show to stream to multiple subscribers. Such a system, however, would have presented an even greater risk of liability. What should we make of this attempt to design technology to exploit a potential "loophole" in the copyright law? The majority rejected the attempt, looking past the details of the technology to how the system looked functionally from the perspective of the subscriber. By contrast, the dissent would have allowed this, applying the law to the particularities of the technology. Should courts look at the overall function of the system, or should they look to the details of the technology at issue?

5. What are the implications of *Aereo* for cloud storage services? For example, imagine that an individual loads a recorded music file from her personal computer onto her cloud storage service, and then later accesses that file via streaming to her smartphone. Would the cloud storage company be liable for publicly performing the copyrighted work? The majority in *Aereo* suggests that such a scenario might be distinguishable, insofar as in the hypothetical, the subscriber owns the copy of the music,

whereas in *Aereo* the subscriber had no ownership interest in the works being streamed. Is this a relevant distinction? If not, does this suggest that many cloud storage services may be liable?

6. Note that, according to the dissent, even if Aereo were not directly liable for publicly performing the copyrighted works, Aereo could potentially be liable for indirect infringement, e.g. for helping or facilitating the infringement of the works by others, in this case the subscribers. We will address these doctrines in more detail in Chapter Seven, *infra*.

7. More generally, *Aereo* presents another example of a new valuable use of existing copyrighted works enabled by a new technology. One way of looking at this case is to ask who should reap the benefits of the new technological use, the copyright owners or the technology companies? From a copyright policy perspective, who should win?

SECTION H. MORAL RIGHTS

Copyright protects specific economic interests that authors have in their works. Of course, authors have non-economic interests as well. For example, writers generally want to be identified as the authors of their works, even if the works are not being sold. Similarly, painters may object if others deface or destroy their works.

A number of countries have laws that specifically protect these non-economic interests. These so-called "moral rights" exist not for the purpose of stimulating the production of creative works, but for the purpose of vindicating the natural rights of authors. Robust conceptions of moral rights achieve this objective by recognizing three distinct rights. First, the right of attribution gives an author the right to insist on being identified as the author of his works. This right also allows an author to remove his name from a work if someone has mutilated or distorted the work. Second, the right of integrity allows an author to control the distortion or destruction of his work. Third, the right of disclosure empowers the author to control how and when her work is publicly presented.

Moral rights occupy an uncertain place in American law. Although the Visual Artists Rights Act of 1990 ("VARA"), now codified at 17 U.S.C. § 106A, gives painters, sculptors, and other visual artists somewhat limited rights of attribution and integrity, federal law contains no other provision specifically designed to vindicate moral rights. This does not mean, however, that courts cannot use existing forms of intellectual property to accomplish such a purpose. Our next case, *Gilliam v. American Broadcasting Cos., Inc.*, represents one of the most sustained judicial considerations of this possibility.

1. GENERALLY

Gilliam v. American Broadcasting Co.
538 F.2d 14 (2d Cir. 1976)

LUMBARD, Circuit Judge:

Plaintiffs, a group of British writers and performers known as "Monty Python," appeal from a denial by Judge Lasker in the Southern District of a preliminary injunction to restrain the American Broadcasting Company (ABC) from broadcasting edited versions of three separate programs originally written and performed by Monty Python for broadcast by the British Broadcasting Corporation (BBC). We agree with Judge Lasker that the appellants have demonstrated that the excising done for ABC impairs the integrity of the original work. We further find that the countervailing injuries that Judge Lasker found might have accrued to ABC as a result of an injunction at a prior date no longer exist. We therefore direct the issuance of a preliminary injunction by the district court.

Since its formation in 1969, the Monty Python group has gained popularity primarily through its thirty-minute television programs created for BBC as part of a comedy series entitled "Monty Python's Flying Circus." In accordance with an agreement between Monty Python and BBC, the group writes and delivers to BBC scripts for use in the television series. This scriptwriters' agreement recites in great detail the procedure to be followed when any alterations are to be made in the script prior to recording of the program. The essence of this section of the agreement is that, while BBC retains final authority to make changes, appellants or their representatives exercise optimum control over the scripts consistent with BBC's authority and only minor changes may be made without prior consultation with the writers. Nothing in the scriptwriters' agreement entitles BBC to alter a program once it has been recorded. The agreement further provides that, subject to the terms therein, the group retains all rights in the script.

Under the agreement, BBC may license the transmission of recordings of the television programs in any overseas territory. The series has been broadcast in this country primarily on non-commercial public broadcasting television stations, although several of the programs have been broadcast on commercial stations in Texas and Nevada. In each instance, the thirty-minute programs have been broadcast as originally recorded and broadcast in England in their entirety and without commercial interruption.

In October 1973, Time-Life Films acquired the right to distribute in the United States certain BBC television programs, including the Monty Python series. Time-Life was permitted to edit the programs only "for insertion of commercials, applicable censorship or governmental . . . rules and regulations, and National Association of Broadcasters and time segment requirements." No similar clause was included in the scriptwriters' agreement between appellants and BBC. Prior to this time, ABC had sought to acquire the right to broadcast excerpts from various Monty Python programs in the spring of 1975, but the group rejected the proposal for such a disjoined format. Thereafter, in July 1975, ABC agreed with Time-Life to broadcast two ninety-minute specials each comprising three thirty-minute Monty Python programs that had not previously been shown in this country.

Correspondence between representatives of BBC and Monty Python reveals that these parties assumed that ABC would broadcast each of the Monty Python programs "in its entirety." On September 5, 1975, however, the group's British representative inquired of BBC how ABC planned to show the programs in their entirety if approximately 24 minutes of each 90 minute program were to be devoted to commercials. BBC replied on September 12, "we can only reassure you that ABC have decided to run the programmes 'back to back,' and that there is a firm undertaking not to segment them."

ABC broadcast the first of the specials on October 3, 1975. Appellants did not see a tape of the program until late November and were allegedly "appalled" at the discontinuity and "mutilation" that had resulted from the editing done by Time-Life for ABC. Twenty-four minutes of the original 90 minutes of recording had been omitted. Some of the editing had been done in order to make time for commercials; other material had been edited, according to ABC, because the original programs contained offensive or obscene matter.

In early December, Monty Python learned that ABC planned to broadcast the second special on December 26, 1975. The parties began negotiations concerning editing of that program and a delay of the broadcast until Monty Python could view it. These negotiations were futile, however, and on December 15 the group filed this action to enjoin the broadcast and for damages. Following an evidentiary hearing, Judge Lasker found that "the plaintiffs have established an impairment of the integrity of their work" which "caused the film or program . . . to lose its iconoclastic verve." According to Judge Lasker, "the damage that has been caused to the plaintiffs is irreparable by its nature." Nevertheless, the judge denied the motion for the preliminary injunction on the grounds that it was unclear who owned the copyright in the programs produced by BBC from the scripts written by Monty Python; that there was a question of whether Time-Life and BBC were indispensable parties to the litigation; that ABC would suffer significant financial loss if it were enjoined a week before the scheduled broadcast; and that Monty Python had displayed a "somewhat disturbing casualness" in their pursuance of the matter.

Judge Lasker granted Monty Python's request for more limited relief by requiring ABC to broadcast a disclaimer during the December 26 special to the effect that the group dissociated itself from the program because of the editing. A panel of this court, however, granted a stay of that order until this appeal could be heard and permitted ABC to broad-cast, at the beginning of the special, only the legend that the program had been edited by ABC. We heard argument on April 13 and, at that time, enjoined ABC from any further broadcast of edited Monty Python programs pending the decision of the court.

I

... We then reach the question whether there is a likelihood that ap-pellants will succeed on the merits. In concluding that there is a likeli-hood of infringement here, we rely especially on the fact that the editing was substantial, i.e., approximately 27 per cent of the original program was omitted, and the editing contravened contractual provisions that limited the right to edit Monty Python material. It should be emphasized that our discussion of these matters refers only to such facts as have been developed upon the hearing for a preliminary injunction. Modified or contrary findings may become appropriate after a plenary trial.

Judge Lasker denied the preliminary injunction in part because he was unsure of the ownership of the copyright in the recorded program. Appellants first contend that the question of ownership is irrelevant be-cause the recorded program was merely a derivative work taken from the script in which they hold the uncontested copyright. Thus, even if BBC owned the copyright in the recorded program, its use of that work would be limited by the license granted to BBC by Monty Python for use of the underlying script. We agree. ...

Since the copyright in the underlying script survives intact despite the incorporation of that work into a derivative work, one who uses the script, even with the permission of the proprietor of the derivative work, may infringe the underlying copyright.

If the proprietor of the derivative work is licensed by the proprietor of the copyright in the underlying work to vend or distribute the deriva-tive work to third parties, those parties will, of course, suffer no liability for their use of the underlying work consistent with the license to the proprietor of the derivative work. Obviously, it was just this type of ar-rangement that was contemplated in this instance. The scriptwriters' agreement between Monty Python and BBC specifically permitted the latter to license the transmission of the recordings made by BBC to dis-tributors such as Time-Life for broadcast in overseas territories.

One who obtains permission to use a copyrighted script in the pro-duction of a derivative work, however, may not exceed the specific pur-pose for which permission was granted. Most of the decisions that have reached this conclusion have dealt with the improper extension of the underlying work into media or time, i. e., duration of the license, not cov-ered by the grant of permission to the derivative work proprietor. Appel-lants herein do not claim that the broadcast by ABC violated media or time restrictions contained in the license of the script to BBC. Rather, they claim that revisions in the script, and ultimately in the program, could be made only after consultation with Monty Python, and that

ABC's broadcast of a program edited after recording and without consultation with Monty Python exceeded the scope of any license that BBC was entitled to grant.

The rationale for finding infringement when a licensee exceeds time or media restrictions on his license—the need to allow the proprietor of the underlying copyright to control the method in which his work is presented to the public—applies equally to the situation in which a licensee makes an unauthorized use of the underlying work by publishing it in a truncated version. Whether intended to allow greater economic exploitation of the work, as in the media and time cases, or to ensure that the copyright proprietor retains a veto power over revisions desired for the derivative work, the ability of the copyright holder to control his work remains paramount in our copyright law. We find, therefore, that unauthorized editing of the underlying work, if proven, would constitute an infringement of the copyright in that work similar to any other use of a work that exceeded the license granted by the proprietor of the copyright.

[The court then analyzed the arrangements between Monty Python, the BBC, and ABC, concluding that ABC did not have permission under any actual or implied licenses to edit the programming as it had.]

Our resolution of these technical arguments serves to reinforce our initial inclination that the copyright law should be used to recognize the important role of the artist in our society and the need to encourage production and dissemination of artistic works by providing adequate legal protection for one who submits his work to the public. We therefore conclude that there is a substantial likelihood that, after a full trial, appellants will succeed in proving infringement of their copyright by ABC's broadcast of edited versions of Monty Python programs. In reaching this conclusion, however, we need not accept appellants' assertion that any editing whatsoever would constitute infringement. Courts have recognized that licensees are entitled to some small degree of latitude in arranging the licensed work for presentation to the public in a manner consistent with the licensee's style or standards. That privilege, however, does not extend to the degree of editing that occurred here especially in light of contractual provisions that limited the right to edit Monty Python material.

II

It also seems likely that appellants will succeed on the theory that, regardless of the right ABC had to broadcast an edited program, the cuts made constituted an actionable mutilation of Monty Python's work. This cause of action, which seeks redress for deformation of an artist's work, finds its roots in the continental concept of droit moral, or moral right, which may generally be summarized as including the right of the artist to have his work attributed to him in the form in which he created it.

American copyright law, as presently written, does not recognize moral rights or provide a cause of action for their violation, since the law seeks to vindicate the economic, rather than the personal, rights of authors. Nevertheless, the economic incentive for artistic and intellectual creation that serves as the foundation for American copyright law cannot be reconciled with the inability of artists to obtain relief for mutilation or misrepresentation of their work to the public on which the artists are financially dependent. Thus courts have long granted relief for misrepresentation of an artist's work by relying on theories outside the statutory law of copyright, such as contract law or the tort of unfair competition. Although such decisions are clothed in terms of proprietary right in one's creation, they also properly vindicate the author's personal right to prevent the presentation of his work to the public in a distorted form.

Here, the appellants claim that the editing done for ABC mutilated the original work and that consequently the broadcast of those programs as the creation of Monty Python violated the Lanham Act § 43(a), 15 U.S.C. § 1125(a).[50] This statute, the federal counterpart to state unfair competition laws, has been invoked to prevent misrepresentations that may injure plaintiff's business or personal reputation, even where no registered trademark is concerned. It is sufficient to violate the Act that a representation of a product, although technically true, creates a false impression of the product's origin. See *Rich v. RCA Corp.*, 390 F. Supp. 530 (S.D.N.Y. 1975) (recent picture of plaintiff on cover of album containing songs recorded in distant past held to be a false representation that the songs were new); *Geisel v. Poynter Products*, Inc., 283 F. Supp. 261, 267 (S.D.N.Y. 1968).

These cases cannot be distinguished from the situation in which a television network broadcasts a program properly designated as having been written and performed by a group, but which has been edited, without the writer's consent, into a form that departs substantially from the original work. "To deform his work is to present him to the public as the creator of a work not his own, and thus makes him subject to criticism for work he has not done." [quoting Roeder, *The Doctrine of Moral Right*, 53 HARV. L. REV. 554, 569 (1940)]. In such a case, it is the writer or performer, rather than the network, who suffers the consequences of the mutilation, for the public will have only the final product by which to evaluate the work. Thus, an allegation that a defendant has presented to the public a "garbled," distorted version of plaintiff's work seeks to redress the very rights sought to be protected by the Lanham Act and should be recognized as stating a cause of action under that statute.

During the hearing on the preliminary injunction, Judge Lasker viewed the edited version of the Monty Python program broadcast on December 26 and the original, unedited version. After hearing argument

---

[50] [Footnote 10] That statute provides in part:
> Any person who shall affix, apply, or annex, or use in connection with any goods or services, . . . a false designation of origin, or any false description or representation . . . and shall cause such goods or services to enter into commerce . . . shall be liable to a civil action by any person . . . who believes that he is or is likely to be damaged by the use of any such false description or representation.

of this appeal, this panel also viewed and compared the two versions. We find that the truncated version at times omitted the climax of the skits to which appellants' rare brand of humor was leading and at other times deleted essential elements in the schematic development of a story line.[51] We therefore agree with Judge Lasker's conclusion that the edited version broadcast by ABC impaired the integrity of appellants' work and represented to the public as the product of appellants what was actually a mere caricature of their talents. We believe that a valid cause of action for such distortion exists and that therefore a preliminary injunction may issue to prevent repetition of the broadcast prior to final determination of the issues. ...

For these reasons we direct that the district court issue the preliminary injunction sought by the appellants.

Notes and Questions

1. What do you think of *Gilliam's* interpretation of copyright? The court candidly stated that American copyright "does not recognize moral rights or provide a cause of action for their violation, since the law seeks to vindicate the economic, rather than the personal, rights of authors." Nevertheless, the court interpreted the law to accomplish precisely the thing American copyright "does not recognize." Can this interpretation be justified as promoting the progress of science and useful arts? If not, does a sufficient alternate justification exist?

2. How far does *Gilliam* extend? ABC lost because its editing distorted the plaintiffs' work, impairing the work's integrity and misrepresenting the nature of the work. Did ABC lose because *any* unauthorized editing constitutes infringement, or because ABC's editing substantially distorted the plaintiffs' work? People do many things that amount to the unlicensed editing of works. Directors may alter scenes from plays when staging them. A writer may quote selectively from the work of another. School chorus directors sometimes abbreviate songs to be sung at public performances and hand out the shortened lyrics to the student performers. A video store may cut and splice videocassettes to remove offensive sexual material before selling the cassettes (with notification of the edits) to people who want to watch "clean" movies. Assuming that these performances or uses of the copyrighted works are otherwise licensed or permitted, can authors who find these activities offensive successfully

---

[51] [Footnote 12] A single example will illustrate the extent of distortion engendered by the editing. In one skit, an upper class English family is engaged in a discussion of the tonal quality of certain words as "woody" or "tinny." The father soon begins to suggest certain words with sexual connotations as either "woody" or "tinny," whereupon the mother fetches a bucket of water and pours it over his head. The skit continues from this point. The ABC edit eliminates this middle sequence so that the father is comfortably dressed at one moment and, in the next moment, is shown in a soaked condition without any explanation for the change in his appearance.

sue for copyright infringement under *Gilliam*? Even if such suits would succeed as a matter of copyright, does the First Amendment limit their scope?

The Family Movie Act of 2005, now codified at 17 U.S.C. § 110(11) partially addresses the removal of movie scenes that viewers may find offensive. The Act allows "a member of a private household" to "make imperceptible" "limited portions" of a motion picture. The Act also makes it legal to sell software or other technology to enable such a result as long as the process does not create a fixed copy of the altered movie. Does the Family Movie Act imply that the spliced videocassettes hypothesized above constitute infringement? Or is it legislative acknowledgement that copyright holders cannot completely control the way others perform or view their works?

3. Disputes of the sort found in *Gilliam* generally arise in the context of licensing. For example, the *Gilliam* defendants had permission to broadcast the shows in question, but they apparently did not have permission to edit the shows as they did. Perhaps then the problems of unauthorized editing could be alleviated by more foresight in the licensing process. This does not, however, obviate the need to consider the extent to which unlicensed editing infringes the derivative work right, for resolution of this issue identifies the party that needs to negotiate for the relevant rights.

If unauthorized editing is infringement, then those purchasing licenses must also obtain permission for any editing they consider necessary, presumably by paying a higher price. If some unauthorized editing is not infringement, then some copyright holders have to convince those who purchase licenses to agree that they will not edit without permission. This would presumably lower the price of licenses.

Finally, it is worth remembering that alteration of works can occur outside the process of licensing. For example, a person who owns a sculpture may decide to alter it physically, perhaps by having it painted. Would this constitute infringement? Or, is a person who owns the physical embodiment of a work entitled to do with it as she wishes? Courts have not agreed about the answer to this question. In *Mirage Editions v. Albuquerque A.R.T. Co.*, 856 F.2d 1341 (9th Cir. 1988), the Ninth Circuit held that a defendant violated the plaintiff's derivative work right by purchasing a book containing images of the plaintiff's work, cutting the images from the book, and fixing them to ceramic tiles for resale. The court reasoned that the tiles with the images constituted another version of the plaintiff's works despite the fact that no reproduction of the works occurred. By contrast, in *Lee v. A.R.T. Company*, 125 F.3d 580 (7th Cir. 1997), the Seventh Circuit ruled the other way on very similar facts. The court rejected the argument that succeeded in *Mirage* because it worried about the consequences:

> Indeed, if Lee is right ..., then any alteration of a work, however slight, requires the author's permission. We asked at oral argu-

ment what would happen if a purchaser jotted a note on one of the note cards, or used it as a coaster for a drink, or cut it in half, or if a collector applied his seal (as is common in Japan); Lee's counsel replied that such changes prepare derivative works, but that as a practical matter artists would not file suit. A definition of derivative work that makes criminals out of art collectors and tourists is jarring despite Lee's gracious offer not to commence civil litigation.

2. VISUAL ARTISTS RIGHTS ACT

Article 6*bis* of the Berne Convention requires member nations to protect the moral rights of authors, particularly the rights of attribution and integrity. This means that the United States arguably did not live up to its treaty obligations in 1989 when the U.S. joined the Berne Convention because American law did not explicitly protect these rights. Congress finessed this problem by taking the position that the United States met its Berne obligations because, as *Gilliam* suggested, American law implicitly recognized moral rights. Nevertheless, proponents of moral rights eventually persuaded Congress to protect moral rights explicitly in the Visual Artists Rights Act of 1990 ("VARA").

VARA may explicitly protect moral rights, but it does not do so comprehensively. As its name applies, VARA protects only a "work of visual art." Such a work is defined in § 101 of the Copyright Act as

(1) a painting, drawing, print, or sculpture, existing in a single copy, in a limited edition of 200 copies or fewer that are signed and consecutively numbered by the author ....; or

(2) a still photographic image produced for exhibition purposes only, existing in a single copy that is signed by the author, or in a limited edition of 200 copies or fewer that are signed and consecutively numbered by the author.

Thus, the VARA essentially covers only works of fine art produced in single copies or limited editions. It does not apply, for example, to an individual's vacation photographs, casual drawings, or . Nor does it apply to many other categories of copyrighted works, such as literary works, musical works, audio-visual works, etc. Also, VARA does not apply to works made for hire.

VARA provides the authors of works of visual art certain rights of attribution and integrity. With respect to attribution, VARA permits authors to: (1) claim authorship of works they created; (2) prevent the use of their names on their works that they did not create; and (3) prevent use of their names when works they created have been distorted in a way that would harm their reputation. With respect to integrity, VARA gives authors the ability to prevent the intentional mutilation or distortion of their works in ways that would harm their reputation. In addition, for "works of recognized stature," VARA allows the author of such a work to prevent the destruction of that work.

Although VARA is part of the Copyright Act, the rights it grants behave differently from other copyright rights. Only the author of a work can own such rights. The author can waive her rights in writing, but cannot transfer them to others. Accordingly, the assignment of copyright in a work neither conveys VARA rights nor constitutes a waiver. Additionally, the rights last only to the end of the author's life, and not an additional 70 years.

Our next case introduces some of the difficulties that VARA presents.

Martin v. City of Indianapolis
192 F.3d 608 (7th Cir. 1998)

HARLINGTON WOOD, JR., Circuit Judge.

We are not art critics, do not pretend to be and do not need to be to decide this case. A large outdoor stainless steel sculpture by plaintiff Jan Martin, an artist, was demolished by the defendant as part of an urban renewal project. Plaintiff brought a one-count suit against the City of Indianapolis (the "City") under the Visual Artists Rights Act of 1990 ("VARA"). The parties filed cross-motions for summary judgment. The district court granted plaintiff's motion and awarded plaintiff statutory damages in the maximum amount allowed for a non-wilful statutory violation.[52] Neither party is satisfied. It is necessary to see how this unique controversy came to be.

I. BACKGROUND

Plaintiff is an artist, but in this instance more with a welding torch than with a brush. He offered evidence to show, not all of it admitted, that his works have been displayed in museums, and other works created for private commissions, including a time capsule for the Indianapolis Museum of Art Centennial. He has also done sculptured jewelry for the Indiana Arts Commission. In 1979, at the Annual Hoosier Salem Art Show, plaintiff was awarded the prize for best of show in any medium. He holds various arts degrees from Purdue University, the Art Institute of Chicago and Bowling Green State University in Ohio. Plaintiff had been employed as production coordinator for Tarpenning-LaFollette Co. (the "Company"), a metal contracting firm in Indianapolis. It was in this position that he turned his artistic talents to metal sculpture fabrication.

In 1984, plaintiff received permission from the Indianapolis Metropolitan Development Commission to erect a twenty-by-forty-foot metal sculpture on land owned by John LaFollette, chairman of the Company.

---

[52] Editors' note: Section 504(c) of the Copyright Act provides for statutory damages up to $30,000 for non-willful infringement of copyright rights, including rights under VARA.

The Company also agreed to furnish the materials. The resulting Project Agreement between the City and the Company granted a zoning variance to permit the erection of plaintiff's proposed sculpture. An attachment to that agreement and the center of this controversy provided as follows:

> Should a determination be made by the Department of Metropolitan Development that the subject sculpture is no longer compatible with the existing land use or that the acquisition of the property is necessary, the owner of the land and the owner of the sculpture will receive written notice signed by the Director of the Department of Metropolitan Development giving the owners of the land and sculpture ninety (90) days to remove said sculpture. Subject to weather and ground conditions.

Plaintiff went to work on the project and in a little over two years it was completed. He named it "Symphony # 1," but as it turns out in view of this controversy, a more suitable musical name might have been "1812 Overture." Because of the possibility that the sculpture might someday have to be removed, as provided for in the Project Agreement, Symphony # 1 was engineered and built by plaintiff so that it could be disassembled for removal and later reassembled. The sculpture did not go unnoticed by the press, public or art community. Favorable comments admitted into evidence and objected to by the City are now an issue on appeal and their admissibility will be considered hereinafter.

The trouble began in April 1992 when the City notified LaFollette that there would be public hearings on the City's proposed acquisition of various properties as part of an urban renewal plan. One of the properties to be acquired was home to Symphony # 1. Kim Martin, president of the Company and plaintiff's brother, responded to the City. He reminded the City that the Company had paid for Symphony # 1, and had signed the agreement with the Metropolitan Development Corporation pertaining to the eventuality of removal. Martin stated that if the sculpture was to be removed, the Company would be willing to donate it to the City provided the City would bear the costs of removal to a new site, but that plaintiff would like some input as to where his sculpture might be placed. Plaintiff also personally appeared before the Metropolitan Development Commission and made the same proposal. This was followed by a letter from plaintiff to the Mayor reiterating the removal proposal. The Mayor responded that he was referring plaintiff's proposal to his staff to see what could be done.

The City thereafter purchased the land. At the closing, plaintiff again repeated his proposal and agreed to assist so Symphony # 1 could be saved and, if necessary, moved without damage. The City's response was that plaintiff would be contacted in the event the sculpture was to be removed. Shortly thereafter, the City awarded a contract to demolish the sculpture, and demolition followed, all without prior notice to plaintiff or the Company. This lawsuit resulted in which summary judgment was allowed for plaintiff. However, his victory was not entirely satisfactory to him, nor was the City satisfied. The City appealed, and plaintiff cross-appealed.

II. ANALYSIS

... VARA seems to be a stepchild of our copyright laws, but does not require copyright registration. Some remedies under the Copyright Act, however, including attorney's fees, are recoverable. 17 U.S.C. §§ 504-05. VARA provides: "[T]he author of a work of visual art ... shall have the right ... to prevent any destruction of a work of *recognized stature,* and any intentional or grossly negligent destruction of that work is a violation of that right." 17 U.S.C. § 106A(a)(3)(B) (emphasis added). The district court considered Symphony # 1 to be of "recognized stature" under the evidence presented and thus concluded that the City had violated plaintiff's rights under VARA. That finding is contested by the City.

"Recognized stature" is a necessary finding under VARA in order to protect a work of visual art from destruction. In spite of its significance, that phrase is not defined in VARA, leaving its intended meaning and application open to argument and judicial resolution. The only case found undertaking to define and apply "recognized stature" is *Carter v. Helmsley-Spear, Inc.,* 861 F. Supp. 202 (S.D.N.Y. 1994). Involved was an unusual work of art consisting of interrelated sculptural elements constructed from recycled materials, mostly metal, to decorate the lobby of a commercial building in a borough of New York City. Part of the work was "a giant hand fashioned from an old school bus, [and] a face made of automobile parts...." Although the Second Circuit reversed the district court and held that the work was not a work of visual art protected by VARA, *id.* at 88, the district court presented an informative discussion in determining whether a work of visual art may qualify as one of "recognized stature." That determination is based greatly on the testimony of experts on both sides of the issue, as would ordinarily be expected.

The stature test formulated by the New York district court required:

> (1) that the visual art in question has "stature," i.e. is viewed as meritorious, and (2) that this stature is "recognized" by art experts, other members of the artistic community, or by some cross-section of society. In making this showing, plaintiffs generally, but not inevitably, will need to call expert witnesses to testify before the trier of fact.

Carter, 861 F. Supp. at 325.

Even though the district court in this present case found that test was satisfied by the plaintiff's evidence, plaintiff argues that the *Carter v. Helmsley-Spear* test may be more rigorous than Congress intended. That may be, but we see no need for the purposes of this case to endeavor to refine that rule. Plaintiff's evidence, however, is not as complete as in *Carter v. Helmsley-Spear,* possibly because Symphony # 1 was destroyed by the City without the opportunity for experts to appraise the sculpture in place.

The City objects to the "stature" testimony that was offered by plaintiff as inadmissible hearsay. If not admitted, it would result in plaintiff's failure to sustain his burden of proof. It is true that plaintiff offered no evidence of experts or others by deposition, affidavit or interrogatories. Plaintiff's evidence of "stature" consisted of certain newspaper and magazine articles, and various letters, including a letter from an art gallery director and a letter to the editor of *The Indianapolis News,* all in support of the sculpture, as well as a program from the show at which a model of the sculpture won "Best of Show." After reviewing the City's objection, the district court excluded plaintiff's "programs and awards" evidence as lacking adequate foundation, but nevertheless found Martin had met his "stature" burden of proof with his other evidence.

Included in the admitted evidence, for example, was a letter dated October 25, 1982 from the Director of the Herron School of Art, Indiana University, Indianapolis. It was written to the Company and says in part, "The proposed sculpture is, in my opinion, an interesting and aesthetically stimulating configuration of forms and structures." *The Indianapolis Star,* in a four-column article by its visual arts editor, discussed public sculpture in Indianapolis. This article included a photograph of Symphony # 1. The article lamented that the City had "been graced by only five pieces of note," but that two more had been added that particular year, one being plaintiff's sculpture. It noted, among other things, that Symphony # 1 had been erected without the aid of "federal grants" and without the help of any committee of concerned citizens. Other public sculptures came in for some criticism in the article. However, in discussing Symphony # 1, the author wrote: "Gleaming clean and abstract, yet domestic in scale and reference, irregularly but securely cabled together, the sculpture shows the site what it might be. It unites the area, providing a nexus, a marker, a designation, an identity and, presumably, a point of pride."

The district judge commented on the City's hearsay objection to plaintiff's admitted evidence as follows:

> The statements contained within the proffered newspaper and magazine articles and letters are offered by Martin to show that respected members of the art community and members of the public at large consider Martin's work to be socially valuable and to have artistic merit, and to show the newsworthiness of Symphony # 1 and Martin's work. *These statements are offered by Martin to show that the declarants said them,* not that the statements are, in fact, true.... The statements contained within the exhibits show how art critics and the public viewed Martin's work, particularly Symphony # 1, and show that the sculpture was a matter worth reporting to the public. Therefore, the statements contained within these challenged exhibits are not hearsay because they are not being offered for the truth of the matters asserted therein.

Martin I, 982 F. Supp. at 630 (emphasis added).

We agree with the assessment made by the district court. ...

Next the City claims that the Project Agreement entered into pre-VARA by plaintiff and the City encompassed many of plaintiff's rights under VARA. Therefore, the City argues, that whereas plaintiff failed to remove his work within the time allowed in the contract, plaintiff waived any cause of action he might have had under VARA. That failure was the City's, not plaintiff's, as under the Agreement the City was obligated to give the owners of the land and the sculpture ninety days to remove the sculpture. The City, after discussing with the Company and plaintiff possible other uses for the tract and the removal proposal, failed to give the required notice and went ahead and demolished the sculpture. Nothing had happened between the parties prior to that which could constitute a waiver of any rights by the Company or plaintiff. Plaintiff had no notice of the City letting a contract for Symphony # 1's demolition and no notice when that demolition would actually occur. After the preliminary and ongoing discussions plaintiff and the Company had with the City, when there was no immediate threat of imminent demolition, plaintiff had the right to continue to rely on the specific notice provided in the Agreement, unless it had been waived, which it was not.

Plaintiff and the Company had proposed a solution if the sculpture was to be moved. That proposal was still pending when the surprise destruction of Symphony # 1 occurred. Prior to the demolition, nothing more had been heard from anyone, including the Mayor. Bureaucratic ineptitude may be the only explanation. Under 17 U.S.C. § 106A(e)(1), an artist may waive VARA rights "in a written instrument signed by the author," specifying to what the waiver applies. There is no written waiver instrument in this case which falls within the VARA requirements. We regard this argument to be without merit.

In spite of the City's conduct resulting in the intentional destruction of the sculpture, we do not believe under all the circumstances, particularly given the fact that the issue of VARA rights had not been raised until this suit, that the City's conduct was "willful," as used in VARA, 17 U.S.C. § 504(c)(2), so as to entitle the plaintiff to enhanced damages. This appears to be a case of bureaucratic failure within the City government, not a willful violation of plaintiff's VARA rights. As far as we can tell from the record, those VARA rights were unknown to the City. The parties proceeded under their pre-VARA agreement which the City breached. However, plaintiff retained his VARA rights. As unfortunate as the City's unannounced demolition of Symphony # 1 was, it does not qualify plaintiff for damages under VARA. ...

Being fully satisfied with the district court's careful resolution of these unique issues and the resulting judgment, the district court's finding is affirmed in all respects.

MANION, Circuit Judge, concurring in part and dissenting in part.

Like my colleagues, I am not an art critic. So I begin with the well-worn adage that one man's junk is another man's treasure. No doubt Jan

Martin treasured what the city's bulldozers treated as junk. At this point in the litigation this court is not in a position to attach either label (or perhaps one falling somewhere in between) to Symphony # 1. For the Martin sculpture to receive protection under the Visual Arts Rights Act (VARA), it has to rise to the statutory level of "recognized stature." Because at this summary judgment stage, at least, it has clearly not merited the protection that goes with that description, I respectfully dissent.

... VARA was not designed to regulate urban renewal, but to protect great works of art from destruction and mutilation, among other things. In order to restrict VARA's reach, the Act was limited to preventing destruction of works of art that had attained a "recognized stature." 17 U.S.C. § 106A(a)(3)(B). The court correctly notes that a natural reading of this term indicates that it has two elements (which correspond to its two words): (1) merit or intrinsic worth; and (2) a public acknowledgment of that merit by society or the art community. As the district court in *Carter v. Helmsley-Spear, Inc.* stated: "the recognized stature requirement is best viewed as a gate-keeping mechanism—protection is afforded only to those works of art that art experts, the art community, or society in general views as possessing stature." So I concur with the court on this point.

I dissent, however, because summary judgment is not appropriate here. A plaintiff cannot satisfy his burden of demonstrating recognized stature through old newspaper articles and unverified letters, some of which do not even address the artwork in question. Rather, as the district court stated in *Carter,* in "making this showing [of recognized stature] plaintiffs generally, but not inevitably, will need to call expert witnesses to testify before the trier of fact." Instances where expert testimony on this point is not necessary will be rare, and this is not one of those exceptional cases where something of unquestioned recognition and stature was destroyed. Furthermore, where newspaper articles are admitted into evidence only to acknowledge recognition but not for the truth of the matter asserted (that the art in question was good or bad), a plaintiff needs more to overcome *a defendant's* motion for summary judgment on a VARA claim, much less prevail on his own summary judgment motion. While the very publication of newspaper articles on a work of art may have bearing on the "recognized" element, there has to be some evidence that the art had stature (i.e., that it met a certain high level of quality). The newspaper articles are hearsay and not admitted for the truth of the matter asserted in them. Construed in the light most favorable to the defendant, they cannot demonstrate by a preponderance of the evidence that the plaintiff's art was of a recognized stature, and that no reasonable jury could find otherwise. Experts need to weigh in here, and the trial court and perhaps this court need to come up with a clearer definition of when works of art achieve "recognized stature."

For now, however, those who are purchasers or donees of art had best beware. To avoid being the perpetual curator of a piece of visual art that has lost (or perhaps never had) its luster, the recipient must obtain at the outset a waiver of the artist's rights under VARA. Before awarding building permits for erection of sculptures, municipalities might be well advised to obtain a written waiver of the artist's rights too. If not, once destroyed, art of questionable value may acquire a minimum worth of $20,000.00 under VARA.

Notes and Questions

1. How many works receive protection against destruction under VARA? *Martin* suggests two ways in which courts might confront this question. First, courts might answer it substantively. The term "work of recognized stature" could identify only a few "great works," or it could refer to a much broader class of "good works." Second, courts might deal with the question procedurally by requiring very specific (and potentially hard to obtain) evidence. With these possibilities in mind, should courts interpret VARA inclusively so many works obtain protection, or should only a few works gain such treatment?

2. A significant theme in the jurisprudence of copyrightable subject matter was the principle of aesthetic neutrality espoused in *Bleistein v. Donaldson Lithographic Co.* You may remember this passage by Justice Holmes:

> It would be a dangerous undertaking for persons trained only to the law to constitute themselves final judges of the worth of pictorial illustrations, outside of the narrowest and most obvious limits. At the one extreme, some works of genius would be sure to miss appreciation. Their very novelty would make them repulsive until the public had learned the new language in which their author spoke. It may be more than doubted, for instance, whether the etchings of Goya or the paintings of Manet would have been sure of protection when seen for the first time. At the other end, copyright would be denied to pictures which appealed to a public less educated than the judge. Yet if they command the interest of any public, they have a commercial value,-it would be bold to say that they have not an aesthetic and educational value,- and the taste of any public is not to be treated with contempt.

By extending protection against destruction only to works of "recognized stature," VARA apparently requires courts to engage in precisely the form of reasoning studiously avoided in *Bleistein*. Do you think that VARA enmeshes courts in the kind of dangers warned against in *Bleistein*, and if so, does that danger affect how courts should interpret the statute? Alternatively, if you conclude that VARA does not create significant problems for courts, does it also mean that *Bleistein*'s concerns are not as serious as Holmes suggested? Should courts become more willing to explicitly consider the aesthetic merits of works in all areas of copyright?

3. VARA becomes particularly tricky when applied to site specific art. Unlike conventional works that are not designed with a particular location in mind, site specific art relates to carefully chosen surroundings. Thus, a sculptor might create shapes specifically intended to incorporate the view from a certain cliff overlooking the ocean. Thus, if those shapes get relocated, they lose their meaning. What happens when the owner of property containing site specific art decides that she no longer wants the art on her property? Does removing the art constitute actionable mutilation or destruction under § 106A(a)(3)? Note that § 106A(c) contains an exception against such a finding for actions related to conservation or public presentation of a work. If the owner of the property removes the shapes with care, does she engage in conservation of the work? Or does she destroy the work because the work is composed of the shapes in a particular surrounding? In *Phillips v. Pembroke Real Estate*, 459 F.3d. 128 (1st Cir. 2006), an artist who had created site specific art sued the property owner when the owner decided to redesign the garden where the art was installed. In ruling for the property owner, the First Circuit held that VARA does not apply to site specific art. Is there a textual basis for such a conclusion? If not, are there compelling reasons to interpret VARA as the First Circuit did?

Chapter Six

FAIR USE AND OTHER DEFENSES

Once a copyright owner establishes a *prima facie* case of infringement, attention shifts to potential defenses that a defendant can raise. Copyright law contains a number of defenses to infringement. The most important of these is the fair use defense, which plays a critical role setting the overall copyright balance. In this Chapter, we will spend a good deal of time exploring the complexities of the fair use doctrine. Copyright also, however, contains a number of other defenses, including copyright misuse, abandonment, statute of limitations, fraud on the copyright office and, increasingly, the First Amendment. In this Chapter we will explore the role that these defenses play in setting the overall balance in copyright law.

SECTION A. FAIR USE

1. ORIGINS

Originally, the Copyright Act contained no fair use defense. However, courts interpreting the Act soon recognized that too strict an application of copyright might hinder its very purposes. For example, copyright could be interpreted to prevent literary critics from quoting passages from works they discuss. These literal reproductions of copyrighted material constitute *prima facie* infringement. However, imposing liability would hinder the dissemination of knowledge that copyright promotes. The case *Folsom v. Marsh* is generally considered the earliest articulation of the fair use doctrine.

Folsom v. Marsh
9 F. Cas. 342 (D. Mass. 1841)

STORY, Circuit Justice.

This is one of those intricate and embarrassing questions, arising in the administration of civil justice, in which it is not, from the peculiar nature and character of the controversy, easy to arrive at any satisfactory conclusion, or to lay down any general principles applicable to all cases. Patents and copyrights approach, nearer than any other class of cases belonging to forensic discussions, to what may be called the metaphysics of the law, where the distinctions are, or at least may be, very subtle and refined, and, sometimes, almost evanescent. ... [I]n cases of copyright, it is often exceedingly obvious, that the whole substance of one work has been copied from another, with slight omissions and formal differences only, which can be treated in no other way than as studied evasions; whereas, in other cases, the identity of the two works in substance, and the question of piracy, often depend upon a nice balance of the comparative use made in one of the materials of the other; the nature, extent, and value of the materials thus used; the objects of each work; and the degree to which each writer may be fairly presumed to have resorted to the same common sources of information, or to have exercised the same common diligence in the selection and arrangement of the materials. Thus, for example, no one can doubt that a reviewer may fairly cite largely from the original work, if his design be really and truly to use the passages for the purposes of fair and reasonable criticism. On the other hand, it is as clear, that if he thus cites the most important parts of the work, with a view, not to criticise, but to supersede the use of the original work, and substitute the review for it, such a use will be deemed in law a piracy. A wide interval might, of course, exist between these two extremes, calling for great caution and involving great difficulty, where the court is approaching the dividing middle line which separates the one from the other ...

In the present case, the work alleged to be pirated, is the Writings of President Washington, in twelve volumes, royal octavo, containing nearly seven thousand pages, of which the first volume contains a life of Washington, by the learned editor, Mr. Sparks, in respect to which no piracy is asserted or proved. The other eleven volumes consist of the letters of Washington, private and official, and his messages and other public acts, with explanatory notes and occasional illustrations by the editor. That the original work is of very great, and, I may almost say, of inestimable value, as the repository of the thoughts and opinions of that great man, no one pretends to doubt. The work of the defendants is in two volumes, duodecimo, containing eight hundred and sixty-six pages. It consists of a Life of Washington, written by the learned defendant, (the Rev. Charles W. Upham), which is formed upon a plan different from that of Mr. Sparks, and in which Washington is made mainly to tell the story of his own life, by inserting therein his letters and his messages, and other written documents, with such connecting lines in the narrative, as may illustrate and explain the times and circumstances, and occasions of writing them. Now, as I have already said, there is no complaint, that Mr. Upham has taken his narrative part, substantially, from the Life by Mr. Sparks. The gravamen is, that he has used the letters of Washington, and inserted, verbatim, copies thereof from the collection of Mr. Sparks. The master finds, by his report, that the whole number of pages in Mr. Upham's work, corresponding and identical with the passages in Mr. Sparks's work, are three hundred and fifty-three pages out of eight hundred and sixty-six, a fraction more than one third of the two volumes of the defendants. Of these three hundred and fifty-three pages, the report finds that three hundred and nineteen pages consist of letters of Washington, which have been taken from Mr. Sparks's work, and have never been published before; namely, sixty-four pages are official letters and documents, and two hundred and fifty-five pages are private letters of Washington. The question, therefore, upon this admitted state of the facts, resolves itself into the point, whether such a use, in the defendants' work, of the letters of Washington, constitutes a piracy of the work of Mr. Sparks.

[Justice Story first holds that: (1) the letters were copyrightable; (2) Washington owned the copyrights in the letters and later assigned those copyrights to the plaintiffs; and (3) the copyright in those letters had not been dedicated to the public.]

The next and leading objection is, that the defendants had a right to abridge and select, and use the materials which they have taken for their work, which, though it embraces the number of letters above stated, is an original and new work, and that it constitutes, in no just sense, a piracy of the work of the plaintiffs. ... It is certainly true, that the defendants' work cannot properly be treated as an abridgment of that of the plaintiffs; neither is it strictly and wholly a mere compilation from the latter. So far as the narrative goes, it is either original, or derived (at least as far as the matter has been brought before the court) from common sources of information, open to all authors. It is not even of the nature of a collection of beauties of an author; for it does not profess to give fugitive extracts, or brilliant passages from particular letters. It is a selection of the entire contents of particular letters, from the whole collection or mass of letters of the work of the plaintiffs. From the known taste and ability of Mr. Upham, it cannot be doubted, that these letters are the most instructive, useful and interesting to be found in that large collection.

The question, then, is, whether this is a justifiable use of the original materials, such as the law recognizes as no infringement of the copyright of the plaintiffs. It is said, that the defendant has selected only such materials, as suited his own limited purpose as a biographer. That is, doubtless, true; and he has produced an exceedingly valuable book. But that is no answer to the difficulty. It is certainly not necessary, to constitute an invasion of copyright, that the whole of a work should be copied, or even a large portion of it, in form or in substance. If so much is taken, that the value of the original is sensibly diminished, or the labors of the original author are substantially to an injurious extent appropriated by another, that is sufficient, in point of law, to constitute a piracy pro tanto. The entirety of the copyright is the property of the author; and it is no defence, that another person has appropriated a part, and not the whole, of any property. Neither does it necessarily depend upon the quantity taken, whether it is an infringement of the copyright or not. It is often affected by other considerations, the value of the materials taken, and the importance of it to the sale of the original work. ... In short, we must often, in deciding questions of this sort, look to the nature and objects of the selections made, the quantity and value of the materials used, and the degree in which the use may prejudice the sale, or diminish the profits, or supersede the objects, of the original work. Many mixed ingredients enter into the discussion of such questions. ...

In the present case, I have no doubt whatever, that there is an invasion of the plaintiffs' copyright; I do not say designedly, or from bad intentions; on the contrary, I entertain no doubt, that it was deemed a perfectly lawful and justifiable use of the plaintiffs' work. But if the defendants may take three hundred and nineteen letters, included in the plaintiffs' copyright, and exclusively belonging to them, there is no reason why another bookseller may not take other five hundred letters, and a third, one thousand letters, and so on, and thereby the plaintiffs' copyright be totally destroyed. Besides; every one must see, that the work of the defendants is mainly founded upon these letters, constituting more than one third of their work, and imparting to it its greatest, nay, its essential value. Without those letters, in its present form the work must fall to the ground. It is not a case, where abbreviated or select passages are taken from particular letters; but the entire letters are taken, and those of most interest and value to the public, as illustrating the life, the acts, and the character of Washington. It seems to me, therefore, that it is a clear invasion of the right of property of the plaintiffs, if the copying of parts of a work, not constituting a major part, can ever be a violation thereof; as upon principle and authority, I have no doubt it may be. If it had been the case of a fair and bona fide abridgment of the work of the plaintiffs, it might have admitted of a very different consideration. ...

I have come to this conclusion, not without some regret, that it may interfere, in some measure, with the very meritorious labors of the defendants, in their great undertaking of a series of works adapted to school libraries. But a judge is entitled in this case, as in others, only to know and to act upon his duty. ... The report of the master must stand confirmed, and a perpetual injunction be awarded. ...

———————

Notes and Questions

1. Justice Story notes at the beginning of the opinion that the line between fair and unfair use is very difficult to determine. What factors did Justice Story consider in deciding whether the defendant's appropriation of Washington's letters constituted fair use? What policy goal guided Justice Story's approach?

2. Do you agree with the *Folsom* result? The defendant did much of his own work writing a biography of Washington and copied none of the plaintiffs' original text, instead only reproducing Washington's letters and documents. Justice Story acknowledges that defendant "produced an exceedingly valuable book," and Story reached his conclusion "not without some regret." If you agree with the result, what could the defendant have done to avoid infringement without changing the character of his book?

In 1976, Congress codified the fair use defense in section 107:

§ 107. Limitations on exclusive rights: Fair use

Notwithstanding the provisions of sections 106 and 106A, the fair use of a copyrighted work, including such use by reproduction in copies or phonorecords or by any other means specified by that section, for purposes such as criticism, comment, news reporting, teaching (including multiple copies for classroom use), scholarship, or research, is not an infringement of copyright. In determining whether the use made of a work in any particular case is a fair use the factors to be considered shall include—

(1) the purpose and character of the use, including whether such use is of a commercial nature or is for nonprofit educational purposes;
(2) the nature of the copyrighted work;
(3) the amount and substantiality of the portion used in relation to the copyrighted work as a whole; and
(4) the effect of the use upon the potential market for or value of the copyrighted work.

The fact that a work is unpublished shall not itself bar a finding of fair use if such finding is made upon consideration of all the above factors.

It is important to note that Congress, in codifying the fair use defense, expected the courts to continue developing fair use in a case-by-case fashion. The purposes of the fair use doctrine, as set forth in section 107, are not exclusive. Similarly, the wording of the section makes clear that the factors listed in section 107 are not exclusive and that courts are free to consider other factors. The legislative history supports this view:

The statement of the fair use doctrine in section 107 offers some guidance to users in determining when the principles of the doctrine apply. However, the endless variety of situations and combinations of circumstances that can rise in particular cases precludes the formulation of exact rules in the statute. The bill endorses the purpose and general scope of the judicial doctrine of fair use, but there is no disposition to freeze the doctrine in the statute, especially during a period of rapid technological change. Beyond a very broad statutory explanation of what fair use is and some of the criteria applicable to it, the courts must be free to adapt the doctrine to particular situations on a case-by-case basis.

H.R. Rep. No. 94-1476, at 9-10 (1976). Thus, fair use remains an equitable, judge-made doctrine courts can use to adjust the copyright balance.

But to what end should courts apply this broad equitable power? What purpose does fair use serve? Because fair use is so broadly defined, it has been the subject of extensive litigation, with cases applying the defense to a wide range of circumstances. It has also been the focus of extensive academic commentary, as scholars and courts seek to find principles to guide application of the broad factors. As you read the cases in this section, examine the rationales that the courts offer for the fair use defense. Are these rationales consistent? Is one more persuasive than the others?

2. CRITICISM, COMMENT, NEWS REPORTING, EDUCATION

Section 107 lists a number of traditionally favored purposes that tend to shield a defendant's use as fair: criticism, comment, news reporting, teaching, scholarship, and research. The legislative history provides a number of non-exclusive examples of fair uses that encompass these purposes:

Quotation of excerpts in a review or criticism for purposes of illustration or comment; quotation of short passages in a scholarly or technical work, for illustration or clarification of the author's observations; use in a parody of some of the content of the work parodied; summary of an address or article, with brief quotations, in a news report; reproduction by a library of a portion of a work to replace part of a damaged copy; reproduction by a teacher or student of a small part of a work to illustrate a lesson; reproduction of a work in legislative or judicial proceedings or reports; incidental and fortuitous reproduction, in a newsreel or broadcast, of a work located in the scene of an event being reported.

H.R. Rep. No. 94-1476, at 66 (1976). These examples are, in some sense, the classic examples of fair use. They involve relatively small-scale, incidental acts of reproduction that support socially valuable endeavors.

Even within this classic category of fair uses, however, difficult questions arise in assessing the scope of such a privilege. Neither the statute nor the courts allow critics, teachers, scholars, or news reporters an unlimited privilege to use copyrighted works. What then are the boundaries of fair use? If a critic can copy short passages from a book in a review, how does he know when he has borrowed too much? What happens if modest copying harms the economic interests of the copyright owner? And how do courts identify and weigh the public interest in copying in questions of fair use?

Let us begin our examination of how favored purposes affect the existence of fair use by studying cases in which the defendant uses the plaintiff's work for the purpose of creating a new work. These uses ostensibly advance social welfare a great deal, for they result in new works that support endeavors that society values. Accordingly, fair use treatment for these uses may seem quite attractive, especially if the defendant argues that the challenged use is vitally important to his work.

However, as we are about to see, courts do not always consider the plausible invocation of a favored purpose sufficient to support fair use. Courts sometimes worry that the defendants overstate the importance and value of alleged favored uses, or that these uses will harm copyright incentives. Courts have therefore denied fair use to defendants whose behavior fits comfortably within the Copyright Act's list of favored purposes. Our first case offers one of the Supreme Court's best-known explanations of how fair use operates in these situations.

Harper & Row Publishers v. Nation Enterprises
471 U.S. 539 (1985)

JUSTICE O'CONNOR delivered the opinion of the Court.

This case requires us to consider to what extent the "fair use" provision of the Copyright Revision Act of 1976 sanctions the unauthorized use of quotations from a public figure's unpublished manuscript. In March 1979, an undisclosed source provided The Nation Magazine with the unpublished manuscript of "A Time to Heal: The Autobiography of Gerald R. Ford." Working directly from the purloined manuscript, an editor of The Nation produced a short piece entitled "The Ford Memoirs—Behind the Nixon Pardon." The piece was timed to "scoop" an article scheduled shortly to appear in Time Magazine. Time had agreed to purchase the exclusive right to print prepublication excerpts from the copyright holders, Harper & Row Publishers, Inc. and Reader's Digest Association, Inc. As a result of The Nation article, Time canceled its agreement. Petitioners brought a successful copyright action against The Nation. On appeal, the Second Circuit reversed the lower court's finding of infringement, holding that The Nation's act was sanctioned as a "fair use" of the copyrighted material. We granted certiorari and we now reverse.

I

In February 1977, shortly after leaving the White House, former President Gerald R. Ford contracted with petitioners Harper & Row and Reader's Digest, to publish his as yet unwritten memoirs. The memoirs were to contain "significant hitherto unpublished material" concerning the Watergate crisis, Mr. Ford's pardon of former President Nixon and "Mr. Ford's reflections on this period of history, and the morality and personalities involved." In addition to the right to publish the Ford memoirs in book form, the agreement gave petitioners the exclusive right to license prepublication excerpts, known in the trade as "first serial rights." Two years later, as the memoirs were nearing completion, petitioners negotiated a prepublication licensing agreement with Time, a weekly news magazine. Time agreed to pay $25,000, $12,500 in advance and an additional $12,500 at publication, in exchange for the right to excerpt 7,500 words from Mr. Ford's account of the Nixon pardon. The issue featuring the excerpts was timed to appear approximately one week before shipment of the full length book version to bookstores. Exclusivity was an important consideration; Harper & Row instituted procedures designed to maintain the confidentiality of the manuscript, and Time retained the right to renegotiate the second payment should the material appear in print prior to its release of the excerpts.

Two to three weeks before the Time article's scheduled release, an unidentified person secretly brought a copy of the Ford manuscript to Victor Navasky, editor of The Nation, a political commentary magazine. Mr. Navasky knew that his possession of the manuscript was not authorized and that the manuscript must be returned quickly to his "source" to avoid discovery. He hastily put together what he believed was "a real hot news story" composed of quotes, paraphrases, and facts drawn exclusively from the manuscript. Mr. Navasky attempted no independent commentary, research or criticism, in part because of the need for speed if he was to "make news" by "publish[ing] in advance of publication of the Ford book. The 2,250-word article appeared on April 3, 1979. As a result of The Nation's article, Time canceled its piece and refused to pay the remaining $12,500. ...

III

A

Fair use was traditionally defined as "a privilege in others than the owner of the copyright to use the copyrighted material in a reasonable manner without his consent." H. Ball, Law of Copyright and Literary Property 260 (1944). The statutory formulation of the defense of fair use in the Copyright Act reflects the intent of Congress to codify the common-law doctrine. Section 107 requires a case-by-case determination whether a particular use is fair, and the statute notes four nonexclusive factors to be considered. ...

Perhaps because the fair use doctrine was predicated on the author's implied consent to "reasonable and customary" use when he released his work for public consumption, fair use traditionally was not recognized as a defense to charges of copying from an author's as yet unpublished works. ... This absolute rule, however, was tempered in practice by the equitable nature of the fair use doctrine. In a given case, factors such as implied consent through *de facto* publication on performance or dissemination of a work may tip the balance of equities in favor of prepublication use. But it has never been seriously disputed that "the fact that the plaintiff's work is unpublished ... is a factor tending to negate the defense of fair use." 3 M. Nimmer, Copyright § 13.05, at 13-62, n. 2. Publication of an author's expression before he has authorized its dissemination seriously infringes the author's right to decide when and whether it will be made public, a factor not present in fair use of published works. ...

We ... find unpersuasive respondents' argument that fair use may be made of a soon-to-be-published manuscript on the ground that the author has demonstrated he has no interest in nonpublication. This argument assumes that the unpublished nature of copyrighted material is only relevant to letters or other confidential writings not intended for dissemination. It is true that common-law copyright was often enlisted in the service of personal privacy. In its commercial guise, however, an author's right to choose when he will publish is no less deserving of protection. The period encompassing the work's initiation, its preparation, and its grooming for public dissemination is a crucial one for any literary endeavor. ... The author's control of first public distribution implicates not only his personal interest in creative control but his property interest in exploitation of prepublication rights, which are valuable in themselves and serve as a valuable adjunct to publicity and marketing. Under ordinary circumstances, the author's right to control the first public appearance of his undisseminated expression will outweigh a claim of fair use.

B

Respondents, however, contend that First Amendment values require a different rule under the circumstances of this case. ... Respondents advance the substantial public import of the subject matter of the Ford memoirs as grounds for excusing a use that would ordinarily not pass muster as a fair use—the piracy of verbatim quotations for the purpose of "scooping" the authorized first serialization. Respondents explain their copying of Mr. Ford's expression as essential to reporting the news story it claims the book itself represents. In respondents' view, not only the facts contained in Mr. Ford's memoirs, but "the precise manner in which [he] expressed himself [were] as newsworthy as what he had to say." Respondents argue that the public's interest in learning this news as fast as possible outweighs the right of the author to control its first publication.

The Second Circuit noted, correctly, that copyright's idea/expression dichotomy "strike[s] a definitional balance between the First Amendment and the Copyright Act by permitting free communication of facts while still protecting an author's expression." No author may copyright his ideas or the facts he narrates. ... But copyright assures those who write and publish factual narratives such as "A Time to Heal" that they may at least enjoy the right to market the original expression contained therein as just compensation for their investment.

Respondents' theory, however, would expand fair use to effectively destroy any expectation of copyright protection in the work of a public figure. Absent such protection, there would be little incentive to create or profit in financing such memoirs, and the public would be denied an important source of significant historical information. The promise of copyright would be an empty one if it could be avoided merely by dubbing the infringement a fair use "news report" of the book.

Nor do respondents assert any actual necessity for circumventing the copyright scheme with respect to the types of works and users at issue here. Where an author and publisher have invested extensive resources in creating an original work and are poised to release it to the public, no legitimate aim is served by pre-empting the right of first publication. The fact that the words the author has chosen to clothe his narrative may of themselves be "newsworthy" is not an independent justification for unauthorized copying of the author's expression prior to publication. ...

In our haste to disseminate news, it should not be forgotten that the Framers intended copyright itself to be the engine of free expression. By establishing a marketable right to the use of one's expression, copyright supplies the economic incentive to create and disseminate ideas. ...

It is fundamentally at odds with the scheme of copyright to accord lesser rights in those works that are of greatest importance to the public. Such a notion ignores the major premise of copyright and injures author and public alike. ...

In view of the First Amendment protections already embodied in the Copyright Act's distinction between copyrightable expression and uncopyrightable facts and ideas, and the latitude for scholarship and comment traditionally afforded by fair use, we see no warrant for expanding the doctrine of fair use to create what amounts to a public figure exception to copyright. Whether verbatim copying from a public figure's manuscript in a given case is or is not fair must be judged according to the traditional equities of fair use.

IV

Fair use is a mixed question of law and fact. ... The factors enumerated in the section are not meant to be exclusive. ... The four factors identified by Congress as especially relevant in determining whether the use was fair are: (1) the purpose and character of the use; (2) the nature of the copyrighted work; (3) the substantiality of the portion used in relation to the copyrighted work as a whole; (4) the effect on the potential market for or value of the copyrighted work. We address each one separately.

Purpose of the Use. The Second Circuit correctly identified news reporting as the general purpose of The Nation's use. News reporting is one of the examples enumerated in § 107. ... This listing was not intended to be exhaustive or to single out any particular use as presumptively a "fair" use. ... The fact that an article arguably is "news" and therefore a productive use is simply one factor in a fair use analysis. ...

The fact that a publication was commercial as opposed to nonprofit is a separate factor that tends to weigh against a finding of fair use. ... In arguing that the purpose of news reporting is not purely commercial, The Nation misses the point entirely. The crux of the profit/nonprofit distinction is not whether the sole motive of the use is monetary gain but whether the user stands to profit from exploitation of the copyrighted material without paying the customary price.

In evaluating character and purpose we cannot ignore The Nation's stated purpose of scooping the forthcoming hardcover and Time abstracts. The Nation's use had not merely the incidental effect but the *intended purpose* of supplanting the copyright holder's commercially valuable right of first publication. ... The trial court found that The Nation knowingly exploited a purloined manuscript. ... Like its competitor newsweekly, it was free to bid for the right of abstracting excerpts from "A Time to Heal." Fair use "distinguishes between 'a true scholar and a chiseler who infringes a work for personal profit.'" *Wainwright Securities Inc. v. Wall Street Transcript Corp.*, 558 F.2d, at 94.

Nature of the Copyrighted Work. Second, the Act directs attention to the nature of the copyrighted work. "A Time to Heal" may be characterized as an unpublished historical narrative or autobiography. The law generally recognizes a greater need to disseminate factual works than works of fiction or fantasy. ...

Some of the briefer quotes from the memoirs are arguably necessary adequately to convey the facts; for example, Mr. Ford's characterization of the White House tapes as the "smoking gun" is perhaps so integral to the idea expressed as to be inseparable from it. But The Nation did not stop at isolated phrases and instead excerpted subjective descriptions and portraits of public figures whose power lies in the author's individualized expression. Such use, focusing on the most expressive elements of the work, exceeds that necessary to disseminate the facts.

The fact that a work is unpublished is a critical element of its "nature." Our prior discussion establishes that the scope of fair use is narrower with respect to unpublished works. While even substantial quotations might qualify as fair use in a review of a published work or a news account of a speech that had been delivered to the public or disseminated to the press, the author's right to control the first public appearance of his expression weighs against such use of the work before its release. The right of first publication encompasses not only the choice whether to publish at all, but also the choices of when, where, and in what form first to publish a work. ...

Amount and Substantiality of the Portion Used. Next, the Act directs us to examine the amount and substantiality of the portion used in relation to the copyrighted work as a whole. In absolute terms, the words actually quoted were an insubstantial portion of "A Time to Heal." The District Court, however, found that "[T]he Nation took what was essentially the heart of the book." We believe the Court of Appeals erred in overruling the District Judge's evaluation of the qualitative nature of the taking. A Time editor described the chapters on the pardon as "the most interesting and moving parts of the entire manuscript." The portions actually quoted were selected by Mr. Navasky as among the most powerful passages in those chapters. He testified that he used verbatim excerpts because simply reciting the information could not adequately convey the "absolute certainty with which [Ford] expressed himself," or show that "this comes from President Ford,"; or carry the "definitive quality" of the original. In short, he quoted these passages precisely because they qualitatively embodied Ford's distinctive expression.

As the statutory language indicates, a taking may not be excused merely because it is insubstantial with respect to the infringing work. As Judge Learned Hand cogently remarked, "no plagiarist can excuse the wrong by showing how much of his work he did not pirate." *Sheldon v. Metro-Goldwyn Pictures Corp.*, 81 F.2d 49, 56 (2d Cir. 1936). Conversely, the fact that a substantial portion of the infringing work was copied verbatim is evidence of the qualitative value of the copied material, both to the originator and to the plagiarist who seeks to profit from marketing someone else's copyrighted expression.

Stripped to the verbatim quotes, the direct takings from the unpublished manuscript constitute at least 13% of the infringing article. The Nation article is structured around the quoted excerpts which serve as its dramatic focal points. In view of the expressive value of the excerpts and their key role in the infringing work, we cannot agree with the Second Circuit that the "magazine took a meager, indeed an infinitesimal amount of Ford's original language."

Effect on the Market. Finally, the Act focuses on "the effect of the use upon the potential market for or value of the copyrighted work." This last factor is undoubtedly the single most important element of fair use. ... The trial court found not merely a potential but an actual effect on the market. Time's cancellation of its projected serialization and its refusal to pay the $12,500 were the direct effect of the infringement. ... Rarely will a case of copyright infringement present such clear-cut evidence of actual damage. Petitioners assured Time that there would be no other authorized publication of any portion of the unpublished manuscript prior to April 23, 1979. Any publication of material from chapters 1 and 3 would permit Time to renegotiate its final payment. Time cited The Nation's article, which contained verbatim quotes from the unpublished manuscript, as a reason for its nonperformance. ...

V

... The Nation conceded that its verbatim copying of some 300 words of direct quotation from the Ford manuscript would constitute an infringement unless excused as a fair use. Because we find that The Nation's use of these verbatim excerpts from the unpublished manuscript was not a fair use, the judgment of the Court of Appeals is reversed, and the case is remanded for further proceedings consistent with this opinion.

It is so ordered.

JUSTICE BRENNAN, with whom JUSTICE WHITE and JUSTICE MARSHALL join, dissenting.

The Court holds that The Nation's quotation of 300 words from the unpublished 200,000-word manuscript of President Gerald R. Ford infringed the copyright in that manuscript, even though the quotations related to a historical event of undoubted significance—the resignation and pardon of President Richard M. Nixon. Although the Court pursues the laudable goal of protecting "the economic incentive to create and disseminate ideas," this zealous defense of the copyright owner's prerogative will, I fear, stifle the broad dissemination of ideas and information copyright is intended to nurture. ... I therefore respectfully dissent. ...

II

... *The Purpose of the Use.* The Nation's purpose in quoting 300 words of the Ford manuscript was, as the Court acknowledges, news reporting. The Ford work contained information about important events of recent history. ... That The Nation objectively reported the information in the Ford manuscript without independent commentary in no way diminishes the conclusion that it was reporting news. A typical newsstory differs from an editorial precisely in that it presents newsworthy information in a straightforward and unelaborated manner. Nor does the source of the information render The Nation's article any less a news report. Often books and manuscripts, solicited and unsolicited, are the subject matter of news reports. Frequently, the manuscripts are unpublished at the time of the news report.

Section 107 lists news reporting as a prime example of fair use of another's expression. Like criticism and all other purposes Congress explicitly approved in § 107, news reporting informs the public; the language of § 107 makes clear that Congress saw the spread of knowledge and information as the strongest justification for a properly limited appropriation of expression. ... In light of the explicit congressional endorsement in § 107, the purpose for which Ford's literary form was borrowed strongly favors a finding of fair use. ...

The Court's reliance on the commercial nature of The Nation's use as "a separate factor that tends to weigh against a finding of fair use," is inappropriate in the present context. Many uses § 107 lists as paradigmatic examples of fair use, including criticism, comment, and news reporting, are generally conducted for profit in this country, a fact of which Congress was obviously aware when it enacted § 107. To negate any argument favoring fair use based on news reporting or criticism because that reporting or criticism was published for profit is to render meaningless the congressional imprimatur placed on such uses. ...

Nor should The Nation's intent to create a "news event" weigh against a finding of fair use. Such a rule, like the Court's automatic presumption against news reporting for profit, would undermine the congressional validation of the news reporting purpose. A news business earns its reputation, and therefore its readership, through consistent prompt publication of news—and often through "scooping" rivals. ...

The Court's reliance on The Nation's putative bad faith is equally unwarranted. No court has found that The Nation possessed the Ford manuscript illegally or in violation of any common-law interest of Harper & Row; all common-law causes of action have been abandoned or dismissed in this case. Even if the manuscript had been "purloined" by someone, nothing in this record imputes culpability to The Nation. On the basis of the record in this case, the most that can be said is that The Nation made use of the contents of the manuscript knowing the copyright owner would not sanction the use.

At several points the Court brands this conduct thievery. This judgment is unsupportable. ... Whether the quotation of 300 words was an infringement or a fair use within the meaning of § 107 is a close question that has produced sharp division in both this Court and the Court of Appeals. If the Copyright Act were held not to prohibit the use, then the copyright owner would have had no basis in law for objecting. The Nation's awareness of an objection that has a significant chance of being adjudged unfounded cannot amount to bad faith. Imputing bad faith on the basis of no more than knowledge of such an objection, the Court impermissibly prejudices the inquiry and impedes arrival at the proper conclusion that the "purpose" factor of the statutorily prescribed analysis strongly favors a finding of fair use in this case.

The Nature of the Copyrighted Work. ... [T]he scope of fair use is generally broader when the source of borrowed expression is a factual or historical work. ... Thus the second statutory factor also favors a finding of fair use in this case.

The Court acknowledges that "[the] law generally recognizes a greater need to disseminate factual works than works of fiction or fantasy," and that "[some] of the briefer quotations from the memoir are arguably necessary to convey the facts." But the Court discounts the force of this consideration, primarily on the ground that "[the] fact that a work is unpublished is a crucial element of its 'nature.'" At this point the Court introduces into analysis of this case a categorical presumption against prepublication fair use.

This categorical presumption is unwarranted on its own terms and unfaithful to congressional intent. Whether a particular prepublication use will impair any interest the Court identifies as encompassed with in the right of first publication, will depend on the nature of the copyrighted work, the timing of prepublication use, the amount of expression used, and the medium in which the second author communicates. Also, certain uses might be tolerable for some purposes but not for others. ...

To the extent the Court purports to evaluate the facts of this case, its analysis relies on sheer speculation. The quotation of 300 words from the manuscript infringed no privacy interest of Mr. Ford. This author intended the words in the manuscript to be a public statement about his Presidency. Lacking, therefore, is the "deliberate choice on the part of the copyright owner" to keep expression confidential. ... What the Court depicts as the copyright owner's "confidentiality" interest is not a privacy interest at all. Rather, it is no more than an economic interest in capturing the full value of initial release of information to the public, and is properly analyzed ... under the fourth statutory factor—the effect on the value of or market for the copyrighted work—and not as a presumed element of the "nature" of the copyright.

The Amount and Substantiality of the Portion Used. More difficult questions arise with respect to judgments about the importance to this case of the amount and substantiality of the quotations used. ... [W]ith respect to the six particular quotes of Mr. Ford's observations and reflections about President Nixon, I agree with the Court's conclusion that The Nation appropriated some literary form of substantial quality. I do not agree, however, that the substantiality of the expression taken was clearly excessive or inappropriate to The Nation's news reporting purpose. ...

With respect to the motivation for the pardon and the insights into the psyche of the fallen President, for example, Mr. Ford's reflections and perceptions are so laden with emotion and deeply personal value judgments that full understanding is immeasurably enhanced by reproducing a limited portion of Mr. Ford's own words. The importance of the work, after all, lies not only in revelation of previously unknown fact but also in revelation of the thoughts, ideas, motivations, and fears of two Presidents at a critical moment in our national history. Thus, while the question is not easily resolved, it is difficult to say that the use of the six quotations was gratuitous in relation to the news reporting purpose. ...

The Effect on the Market. ... The Nation's publication indisputably precipitated Time's eventual cancellation. But that does not mean that The Nation's use of the 300 quoted words caused this injury to Harper & Row. Wholly apart from these quoted words, The Nation published significant information and ideas from the Ford manuscript. If it was this publication of information, and not the publication of the few quotations, that caused Time to abrogate its serialization agreement, then whatever the negative effect on the serialization market, that effect was the product of wholly legitimate activity.

Because The Nation was the first to convey the information in this case, it did perhaps take from Harper & Row some of the value that publisher sought to garner for itself through the contractual arrangement with Ford and the license to Time. Harper & Row had every right to seek to monopolize revenue from that potential market through contractual arrangements but it has no right to set up copyright as a shield from competition in that market because copyright does not protect information. The Nation had every right to seek to be the first to publish that information.

Notes and Questions

1. The Court's opinion illustrates how the four factors are often applied in fair use cases:

a. Purpose and character of the use. Courts often look to whether the use is commercial or non-commercial. Commercial uses count against fair use, while non-commercial uses support a finding of fair use. Courts will also look at whether the use is transformative or non-transformative.

b. Nature of the work. Creative works are entitled to more protection, whereas works that are more factual in nature typically receive less protection. In addition, unpublished works often receive more protection. *See Salinger v. Random House*, 811 F.2d 90 (2d Cir. 1987), *cert. denied*, 484 U.S. 890 (1987) (no fair use of excerpts of private, unpublished letters of J.D. Salinger in an unauthorized biography).

c. Amount copied. In assessing the amount of the work copied, the measure is both quantitative and qualitative. In absolute terms, the amount of copying in *Harper & Row* was minimal compared to the size of the overall work. However, the Court noted that qualitatively, the Nation took the most important sections of the work.

d. Impact on the market. In assessing the harm to the market, the court looked at both the immediate market for excerpts and the subsequent market for sales of the book. In this case, it was relatively easy for the plaintiff to establish harm. As we will see in later cases, this issue is often not so clear cut.

2. What should the Nation have done in order to avoid liability? How much of the book could the Nation have taken and still been privileged under the fair use defense? If you had been counsel to the Nation after they received the manuscript and prior to their publication of the article, what advice would you have given your client? Would the result in this case have been different if the Nation had published exactly the same excerpts, but one month after publication of the book?

3. The Court rejects the argument that any categorical exception to copyright liability exists for works that are particularly newsworthy and instead relies upon a balancing of the four fair use factors. Did the Court weigh these factors appropriately? Do you agree that there should be no categorical exception for newsworthy works? How should newsworthiness be factored in, if at all, into fair use analysis? On this point, consider *Nunez v. Caribbean International News Corp.*, 235 F.3d 18 (1st Cir. 2000) (finding fair use where local newspaper published, without authorization, revealing photographs of Miss Puerto Rico Universe 1997 during controversy over her fitness to retain her crown).

4. *Harper & Row* squarely presented the Court with a conflict between the interests of a copyright holder and those of an author who claimed to serve public interest through its writing. In this case, the Court resolved this conflict in the copyright holder's favor. How broad are the implications of this resolution? Should we understand *Harper* as a signal to generally favor the interests of copyright holders in fair use cases? Or, did *Harper* address only the peculiar context in which the Nation acted?

Problem

You are counsel for a local television station in a city marked by tensions between racial minorities and the local police. Yesterday, a major news story broke when one of your competitors broadcast a cell-phone video showing a group of seven police officers appearing to use excessive force, repeatedly striking an African-American man. Your competitor obtained the video from an individual, paying the individual a substantial sum for an exclusive license to broadcast the video. This is an issue of critical importance to the community, and your television station desperately wants to broadcast the video. What advice do you give about whether you can broadcast the video without a license?

New Era Publications v. Carol Publishing Group
904 F.2d 152 (2d Cir. 1990)

FEINBERG, Circuit Judge.

Defendant Carol Publishing Group appeals from a ... judgment ... permanently enjoining it from publishing a biography in its present form, on grounds of copyright infringement. [T]he district court held that the biography's quotations from its subject's writings—all of which had been published—did not constitute "fair use." We disagree. ...

Background

The biography at issue in this appeal is entitled *A Piece of Blue Sky: Scientology, Dianetics and L. Ron Hubbard Exposed*, and was written by Jonathan Caven-Atack. The subject of the book is L. Ron Hubbard, the controversial founder of the Church of Scientology, who died in 1986.

The author joined the Church when he was 19 and was a member for almost nine years. In 1983, however, according to the author, his faith in the Church was shaken by what he saw as the Church's repressive practices toward dissident members. The author subsequently resigned from the Church, but undertook a thorough investigation into the Church and Hubbard. During the course of this inquiry, the author became convinced that the Church was a dangerous cult, and that Hubbard was a vindictive and profoundly disturbed man.

The author's investigation culminated in the book, which, in its present manuscript form, is 527 double-spaced pages in length. As its title makes plain, the book is an unfavorable biography of Hubbard and a strong attack on Scientology; the author's purpose is to expose what he believes is the pernicious nature of the Church and the deceit that is the foundation of its teachings. The book paints a highly unflattering portrait of Hubbard as a thoroughgoing charlatan who lied relentlessly about his accomplishments. The author's attitude toward his subject can be gauged by his descriptions of Hubbard as "an arrogant, amoral egomaniac," "a paranoid, power hungry, petty sadist," and—perhaps ironically in light of the claims in this case—"an outright plagiarist." The book quotes widely from Hubbard's works, using passages from Hubbard's writings both in the body of the text and at the beginning of many chapters. The author had a rich vein of material to mine, because Hubbard wrote prolifically on a wide variety of subjects, including science fiction, philosophy and religion. ...

Plaintiff New Era Publications International is the exclusive licensee of Hubbard's works. After learning that appellant Carol Publishing Group intended to publish the book, appellee sued appellant in the district court. Appellee claimed that the book copied "substantial portions" of certain of Hubbard's works in violation of its exclusive copyright rights under 17 U.S.C. § 106, and accused appellant of willful copyright infringement. ... In particular, appellee argued that 121 passages of the book were drawn from 48 of Hubbard's works. The complaint sought, among other things, an injunction to stop publication of the book. ...

The district court granted a permanent injunction. ... Appellant now appeals. ...

Discussion

1. Fair Use

    ...

    A. Factor One: Purpose and Character of the Use

    As noted above, the book is an unfavorable biography. Section 107 provides that use of copyrighted materials for "purposes such as criticism, ... scholarship, or research, is not an infringement of copyright." Our cases establish that biographies in general, and critical biographies in particular, fit "comfortably within" these statutory categories "of uses illustrative of uses that can be fair." *Salinger v. Random House, Inc.*, 811 F.2d at 96. ...

    True, the Supreme Court in *Harper & Row* did not end its analysis of factor one once it had determined that the allegedly infringing use (news reporting) was listed in § 107 as an example of fair use. However, what the Court went on to consider was the infringer's knowing exploitation of the copyrighted material—obtained in an underhanded manner—for an undeserved economic profit. The present case, by contrast, does not involve "an attempt to rush to the market just ahead of the copyright holder's imminent publication, as occurred in *Harper & Row*." *Salinger*, 811 F.2d at 96. Instead, as the author explained in detail in an affidavit submitted below, discussing the reason why he included each quote, the author uses Hubbard's works for the entirely legitimate purpose of making his point that Hubbard was a charlatan and the Church a dangerous cult. To be sure, the author and appellant want to make a profit in publishing the book. But the author's use of material "to enrich" his biography is protected fair use, "notwithstanding that he and his publisher anticipate profits." *Id.*

    We hold that factor one favors appellant.

    B. Factor Two: Nature of the Copyrighted Work

    The district court found that all of the works from which the author quoted had been published. Whether or not a work is published is critical to its nature under factor two, because "the scope of fair use is narrower with respect to unpublished works." *Harper & Row*, 471 U.S. at 564. ...

    Furthermore, the scope of fair use is greater with respect to factual than non-factual works. While there is no bright-line test for distinguishing between these two categories, we have referred to the former as works that are "essentially factual in nature," *Maxtone-Graham v. Burtchaell*, 803 F.2d at 1263, or "primarily informational rather than creative." *Consumers Union of United States, Inc. v. General Signal Corp.*, 724 F.2d 1044, 1049 (2d Cir. 1983). We have some hesitation in trying to characterize Hubbard's diverse body of writings as solely "factual" or "non-factual," but on balance, we believe that the quoted works—which deal with Hubbard's life, his views on religion, human relations, the Church, etc.—are more properly viewed as factual or informational. ...

We conclude that factor two favors appellant.

C.   Factor Three: Volume of Quotation

... Here, the book uses overall a small percentage of Hubbard's works. Appellant calculates that the book quotes only a minuscule amount of 25 of the 48 works that appellee claimed were infringed, 5-6% of 12 other works and 8% or more of 11 works, each of the 11 being only a few pages in length. In the context of quotation from published works, where a greater amount of copying is allowed, this is not so much as to be unfair.

Nor is the use qualitatively unfair. Appellee asserts that "key portions" of Hubbard's works are taken "[i]n many cases." But the district court found that the quotations in the book's text—which amount to the bulk of the allegedly infringing passages—do not take essentially the heart of Hubbard's works. And our review of the remaining 17 passages, which are "set off by themselves at the beginning of a part or chapter" and "set the tone for the sections they precede," persuades us that they too do not take essentially the heart of Hubbard's works. ...

We find that factor three favors appellant.

D.   Factor Four: Effect on the Market

... Appellee argues strenuously that factor four favors it, asserting that it intends to publish an authorized biography of Hubbard that will include excerpts from all of his works, including material as yet unpublished, and that the book will discourage potential readers of the authorized biography by conveying the flavor of Hubbard's writings. ...

We do not find [this] argument persuasive. ... [W]e are skeptical here that potential customers for the authorized favorable biography of Hubbard in the future will be deterred from buying because the author's unfavorable biography quotes from Hubbard's works. Indeed, it is not "beyond the realm of possibility that" the book "might stimulate further interest" in the authorized biography. *Maxtone-Graham v. Burtchaell*, 803 F.2d at 1264.

Furthermore, even assuming that the book discourages potential purchasers of the authorized biography, this is not necessarily actionable under the copyright laws. Such potential buyers might be put off because the book persuaded them (as it clearly hopes to) that Hubbard was a charlatan, but the copyright laws do not protect against that sort of injury. Harm to the market for a copyrighted work or its derivatives caused by a "devastating critique" that "diminished sales by convincing the public that the original work was of poor quality" is not "within the scope of copyright protection." *Consumers Union of United States, Inc. v. General Signal Corp.*, 724 F.2d at 1051. This is so because the critique and the copyrighted work serve "fundamentally different functions, by virtue" of, among other things, "their opposing viewpoints." *Maxtone-Graham*, 803 F.2d at 1264. "Where the copy does not compete in any way with the original," copyright's central concern—"that creation will be discouraged if demand can be undercut by copiers"—is absent. *Consumers Union*, 724 F.2d at 1051. Here, the purpose of the book is diametrically opposed to that of the authorized biography; the former seeks to unmask Hubbard and the Church, while the latter presumably will be designed to promote public interest in Hubbard and the Church. Thus, even if the book ultimately harms sales of the authorized biography, this would not result from unfair infringement forbidden by the copyright laws, but rather from a convincing work that effectively criticizes Hubbard, the very type of work that the Copyright Act was designed to protect and encourage. ...

We conclude that factor four favors appellant.

E.   Other Factors

... In sum, balancing all of the relevant factors, we believe that the present case presents a strong set of facts for invoking the fair use defense: The book is a critical biography, designed to educate the public about Hubbard, a public figure who sought public attention, albeit on his own terms; the book quotes from merely a small portion of Hubbard's works and from only those that have been published; and, it will cause no adverse impact protected by the copyright law on the market for Hubbard's writings. In these circumstances, we conclude that the book's use of passages from Hubbard's work is protected fair use.

Notes and Questions

1.   Like *Harper*, *New Era* presents a conflict between the interests of a copyright holder and a writer who claimed to serve the public interest by using copyrighted material. Yet, unlike *Harper*, *New Era* resolves the conflict against the copyright holder. Why did this happen? Does your answer to this question affect how broadly you understand *Harper*'s preference for the interests of copyright holders?

2.   *New Era* introduces a theme—criticism of the author—that plays an important role in many fair use cases. Why should it matter that Mr. Caven-Atack's biography criticized L. Ron Hubbard? Does the court's emphasis on the critical nature of the biography mean that a biographer favorably inclined towards Hubbard has less freedom to borrow from Hubbard's work than a critical biographer?

3.   According to *Harper*, "The fact that a work is unpublished is a critical element of its 'nature.'" Of course, biographers frequently want to quote—sometimes liberally—from the unpublished writings of their subjects. Does *Harper* mean that individuals can influence what is written about them by denying biographers the ability to quote from unpublished writings? Or, does *New Era* express a theory of fair use that

gives biographers the ability to quote with relative impunity? If you believe that this is the case, you may wish to consider *Salinger v. Random House*, 811 F.2d 90 (2d Cir. 1987). In *Salinger*, the defendant wrote an unauthorized biography of the famously reclusive author J.D. Salinger. The defendant found collections of Salinger's unpublished letters in a number of publicly accessible libraries. Originally, the defendant included passages from various letters in the biography, but when threatened with by Salinger, changed these passages to paraphrases rather than direct quotes. These changes failed to satisfy Salinger, who sued in copyright. The district court rejected Salinger's motion for a preliminary injunction, but the Second Circuit reversed, holding that the use of these passages did not constitute fair use in large part because the letters were unpublished. In your opinion, did *Salinger* correctly interpret *Harper*?

3. PARODY AND TRANSFORMATIVE USES

We have seen that the purpose attributed to a defendant's use greatly influences whether the use is fair. However, it is not always easy to identify a single purpose behind a defendant's use. For example, in *Harper*, the Supreme Court recognized the news reporting purpose behind the Nation's story, but it also characterized that use as commercial because the Nation clearly wanted to profit from selling the story. What should courts do when defendants claim to use copyrighted material for favored purposes but profit financially from the uses in question? How quickly should courts attribute a favored purpose to a defendant's work, and how easily should commercial activity prevent a finding of fair use? Our next case considers these questions in the context of yet another favored use—parody.

Campbell v. Acuff-Rose Music
510 U.S. 569 (1994)

JUSTICE SOUTER delivered the opinion of the Court.

We are called upon to decide whether 2 Live Crew's commercial parody of Roy Orbison's song, "Oh, Pretty Woman," may be a fair use within the meaning of the Copyright Act of 1976. Although the District Court granted summary judgment for 2 Live Crew, the Court of Appeals reversed, holding the defense of fair use barred by the song's commercial character and excessive borrowing. Because we hold that a parody's commercial character is only one element to be weighed in a fair use enquiry, and that insufficient consideration was given to the nature of parody in weighing the degree of copying, we reverse and remand.

I

In 1964, Roy Orbison and William Dees wrote a rock ballad called "Oh, Pretty Woman" and assigned their rights in it to respondent Acuff-Rose Music, Inc. Acuff-Rose registered the song for copyright protection.

Petitioners Luther R. Campbell, Christopher Wongwon, Mark Ross, and David Hobbs are collectively known as 2 Live Crew, a popular rap music group. In 1989, Campbell wrote a song entitled "Pretty Woman," which he later described in an affidavit as intended, "through comical lyrics, to satirize the original work...." On July 5, 1989, 2 Live Crew's manager informed Acuff-Rose that 2 Live Crew had written a parody of "Oh, Pretty Woman," that they would afford all credit for ownership and authorship of the original song to Acuff-Rose, Dees, and Orbison, and that they were willing to pay a fee for the use they wished to make of it. Enclosed with the letter were a copy of the lyrics and a recording of 2 Live Crew's song. Acuff-Rose's agent refused permission, stating that "I am aware of the success enjoyed by 'The 2 Live Crews', but I must inform you that we cannot permit the use of a parody of 'Oh, Pretty Woman.'" Nonetheless, in June or July 1989, 2 Live Crew released records, cassette tapes, and compact discs of "Pretty Woman" in a collection of songs entitled "As Clean As They Wanna Be." The albums and compact discs identify the authors of "Pretty Woman" as Orbison and Dees and its publisher as Acuff-Rose.

Almost a year later, after nearly a quarter of a million copies of the recording had been sold, Acuff-Rose sued 2 Live Crew and its record company, Luke Skyywalker Records, for copyright infringement. ... We granted certiorari to determine whether 2 Live Crew's commercial parody could be a fair use.

II

It is uncontested here that 2 Live Crew's song would be an infringement of Acuff-Rose's rights in "Oh, Pretty Woman," under the Copyright Act of 1976, but for a finding of fair use through parody. ...

A

... The first factor in a fair use enquiry is "the purpose and character of the use, including whether such use is of a commercial nature or is for nonprofit educational purposes." The enquiry here may be guided by the examples given in the preamble to § 107, looking to whether the use is for criticism, or comment, or news reporting, and the like. The central purpose of this investigation is to see, in Justice Story's words, whether the new work merely "supersede[s] the objects" of the original creation, or instead adds something new, with a further purpose or different character, altering the first with new expression, meaning, or message; it asks, in other words, whether and to what extent the new work is "transformative." Although such transformative use is not absolutely necessary for a finding of fair use, the goal of copyright, to promote science and the arts, is generally furthered by the creation of transformative works.

Such works thus lie at the heart of the fair use doctrine's guarantee of breathing space within the confines of copyright, and the more transformative the new work, the less will be the significance of other factors, like commercialism, that may weigh against a finding of fair use.

This Court has only once before even considered whether parody may be fair use, and that time issued no opinion because of the Court's equal division. Suffice it to say now that parody has an obvious claim to transformative value, as Acuff-Rose itself does not deny. Like less ostensibly humorous forms of criticism, it can provide social benefit, by shedding light on an earlier work, and, in the process, creating a new one. We thus line up with the courts that have held that parody, like other comment or criticism, may claim fair use under § 107.

The germ of parody lies in the definition of the Greek *parodeia*, quoted in Judge Nelson's Court of Appeals dissent, as "a song sung alongside another." Modern dictionaries accordingly describe a parody as a "literary or artistic work that imitates the characteristic style of an author or a work for comic effect or ridicule," or as a "composition in prose or verse in which the characteristic turns of thought and phrase in an author or class of authors are imitated in such a way as to make them appear ridiculous." [11 OXFORD ENGLISH DICTIONARY 247 (2d ed. 1989).] For the purposes of copyright law, the nub of the definitions, and the heart of any parodist's claim to quote from existing material, is the use of some elements of a prior author's composition to create a new one that, at least in part, comments on that author's works. If, on the contrary, the commentary has no critical bearing on the substance or style of the original composition, which the alleged infringer merely uses to get attention or to avoid the drudgery in working up something fresh, the claim to fairness in borrowing from another's work diminishes accordingly (if it does not vanish), and other factors, like the extent of its commerciality, loom larger. Parody needs to mimic an original to make its point, and so has some claim to use the creation of its victim's (or collective victims') imagination, whereas satire can stand on its own two feet and so requires justification for the very act of borrowing.

The fact that parody can claim legitimacy for some appropriation does not, of course, tell either parodist or judge much about where to draw the line. Like a book review quoting the copyrighted material criticized, parody may or may not be fair use, and petitioners' suggestion that any parodic use is presumptively fair has no more justification in law or fact than the equally hopeful claim that any use for news reporting should be presumed fair. The Act has no hint of an evidentiary preference for parodists over their victims, and no workable presumption for parody could take account of the fact that parody often shades into satire when society is lampooned through its creative artifacts, or that a work may contain both parodic and nonparodic elements. Accordingly, parody, like any other use, has to work its way through the relevant factors, and be judged case by case, in light of the ends of the copyright law.

Here, the District Court held, and the Court of Appeals assumed, that 2 Live Crew's "Pretty Woman" contains parody, commenting on and criticizing the original work, whatever it may have to say about society at large. As the District Court remarked, the words of 2 Live Crew's song copy the original's first line, but then "quickly degenerat[e] into a play on words, substituting predictable lyrics with shocking ones ... [that] derisively demonstrat[e] how bland and banal the Orbison song seems to them." Judge Nelson, dissenting below, came to the same conclusion, that the 2 Live Crew song "was clearly intended to ridicule the white-bread original" and "reminds us that sexual congress with nameless streetwalkers is not necessarily the stuff of romance and is not necessarily without its consequences. The singers (there are several) have the same thing on their minds as did the lonely man with the nasal voice, but here there is no hint of wine and roses." Although the majority below had difficulty discerning any criticism of the original in 2 Live Crew's song, it assumed for purposes of its opinion that there was some.

We have less difficulty in finding that critical element in 2 Live Crew's song than the Court of Appeals did, although having found it we will not take the further step of evaluating its quality. The threshold question when fair use is raised in defense of parody is whether a parodic character may reasonably be perceived. Whether, going beyond that, parody is in good taste or bad does not and should not matter to fair use.

While we might not assign a high rank to the parodic element here, we think it fair to say that 2 Live Crew's song reasonably could be perceived as commenting on the original or criticizing it, to some degree. 2 Live Crew juxtaposes the romantic musings of a man whose fantasy comes true, with degrading taunts, a bawdy demand for sex, and a sigh of relief from paternal responsibility. The later words can be taken as a comment on the naiveté of the original of an earlier day, as a rejection of its sentiment that ignores the ugliness of street life and the debasement that it signifies. It is this joinder of reference and ridicule that marks off the author's choice of parody from the other types of comment and criticism that traditionally have had a claim to fair use protection as transformative works.

The Court of Appeals, however, immediately cut short the enquiry into 2 Live Crew's fair use claim by confining its treatment of the first factor essentially to one relevant fact, the commercial nature of the use. The court then inflated the significance of this fact by applying a presumption ostensibly culled from *Sony*, that "every commercial use of copyrighted material is presumptively ... unfair...." *Sony*, 464 U.S., at 451. In giving virtually dispositive weight to the commercial nature of the parody, the Court of Appeals erred.

The language of the statute makes clear that the commercial or non-profit educational purpose of a work is only one element of the first factor enquiry into its purpose and character. Section 107(1) uses the term "including" to begin the dependent clause referring to commercial use, and the main clause speaks of a broader investigation into "purpose and character." As we explained in *Harper & Row*, Congress resisted attempts to narrow the ambit of this traditional enquiry by adopting categories of presumptively fair use, and it urged courts to preserve the breadth of their traditionally ample view of the universe of relevant evidence[Accordingly, the mere fact that a use is educational and not for profit does not insulate it from a finding of infringement,]any more than the commercial character of a use bars a finding of fairness. If, indeed, commerciality carried presumptive force against a finding of fairness, the presumption would swallow nearly all of the illustrative uses listed in the preamble paragraph of § 107, including news reporting, comment, criticism, teaching, scholarship, and research, since these activities "are generally conducted for profit in this country." *Harper & Row*, *supra*, at 592 (Brennan, J., dissenting). Congress could not have intended such a rule, which certainly is not inferable from the common-law cases, arising as they did from the world of letters in which Samuel Johnson could pronounce that "[n]o man but a blockhead ever wrote, except for money." 3 BOSWELL'S LIFE OF JOHNSON 19 (G. Hill ed. 1934).

B

The second statutory factor, "the nature of the copyrighted work," ... calls for recognition that some works are closer to the core of intended copyright protection than others, with the consequence that fair use is more difficult to establish when the former works are copied. We agree with both the District Court and the Court of Appeals that the Orbison original's creative expression for public dissemination falls within the core of the copyright's protective purposes. This fact, however, is not much help in this case, or ever likely to help much in separating the fair use sheep from the infringing goats in a parody case, since parodies almost invariably copy publicly known, expressive works.

C

The third factor asks whether "the amount and substantiality of the portion used in relation to the copyrighted work as a whole," are reasonable in relation to the purpose of the copying. Here, attention turns to the persuasiveness of a parodist's justification for the particular copying done, and the enquiry will harken back to the first of the statutory factors, for, as in prior cases, we recognize that the extent of permissible copying varies with the purpose and character of the use. The facts bearing on this factor will also tend to address the fourth, by revealing the degree to which the parody may serve as a market substitute for the original or potentially licensed derivatives.

The District Court considered the song's parodic purpose in finding that 2 Live Crew had not helped themselves overmuch. The Court of Appeals disagreed, stating that "[w]hile it may not be inappropriate to find that no more was taken than necessary, the copying was qualitatively substantial. ... We conclude that taking the heart of the original and making it the heart of a new work was to purloin a substantial portion of the essence of the original."

The Court of Appeals is of course correct that this factor calls for thought not only about the quantity of the materials used, but about their quality and importance, too. In *Harper & Row*, for example, the Nation had taken only some 300 words out of President Ford's memoirs, but we signaled the significance of the quotations in finding them to amount to "the heart of the book," the part most likely to be newsworthy and important in licensing serialization. We also agree with the Court of Appeals that whether "a substantial portion of the infringing work was copied verbatim" from the copyrighted work is a relevant question, for it may reveal a dearth of transformative character or purpose under the first factor, or a greater likelihood of market harm under the fourth; a work composed primarily of an original, particularly its heart, with little added or changed, is more likely to be a merely superseding use, fulfilling demand for the original.

Where we part company with the court below is in applying these guides to parody, and in particular to parody in the song before us. Parody presents a difficult case. Parody's humor, or in any event its comment, necessarily springs from recognizable allusion to its object through distorted imitation. Its art lies in the tension between a known original and its parodic twin. When parody takes aim at a particular original work, the parody must be able to "conjure up" at least enough of that original to make the object of its critical wit recognizable. What makes for this recognition is quotation of the original's most distinctive or memorable features, which the parodist can be sure the audience will know. Once enough has been taken to assure identification, how much more is reasonable will depend, say, on the extent to which the song's overriding purpose and character is to parody the original or, in contrast, the likelihood that the parody may serve as a market substitute for the original. But using some characteristic features cannot be avoided.

We think the Court of Appeals was insufficiently appreciative of parody's need for the recognizable sight or sound when it ruled 2 Live Crew's use unreasonable as a matter of law. It is true, of course, that 2 Live Crew copied the characteristic opening bass riff (or musical phrase) of the original, and true that the words of the first line copy the Orbison lyrics. But if quotation of the opening riff and the first line may be said to go to the "heart" of the original, the heart is also what most readily conjures up the song for parody, and it is the heart at which parody takes aim. Copying does not become excessive in relation to parodic purpose merely because the portion taken was the original's heart. If 2 Live Crew had copied a significantly less memorable part of the original, it is difficult to see how its parodic character would have come through.

This is not, of course, to say that anyone who calls himself a parodist can skim the cream and get away scot free. In parody, as in news reporting, context is everything, and the question of fairness asks what else the parodist did besides go to the heart of the original. It is significant that 2 Live Crew not only copied the first line of the original, but thereafter departed markedly from the Orbison lyrics for its own ends. 2 Live

Crew not only copied the bass riff and repeated it, but also produced otherwise distinctive sounds, interposing "scraper" noise, overlaying the music with solos in different keys, and altering the drum beat. This is not a case, then, where "a substantial portion" of the parody itself is composed of a "verbatim" copying of the original. It is not, that is, a case where the parody is so insubstantial, as compared to the copying, that the third factor must be resolved as a matter of law against the parodists.

Suffice it to say here that, as to the lyrics, we think the Court of Appeals correctly suggested that "no more was taken than necessary," but just for that reason, we fail to see how the copying can be excessive in relation to its parodic purpose, even if the portion taken is the original's "heart." As to the music, we express no opinion whether repetition of the bass riff is excessive copying, and we remand to permit evaluation of the amount taken, in light of the song's parodic purpose and character, its transformative elements, and considerations of the potential for market substitution sketched more fully below.

D

The fourth fair use factor is "the effect of the use upon the potential market for or value of the copyrighted work." It requires courts to consider not only the extent of market harm caused by the particular actions of the alleged infringer, but also "whether unrestricted and widespread conduct of the sort engaged in by the defendant ... would result in a substantially adverse impact on the potential market" for the original. The enquiry "must take account not only of harm to the original but also of harm to the market for derivative works." *Harper & Row, supra*, 471 U.S. at 568.

Since fair use is an affirmative defense, its proponent would have difficulty carrying the burden of demonstrating fair use without favorable evidence about relevant markets. In moving for summary judgment, 2 Live Crew left themselves at just such a disadvantage when they failed to address the effect on the market for rap derivatives, and confined themselves to uncontroverted submissions that there was no likely effect on the market for the original. They did not, however, thereby subject themselves to the evidentiary presumption applied by the Court of Appeals. In assessing the likelihood of significant market harm, the Court of Appeals quoted from language in *Sony* that "'[i]f the intended use is for commercial gain, that likelihood may be presumed. But if it is for a noncommercial purpose, the likelihood must be demonstrated.'" The court reasoned that because "the use of the copyrighted work is wholly commercial, ... we presume that a likelihood of future harm to Acuff-Rose exists." In so doing, the court resolved the fourth factor against 2 Live Crew, just as it had the first, by applying a presumption about the effect of commercial use, a presumption which as applied here we hold to be error.

No "presumption" or inference of market harm that might find support in *Sony* is applicable to a case involving something beyond mere duplication for commercial purposes. *Sony*'s discussion of a presumption contrasts a context of verbatim copying of the original in its entirety for commercial purposes, with the noncommercial context of *Sony* itself (home copying of television programming). In the former circumstances, what *Sony* said simply makes common sense: when a commercial use amounts to mere duplication of the entirety of an original, it clearly "supersede[s] the objects," *Folsom v. Marsh, supra,* at 348, of the original and serves as a market replacement for it, making it likely that cognizable market harm to the original will occur. But when, on the contrary, the second use is transformative, market substitution is at least less certain, and market harm may not be so readily inferred. Indeed, as to parody pure and simple, it is more likely that the new work will not affect the market for the original in a way cognizable under this factor, that is, by acting as a substitute for it. This is so because the parody and the original usually serve different market functions.

We do not, of course, suggest that a parody may not harm the market at all, but when a lethal parody, like a scathing theater review, kills demand for the original, it does not produce a harm cognizable under the Copyright Act. Because "parody may quite legitimately aim at garroting the original, destroying it commercially as well as artistically," B. Kaplan, AN UNHURRIED VIEW OF COPYRIGHT 69 (1967), the role of the courts is to distinguish between "[b]iting criticism [that merely] suppresses demand [and] copyright infringement[, which] usurps it." *Fisher v. Dees,* 794 F.2d, at 438.

This distinction between potentially remediable displacement and unremediable disparagement is reflected in the rule that there is no protectible derivative market for criticism. The market for potential derivative uses includes only those that creators of original works would in general develop or license others to develop. Yet the unlikelihood that creators of imaginative works will license critical reviews or lampoons of their own productions removes such uses from the very notion of a potential licensing market. "People ask ... for criticism, but they only want praise." S. Maugham, OF HUMAN BONDAGE 241 (Penguin ed. 1992). Thus, to the extent that the opinion below may be read to have considered harm to the market for parodies of "Oh, Pretty Woman," the court erred.

In explaining why the law recognizes no derivative market for critical works, including parody, we have, of course, been speaking of the later work as if it had nothing but a critical aspect. But the later work may have a more complex character, with effects not only in the arena of criticism but also in protectible markets for derivative works, too. In that sort of case, the law looks beyond the criticism to the other elements of the work, as it does here. 2 Live Crew's song comprises not only parody but also rap music, and the derivative market for rap music is a proper focus of enquiry. Evidence of substantial harm to it would weigh against a finding of fair use, because the licensing of derivatives is an important economic incentive to the creation of originals. Of course, the only harm to derivatives that need concern us, as discussed above, is the harm of market substitution. The fact that a parody may impair the market for derivative uses by the very effectiveness of its critical commentary is no more relevant under copyright than the like threat to the original market.

Although 2 Live Crew submitted uncontroverted affidavits on the question of market harm to the original, neither they, nor Acuff-Rose, introduced evidence or affidavits addressing the likely effect of 2 Live Crew's parodic rap song on the market for a nonparody, rap version of "Oh, Pretty Woman." And while Acuff-Rose would have us find evidence of a rap market in the very facts that 2 Live Crew recorded a rap parody of "Oh, Pretty Woman" and another rap group sought a license to record a rap derivative, there was no evidence that a potential rap market was harmed in any way by 2 Live Crew's parody, rap version. The fact that 2 Live Crew's parody sold as part of a collection of rap songs says very little about the parody's effect on a market for a rap version of the original, either of the music alone or of the music with its lyrics. The District Court essentially passed on this issue, observing that Acuff-Rose is free to record "whatever version of the original it desires"; the Court of Appeals went the other way by erroneous presumption. Contrary to each treatment, it is impossible to deal with the fourth factor except by recognizing that a silent record on an important factor bearing on fair use disentitled the proponent of the defense, 2 Live Crew, to summary judgment. The evidentiary hole will doubtless be plugged on remand.

III

It was error for the Court of Appeals to conclude that the commercial nature of 2 Live Crew's parody of "Oh, Pretty Woman" rendered it presumptively unfair. No such evidentiary presumption is available to address either the first factor, the character and purpose of the use, or the fourth, market harm, in determining whether a transformative use, such as parody, is a fair one. The court also erred in holding that 2 Live Crew had necessarily copied excessively from the Orbison original, considering the parodic purpose of the use. We therefore reverse the judgment of the Court of Appeals and remand the case for further proceedings consistent with this opinion.

It is so ordered.

APPENDIX A TO OPINION OF THE COURT

"Oh, Pretty Woman" by Roy Orbison and William Dees
Pretty Woman, walking down the street,
Pretty Woman, the kind I like to meet,
Pretty Woman, I don't believe you, you're not the truth,
No one could look as good as you
Mercy
Pretty Woman, won't you pardon me,

Pretty Woman, I couldn't help but see,
Pretty Woman, that you look lovely as can be
Are you lonely just like me?
Pretty Woman, stop a while,
Pretty Woman, talk a while,
Pretty Woman give your smile to me
Pretty Woman, yeah, yeah, yeah
Pretty Woman, look my way,
Pretty Woman, say you'll stay with me
'Cause I need you, I'll treat you right
Come to me baby, Be mine tonight
Pretty Woman, don't walk on by,
Pretty Woman, don't make me cry,
Pretty Woman, don't walk away,
Hey, O.K.
If that's the way it must be, O.K.
I guess I'll go on home, it's late
There'll be tomorrow night, but wait!
What do I see
Is she walking back to me?
Yeah, she's walking back to me!
Oh, Pretty Woman.

APPENDIX B TO OPINION OF THE COURT

"Pretty Woman" as Recorded by 2 Live Crew
Pretty woman walkin' down the street
Pretty woman girl you look so sweet
Pretty woman you bring me down to that knee
Pretty woman you make me wanna beg please
Oh, pretty woman
Big hairy woman you need to shave that stuff
Big hairy woman you know I bet it's tough
Big hairy woman all that hair it ain't legit
'Cause you look like 'Cousin It'
Big hairy woman
Bald headed woman girl your hair won't grow
Bald headed woman you got a teeny weeny afro
Bald headed woman you know your hair could look nice
Bald headed woman first you got to roll it with rice
Bald headed woman here, let me get this hunk of biz for ya
Ya know what I'm saying you look better than rice a roni
Oh bald headed woman
Big hairy woman come on in
And don't forget your bald headed friend
Hey pretty woman let the boys
Jump in
Two timin' woman girl you know you ain't right
Two timin' woman you's out with my boy last night
Two timin' woman that takes a load off my mind

Two timin' woman now I know the baby ain't mine
Oh, two timin' woman
Oh pretty woman

Notes and Questions

1. You can listen to excerpts of the two songs at issue in this case at this URL:

   http://mcir.usc.edu/cases/1990-1999/Pages/campbellacuffrose.html

2. The Court of Appeals decided against 2LiveCrew in large part because 2LiveCrew sold its work commercially. What did the Supreme Court find wrong with this construction of fair use? A defendant making nonprofit use of a work presumably has no profits from which to pay a license fee to a copyright holder. Fair use allows such a user to create a new work without suffering a financial loss. By contrast, a defendant making a for-profit use raises revenue from which she could pay a license fee. Shouldn't copyright law require such payment?

3. The Court places great weight on its conclusion that the 2LiveCrew version of Pretty Woman is transformative. According to the Court, transformative uses "lie at the heart of the fair use doctrine's guarantee of breathing space within the confines of copyright." How should we understand the significance of transformative use? Consider two possibilities. First, the concept could be binary. A derivative work that accomplishes a certain amount of transformation gains a strong, if not conclusive, presumption of fair use. Second, the concept could be fluid, one of many factors affecting fair use on a case by case basis. *Campbell* operates on the second of these possibilities, stating that "the more transformative the new work, the less will be the significance of other factors, like commercialism, that may weigh against a finding of fair use." Is this wise? How should a court measure the degree of transformation accomplished by any work, and can a court accomplish the task without getting drawn into subjective determinations of the sort that *Bleistein* cautioned against?

4. *Campbell* raises again the role of criticism in fair use. The opinion (and indeed copyright doctrine generally) gives parodies that comment on and criticize the original work much more generous fair use treatment than works that do not. Why is this so, and is this distinction justified? If transformation goes a long way to establishing fair use, presumably a use could be highly transformative without criticizing the borrowed work. Shouldn't such a work get generous fair use treatment? What would happen to parody as an art form if courts required parodists to obtain licenses from copyright holders?

5. Compare the application of the third fair use factor in *Campbell* with the application of that same factor in *Harper & Row*. Is the applica-

tion consistent? In *Harper & Row*, the Court emphasized that the defendant copied the "heart" of the work. In *Campbell*, the Court acknowledged that 2LiveCrew had copied the heart of the work, yet gave this little weight. Consider also the treatment of the second factor, the nature of the work. What accounts for the different treatment?

6. *Campbell* rejected the argument that fair use analysis should count harm to the market resulting from the communicative impact of a parody. The Court claimed that a market for critical parodies of copyrighted works would be unlikely to develop. However, the Court suggested that there might be a market for non-parodic derivative works, and that an open question existed as to the potential harm to this market. The Court therefore remanded the case, and it was ultimately settled by the parties. Do you agree with the Court's observation about markets for critical parodies? If such markets exist, does that undermine the Court's conclusion that the communicative impact of parodies does not affect the market for the copyrighted work?

7. *Campbell* discusses the fair use treatment of parody at great length, but it never delivers the punch line. Instead of deciding whether 2LiveCrew's work was a fair use, the Court remands the case for further proceedings. The parties ultimately settled the case. Did 2LiveCrew's work constitute fair use?

Rogers v. Koons
960 F.2d 301 (2d Cir. 1992)

CARDAMONE, Circuit Judge,

The key to this copyright infringement suit, brought by a plaintiff photographer against a defendant sculptor and the gallery representing him, is defendants' borrowing of plaintiff's expression of a typical American scene—a smiling husband and wife holding a litter of charming puppies. The copying was so deliberate as to suggest that defendants resolved so long as they were significant players in the art business, and the copies they produced bettered the price of the copied work by a thousand to one, their piracy of a less well-known artist's work would escape being sullied by an accusation of plagiarism.

BACKGROUND FACTS

A. Rogers

We think it helpful to understanding this appeal to set forth the principals' professional backgrounds. Plaintiff, Art Rogers, a 43-year-old professional artist-photographer, has a studio and home at Point Reyes, California, where he makes his living by creating, exhibiting, publishing and otherwise making use of his rights in his photographic works. Exhibitions of his photographs have been held in California and as far away as Maine, Florida and New York. His work has been described in French, British and numerous American publications, including the *Journal of American Photography*, Polaroid's *Close-Up Magazine* and the *Popular Photography Annual*. Rogers' photographs are part of the permanent collection of the San Francisco Museum of Modern Art, the Center for Creative Photography at the University of Arizona and Joseph E. Seagrams and Sons in New York City. He has taught photography at the San Francisco Museum of Modern Art.

B.   Creating The Photograph "Puppies"

In 1980 an acquaintance, Jim Scanlon, commissioned Rogers to photograph his eight new German Shepherd puppies. When Rogers went to his home on September 21, 1980 he decided that taking a picture of the puppies alone would not work successfully, and chose instead to include Scanlon and his wife holding them. Substantial creative effort went into both the composition and production of "Puppies," a black and white photograph. At the photo session, and later in his lab, Rogers drew on his years of artistic development. He selected the light, the location, the bench on which the Scanlons are seated and the arrangement of the small dogs. He also made creative judgments concerning technical matters with his camera and the use of natural light. He prepared a set of "contact sheets," containing 50 different images, from which one was selected.

After the Scanlons purchased their prints for $200, "Puppies" became part of Rogers' catalogue of images available for further use, from which he, like many professional photographers, makes his living. "Puppies" has been used and exhibited a number of times. A signed print of it has been sold to a private collector, and in 1989 it was licensed for use in an anthology called "Dog Days." Rogers also planned to use the picture in a series of hand-tinted prints of his works. In 1984 Rogers had licensed "Puppies", along with other works, to Museum Graphics, a company that produces and sells notecards and postcards with high quality reproductions of photographs by well-respected American photographers including, for example, Ansel Adams. Museum Graphics has produced and distributed the "Puppies" notecard since 1984. The first printing was of 5,000 copies and there has been a second similar size printing.

C.   Koons

Defendant Jeff Koons is a 37-year-old artist and sculptor residing in New York City. After receiving a Bachelor of Fine Arts degree from Maryland Institute College of Art in 1976, he worked at a number of jobs, principally membership development at the Museum of Modern Art in New York. While pursuing his career as an artist, he also worked until 1984 as a mutual funds salesman, a registered commodities salesman and broker, and a commodities futures broker. In the ten years from 1980 to 1990 Koons has exhibited his works in approximately 100 Group Exhibitions and in eleven one-man shows. His bibliography is extensive. Koons is represented by Sonnabend Gallery, New York, Donald Young

Gallery, Chicago, and Galerie Max Hetzler, Cologne, Germany. His works sell at very substantial prices, over $100,000. He is a controversial artist hailed by some as a "modern Michelangelo," while others find his art "truly offensive." A New York Times critic complained that "Koons is pushing the relationship between art and money so far that everyone involved comes out looking slightly absurd."

D. Creating the Sculpture "String of Puppies"

After a successful Sonnabend show in 1986, Koons began creating a group of 20 sculptures for a 1988 exhibition at the same gallery that he called the "Banality Show." He works in an art tradition dating back to the beginning of the twentieth century. This tradition defines its efforts as follows: when the artist finishes his work, the meaning of the original object has been extracted and an entirely new meaning set in its place. An example is Andy Warhol's reproduction of multiple images of Campbell's soup cans. Koons' most famous work in this genre is a stainless steel casting of an inflatable rabbit holding a carrot. During 1986 and 1987 the sculptor traveled widely in Europe looking at materials and workshops where he might fabricate materials for the Banality Show. He decided to use porcelain, mirrors and wood as mediums. Certain European studios were chosen to execute his porcelain works, other studios chosen for the mirror pieces, and the small Demetz Studio, located in the northern hill country town of Ortessi, Italy, was selected to carve the wood sculptures.

Koons acknowledges that the source for "String of Puppies" was a Museum Graphics notecard of "Puppies" which he purchased in a "very commercial, tourist-like card shop" in 1987. After buying the card, he tore off that portion showing Rogers' copyright of "Puppies." Koons saw certain criteria in the notecard that he thought made it a workable source. He believed it to be typical, commonplace and familiar. The notecard was also similar to other images of people holding animals that Koons had collected. Thus, he viewed the picture as part of the mass culture—"resting in the collective sub-consciousness of people regardless of whether the card had actually ever been seen by such people."

Appellant gave his artisans one of Rogers' notecards and told them to copy it. But in order to guide the creation of a three-dimensional sculptural piece from the two-dimensional photograph, Koons communicated extensively with the Demetz Studio. He visited it once a week during the period the piece was being carved by the workers and gave them written instructions. In his "production notes" Koons stressed that he wanted "Puppies" copied faithfully in the sculpture. For example, he told his artisans the "work must be just like photo—features of photo must be captured;" later, "puppies need detail in fur. Details—Just Like Photo!;" other notes instruct the artisans to "keep man in angle of photo—mild lean to side & mildly forward—same for woman," to "keep woman's big smile," and to "keep [the sculpture] very, very realistic;" others state, "Girl's nose is too small. Please make larger as per photo;" another reminds the artisans that "The puppies must have variation in fur as per photo—not just large area of paint—variation as per photo."

To paint the polychromed wood "String of Puppies" sculptures, Koons provided a chart with an enlarged photocopy of "Puppies" in the center; painting directions were noted in the margin with arrows drawn to various areas of the photograph. The chart noted, "Puppies, painted in shades of blue. Variation of light-to-dark as per photo. Paint realistic as per photo, but in blues." and "Man's hair, white with shades of grey as per black and white photo!"

When it was finished, "String of Puppies" was displayed at the Sonnabend Gallery, which opened the Banality Show on November 19, 1988. Three of the four copies made were sold to collectors for a total of $367,000; the fourth or artist's copy was kept by Koons. Defendant Koons' use of "Puppies" to create "String of Puppies" was not authorized by plaintiff. Rogers learned of Koons' unauthorized use of his work through Jim Scanlon, the man who had commissioned Rogers to create "Puppies." A friend of Scanlon's, who was familiar with the photograph, called to tell him that what she took to be a "colorized" version of "Puppies" was on the front page of the calendar section of the May 7, 1989 Sunday Los Angeles Times. In fact, as she and Scanlon later learned, the newspaper actually depicted Koons' "String of Puppies" in connection with an article about its exhibition at the Los Angeles Museum of Contemporary Art.

DISCUSSION

III The Fair Use Doctrine

Defendant Koons ... defends his use of Rogers' work "Puppies" to craft "String of Puppies" under a claim of a privilege of "fair use."

1. Purpose and Character of the Use

The first factor, purpose and character of the use, asks whether the original was copied in good faith to benefit the public or primarily for the commercial interests of the infringer. Knowing exploitation of a copyrighted work for personal gain militates against a finding of fair use. And—because it is an equitable doctrine—wrongful denial of exploitative conduct towards the work of another may bar an otherwise legitimate fair use claim. Relevant to this issue is Koons' conduct, especially his action in tearing the copyright mark off of a Rogers notecard prior to sending it to the Italian artisans. This action suggests bad faith in defendant's use of plaintiff's work, and militates against a finding of fair use.

The Supreme Court has held that copies made for commercial or profit-making purposes are presumptively unfair.[53] We have stated that,

---

[53] Editors' note: This holding occurs in the case of *Sony Corporation of America v. Universal City Studios*, 464 U.S. 417 (1984), which we will study below. For now, it is sufficient to

though it is a significant factor, whether the profit element of the fair use calculus affects the ultimate determination of whether there is a fair use depends on the totality of the factors considered; it is not itself controlling. Thus, while we note that Koons' substantial profit from his intentionally exploitive use of Rogers' work also militates against the finding of fair use, we turn next to consider his contention that the primary purpose of the use was for social comment.

Parody or Satire as Fair Use: The Act expressly provides that comment on or criticism of a copyrighted work may be a valid use under the fair use doctrine. We must analyze therefore whether "String of Puppies" is properly considered a comment on or criticism of the photograph "Puppies." Koons argues that his sculpture is a satire or parody of society at large. He insists that "String of Puppies" is a fair social criticism and asserts to support that proposition that he belongs to the school of American artists who believe the mass production of commodities and media images has caused a deterioration in the quality of society, and this artistic tradition of which he is a member proposes through incorporating these images into works of art to comment critically both on the incorporated object and the political and economic system that created it. These themes, Koons states, draw upon the artistic movements of Cubism and Dadaism, with particular influence attributed to Marcel Duchamp, who in 1913 became the first to incorporate manufactured objects (readymades) into a work of art, directly influencing Koons' work and the work of other contemporary American artists. We accept this definition of the objective of this group of American artists.

To analyze Koons' parody defense, we must first define it. Parody or satire, as we understand it, is when one artist, for comic effect or social commentary, closely imitates the style of another artist and in so doing creates a new art work that makes ridiculous the style and expression of the original. Under our cases parody and satire are valued forms of criticism, encouraged because this sort of criticism itself fosters the creativity protected by the copyright law. We have consistently held that a parody entitles its creator under the fair use doctrine to more extensive use of the copied work than is ordinarily allowed under the substantial similarity test.

Hence, it must first be determined whether "String of Puppies" is a parody of Rogers' work for purposes of the fair use doctrine. We agree with the district court that it is not. It is the rule in this Circuit that though the satire need not be only of the copied work and may, as appellants urge of "String of Puppies," also be a parody of modern society, the copied work must be, at least in part, an object of the parody, otherwise there would be no need to conjure up the original work.

We think this is a necessary rule, as were it otherwise there would be no real limitation on the copier's use of another's copyrighted work to

---

remember that *Campbell v. Acuff-Rose* criticized the 6th Circuit for its rigid application of this presumption.

make a statement on some aspect of society at large. If an infringement of copyrightable expression could be justified as fair use solely on the basis of the infringer's claim to a higher or different artistic use— without insuring public awareness of the original work—there would be no practicable boundary to the fair use defense. Koons' claim that his infringement of Rogers' work is fair use solely because he is acting within an artistic tradition of commenting upon the commonplace thus cannot be accepted. The rule's function is to insure that credit is given where credit is due. By requiring that the copied work be an object of the parody, we merely insist that the audience be aware that underlying the parody there is an original and separate expression, attributable to a different artist. This awareness may come from the fact that the copied work is publicly known or because its existence is in some manner acknowledged by the parodist in connection with the parody. Of course, while our view of this matter does not necessarily prevent Koons' expression, although it may, it does recognize that any such exploitation must at least entail "paying the customary price." *Harper & Row Publishers, Inc.*, 471 U.S. at 562.

The problem in the instant case is that even given that "String of Puppies" is a satirical critique of our materialistic society, it is difficult to discern any parody of the photograph "Puppies" itself. We conclude therefore that this first factor of the fair use doctrine cuts against a finding of fair use. The circumstances of this case indicate that Koons' copying of the photograph "Puppies" was done in bad faith, primarily for profit-making motives, and did not constitute a parody of the original work.

2. Nature of the Copyrighted Work

The next fair use factor asks what is the nature of the work that has been copied. Where the original work is factual rather than fictional the scope of fair use is broader. Whether the original is creative, imaginative, or represents an investment of time in anticipation of a financial return also should be considered. Here "Puppies" was a published work of art. As an original expression it has more in common with fiction than with works based on facts, such as, for example, biographies or telephone directories. Since "Puppies" was creative and imaginative and Rogers, who makes his living as a photographer, hopes to gain a financial return for his efforts with this photograph, this factor militates against a finding of fair use.

3. Amount and Substantiality of Work Used

Where the amount of copying exceeds permissible levels, summary judgment has been upheld. To a large degree, this factor involves the same analysis as that used when determining if the copy is substantially similar to the original. Sometimes wholesale copying may be permitted, while in other cases taking even a small percentage of the original work has been held unfair use. It is not fair use when more of the original is copied than necessary. Even more critical than the quantity is the qualitative degree of the copying: what degree of the essence of the original is copied in relation to its whole.

Appellants claim that under a parody defense their use of Rogers' work did not exceed the level permitted under the fair use doctrine. As discussed previously, this Circuit has traditionally afforded parodists significant leeway with respect to the extent and nature of their copying. Yet, even under such a defense there are limitations on what constitutes fair use. Here, the essence of Rogers' photograph was copied nearly *in toto*, much more than would have been necessary even if the sculpture had been a parody of plaintiff's work. In short, it is not really the parody flag that appellants are sailing under, but rather the flag of piracy. Moreover, because we have already determined that "String of Puppies" is not a parody of Rogers' work, appellants cannot avail themselves of this heightened tolerance under a parody defense.

4.   Effect of the Use on the Market Value of the Original

The fourth factor looks at the effect of the use on the market value of the original. Under this factor a balance must be struck between the benefit gained by the copyright owner when the copying is found an unfair use and the benefit gained by the public when the use is held to be fair. The less adverse impact on the owner, the less public benefit need be shown to sustain non-commercial fair use. It is plain that where a use has no demonstrable impact on a copyright owners' potential market, the use need not be prohibited to protect the artist's incentive to pursue his inventive skills. Yet where the use is intended for commercial gain some meaningful likelihood of future harm is presumed.

A critical inquiry under this factor then is whether defendants Koons and Sonnabend planned to profit from their exploitation of "Puppies" without paying Rogers for their use of his photo—that is, whether Koons' work is primarily commercial in nature. We have already concluded that it is. In this case, of course, the copy was in a different medium than the original: one was a three-dimensional piece of sculpture, and the other a two-dimensional black and white photo. But the owner of a copyright with respect to this market-factor need only demonstrate that if the unauthorized use becomes "widespread" it would prejudice his potential market for his work. The reason for this rule relates to a central concern of copyright law that unfair copying undercuts demand for the original work and, as an inevitable consequence, chills creation of such works. Hence the inquiry considers not only harm to the market for the original photograph, but also harm to the market for derivative works. It is obviously not implausible that another artist, who would be willing to purchase the rights from Rogers, would want to produce a sculpture like Rogers' photo and, with Koons' work extant, such market is reduced. Similarly, defendants could take and sell photos of "String of Puppies," which would prejudice Rogers' potential market for the sale of the "Puppies" notecards, in addition to any other derivative use he might plan.

Here there is simply nothing in the record to support a view that Koons produced "String of Puppies" for anything other than sale as high-priced art. Hence, the likelihood of future harm to Rogers' photograph is presumed, and plaintiff's market for his work has been prejudiced.

CONCLUSION

Accordingly, the judgment of the district court is affirmed in all respects.

Art Rogers, "Puppies"

Jeff Koons, "String of Puppies"[54]

---

[54] A color image of "String of Puppies" may be seen at:
http://www.jeffkoons.com/artwork/banality/string-puppies

_____

Notes and Questions

1. *Rogers v. Koons* predates *Campbell v. Acuff-Rose* by two years, but it presents challenges that remain vexing despite the Supreme Court's efforts to clarify the fair use treatment of parodies. Let us begin with the identification of parodies. The *Rogers* court concluded that Koons' sculpture was not a parody because it did not comment upon the original work. Why did the court reach this conclusion? Did it simply not believe that Koons' work said anything about Rogers' photograph, or did the court adopt a particular conception of parody that rendered Koons' comments about Rogers' photograph irrelevant for purposes of fair use? What, if anything, should we make of the fact that Rogers's photograph was not particularly famous or well known? What standard did the Supreme Court in *Campbell* later lay out for when a work is considered a parody? Would Koons's sculpture have satisfied this standard?

2. Accepting for the moment that Koons' work was not a parody within the meaning of copyright law, there remains the question of whether the work has transformative value sufficient to tip the fair analysis use in Koons' favor. Obviously the court did not think so, but consider some of the reasons that might have supported such a conclusion. The court could have believed that "String of Puppies" merely reproduced Rogers' photograph as a sculpture and therefore had minimal transformative value. Alternatively, the court might have understood "String of Puppies" as a serious artistic statement about banality whose value still could not tip the fair use calculation. Did the court choose one of these reasons, and if so, what are the implications of that choice for the strength of the case against Koons?

3. The court found that Koons' work harmed the market for Rogers' photograph. The court stated that a "critical inquiry" behind its reasoning was Koons' commercial motivation. This led to the conclusion that it is "obviously not implausible" that another artist would want to license Rogers' photograph as the basis for a sculpture. Do you think that this relatively tepid statement about market harm ought to tip the fair use analysis against Koons? Does Koons' intention to profit truly affect whether his work undermined the market for Rogers' work? What if Koons had created "String of Puppies" at no charge for a charity? Finally, do you think that other artists want to use photographs like Rogers' for the kind of use made by Koons? If they do, would Rogers willingly license his photograph to them?

4. *Rogers v. Koons* is one of a number of controversial cases that turn on judicial perception of whether a work criticizes or comments upon a copyrighted original. For example, in *Dr. Seuss Enterprises v. Penguin Books, U.S.A.*, 109 F.3d 1394 (9th Cir. 1997), the Ninth Circuit denied fair use treatment for the defendant's Dr. Seuss-style story depict-

ing the O.J. Simpson murder trial. The court reached this result, in part, by concluding that the story was a satirical comment on the trial, and not a parody commenting upon the underlying work. Other courts, however, have rejected a hard and fast distinction between satire and parody. *See, e.g., Blanch v. Koons*, 467 F.3d 244 (2d Cir. 2006) (discussed *infra*). If the use is both transformative and critical, why should the particular target of the critical commentary matter?

5. Even if the target of the criticism matters, are we confident that courts can tell when a particular use of a copyrighted work is criticizing that work? Consider, for example, *Salinger v. Colting*, 617 F.3d 68 (2d Cir. 2010), which involved a novel using characters from J. D. Salinger's *Catcher in the Rye* to tell a story 60 years after the events in the original novel. The Second Circuit in that case rejected the defendant's argument (supported by a number of literature professors) that the novel contained critical commentary about *Catcher in the Rye*, and ultimately concluded that the novel was merely an unauthorized sequel. By contrast, in *Suntrust Bank v. Houghton Mifflin Company*, 268 F.3d 1257 (11th Cir. 2001), the Eleventh Circuit found that a book re-telling the story *Gone With the Wind* from the perspective of a slave on the plantation contained a critique of the original work and was therefore fair use.

How much deference should courts give to an author's claim that her work comments upon the original? Too little deference, and courts will make impossible critiques that are subtle or indirect. Too much deference, and courts will enable thinly-disguised sequels that seek merely build upon the original without paying compensation. How should courts make these determinations? What result best furthers the broader policies underlying copyright?

6. Fourteen years after *Rogers v. Koons*, the artist Jeff Koons was again sued and the Second Circuit issued yet another fair use opinion regarding his work. In *Blanch v. Koons*, 467 F.3d 244 (2d Cir. 2006), Koons created a painting, "Niagara," which appropriated a preexisting photograph of a woman's feet, taken by fashion photographer Andrea Blanch. Koons placed the photograph, along with other similar photographs, against a background that included images of hamburgers, donuts, and other fast food. According to Koons, the painting was a commentary on commercial imagery and culture. (The original photograph is reproduced below on the left, and Koons's painting is reproduced below on the right).

The Second Circuit held that Koons's use was fair. The court held that the purpose of Koons's use was transformative, insofar as it commented upon the social and aesthetic consequences of mass media. The court also rejected the need to determine whether Koons's use was parody or satire. Instead, the relevant question was whether the use was necessary to the artist's purpose, and in determing this, the court gave significant deference to Koons's owns statements on this score.

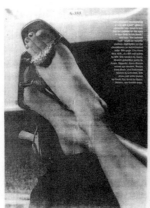

Can you square this decision with the very same court's earlier decision in *Rogers*?

———————

Problem

A group of cartoonists create two issues of an underground, adult-oriented comic book called *Air Pirates Funnies*. The comic books use the cartoon characters Mickey and Minnie Mouse, whose copyrights are held by the Disney Corp. These comic books are decidedly not intended for children, and depict Mickey and Minnie Mouse as promiscuous, drug-dealing mice. Disney Corp. sues the cartoonists. Is this fair use?

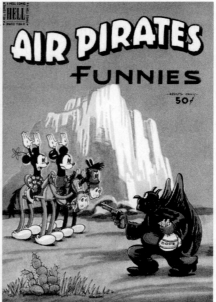

4. DUPLICATION OF COPYRIGHTED WORKS

So far, the fair use cases we have examined involve defendants whose claim to fair use rested in part on the value of new works they created. We now turn to cases in which the defendant claims fair use, but does not use the copyrighted original to create a new work. Fact patterns like these present less obvious cases for fair use. Without the creation of new work, it is not always clear if society benefits enough from the use to justify fair use treatment. However, it is possible that the uses in question strongly promote favored purposes, or that their impact on the market for copyrighted works is low. If so, then fair use treatment for those uses would still make sense. We begin with perhaps the Supreme Court's most famous opinion concerning copyright.

Sony v. Universal City Studios
464 U.S. 417 (1984)

JUSTICE STEVENS delivered the opinion of the Court.

Petitioners manufacture and sell home video tape recorders (VTRs). Respondents own the copyrights on some of the television programs that are broadcast on the public airwaves. Some members of the general public use video tape recorders sold by petitioners to record some of these broadcasts, as well as a large number of other broadcasts. The question presented is whether the sale of petitioners' copying equipment to the general public violates any of the rights conferred upon respondents by the Copyright Act. ...

I

The two respondents in this action, Universal Studios, Inc. and Walt Disney Productions, produce and hold the copyrights on a substantial number of motion pictures and other audiovisual works. In the current marketplace, they can exploit their rights in these works in a number of ways: by authorizing theatrical exhibitions, by licensing limited showings on cable and network television, by selling syndication rights for repeated airings on local television stations, and by marketing programs on prerecorded videotapes or videodiscs. Some works are suitable for exploitation through all of these avenues, while the market for other works is more limited.

Petitioner Sony manufactures millions of Betamax video tape recorders and markets these devices through numerous retail establishments. Sony's Betamax VTR is a mechanism consisting of three basic components: (1) a tuner, which receives electromagnetic signals transmitted over the television band of the public airwaves and separates them into audio and visual signals; (2) a recorder, which records such signals on a magnetic tape; and (3) an adapter, which converts the audio and visual signals on the tape into a composite signal that can be received by a television set. ...

The respondents and Sony both conducted surveys of the way the Betamax machine was used by several hundred owners during a sample period in 1978. Although there were some differences in the surveys, they both showed that the primary use of the machine for most owners was "time-shifting"—the practice of recording a program to view it once at a later time, and thereafter erasing it. Time-shifting enables viewers to see programs they otherwise would miss because they are not at home, are occupied with other tasks, or are viewing a program on another station at the time of a broadcast that they desire to watch. Both surveys also showed, however, that a substantial number of interviewees had accumulated libraries of tapes. Sony's survey indicated that over 80% of the interviewees watched at least as much regular television as they had before owning a Betamax. Respondents offered no evidence of decreased television viewing by Betamax owners.

Sony introduced considerable evidence describing television programs that could be copied without objection from any copyright holder, with special emphasis on sports, religious, and educational programming. For example, their survey indicated that 7.3% of all Betamax use is to record sports events, and representatives of professional baseball, football, basketball, and hockey testified that they had no objection to the recording of their televised events for home use.

Respondents offered opinion evidence concerning the future impact of the unrestricted sale of VTR's on the commercial value of their copyrights. The District Court found, however, that they had failed to prove any likelihood of future harm from the use of VTR's for time-shifting. ...

II

Article I, Sec. 8 of the Constitution provides that: "The Congress shall have Power ... to Promote the Progress of Science and useful Arts, by securing for limited Times to Authors and Inventors the exclusive Right to their respective Writings and Discoveries."

The monopoly privileges that Congress may authorize are neither unlimited nor primarily designed to provide a special private benefit. Rather, the limited grant is a means by which an important public purpose may be achieved. It is intended to motivate the creative activity of authors and inventors by the provision of a special reward, and to allow the public access to the products of their genius after the limited period of exclusive control has expired. ...

From its beginning, the law of copyright has developed in response to significant changes in technology. Indeed, it was the invention of a new form of copying equipment—the printing press—that gave rise to the original need for copyright protection. Repeatedly, as new developments have occurred in this country, it has been the Congress that has fashioned the new rules that new technology made necessary. ...

The judiciary's reluctance to expand the protections afforded by the copyright without explicit legislative guidance is a recurring theme. Sound policy, as well as history, supports our consistent deference to Congress when major technological innovations alter the market for copyrighted materials. Congress has the constitutional authority and the institutional ability to accommodate fully the varied permutations of competing interests that are inevitably implicated by such new technology.

In a case like this, in which Congress has not plainly marked our course, we must be circumspect in construing the scope of rights created by a legislative enactment which never contemplated such a calculus of interests. ...

Copyright protection ... has never accorded the copyright owner complete control over all possible uses of his work. Rather, the Copyright Act grants the copyright holder "exclusive" rights to use and to authorize the use of his work in five qualified ways, including reproduction of the copyrighted work in copies. All reproductions of the work, however, are not within the exclusive domain of the copyright owner; some are in the public domain. Any individual may reproduce a copyrighted work for a "fair use;" the copyright owner does not possess the exclusive right to such a use. ...

The two respondents in this case do not seek relief against the Betamax users who have allegedly infringed their copyrights. ... It is, however, the taping of respondents own copyrighted programs that provides them with standing to charge Sony with contributory infringement. To prevail, they have the burden of proving that users of the Betamax have infringed their copyrights and that Sony should be held responsible for that infringement.

III

[In this section of the opinion, the Court analyzes third-party liability doctrines in copyright law and concludes that Sony will not be held liable for selling the Betamax if the product "is widely used for legitimate, unobjectionable purposes. Indeed, it need merely be capable of substantial noninfringing uses." The issue of third-party liability will be discussed *infra* in Chapter Seven of the casebook. For present purposes, simply note that Sony will not be liable if the Betamax is capable of substantial noninfringing uses.]

IV

The question is thus whether the Betamax is capable of commercially significant noninfringing uses. In order to resolve that question, we need not explore all the different potential uses of the machine and determine whether or not they would constitute infringement. Rather, we need only consider whether on the basis of the facts as found by the district court a significant number of them would be non-infringing. Moreover, in order to resolve this case we need not give precise content to the question of how much use is commercially significant. For one potential use of the Betamax plainly satisfies this standard, however it is understood: private, noncommercial time-shifting in the home. It does so both (A) because respondents have no right to prevent other copyright holders from authorizing it for their programs, and (B) because the District Court's factual findings reveal that even the unauthorized home time-shifting of respondents' programs is legitimate fair use.

A. Authorized Time Shifting

[The Court finds ample support for the district court's finding that many copyright owners authorize end-users to engage in time-shifting].

B. Unauthorized Time-Shifting

Even unauthorized uses of a copyrighted work are not necessarily infringing. An unlicensed use of the copyright is not an infringement unless it conflicts with one of the specific exclusive rights conferred by the copyright statute. Moreover, the definition of exclusive rights in § 106 of the present Act is prefaced by the words "subject to sections 107 through 118." Those sections describe a variety of uses of copyrighted material that "are not infringements of copyright notwithstanding the provisions of § 106." The most pertinent in this case is § 107, the legislative endorsement of the doctrine of "fair use."

That section identifies various factors that enable a Court to apply an "equitable rule of reason" analysis to particular claims of infringement. Although not conclusive, the first factor requires that "the commercial or nonprofit character of an activity" be weighed in any fair use decision. If the Betamax were used to make copies for a commercial or profit-making purpose, such use would presumptively be unfair. The contrary presumption is appropriate here, however, because the District Court's findings plainly establish that time-shifting for private home use must be characterized as a noncommercial, nonprofit activity. Moreover, when one considers the nature of a televised copyrighted audiovisual work, and that timeshifting merely enables a viewer to see such a work which he had been invited to witness in its entirety free of charge, the fact that the entire work is reproduced, does not have its ordinary effect of militating against a finding of fair use.

This is not, however, the end of the inquiry because Congress has also directed us to consider "the effect of the use upon the potential market for or value of the copyrighted work." [17 U.S.C. § 107(4).] The purpose of copyright is to create incentives for creative effort. Even copying for noncommercial purposes may impair the copyright holder's ability to obtain the rewards that Congress intended him to have. But a use that has no demonstrable effect upon the potential market for, or the value of, the copyrighted work need not be prohibited in order to protect the author's incentive to create. The prohibition of such noncommercial uses would merely inhibit access to ideas without any countervailing benefit.

Thus, although every commercial use of copyrighted material is presumptively an unfair exploitation of the monopoly privilege that belongs to the owner of the copyright, noncommercial uses are a different matter. A challenge to a noncommercial use of a copyrighted work requires proof either that the particular use is harmful, or that if it should become widespread, it would adversely affect the potential market for the copyrighted work. Actual present harm need not be shown; such a requirement would leave the copyright holder with no defense against predictable damage. Nor is it necessary to show with certainty that future harm will result. What is necessary is a showing by a preponderance of the evidence that some meaningful likelihood of future harm exists. If the intended use is for commercial gain, that likelihood may be presumed. But if it is for a noncommercial purpose, the likelihood must be demonstrated.

In this case, respondents failed to carry their burden with regard to home time-shifting. The District Court described respondents' evidence as follows:

> Plaintiffs' experts admitted at several points in the trial that the time-shifting without librarying would result in "not a great deal of harm." Plaintiffs' greatest concern about time-shifting is with "a point of important philosophy that transcends even commercial judgment." They fear that with any Betamax usage, "invisible boundaries" are passed: "the copyright owner has lost control over his program."

> ... There was no need for the District Court to say much about past harm. "Plaintiffs have admitted that no actual harm to their copyrights has occurred to date."

On the question of potential future harm from time-shifting, the District Court offered a more detailed analysis of the evidence. It rejected respondents' "fear that persons 'watching' the original telecast of a program will not be measured in the live audience and the ratings and revenues will decrease," by observing that current measurement technology allows the Betamax audience to be reflected. It rejected respondents' prediction "that live television or movie audiences will decrease as more people watch Betamax tapes as an alternative," with the observation that "[t]here is no factual basis for [the underlying] assumption." It rejected respondents' "fear that time-shifting will reduce audiences for telecast reruns," and concluded instead that "given current market practices, this should aid plaintiffs rather than harm them." And it declared that respondents' suggestion "that theater or film rental exhibition of a program will suffer because of time-shift recording of that program" "lacks merit." ...

When these factors are all weighed in the "equitable rule of reason" balance, we must conclude that this record amply supports the District Court's conclusion that home time-shifting is fair use.

In summary, the record and findings of the District Court lead us to two conclusions. First, Sony demonstrated a significant likelihood that substantial numbers of copyright holders who license their works for broadcast on free television would not object to having their broadcasts time-shifted by private viewers. And second, respondents failed to demonstrate that time-shifting would cause any likelihood of nonminimal harm to the potential market for, or the value of, their copyrighted works. The Betamax is, therefore, capable of substantial noninfringing uses. Sony's sale of such equipment to the general public does not constitute contributory infringement of respondent's copyrights. ...

JUSTICE BLACKMUN, with whom JUSTICE MARSHALL, JUSTICE POWELL, and JUSTICE REHNQUIST join, dissenting.

...

VI

... The Court's second stated reason for finding that Sony is not liable for contributory infringement is its conclusion that even unauthorized time-shifting is fair use. This conclusion is ... troubling. The Court begins by suggesting that the fair use doctrine operates as a general "equitable rule of reason." That interpretation mischaracterizes the doctrine, and simply ignores the language of the statute. Section 107 establishes the fair use doctrine "for purposes such as criticism, comment, news reporting, teaching, ... scholarship, or research." These are all productive uses. It is true that the legislative history states repeatedly that the doctrine must be applied flexibly on a case-by-case basis, but those references were only in the context of productive uses. Such a limitation on fair use comports with its purpose, which is to facilitate the creation of new works. There is no indication that the fair use doctrine has any application for purely personal consumption on the scale involved in this case, and the Court's application of it here deprives fair use of the major cohesive force that has guided evolution of the doctrine in the past.

Having bypassed the initial hurdle for establishing that a use is fair, the Court then purports to apply to time-shifting the four factors explicitly stated in the statute. The first is "the purpose and character of the use, including whether such use is of a commercial nature or is for nonprofit educational purposes." The Court confidently describes timeshifting as a noncommercial, nonprofit activity. It is clear, however, that personal use of programs that have been copied without permission is not what § 107(1) protects. The intent of the section is to encourage users to engage in activities the primary benefit of which accrues to others. Time-shifting involves no such humanitarian impulse. It is likewise something of a mischaracterization of time-shifting to describe it as noncommercial in the sense that that term is used in the statute. As one commentator has observed, time-shifting is noncommercial in the same sense that stealing jewelry and wearing it—instead of reselling it—is noncommercial. Purely consumptive uses are certainly not what the fair use doctrine was designed to protect, and the awkwardness of applying the statutory language to time-shifting only makes clearer that fair use was designed to protect only uses that are productive.

The next two statutory factors are all but ignored by the Court—though certainly not because they have no applicability. The second factor—"the nature of the copyrighted work"—strongly supports the view that time-shifting is an infringing use. The rationale guiding application of this factor is that certain types of works, typically those involving "more of diligence than of originality or inventiveness," require less copyright protection than other original works. Thus, for example, informational works, such as news reports, that readily lend themselves to productive use by others, are less protected than creative works of entertainment. Sony's own surveys indicate that entertainment shows account for more than 80 percent of the programs recorded by Betamax owners.

The third statutory factor—"the amount and substantiality of the portion used"—is even more devastating to the Court's interpretation. It is undisputed that virtually all VTR owners record entire works, thereby creating an exact substitute for the copyrighted original. Fair use is intended to allow individuals engaged in productive uses to copy small portions of original works that will facilitate their own productive endeavors. Time-shifting bears no resemblance to such activity, and the complete duplication that it involves might alone be sufficient to preclude a finding of fair use. It is little wonder that the Court has chosen to ignore this statutory factor.

The fourth factor requires an evaluation of "the effect of the use upon the potential market for or value of the copyrighted work." This is the factor upon which the Court focuses, but once again, the Court has misread the statute. As mentioned above, the statute requires a court to consider the effect of the use on the potential market for the copyrighted work. The Court has struggled mightily to show that VTR use has not reduced the value of the Studios' copyrighted works in their present markets. Even if true, that showing only begins the proper inquiry. The development of the VTR has created a new market for the works produced by the Studios. That market consists of those persons who desire to view television programs at times other than when they are broadcast, and who therefore purchase VTR recorders to enable them to time-shift. Because time-shifting of the Studios' copyrighted works involves the copying of them, however, the Studios are entitled to share in the benefits of that new market. Those benefits currently go to Sony through Betamax sales. Respondents therefore can show harm from VTR use simply by showing that the value of their copyrights would increase if they were compensated for the copies that are used in the new market. The existence of this effect is self-evident. ...

Notes and Questions

1. The majority and dissent differ significantly over whether personal, consumptive uses should even qualify for consideration under the fair use defense. The dissent, in particular, argues that such personal uses are not consistent with the other purposes listed in section 107, namely, "criticism, comment, news reporting, teaching (including multiple copies for classroom use), scholarship, or research," insofar as such uses are purely consumptive. Is the dissent right? How does taping a television sit-com for later viewing further the "progress of science and the useful arts"? What theory of fair use underlies the majority's opinion? The dissent's?

2. The Court indicates that noncommercial uses are good candidates for fair use treatment, especially when compared to commercial uses. What is a noncommercial use? If that term encompasses behavior that does not involve the sale of a good or service, there are many personal uses that appear to qualify—taping television shows to build a library of tapes, giving a copy of a digital music file to a friend, or downloading and printing photographs from the Internet to decorate a room. Are these really noncommercial uses that receive favorable fair use treatment? Or, are they commercial because they allow consumers to avoid paying for something that copyright holders would be willing to sell?

3. *Sony* also states that, "A challenge to a noncommercial use of a copyrighted work requires proof either that the particular use is harmful, or that if it should become widespread, it would adversely affect the potential market for the copyrighted work." What does it mean to adversely affect the market or potential market for a copyrighted work? For example, copyright holders did not charge viewers for making copies of television shows on VTRs, but they might have been interested in doing so. Doesn't this mean that home videotaping affected a potential market for the copyrighted work? If not, how does one identify whether a challenged use affects a potential market for a copyrighted work?

4. One very influential response to the above question has been to view the fair use analysis in *Sony* as a response to market failure. *See* Wendy Gordon, *Fair Use as Market Failure: A Structural and Economic Analysis of the Betamax Case and its Predecessors*, 82 COLUM. L. REV. 1600 (1982). In certain situations, personal uses like time-shifting will be so modest in value that the transaction costs of licensing such uses would exceed the value of the use itself. Thus, for example, locating the owner of the copyright in the television broadcast and negotiating a license for a personal use would greatly exceed the value of that use to the consumer. Under such circumstances, a mutually-beneficial exchange would be prevented, and the market would fail. Under this view, fair use steps in to transfer the entitlement from the copyright owner to the user, mimicking the result that would obtain in the absence of market failure.

If fair use is a response to market failure, then what should the scope of fair use be in an environment of low transactions costs? For example, copyright holders could use the Internet to license small, seemingly inconsequential uses of works. Thus, a teacher who wanted to print a few copies of an online article for class could use a credit card to pay whatever price the copyright holder wanted to charge for the use. If such licensing schemes could be implemented, should uses like this be denied fair use treatment? If so, do you believe that low cost licensing schemes should reduce the scope of fair use from whatever it is today?

Or take the facts of *Sony* itself. Today, many television episodes are available for viewing on the Internet, for a small fee or subscription. In the not-to-distant future, it may be the case that nearly every episode of every television show is available on-demand over the Internet, for a small fee. If this is the case, then will time-shifting no longer be fair use? More generally, can changes in technology alter the scope of fair use?

5. Who bears the burden of proving that there will be harm to the market for the work? In some cases, particularly ones involving future markets, it may be difficult to establish whether there will be harm to the market. In these cases, the burden of proof may be dispositive. In *Sony*, the Court indicated that harm can be presumed when the use is commercial, but must be established by the copyright owner when the use is non-commercial.

In cases where the use is commercial, what kind of evidence would a defendant present to prove that the market would not be harmed? Recall that Pretty Woman parody in *Campbell* was a commercial use. Thus, on remand, the defendants bore the burden of proving that their parody would have no impact on the market for non-parodic rap derivatives of the work. How could the defendants have satisfied this burden?

6. Are personal copies of recorded music fair use? Despite the similarities to the *Sony* case, the issue has never been definitively resolved by the courts. Instead, Congress settled the issue legislatively by passing the Audio Home Recording Act of 1992 (AHRA). Shortly before the Act was passed, the consumer electronics industry was about to introduce digital audio tape, which would have allowed consumers to make perfect digital copies of music. Introduction of the technology was delayed by the prospect of copyright infringement lawsuits similar to *Sony*. The impasse was resolved when Congress passed the AHRA. The AHRA exempted from copyright liability consumers who made analog or digital copies of recorded music for noncommercial purposes. 17 U.S.C. § 1008. In exchange, consumer electronics companies were required to place certain copy-protection technologies in their digital audio tape decks. In addition, a statutory royalty was imposed on sales of both digital audio tapes and tape decks, which was to be redistributed to music copyright owners. Thus, home taping of music is privileged by the AHRA.

American Geophysical Union v. Texaco
60 F.3d 913 (2d Cir. 1994)

JON O. NEWMAN, Chief Judge:

This interlocutory appeal presents the issue of whether, under the particular circumstances of this case, the fair use defense to copyright infringement applies to the photocopying of articles in a scientific journal. ... Though not for precisely the same reasons, we agree with the District Court's conclusion that this particular copying was not fair use and therefore affirm.

Background

Plaintiffs American Geophysical Union and 82 other publishers of scientific and technical journals brought a class action claiming that Texaco's unauthorized photocopying of articles from their journals constituted copyright infringement. Among other defenses, Texaco claimed that its copying was fair use under section 107 of the Copyright Act. Since it appeared likely that the litigation could be resolved once the fair use defense was adjudicated, the parties agreed that an initial trial should be limited to whether Texaco's copying was fair use, and further agreed that this issue would be submitted for decision on a written record.

Although Texaco employs 400 to 500 research scientists, of whom all or most presumably photocopy scientific journal articles to support their Texaco research, the parties stipulated—in order to spare the enormous expense of exploring the photocopying practices of each of them—that one scientist would be chosen at random as the representative of the entire group. The scientist chosen was Dr. Donald H. Chickering, II, a scientist at Texaco's research center in Beacon, New York. For consideration at trial, the publishers selected from Chickering's files photocopies of eight particular articles from the *Journal of Catalysis*. ...

Employing between 400 and 500 researchers nationwide, Texaco conducts considerable scientific research seeking to develop new products and technology primarily to improve its commercial performance in the petroleum industry. As part of its substantial expenditures in support of research activities at its Beacon facility, Texaco subscribes to many scientific and technical journals and maintains a sizable library with these materials. Among the periodicals that Texaco receives at its Beacon research facility is the *Journal of Catalysis*, a monthly publication produced by Academic Press, Inc., a major publisher of scholarly journals and one of the plaintiffs in this litigation. Texaco had initially purchased one subscription to *Catalysis* for its Beacon facility, and increased its total subscriptions to two in 1983. Since 1988, Texaco has maintained three subscriptions to *Catalysis*.

Each issue of *Catalysis* contains articles, notes, and letters , ranging in length from two to twenty pages. All of the articles are received by the journal's editors through unsolicited submission by various authors. Authors are informed that they must transfer the copyright in their writings to Academic Press if one of their articles is accepted for publication, and no form of money payment is ever provided to authors whose works are published. Academic Press typically owns the copyright for each individual article published in *Catalysis*, and every issue of the journal includes a general statement that no part of the publication is to be reproduced without permission from the copyright owner. The average monthly issue of *Catalysis* runs approximately 200 pages and comprises 20 to 25 articles.

Chickering, a chemical engineer at the Beacon research facility, has worked for Texaco since 1981 conducting research in the field of catalysis, which concerns changes in the rates of chemical reactions. To keep abreast of developments in his field, Chickering must review works published in various scientific and technical journals related to his area of research. Texaco assists in this endeavor by having its library circulate current issues of relevant journals to Chickering when he places his name on the appropriate routing list.

The copies of the eight articles from *Catalysis* found in Chickering's files that the parties have made the exclusive focus of the fair use trial were photocopied in their entirety by Chickering or by other Texaco employees at Chickering's request. Chickering apparently believed that the material and data found within these articles would facilitate his current or future professional research. The evidence developed at trial indicated that Chickering did not generally use the *Catalysis* articles in his research immediately upon copying, but placed the photocopied articles in his files to have them available for later reference as needed. Chickering became aware of six of the photocopied articles when the original issues of *Catalysis* containing the articles were circulated to him. He learned of the other two articles upon seeing a reference to them in another published article. As it turned out, Chickering did not have occasion to make use of five of the articles that were copied.

Discussion

I. The Nature of the Dispute

The parties and many of the *amici curiae* have approached this case as if it concerns the broad issue of whether photocopying of scientific articles is fair use, or at least the only slightly more limited issue of whether photocopying of such articles is fair use when undertaken by a research scientist engaged in his own research. Such broad issues are not before us. Rather, we consider whether Texaco's photocopying by 400 or 500 scientists, as represented by Chickering's example, is a fair use. This includes the question whether such institutional, systematic copying increases the number of copies available to scientists while avoiding the necessity of paying for license fees or for additional subscriptions. We do not deal with the question of copying by an individual, for personal use in research or otherwise (not for resale), recognizing that under the fair use doctrine or the *de minimis* doctrine, such a practice by an individual might well not constitute an infringement. In other words, our opinion does not decide the case that would arise if Chickering were a professor or an independent scientist engaged in copying and creating files for independent research, as opposed to being employed by an institution in the pursuit of his research on the institution's behalf. ...

A. Fair Use and Photocopying

We consider initially the doctrine of fair use and its application to photocopying of documents. ...

As with the development of other easy and accessible means of mechanical reproduction of documents, the invention and widespread availability of photocopying technology threatens to disrupt the delicate balances established by the Copyright Act. As a leading commentator astutely notes, the advent of modern photocopying technology creates a pressing need for the law "to strike an appropriate balance between the authors' interest in preserving the integrity of copyright, and the public's right to enjoy the benefits that photocopying technology offers." 3 NIMMER ON COPYRIGHT § 13.05 [E][1], at 13-226. ...

II. The Enumerated Fair Use Factors of Section 107

A. First Factor: Purpose and Character of Use

The first factor listed in section 107 is "the purpose and character of the use, including whether such use is of a commercial nature or is for nonprofit educational purposes." Especially pertinent to an assessment of the first fair use factor are the precise circumstances under which copies of the eight *Catalysis* articles were made. After noticing six of these articles when the original copy of the journal issue containing each of them was circulated to him, Chickering had them photocopied, at least initially, for the same basic purpose that one would normally seek to obtain the original—to have it available on his shelf for ready reference if and when he needed to look at it. The library circulated one copy and invited all the researchers to make their own photocopies. It is a reasonable inference that the library staff wanted each journal issue moved around the building quickly and returned to the library so that it would be available for others to look at. Making copies enabled all researchers who might one day be interested in examining the contents of an article in the issue to have the article readily available in their own offices. In Chickering's own words, the copies of the articles were made for "my personal convenience," since it is "far more convenient to have access in my office to a photocopy of an article than to have to go to the library each time I wanted to refer to it." Significantly, Chickering did not even have occasion to use five of the photocopied articles at all, further revealing that the photocopies of the eight *Catalysis* articles were primarily made just for "future retrieval and reference."

It is true that photocopying these articles also served other purposes. The most favorable for Texaco is the purpose of enabling Chickering, if the need should arise, to go into the lab with pieces of paper that (a) were not as bulky as the entire issue or a bound volume of a year's issues, and (b) presented no risk of damaging the original by exposure to chemicals. And these purposes might suffice to tilt the first fair use factor in favor of Texaco if these purposes were dominant. For example, if Chickering had asked the library to buy him a copy of the pertinent issue of *Catalysis* and had placed it on his shelf, and one day while reading it had noticed a chart, formula, or other material that he wanted to take right into the lab, it might be a fair use for him to make a photocopy, and use that copy in the lab (especially if he did not retain it and build up a mini-library of photocopied articles). This is the sort of "spontaneous" copying that is part of the test for permissible nonprofit classroom copying. But that is not what happened here as to the six items copied from the circulated issues. ...

The photocopying of these eight *Catalysis* articles may be characterized as "archival"—*i.e.*, done for the primary purpose of providing numerous Texaco scientists (for whom Chickering served as an example) each with his or her own personal copy of each article without Texaco's having to purchase another original journal. The photocopying "merely 'supersede[s] the objects' of the original creation," *Campbell*, 510 U.S. at ---- (quoting *Folsom v. Marsh*, 9 F.Cas. 342, 348 (No. 4,901) (C.C.D. Mass. 1841)), and tilts the first fair use factor against Texaco. We do not mean to suggest that no instance of archival copying would be fair use, but the first factor tilts against Texaco in this case because the making of copies to be placed on the shelf in Chickering's office is part of a systematic process of encouraging employee researchers to copy articles so as to multiply available copies while avoiding payment. ...

1. *Commercial use.* We generally agree with Texaco's contention that the District Court placed undue emphasis on the fact that Texaco is a for-profit corporation conducting research primarily for commercial gain. Since many, if not most, secondary users seek at least some measure of commercial gain from their use, unduly emphasizing the commercial motivation of a copier will lead to an overly restrictive view of fair use. Though the Supreme Court had stated in *Sony* that every commercial use was "presumptively" unfair, that Court and lower courts have come to explain that the commercial nature of a secondary use simply "'tends to weigh against a finding of fair use.'" *Campbell*, 510 U.S. at ---- (quoting *Harper & Row*, 471 U.S. at 562).

Indeed, *Campbell* warns against "elevat[ing] ... to a *per se* rule" *Sony*'s language about a presumption against fair use arising from commercial use. *Campbell* discards that language in favor of a more subtle, sophisticated approach, which recognizes that "the more transformative the new work, the less will be the significance of other factors, like commercialism, that may weigh against a finding of fair use." *Id.* [at ----, 114 S.Ct.] at 1171. The Court states that "the commercial or nonprofit educational purpose of a work is only one element of the first factor enquiry" and points out that "[i]f, indeed, commerciality carried presumptive force against a finding of fairness, the presumption would swallow nearly all of the illustrative uses listed in the preamble paragraph of § 107...." *Id.*

We do not mean to suggest that the District Court overlooked these principles; in fact, the Court discussed them insightfully. Rather, our concern here is that the Court let the for-profit nature of Texaco's activity weigh against Texaco without differentiating between a direct commercial use and the more indirect relation to commercial activity that occurred here. Texaco was not gaining direct or immediate commercial advantage from the photocopying at issue in this case—*i.e.*, Texaco's profits, revenues, and overall commercial performance were not tied to its making copies of eight *Catalysis* articles for Chickering. Rather, Texaco's photocopying served, at most, to facilitate Chickering's research, which in turn might have led to the development of new products and technology that could have improved Texaco's commercial performance. ...

We do not consider Texaco's status as a for-profit company irrelevant to the fair use analysis. Though Texaco properly contends that a court's focus should be on the use of the copyrighted material and not simply on the user, it is overly simplistic to suggest that the "purpose and character of the use" can be fully discerned without considering the nature and objectives of the user. ...

As noted before, in this particular case the link between Texaco's commercial gain and its copying is somewhat attenuated: the copying, at most, merely facilitated Chickering's research that might have led to the production of commercially valuable products. Thus, it would not be accurate to conclude that Texaco's copying of eight particular *Catalysis* articles amounted to "commercial exploitation," especially since the immediate goal of Texaco's copying was to facilitate Chickering's research in the sciences, an objective that might well serve a broader public purpose. Still, we need not ignore the for-profit nature of Texaco's enterprise, especially since we can confidently conclude that Texaco reaps at least some indirect economic advantage from its photocopying. As the publishers emphasize, Texaco's photocopying for Chickering could be regarded simply as another "factor of production" utilized in Texaco's efforts to develop profitable products. Conceptualized in this way, it is not obvious why it is fair for Texaco to avoid having to pay at least some price to copyright holders for the right to photocopy the original articles.

2. *Transformative Use.* The District Court properly emphasized that Texaco's photocopying was not "transformative." After the District Court issued its opinion, the Supreme Court explicitly ruled that the concept of a "transformative use" is central to a proper analysis under the first factor. The Court explained that though a "transformative use is not absolutely necessary for a finding of fair use, ... the more transformative the new work, the less will be the significance of other factors, like commercialism, that may weigh against a finding of fair use." ...

Texaco suggests that its conversion of the individual *Catalysis* articles through photocopying into a form more easily used in a laboratory might constitute a transformative use. However, Texaco's photocopying merely transforms the material object embodying the intangible article that is the copyrighted original work. Texaco's making of copies cannot properly be regarded as a transformative use of the copyrighted material.

Even though Texaco's photocopying is not technically a transformative use of the copyrighted material, we should not overlook the significant independent value that can stem from conversion of original journal articles into a format different from their normal appearance. As previously explained, Texaco's photocopying converts the individual *Catalysis* articles into a useful format. Before modern photocopying, Chickering probably would have converted the original article into a more serviceable form by taking notes, whether cursory or extended; today he can do so with a photocopying machine. Nevertheless, whatever independent value derives from the more usable format of the photocopy does not mean that every instance of photocopying wins on the first factor. In this case, the predominant archival purpose of the copying tips the first factor against the copier, despite the benefit of a more usable format. ...

On balance, we agree with the District Court that the first factor favors the publishers, primarily because the dominant purpose of the use is a systematic institutional policy of multiplying the available number of copies of pertinent copyrighted articles by circulating the journals among employed scientists for them to make copies, thereby serving the same purpose for which additional subscriptions are normally sold, or, as will be discussed, for which photocopying licenses may be obtained.

B. Second Factor: Nature of Copyrighted Work

The second statutory fair use factor is "the nature of the copyrighted work." ...

Though a significant measure of creativity was undoubtedly used in the creation of the eight articles copied from *Catalysis*, even a glance at their content immediately reveals the predominantly factual nature of these works. Moreover, though we have previously recognized the importance of strong copyright protection to provide sufficient incentives for the creation of scientific works, nearly every category of copyrightable works could plausibly assert that broad copyright protection was essential to the continued vitality of that category of works.

Ultimately, then, the manifestly factual character of the eight articles precludes us from considering the articles as "within the core of the copyright's protective purposes." Thus, in agreement with the District Court, we conclude that the second factor favors Texaco.

C. Third Factor: Amount and Substantiality of Portion Used

The third statutory fair use factor is "the amount and substantiality of the portion used in relation to the copyrighted work as a whole." The

District Court concluded that this factor clearly favors the publishers because Texaco copied the eight articles from *Catalysis* in their entirety. ...

Texaco's suggestion that we consider that it copied only a small percentage of the total compendium of works encompassed within *Catalysis* is superficially intriguing, especially since *Catalysis* is traditionally marketed only as a periodical by issue or volume. However, as the District Court recognized, each of the eight articles in *Catalysis* was separately authored and constitutes a discrete "original work[ ] of authorship." As we emphasized at the outset, each article enjoys independent copyright protection, which the authors transferred to Academic Press, and what the publishers claim has been infringed is the copyright that subsists in each individual article—not the distinct copyright that may subsist in each journal issue or volume by virtue of the publishers' original compilation of these articles. ...

Despite Texaco's claims that we consider its amount of copying "minuscule" in relation to the entirety of *Catalysis*, we conclude, as did the District Court, that Texaco has copied entire works. Though this conclusion does not preclude a finding of fair use, it militates against such a finding and weights the third factor in favor of the publishers. ...

D.   Fourth Factor: Effect Upon Potential Market or Value

The fourth statutory fair use factor is "the effect of the use upon the potential market for or value of the copyrighted work." ...

In analyzing the fourth factor, it is important (1) to bear in mind the precise copyrighted works, namely the eight journal articles, and (2) to recognize the distinctive nature and history of "the potential market for or value of" these particular works. Specifically, though there is a traditional market for, and hence a clearly defined value of, journal issues and volumes, in the form of per-issue purchases and journal subscriptions, there is neither a traditional market for, nor a clearly defined value of, individual journal articles. As a result, analysis of the fourth factor cannot proceed as simply as would have been the case if Texaco had copied a work that carries a stated or negotiated selling price in the market.

Like most authors, writers of journal articles do not directly seek to capture the potential financial rewards that stem from their copyrights by personally marketing copies of their writings. Rather, like other creators of literary works, the author of a journal article "commonly sells his rights to publishers who offer royalties in exchange for their services in producing and marketing the author's work." *Harper & Row*, 471 U.S. at 547. In the distinctive realm of academic and scientific articles, however, the only form of royalty paid by a publisher is often just the reward of being published, publication being a key to professional advancement and prestige for the author. The publishers in turn incur the costs and labor of producing and marketing authors' articles, driven by the prospect of capturing the economic value stemming from the copyrights in the original works, which the authors have transferred to them. Ultimately, the monopoly privileges conferred by copyright protection and the potential financial rewards therefrom are not directly serving to motivate authors to write individual articles; rather, they serve to motivate publishers to produce journals, which provide the conventional and often exclusive means for disseminating these individual articles. It is the prospect of such dissemination that contributes to the motivation of these authors.

Significantly, publishers have traditionally produced and marketed authors' individual articles only in a journal format, *i.e.*, in periodical compilations of numerous articles. In other words, publishers have conventionally sought to capture the economic value from the "exclusive rights" to "reproduce" and "distribute copies" of the individual articles, solely by compiling many such articles together in a periodical journal and then charging a fee to subscribe. Publishers have not traditionally provided a simple or efficient means to obtain single copies of individual articles; reprints are usually available from publishers only in bulk quantities and with some delay. ...

1. *Sales of Additional Journal Subscriptions, Back Issues, and Back Volumes.* Since we are concerned with the claim of fair use in copying the eight individual articles from *Catalysis*, the analysis under the fourth factor must focus on the effect of Texaco's photocopying upon the potential market for or value of these individual articles. Yet, in their respective discussions of the fourth statutory factor, the parties initially focus on the impact of Texaco's photocopying of individual journal articles upon the market for *Catalysis* journals through sales of *Catalysis* subscriptions, back issues, or back volumes. ...

On this record, however, the evidence is not resounding for either side. The District Court specifically found that, in the absence of photocopying, (1) "Texaco would not ordinarily fill the need now being supplied by photocopies through the purchase of back issues or back volumes ... [or] by enormously enlarging the number of its subscriptions," but (2) Texaco still "would increase the number of subscriptions somewhat." This moderate conclusion concerning the actual effect on the marketability of journals, combined with the uncertain relationship between the market for journals and the market for and value of individual articles, leads us to conclude that the evidence concerning sales of additional journal subscriptions, back issues, and back volumes does not strongly support either side with regard to the fourth factor. At best, the loss of a few journal subscriptions tips the fourth factor only slightly toward the publishers because evidence of such loss is weak evidence that the copied articles themselves have lost any value.

2. *Licensing Revenues and Fees.* The District Court, however, went beyond discussing the sales of additional journal subscriptions in holding that Texaco's photocopying affected the value of the publishers' copyrights. Specifically, the Court pointed out that, if Texaco's unauthorized photocopying was not permitted as fair use, the publishers' revenues would increase significantly since Texaco would (1) obtain articles from

document delivery services (which pay royalties to publishers for the right to photocopy articles), (2) negotiate photocopying licenses directly with individual publishers, and/or (3) acquire some form of photocopying license from the Copyright Clearance Center Inc. ("CCC").[55] Texaco claims that the District Court's reasoning is faulty because, in determining that the value of the publishers' copyrights was affected, the Court assumed that the publishers were entitled to demand and receive licensing royalties and fees for photocopying. Yet, continues Texaco, whether the publishers can demand a fee for permission to make photocopies is the very question that the fair use trial is supposed to answer.

It is indisputable that, as a general matter, a copyright holder is entitled to demand a royalty for licensing others to use its copyrighted work, and that the impact on potential licensing revenues is a proper subject for consideration in assessing the fourth factor.

However, not every effect on potential licensing revenues enters the analysis under the fourth factor. Specifically, courts have recognized limits on the concept of "potential licensing revenues" by considering only traditional, reasonable, or likely to be developed markets when examining and assessing a secondary use's "effect upon the potential market for or value of the copyrighted work." ...

Though the publishers still have not established a conventional market for the direct sale and distribution of individual articles, they have created, primarily through the CCC, a workable market for institutional users to obtain licenses for the right to produce their own copies of individual articles via photocopying. The District Court found that many major corporations now subscribe to the CCC systems for photocopying licenses. Indeed, it appears from the pleadings, especially Texaco's counterclaim, that Texaco itself has been paying royalties to the CCC. Since the Copyright Act explicitly provides that copyright holders have the "exclusive rights" to "reproduce" and "distribute copies" of their works, and since there currently exists a viable market for licensing these rights for individual journal articles, it is appropriate that potential licensing revenues for photocopying be considered in a fair use analysis.

Despite Texaco's claims to the contrary, it is not unsound to conclude that the right to seek payment for a particular use tends to become legally cognizable under the fourth fair use factor when the means for paying for such a use is made easier. This notion is not inherently troubling: it is sensible that a particular unauthorized use should be considered "more fair" when there is no ready market or means to pay for the use, while such an unauthorized use should be considered "less fair" when there is a ready market or means to pay for the use. The vice of circular

---

[55] [Footnote 16] The CCC is a central clearing-house established in 1977 primarily by publishers to license photocopying. The CCC offers a variety of licensing schemes; fees can be paid on a per copy basis or through blanket license arrangements. Most publishers are registered with the CCC, but the participation of for-profit institutions that engage in photocopying has been limited, largely because of uncertainty concerning the legal questions at issue in this lawsuit.

reasoning arises only if the availability of payment is conclusive against fair use. Whatever the situation may have been previously, before the development of a market for institutional users to obtain licenses to photocopy articles, it is now appropriate to consider the loss of licensing revenues in evaluating "the effect of the use upon the potential market for or value of" journal articles. It is especially appropriate to do so with respect to copying of articles from *Catalysis*, a publication as to which a photocopying license is now available. We do not decide how the fair use balance would be resolved if a photocopying license for *Catalysis* articles were not currently available.

Primarily because of lost licensing revenue, and to a minor extent because of lost subscription revenue, we agree with the District Court that "the publishers have demonstrated a substantial harm to the value of their copyrights through [Texaco's] copying," and thus conclude that the fourth statutory factor favors the publishers.

E. Aggregate Assessment

We conclude that three of the four statutory factors, including the important first and the fourth factors, favor the publishers. We recognize that the statutory factors provide a nonexclusive guide to analysis, but to whatever extent more generalized equitable considerations are relevant, we are in agreement with the District Court's analysis of them. We therefore agree with the District Court's conclusion that Texaco's photocopying of eight particular articles from the Journal of *Catalysis* was not fair use.

JACOBS, CIRCUIT JUDGE, dissenting:

...

B. Effect Upon Potential Market or Value

In gauging the effect of Dr. Chickering's photocopying on the potential market or value of the copyrighted work, the majority properly considers two separate means of marketing: (1) journal subscriptions and sales, and (2) licensing revenues and fees.

(1) *Subscriptions and sales.* The majority makes clear that, considered solely in terms of journal subscriptions and sales, this factor is a toss-up that may tip in the publisher's favor, but only after teetering for a while: "At best, the loss of a few journal subscriptions tips the fourth factor only slightly toward the publishers because evidence of such loss is weak evidence that the copied articles themselves have lost any value." The majority pointedly observes that no evidence is offered that the photocopying at issue here, "if widespread, would impair the marketability of journals...." Since Dr. Chickering's use maximizes the utility of a *Catalysis* subscription for the only audience it is ever likely to capture, I do not consider that the failure of proof in this respect is an oversight by the publishers or their able counsel.

As to the individual articles photocopied by Dr. Chickering, I agree with the majority—as I read the opinion—that one cannot put a finger on any loss suffered by the publisher in the value of the individual articles or in the traditional market for subscriptions and back issues. The district court found that Texaco would not purchase back-issues or back volumes in the numbers needed to supply individual copies of articles to individual scientists.

Finally, the circulation of *Catalysis* among a number of Texaco scientists can come as no surprise to the publisher of *Catalysis*, which charges double the normal subscription rate to institutional subscribers. The publisher must therefore assume that, unless they are reading *Catalysis* for pleasure or committing it to memory, the scientists will extract what they need and arrange to copy it for personal use before passing along the institutional copies.

(2) *Licensing Revenues and Fees*. The majority states that "[o]nly an impact on potential licensing revenues for traditional, reasonable, or likely to be developed markets should be legally cognizable when evaluating a secondary use's 'effect upon the potential market for or value of the copyrighted work.'" That statement of the law, with which I fully agree, supports the conclusion that the availability of a CCC license has little to do with fair use. ...

In this case the only harm to a market is to the supposed market in photocopy licenses. The CCC scheme is neither traditional nor reasonable; and its development into a real market is subject to substantial impediments. There is a circularity to the problem: the market will not crystallize unless courts reject the fair use argument that Texaco presents; but, under the statutory test, we cannot declare a use to be an infringement unless (assuming other factors also weigh in favor of the secondary user) there is a market to be harmed. At present, only a fraction of journal publishers have sought to exact these fees. I would hold that this fourth factor decisively weighs in favor of Texaco, because there is no normal market in photocopy licenses, and no real consensus among publishers that there ought to be one.

The majority holds that photocopying journal articles without a license is an infringement. Yet it is stipulated that (a) institutions such as Texaco subscribe to numerous journals, only 30 percent of which are covered by a CCC license; (b) not all publications of each CCC member are covered by the CCC licenses; and (c) not all the articles in publications covered by the CCC are copyrighted. It follows that no CCC license can assure a scientist that photocopying any given article is legal. ...

Under a transactional license, the user must undertake copyright research every time an article is photocopied. First, one must consult a directory to determine whether or not the publisher of the journal is a member of the CCC. If it is, one must ascertain whether the particular publication is one that is covered by the CCC arrangement, because not all publications of participating publishers are covered. Then one must somehow determine whether the actual article is one in which the publisher actually holds a copyright, since there are many articles that, for such reasons as government sponsorship of the research, are not subject to copyright. The production director of plaintiff Springer-Verlag testified at trial that it is almost impossible to tell which articles might be covered by a copyright. Since even an expert has difficulty making such a determination, the transactional scheme would seem to require that an intellectual property lawyer be posted at each copy machine. Finally, once it is determined that the specific article is covered, the copyist will need to record in a log the date, name of publication, publisher, title and author of article, and number of pages copied. ...

The fourth factor tips decidedly in Texaco's favor because there is no appreciable impairment of the publishing revenue from journal subscriptions and sales; because the publisher captures additional revenue from institutional users by charging a double subscription price (and can presumably charge any price the users will pay); and because the market for licensing is cumbersome and unrealized. ...

Notes and Questions

1.   How does *Texaco* square with *Sony*? In *Sony*, the Supreme Court found fair use for reproduction of copyrighted works without connection to the favored purposes enumerated in § 107 of the Copyright Act. Yet, in *Texaco*, the Second Circuit finds no fair use despite an obvious connection to scientific research. Did *Texaco* misunderstand the impact of *Sony*? Does *Sony* apply only to its specific facts (namely time-shifting of over-the-air television programming)? Or, was *Sony* wrongly decided?

2.   The *Texaco* court recognized Chickering's purpose as research, yet it also noted Texaco's status as a for-profit corporation. Would the court's ultimate conclusion have been different if Chickering had worked for a non-profit institution such as a university? If so, does it now matter that universities often commercially exploit the results of their scientists' inventions?

3.   The majority and dissent in *Texaco* adopt two somewhat different perspectives on the fair use defense. The dissent adopts the more traditional view of fair use as a mechanism for furthering knowledge and research, and on this score places great weight on the research purpose. The majority, by contrast, gives this factor less weight, instead emphasizing the fact that a market apparently existed for the smaller scale uses. Which perspective do you find more persuasive?

4.   The majority opinion in *Texaco*, applying the fourth factor (impact on the market), acknowledged that there was little evidence of harm to sales of journal subscriptions. However, it found harm to the developing market for photocopying licenses. The copyright statute expressly

directs courts to consider, not only actual markets, but "potential markets" in determining market harm. Are there any limits to the definition of a "potential market?" The dissent argues that the majority's broad definition of potential market makes fair use analysis entirely circular. What is the majority's response? Do you find it persuasive?

5. Under a market failure perspective, how can we tell whether a market has failed? In *Texaco*, did a functioning market exist? The dissent argued that it did not, and that the CCC was not a sufficient solution. By contrast, the majority found the CCC to be sufficient. What about cases involving a new technology, where a market may not have developed yet? For example, some have argued that the *Sony* decision was wrongly decided because licensing schemes might well have developed for time-shifting and the decision effectively prevented such market solutions from developing. Do you find this argument persuasive? What should courts do in situations involving new technologies?

6. The Copyright Act's legislative history indicates that "reproduction by a teacher or student of a small part of a work to illustrate a lesson" should constitute a fair use. The legislative history also contains a set of fair use "guidelines" for classroom photocopying of books and periodicals. These guidelines emerged from a working group of publishers and other interests assembled by Congress in the run-up to the 1976 Act. According to the guidelines, teachers may, under certain circumstances, make single copies of works for their own use, or multiple copies for distribution to students. Uses that fall within the guidelines should generally be considered fair use. However, the guidelines contemplate that the courts will continue to adjust fair use law in response to new circumstances, and that there may be uses outside the guidelines that nevertheless constitute fair use.[56]

Despite the guidelines, substantial uncertainty continues to exist regarding the scope of permissible educational copying. For example, what about "coursepacks" in which teachers assemble and photocopy portions from a number of different works? In *Princeton University Press v. Michigan Document Services*, 99 F.3d 1381 (6th Cir. 1996), a divided Sixth Circuit, sitting *en banc*, found that production of coursepacks by commercial copyshops was not fair use, in part because a licensing market existed. *See also, Basic Books v. Kinko's Graphic Corp.*, 758 F. Supp. 1522 (S.D.N.Y. 1991) (reaching largely the same result).

A modern variant of this same issue involves the increasingly popular practice of making excerpts of readings available to students electronically, via web-based "e-reserves." Many colleges permit instructors to upload portions of copyrighted articles and books onto websites for electronic distribution to their students. Is this practice fair use? Is it more akin to in-class distribution of photocopies, or more akin to distribution of a "coursepack"? In *Cambridge University Press v. Becker*, 863 F.Supp.2d 1190 (N.D. Ga. 2012), the court addressed Georgia State Uni-

---

[56] These guidelines may be found in H.R. Rep. No. 94-1476, at 68-69.

versity's practice of allowing faculty to post excerpts of copyrighted works on web-based e-reserves and held that, in the majority of instances, this constituted fair use. On appeal, the court in *Cambridge Univ. Press. v. Patton*, 769 F.3d 1232 (11th Cir. 2014) affirmed some portions of the district court's fair use analysis, rejected others, and remanded for further proceedings.

7.   In addition to fair use, the Copyright Act contains a specific statutory privilege that allows certain libraries and archives to make limited, non-commercial reproductions of material in their collections for preservation and other related purposes. 17 U.S.C. § 108.

5. AGGREGATIVE USES

In addition to enabling the easy literal duplication of copyrighted works, new technologies have allowed individuals and companies to combine and exploit copyrighted works in interesting new ways. For example, digital technology allows individuals to easily combine and incorporate copyrighted materials into new works, in ways that were difficult before. Similarly, new technologies have allowed companies to efficiently assemble and aggregate large collections of copyrighted works, for various purposes not originally contemplated by the author. How should copyright law address these new uses, particularly when the copying is very literal? How should courts apply the precedents from the preceding section to such situations?

Bill Graham Archives v. Dorling Kindersley Ltd.
448 F.3d 605 (2d Cir. 2006)

RESTANI, Judge.

This appeal concerns the scope of copyright protection afforded artistic concert posters reproduced in reduced size in a biography of the musical group the Grateful Dead.

BACKGROUND

In October of 2003, [defendant Dorling Kindersley Limited ("DK")] published GRATEFUL DEAD: THE ILLUSTRATED TRIP ("Illustrated Trip"), in collaboration with Grateful Dead Productions, intended as a cultural history of the Grateful Dead. The resulting 480-page coffee table book tells the story of the Grateful Dead along a timeline running continuously through the book, chronologically combining over 2000 images representing dates in the Grateful Dead's history with explanatory text. A typical page of the book features a collage of images, text, and graphic art designed to simultaneously capture the eye and inform the reader. Plaintiff [Bill Graham Archives ("BGA")] claims to own the copyright to seven images displayed in Illustrated Trip, which DK reproduced without BGA's permission.

Initially, DK sought permission from BGA to reproduce the images. In May of 2003, the CEO of Grateful Dead Productions sent a letter to BGA seeking permission for DK to publish the images. BGA responded by offering permission in exchange for Grateful Dead Productions' grant of permission to BGA to make CDs and DVDs out of concert footage in BGA's archives. Next, DK directly contacted BGA seeking to negotiate a license agreement, but the parties disagreed as to an appropriate license fee. Nevertheless, DK proceeded with publication of Illustrated Trip without entering a license fee agreement with BGA. Specifically, DK reproduced seven artistic images originally depicted on Grateful Dead event posters and tickets. BGA's seven images are displayed in significantly reduced form and are accompanied by captions describing the concerts they represent.

When DK refused to meet BGA's post-publication license fee demands, BGA filed suit for copyright infringement....

DISCUSSION

... We agree with the district court that DK's use of the copyrighted images is protected as fair use.

I. Purpose and Character of Use

We first address "the purpose and character of the use, including whether such use is of a commercial nature or is for nonprofit educational purposes." 17 U.S.C. § 107(1). Most important to the court's analysis of the first factor is the "transformative" nature of the work. The question is "whether the new work merely supersede[s] the objects of the original creation, or instead adds something new, with a further purpose or different character, altering the first with new expression, meaning, or message." *Campbell v. Acuff-Rose Music, Inc.*, 510 U.S. 569, 579 (1994).

Here, the district court determined that Illustrated Trip is a biographical work, and the original images are not, and therefore accorded a strong presumption in favor of DK's use. In particular, the district court concluded that DK's use of images placed in chronological order on a timeline is transformatively different from the mere expressive use of images on concert posters or tickets. Because the works are displayed to commemorate historic events, arranged in a creative fashion, and displayed in significantly reduced form, the district court held that the first fair use factor weighs heavily in favor of DK.

Appellant challenges the district court's strong presumption in favor of fair use based on the biographical nature of Illustrated Trip. Appellant argues that based on this purported error the district court failed to examine DK's justification for its use of each of the images. Moreover, Appellant argues that as a matter of law merely placing poster images along a timeline is not a transformative use. Appellant asserts that each reproduced image should have been accompanied by comment or criticism related to the artistic nature of the image.

We disagree with Appellant's limited interpretation of transformative use and we agree with the district court that DK's actual use of each image is transformatively different from the original expressive purpose. Preliminarily, we recognize, as the district court did, that Illustrated Trip is a biographical work documenting the 30-year history of the Grateful Dead. While there are no categories of presumptively fair use, courts have frequently afforded fair use protection to the use of copyrighted material in biographies, recognizing such works as forms of historic scholarship, criticism, and comment that require incorporation of original source material for optimum treatment of their subjects. No less a recognition of biographical value is warranted in this case simply because the subject made a mark in pop culture rather than some other area of human endeavor.

In the instant case, DK's purpose in using the copyrighted images at issue in its biography of the Grateful Dead is plainly different from the original purpose for which they were created. Originally, each of BGA's images fulfilled the dual purposes of artistic expression and promotion. The posters were apparently widely distributed to generate public interest in the Grateful Dead and to convey information to a large number people about the band's forthcoming concerts. In contrast, DK used each of BGA's images as historical artifacts to document and represent the actual occurrence of Grateful Dead concert events featured on Illustrated Trip's timeline.

In some instances, it is readily apparent that DK's image display enhances the reader's understanding of the biographical text. In other instances, the link between image and text is less obvious; nevertheless, the images still serve as historical artifacts graphically representing the fact of significant Grateful Dead concert events selected by the Illustrated Trip's author for inclusion in the book's timeline. We conclude that both types of uses fulfill DK's transformative purpose of enhancing the biographical information in Illustrated Trip, a purpose separate and distinct from the original artistic and promotional purpose for which the images were created. In sum, because DK's use of the disputed images is transformative both when accompanied by referencing commentary and when standing alone, we agree with the district court that DK was not required to discuss the artistic merits of the images to satisfy this first factor of fair use analysis.

This conclusion is strengthened by the manner in which DK displayed the images. First, DK significantly reduced the size of the reproductions. While the small size is sufficient to permit readers to recognize the historical significance of the posters, it is inadequate to offer more than a glimpse of their expressive value. In short, DK used the minimal image size necessary to accomplish its transformative purpose.

Second, DK minimized the expressive value of the reproduced images by combining them with a prominent timeline, textual material, and original graphical artwork, to create a collage of text and images on each page of the book. To further this collage effect, the images are displayed at angles and the original graphical artwork is designed to blend with the images and text. Overall, DK's layout ensures that the images at issue are employed only to enrich the presentation of the cultural history of the Grateful Dead, not to exploit copyrighted artwork for commercial gain.

③Third, BGA's images constitute an inconsequential portion of Illustrated Trip.... In the instant case, the book is 480 pages long, while the BGA images appear on only seven pages. Although the original posters range in size from 13″ x 19″ to more than 19″ x 27,″ the largest reproduction of a BGA image in Illustrated Trip is less than 3″ x 4 ½,″ less than 1/20 the size of the original. And no BGA image takes up more than one-eighth of a page in a book or is given more prominence than any other image on the page. In total, the images account for less than one-fifth of one percent of the book....

④Finally, as to this first factor, we briefly address the commercial nature of Illustrated Trip. Even though Illustrated Trip is a commercial venture, we recognize that "nearly all of the illustrative uses listed in the preamble paragraph of § 107 ... are generally conducted for profit ...." *Campbell*, 510 U.S. at 584. Moreover, "[t]he crux of the profit/nonprofit distinction is not whether the sole motive of the use is monetary gain but whether the user stands to profit from exploitation of the copyrighted material without paying the customary price." *Harper*, 471 U.S. at 562. Here, Illustrated Trip does not exploit the use of BGA's images as such for commercial gain. Significantly, DK has not used any of BGA's images in its commercial advertising or in any other way to promote the sale of the book. Illustrated Trip merely uses pictures and text to describe the life of the Grateful Dead. By design, the use of BGA's images is incidental to the commercial biographical value of the book.

Accordingly, we conclude that the first fair use factor weighs in favor of DK because DK's use of BGA's images is transformatively different from the images' original expressive purpose and DK does not seek to exploit the images' expressive value for commercial gain.

II. Nature of the Copyrighted Work

The second factor in a fair use determination is "the nature of the copyrighted work." 17 U.S.C. § 107(2)....

We agree with the district court that the creative nature of artistic images typically weighs in favor of the copyright holder. We recognize, however, that the second factor may be of limited usefulness where the creative work of art is being used for a transformative purpose.... Here, we conclude that DK is using BGA's images for the transformative purpose of enhancing the biographical information provided in Illustrated Trip. Accordingly, we hold that even though BGA's images are creative works, which are a core concern of copyright protection, the second factor has limited weight in our analysis because the purpose of DK's use was to emphasize the images' historical rather than creative value.

III. Amount and Substantiality of the Portion Used

The third fair use factor asks the court to examine "the amount and substantiality of the portion used in relation to the copyrighted work as a whole." 17 U.S.C. § 107(3)....

Here, DK used BGA's images because the posters and tickets were historical artifacts that could document Grateful Dead concert events and provide a visual context for the accompanying text. To accomplish this use, DK displayed reduced versions of the original images and intermingled these visuals with text and original graphic art. As a consequence, even though the copyrighted images are copied in their entirety, the visual impact of their artistic expression is significantly limited because of their reduced size. We conclude that such use by DK is tailored to further its transformative purpose because DK's reduced size reproductions of BGA's images in their entirety displayed the minimal image size and quality necessary to ensure the reader's recognition of the images as historical artifacts of Grateful Dead concert events. Accordingly, the third fair use factor does not weigh against fair use.

IV. Effect of the Use upon the Market for or Value of the Original

The fourth factor is "the effect of the use upon the potential market for or value of the copyrighted work." 17 U.S.C. § 107(4)....

In the instant case, the parties agree that DK's use of the images did not impact BGA's primary market for the sale of the poster images. Instead, we look to whether DK's unauthorized use usurps BGA's potential to develop a derivative market. Appellant argues that DK interfered with the market for licensing its images for use in books. Appellant contends that there is an established market for licensing its images and it suffered both the loss of royalty revenue directly from DK and the opportunity to obtain royalties from others.

"It is indisputable that, as a general matter, a copyright holder is entitled to demand a royalty for licensing others to use its copyrighted work, and that the impact on potential licensing revenues is a proper subject for consideration in assessing the fourth factor." *Texaco*, 60 F.3d at 929. We have noted, however, that "were a court automatically to conclude in every case that potential licensing revenues were impermissibly impaired simply because the secondary user did not pay a fee for the right to engage in the use, the fourth fair use factor would always favor the copyright holder." *Id.* at 930 n. 17.... Accordingly, we do not find a harm to BGA's license market merely because DK did not pay a fee for BGA's copyrighted images.

Instead, we look at the impact on potential licensing revenues for "traditional, reasonable, or likely to be developed markets." *Texaco*, 60 F.3d at 930. In order to establish a traditional license market, Appellant points to the fees paid to other copyright owners for the reproduction of their images in Illustrated Trip. Moreover, Appellant asserts that it established a market for licensing its images, and in this case expressed a willingness to license images to DK. Neither of these arguments shows impairment to a traditional, as opposed to a transformative market.

Here, unlike in *Texaco*, we hold that DK's use of BGA's images is transformatively different from their original expressive purpose. In a case such as this, a copyright holder cannot prevent others from entering fair use markets merely "by developing or licensing a market for parody, news reporting, educational or other transformative uses of its own creative work." *Castle Rock*, 150 F.3d at 146 n. 11. "[C]opyright owners may not preempt exploitation of transformative markets ...." *Id*. Moreover, a publisher's willingness to pay license fees for reproduction of images does not establish that the publisher may not, in the alternative, make fair use of those images. *Campbell*, 510 U.S. at 585 n. 18 (stating that "being denied permission to use [or pay license fees for] a work does not weigh against a finding of fair use"). Since DK's use of BGA's images falls within a transformative market, BGA does not suffer market harm due to the loss of license fees.

V. Balance of Factors

On balance, we conclude, as the district court did, that the fair use factors weigh in favor of DK's use....

Notes and Questions

1. Analyzing the first factor, the court concluded that the use was transformative, insofar as the defendants placed the copyrighted posters

in chronological order along a timeline. Yet although the context surrounding the posters was certainly quite different from the original context, the posters themselves were not transformed in any way (other than reduced in size). Contrast the song in *Campbell*, which was itself transformed. In what sense, then, did the court use the term "transformative," if not in reference to transformation of the work itself? Is this definition of "transformative" consistent with the definition set forth in *Texaco* and *Campbell supra*?

2.   Analyzing the fourth factor, the court concluded that BGA's use was unlikely to harm the market for the work, and that that this factor therefore favored fair use. In reaching this conclusion, the court rejected DK's argument that there existed an established market for licensing these kinds of uses of these images. However, DK was fully willing to license the use and had in the past granted similar licenses to others. Moreover, BGA had agreed to license its use of the works of other copyright owners in its book. Thus, there appeared to be a way for BGA to secure a license, and DK could plausibly argue that it lost revenue as a result of the uncompensated use.

Was the court's rejection of DK's argument consistent with the result in *Texaco supra*? The court in *Bill Graham Archives* cited *Texaco*'s language that only "traditional, reasonable, or likely to be developed markets" for licensing should be considered under the fourth factor. However, the court held that this did not apply to "transformative" markets, and that because this was a transformative use, the loss of licensing revenue should not be counted as market harm. Does this distinction between "traditional" and "transformative" markets work? Consider, for example, the very traditional, but very transformative, market for licensing movie rights of books. After *Bill Graham Archives*, how do we decide which licensing markets count of purposes of the fourth factor?

3.   Do you agree with the result in *Bill Graham Archives*? What theory of fair use underlies your opinion?

Problem

You have a client who is a film-maker, interested in making a documentary about the history of the Grateful Dead. Your client would like to include in the documentary sound recordings of many of the Grateful Dead's most popular and famous songs. The copyright holder in the sound recordings is willing to license these uses, but at a cost that greatly exceeds what your client is able to pay. Your client would like to go ahead and use the sound recordings without a license. What advice would you give her?

Authors Guild v. Google
– F.3d – (2d Cir. 2015)

LEVAL, Circuit Judge.

This copyright dispute tests the boundaries of fair use. Plaintiffs, who are authors of published books under copyright, sued Google, Inc. for copyright infringement.... Through its Library Project and its Google Books project, acting without permission of rights holders, Google has made digital copies of tens of millions of books, including Plaintiffs', that were submitted to it for that purpose by major libraries.... Plaintiffs sought injunctive and declaratory relief as well as damages.

Google defended on the ground that its actions constitute "fair use" .... The district court agreed. Plaintiffs brought this appeal.....

BACKGROUND

...

II. Google Books and the Google Library Project

Google's Library Project, which began in 2004, involves bi-lateral agreements between Google and a number of the world's major research libraries.[57] Under these agreements, the participating libraries select books from their collections to submit to Google for inclusion in the project. Google makes a digital scan of each book, extracts a machine-readable text, and creates an index of the machine-readable text of each book. Google retains the original scanned image of each book, in part so as to improve the accuracy of the machine-readable texts and indices as image-to-text conversion technologies improve.

Since 2004, Google has scanned, rendered machine-readable, and indexed more than 20 million books, including both copyrighted works and works in the public domain. The vast majority of the books are non-fiction, and most are out of print. All of the digital information created by Google in the process is stored on servers protected by the same security systems Google uses to shield its own confidential information.

The digital corpus created by the scanning of these millions of books enables the Google Books search engine. Members of the public who access the Google Books website can enter search words or terms of their own choice, receiving in response a list of all books in the database in which those terms appear, as well as the number of times the term appears in each book. A brief description of each book, entitled "About the Book," gives some rudimentary additional information, including a list of the words and terms that appear with most frequency in the book. It

---

[57] [Footnote 3] Libraries participating in the Library Project at the time the suit was filed included the University of Michigan, the University of California, Harvard University, Stanford University, Oxford University, Columbia University, Princeton University, Ghent University, Keio University, the Austrian National Library, and the New York Public Library.

sometimes provides links to buy the book online and identifies libraries where the book can be found.[58] The search tool permits a researcher to identify those books, out of millions, that do, as well as those that do not, use the terms selected by the researcher. Google notes that this identifying information instantaneously supplied would otherwise not be obtainable in lifetimes of searching.

No advertising is displayed to a user of the search function. Nor does Google receive payment by reason of the searcher's use of Google's link to purchase the book....

The Google Books search function also allows the user a limited viewing of text. In addition to telling the number of times the word or term selected by the searcher appears in the book, the search function will display a maximum of three "snippets" containing it. A snippet is a horizontal segment comprising ordinarily an eighth of a page.... Each search for a particular word or term within a book will reveal the same three snippets, regardless of the number of computers from which the search is launched. Only the first usage of the term on a given page is displayed.... Google's program does not allow a searcher to increase the number of snippets revealed by repeated entry of the same search term or by entering searches from different computers. A searcher can view more than three snippets of a book by entering additional searches for different terms. However, Google makes permanently unavailable for snippet view one snippet on each page and one complete page out of every ten—a process Google calls "blacklisting."

Google also disables snippet view entirely for types of books for which a single snippet is likely to satisfy the searcher's present need for the book, such as dictionaries, cookbooks, and books of short poems. Finally, since 2005, Google will exclude any book altogether from snippet view at the request of the rights holder by the submission of an online form.

Under its contracts with the participating libraries, Google allows each library to download copies—of both the digital image and machine-readable versions—of the books that library submitted to Google for scanning (but not of books submitted by other libraries).... The agreements between Google and the libraries, although not in all respects uniform, require the libraries to abide by copyright law in utilizing the digital copies they download and to take precautions to prevent dissemination of their digital copies to the public at large.....

DISCUSSION

...

II. The Search and Snippet View Functions

---

[58] [Footnote 4] Appendix A exhibits, as an example, a web page that would be revealed to a searcher who entered the phase "fair use," showing snippets from Alan Latman, Robert A. Gorman, & Jane C. Ginsburg, COPYRIGHT FOR THE EIGHTIES (1985).

A. Factor One

(1) *Transformative purpose.* [T]ransformative uses tend to favor a fair use finding because a transformative use is one that communicates something new and different from the original or expands its utility, thus serving copyright's overall objective of contributing to public knowledge.

The word "transformative" cannot be taken too literally as a sufficient key to understanding the elements of fair use. It is rather a suggestive symbol for a complex thought, and does not mean that any and all changes made to an author's original text will necessarily support a finding of fair use. ... [T]he would-be fair user of another's work must have justification for the taking ....

A further complication that can result from oversimplified reliance on whether the copying involves transformation is that the word "transform" also plays a role in defining "derivative works," over which the original rights holder retains exclusive control. Section 106 of the Act specifies the "exclusive right[ ]" of the copyright owner "(2) to prepare derivative works based upon the copyrighted work." The statute defines derivative works largely by example, rather than explanation. The examples include "translation, musical arrangement, dramatization, fictionalization, motion picture version, sound recording, art reproduction, abridgement, condensation," to which list the statute adds "any other form in which a work may be ... transformed." ... While such changes can be described as transformations, they do not involve the kind of transformative purpose that favors a fair use finding. The statutory definition suggests that derivative works generally involve transformations in the nature of changes of form. By contrast, copying from an original for the purpose of criticism or commentary on the original or provision of information about it, tends most clearly to satisfy *Campbell's* notion of the "transformative" purpose involved in the analysis of Factor One.

With these considerations in mind, we first consider whether Google's search and snippet views functions satisfy the first fair use factor with respect to Plaintiffs' rights in their books....

(2) *Search Function.* We have no difficulty concluding that Google's making of a digital copy of Plaintiffs' books for the purpose of enabling a search for identification of books containing a term of interest to the searcher involves a highly transformative purpose, in the sense intended by Campbell. Our court's exemplary discussion in *Author's Guild v. HathiTrust* [755 F.3d 87 (2d Cir. 2014)] informs our ruling. That case involved a dispute that is closely related, although not identical, to this one. Authors brought claims of copyright infringement against HathiTrust, an entity formed by libraries participating in the Google Library Project to pool the digital copies of their books created for them by Google. The suit challenged various usages HathiTrust made of the digital copies. Among the challenged uses was HathiTrust's offer to its patrons of "full-text searches," which, very much like the search offered by

Google Books to Internet users, permitted patrons of the libraries to locate in which of the digitized books specific words or phrases appeared.
(HathiTrust's search facility did not include the snippet view function, or
any other display of text.) We concluded that both the making of the digital copies and the use of those copies to offer the search tool were fair
uses.

Notwithstanding that the libraries had downloaded and stored complete digital copies of entire books, we noted that such copying was essential to permit searchers to identify and locate the books in which
words or phrases of interest to them appeared. We concluded "that the
creation of a full-text searchable database is a quintessentially transformative use ... [as] the result of a word search is different in purpose,
character, expression, meaning, and message from the page (and the
book) from which it is drawn."...

As with *HathiTrust* ..., the purpose of Google's copying of the original copyrighted books is to make available significant information about
those books, permitting a searcher to identify those that contain a word
or term of interest, as well as those that do not include reference to it. In
addition,... Google allows readers to learn the frequency of usage of selected words in the aggregate corpus of published books in different historical periods. We have no doubt that the purpose of this copying is the
sort of transformative purpose described in Campbell as strongly favoring satisfaction of the first factor.

We recognize that our case differs from *HathiTrust* in two potentially
significant respects. First, HathiTrust did not "display to the user any
text from the underlying copyrighted work," whereas Google Books provides the searcher with snippets containing the word that is the subject
of the search. Second, HathiTrust was a nonprofit educational entity,
while Google is a profit-motivated commercial corporation. We discuss
those differences below.

(3) *Snippet View*. Plaintiffs correctly point out that this case is significantly different from *HathiTrust* in that the Google Books search function allows searchers to read snippets from the book searched, whereas
HathiTrust did not allow searchers to view any part of the book. Snippet
view adds important value to the basic transformative search function,
which tells only whether and how often the searched term appears in the
book. Merely knowing that a term of interest appears in a book does not
necessarily tell the searcher whether she needs to obtain the book, because it does not reveal whether the term is discussed in a manner or
context falling within the scope of the searcher's interest....

Google's division of the page into tiny snippets is designed to show
the searcher just enough context surrounding the searched term to help
her evaluate whether the book falls within the scope of her interest
(without revealing so much as to threaten the author's copyright interests). Snippet view thus adds importantly to the highly transformative
purpose of identifying books of interest to the searcher. With respect to

the first factor test, it favors a finding of fair use (unless the value of its transformative purpose is overcome by its providing text in a manner that offers a competing substitute for Plaintiffs' books, which we discuss under factors three and four below).

(4) *Google's Commercial Motivation.* Plaintiffs also contend that Google's commercial motivation weighs in their favor under the first factor. Google's commercial motivation distinguishes this case from *HathiTrust*, as the defendant in that case was a non-profit entity founded by, and acting as the representative of, libraries. Although Google has no revenues flowing directly from its operation of the Google Books functions, Plaintiffs stress that Google is profit-motivated and seeks to use its dominance of book search to fortify its overall dominance of the Internet search market, and that thereby Google indirectly reaps profits from the Google Books functions....

Our court has since repeatedly rejected the contention that commercial motivation should outweigh a convincing transformative purpose and absence of significant substitutive competition with the original.... While we recognize that in some circumstances, a commercial motivation on the part of the secondary user will weigh against her, especially, as the Supreme Court suggested, when a persuasive transformative purpose is lacking, we see no reason in this case why Google's overall profit motivation should prevail as a reason for denying fair use over its highly convincing transformative purpose, together with the absence of significant substitutive competition, as reasons for granting fair use. Many of the most universally accepted forms of fair use, such as news reporting and commentary, quotation in historical or analytic books, reviews of books, and performances, as well as parody, are all normally done commercially for profit.

B. Factor Two

The second fair use factor directs consideration of the "nature of the copyrighted work."...

In considering the second factor in *HathiTrust*, we concluded that it was "not dispositive," commenting that courts have hardly ever found that the second factor in isolation played a large role in explaining a fair use decision. The same is true here. While each of the three Plaintiffs' books in this case is factual, we do not consider that as a boost to Google's claim of fair use.... To the extent that the "nature" of the original copyrighted work necessarily combines with the "purpose and character" of the secondary work to permit assessment of whether the secondary work uses the original in a "transformative" manner, as the term is used in *Campbell*, the second factor favors fair use not because Plaintiffs' works are factual, but because the secondary use transformatively provides valuable information about the original, rather than replicating protected expression in a manner that provides a meaningful substitute for the original.

C. Factor Three

The third statutory factor instructs us to consider "the amount and substantiality of the portion used in relation to the copyrighted work as a whole."....

(1) *Search Function.* The Google Books program has made a digital copy of the entirety of each of Plaintiffs' books. Notwithstanding the reasonable implication of Factor Three that fair use is more likely to be favored by the copying of smaller, rather than larger, portions of the original, courts have rejected any categorical rule that a copying of the entirety cannot be a fair use. Complete unchanged copying has repeatedly been found justified as fair use when the copying was reasonably appropriate to achieve the copier's transformative purpose and was done in such a manner that it did not offer a competing substitute for the original....

In *HathiTrust*, our court concluded in its discussion of the third factor that "[b]ecause it was reasonably necessary for the [HathiTrust Digital Library] to make use of the entirety of the works in order to enable the full-text search function, we do not believe the copying was excessive." As with *HathiTrust*, not only is the copying of the totality of the original reasonably appropriate to Google's transformative purpose, it is literally necessary to achieve that purpose. If Google copied less than the totality of the originals, its search function could not advise searchers reliably whether their searched term appears in a book (or how many times).

While Google makes an unauthorized digital copy of the entire book, it does not reveal that digital copy to the public. The copy is made to enable the search functions to reveal limited, important information about the books. With respect to the search function, Google satisfies the third factor test, as illuminated by the Supreme Court in *Campbell*.

(2) *Snippet View.* Google's provision of snippet view makes our third factor inquiry different from that inquiry in *HathiTrust*. What matters in such cases is not so much "the amount and substantiality of the portion used" in making a copy, but rather the amount and substantiality of what is thereby made accessible to a public for which it may serve as a competing substitute. In *HathiTrust*, notwithstanding the defendant's full-text copying, the search function revealed virtually nothing of the text of the originals to the public. Here, through the snippet view, more is revealed to searchers than in *HathiTrust*.

Without doubt, enabling searchers to see portions of the copied texts could have determinative effect on the fair use analysis. The larger the quantity of the copyrighted text the searcher can see and the more control the searcher can exercise over what part of the text she sees, the greater the likelihood that those revelations could serve her as an effective, free substitute for the purchase of the plaintiff's book. We nonetheless conclude that, at least as presently structured by Google, the snippet view does not reveal matter that offers the marketplace a significantly competing substitute for the copyrighted work.

Google has constructed the snippet feature in a manner that substantially protects against its serving as an effectively competing substitute for Plaintiffs' books. In the Background section of this opinion, we describe a variety of limitations Google imposes on the snippet function.... The result of these restrictions is, so far as the record demonstrates, that a searcher cannot succeed, even after long extended effort to multiply what can be revealed, in revealing through a snippet search what could usefully serve as a competing substitute for the original....

D. Factor Four

The fourth fair use factor, "the effect of the [copying] use upon the potential market for or value of the copyrighted work," focuses on whether the copy brings to the marketplace a competing substitute for the original, or its derivative, so as to deprive the rights holder of significant revenues because of the likelihood that potential purchasers may opt to acquire the copy in preference to the original. Because copyright is a commercial doctrine whose objective is to stimulate creativity among potential authors by enabling them to earn money from their creations, the fourth factor is of great importance in making a fair use assessment.

Campbell stressed the close linkage between the first and fourth factors, in that the more the copying is done to achieve a purpose that differs from the purpose of the original, the less likely it is that the copy will serve as a satisfactory substitute for the original. Consistent with that observation, the *HathiTrust* court found that the fourth factor favored the defendant and supported a finding of fair use because the ability to search the text of the book to determine whether it includes selected words "does not serve as a substitute for the books that are being searched."

However, *Campbell's* observation as to the likelihood of a secondary use serving as an effective substitute goes only so far. Even if the purpose of the copying is for a valuably transformative purpose, such copying might nonetheless harm the value of the copyrighted original if done in a manner that results in widespread revelation of sufficiently significant portions of the original as to make available a significantly competing substitute. The question for us is whether snippet view, notwithstanding its transformative purpose, does that. We conclude that, at least as snippet view is presently constructed, it does not.

Especially in view of the fact that the normal purchase price of a book is relatively low in relation to the cost of manpower needed to secure an arbitrary assortment of randomly scattered snippets, we conclude that the snippet function does not give searchers access to effectively competing substitutes. Snippet view, at best and after a large commitment of manpower, produces discontinuous, tiny fragments, amounting in the aggregate to no more than 16% of a book. This does not threaten the rights holders with any significant harm to the value of their copyrights or diminish their harvest of copyright revenue.

We recognize that the snippet function can cause some loss of sales. There are surely instances in which a searcher's need for access to a text will be satisfied by the snippet view, resulting in either the loss of a sale to that searcher, or reduction of demand on libraries for that title, which might have resulted in libraries purchasing additional copies. But the possibility, or even the probability or certainty, of some loss of sales does not suffice to make the copy an effectively competing substitute that would tilt the weighty fourth factor in favor of the rights holder in the original. There must be a meaningful or significant effect "upon the potential market for or value of the copyrighted work." 17 U.S .C. § 107(4).

Furthermore, the type of loss of sale envisioned above will generally occur in relation to interests that are not protected by the copyright. A snippet's capacity to satisfy a searcher's need for access to a copyrighted book will at times be because the snippet conveys a historical fact that the searcher needs to ascertain. For example, a student writing a paper on Franklin D. Roosevelt might need to learn the year Roosevelt was stricken with polio. By entering "Roosevelt polio" in a Google Books search, the student would be taken to (among numerous sites) a snippet from page 31 of Richard Thayer Goldberg's THE MAKING OF FRANKLIN D. ROOSEVELT (1981), telling that the polio attack occurred in 1921. This would satisfy the searcher's need for the book, eliminating any need to purchase it or acquire it from a library. But what the searcher derived from the snippet was a historical fact. Author Goldberg's copyright does not extend to the facts communicated by his book. It protects only the author's manner of expression. Google would be entitled, without infringement of Goldberg's copyright, to answer the student's query about the year Roosevelt was afflicted, taking the information from Goldberg's book. The fact that, in the case of the student's snippet search, the information came embedded in three lines of Goldberg's writing, which were superfluous to the searcher's needs, would not change the taking of an unprotected fact into a copyright infringement.

Even if the snippet reveals some authorial expression, because of the brevity of a single snippet and the cumbersome, disjointed, and incomplete nature of the aggregation of snippets made available through snippet view, we think it would be a rare case in which the searcher's interest in the protected aspect of the author's work would be satisfied by what is available from snippet view, and rarer still—because of the cumbersome, disjointed, and incomplete nature of the aggregation of snippets made available through snippet view—that snippet view could provide a significant substitute for the purchase of the author's book.

Accordingly, considering the four fair use factors in light of the goals of copyright, we conclude that Google's making of a complete digital copy of Plaintiffs' works for the purpose of providing the public with its search and snippet view functions (at least as snippet view is presently designed) is a fair use and does not infringe Plaintiffs' copyrights in their books.

III. Derivative Rights in Search and Snippet View

Plaintiffs next contend that, under Section 106(2), they have a derivative right in the application of search and snippet view functions to their works, and that Google has usurped their exclusive market for such derivatives.

There is no merit to this argument. As explained above, Google does not infringe Plaintiffs' copyright in their works by making digital copies of them, where the copies are used to enable the public to get information about the works, such as whether, and how often they use specified words or terms (together with peripheral snippets of text, sufficient to show the context in which the word is used but too small to provide a meaningful substitute for the work's copyrighted expression). The copyright resulting from the Plaintiffs' authorship of their works does not include an exclusive right to furnish the kind of information about the works that Google's programs provide to the public. For substantially the same reasons, the copyright that protects Plaintiffs' works does not include an exclusive derivative right to supply such information through query of a digitized copy.

The extension of copyright protection beyond the copying of the work in its original form to cover also the copying of a derivative reflects a clear and logical policy choice. An author's right to control and profit from the dissemination of her work ought not to be evaded by conversion of the work into a different form. The author of a book written in English should be entitled to control also the dissemination of the same book translated into other languages, or a conversion of the book into a film. The copyright of a composer of a symphony or song should cover also conversions of the piece into scores for different instrumentation, as well as into recordings of performances.

This policy is reflected in the statutory definition, which explains the scope of the "derivative" largely by examples—including "a translation, musical arrangement, dramatization, fictionalization, motion picture version, sound recording, art reproduction, abridgement, [or] condensation"—before adding, "or any other form in which a work may be recast, transformed, or adapted." 17 U.S.C. § 101. As noted above, this definition, while imprecise, strongly implies that derivative works over which the author of the original enjoys exclusive rights ordinarily are those that re-present the protected aspects of the original work, i.e., its expressive content, converted into an altered form, such as the conversion of a novel into a film, the translation of a writing into a different language, the reproduction of a painting in the form of a poster or post card, recreation of a cartoon character in the form of a three-dimensional plush toy, adaptation of a musical composition for different instruments, or other similar conversions. If Plaintiffs' claim were based on Google's converting their books into a digitized form and making that digitized version accessible to the public, their claim would be strong. But as noted above, Google safeguards from public view the digitized copies it makes and allows access only to the extent of permitting the public to search for the very limited information accessible through the search function and snippet view. The program does not allow access in any substantial way to a book's expressive content. Nothing in the statutory definition of a derivative work, or of the logic that underlies it, suggests that the author of an original work enjoys an exclusive derivative right to supply information about that work of the sort communicated by Google's search functions.

Plaintiffs seek to support their derivative claim by a showing that there exist, or would have existed, paid licensing markets in digitized works, such as those provided by the Copyright Clearance Center or the previous, revenue-generating version of the Google Partners Program. Plaintiffs also point to the proposed settlement agreement rejected by the district court in this case, according to which Google would have paid authors for its use of digitized copies of their works. The existence or potential existence of such paid licensing schemes does not support Plaintiffs' derivative argument. The access to the expressive content of the original that is or would have been provided by the paid licensing arrangements Plaintiffs cite is far more extensive than that which Google's search and snippet view functions provide. Those arrangements allow or would have allowed public users to read substantial portions of the book. Such access would most likely constitute copyright infringement if not licensed by the rights holders. Accordingly, such arrangements have no bearing on Google's present programs, which, in a non-infringing manner, allow the public to obtain limited data about the contents of the book, without allowing any substantial reading of its text.

Plaintiffs also seek to support their derivative claim by a showing that there is a current unpaid market in licenses for partial viewing of digitized books, such as the licenses that publishers currently grant to the Google Partners program and Amazon's Search Inside the Book program to display substantial portions of their books. Plaintiffs rely on *Infinity Broadcast Corporation v. Kirkwood*, 150 F.3d 104 (2nd Cir.1998) and *United States v. American Society of Composers, Authors and Publishers (ASCAP)*, 599 F.Supp.2d 415 (S.D.N.Y.2009) for the proposition that "a secondary use that replaces a comparable service licensed by the copyright holder, even without charge, may cause market harm." In the cases cited, however, the purpose of the challenged secondary uses was not the dissemination of information about the original works, which falls outside the protection of the copyright, but was rather the retransmission, or re-dissemination, of their expressive content. Those precedents do not support the proposition Plaintiffs assert—namely that the availability of licenses for providing unprotected information about a copyrighted work, or supplying unprotected services related to it, gives the copyright holder the right to exclude others from providing such information or services....

APPENDIX A

Notes and Questions

1. In its analysis of the first factor, the court in *Google* held that Google's literal copying of millions of books was "transformative" and therefore weighed in favor of fair use. The court's opinion was thus consistent with an understanding, reflected in *Bill Graham Archives*, that in analyzing the first factor, courts should look not solely at whether the work itself has been transformed, but whether the new use serves a transformative purpose, i.e. a purpose different from the one originally served by the copyrighted work. Do you agree with this understanding? Does it apply equally to cases like *Rogers v. Koons*, discussed *supra*, where the artist reproduced the original postcard rather literally, but

used it for a very different purpose? *See* Mahita Gajanan, "Controversial Artist Richard Prince Sued for Copyright Infringement," THE GUARDIAN (Jan. 4, 2016) (appropriationist artist prints, frames, and displays in an art gallery copyrighted photos downloaded from other individuals' Instagram accounts).

2. What is the difference between a transformative fair use (which results in no liability) and a transformative derivative work (which belongs to the copyright holder)? Since transformation is an element in both fair use and the definition of a derivative work, where do we draw the line? The court in *Google* suggests a distinction based on the illustrative list in the statutory definition of "derivative work":

> [D]erivative works over which the author of the original enjoys exclusive rights ordinarily are those that re-present the protected aspects of the original work, i.e., its expressive content, converted into an altered form, such as the conversion of a novel into a film, the translation of a writing into a different language, the reproduction of a painting in the form of a poster or post card, recreation of a cartoon character in the form of a three-dimensional plush toy, adaptation of a musical composition for different instruments, or other similar conversions.

This suggests that works that do more than simply "re-present the … expressive content" of the work in a different form may fall outside the scope of the derivative work right. Does this seem like a workable distinction? How did the court apply this distinction to the facts in *Google*?

3. The court rejected plaintiffs' argument that there was an available licensing market for search and for the snippets. Indeed, as the court acknowledged, the parties had at one point agreed to a proposed settlement (which the trial court later refused to approve), under which Google would have paid the plaintiffs a license for permission to copy, index, and make available plaintiffs' copyrighted works through its Book Search program. Why isn't this evidence, under *Texaco*, that there was a valid potential licensing market and thus harm to the potential market? Does this suggest that, under a market failure theory of fair use, the case was wrongly decided? Did you find the court's rejection of this argument persuasive? What should we make of the fact that the court considered this argument separately as a claim for violation of the derivative work right, rather than under the fourth factor of the fair use analysis?

4. Google took several steps to make sure that its service would have a limited impact on the market for the books themselves, including reproducing only the same snippets for each term searched, "blacklisting" certain results and pages, making unavailable snippets for certain works that could be particularly adversely affected by the service, etc. To what extent could Google relax any of these measures and still fall within the fair use defense? What if Google began aggressively selling advertising on its Book Search service? Would that make a difference?

5.   The Second Circuit's opinion in *Google* followed a number of prior cases involving similar, though not identical, facts. The opinion repeatedly references the Second Circuit's own prior opinion in *Authors Guild v. HathiTrust,* 755 F.3d 87 (2d Cir. 2014), which involved a nonprofit entity established by the participating libraries in the Google Books Project, which enabled library users to conduct text searches on the database of scanned books provided to the libraries under the Google Books Project. *HathiTrust* thus involved a very similar fair use defense, at least with respect to the search function (though not the snippet view, as noted by the *Google* court).

6.   Another important earlier case was *Kelly v. Arriba Soft Corp.,* 280 F.3d 934 (9th Cir. 2002), which involved a copyright claim brought against an image search engine. The defendant Arriba Soft provided a web-based search engine which allowed users to search for specific images on the internet. To provide this service, Arriba Soft programmed its computers to visit webpages on the internet and download and store any images found on those webpages, along with associated information that indicated the subject of that image. This information was stored in a database, which could be searched by users through Arriba Soft's website. In response to a search, Arriba Soft would display a results page with smaller, thumbnail-sized versions of the images.

The Ninth Circuit held that Arriba Soft's activities constituted fair use. In reaching this result, the panel held that Arriba Soft's copying of the original images and display of the reduced-size thumbnails was transformative insofar as it served a very different purpose from the originals. The court also held that there was little risk of any harm to the market, as the thumbnail-sized images were not substitutes for the original full-sized versions. *See also Perfect 10 v. Amazon.com,* 487 F.3d 701 (9th Cir. 2007) (finding fair use in a similar case involving an image search engine, despite evidence that the copyright owner licensed thumbnail versions of images for use on cellphones).

7.   If Google had lost the case, it is hard to see how it could have legitimately licensed the ability to scan and copy all of the millions of books in the collections of the various libraries, given the costs associated with identifying all of the copyright owners and reaching individual licensing agreements. Thus, practically speaking, a contrary result would likely have made the project impracticable (or at least resulted in significant gaps in the database).

The Google Book Search litigation thus drew increased attention to the problem of so-called orphan works. Orphan works are works that are still copyrighted, but whose copyright owners are difficult to identify and locate. This may be due to lack of any identifying information on the work itself, due to the multiple transfers of the copyright interest via license or inheritance, or simply through the passage of time and lack of good records. Because the rights holders of such works are difficult to identify, those who wish to license these works face serious obstacles. They may refrain from using the work because of uncertainty and the risk that a copyright owner could later emerge and sue for damages or injunctive relief. In the case of mass digitization efforts like Google Book Search, these obstacles would make it prohibitively expensive to acquire all of the licenses necessary to undertake its project.

The Copyright Office has concluded that the problem of orphan works is "widespread and significant," and has proposed legislation that would limit the liability of users of copyrighted works in cases where they made a good faith attempt, but were ultimately unable, to identify the copyright owners. The legislation would define what constituted a good faith diligent search, and would also limit both monetary and injunctive relief in cases where the user had engaged in such a search. The Copyright Office considered, but ultimately rejected, other possible responses, such as modifying the fair use defense, enacting an orphan-works exception, or creating a government-run licensing program. As yet, Congress has not passed any legislation responding to the orphan works problem.

6. INTEROPERABILITY

Fair use also plays an important and unique role in setting copyright entitlements in computer software. Earlier in this book, we explored how courts have adopted doctrines such as infringement and the idea/expression dichotomy to the special circumstances surrounding computer software. Here, we examine a similar process with the fair use doctrine. In particular, courts have grappled with whether copying of software in the course of making interoperable programs can constitute fair use.

Sega Enterprises v. Accolade
977 F.2d 1510 (9th Cir. 1993)

REINHARDT, Circuit Judge:

We are asked to determine … whether the Copyright Act permits persons who are neither copyright holders nor licensees to disassemble a copyrighted computer program in order to gain an understanding of the unprotected functional elements of the program. In light of the public policies underlying the Act, we conclude that, when the person seeking the understanding has a legitimate reason for doing so and when no other means of access to the unprotected elements exists, such disassembly is as a matter of law a fair use of the copyrighted work. …

I. Background

Plaintiff-appellee Sega Enterprises, Ltd., a Japanese corporation, and its subsidiary, Sega of America, develop and market video entertainment systems, including the "Genesis" console and video game cartridges. Defendant-appellant Accolade, Inc., is an independent developer, manufacturer, and marketer of computer entertainment software, including game cartridges that are compatible with the Genesis console, as well as game cartridges that are compatible with other computer systems.

Sega licenses its copyrighted computer code and its "SEGA" trademark to a number of independent developers of computer game software. Those licensees develop and sell Genesis-compatible video games in competition with Sega. Accolade is not and never has been a licensee of Sega. Prior to rendering its own games compatible with the Genesis console, Accolade explored the possibility of entering into a licensing agreement with Sega, but abandoned the effort because the agreement would have required that Sega be the exclusive manufacturer of all games produced by Accolade.

Accolade used a two-step process to render its video games compatible with the Genesis console. First, it "reverse engineered" Sega's video game programs in order to discover the requirements for compatibility with the Genesis console. As part of the reverse engineering process, Accolade transformed the machine-readable object code contained in commercially available copies of Sega's game cartridges into human-readable source code using a process called "disassembly" or "decompilation."[59] Accolade purchased a Genesis console and three Sega game cartridges, wired a decompiler into the console circuitry, and generated printouts of the resulting source code. Accolade engineers studied and annotated the printouts in order to identify areas of commonality among the three game programs. They then loaded the disassembled code back into a computer, and experimented to discover the interface specifications for the Genesis console by modifying the programs and studying the results. At the end of the reverse engineering process, Accolade created a development manual that incorporated the information it had discovered about the requirements for a Genesis-compatible game. According to the Accolade employees who created the manual, the manual contained only functional descriptions of the interface requirements and did not include any of Sega's code.

In the second stage, Accolade created its own games for the Genesis. According to Accolade, at this stage it did not copy Sega's programs, but relied only on the information concerning interface specifications for the Genesis that was contained in its development manual. Accolade main-

---

[59] [Footnote 2] Computer programs are written in specialized alphanumeric languages, or "source code". In order to operate a computer, source code must be translated into computer readable form, or "object code". Object code uses only two symbols, 0 and 1, in combinations which represent the alphanumeric characters of the source code. A program written in source code is translated into object code using a computer program called an "assembler" or "compiler", and then imprinted onto a silicon chip for commercial distribution. Devices called "disassemblers" or "decompilers" can reverse this process by "reading" the electronic signals for "0" and "1" that are produced while the program is being run, storing the resulting object code in computer memory, and translating the object code into source code. Both assembly and disassembly devices are commercially available, and both types of devices are widely used within the software industry.

tains that with the exception of the interface specifications, none of the code in its own games is derived in any way from its examination of Sega's code. In 1990, Accolade released "Ishido", a game which it had originally developed and released for use with the Macintosh and IBM personal computer systems, for use with the Genesis console. ...

III. Copyright Issues

Accolade raises four arguments in support of its position that disassembly of the object code in a copyrighted computer program does not constitute copyright infringement. First, it maintains that intermediate copying does not infringe the exclusive rights granted to copyright owners in section 106 of the Copyright Act unless the end product of the copying is substantially similar to the copyrighted work. ... Finally, Accolade contends that disassembly of object code in order to gain an understanding of the ideas and functional concepts embodied in the code is a fair use that is privileged by section 107 of the Act.

Neither the language of the Act nor the law of this circuit supports Accolade's first three arguments. Accolade's fourth argument, however, has merit. Although the question is fairly debatable, we conclude based on the policies underlying the Copyright Act that disassembly of copyrighted object code is, as a matter of law, a fair use of the copyrighted work if such disassembly provides the only means of access to those elements of the code that are not protected by copyright and the copier has a legitimate reason for seeking such access. Accordingly, we hold that Sega has failed to demonstrate a likelihood of success on the merits of its copyright claim. Because on the record before us the hardships do not tip sharply (or at all) in Sega's favor, the preliminary injunction issued in its favor must be dissolved, at least with respect to that claim.

A.   Intermediate Copying

We have previously held that the Copyright Act does not distinguish between unauthorized copies of a copyrighted work on the basis of what stage of the alleged infringer's work the unauthorized copies represent. Our holding ... was based on the plain language of the Act. Section 106 grants to the copyright owner the exclusive rights "to reproduce the work in copies," "to prepare derivative works based upon the copyrighted work," and to authorize the preparation of copies and derivative works. 17 U.S.C. § 106(1)-(2). Section 501 provides that "[a]nyone who violates any of the exclusive rights of the copyright owner as provided by sections 106 through 118 ... is an infringer of the copyright." On its face, that language unambiguously encompasses and proscribes "intermediate copying".

In order to constitute a "copy" for purposes of the Act, the allegedly infringing work must be fixed in some tangible form, "from which the work can be perceived, reproduced, or otherwise communicated, either directly or with the aid of a machine or device." 17 U.S.C. Section 101. The computer file generated by the disassembly program, the printouts of the disassembled code, and the computer files containing Accolade's modifications of the code that were generated during the reverse engineering process all satisfy that requirement. The intermediate copying done by Accolade therefore falls squarely within the category of acts that are prohibited by the statute. ...

D. Fair Use

Accolade contends, finally, that its disassembly of copyrighted object code as a necessary step in its examination of the unprotected ideas and functional concepts embodied in the code is a fair use that is privileged by section 107 of the Act. Because, in the case before us, disassembly is the only means of gaining access to those unprotected aspects of the program, and because Accolade has a legitimate interest in gaining such access (in order to determine how to make its cartridges compatible with the Genesis console), we agree with Accolade. Where there is good reason for studying or examining the unprotected aspects of a copyrighted computer program, disassembly for purposes of such study or examination constitutes a fair use. ...

2.

...

(a)

With respect to the first statutory factor, we observe initially that the fact that copying is for a commercial purpose weighs against a finding of fair use. However, the presumption of unfairness that arises in such cases can be rebutted by the characteristics of a particular commercial use. ...

Sega argues that because Accolade copied its object code in order to produce a competing product, the *Harper & Row* presumption applies and precludes a finding of fair use. That analysis is far too simple and ignores a number of important considerations. We must consider other aspects of "the purpose and character of the use" as well. As we have noted, the use at issue was an intermediate one only and thus any commercial "exploitation" was indirect or derivative.

The declarations of Accolade's employees indicate, and the district court found, that Accolade copied Sega's software solely in order to discover the functional requirements for compatibility with the Genesis console—aspects of Sega's programs that are not protected by copyright. With respect to the video game programs contained in Accolade's game cartridges, there is no evidence in the record that Accolade sought to avoid performing its own creative work. Indeed, most of the games that Accolade released for use with the Genesis console were originally developed for other hardware systems. Moreover, with respect to the interface procedures for the Genesis console, Accolade did not seek to avoid paying a customarily charged fee for use of those procedures, nor did it simply copy Sega's code; rather, it wrote its own procedures based on what it had learned through disassembly. Taken together, these facts indicate that although Accolade's ultimate purpose was the release of Genesis-compatible games for sale, its direct purpose in copying Sega's code, and thus its direct use of the copyrighted material, was simply to study the functional requirements for Genesis compatibility so that it could modify existing games and make them usable with the Genesis console. Moreover, as we discuss below, no other method of studying those requirements was available to Accolade. On these facts, we conclude that Accolade copied Sega's code for a legitimate, essentially non-exploitative purpose, and that the commercial aspect of its use can best be described as of minimal significance.

We further note that we are free to consider the public benefit resulting from a particular use notwithstanding the fact that the alleged infringer may gain commercially. Public benefit need not be direct or tangible, but may arise because the challenged use serves a public interest. In the case before us, Accolade's identification of the functional requirements for Genesis compatibility has led to an increase in the number of independently designed video game programs offered for use with the Genesis console. It is precisely this growth in creative expression, based on the dissemination of other creative works and the unprotected ideas contained in those works, that the Copyright Act was intended to promote. The fact that Genesis-compatible video games are not scholarly works, but works offered for sale on the market, does not alter our judgment in this regard. We conclude that given the purpose and character of Accolade's use of Sega's video game programs, the presumption of unfairness has been overcome and the first statutory factor weighs in favor of Accolade.

(b)

As applied, the fourth statutory factor, effect on the potential market for the copyrighted work, bears a close relationship to the "purpose and character" inquiry in that it, too, accommodates the distinction between the copying of works in order to make independent creative expression possible and the simple exploitation of another's creative efforts. We must, of course, inquire whether, "if [the challenged use] should become widespread, it would adversely affect the potential market for the copyrighted work," *Sony Corp. v. Universal City Studios*, 464 U.S. 417, 451 (1984), by diminishing potential sales, interfering with marketability, or usurping the market. If the copying resulted in the latter effect, all other considerations might be irrelevant. The *Harper & Row* Court found a use that effectively usurped the market for the copyrighted work by supplanting that work to be dispositive. However, the same consequences do not and could not attach to a use which simply enables the copier to enter the market for works of the same type as the copied work.

Unlike the defendant in *Harper & Row*, which printed excerpts from President Ford's memoirs verbatim with the stated purpose of "scooping" a Time magazine review of the book, Accolade did not attempt to "scoop" Sega's release of any particular game or games, but sought only to become a legitimate competitor in the field of Genesis-compatible video games. Within that market, it is the characteristics of the game program as experienced by the user that determine the program's commercial success. As we have noted, there is nothing in the record that suggests that Accolade copied any of those elements.

By facilitating the entry of a new competitor, the first lawful one that is not a Sega licensee, Accolade's disassembly of Sega's software undoubtedly "affected" the market for Genesis-compatible games in an indirect fashion. We note, however, that while no consumer except the most avid devotee of President Ford's regime might be expected to buy more than one version of the President's memoirs, video game users typically purchase more than one game. There is no basis for assuming that Accolade's "Ishido" has significantly affected the market for Sega's "Altered Beast", since a consumer might easily purchase both; nor does it seem unlikely that a consumer particularly interested in sports might purchase both Accolade's "Mike Ditka Power Football" and Sega's "Joe Montana Football", particularly if the games are, as Accolade contends, not substantially similar. In any event, an attempt to monopolize the market by making it impossible for others to compete runs counter to the statutory purpose of promoting creative expression and cannot constitute a strong equitable basis for resisting the invocation of the fair use doctrine. Thus, we conclude that the fourth statutory factor weighs in Accolade's, not Sega's, favor, notwithstanding the minor economic loss Sega may suffer.

(c)

The second statutory factor, the nature of the copyrighted work, reflects the fact that not all copyrighted works are entitled to the same level of protection. The protection established by the Copyright Act for original works of authorship does not extend to the ideas underlying a work or to the functional or factual aspects of the work. To the extent that a work is functional or factual, it may be copied, as may those expressive elements of the work that "must necessarily be used as incident to" expression of the underlying ideas, functional concepts, or facts. *Baker v. Selden,* 101 U.S. 99, 104 (1879). Works of fiction receive greater protection than works that have strong factual elements, such as historical or biographical works, or works that have strong functional elements, such as accounting textbooks. Works that are merely compilations of fact are copyrightable, but the copyright in such a work is "thin."

Computer programs pose unique problems for the application of the "idea/expression distinction" that determines the extent of copyright protection. To the extent that there are many possible ways of accomplishing a given task or fulfilling a particular market demand, the programmer's choice of program structure and design may be highly creative and idiosyncratic. However, computer programs are, in essence, utilitarian articles—articles that accomplish tasks. As such, they contain many logical, structural, and visual display elements that are dictated by the function to be performed, by considerations of efficiency, or by external factors such as compatibility requirements and industry demands. In some circumstances, even the exact set of commands used by the programmer is deemed functional rather than creative for purposes of copyright. ...

Sega argues that even if many elements of its video game programs are properly characterized as functional and therefore not protected by copyright, Accolade copied protected expression. Sega is correct. The record makes clear that disassembly is wholesale copying. Because computer programs are also unique among copyrighted works in the form in which they are distributed for public use, however, Sega's observation does not bring us much closer to a resolution of the dispute.

The unprotected aspects of most functional works are readily accessible to the human eye. The systems described in accounting textbooks or the basic structural concepts embodied in architectural plans, to give two examples, can be easily copied without also copying any of the protected, expressive aspects of the original works. Computer programs, however, are typically distributed for public use in object code form, embedded in a silicon chip or on a floppy disk. For that reason, humans often cannot gain access to the unprotected ideas and functional concepts contained in object code without disassembling that code—*i.e.*, making copies.

Sega argues that the record does not establish that disassembly of its object code is the only available method for gaining access to the interface specifications for the Genesis console, and the district court agreed. An independent examination of the record reveals that Sega misstates its contents, and demonstrates that the district court committed clear error in this respect.

First, the record clearly establishes that humans cannot read object code. Sega makes much of Mike Lorenzen's statement that a reverse engineer can work directly from the zeros and ones of object code but "[i]t's not as fun." In full, Lorenzen's statements establish only that the use of an electronic decompiler is not absolutely necessary. Trained programmers can disassemble object code by hand. Because even a trained programmer cannot possibly remember the millions of zeros and ones that make up a program, however, he must make a written or computerized copy of the disassembled code in order to keep track of his work. The relevant fact for purposes of Sega's copyright infringement claim and Accolade's fair use defense is that translation of a program from object code into source code cannot be accomplished without making copies of the code.

Second, the record provides no support for a conclusion that a viable alternative to disassembly exists. The district court found that Accolade could have avoided a copyright infringement claim by "peeling" the chips contained in Sega's games or in the Genesis console, as authorized by section 906 of the SCPA, 17 U.S.C. § 906. Even Sega's *amici* agree that this finding was clear error. The declaration of Dr. Harry Tredennick, an expert witness for Accolade, establishes that chip peeling yields only a physical diagram of the object code embedded in a ROM chip.

The district court also suggested that Accolade could have avoided a copyright infringement suit by programming in a "clean room." That finding too is clearly erroneous. A "clean room" is a procedure used in the computer industry in order to prevent direct copying of a competitor's code during the development of a competing product. Programmers in clean rooms are provided only with the functional specifications for the desired program. As Dr. Tredennick explained, the use of a clean room would not have avoided the need for disassembly because disassembly was necessary in order to discover the functional specifications for a Genesis-compatible game.

In summary, the record clearly establishes that disassembly of the object code in Sega's video game cartridges was necessary in order to understand the functional requirements for Genesis compatibility. The interface procedures for the Genesis console are distributed for public use only in object code form, and are not visible to the user during operation of the video game program. Because object code cannot be read by humans, it must be disassembled, either by hand or by machine. Disassembly of object code necessarily entails copying. Those facts dictate our analysis of the second statutory fair use factor. If disassembly of copyrighted object code is *per se* an unfair use, the owner of the copyright gains a *de facto* monopoly over the functional aspects of his work— aspects that were expressly denied copyright protection by Congress. In order to enjoy a lawful monopoly over the idea or functional principle underlying a work, the creator of the work must satisfy the more stringent standards imposed by the patent laws. Sega does not hold a patent on the Genesis console.

Because Sega's video game programs contain unprotected aspects that cannot be examined without copying, we afford them a lower degree of protection than more traditional literary works. In light of all the considerations discussed above, we conclude that the second statutory factor also weighs in favor of Accolade.

(d)

As to the third statutory factor, Accolade disassembled entire programs written by Sega. Accordingly, the third factor weighs against Accolade. The fact that an entire work was copied does not, however, preclude a finding a fair use. In fact, where the ultimate (as opposed to direct) use is as limited as it was here, the factor is of very little weight.

(e)

In summary, careful analysis of the purpose and characteristics of Accolade's use of Sega's video game programs, the nature of the computer programs involved, and the nature of the market for video game cartridges yields the conclusion that the first, second, and fourth statutory fair use factors weigh in favor of Accolade, while only the third weighs in favor of Sega, and even then only slightly. Accordingly, Accolade clearly has by far the better case on the fair use issue.

We are not unaware of the fact that to those used to considering copyright issues in more traditional contexts, our result may seem incongruous at first blush. To oversimplify, the record establishes that Accolade, a commercial competitor of Sega, engaged in wholesale copying of Sega's copyrighted code as a preliminary step in the development of a competing product. However, the key to this case is that we are dealing with computer software, a relatively unexplored area in the world of copyright law. We must avoid the temptation of trying to force "the proverbial square peg in[to] a round hole." *Computer Associates Int'l, Inc. v. Altai*, 23 U.S.P.Q.2d 1241, 1257 (2d Cir. 1992). ...

Sega argues that the considerable time, effort, and money that went into development of the Genesis and Genesis-compatible video games militate against a finding of fair use. Borrowing from antitrust principles, Sega attempts to label Accolade a "free rider" on its product development efforts. In *Feist Publications*, however, the Court unequivocally rejected the "sweat of the brow" rationale for copyright protection. Under the Copyright Act, if a work is largely functional, it receives only weak protection. "This result is neither unfair nor unfortunate. It is the means by which copyright advances the progress of science and art." *Feist,* 499 U.S. at 350. Here, while the work may not be largely functional, it incorporates functional elements which do not merit protection. The equitable considerations involved weigh on the side of public access. Accordingly, we reject Sega's argument.

[The court's discussion of trademark issues is omitted.]

Notes and Questions

1. Compare the court's treatment of the four fair use factors to the decisions of courts in non computer software cases. Is the court's treatment of these factors (particularly the first and fourth factors) consistent with the treatment in other cases? In what ways does the treatment differ? And are these differences justified?

2. Reverse engineering is a common practice in many industries with products involving know-how. Companies will routinely purchase competing products and take them apart in order to study how the products were put together. They can then learn from these products and incorporate innovations into their own products. This activity is generally permissible under both trade secret law and patent law.

In software markets, companies reverse engineer products, not only for the above reasons, but additionally to create compatible products. This ability to create compatible products is particularly important in software markets because of so-called network effects. A product exhibits network effects when its value to the consumer depends on the number of other consumers who also use the product. For example, a telephone has relatively little value if only a single person owns one. However, the value rises steeply if many people do so. Because of network effects, software markets can often tip toward a dominant producer, particularly if compatibility is important to users. You may have experienced the challenges of adopting a new word processing program when the new program cannot read files written by those who use other, more established software. Indeed, you may have decided that it is "not worth it" to use the new software, even if it has attractive features that the more established programs lack. Accordingly, software companies generally have to ensure that their new products are compatible with existing dominant platforms, or their sales will suffer.

3. The market for video game consoles is intensely competitive and subject to strong network effects. Console manufacturers often adopt a strategy of selling consoles below cost in order to establish a wide network of consoles, and then recouping their profits via sales of cartridges. (This is similar to strategies adopted by camera companies, razor blade companies, printer companies, etc.). This practice also allows such companies to engage in price discrimination, i.e. to charge consumers differentially based upon how much they value the system as a whole. Accolade's practice of selling unauthorized games for the Genesis thus kept Sega from undertaking this strategy.

From a policy standpoint, then, one question is whether such a result is socially undesirable. The court in *Sega* seemed to find Sega's attempt to restrict competition problematic. Do you agree? What is so bad about Sega's strategy? And what role, if any, should copyright law play?

4. Can software publishers contract around the reverse engineering privilege? For example, if a software company included, in its shrink-wrap agreement, a clause prohibiting reverse engineering, would this be enforceable? On this point, see the discussion *infra* Chapter Ten on preemption.

SECTION B. FIRST AMENDMENT

Increasingly, defendants have begun to raise claims that parts of the Copyright Act, or particular applications of the Act, violate the defendants' First Amendment rights. Defendants sometimes argue that copyright prohibits people from engaging in behavior that would normally be considered free speech. As we have seen throughout this book, copyright prohibits some people from printing and selling texts, performing music, writing certain stories, and displaying works of art. If Congress passed a law generally prohibiting people from doing these things, it is easy to imagine that the Supreme Court would use the First Amendment to invalidate the statute. Why then should such prohibitions be tolerated in the name of copyright?

As a general rule, courts reject the notion that copyright violates the First Amendment. This does not mean, however, that the First Amendment is irrelevant to copyright. Our next case contains a recent Supreme Court analysis of copyright's relationship to the First Amendment.

Eldred v. Ashcroft
537 U.S. 186 (2003)

JUSTICE GINSBURG delivered the opinion of the Court.

[This case involves a constitutional challenge to the Copyright Term Extension Act (CTEA), which added 20 years to the term of existing and future copyrighted works. The facts of the case, along with the Court's discussion of the argument that the CTEA violates Article I of the U.S. Constitution, are presented earlier in Chapter Four.]

III

Petitioners separately argue that the CTEA is a content-neutral regulation of speech that fails heightened judicial review under the First Amendment. We reject petitioners' plea for imposition of uncommonly strict scrutiny on a copyright scheme that incorporates its own speech-protective purposes and safeguards. The Copyright Clause and First Amendment were adopted close in time. This proximity indicates that, in the Framers' view, copyright's limited monopolies are compatible with free speech principles. Indeed, copyright's purpose is to promote the creation and publication of free expression. As *Harper & Row* observed: "[T]he Framers intended copyright itself to be the engine of free expression. By establishing a marketable right to the use of one's expression, copyright supplies the economic incentive to create and disseminate ideas."

In addition to spurring the creation and publication of new expression, copyright law contains built-in First Amendment accommodations. First, it distinguishes between ideas and expression and makes only the latter eligible for copyright protection. Specifically, 17 U.S.C. § 102(b) provides: "In no case does copyright protection for an original work of authorship extend to any idea, procedure, process, system, method of operation, concept, principle, or discovery, regardless of the form in which it is described, explained, illustrated, or embodied in such work." As we said in *Harper & Row*, this "idea/expression dichotomy strike[s] a definitional balance between the First Amendment and the Copyright Act by permitting free communication of facts while still protecting an author's expression." Due to this distinction, every idea, theory, and fact in a copyrighted work becomes instantly available for public exploitation at the moment of publication.

Second, the "fair use" defense allows the public to use not only facts and ideas contained in a copyrighted work, but also expression itself in certain circumstances. Codified at 17 U.S.C. § 107, the defense provides:

"[T]he fair use of a copyrighted work, including such use by reproduction in copies ..., for purposes such as criticism, comment, news reporting, teaching (including multiple copies for classroom use), scholarship, or research, is not an infringement of copyright." The fair use defense affords considerable "latitude for scholarship and comment." *Harper & Row*, 471 U.S. at 560. ...

Finally, the case petitioners principally rely upon for their First Amendment argument, *Turner Broadcasting System, Inc. v. FCC*, 522 U.S. 622 (1994), bears little on copyright. The statute at issue in *Turner* required cable operators to carry and transmit broadcast stations through their proprietary cable systems. Those "must-carry" provisions, we explained, implicated "the heart of the First Amendment," namely, "the principle that each person should decide for himself or herself the ideas and beliefs deserving of expression, consideration, and adherence." *Id.* at 641.

The CTEA, in contrast, does not oblige anyone to reproduce another's speech against the carrier's will. Instead, it protects authors' original expression from unrestricted exploitation. Protection of that order does not raise the free speech concerns present when the government compels or burdens the communication of particular facts or ideas. The First Amendment securely protects the freedom to make—or decline to make—one's own speech; it bears less heavily when speakers assert the right to make other people's speeches. To the extent such assertions raise First Amendment concerns, copyright's built-in free speech safeguards are generally adequate to address them. We recognize that the D.C. Circuit spoke too broadly when it declared copyrights "categorically immune from challenges under the First Amendment." But when, as in this case, Congress has not altered the traditional contours of copyright protection, further First Amendment scrutiny is unnecessary.

Notes and Questions

1. *Eldred* states that copyright law's "built-in free speech safeguards" are "generally adequate" to deal with any First Amendment issues. Accordingly, when Congress "has not altered the traditional contours of copyright protection," independent First Amendment scrutiny is unnecessary. What would it mean for Congress to alter "the traditional contours of copyright protection," and what would be the consequences? For example, would the First Amendment affect Congress' ability to repeal the fair use doctrine? *Cf. Universal City Studios, Inc. v. Corley*, 273 F.3d 429 (2d Cir. 2001) (rejecting First Amendment challenge to portions of the DMCA).

2. Does *Eldred*'s statement about changing the contours of copyright have implications for how judges decide ordinary copyright cases? For example, should courts make reference to First Amendment cases or

values when applying the fair use doctrine, or should courts ignore those things and rely solely on "internal" copyright principles? Here again, courts have generally discounted the need for explicit consideration of the First Amendment in copyright cases.[60] Do you agree?

3.   The U.S. Supreme Court revisited this issue in *Golan v. Holder*, 132 S. Ct. 873 (2011), shedding additional light on what constitutes "the traditional contours of copyright protection." In *Golan,*, the plaintiffs brought a constitutional challenge against the Uruguay Round Agreements Act (URAA). The URAA restored copyright protection for certain foreign films that had passed into the public domain as a result of a failure to comply with U.S. copyright formalities. The plaintiffs challenged the URAA, arguing that it "altered the traditional contours of copyright protection," by for the first time protecting works that had already passed into the public domain. The Supreme Court disagreed, holding that the URAA did not alter the "traditional countours" of copyright protection, insofar as it left intact both the fair use defense and the idea/expression dichotomy. In the wake of *Golan*, what sorts of changes would alter the "traditional contours" of copyright protection so as to trigger additional First Amendment scrutiny?

SECTION C. COPYRIGHT MISUSE

In recent years, some courts have begun to recognize a new defense to a copyright infringement suit: copyright misuse. The defense applies in cases where a copyright owner seeks, typically through licensing, to use the copyright to gain rights beyond those granted by the Act, in a way that violates public policy. If a court finds that the copyright owner has engaged in misuse, then the copyright will be unenforceable until the effects of the misuse have dissipated.

The defense does not appear anywhere in the text of the Copyright Act. Instead, it is an equitable defense, which courts have created by drawing an analogy to the more well-recognized doctrine of patent misuse. Patent misuse occurs when a patent holder attempts to leverage the patent to restrain competition in a separate market. In *Morton Salt v. G. S. Suppiger*, 314 U.S. 488 (1942), for example, the plaintiff Morton owned a patent on a salt-depositing machine and licensed the machine on the condition that licensees only use salt tablets sold by Morton. The Court found that this constituted patent misuse, insofar as it was an attempt by Morton to expand the scope of its patent to control the market for unpatented salt tablets. The Court found that this violated policies underlying the patent act.

---

[60] One notable exception is *Suntrust Bank v. Houghton Mifflin Co.*, 268 F.3d 1257 (11th Cir. 2001), in which the court reversed a district court's preliminary injunction barring sale of an allegedly infringing book on the grounds that the injunction was an unlawful prior restraint on a use which was likely to get fair use treatment. In so doing, the court stated that it was important to "remain cognizant of the First Amendment protection interwoven into copyright." *Id.* at 1265.

In *Lasercomb America v. Reynolds*, 911 F.2d 970, 972 (4th Cir. 1990), the court extended this reasoning, by analogy, to copyright cases. In *Lasercomb*, the plaintiff owned a copyright in a piece of die-making software and licensed it on the condition that licensees refrain from developing any competing die-making software. The *Lasercomb* court held that this was an attempt to control expression of the unprotected idea embodied in the software. The court accordingly refused to enforce the copyright on grounds of copyright misuse.

In *Alcatel USA v. DGI Technologies*, 166 F.3d 772 (5th Cir. 1999), the court found misuse in a case involving a software license that effectively prevented a competitor from reverse engineering the software to create a compatible piece of computer hardware. In that case, the plaintiff made and sold computerized switching systems used by long-distance telephone companies. The defendant made a piece of compatible hardware for these systems. In order to create this compatible hardware, the defendant downloaded from the switching system a copy of the plaintiff's operating system, which was subject to a restrictive license. Although the license did not expressly forbid other companies from making compatible products, the court held that the restrictive license had the same practical effect by limiting the ability of third parties to copy and analyze the operating system software. The court concluded that this was an improper attempt to use copyright law to restrict competition in the market for unprotected hardware, and that this constituted misuse.

Notes and Questions

1.   The precise scope of the misuse defense remains somewhat uncertain. Many copyright licensing agreements restrict the activities of the licensees in various ways. What kinds of restrictions improperly extend the copyright in ways that violate public policy?

In *Lasercomb*, mentioned above, the court found misuse when the software license barred the licensee from writing its own competitive software, holding that the license improperly allowed the copyright owner to protect the idea of the software. What other kinds of licensing agreements would constitute misuse? What about a license that required a licensee not to disclose proprietary information found in the software? What about a license that required a licensee to give up certain fair use rights, such as reverse engineering?

On this score, consider *Video Pipeline v. Buena Vista Home Entertainment*, 342 F.3d 191 (3d Cir. 2003). In that case, Disney entered into licensing agreements with a number of websites, under which such sites could deliver preview trailers of Disney movies via hyperlinks. As part of the license, the websites promised that: "The Website in which the Trailers are used may not be derogatory or critical of the entertainment industry or of [Disney] ... or of any motion picture produced or distributed by [Disney]. ... The defendant argued that the clause represented copyright misuse, insofar as it sought to suppress criticism and free speech.

The court recognized that an attempt to suppress criticism could potentially subvert and undermine broader policies underlying copyright law more generally. In this case, however, the court found no grounds to believe that the provision in question would have the effect of hindering creative expression to such an extent as to amount to misuse.

2. How is misuse related to antitrust law? To some extent, misuse gets at some of the same concerns about anti-competitive conduct. Yet it is clear that copyright misuse encompasses activities that would not otherwise constitute an antitrust violation. Some commentators have argued that courts should do away with misuse and rely solely upon antitrust law to police the behavior of copyright owners.

3. The misuse doctrine has not been recognized by all circuits. The doctrine was applied by the Ninth Circuit in a more typical copyright case: *Practice Management Information Corp. v. American Medical Assoc.*, 121 F.3d 516 (9th Cir. 1997). In that case, the AMA asserted a copyright over a coding system for medical procedures. It licensed the system to the federal Health Care Financing Administration on the condition that the agency not use any competing system. The AMA then sued a company that sought to publish the coding system without authorization. The court in that case held that the AMA had engaged in copyright misuse. Other courts, however, have expressed some skepticism regarding the viability of copyright misuse. *See, e.g., Saturday Evening Post v. Rumbleseat Press*, 816 F.2d 1191, 1200 (7th Cir. 1987) (expressing some doubt as to extending copyright misuse beyond what would be proscribed under anti-trust laws).

4. Copyright misuse is a defense to an infringement action. It should be noted that the defendant need not be subject to the improper licensing term that forms the basis for the misuse allegation. That is, a defendant can point to a licensing agreement with a third party as the grounds for misuse, as was the case in *Alcatel* above. Note also that a successful misuse defense does not invalidate the copyright. The copyright is still valid. However, the plaintiff cannot enforce it until the effects of the misuse have been dissipated.

SECTION D. OTHER DEFENSES

In addition to the major defenses noted above, copyright law also contains a number of additional defenses that are worth mentioning briefly here.

1. ABANDONMENT

If a copyright owner abandons his or her copyright, then that owner can no longer enforce the copyright. The requirements for abandonment, however, are quite strict. There must be an intent to abandon the copyright, usually evinced by some overt act, such as a statement to that effect. Merely posting the work on the Internet, distributing it for free, or failing to enforce the copyright is not generally sufficient to amount to abandonment. Thus, copyright is unlike trademark law, where failure to enforce the mark can often lead to abandonment.

2. STATUTE OF LIMITATIONS

Section 507(b) of the Copyright Act states: "No civil action shall be maintained under the [Act] unless it is commenced within three years after the claim accrued."[61] The Copyright Act thus establishes a three-year statute of limitations period for civil copyright claims.

This might lead one to think that, once a copyright owner is made aware of an act of infringement, he or she must take action within three years or lose the right to bring a claim forever. However, under the "separate accrual" rule, a new claim accrues each time the defendant engages in a new act of infringement. Thus, even if a defendant first infringed upon a copyrighted work 20 years ago (say, by creating an unauthorized movie version of a literary work), if that defendant continues to infringe upon an exclusive right today (say, by selling a copy of that movie to the public), each new act of infringement starts a new three-year limitations period. The practical effect is to make it possible to bring a civil suit based on a long-past initial act of infringement, so long as the infringing work continues to be exploited today.

Note that the three-year limitations period does have the effect of limiting the relief available to the plaintiff. The plaintiff will only be able to recover damages for acts that occurred within three years prior to the filing of the suit, since any claims based on earlier acts of infringement would be barred by the limitations period. Thus, if the work had been exploited for 20 years, the plaintiff may only be entitled to damages for the most recent three years. However, prospective injunctive relief would certainly still be available, e.g. an order barring future exploitation of the infringing work.

Recently, the U.S. Supreme Court considered whether a long delay might bar a civil suit under the separate equitable doctrine of laches, which generally prevents parties from bringing certain types of civil claims when a delay unfairly prejudices the defendant. The case, *Petrella v. Metro-Goldwyn-Mayer*, 134 S.Ct. 1962 (2014), involved the movie

---

[61] Note that this provision sets forth a separate five-year statute of limitations period for criminal actions.

"Raging Bull," directed by Martin Scorsese, starring Robert DeNiro, and based on a screenplay written by Frank Petrella. Petrella wrote the screenplay in 1963 and assigned the copyright to MGM, which then released the movie in 1980 and continued to market the film in subsequent years. Petrella died during the initial copyright term, and the renewal right passed to his daughter, who renewed the copyright in 1991, thus effectively terminating the assignment to MGM. Even though MGM continued to exploit the work after renewal, the daughter did not file suit until 2009, nearly 18 years after her claim first accrued.

Under the separate accrual rule, Petrella (the daughter) could still bring suit for damages incurred during the preceding three years, as well as for an injunction barring future distribution and use of the movie. MGM argued that, even if the suit was not barred by the statute of limitations, it should be barred by the equitable doctrine of laches, because the delay had prejudiced MGM's interests. The Supreme Court, however, disagreed. With respect to the claim for damages, the Court refused to impose a limitation via laches where Congress had expressly set forth a limitations period in the Copyright Act. The Court noted that the limitations period, by imposing a three-year limit on retrospective damages, already took into account any concerns about prejudicial delay in bringing a lawsuit.

With respect to injunctive relief, the Court left open the possibility that, in extraordinary circumstances, a long unjustified delay could affect or curtail the equitable relief available to the plaintiff. Thus, for example, where a plaintiff, although aware of a potential infringement, sits back and allows the defendant to invest significantly in the infringing work, only to later sue for impoundment and destruction of all copies of the infringing work, a court may properly refuse to order such relief. Absent such circumstances, however, laches would not ordinarily stand in the way of prospective injunctive relief.

3. FRAUD ON THE COPYRIGHT OFFICE

Fraudulent statements made to the copyright office during the registration of a work can also be a defense to a copyright infringement action. Such fraudulent statements can be sufficient to invalidate the copyright registration. Since registration is a pre-requisite to filing an infringement action, such a fraud can effectively prevent enforcement of the copyright.

Chapter Seven

THIRD PARTY LIABILITY

Thus far, we have focused on doctrines that impose copyright liability on parties that engage in acts of infringement. In this chapter, we consider doctrines that impose copyright liability on parties who do not commit infringement themselves, but assist or are otherwise connected to acts that are infringing. Although the Copyright Act does not explicitly provide for third party copyright liability, the courts created such liability by analogizing to similar doctrines in tort law and agency law. Congress has since accepted the long standing judicial practice of imposing such liability in certain circumstances.

Understanding third party copyright liability requires appreciation of how its doctrines have developed in response to various types of disputes. When the courts first developed the doctrines, the typical dispute involved a defendant who did business with one or more persons who committed copyright infringement. In most of these cases, the amount of infringement was relatively limited. As you will soon see, the seminal cases involved actions against a chain of department stores and an agency that represented and promoted performing artists. Vicarious and contributory liability did a reasonable, if not perfect, job of handling these cases.

All of this changed in the late 20th century as the rise of modern electronics made it possible for a single business to facilitate thousands, if not millions, of infringers. Increasing sales of photocopy machines and video cassette recorders made it easy for ordinary individuals to make unauthorized copies of copyrighted works on demand. This problem has become even more widespread with the development of personal computers and the Internet, particularly because these technologies make the mass duplication and distribution of copyrighted works extremely fast and inexpensive.

The difficulty of enforcing copyrights against numerous and often anonymous individual infringers has led copyright owners to assert claims against intermediaries that facilitate or are in some way connected with infringing activity. Why sue thousands, or even millions, of elusive Internet users when a single action against an Internet service provider ("ISP") or the manufacturer of a copying technology like the VCR could achieve equal or superior results? Imposing liability on third parties such as ISPs would, in many cases, effectively reduce infringement because entities like ISPs will respond to the threat of liability by controlling the behavior of their customers. At the same time, however, it must be noted that the very products and services that support infringement also facilitate entirely legitimate activities. If third parties respond to the threat of liability by withdrawing services or products from the market, it is entirely possible that they will simultaneously reduce infringement and legitimate, perfectly legal behavior.

Not surprisingly, the controversy surrounding modern third party copyright liability place considerable pressure on the doctrines of vicarious and contributory liability. This chapter presents these doctrines, along with the basic policy questions they raise. It then explores the challenges posed by modern electronics and the Internet before turning to legislative responses that may or may not adequately deal with the problems in question.

SECTION A. VICARIOUS LIABILITY

Shapiro, Bernstein & Co. v. H. L. Green Co.
316 F.2d 304 (2d Cir. 1963)

KAUFMAN, Circuit Judge.

This action for copyright infringement presents us with a picture all too familiar in copyright litigation: a legal problem vexing in its difficulty, a dearth or squarely applicable precedents, a business setting so common that the dearth of precedents seems inexplicable, and an almost complete absence of guidance from the terms of the Copyright Act. The plaintiffs in the court below, appellants here, are the copyright proprietors of several musical compositions, recordings of which have met with considerable popularity, especially amongst the younger set. ...

Jalen operated the phonograph record department as concessionaire in twenty-three stores of defendant H. L. Green Co., Inc., pursuant to written licenses from the Green Company. The complaint alleged that Green was liable for copyrights infringement because it "sold, or contributed to and participated actively in the sale of" the so-called "bootleg" records manufactured by Jalen and sold by Jalen in the Green stores.

The District Judge, after trial, found Jalen liable as manufacturer of the "bootleg" records. ... He concluded, however, that Green had not sold any of the phonograph records and was not liable for any sales made by Jalen; he accordingly dismissed the complaint as to Green. Jalen takes no appeal, but plaintiffs come before us to challenge the dismissal of the claims asserted against Green. The validity of those claims depends upon a detailed examination of the relationship between Green and the conceded infringer Jalen.

At the time of suit, Jalen had been operating under license from Green the phonograph record department in twenty-three of its stores, in some for as long as thirteen years. The licensing agreements provided that Jalen and its employees were to "abide by, observe and obey all rules and regulations promulgated from time to time by H. L. Green Company, Inc. * * *" Green, in its "unreviewable discretion", had the authority to discharge any employee believed to be conducting himself improperly. Jalen, in turn, agreed to save Green harmless from any claims arising in connection with the conduct of the phonograph record concession. Significantly, the licenses provided that Green was to receive a percentage—in some cases 10%, in others 12%—of Jalen's gross receipts from the sale of records, as its full compensation as licensor.

In the actual day-to-day functioning of the record department, Jalen ordered and purchased all records, was billed for them, and paid for them. All sales were made by Jalen employees, who, as the District Court found, were under the effective control and supervision of Jalen. All of the daily proceeds from record sales went into Green's cash registers and were removed therefrom by the cashier of the store. At regular accounting periods, Green deducted its 10% or 12% Commission and deducted the salaries of the Jalen employees, which salaries were handed over by the Green cashier to one of Jalen's employees to be distributed to the others. Social security and withholding taxes were withheld from the salaries of the employees by Green, and the withholdings then turned over to Jalen. Only then was the balance of the gross receipts of the record department given to Jalen. Customers purchasing records were given a receipt on a printed form marked "H. L. Green Company, Inc."; Jalen's name was wholly absent from the premises. The District Judge found that Green did not actively participate in the sale of the records and that it had no knowledge of the unauthorized manufacture of the records.

... [W]e hold that appellee Green is liable for the sale of the infringing "bootleg" records, and we therefore reverse the judgment dismissing the complaint and remand for a determination of damages.

Section 101(e) of the Copyright Act makes unlawful the "unauthorized manufacture, use, or sale" of phonograph records. Because of the open-ended terminology of the section, and the related section 1(e), courts have had to trace, case by case, a pattern of business relationships which would render one person liable for the infringing conduct of another. It is quite clear, for example, that the normal agency rule of *respondeat superior* applies to copyright infringement by a servant within the scope of his employment. Realistically, the courts have not drawn a rigid line between the strict cases of agency, and those of independent contract, license, and lease. Many of the elements which have given rise to the doctrine of *respondeat superior* may also be evident in factual settings other than that of a technical employer-employee relationship. When the right and ability to supervise coalesce with an obvious and direct financial interest in the exploitation of copyrighted materials— even in the absence of actual knowledge that the copyright monopoly is being impaired, the purposes of copyright law may be best effectuated by the imposition of liability upon the beneficiary of that exploitation.

The two lines of precedent most nearly relevant to the case before us are those which deal, on the one hand, with the landlord leasing his property at a fixed rental to a tenant who engages in copyright-infringing conduct on the leased premises and, on the other hand, the proprietor or manager of a dance hall or music hall leasing his premises to or hiring a dance band, which brings in customers and profits to the proprietor by performing copyrighted music but without complying with the terms of the Copyright Act. If the landlord lets his premises without knowledge of the impending infringement by his tenant, exercises no supervision over him, charges a fixed rental and receives no other benefit from the infringement, and contributes in no way to it, it has been held that the landlord is not liable for his tenant's wrongdoing. But, the cases are legion which hold the dance hall proprietor liable for the infringement of copyright resulting from the performance of a musical composition by a band or orchestra whose activities provide the proprietor with a source of customers and enhanced income. He is liable whether the bandleader is considered, as a technical matter, an employee or an independent contractor, and whether or not the proprietor has knowledge of the compositions to be played or any control over their selection.

We believe that the principle which can be extracted from the dance hall cases is a sound one and, under the facts of the cases before us, is here applicable. Those cases and this one lie closer on the spectrum to the employer-employee model than to the landlord-tenant model. Green licensed one facet of its variegated business enterprise, for some thirteen years, to the Jalen Amusement Company. Green retained the ultimate right of supervision over the conduct of the record concession and its employees. By reserving for itself a proportionate share of the gross receipts from Jalen's sales of phonograph records, Green had a most definite financial interest in the success of Jalen's concession; 10% or 12% of the sales price of every record sold by Jalen, whether "bootleg" or legitimate, found its way—both literally and figuratively—into the coffers of the Green Company. We therefore conclude, on the particular facts before us, that Green's relationship to its infringing licensee, as well as its strong concern for the financial success of the phonograph record concession, renders it liable for the unauthorized sales of the "bootleg" records.

The imposition of liability upon the Green Company, even in the absence of an intention to infringe or knowledge of infringement, is not unusual. As one observer has noted, "Although copyright infringements are quite generally termed piracy, only a minority of infringers fly the Jolly Roger." While there have been some complaints concerning the harshness of the principle of strict liability in copyright law, courts have consistently refused to honor the defense of absence of knowledge or intention. The reasons have been variously stated. "The protection accorded literary property would be of little value if * * * insulation from payment of damages could be secured * * * by merely refraining from making inquiry." *De Acosta v. Brown*, 146 F.2d at 412. "It is the innocent infringer who must suffer, since he, unlike the copyright owner, either has an opportunity to guard against the infringement (by diligent inquiry), or at least the ability to guard against the infringement (by an indemnity agreement * * * and/or by insurance)." Letter from Melville B. Nimmer to the Copyright Office, in Study No. 25 Prepared for the Subcommittee on Patents, Trademarks, and Copyrights of the Senate Comm. on the Judiciary, 86th Cong., 2nd Sess. 169 (Latman & Tager, "Liability of Innocent Infringers of Copyrights.")

For much the same reasons, the imposition of vicarious liability in the case before us cannot be deemed unduly harsh or unfair. Green has the power to police carefully the conduct of its concessionaire Jalen; our judgment will simply encourage it to do so, thus placing responsibility where it can and should be effectively exercised. Green's burden will not be unlike that quite commonly imposed upon publishers, printers, and vendors of copyrighted materials. Indeed, the record in this case reveals that the "bootleg" recordings were somewhat suspicious on their face; they bore no name of any manufacturer upon the labels or on the record jackets, as is customary in the trade. Moreover, plaintiffs' agent and attorneys wrote to Green in March and April 1958, requesting information regarding certain of the "bootleg" records and finally, upon receiving no reply from Green, threatening to institute suit for copyright infringement. The suit was in fact commenced the following month. Although these last-recited facts are not essential to our holding of copyright infringement by Green, they reinforce our conclusion that in many cases, the party found strictly liable is in a position to police the conduct of the "primary" infringer. Were we to hold otherwise, we might foresee the prospect—not wholly unreal—of large chain and department stores establishing "dummy" concessions and shielding their own eyes from the possibility of copyright infringement, thus creating a buffer against liability while reaping the proceeds of infringement.

Even if a fairly constant system of surveillance is thought too burdensome, Green is in the position to safeguard itself in a less arduous manner against liability resulting from the conduct of its concessionaires. It has in fact done so, by incorporating a save-harmless provision in its licensing agreements with Jalen. Surely the beneficent purposes of the copyright law would be advanced by placing the jeopardy of Jalen's insolvency upon Green rather than upon the proprietor of the copyright. ...

Reversed and remanded.

Notes and Questions

1. This chapter presents vicarious liability first because its elements and rationale are relatively clear. Nevertheless, the complexities and challenges associated with third party copyright liability emerge quickly. Courts routinely cite *Shapiro* for the proposition that vicarious liability depends on the defendant's "right and ability to supervise" the primary infringer and "an obvious and direct financial interest" in the infringement. These elements do not, in and of themselves, define the scope of liability. At one end of a spectrum, courts could limit liability to cases where the defendant has a relationship with the primary infringer similar to the principal/agent relationship that establishes *respondeat superior* liability. At the other end of the spectrum, courts could extend liability to any defendant who has the ability to influence an infringer as part of a business relationship motivated by profit. Where along this spectrum does *Shapiro* place the law of vicarious copyright liability? The Second Circuit compared the well-accepted precedents of dance hall cases and landlord/tenant cases. What distinguishes dance hall proprietors from landlords for purposes of vicarious liability, and how, if at all, does this limit the scope of such liability?

2. Regardless of how you interpret *Shapiro*, be aware that courts have not agreed about the scope of vicarious liability. For example, they have imposed and refused to impose liability on corporate parents for infringement by subsidiaries and trade show organizers for infringement by exhibitors. Accordingly, copyright lawyers must become familiar with the reasons courts might prefer to restrict or expand the scope of vicarious liability because they will have to persuade courts that certain lines of precedent are normatively superior to others. Do you favor expanding or restricting the scope of vicarious liability, and why? The following case will give you some food for thought.

Polygram International Publishing v. Nevada/Tig
855 F. Supp. 1314 (D. Mass 1994)

KEETON, District Judge.

... Plaintiffs are members of the American Society of Composers, Authors, and Publishers (ASCAP) and are the copyright holders of ten songs played by various exhibitors and entertainers at a computer trade show and awards ceremony. Defendants organized the trade show and co-sponsored the awards ceremony. Plaintiffs seek to hold defendants liable under the federal Copyright Act, 17 U.S.C. § 101 *et. seq.*, for ten counts of copyright infringement based on performances of copyrighted music by the exhibitors and entertainers. ...

[Editors' note: The court held that no liability existed because the plaintiff did not have sufficient evidence of underlying infringement by exhibitors. Nevertheless, because of the possibility of reversal on this issue, the court also issued a ruling on the issue of vicarious liability.]

II. Findings of Historical Fact

Defendant Nevada/TIG, Inc. was dismissed from this case by stipulation (Docket No. 21). The two remaining defendants, Interface Group-Massachusetts, Inc. and Interface Group-Nevada, Inc. (collectively "Interface") organize and promote major conventions and trade shows, including the world's largest trade show for the computer industry, "COMDEX/Fall."

The plaintiffs are members of the American Society of Composers, Authors, and Publishers (ASCAP), and have granted to ASCAP the non-exclusive right to license public performances of their copyrighted musical compositions. ...

Almost two years before the COMDEX/Fall show, ASCAP communicated with Interface in the hope of entering into a license agreement that would authorize performances of any of the copyrighted music in the ASCAP repertory at Interface's trade shows. ASCAP has licensed other trade show organizers, but despite repeated offers by ASCAP, Interface did not obtain a similar trade show license, which would have cost about $ 4,000 for the COMDEX/Fall show. Interface states that it believed no license was necessary for the COMDEX/Fall show because Interface itself did not intend to perform any music.

The COMDEX/Fall show was held in October, 1991, in Las Vegas. The show occupied over 2.5 million square feet in seven separate convention centers and hotels. Over 2,000 exhibitors rented space from Interface for exhibition booths from which they could display their wares. Exhibitors were responsible for the content of their booths, but they were required to abide by the general Rules and Regulations established by Interface. Rule 1 of these Rules and Regulations forbids exhibitors from using music at a volume that might intrude upon adjacent exhibit areas, and advises exhibitors that it is their responsibility to obtain proper copyright licenses from ASCAP or other licensing authorities for any music played.

During the five days of the show, about 132,000 persons attended. Two of these attendees were investigators for ASCAP, who overheard copyrighted music of the plaintiffs being performed at five exhibition booths. ...

Interface derived its profit from COMDEX/Fall from three sources: booth rentals at $35.95 per square foot, admission fee charges of $75 per person for attendees, and advertising revenues. Gross revenues from these three sources at COMDEX/Fall exceeded $44 million. Interface did not earn any revenue directly from any business activity generated at exhibitors' booths. ...

IV. Vicarious Liability

 A. In General

In *Shapiro, Bernstein & Co. v. H.L. Green Co.*, 316 F.2d 304 (2d Cir. 1963), the Second Circuit articulated what has become the acknowledged standard for a finding of vicarious liability in the context of copyright infringement:

> When the right and ability to supervise coalesce with an obvious and direct financial interest in the exploitation of copyrighted materials—even in the absence of actual knowledge that the copyright monopoly is being impaired—the purposes of copyright law may be best effectuated by the imposition of liability upon the beneficiary of that exploitation.

The court derived these two elements—the right and ability to supervise and an obvious and direct financial interest—from two contrasting lines of precedent under the copyright laws. Under one set of cases, in which landlords were exempted from liability for the copyright infringements of their tenants, the court noted that the landlords received only a fixed rental fee from the tenants, did not know of the tenants' copyright infringements, did not supervise the tenants, and received no financial benefit from the infringements.

Under the other line of cases, the so-called "dance hall cases," the owners of nightclubs and similar establishments were held vicariously liable for the infringement of musical copyrights by bands performing at the club. ...

The court in *Shapiro, Bernstein* was faced with a question similar to the one before this court: where along the spectrum of fact patterns from nightclub to landlord does the defendant stand? ...

Like the court in *Shapiro, Bernstein*, I conclude that the defendant in this case, in its relation to the exhibitors, lies closer on the spectrum to the nightclub and department store than to the landlord. Indeed, although Interface's computer show may not evoke this image, another trade show organizer and its exhibitors might aptly fit the model foreseen by the Second Circuit of a large organization establishing "dummy" concessions that buffer the organization from liability for profitable infringements. Picture, for example, a fashion trade show at which each exhibitor played copyrighted music while its models walked the runway. If the organizer of this hypothetical trade show had contractual control over its exhibitors, arranged the audience for the exhibitors, and derived a profit from the exhibitors through rents, a cover charge, and advertising, it would be well within the precedents to hold the organizer vicariously liable for the copyright infringements of its exhibitors. Interface is in a position not materially different.

Before demonstrating how the elements of benefit and control apply to the facts of this case, I pause briefly to examine, first, the history and the policy justifications behind the legal theory of vicarious liability, second, a description of vicarious liability in the context of copyright infringement that appears in the House Report on the Copyright Act of 1976, and third, questions arising from the development of this view of vicarious liability for copyright infringement.

B. History of and Justification for Vicarious Liability

The *Shapiro, Bernstein* court's inclusion of a policy justification for vicarious liability along with its discussion of the two elements of benefit and control reflects the now common recognition in other areas of the law that vicarious liability rests, in part at least, on a policy foundation relating to risk allocation. Even in copyright cases, in which the touchstones of benefit and control have become the defining elements for vicarious liability, we nevertheless are considering "the broader problem of identifying the circumstances in which it is just to hold one individual accountable for the acts of another." *Sony Corp. of America v. Universal City Studios, Inc.*, 464 U.S. 417, 435 (1984).

The theory of vicarious liability developed from the law of agency, specifically employer-employee relationships, in which the "master" was held strictly liable for the torts of a "servant." Various legal concepts were fashioned to explain this liability, including the concepts of "control," "right to control," and "manner and means of performance." *See* Restatement (Second) of Agency, § 220(2).

Modern decisions, when explaining policy justifications for vicarious liability rather than merely citing precedent, commonly refer to risk allocation. When an individual seeks to profit from an enterprise in which identifiable types of losses are expected to occur, it is ordinarily fair and reasonable to place responsibility for those losses on the person who profits, even if that person makes arrangements for others to perform the acts that foreseeably cause the losses. The law of vicarious liability treats the expected losses as simply another cost of doing business. The enterprise and the person profiting from it are better able than either the innocent injured plaintiff or the person whose act caused the loss to distribute the costs and to shift them to others who have profited from the enterprise. In addition, placing responsibility for the loss on the enterprise has the added benefit of creating a greater incentive for the enterprise to police its operations carefully to avoid unnecessary losses.

This background of policy justifications for vicarious liability serves to place in context the two elements of benefit and control derived from the previous case law by the court in *Shapiro, Bernstein*. By focusing on benefit received from and control over an enterprise, a court can evaluate the defendant's ability to spread losses and police conduct within the enterprise, as well as the underlying fairness of holding the defendant liable.

The distinctive version of vicarious liability that has developed in the context of copyright omits the requirement, common elsewhere in the law of vicarious liability, that the right and ability to control extend to the "manner and means of performance." This distinctive variation is understandable, however, and is consistent with the policy foundations, as long as the right of control extends far enough to give the person (or entity) who is to be held vicariously liable a veto over performing any music at all, if authorization of the copyright holder can not be established. ...

E.   The Right and Ability to Supervise or Control

In determining that a defendant meets the "control" (or "supervision") prong of the test for vicarious liability, courts have ... adopted terms similar to those described in the legislative record of the amendments to the Copyright Act of 1976. That is, defendants are found to have "control" over a performance if they "either actively operate or supervise the operation of the place wherein the performances occur, *or* control the content of the infringing program." House Report, 159-60 (emphasis added).

Taking into consideration this body of case law, I find, as a factfinder engaged in adjudicative fact finding, that Interface had a right and ability to control and supervise its exhibitors, as those terms are used in the context of vicarious liability in copyright cases.

I base this finding in part on my evaluation of the weight and materiality of the stipulated facts that (1) Interface exercised authority and control over its exhibitors through its Rules and Regulations and (2) the exhibitors were bound to follow these rules. Also, I base this finding in part on my evaluation of the weight and materiality of the following facts drawn from submitted affidavits and depositions.

First, the vice-president of Interface, Richard Schwab, acknowledged in his deposition that Interface could have altered its Rules and Regulations to prohibit music at COMDEX/Fall, but it did not. Instead, Interface chose only to prohibit music at levels that were intrusive to other exhibitors, and advised exhibitors to obtain proper licenses for any music they did play.

Second, Mr. Schwab states in his affidavit that during the COMDEX/Fall show, 10 to 12 Interface employees walked the aisles to ensure "rules compliance." Although Mr. Schwab believes it would be impractical to police the show for all rules violations, it is clear from Mr. Schwab's statement that Interface was actively involved in managing the show and did not function as an absentee landlord. For example, Interface employees were available during the show to address exhibitor needs and to answer exhibitor complaints, including complaints about exhibitors encroaching on other space or blocking aisles during the show.

Third, the COMDEX Rules and Regulations further demonstrate the extent of Interface's control over its exhibitors. Under these rules, Interface could restrict exhibits that "because of noise, method of operation, materials or any other reason become objectionable." (Exhibit 1, p. 2-2.) In addition, Interface reserved the right to police exhibitors during the show:

> Show Management may prohibit or remove any Exhibit which, in the opinion of Show Management, detracts from the general character of the Exposition as a whole, or consists of products or services inconsistent with the purpose of the Exposition.

> This reservation includes persons, things, conduct, printed matter and anything of a character which Show Management determines objectionable.

Exhibit 1, p. 2-2. Interface also exercised control over details such as the distribution of food and drink from booths, the design and construction of booths, and the use of video cameras. *Id.* pp. 2-3 to 2-22.

Based on my evaluation of all the evidence before me, I find that Interface actively supervised the COMDEX/Fall show where the five allegedly infringing performances occurred at exhibitor booths. In addition, I find that Interface had the contractual ability to control these allegedly infringing performances. ...

F. Financial Benefit

The second prong of the test for vicarious liability, as stated in *Shapiro, Bernstein*, requires that the defendant have a "direct financial interest in the exploitation of copyrighted materials." 316 F.2d at 307. As with determinations of "control," courts have not formulated an explicit test for determining whether a benefit to a defendant is "direct," perhaps in part because, as the case law demonstrates, it is difficult to define and measure the "direct" financial benefit that a performance of music confers.

For example, in cases interpreting the earlier Copyright Act that included a requirement that the infringing public performance be for profit, courts determined that profit could be inferred from the very fact of playing music in a profit-making establishment. ...

The primary formulation of the requirement that the financial benefit be "direct" appears in *Shapiro, Bernstein*, in which the infringement involved the sale of records rather than the performance of music. The court in that case was able to conclude that the defendant had a direct financial interest in the infringing activity based on defendant's receipt of a percentage of the sales. In cases involving the performance of music, however, courts have sometimes relied on an inferred, overall benefit that a performance of music confers on an establishment, rather than attempting to discern the "direct" benefit. ...

Perhaps courts have assumed that music provides an overall benefit to an establishment and have avoided exploring the "direct" benefit from an exploited copyright because, in the particular case of music, the benefit from a performance, though clearly existing, is often unmeasurable. For example, it is widely accepted that restaurant owners may be held vicariously liable for infringing performances by musicians, but how many minutes of music per meal does it take to show that the financial benefit to a restaurant is "direct"? Or, as another example, in this circuit the infringing performances of a band resulted in liability for a race track owner that wanted to "entertain its patrons when they were not absorbed in watching the races." *Famous Music*, 554 F.2d at 1214. If the vicarious liability standard of *Shapiro, Bernstein* were applied, would the adequacy of proof that the financial benefit is "direct" depend on evidence about the length of the musical interludes and how many patrons, if any, listened to the music?

Rather than purporting to measure the benefits of a musical performance and determine whether they are "direct," some courts, it appears, have implicitly adopted a position like that described in the legislative history of the 1976 amendments to the Copyright Act. Instead of rigidly requiring that a financial interest be "direct," these courts have imposed vicarious liability based on a determination that the defendants "expect commercial gain from the operation and either direct or indirect benefit from the infringing performance." House Report, 159-60. This two-part test—commercial gain from the overall operation and either a direct or indirect financial benefit from the infringement itself—serves to limit vicarious infringement to the activities of those who in some measure profit from the infringement, while at the same time defining the benefit from the infringing activity itself in a manner that allows the court to acknowledge the more intangible, indirect benefits from performances.

Having reviewed the case law, I find as an adjudicative fact that Interface derived a financial benefit from the infringing performances of its exhibitors, and that this benefit was of a kind that meets the requirement that it be "direct," in the sense in which that term appears in the cases that phrase the requirement as one of "direct financial benefit." I find also that Interface expected commercial gain from the COMDEX/Fall show and received from the performances by exhibitors a benefit of a kind called "direct" in some of the precedents, though more likely to be perceived as "indirect" by a person unfamiliar with the precedents.

I reach these evaluative findings for the following reasons: First, Interface expected commercial benefit from the COMDEX/Fall show and received over $44 million in gross revenues. Second, Interface's Trade Show President Jason Chudnofsky acknowledged that at many other trade shows, music is an "integral part of the production." Although he does not believe music is important at COMDEX shows, I reach a different finding based on the deposition testimony of Richard Schwab, who asserted that banning music at COMDEX/Fall would be "a dramatic change from our standard operating procedure" and therefore would have been "non-competitive and unnecessarily irksome to exhibitors."

Third, I infer from Mr. Schwab's statement about communication that music may be used "to communicate with attendees" at the show. Since communicating with attendees and cultivating their interest in one's products is the entire purpose for exhibitors at the trade show, I find that when music assists in this communication, it provides a financial benefit to the show of a kind that satisfies the financial benefit prong of the test for vicarious liability, just as music that enhances a meal provides that kind of benefit to a restaurant. ...

Based on the lean record in this case, I find as an adjudicative fact that Interface derived a benefit from the exhibitors' music that was substantial enough to be considered significant in determining whether the financial benefit prong of the test for vicarious liability has been satisfied. ...

Notes and Questions

1. Is *Polygram* consistent with *Shapiro*? In particular, did *Polygram* leave the elements of vicarious liability unchanged from *Shapiro*, or did it alter them, however subtly? With respect to control, Judge Keeton paid considerable attention to hypothetical contractual provisions the defendants could have insisted upon. With respect to financial benefit, Judge Keeton asserted that the defendants had the necessary interest in the exhibitors' infringements because music assisted the exhibitors' communication with conference attendees, thereby making the overall show more successful. Was Judge Keeton right in giving significance to these items, and if so, what were the consequences of doing so for the scope of vicarious liability?

2. *Polygram* offered justifications for vicarious liability similar to those given for enterprise liability in modern tort law. One set of arguments noted the beneficial consequences of liability. Judge Keeton asserted that the enterprises held liable are better than injured copyright holders at raising compensation for infringement and spreading losses. Vicarious liability also gives those held liable the incentive to prevent infringement. Do you agree with Judge Keeton, and if so, to what extent? If you are skeptical about the benefits of vicarious liability, do you doubt the truth of Judge Keeton's arguments, or are you worried that vicarious liability sometimes imposes social costs that offset these benefits? How might such costs arise?

3. *Polygram* also justified its result as a matter of fairness. According to Judge Keeton, "[w]hen an individual seeks to profit from an enterprise in which identifiable losses are expected to occur, it is ordinarily fair and reasonable to place responsibility for those losses on the person who profits." What exactly does this statement mean, and do you agree with it? For example, consider the number of for-profit enterprises that will eventually facilitate copyright infringement by others. An Internet

service provider will eventually have a subscriber who commits infringement. Manufacturers of personal music players will eventually sell to people who load infringing copies of music onto their players. Office supply stores will eventually sell paper and computer disks to people who commit infringement. Even the electric company will inevitably sell electricity to people who use it to commit infringement. Is it "fair and reasonable" to place responsibility for infringement on these enterprises?

4. Consider the factual scenarios that support enterprise liability in tort, such as *respondeat superior* and strict products liability. Are these scenarios truly similar to those that arise in copyright? If you can think of situations in which the justifications offered by *Polygram* truly support liability, do the elements of control and financial interest effectively identify those situations for courts and potential litigants?

SECTION B. CONTRIBUTORY LIABILITY

A & M Records v. Abdallah
948 F. Supp. 1449 (C.D. Cal. 1996)

LAUGHLIN E. WATERS, Senior District Judge.

On February 24, 1994, twenty-six major record companies sued numerous corporations and individuals, including Mohammed Abdallah, who were allegedly engaging in copyright and trademark infringement. The other defendants either failed to respond to the complaint or settled, but the case against Mr. Abdallah proceeded to trial. Mr. Abdallah is the president and sole owner of defendant General Audio Video Cassettes, Inc. ("GAVC"), a California corporation that sells blank audiotapes and duplicating equipment. ...

Plaintiffs are twenty-six major record companies in the United States, doing business in Los Angeles, California. Together they own the copyrights and trademarks for the 156 sound recordings and 24 trade names that are listed in Appendices A and B attached hereto.

Defendant Mohammed Abdallah is the president and sole owner of GAVC. GAVC is a California corporation doing business in California, with a branch office in New Jersey. GAVC sells empty cassette cartridges, spools of blank recording tape, audio duplicating equipment, and "time-loaded" audio tapes. A "time-loaded" audio tape is a tape that runs for a certain time period that is specified by the customer. For example, a customer would order 10,000 tapes with a playing time of 27 minutes and 45 seconds, and GAVC would then assemble 10,000 cassette tapes of that length out of blank recording tape and empty cassette cartridges using tape loading machines.

Between 1990 and 1992, GAVC sold time-loaded audio tapes to defendants Rizik Muslet, Mohammed Issa Halisi, and Mohammed Alabed. These individuals used the time-loaded audio tapes to illegally counterfeit the plaintiffs' copyrighted works. ... These individuals also packaged these counterfeit tapes in cassette cartridges using insert cards with the plaintiffs' trademarks. The counterfeiters were never licensed to use the plaintiffs' copyrights or trademarks.

Audiocassette counterfeiters such as Mr. Muslet, Mr. Halisi, and Mr. Alabed must have blank cassettes timed to specific lengths in order to produce marketable counterfeit tapes. Tapes of standard lengths (e.g. 30 or 60 minutes) are unacceptable because they either cut off the music of the sound recording or leave large amounts of silent time on each side of the tape. Therefore, counterfeiters are dependent on suppliers such as GAVC to acquire blank tapes that are timed to the specific length of the sound recording that they wish to counterfeit.

In September of 1991, Mr. Muslet was searching for a new supplier of time-loaded tapes for his counterfeiting operation. He met with Mr. Abdallah and informed him about the nature of the counterfeit operation, and the two agreed on a price for blank time-loaded cassettes. Mr. Muslet also needed a new supplier for insert cards for the counterfeit tapes, and asked Mr. Abdallah to assist him in that regard. Mr. Abdallah said that he would have somebody contact Mr. Muslet, and a few days later a supplier called Mr. Muslet having been referred by Mr. Abdallah.

Throughout their business relationship, Mr. Muslet sent Mr. Abdallah numerous "legitimate" tapes (i.e., non-counterfeit tapes of sound recordings) to time. Mr. Abdallah would time these cassettes and send them back to Mr. Muslet with the time of the cassette written on it. Mr. Muslet would then use these times when ordering blank tapes from Mr. Abdallah.

From September of 1991 to October of 1992, Mr. Muslet purchased over 300,000 blank cassettes and a tape duplicating machine from GAVC. In October of 1992, Mr. Muslet's counterfeiting operation was raided by the police and he was arrested.

Mr. Abdallah's knowledge of his customer's counterfeiting activities was also demonstrated by his conversations with his employee, Asmar Chabbo. Mr. Chabbo worked for GAVC from July 1990 until July 1992. During that period, he became Mr. Abdallah's office manager in GAVC's branch office in New Jersey. Mr. Chabbo testified that Mr. Abdallah explained to him that some of GAVC's customers used the blank time-loaded tapes to counterfeit legitimate sound recordings, and also explained the methods that his customers used to counterfeit tapes.

Mr. Chabbo further testified to Mr. Abdallah's relationship with Mohammed Halisi, GAVC's largest customer. At one point Mr. Abdallah mentioned that he was worried about the credit he had extended to Mr. Halisi, because Mr. Halisi had been raided by the police for counterfeiting activities and all his merchandise had been seized. On another occasion, Mr. Halisi complained to Mr. Abdallah that the time-loaded cassettes he had purchased from GAVC were too short for the "Michael Jackson cassette." These and other episodes related by Mr. Chabbo made it clear that Mr. Abdallah was aware of Mr. Halisi's illegal counterfeiting activities and yet still continued to supply him with time-loaded audio cassettes.

Mr. Chabbo also testified that Mr. Abdallah frequently timed new legitimate cassettes for his customers. Sometimes, as Mr. Muslet had previously explained, the customer would send in the legitimate cassette and Mr. Abdallah would time it, write the time on the cassette, and send the cassette back to the customer. On other occasions, the customer would send Mr. Abdallah the legitimate cassette and an order for time-loaded cassettes. Mr. Abdallah would then time the legitimate cassette and manufacture thousands of blank time-loaded cassettes based on the time of the legitimate cassette. The blank time-loaded cassettes were sent back to the customer along with the original legitimate cassette.

To support this contention, plaintiffs introduced numerous legitimate cassettes that had been seized from a raid on Mr. Muslet's warehouse. These cassettes had their time written on them in Mr. Abdallah's handwriting, as identified by both Mr. Chabbo and an independent handwriting expert. Thus, there was credible evidence from three different sources that Mr. Abdallah had timed legitimate cassettes for his customers. This fact strongly indicates that Mr. Abdallah knew what his counterfeiting customers were doing with the tapes that he sold them.

In conclusion, this Court finds that at least three of Mr. Abdallah's customers engaged in a substantial amount of counterfeiting and trademark infringement, including the 156 copyrighted sound recordings and 24 trade names listed in Appendices A an B, respectively. This Court further finds that the time-loaded cassettes which Mr. Abdallah sold to these customers was a material contribution to their counterfeiting activities, since audiotape counterfeiters must have blank tapes timed to specific lengths. Finally, and most critically, this Court concludes that Mr. Abdallah had actual knowledge of the counterfeiting and trademark infringement being done by his customers, and that, notwithstanding that knowledge, he continued to supply these customers with the time-loaded audiocassettes necessary to continue their counterfeiting activities.

There was no evidence that Mr. Abdallah or anyone at GAVC ever copied any sound recordings themselves. ...

Since it is undisputed that Mr. Abdallah did not participate in any copyright or trademark violations directly, the plaintiff's only basis for liability rests on a theory of contributory liability. This theory was outlined in *Gershwin Publishing Corp. v. Columbia Artists Management*, which stated that "one who, with knowledge of the infringing activity, induces, causes or materially contributes to the infringing conduct of another" is "equally liable with the direct infringer."

In the present case, the plaintiffs have established every element set out by *Gershwin*. ... This Court has concluded that Mr. Abdallah had actual knowledge of his customer's counterfeit activity and continued to provide them with time-loaded cassettes. And finally, the Court has found that Mr. Abdallah's provision of time-loaded cassettes was a material contribution to his customers' counterfeiting activities. ... Therefore, the plaintiffs have successfully demonstrated that Mr. Abdallah is liable for contributory copyright infringement.

... [The Court's discussion of damages, attorneys' fees, and trademark infringement is omitted.]

Notes and Questions

1. *Abdallah* cited the seminal case for contributory copyright liability, *Gershwin Publishing Corp. v. Columbia Artists Management*, 443 F.2d 1159 (2d. Cir. 1971). In that case, the defendant Columbia Artists Management acted as manager for a number of performing artists. As part of its activities, Columbia organized a number of local non-profit organizations that sponsored concerts at which Columbia would book its artists. Columbia then assisted these organizations with budget matters, selection of artists, and printing of concert programs. Columbia knew that neither the local organizations nor their artists had obtained licenses for the performance of copyrighted works at these concerts. The plaintiffs, who held copyright in a number of popular songs, sued Columbia for both vicarious and contributory infringement. The district court found Columbia liable on both theories, and the Second Circuit affirmed.

The *Gershwin* opinion contains a fairly terse analysis of contributory liability. However, courts repeatedly cite the case for its statement that "one who, with knowledge of the infringing activity, induces, causes or materially contributes to the infringing conduct of another, may be held liable as a "'contributory' infringer." Admittedly, this statement also mentioned inducement and causation as other methods of establishing liability. However, case law after *Gershwin* generally focused on the role of knowledge and material contribution until the *Grokster* case in 2005. *Abdallah* offers a straightforward example of contributory liability in the wake of *Gershwin*.

2. Contributory liability's elements differ from those of vicarious liability. This implies that contributory liability exists for different reasons than vicarious liability. What intuition or policy does contributory liability implement, and how does it differ from the policy expressed in vicarious liability? You may recall that courts identified vicarious liability as an outgrowth of the strict liability doctrine *respondeat superior*. Does contributory liability also implement a form of strict liability?

3. As was the case with vicarious liability, it is not immediately clear how far contributory liability extends. Liability could be fairly limited if courts require that a defendant actually know of a specific infringer's behavior and actively assist the infringement. Thus, in *Abdallah*,

liability existed because the defendant engaged in particular form of behavior with knowledge of its consequences. Ordinarily, selling blank cassette tapes to someone would not by itself make the seller liable for any
infringement that followed. However, Abdallah knew exactly what his
customers were doing, timed the programming to be duplicated, produced tapes of the desired length, and even financed his customers after
a police raid against them. By contrast, no liability existed in *Demetri-
ades v. Kauffman*, 690 F. Supp. 289 (S.D.N.Y. 1988), a case in which the
plaintiff claimed that the defendants were liable for infringement of the
plaintiff's architectural plans because the defendants acted as real estate
brokers for the sale of property on which the infringing house was built.
The court in that case rejected liability because "something more" than
selling property to the infringer was necessary to create liability, even if
the defendant knew about the impending infringement.

Alternatively, liability could be quite broad if courts decide that unverified complaints about infringement establish knowledge and that
any facilitation of infringement constitutes material contribution. What
kind of contributory liability regime should courts implement? Would
you support making it easier to hold defendants contributorily liable for
the infringement of others? Consider the issues raised by the following
case.

UMG Recordings v. Sinnott
300 F. Supp. 2d 993 (E.D. Cal. 2004)

MORRISON C. ENGLAND, JR., United States District Judge.

Plaintiffs, twenty three recording companies, filed this suit against
Defendant Richard Sinnott ("Sinnott"), owner and operator of the
Marysville Flea Market ("MFM"), seeking to hold him responsible for the
infringement of many of the copyrights Plaintiffs own. The infringement
was committed not by Sinnott directly, but rather by several MFM vendors who were selling pirated or counterfeit music. By this motion,
Plaintiffs contend that they are entitled to summary judgment as to
Sinnott's liability, leaving only the issue of damages to be decided at trial. As explained below, the Court agrees with Plaintiffs, and therefore
the motion is GRANTED.

BACKGROUND

Plaintiffs are owners of the copyrights to some of the most popular
sound recordings in the world. Plaintiffs are also members of the Recording Industry Association of America ("RIAA"), an organization which,
among other things, is charged with combating the problem of counterfeit sound recordings in the United States. Toward that end, the RIAA
investigated the sale of counterfeit compact discs ("CDs") and cassettes
by vendors at the Marysville Flea Market.

Sinnott has been the sole owner of the MFM since 1992. The MFM operates every Sunday, weather permitting, and has the capacity to accommodate about 200 vendor booths, although there are generally some booths left empty. Sinnott. Each vendor pays Sinnott a fee to rent a booth to sell merchandise to MFM customers. Sinnott provides security, utilities, restrooms, and a clean environment in which to sell merchandise to the approximately 1,500 customers that attend the flea market each week. Sinnott also operates concession stands at the MFM, and he is the only authorized seller of food or beverages on the premises. Sinnott recently opened and operates a go-kart track at the property.

Sinnott runs the day-to-day operations of the MFM, sets all rules and regulations, and is generally present during operating hours. Sinnott reserves the "right to inspect all merchandise, and also the right to refuse or cancel space rental." There are also rules restricting the types of merchandise that may be sold, such as prohibiting the sale of alcohol, and also food and drinks that can readily be consumed on the premises. The rules also add special requirements for vendors that sell produce. MFM employs security personnel that patrol the grounds and enforce these rules. MFM security personnel can, and have, ejected both customers and vendors for violating these rules.

On September 3, 2000, RIAA sent investigators to the MFM. There they found three vendors collectively offering approximately 3000 counterfeit CDs and cassettes for sale. The investigators went to the MFM office, and explained to Sinnott that several of his venders were selling CDs in violation of Plaintiffs' copyrights, and sought his assistance in putting a stop to these infringing sales. They also offered to train MFM employees on simple methods of detecting pirated and counterfeit CDs and cassettes, and on ways to distinguish these from original recordings. In response, Sinnott "threw (the RIAA investigators) out of [his] office and told them not to come back on [his] property without [his] permission." He did allow the investigators to deliver cease and desist letters to the vendors before leaving, however.

RIAA investigators visited the MFM at least six more times between September of 2000 and September of 2003, each time encountering vendors offering infringing CDs and cassettes for sale. Several of the vendors were quite candid in admitting that the CDs and cassettes they offered for sale were not original recordings. In all, a total of approximately 20,000 infringing CDs and cassettes were seen by RIAA investigators as being offered for sale during these visits, and investigators purchased 151 of these infringing CDs and cassettes.

Between September of 2000 and August of 2002, Charles Hausman, Anti-Piracy Counsel for RIAA, sent Sinnott four letters advising him of the infringing activity conducted by his vendors and explaining his potential liability. Each letter contained an offer to train MFM personnel on ways to detect and prevent the sale of counterfeit merchandise. Sinnott did not respond to any of these letters, and while acknowledging receipt, claims that he did not read them.

Plaintiffs, having failed to secure Sinnott's voluntary cooperation and assistance in preventing the infringing sales, filed this suit seeking to enforce their copyrights. Plaintiffs now move for summary judgment on the issue of Sinnott's contributory and vicarious liability for the MFM vendors' direct copyright infringement. ...

ANALYSIS

... [The court concluded that the vendors of the CDs in question had committed copyright infringement.]

2.   Contributory Copyright Infringement

The theory of contributory liability was applied to copyright infringement by the Second Circuit in *Gershwin Publ'g Corp. v. Columbia Artists Mgmt., Inc.*, 443 F.2d 1159 (2d Cir. 1971). In the classic statement of the theory, "one who, with knowledge of the infringing activity, induces, causes or materially contributes to the infringing conduct of another, may be held liable as a 'contributory' infringer."

A.   Knowledge of Direct Infringement

To hold Sinnott liable for contributory infringement, Plaintiffs must show that Sinnott "'[knew] or had reason to know' of direct infringement." Sinnott strenuously argues that actual knowledge, rather than constructive knowledge, is required to hold him liable for contributory infringement. He further contends that he neither knew, nor had reason to know, of the direct infringing activities of his vendors.

It is clear that Sinnott had both actual and constructive knowledge of the MFM vendors' direct infringement. Actual knowledge is established by Sinnott's admission that RIAA investigators personally told him of the infringement on September 3, 2000. RIAA investigators Victor Ayala and Kris Buckner identified themselves to Sinnott, and explained that three MFM vendors were selling infringing CDs or cassettes, requested his assistance in putting a stop to the infringing activity, explained Sinnott's potential liability, and offered to train Sinnott and his staff to recognize infringing sound recordings. Sinnott refused to assist the investigators, and he called security to have them escorted outside. Sinnott did allow the investigators to deliver cease and desist letters to three vendors with his security guard present, but he refused to accept copies of those letters himself.

Sinnott claims this is insufficient to establish actual knowledge because he did not know who or what RIAA was, and claims to have felt threatened by the investigators. What he does not claim, however, is that he did not receive and understand the message the investigators delivered. He admits he understood the investigators explained both the direct infringement being committed by his vendors and his possible personal liability for that infringement. The fact that he was not personally acquainted with the messenger does not mean that he can ignore the message and claim ignorance of its contents.

Further, Sinnott claims that he cannot be held to knowledge of the direct infringement because no law enforcement personnel came to MFM to confiscate infringing sound recordings or otherwise inform him that the vendors were, in fact, infringing Plaintiffs' copyrights. The fact that law enforcement did not seize any CDs or cassettes does not establish that Sinnott did not have notice of the infringing activity. Sinnott does not explain how a Sheriff's deputy is more qualified to point out examples of infringing recordings than trained investigators representing the copyright holders themselves.

Finally, Sinnott claims he was not provided specific information regarding the identity of the infringing vendors or the specific CDs or cassettes which were being sold in violation of Plaintiffs' copyright. The RIAA investigators attempted to show Sinnott the actual infringing recordings in person, and asked his assistance in allowing the investigators to request the vendors voluntarily surrender the counterfeit CDs and cassettes. Sinnott refused, claiming "it's not my problem."

These arguments that Sinnott did not have actual knowledge are without merit. There was more than a "bare" or "unsupported" assertion of infringement here. Sinnott purposefully refused to witness the infringement, and chose not to act on to the personal notification he received. This does not allow him to disavow knowledge of the infringement, however.

In addition, between September of 2000 and August of 2002, a time period starting shortly after Sinnott received personal notification of the direct infringement, the RIAA sent Sinnott four letters explaining his vendors' infringing activities. These letters also explained Sinnott's potential personal liability for the vendors' direct infringement. Attached to one of these letters were copies of the cease and desist letters the investigators gave to the three MFM vendors on September 3, 2000. Each cease and desist letter contained the name and address of the vendor that was selling infringing material. Sinnott acknowledges that he received these letters sent by the RIAA, but claims he did not read them.

Sinnott cannot, however, disavow the knowledge he would have had by reading the letters merely because he chose not to read them. Sinnott was aware the RIAA was investigating copyright infringement by MFM vendors, and the RIAA had previously advised him he could be held liable for their infringing activities. This is analogous to the situation in *Erhard v. Commissioner*, 87 F.3d 273 (9th Cir. 1996), in which the plaintiff received a deficiency notice from the Internal Revenue Service but refused to open it. The taxpayer had received similar notices for prior years, and was held to actual notice of the contents of this notice also. Similarly, Sinnott was expected to open the letters he received from RIAA after RIAA investigators had personally explained his potential liability to him. Thus, Sinnott is held to actual knowledge of the information contained in the letters.

Sinnott also had constructive knowledge of the direct infringement at MFM. At least one MFM employee was aware that vendors were selling infringing material. When the RIAA investigators delivered the three cease and desist letters on September 3, 2000, an MFM employee accompanied the investigators and insisted on reading the letters himself prior to allowing Ayala to give the letter to the vendor. Additionally, on other occasions when investigators visited MFM without disclosing their identity, MFM employees told investigators that Sinnott had received letters from RIAA regarding the counterfeit CDs being sold at MFM.

Accordingly, the Court finds that Sinnott had knowledge of the direct infringement by MFM vendors. Therefore, Sinnott is liable for contributory infringement if he materially contributed to the direct infringement.

B. Material Contribution to Direct Infringement

Operating a flea market or swap meet involves providing vendors with support services such as "the provision of space, utilities, parking, advertising, plumbing, and customers." This is all that is required to satisfy the requirement of material contribution necessary to establish contributory liability. ... Merely "providing the site and facilities for known infringing activities is sufficient to establish contributory liability." As explained above, Sinnott had knowledge of the vendors' infringing activity, yet continued to provide the site and facilities to allow the vendors to continue to sell counterfeit CDs and cassettes. The fact that these vendors were given no special benefit above and beyond non-infringing vendors does not allow Sinnott to escape liability.

Therefore, Sinnott, with knowledge of the vendors' infringing activity, materially contributed to the infringement. Accordingly, Plaintiffs have established Sinnott's liability for contributory infringement of Plaintiffs' copyrights.

[The court went on to hold the defendant vicariously liable as well.]

CONCLUSION

For the reasons explained more fully above, Plaintiffs' Motion for Summary Judgment of Sinnott's liability is GRANTED. Plaintiffs' damages remain undecided.

IT IS SO ORDERED.

Notes and Questions

1. *UMG* presses the question of how far to extend contributory liability. Although it is not the "high water mark" of how far courts have taken contributory liability, it does extend the doctrine beyond factual scenarios of the sort found in *Abdallah* or *Gershwin*. The court determined that Sinnott had the necessary knowledge because the plaintiff

had delivered cease and desist letters to him, and the court found that Sinnott's renting of booths to infringers established material contribution. Does delivering a complaint to a potential defendant establish her knowledge, and does her provision of a useful resource establish material contribution?

Think for a moment about the consequences of interpreting contributory liability this way. Consider an online auction website like eBay. Suppose one of eBay's subscribers begins selling counterfeit music recordings. Should delivery of a cease and desist letter to eBay be enough to make eBay liable for any infringement occurring after the complaint, since eBay provides facilities used by the infringer to sell its counterfeit goods? What should eBay do in response to receiving complaints like these, especially if the eBay seller contends that the recordings in question are not counterfeits?

2.   Regardless of how cases like this get decided, either the plaintiff or defendant will get saddled with burdens it does not want to bear. If plaintiffs win, defendants will have to bear the costs of investigating complaints about infringement, monitoring and disrupting the business of their customers, and paying for any infringement committed. If defendants win, plaintiffs will find it harder to stop infringement because they will have pursue individual infringers who may not be easy to locate, and plaintiffs will suffer financial losses if infringers prove impecunious. Who should bear the risk of loss in cases like this, and why? And, is it better to use principles of vicarious liability or contributory liability to decide?

SECTION C. MODERN TECHNOLOGY AND THIRD PARTY LIABILITY

Having acquainted ourselves with the traditional doctrines of third party copyright liability, we now examine them in the context of modern technology. As we have seen in other contexts, modern technology raises the stakes in copyright by enabling infringement on a large scale. Copyright holders could theoretically sue every person who misuses modern technology to commit infringement, but a number of practical obstacles exist. It is frequently difficult, if not impossible, to identify the users of modern technology. Even if found, infringers may have insufficient assets to pay judgments against them. Finally, the logistical nightmare of managing thousands, if not millions, of infringement actions means that aggrieved copyright holders will recover damages from only a fraction of all who have infringed their works.

Third party copyright actions could solve this problem for copyright holders. If the law imposes liability on those who provide technology to infringers, one of two things will happen. Technology providers will either compensate copyright holders for infringing misuse of technology, or they will stop infringement, perhaps by monitoring the behavior of their customers or taking technology off of the market. Of course, interpreting the law this way is controversial from both doctrinal and policy perspectives. We begin our examination of these issues with the first of two Supreme Court opinions concerning third party copyright liability.

Sony Corporation of America v. Universal City Studios
464 U.S. 417 (1984)

JUSTICE STEVENS delivered the opinion of the Court.

Petitioners manufacture and sell home video tape recorders. Respondents own the copyrights on some of the television programs that are broadcast on the public airwaves. Some members of the general public use video tape recorders sold by petitioners to record some of these broadcasts, as well as a large number of other broadcasts. The question presented is whether the sale of petitioners' copying equipment to the general public violates any of the rights conferred upon respondents by the Copyright Act.

After a lengthy trial, the District Court denied respondents all the relief they sought and entered judgment for petitioners. The United States Court of Appeals for the Ninth Circuit reversed the District Court's judgment on respondents' copyright claim, holding petitioners liable for contributory infringement and ordering the District Court to fashion appropriate relief. We granted certiorari; since we had not completed our study of the case last Term, we ordered reargument. We now reverse.

An explanation of our rejection of respondents' unprecedented attempt to impose copyright liability upon the distributors of copying equipment requires a quite detailed recitation of the findings of the District Court. In summary, those findings reveal that the average member of the public uses a VTR principally to record a program he cannot view as it is being televised and then to watch it once at a later time. This practice, known as "time-shifting," enlarges the television viewing audience. For that reason, a significant amount of television programming may be used in this manner without objection from the owners of the copyrights on the programs. For the same reason, even the two respondents in this case, who do assert objections to time-shifting in this litigation, were unable to prove that the practice has impaired the commercial value of their copyrights or has created any likelihood of future harm. Given these findings, there is no basis in the Copyright Act upon which respondents can hold petitioners liable for distributing VTR's to the general public. The Court of Appeals' holding that respondents are entitled to enjoin the distribution of VTR's, to collect royalties on the sale of such equipment, or to obtain other relief, if affirmed, would enlarge the scope of respondents' statutory monopolies to encompass control over an article of commerce that is not the subject of copyright protection. Such an expansion of the copyright privilege is beyond the limits of the grants authorized by Congress.

I

... From its beginning, the law of copyright has developed in response to significant changes in technology. Indeed, it was the invention of a new form of copying equipment—the printing press—that gave rise to the original need for copyright protection. Repeatedly, as new developments have occurred in this country, it has been the Congress that has fashioned the new rules that new technology made necessary. Thus, long before the enactment of the Copyright Act of 1909, 35 Stat. 1075, it was settled that the protection given to copyrights is wholly statutory. The remedies for infringement "are only those prescribed by Congress." *Thompson v. Hubbard*, 131 U.S. 123, 151 (1889).

The judiciary's reluctance to expand the protections afforded by the copyright without explicit legislative guidance is a recurring theme. Sound policy, as well as history, supports our consistent deference to Congress when major technological innovations alter the market for copyrighted materials. Congress has the constitutional authority and the institutional ability to accommodate fully the varied permutations of competing interests that are inevitably implicated by such new technology. ...

III

The Copyright Act does not expressly render anyone liable for infringement committed by another. In contrast, the Patent Act expressly brands anyone who "actively induces infringement of a patent" as an infringer, 35 U. S. C. § 271(b), and further imposes liability on certain individuals labeled "contributory" infringers, § 271(c). The absence of such express language in the copyright statute does not preclude the imposition of liability for copyright infringements on certain parties who have not themselves engaged in the infringing activity. For vicarious liability is imposed in virtually all areas of the law, and the concept of contributory infringement is merely a species of the broader problem of identifying the circumstances in which it is just to hold one individual accountable for the actions of another. ...

Respondents argue that ... supplying the "means" to accomplish an infringing activity and encouraging that activity through advertisement are sufficient to establish liability for copyright infringement. This argument rests on a gross generalization that cannot withstand scrutiny. ...

If vicarious liability is to be imposed on Sony in this case, it must rest on the fact that it has sold equipment with constructive knowledge of the fact that its customers may use that equipment to make unauthorized copies of copyrighted material. There is no precedent in the law of copyright for the imposition of vicarious liability on such a theory. The closest analogy is provided by the patent law cases to which it is appropriate to refer because of the historic kinship between patent law and copyright law.

In the Patent Act both the concept of infringement and the concept of contributory infringement are expressly defined by statute. The prohibition against contributory infringement is confined to the knowing sale of a component especially made for use in connection with a particular patent. There is no suggestion in the statute that one patentee may object to the sale of a product that might be used in connection with other patents. Moreover, the Act expressly provides that the sale of a "staple article or commodity of commerce suitable for substantial noninfringing use" is not contributory infringement. 35 U. S. C. § 271(c).

When a charge of contributory infringement is predicated entirely on the sale of an article of commerce that is used by the purchaser to infringe a patent, the public interest in access to that article of commerce is necessarily implicated. A finding of contributory infringement does not, of course, remove the article from the market altogether; it does, however, give the patentee effective control over the sale of that item. Indeed, a finding of contributory infringement is normally the functional equivalent of holding that the disputed article is within the monopoly granted to the patentee.

For that reason, in contributory infringement cases arising under the patent laws the Court has always recognized the critical importance of not allowing the patentee to extend his monopoly beyond the limits of his specific grant. These cases deny the patentee any right to control the distribution of unpatented articles unless they are "unsuited for any commercial noninfringing use." *Dawson Chemical Co. v. Rohm & Hass Co.*, 448 U.S. 176, 198 (1980). Unless a commodity "has no use except through practice of the patented method," *id.*, at 199, the patentee has no right to claim that its distribution constitutes contributory infringement. ...

We recognize there are substantial differences between the patent and copyright laws. But in both areas the contributory infringement doctrine is grounded on the recognition that adequate protection of a monopoly may require the courts to look beyond actual duplication of a device or publication to the products or activities that make such duplication possible. The staple article of commerce doctrine must strike a balance between a copyright holder's legitimate demand for effective—not merely symbolic—protection of the statutory monopoly, and the rights of others freely to engage in substantially unrelated areas of commerce. Accordingly, the sale of copying equipment, like the sale of other articles of commerce, does not constitute contributory infringement if the product is widely used for legitimate, unobjectionable purposes. Indeed, it need merely be capable of substantial noninfringing uses.

IV

The question is thus whether the Betamax is capable of commercially significant noninfringing uses. In order to resolve that question, we need not explore all the different potential uses of the machine and determine whether or not they would constitute infringement. Rather, we need only consider whether on the basis of the facts as found by the District Court a significant number of them would be noninfringing. Moreover, in order to resolve this case we need not give precise content to the question of how much use is commercially significant. For one potential use of the Betamax plainly satisfies this standard, however it is understood: private, noncommercial time-shifting in the home. It does so both (A) because respondents have no right to prevent other copyright holders from authorizing it for their programs, and (B) because the District Court's factual findings reveal that even the unauthorized home time-shifting of respondents' programs is legitimate fair use.

[The Court's discussion of time-shifting and fair use is omitted here, but reproduced earlier in Chapter Six.]

In summary, the record and findings of the District Court lead us to two conclusions. First, Sony demonstrated a significant likelihood that substantial numbers of copyright holders who license their works for broadcast on free television would not object to having their broadcasts time-shifted by private viewers. And second, respondents failed to demonstrate that time-shifting would cause any likelihood of nonminimal harm to the potential market for, or the value of, their copyrighted works. The Betamax is, therefore, capable of substantial noninfringing uses. Sony's sale of such equipment to the general public does not constitute contributory infringement of respondents' copyrights.

V

"The direction of Art. I is that Congress shall have the power to promote the progress of science and the useful arts. When, as here, the Constitution is permissive, the sign of how far Congress has chosen to go can come only from Congress." *Deepsouth Packing Co. v. Laitram Corp.*, 406 U.S. 518, 530 (1972).

One may search the Copyright Act in vain for any sign that the elected representatives of the millions of people who watch television every day have made it unlawful to copy a program for later viewing at home, or have enacted a flat prohibition against the sale of machines that make such copying possible.

It may well be that Congress will take a fresh look at this new technology, just as it so often has examined other innovations in the past. But it is not our job to apply laws that have not yet been written. Applying the copyright statute, as it now reads, to the facts as they have been developed in this case, the judgment of the Court of Appeals must be reversed.

It is so ordered.

JUSTICE BLACKMUN, with whom JUSTICE MARSHALL, JUSTICE POWELL, and JUSTICE REHNQUIST join, dissenting.

A restatement of the facts and judicial history of this case is necessary, in my view, for a proper focus upon the issues. Respondents' position is hardly so "unprecedented" in the copyright law, nor does it really embody a "gross generalization," or a "novel theory of liability," and the like, as the Court, in belittling their claims, describes the efforts of respondents.

[The dissent's conclusion that time-shifting is not fair use is omitted. It is reproduced in part earlier in Chapter Six.]

V

Contributory Infringement

From the Studios' perspective, the consequences of home VTR recording are the same as if a business had taped the Studios' works off the air, duplicated the tapes, and sold or rented them to members of the public for home viewing. The distinction is that home VTR users do not record for commercial advantage; the commercial benefit accrues to the manufacturer and distributors of the Betamax. I thus must proceed to discuss whether the manufacturer and distributors can be held contributorily liable if the product they sell is used to infringe. ...

B

... Sony argues that the manufacturer or seller of a product used to infringe is absolved from liability whenever the product can be put to any substantial noninfringing use. The District Court so held, borrowing the "staple article of commerce" doctrine governing liability for contributory infringement of patents. This Court today is much less positive. I do not agree that this technical judge-made doctrine of patent law, based in part on considerations irrelevant to the field of copyright should be imported wholesale into copyright law. Despite their common constitutional source, patent and copyright protections have not developed in a parallel fashion, and this Court in copyright cases in the past has borrowed patent concepts only sparingly.

I recognize, however, that many of the concerns underlying the "staple article of commerce" doctrine are present in copyright law as well. As the District Court noted, if liability for contributory infringement were imposed on the manufacturer or seller of every product used to infringe—a typewriter, a camera, a photocopying machine—the "wheels of commerce" would be blocked.

I therefore conclude that if a significant portion of the product's use is noninfringing, the manufacturers and sellers cannot be held contributorily liable for the product's infringing uses. If virtually all of the product's use, however, is to infringe, contributory liability may be imposed; if no one would buy the product for noninfringing purposes alone, it is clear that the manufacturer is purposely profiting from the infringement, and that liability is appropriately imposed. In such a case, the copyright owner's monopoly would not be extended beyond its proper bounds; the manufacturer of such a product contributes to the infringing activities of others and profits directly thereby, while providing no benefit to the public sufficient to justify the infringement.

The Court of Appeals concluded that Sony should be held liable for contributory infringement, reasoning that "[videotape] recorders are manufactured, advertised, and sold for the primary purpose of reproducing television programming," and "[virtually] all television programming is copyrighted material." While I agree with the first of these propositions, the second, for me, is problematic. The key question is not the amount of television programming that is copyrighted, but rather the amount of VTR usage that is infringing. Moreover, the parties and their *amici* have argued vigorously about both the amount of television programming that is covered by copyright and the amount for which permission to copy has been given. The proportion of VTR recording that is infringing is ultimately a question of fact, and the District Court specifically declined to make findings on the "percentage of legal versus illegal home-use recording." 480 F. Supp., at 468. In light of my view of the law, resolution of this factual question is essential. I therefore would remand the case for further consideration of this by the District Court.

VI

The Court has adopted an approach very different from the one I have outlined. It is my view that the Court's approach alters dramatically the doctrines of fair use and contributory infringement as they have been developed by Congress and the courts. Should Congress choose to respond to the Court's decision, the old doctrines can be resurrected. As it stands, however, the decision today erodes much of the coherence that these doctrines have struggled to achieve.

The Court's disposition of the case turns on its conclusion that time-shifting is a fair use. Because both parties agree that time-shifting is the primary use of VTR's, that conclusion, if correct, would settle the issue of Sony's liability under almost any definition of contributory infringement. The Court concludes that time-shifting is fair use for two reasons. Each is seriously flawed.

[The dissent's discussion of the majority's fair use reasoning is omitted.]

Because of the Court's conclusion concerning the legality of time-shifting, it never addresses the amount of noninfringing use that a manufacturer must show to absolve itself from liability as a contributory infringer. Thus, it is difficult to discuss how the Court's test for contributory infringement would operate in practice under a proper analysis of time-shifting. One aspect of the test as it is formulated by the Court, however, particularly deserves comment. The Court explains that a manufacturer of a product is not liable for contributory infringement as long as the product is "*capable* of substantial noninfringing uses." *Ante,* at 442 (emphasis supplied). Such a definition essentially eviscerates the concept of contributory infringement. Only the most unimaginative manufacturer would be unable to demonstrate that a image-duplicating product is "capable" of substantial noninfringing uses. Surely Congress desired to prevent the sale of products that are used almost exclusively to infringe copyrights; the fact that noninfringing uses exist presumably would have little bearing on that desire.

More importantly, the rationale for the Court's narrow standard of contributory infringement reveals that, once again, the Court has confused the issue of liability with that of remedy. The Court finds that a narrow definition of contributory infringement is necessary in order to protect "the rights of others freely to engage in substantially unrelated areas of commerce." *Ante*, at 442. But application of the contributory infringement doctrine implicates such rights only if the remedy attendant upon a finding of liability were an injunction against the manufacture of the product in question. The issue of an appropriate remedy is not before the Court at this time, but it seems likely that a broad injunction is not the remedy that would be ordered. It is unfortunate that the Court has allowed its concern over a remedy to infect its analysis of liability.

VII

... Like so many other problems created by the interaction of copyright law with a new technology, "[there] can be no really satisfactory solution to the problem presented here, until Congress acts." *Twentieth Century Music Corp. v. Aiken*, 422 U.S., at 167 (dissenting opinion). But in the absence of a congressional solution, courts cannot avoid difficult problems by refusing to apply the law. We must "take the Copyright Act . . . as we find it," *Fortnightly Corp. v. United Artists Television, Inc.*, 392 U.S., at 401-402, and "do as little damage as possible to traditional copyright principles . . . until the Congress legislates." *Id.*, at 404 (dissenting opinion).

Notes and Questions

1. *Sony* is a difficult and controversial opinion. The opinion is famous for its conclusion that "the sale of copying equipment, like the sale of other articles of commerce, does not constitute contributory infringement if the product is widely used for legitimate, unobjectionable purposes. Indeed, it need merely be capable of substantial noninfringing uses." However, it is unclear how this statement affects the law of third party copyright liability. Let us start by examining *Sony* at the doctrinal level. The plaintiffs might have prevailed on either of the two theories extant at the time of the case, vicarious liability or contributory liability. Did the Court address both of these theories, and if so, how?

The answer to this question has great practical significance. If *Sony* affected both vicarious and contributory liability, then sellers of copying equipment became immune from third party liability as long as their equipment was "capable of substantial noninfringing use." However, if *Sony* affected only one of these doctrines, then sellers of copying equipment still had to worry about being sued under the unaffected doctrine. Can you trace the Court's reasoning about vicarious or contributory liability? If so, what elements of the claims were addressed, or did *Sony* announce an exception to otherwise unaffected doctrines?

2. Regardless of the doctrines that *Sony* affected, there is also the question of what kind of defendant can claim *Sony*'s protection. *Sony*'s exemption applies to "the sale of copying equipment," but just what does this term encompass? It obviously applies to videotape recorders and similar devices such as photocopying machines. But what about the distribution of copying technology that is arguably not "the sale of equipment"? For example, would courts perceive software as "equipment" in the same sense as a photocopy machine, and what about the fact that software is generally licensed, and not sold, to users? If you are inclined to apply *Sony* to the distribution of software, what about the provision of services that facilitate copying such as Internet service?

3. How easy should it be for a defendant to show that its goods or services are capable of substantial noninfringing use? If the requirement is easy to meet, many (if not most) technology providers will be able to design and sell products with relatively little attention to copyright. Would such a state of affairs be beneficial, or would the door be open to the cynical businesses who know that their activity facilitates infringement, but feign ignorance in the name of profit?

4. Was *Sony* correctly decided? The plaintiffs' case was fairly plausible as a matter of existing doctrine. For contributory liability, *Sony* surely knew that many of its purchasers committed infringement, yet it continued selling videorecorders. For vicarious liability, *Sony* could have stopped the infringement by discontinuing sales, and it surely profited from those sales. Moreover, the vicarious liability rationales expressed in *Polygram* support the extension of liability because Sony could raise the price of videorecorders to cover the cost of infringements it could not prevent.

Your answer to this question may depend on whether you agree with the policies the Court used to support its decision. The Court apparently considered it unwise to impose liability on defendants like Sony in the absence of clear Congressional intent. Do you find this reasoning persuasive, especially in light of the common law origins of third party copyright liability in judge-made law?

The Court also expressed concern that imposing liability on Sony might adversely affect "unrelated areas of commerce." By doing so, the Court essentially balanced the value of increasing the security of copyright against the value of losses that might follow in those unrelated areas of commerce, and it struck a balance that strongly favored potential copyright defendants. After all, defendants who can claim the protection of *Sony* are immune from liability as long as their equipment is capable of substantial noninfringing use. This allows defendants to sell with impunity equipment that causes real, present losses to the security of copyrights while being only capable of substantial non-infringing use. Why did the Supreme Court consider this good for society, and do you agree? If you do not agree, would you adopt the dissent's position about the type of equipment that could be sold without risk of third party copyright liability? Are your answers to these questions affected at all by the fact that revenue from home video sales and rentals now greatly increases the economic viability of movies that prove unsuccessful at the box office? Or, has *Sony* become a "mistake" in light of the Internet's great potential for infringement?

Metro-Goldwyn-Mayer Studios v. Grokster
545 U.S. 913 (2005)

JUSTICE SOUTER delivered the opinion of the Court.

The question is under what circumstances the distributor of a product capable of both lawful and unlawful use is liable for acts of copyright infringement by third parties using the product. We hold that one who distributes a device with the object of promoting its use to infringe copyright, as shown by clear expression or other affirmative steps taken to foster infringement, is liable for the resulting acts of infringement by third parties.

I

A

Respondents, Grokster, Ltd., and StreamCast Networks, Inc., defendants in the trial court, distribute free software products that allow computer users to share electronic files through peer-to-peer networks, so called because users' computers communicate directly with each other, not through central servers. The advantage of peer-to-peer networks over information networks of other types shows up in their substantial and growing popularity. Because they need no central computer server to mediate the exchange of information or files among users, the high-bandwidth communications capacity for a server may be dispensed with, and the need for costly server storage space is eliminated. Since copies of a file (particularly a popular one) are available on many users' computers, file requests and retrievals may be faster than on other types of networks, and since file exchanges do not travel through a server, communications can take place between any computers that remain connected to the network without risk that a glitch in the server will disable the network in its entirety. Given these benefits in security, cost, and efficiency, peer-to-peer networks are employed to store and distribute electronic files by universities, government agencies, corporations, and libraries, among others.

Other users of peer-to-peer networks include individual recipients of Grokster's and StreamCast's software, and although the networks that they enjoy through using the software can be used to share any type of digital file, they have prominently employed those networks in sharing copyrighted music and video files without authorization. A group of copyright holders (MGM for short, but including motion picture studios, recording companies, songwriters, and music publishers) sued Grokster and StreamCast for their users' copyright infringements, alleging that they knowingly and intentionally distributed their software to enable users to reproduce and distribute the copyrighted works in violation of the Copyright Act. MGM sought damages and an injunction.

Discovery during the litigation revealed the way the software worked, the business aims of each defendant company, and the predilections of the users. Grokster's eponymous software employs what is known as FastTrack technology, a protocol developed by others and licensed to Grokster. StreamCast distributes a very similar product except that its software, called Morpheus, relies on what is known as Gnutella technology. A user who downloads and installs either software possesses the protocol to send requests for files directly to the computers of others using software compatible with FastTrack or Gnutella. On the FastTrack network opened by the Grokster software, the user's request goes to a computer given an indexing capacity by the software and designated a supernode, or to some other computer with comparable power and capacity to collect temporary indexes of the files available on the computers of users connected to it. The supernode (or indexing computer) searches its own index and may communicate the search request to other supernodes. If the file is found, the supernode discloses its location to the computer requesting it, and the requesting user can download the file directly from the computer located. The copied file is placed in a designated sharing folder on the requesting user's computer, where it is available for other users to download in turn, along with any other file in that folder.

In the Gnutella network made available by Morpheus, the process is mostly the same, except that in some versions of the Gnutella protocol there are no supernodes. In these versions, peer computers using the protocol communicate directly with each other. When a user enters a search request into the Morpheus software, it sends the request to computers connected with it, which in turn pass the request along to other connected peers. The search results are communicated to the requesting computer, and the user can download desired files directly from peers' computers. As this description indicates, Grokster and StreamCast use no servers to intercept the content of the search requests or to mediate the file transfers conducted by users of the software, there being no central point through which the substance of the communications passes in either direction.

Although Grokster and StreamCast do not therefore know when particular files are copied, a few searches using their software would show what is available on the networks the software reaches. MGM commissioned a statistician to conduct a systematic search, and his study showed that nearly 90% of the files available for download on the FastTrack system were copyrighted works. Grokster and StreamCast dispute this figure, raising methodological problems and arguing that free copying even of copyrighted works may be authorized by the rightholders. They also argue that potential noninfringing uses of their software are significant in kind, even if infrequent in practice. Some musical performers, for example, have gained new audiences by distributing their copyrighted works for free across peer-to-peer networks, and some distributors of unprotected content have used peer-to-peer networks to disseminate files, Shakespeare being an example. Indeed, StreamCast has given Morpheus users the opportunity to download the briefs in this very case, though their popularity has not been quantified.

As for quantification, the parties' anecdotal and statistical evidence entered thus far to show the content available on the FastTrack and Gnutella networks does not say much about which files are actually downloaded by users, and no one can say how often the software is used to obtain copies of unprotected material. But MGM's evidence gives reason to think that the vast majority of users' downloads are acts of infringement, and because well over 100 million copies of the software in question are known to have been downloaded, and billions of files are shared across the FastTrack and Gnutella networks each month, the probable scope of copyright infringement is staggering.

Grokster and StreamCast concede the infringement in most downloads, and it is uncontested that they are aware that users employ their software primarily to download copyrighted files, even if the decentralized FastTrack and Gnutella networks fail to reveal which files are being copied, and when. From time to time, moreover, the companies have learned about their users' infringement directly, as from users who have sent e-mail to each company with questions about playing copyrighted movies they had downloaded, to whom the companies have responded with guidance. And MGM notified the companies of 8 million copyrighted files that could be obtained using their software.

Grokster and StreamCast are not, however, merely passive recipients of information about infringing use. The record is replete with evidence that from the moment Grokster and StreamCast began to distribute their free software, each one clearly voiced the objective that recipients use it to download copyrighted works, and each took active steps to encourage infringement.

After the notorious file-sharing service, Napster, was sued by copyright holders for facilitation of copyright infringement, *A & M Records,*

Inc. v. Napster, Inc., 114 F. Supp. 2d 896 (N.D. Cal. 2000), StreamCast gave away a software program of a kind known as OpenNap, designed as compatible with the Napster program and open to Napster users for downloading files from other Napster and OpenNap users' computers. Evidence indicates that "[i]t was always [StreamCast's] intent to use [its OpenNap network] to be able to capture email addresses of [its] initial target market so that [it] could promote [its] StreamCast Morpheus interface to them,"; indeed, the OpenNap program was engineered "to leverage Napster's 50 million user base."

StreamCast monitored both the number of users downloading its OpenNap program and the number of music files they downloaded. It also used the resulting OpenNap network to distribute copies of the Morpheus software and to encourage users to adopt it. Internal company documents indicate that StreamCast hoped to attract large numbers of former Napster users if that company was shut down by court order or otherwise, and that StreamCast planned to be the next Napster. A kit developed by StreamCast to be delivered to advertisers, for example, contained press articles about StreamCast's potential to capture former Napster users, and it introduced itself to some potential advertisers as a company "which is similar to what Napster was." It broadcast banner advertisements to users of other Napster-compatible software, urging them to adopt its OpenNap. An internal e-mail from a company executive stated: "We have put this network in place so that when Napster pulls the plug on their free service ... or if the Court orders them shut down prior to that ... we will be positioned to capture the flood of their 32 million users that will be actively looking for an alternative."

Thus, StreamCast developed promotional materials to market its service as the best Napster alternative. One proposed advertisement read: "Napster Inc. has announced that it will soon begin charging you a fee. That's if the courts don't order it shut down first. What will you do to get around it?" Another proposed ad touted StreamCast's software as the "# 1 alternative to Napster" and asked "[w]hen the lights went off at Napster ... where did the users go?" StreamCast even planned to flaunt the illegal uses of its software; when it launched the OpenNap network, the chief technology officer of the company averred that "[t]he goal is to get in trouble with the law and get sued. It's the best way to get in the new[s]."

The evidence that Grokster sought to capture the market of former Napster users is sparser but revealing, for Grokster launched its own OpenNap system called Swaptor and inserted digital codes into its Web site so that computer users using Web search engines to look for "Napster" or "[f]ree filesharing" would be directed to the Grokster Web site, where they could download the Grokster software. And Grokster's name is an apparent derivative of Napster.

StreamCast's executives monitored the number of songs by certain commercial artists available on their networks, and an internal communication indicates they aimed to have a larger number of copyrighted songs available on their networks than other file-sharing networks. The point, of course, would be to attract users of a mind to infringe, just as it would be with their promotional materials developed showing copyrighted songs as examples of the kinds of files available through Morpheus. Morpheus in fact allowed users to search specifically for "Top 40" songs, which were inevitably copyrighted. Similarly, Grokster sent users a newsletter promoting its ability to provide particular, popular copyrighted materials.

In addition to this evidence of express promotion, marketing, and intent to promote further, the business models employed by Grokster and StreamCast confirm that their principal object was use of their software to download copyrighted works. Grokster and StreamCast receive no revenue from users, who obtain the software itself for nothing. Instead, both companies generate income by selling advertising space, and they stream the advertising to Grokster and Morpheus users while they are employing the programs. As the number of users of each program increases, advertising opportunities become worth more. While there is doubtless some demand for free Shakespeare, the evidence shows that substantive volume is a function of free access to copyrighted work. Users seeking Top 40 songs, for example, or the latest release by Modest Mouse, are certain to be far more numerous than those seeking a free Decameron, and Grokster and StreamCast translated that demand into dollars.

Finally, there is no evidence that either company made an effort to filter copyrighted material from users' downloads or otherwise impede the sharing of copyrighted files. Although Grokster appears to have sent e-mails warning users about infringing content when it received threatening notice from the copyright holders, it never blocked anyone from continuing to use its software to share copyrighted files. StreamCast not only rejected another company's offer of help to monitor infringement, but blocked the Internet Protocol addresses of entities it believed were trying to engage in such monitoring on its networks.

B

After discovery, the parties on each side of the case cross-moved for summary judgment. The District Court limited its consideration to the asserted liability of Grokster and StreamCast for distributing the current versions of their software, leaving aside whether either was liable "for damages arising from past versions of their software, or from other past activities." The District Court held that those who used the Grokster and Morpheus software to download copyrighted media files directly infringed MGM's copyrights, a conclusion not contested on appeal, but the court nonetheless granted summary judgment in favor of Grokster and StreamCast as to any liability arising from distribution of the then current versions of their software. Distributing that software gave rise to no liability in the court's view, because its use did not provide the distributors with actual knowledge of specific acts of infringement.

The Court of Appeals affirmed. In the court's analysis, a defendant was liable as a contributory infringer when it had knowledge of direct infringement and materially contributed to the infringement. But the court read [*Sony*] as holding that distribution of a commercial product capable of substantial noninfringing uses could not give rise to contributory liability for infringement unless the distributor had actual knowledge of specific instances of infringement and failed to act on that knowledge. The fact that the software was capable of substantial noninfringing uses in the Ninth Circuit's view meant that Grokster and StreamCast were not liable, because they had no such actual knowledge, owing to the decentralized architecture of their software. The court also held that Grokster and StreamCast did not materially contribute to their users' infringement because it was the users themselves who searched for, retrieved, and stored the infringing files, with no involvement by the defendants beyond providing the software in the first place.

The Ninth Circuit also considered whether Grokster and StreamCast could be liable under a theory of vicarious infringement. The court held against liability because the defendants did not monitor or control the use of the software, had no agreed-upon right or current ability to supervise its use, and had no independent duty to police infringement. We granted certiorari.

II

A

MGM and many of the *amici* fault the Court of Appeals's holding for upsetting a sound balance between the respective values of supporting creative pursuits through copyright protection and promoting innovation in new communication technologies by limiting the incidence of liability for copyright infringement. The more artistic protection is favored, the more technological innovation may be discouraged; the administration of copyright law is an exercise in managing the trade-off.

The tension between the two values is the subject of this case, with its claim that digital distribution of copyrighted material threatens copyright holders as never before, because every copy is identical to the original, copying is easy, and many people (especially the young) use file-sharing software to download copyrighted works. This very breadth of the software's use may well draw the public directly into the debate over copyright policy, and the indications are that the ease of copying songs or movies using software like Grokster's and Napster's is fostering disdain for copyright protection. As the case has been presented to us, these fears are said to be offset by the different concern that imposing liability, not only on infringers but on distributors of software based on its potential for unlawful use, could limit further development of beneficial technologies.

The argument for imposing indirect liability in this case is, however, a powerful one, given the number of infringing downloads that occur every day using StreamCast's and Grokster's software. When a widely shared service or product is used to commit infringement, it may be impossible to enforce rights in the protected work effectively against all direct infringers, the only practical alternative being to go against the distributor of the copying device for secondary liability on a theory of contributory or vicarious infringement.

One infringes contributorily by intentionally inducing or encouraging direct infringement, see *Gershwin Pub. Corp. v. Columbia Artists Management, Inc.*, 443 F.2d 1159, 1162 (C.A.2 1971), and infringes vicariously by profiting from direct infringement while declining to exercise a right to stop or limit it, *Shapiro, Bernstein & Co. v. H.L. Green Co.*, 316 F.2d 304, 307 (C.A.2 1963). Although "[t]he Copyright Act does not expressly render anyone liable for infringement committed by another," *Sony Corp. v. Universal City Studios*, 464 U.S., at 434, these doctrines of secondary liability emerged from common law principles and are well established in the law.

Rules

B

Despite the currency of these principles of secondary liability, this Court has dealt with secondary copyright infringement in only one recent case, and because MGM has tailored its principal claim to our opinion there, a look at our earlier holding is in order. In *Sony Corp. v. Universal City Studios*, this Court addressed a claim that secondary liability for infringement can arise from the very distribution of a commercial product. There, the product, novel at the time, was what we know today as the videocassette recorder or VCR. Copyright holders sued Sony as the manufacturer, claiming it was contributorily liable for infringement that occurred when VCR owners taped copyrighted programs because it supplied the means used to infringe, and it had constructive knowledge that infringement would occur. At the trial on the merits, the evidence showed that the principal use of the VCR was for "time-shifting," or taping a program for later viewing at a more convenient time, which the Court found to be a fair, not an infringing, use. There was no evidence that Sony had expressed an object of bringing about taping in violation of copyright or had taken active steps to increase its profits from unlawful taping. Although Sony's advertisements urged consumers to buy the VCR to "record favorite shows" or "build a library" of recorded programs, neither of these uses was necessarily infringing.

On those facts, with no evidence of stated or indicated intent to promote infringing uses, the only conceivable basis for imposing liability was on a theory of contributory infringement arising from its sale of VCRs to consumers with knowledge that some would use them to infringe. But because the VCR was "capable of commercially significant noninfringing uses," we held the manufacturer could not be faulted solely on the basis of its distribution.

This analysis reflected patent law's traditional staple article of commerce doctrine, now codified, that distribution of a component of a patented device will not violate the patent if it is suitable for use in other ways. The doctrine was devised to identify instances in which it may be presumed from distribution of an article in commerce that the distributor intended the article to be used to infringe another's patent, and so may justly be held liable for that infringement. ...

In sum, where an article is "good for nothing else" but infringement, there is no legitimate public interest in its unlicensed availability, and there is no injustice in presuming or imputing an intent to infringe. Conversely, the doctrine absolves the equivocal conduct of selling an item with substantial lawful as well as unlawful uses, and limits liability to instances of more acute fault than the mere understanding that some of one's products will be misused. It leaves breathing room for innovation and a vigorous commerce.

The parties and many of the *amici* in this case think the key to resolving it is the *Sony* rule and, in particular, what it means for a product to be "capable of commercially significant noninfringing uses." MGM advances the argument that granting summary judgment to Grokster and StreamCast as to their current activities gave too much weight to the value of innovative technology, and too little to the copyrights infringed by users of their software, given that 90% of works available on one of the networks was shown to be copyrighted. Assuming the remaining 10% to be its noninfringing use, MGM says this should not qualify as "substantial," and the Court should quantify *Sony* to the extent of holding that a product used "principally" for infringement does not qualify. As mentioned before, Grokster and StreamCast reply by citing evidence that their software can be used to reproduce public domain works, and they point to copyright holders who actually encourage copying. Even if infringement is the principal practice with their software today, they argue, the noninfringing uses are significant and will grow.

We agree with MGM that the Court of Appeals misapplied *Sony*, which it read as limiting secondary liability quite beyond the circumstances to which the case applied. *Sony* barred secondary liability based on presuming or imputing intent to cause infringement solely from the design or distribution of a product capable of substantial lawful use, which the distributor knows is in fact used for infringement. The Ninth Circuit has read *Sony*'s limitation to mean that whenever a product is capable of substantial lawful use, the producer can never be held contributorily liable for third parties' infringing use of it; it read the rule as being this broad, even when an actual purpose to cause infringing use is shown by evidence independent of design and distribution of the product, unless the distributors had "specific knowledge of infringement at a time at which they contributed to the infringement, and failed to act upon that information," (internal quotation marks and alterations omitted). Because the Circuit found the StreamCast and Grokster software capable of substantial lawful use, it concluded on the basis of its reading of *Sony* that neither company could be held liable, since there was no showing that their software, being without any central server, afforded them knowledge of specific unlawful uses.

This view of *Sony*, however, was error, converting the case from one about liability resting on imputed intent to one about liability on any theory. Because *Sony* did not displace other theories of secondary liability, and because we find below that it was error to grant summary judgment to the companies on MGM's inducement claim, we do not revisit *Sony* further, as MGM requests, to add a more quantified description of the point of balance between protection and commerce when liability rests solely on distribution with knowledge that unlawful use will occur. It is enough to note that the Ninth Circuit's judgment rested on an erroneous understanding of *Sony* and to leave further consideration of the *Sony* rule for a day when that may be required.

C

Sony's rule limits imputing culpable intent as a matter of law from the characteristics or uses of a distributed product. But nothing in *Sony* requires courts to ignore evidence of intent if there is such evidence, and the case was never meant to foreclose rules of fault-based liability derived from the common law. Thus, where evidence goes beyond a product's characteristics or the knowledge that it may be put to infringing uses, and shows statements or actions directed to promoting infringement, *Sony*'s staple-article rule will not preclude liability.

The classic case of direct evidence of unlawful purpose occurs when one induces commission of infringement by another, or "entic[es] or persuad[es] another" to infringe, Black's Law Dictionary 790 (8th ed. 2004), as by advertising. Thus at common law a copyright or patent defendant who "not only expected but invoked [infringing use] by advertisement" was liable for infringement "on principles recognized in every part of the law." *Kalem Co. v. Harper Brothers*, 222 U.S., at 62-63 (copyright infringement).

The rule on inducement of infringement as developed in the early cases is no different today. Evidence of "active steps ... taken to encourage direct infringement," *Oak Industries, Inc. v. Zenith Electronics Corp.*, 697 F. Supp. 988, 992 (N.D. Ill. 1988), such as advertising an infringing use or instructing how to engage in an infringing use, show an affirmative intent that the product be used to infringe, and a showing that infringement was encouraged overcomes the law's reluctance to find liability when a defendant merely sells a commercial product suitable for some lawful use.

For the same reasons that *Sony* took the staple-article doctrine of patent law as a model for its copyright safe-harbor rule, the inducement rule, too, is a sensible one for copyright. We adopt it here, holding that one who distributes a device with the object of promoting its use to infringe copyright, as shown by clear expression or other affirmative steps taken to foster infringement, is liable for the resulting acts of infringement by third parties. We are, of course, mindful of the need to keep from trenching on regular commerce or discouraging the development of technologies with lawful and unlawful potential. Accordingly, just as

Sony did not find intentional inducement despite the knowledge of the VCR manufacturer that its device could be used to infringe, mere knowledge of infringing potential or of actual infringing uses would not be enough here to subject a distributor to liability. Nor would ordinary acts incident to product distribution, such as offering customers technical support or product updates, support liability in themselves. The inducement rule, instead, <u>premises liability</u> on purposeful, culpable expression and conduct, and thus does nothing to compromise legitimate commerce or discourage innovation having a lawful promise.

III

A

The only apparent question about treating MGM's evidence as sufficient to withstand summary judgment under the theory of inducement goes to the need on MGM's part to adduce evidence that StreamCast and Grokster <u>communicated an inducing message to their software users</u>. The classic instance of inducement is by advertisement or solicitation that broadcasts a message designed to stimulate others to commit violations. MGM claims that such a message is shown here. It is undisputed that StreamCast beamed onto the computer screens of users of Napster-compatible programs ads urging the adoption of its OpenNap program, which was designed, as its name implied, to invite the custom of patrons of Napster, then under attack in the courts for facilitating massive infringement. Those who accepted StreamCast's OpenNap program were offered software to perform the same services, which a factfinder could conclude would readily have been understood in the Napster market as the ability to download copyrighted music files. Grokster distributed an electronic newsletter containing links to articles promoting its software's ability to access popular copyrighted music. And anyone whose Napster or free file-sharing searches turned up a link to Grokster would have understood Grokster to be offering the same file-sharing ability as Napster, and to the same people who probably used Napster for infringing downloads; that would also have been the understanding of anyone offered Grokster's suggestively named Swaptor software, its version of OpenNap. And both companies communicated a clear message by responding <u>affirmatively to requests for help in locating and playing copyrighted materials</u>.

In StreamCast's case, of course, the evidence just described was supplemented by other unequivocal indications of unlawful purpose in the internal communications and advertising designs aimed at Napster users ("When the lights went off at Napster ... where did the users go?"). Whether the messages were communicated is not to the point on this record. The function of the message in the theory of inducement is to prove by a defendant's own statements that his unlawful purpose disqualifies him from claiming protection (and incidentally to point to actual violators likely to be found among those who hear or read the message). Proving that a message was sent out, then, is the preeminent but not exclusive way of showing that active steps were taken with the purpose of bringing about infringing acts, and of showing that infringing acts took place by using the device distributed. Here, the summary judgment record is replete with other evidence that Grokster and StreamCast, unlike the manufacturer and distributor in *Sony*, acted with a purpose to cause copyright violations by use of software suitable for illegal use.

Three features of this evidence of intent are particularly notable. First, each company showed itself to be aiming to satisfy a known source of demand for copyright infringement, the market comprising former Napster users. StreamCast's internal documents made constant reference to Napster, it initially distributed its Morpheus software through an OpenNap program compatible with Napster, it advertised its Open-Nap program to Napster users, and its Morpheus software functions as Napster did except that it could be used to distribute more kinds of files, including copyrighted movies and software programs. Grokster's name is apparently derived from Napster, it too initially offered an OpenNap program, its software's function is likewise comparable to Napster's, and it attempted to divert queries for Napster onto its own Web site. Grokster and StreamCast's efforts to supply services to former Napster users, deprived of a mechanism to copy and distribute what were overwhelmingly infringing files, indicate a principal, if not exclusive, intent on the part of each to bring about infringement.

Second, this evidence of unlawful objective is given added significance by MGM's showing that neither company attempted to develop filtering tools or other mechanisms to diminish the infringing activity using their software. While the Ninth Circuit treated the defendants' failure to develop such tools as irrelevant because they lacked an independent duty to monitor their users' activity, we think this evidence underscores Grokster's and StreamCast's intentional facilitation of their users' infringement.[62]

Third, there is a further complement to the direct evidence of unlawful objective. It is useful to recall that StreamCast and Grokster make money by selling advertising space, by directing ads to the screens of computers employing their software. As the record shows, the more the software is used, the more ads are sent out and the greater the advertising revenue becomes. Since the extent of the software's use determines the gain to the distributors, the commercial sense of their enterprise turns on high-volume use, which the record shows is infringing. This evidence alone would not justify an inference of unlawful intent, but viewed in the context of the entire record its import is clear. The unlawful objective is unmistakable.

---

[62] [Footnote 12] Of course, in the absence of other evidence of intent, a court would be unable to find contributory infringement liability merely based on a failure to take affirmative steps to prevent infringement, if the device otherwise was capable of substantial noninfringing uses. Such a holding would tread too close to the *Sony* safe harbor.

B

In addition to intent to bring about infringement and distribution of a device suitable for infringing use, the inducement theory of course requires evidence of actual infringement by recipients of the device, the software in this case. As the account of the facts indicates, there is evidence of infringement on a gigantic scale, and there is no serious issue of the adequacy of MGM's showing on this point in order to survive the companies' summary judgment requests. Although an exact calculation of infringing use, as a basis for a claim of damages, is subject to dispute, there is no question that the summary judgment evidence is at least adequate to entitle MGM to go forward with claims for damages and equitable relief. ...

In sum, this case is significantly different from *Sony* and reliance on that case to rule in favor of StreamCast and Grokster was error. *Sony* dealt with a claim of liability based solely on distributing a product with alternative lawful and unlawful uses, with knowledge that some users would follow the unlawful course. The case struck a balance between the interests of protection and innovation by holding that the product's capability of substantial lawful employment should bar the imputation of fault and consequent secondary liability for the unlawful acts of others.

MGM's evidence in this case most obviously addresses a different basis of liability for distributing a product open to alternative uses. Here, evidence of the distributors' words and deeds going beyond distribution as such shows a purpose to cause and profit from third-party acts of copyright infringement. If liability for inducing infringement is ultimately found, it will not be on the basis of presuming or imputing fault, but from inferring a patently illegal objective from statements and actions showing what that objective was.

There is substantial evidence in MGM's favor on all elements of inducement, and summary judgment in favor of Grokster and StreamCast was error. On remand, reconsideration of MGM's motion for summary judgment will be in order.

The judgment of the Court of Appeals is vacated, and the case is remanded for further proceedings consistent with this opinion.

It is so ordered.

JUSTICE GINSBURG, with whom THE CHIEF JUSTICE and JUSTICE KENNEDY join, concurring.

I concur in the Court's decision, which vacates in full the judgment of the Court of Appeals for the Ninth Circuit, and write separately to clarify why I conclude that the Court of Appeals misperceived, and hence misapplied, our holding in *Sony Corp. of America v. Universal City Studios, Inc.*, 464 U.S. 417 (1984). ...

"The staple article of commerce doctrine" applied to copyright, the [*Sony*] Court stated, "must strike a balance between a copyright holder's legitimate demand for effective–not merely symbolic–protection of the statutory monopoly, and the rights of others freely to engage in substantially unrelated areas of commerce." *Sony*, 464 U.S., at 442. "Accordingly," the Court held, "the sale of copying equipment, like the sale of other articles of commerce, does not constitute contributory infringement if the product is widely used for legitimate, unobjectionable purposes. Indeed, it need merely be capable of substantial noninfringing uses." *Ibid.* Thus, to resolve the *Sony* case, the Court explained, it had to determine "whether the Betamax is capable of commercially significant noninfringing uses." *Ibid.*

To answer that question, the Court considered whether "a significant number of [potential uses of the Betamax were] noninfringing." The Court homed in on one potential use–private, noncommercial time-shifting of television programs in the home (*i.e.*, recording a broadcast TV program for later personal viewing). Time-shifting was noninfringing, the Court concluded, because in some cases trial testimony showed it was authorized by the copyright holder, and in others it qualified as legitimate fair use. Most purchasers used the Betamax principally to engage in time-shifting, a use that "plainly satisfie[d]" the Court's standard. Thus, there was no need in *Sony* to "give precise content to the question of how much [actual or potential] use is commercially significant." Further development was left for later days and cases.

The Ninth Circuit went astray, I will endeavor to explain, when that court granted summary judgment to Grokster and StreamCast on the charge of contributory liability based on distribution of their software products. ... The appeals court pointed to the band Wilco, which made one of its albums available for free downloading, to other recording artists who may have authorized free distribution of their music through the Internet, and to public domain literary works and films available through Grokster's and StreamCast's software. Although it acknowledged MGM's assertion that "the vast majority of the software use is for copyright infringement," the court concluded that Grokster's and StreamCast's proffered evidence met *Sony*'s requirement that "a product need only be capable of substantial noninfringing uses." 380 F.3d, at 1162.

This case differs markedly from *Sony*. Here, there has been no finding of any fair use and little beyond anecdotal evidence of noninfringing uses. In finding the Grokster and StreamCast software products capable of substantial noninfringing uses, the District Court and the Court of Appeals appear to have relied largely on declarations submitted by the defendants. These declarations include assertions (some of them hearsay) that a number of copyright owners authorize distribution of their works on the Internet and that some public domain material is available through peer-to-peer networks including those accessed through Grokster's and StreamCast's software. ...

Even if the absolute number of noninfringing files copied using the Grokster and StreamCast software is large, it does not follow that the products are therefore put to substantial noninfringing uses and are thus immune from liability. The number of noninfringing copies may be reflective of, and dwarfed by, the huge total volume of files shared. Further, the District Court and the Court of Appeals did not sharply distinguish between uses of Grokster's and StreamCast's software products (which this case is about) and uses of peer-to-peer technology generally (which this case is not about).

In sum, when the record in this case was developed, there was evidence that Grokster's and StreamCast's products were, and had been for some time, overwhelmingly used to infringe, and that this infringement was the overwhelming source of revenue from the products. Fairly appraised, the evidence was insufficient to demonstrate, beyond genuine debate, a reasonable prospect that substantial or commercially significant noninfringing uses were likely to develop over time. On this record, the District Court should not have ruled dispositively on the contributory infringement charge by granting summary judgment to Grokster and StreamCast.

If, on remand, the case is not resolved on summary judgment in favor of MGM based on Grokster and StreamCast actively inducing infringement, the Court of Appeals, I would emphasize, should reconsider, on a fuller record, its interpretation of *Sony*'s product distribution holding.

JUSTICE BREYER, with whom JUSTICE STEVENS and JUSTICE O'CONNOR join, concurring.

I agree with the Court that the distributor of a dual-use technology may be liable for the infringing activities of third parties where he or she actively seeks to advance the infringement. I further agree that, in light of our holding today, we need not now "revisit" *Sony Corp. of America v. Universal City Studios, Inc.*, 464 U.S. 417 (1984). Other Members of the Court, however, take up the *Sony* question: whether Grokster's product is "capable of 'substantial' or 'commercially significant' noninfringing uses." (Ginsburg, J., concurring) (quoting *Sony, supra*, at 442). And they answer that question by stating that the Court of Appeals was wrong when it granted summary judgment on the issue in Grokster's favor. I write to explain why I disagree with them on this matter.

I

...

B

When measured against *Sony*'s underlying evidence and analysis, the evidence now before us shows that Grokster passes *Sony*'s test—that is, whether the company's product is capable of substantial or commercially significant noninfringing uses. For one thing, petitioners' (hereinafter MGM) own expert declared that 75% of current files available on Grokster are infringing and 15% are "likely infringing." That leaves some number of files near 10% that apparently are noninfringing, a figure very similar to the 9% or so of authorized time-shifting uses of the VCR that the Court faced in *Sony*. ...

Importantly, *Sony* also used the word "capable," asking whether the product is "capable of" substantial noninfringing uses. Its language and analysis suggest that a figure like 10%, if fixed for all time, might well prove insufficient, but that such a figure serves as an adequate foundation where there is a reasonable prospect of expanded legitimate uses over time. And its language also indicates the appropriateness of looking to potential future uses of the product to determine its "capability."

Here the record reveals a significant future market for noninfringing uses of Grokster-type peer-to-peer software. Such software permits the exchange of any sort of digital file–whether that file does, or does not, contain copyrighted material. As more and more uncopyrighted information is stored in swappable form, it seems a likely inference that lawful peer-to-peer sharing will become increasingly prevalent. ...

There may be other now-unforeseen noninfringing uses that develop for peer-to-peer software, just as the home-video rental industry (unmentioned in *Sony*) developed for the VCR. But the foreseeable development of such uses, when taken together with an estimated 10% noninfringing material, is sufficient to meet *Sony*'s standard. ...

II

The real question here, I believe, is not whether the record evidence satisfies *Sony*. ... Instead, the real question is whether we should modify the *Sony* standard, as MGM requests, or interpret *Sony* more strictly, as I believe Justice Ginsburg's approach would do in practice.

... *Sony* itself sought to "strike a balance between a copyright holder's legitimate demand for effective–not merely symbolic–protection of the statutory monopoly, and the rights of others freely to engage in substantially unrelated areas of commerce." [*Sony*], at 442. Thus, to determine whether modification, or a strict interpretation, of *Sony* is needed, I would ask whether MGM has shown that *Sony* incorrectly balanced copyright and new-technology interests. In particular: (1) Has *Sony* (as I interpret it) worked to protect new technology? (2) If so, would modification or strict interpretation significantly weaken that protection? (3) If so, would new or necessary copyright-related benefits outweigh any such weakening?

A

The first question is the easiest to answer. *Sony*'s rule, as I interpret it, has provided entrepreneurs with needed assurance that they will be shielded from copyright liability as they bring valuable new technologies to market. ...

B

The second, more difficult, question is whether a modified *Sony* rule (or a strict interpretation) would significantly weaken the law's ability to protect new technology. Justice Ginsburg's approach would require defendants to produce considerably more concrete evidence—more than was presented here—to earn *Sony*'s shelter. That heavier evidentiary demand, and especially the more dramatic (case-by-case balancing) modifications that MGM and the Government seek, would, I believe, undercut the protection that *Sony* now offers.

To require defendants to provide, for example, detailed evidence—say business plans, profitability estimates, projected technological modifications, and so forth—would doubtless make life easier for copyrightholder plaintiffs. But it would simultaneously increase the legal uncertainty that surrounds the creation or development of a new technology capable of being put to infringing uses. Inventors and entrepreneurs (in the garage, the dorm room, the corporate lab, or the boardroom) would have to fear (and in many cases endure) costly and extensive trials when they create, produce, or distribute the sort of information technology that can be used for copyright infringement. They would often be left guessing as to how a court, upon later review of the product and its uses, would decide when necessarily rough estimates amounted to sufficient evidence. They would have no way to predict how courts would weigh the respective values of infringing and noninfringing uses; determine the efficiency and advisability of technological changes; or assess a product's potential future markets. The price of a wrong guess—even if it involves a good-faith effort to assess technical and commercial viability—could be large statutory damages (not less than $750 and up to $30,000 per infringed work). 17 U.S.C. § 504(c)(1). The additional risk and uncertainty would mean a consequent additional chill of technological development.

C

The third question—whether a positive copyright impact would outweigh any technology-related loss—I find the most difficult of the three. I do not doubt that a more intrusive *Sony* test would generally provide greater revenue security for copyright holders. But it is harder to conclude that the gains on the copyright swings would exceed the losses on the technology roundabouts.

For one thing, the law disfavors equating the two different kinds of gain and loss; rather, it leans in favor of protecting technology. As *Sony* itself makes clear, the producer of a technology which permits unlawful copying does not himself engage in unlawful copying—a fact that makes the attachment of copyright liability to the creation, production, or distribution of the technology an exceptional thing. Moreover, *Sony* has been the law for some time. And that fact imposes a serious burden upon copyright holders like MGM to show a need for change in the current rules of the game, including a more strict interpretation of the test.

In any event, the evidence now available does not, in my view, make out a sufficiently strong case for change. To say this is not to doubt the basic need to protect copyrighted material from infringement. The Constitution itself stresses the vital role that copyright plays in advancing the "useful Arts." Art. I, § 8, cl. 8. No one disputes that "reward to the author or artist serves to induce release to the public of the products of his creative genius." *United States v. Paramount Pictures, Inc.*, 334 U.S. 131, 158 (1948). And deliberate unlawful copying is no less an unlawful taking of property than garden-variety theft. But these highly general principles cannot by themselves tell us how to balance the interests at issue in *Sony* or whether *Sony*'s standard needs modification. And at certain key points, information is lacking.

Will an unmodified *Sony* lead to a significant diminution in the amount or quality of creative work produced? Since copyright's basic objective is creation and its revenue objectives but a means to that end, this is the underlying copyright question. And its answer is far from clear.

Unauthorized copying likely diminishes industry revenue, though it is not clear by how much. ... More importantly, copyright holders at least potentially have other tools available to reduce piracy and to abate whatever threat it poses to creative production. As today's opinion makes clear, a copyright holder may proceed against a technology provider where a provable specific intent to infringe (of the kind the Court describes) is present. Services like Grokster may well be liable under an inducement theory.

In addition, a copyright holder has always had the legal authority to bring a traditional infringement suit against one who wrongfully copies. Indeed, since September 2003, the Recording Industry Association of America (RIAA) has filed "thousands of suits against people for sharing copyrighted material." Walker, *New Movement Hits Universities: Get Legal Music*, WASHINGTON POST, Mar. 17, 2005, p. E1. These suits have provided copyright holders with damages; have served as a teaching tool, making clear that much file sharing, if done without permission, is unlawful; and apparently have had a real and significant deterrent effect.

Further, copyright holders may develop new technological devices that will help curb unlawful infringement. Some new technology, called "digital 'watermarking'" and "digital fingerprint[ing]," can encode within the file information about the author and the copyright scope and date, which "fingerprints" can help to expose infringers.

At the same time, advances in technology have discouraged unlawful copying by making lawful copying (e.g., downloading music with the copyright holder's permission) cheaper and easier to achieve. Several services now sell music for less than $1 per song. (Walmart.com, for example, charges $0.88 each). Consequently, many consumers initially attracted to the convenience and flexibility of services like Grokster are now migrating to lawful paid services (services with copying permission) where they can enjoy at little cost even greater convenience and flexibility without engaging in unlawful swapping.

Thus, lawful music downloading services—those that charge the customer for downloading music and pay royalties to the copyright holder—

have continued to grow and to produce substantial revenue. And more advanced types of non-music-oriented P2P networks have also started to develop, drawing in part on the lessons of Grokster.

Finally, as *Sony* recognized, the legislative option remains available. Courts are less well suited than Congress to the task of "accommodat[ing] fully the varied permutations of competing interests that are inevitably implicated by such new technology." *Sony*, 464 U.S., at 431.

I do not know whether these developments and similar alternatives will prove sufficient, but I am reasonably certain that, given their existence, a strong demonstrated need for modifying *Sony* (or for interpreting *Sony*'s standard more strictly) has not yet been shown. That fact, along with the added risks that modification (or strict interpretation) would impose upon technological innovation, leads me to the conclusion that we should maintain *Sony*, reading its standard as I have read it. As so read, it requires affirmance of the Ninth Circuit's determination of the relevant aspects of the *Sony* question....

For these reasons, I disagree with Justice Ginsburg, but I agree with the Court and join its opinion.

Notes and Questions

1. Before *Grokster*, the overwhelming majority of third party copyright liability cases, including *Sony*, were litigated under conventional theories of vicarious and contributory liability. *Grokster*, however, was decided on the basis on inducement. Why did the Court hold the *Grokster* defendants liable for inducement instead of conventional vicarious or contributory liability? Can you identify difficulties associated with *Sony* that made inducement a desirable basis for liability in *Grokster*?

2. What is the rationale or policy behind inducement, and how would you compare inducement's rationale or policy to those of vicarious and contributory liability as articulated in cases like *Shapiro* and *Abdallah*? It may be difficult to discern the rationale behind each form of third party copyright liability, but doing so will help you make sense of how various doctrinal pieces fit together. For example, consider *Sony*'s limitation on third party copyright liability. *Grokster* states, "One infringes contributorily by intentionally inducing or encouraging direct infringement." This classifies inducement as a species of contributory liability. Prior to *Grokster*, many understood *Sony* as a limit on the scope of contributory liability. Nevertheless, in Part IIC of its opinion, the Court clearly states that *Sony* does not limit inducement. Does inducement's rationale explain why *Sony* does not limit inducement actions?

3. What does it mean for a defendant to induce infringement? *Grokster* involved defendants who apparently distributed technology hoping that others would use it to infringe. Courts could limit induce-

ment to cases like this, where defendants act with the specific intent and purpose of causing others to infringe. However, courts could also extend inducement to defendants who are certain that their behavior will lead to infringement, but whose desire to cause infringement is somewhat equivocal. For example, consider the designer of peer-to-peer software that makes it easy for college students to share class notes and who distributes the software on college campuses. What if this designer knew that students could just as easily share music as class notes and distributes the software knowing that college students are particularly likely to swap infringing copies of music? Does she intend to cause infringement under *Grokster* by distributing her software with knowledge that infringement would surely follow? Alternatively, what about Apple Computer, which sold its popular iPod players under the advertising campaign "Rip. Mix. Burn."? Why might a court want to extend inducement liability to such defendants, and why might a court want to refrain from doing so?

4. When the Supreme Court granted certiorari in *Grokster*, many observers thought the Court would clarify the amount of noninfringing use required to shield a technology provider under *Sony*. As we have now seen, the Court disappointed those who hoped for such a clarification. Justice Souter's opinion, although unanimous, simply affirms the Court's support of the *Sony* rule, but it says nothing about how easily copying technology can satisfy the requirement of being capable of substantial noninfringing use. However, 6 members of the Court were willing to speak at greater length about *Sony*, but their views were evenly divided. What distinguishes the two concurrences, and which of the concurring opinions do you think interpreted *Sony* correctly?

Perfect 10 v. Visa International Service Association
494 F.3d 788 (9th Cir. 2007)

MILAN J. SMITH, JR., Circuit Judge:

Perfect 10, Inc. (Perfect 10) sued Visa International Service Association, MasterCard International Inc., and several affiliated banks and data processing services (collectively, the Defendants), alleging secondary liability under federal copyright and trademark law and liability under California statutory and common law. It sued because Defendants continue to process credit card payments to websites that infringe Perfect 10's intellectual property rights after being notified by Perfect 10 of infringement by those websites. The district court dismissed all causes of action under Federal Rule of Civil Procedure 12(b)(6) for failure to state a claim upon which relief can be granted. We affirm the decision of the district court.

FACTS AND PRIOR PROCEEDINGS

Perfect 10 publishes the magazine "PERFECT10" and operates the subscription website www.perfect10.com, both of which "feature tasteful copyrighted images of the world's most beautiful natural models." ... Perfect 10 alleges that numerous websites based in several countries have stolen its proprietary images, altered them, and illegally offered them for sale online.

Instead of suing the direct infringers in this case, Perfect 10 sued Defendants, financial institutions that process certain credit card payments to the allegedly infringing websites. The Visa and MasterCard entities are associations of member banks that issue credit cards to consumers, automatically process payments to merchants authorized to accept their cards, and provide information to the interested parties necessary to settle the resulting debits and credits. Defendants collect fees for their services in these transactions. Perfect 10 alleges that it sent Defendants repeated notices specifically identifying infringing websites and informing Defendants that some of their consumers use their payment cards to purchase infringing images. Defendants admit receiving some of these notices, but they took no action in response to the notices after receiving them. ...

DISCUSSION

SECONDARY LIABILITY UNDER FEDERAL COPYRIGHT AND TRADEMARK LAW

A. Secondary Liability for Copyright Infringement

... We evaluate Perfect 10's claims with an awareness that credit cards serve as the primary engine of electronic commerce and that Congress has determined it to be the "policy of the United States—(1) to promote the continued development of the Internet and other interactive computer services and other interactive media [and] (2) to preserve the vibrant and competitive free market that presently exists for the Internet and other interactive computer services, unfettered by Federal or State regulation."[63] 47 U.S.C. §§ 230(b)(1), (2).[64]

1. Contributory Copyright Infringement

Contributory copyright infringement is a form of secondary liability with roots in the tort-law concepts of enterprise liability and imputed intent. This court and the United States Supreme Court (Supreme Court) have announced various formulations of the same basic test for such liability. ... We understand these several [formulations] to be non-contradictory variations on the same basic test, *i.e.*, that one contributorily infringes when he (1) has knowledge of another's infringement and

---

[63] Editors' note: The quoted passage comes from the Communications Decency Act.

[64] [Footnote 2] Congress expressed similar sentiments when it enacted the Digital Millennium Copyright Act (DMCA), one of the stated purposes of which was to "facilitate the robust development and worldwide expansion of electronic commerce, communications, research, development, and education in the digital age." S. Rep. 105-190, at 1-2 (1998).

(2) either (a) materially contributes to or (b) induces that infringement. Viewed in isolation, the language of the tests described is quite broad, but when one reviews the details of the actual "cases and controversies" before the relevant court in each of the test-defining cases and the actual holdings in those cases, it is clear that the factual circumstances in this case are not analogous. To find that Defendants' activities fall within the scope of such tests would require a radical and inappropriate expansion of existing principles of secondary liability and would violate the public policy of the United States.

a. Knowledge of the Infringing Activity

Because we find that Perfect 10 has not pled facts sufficient to establish that Defendants induce or materially contribute to the infringing activity, Perfect 10's contributory copyright infringement claim fails and we need not address the Defendants' knowledge of the infringing activity.

b. Material Contribution, Inducement, or Causation

To state a claim of contributory infringement, Perfect 10 must allege facts showing that Defendants induce, cause, or materially contribute to the infringing conduct. Three key cases found defendants contributorily liable under this standard: *Fonovisa, Inc. v. Cherry Auction, Inc.*, 76 F.3d 259 (9th Cir. 1996), *A & M Records, Inc. v. Napster, Inc.*, 239 F.3d 1004 (9th Cir. 2001), and *Metro-Goldwyn-Mayer Studios, Inc. v. Grokster, Ltd.*, 545 U.S. 913 (2005). In *Fonovisa,* we held a swap meet operator contributorily liable for the sale of pirated works at the swap meet. In *Napster,* we held the operator of an electronic file sharing system liable when users of that system employed it to exchange massive quantities of copyrighted music. In *Grokster,* the Supreme Court found liability for the substantially similar act of distributing software that enabled exchange of copyrighted music on a peer-to-peer, rather than a centralized basis.[65] Perfect 10 argues that by continuing to process credit card payments to the infringing websites despite having knowledge of ongoing infringement, Defendants induce, enable and contribute to the infringing activity in the same way the defendants did in *Fonovisa*, *Napster*, and *Grokster*. We disagree.

1. Material Contribution

The credit card companies cannot be said to materially contribute to the infringement in this case because they have no direct connection to that infringement. ... While Perfect 10 has alleged that Defendants make it easier for websites to profit from this infringing activity, the issue here is reproduction, alteration, display and distribution, which can occur without payment. Even if infringing images were not paid for, there would still be infringement.

---

[65] [Footnote 5] Because the *Grokster* court focused primarily on an "inducement" theory rather than a "material contribution" theory, our primary discussion of *Grokster* is located below in the "inducement" section of this opinion.

Our analysis is fully consistent with this court's recent decision in *Perfect 10 v. Amazon.com*, 483 F.3d 701 (9th Cir. 2007), where we found that [the search engine company] "Google could be held contributorily liable if it had knowledge that infringing Perfect 10 images were available using its search engine, could take simple measures to prevent further damage to Perfect 10's copyrighted works, and failed to take such steps."[66] The dissent claims this statement applies squarely to Defendants if we just substitute "payment systems" for "search engine." But this is only true if search engines and payment systems are equivalents for these purposes, and they are not. The salient distinction is that Google's search engine itself assists in the distribution of infringing content to Internet users, while Defendants' payment systems do not. ...

Our holding is also fully consistent with and supported by this court's previous holdings in *Fonovisa* and *Napster*. While there are some limited similarities between the factual scenarios in *Fonovisa* and *Napster* and the facts in this case, the differences in those scenarios are substantial, and, in our view, dispositive. In *Fonovisa,* we held a flea market proprietor liable as a contributory infringer when it provided the facilities for and benefited from the sale of pirated works. ...

In *Napster,* this court found the designer and distributor of a software program liable for contributory infringement. Napster was a file-sharing program which, while capable of non-infringing use, was expressly engineered to enable the easy exchange of pirated music and was widely so used. Citing the *Fonovisa* standard, the *Napster* court found that Napster materially contributes to the users' direct infringement by knowingly providing the "site and facilities" for that infringement.

Seeking to draw an analogy to *Fonovisa* and, by extension, *Napster*, Perfect 10 pleads that Defendants materially contribute to the infringement by offering services that allow it to happen on a larger scale than would otherwise be possible. ... [Perfect 10 argues] for an extremely broad conception of the term "site and facilities" that bears no relationship to the holdings in the actual "cases and controversies" decided in *Fonovisa* and *Napster*. Taken literally, Perfect 10's theory appears to include any tangible or intangible component related to any transaction in which infringing material is bought and sold. But *Fonovisa* and *Napster* do not require or lend themselves to such a construction. The actual display, location, and distribution of infringing images in this case occurs on websites that organize, display, and transmit information over the wires and wireless instruments that make up the Internet. The *websites* are the "site" of the infringement, not Defendants' payment networks. Defendants do not create, operate, advertise, or otherwise promote these websites. They do not operate the servers on which they reside. Unlike

---

[66] Editors' note: In *Perfect 10 v. Amazon,* Perfect 10 sued a number of search engines, including Google, for facilitating infringement of Perfect 10's images. The district court concluded, among other things, that Perfect 10 would likely not prevail on its contributory liability claim and therefore denied injunctive relief. The Ninth Circuit reversed and remanded the case to the district court.

the *Napster* (and *Grokster*) defendants, they do not provide users the tools to locate infringing material, nor does any infringing material ever reside on or pass through any network or computer Defendants operate. Defendants merely provide a method of payment, not a "site" or "facility" of infringement. Any conception of "site and facilities" that encompasses Defendants would also include a number of peripherally-involved third parties, such as computer display companies, storage device companies, and software companies that make the software necessary to alter and view the pictures and even utility companies that provide electricity to the Internet.

Perfect 10 seeks to side-step this reality by alleging that Defendants are still contributory infringers because they could refuse to process payments to the infringing websites and thereby undermine their commercial viability. Even though we must take this factual allegation as true, that Defendants have the power to undermine the commercial viability of infringement does not demonstrate that the Defendants materially contribute to that infringement. As previously noted, the direct infringement here is the reproduction, alteration, display and distribution of Perfect 10's images over the Internet. Perfect 10 has not alleged that any infringing material passes over Defendants' payment networks or through their payment processing systems, or that Defendants designed or promoted their payment systems as a means to infringe. While Perfect 10 has alleged that Defendants make it easier for websites to profit from this infringing activity, the infringement stems from the failure to obtain a license to distribute, not the processing of payments.

2. Inducement

In *Grokster*, the Supreme Court applied the patent law concept of "inducement" to a claim of contributory infringement against a file-sharing program. The court found that "one who distributes a device with the object of promoting its use to infringe copyright, as shown by clear expression or other affirmative steps taken to foster infringement, is liable for the resulting acts of infringement by third parties." Perfect 10 claims that *Grokster* is analogous because Defendants induce customers to use their cards to purchase goods and services, and are therefore guilty of specifically inducing infringement if the cards are used to purchase images from sites that have content stolen from Perfect 10. This is mistaken. Because Perfect 10 alleges no "affirmative steps taken to foster infringement" and no facts suggesting that Defendants promoted their payment system as a means to infringe, its claim is premised on a fundamental misreading of *Grokster* that would render the concept of "inducement" virtually meaningless.

The *Grokster* court announced that the standard for inducement liability is providing a service "with the object of promoting its use to infringe copyright." "[M]ere knowledge of infringing potential or actual infringing uses would not be enough here to subject [a defendant] to liability." Instead, inducement "premises liability on purposeful, culpable expression and conduct, and thus does nothing to compromise legitimate commerce or discourage innovation having a lawful promise." Moreover, to establish inducement liability, it is crucial to establish that the distributors "communicated an inducing message to their ... users," the classic example of which is an "advertisement or solicitation that broadcasts a message designed to stimulate others to commit violations." The *Grokster* court summarized the "inducement" rule as follows:

> In sum, where an article is good for nothing else but infringement, there is no legitimate public interest in its unlicensed availability, and there is no injustice in presuming or imputing an intent to infringe. Conversely, the doctrine absolves the equivocal conduct of selling an item with substantial lawful as well as unlawful uses, and limits liability to instances of more acute fault than the mere understanding that some of one's products will be misused. It leaves breathing room for innovation and a vigorous commerce.

Perfect 10 has not alleged that any of these standards are met or that any of these considerations are present here. Defendants do, of course, market their credit cards as a means to pay for goods and services, online and elsewhere. But it does not follow that Defendants affirmatively promote each product that their cards are used to purchase. The software systems in *Napster* and *Grokster* were engineered, disseminated, and promoted explicitly for the purpose of facilitating piracy of copyrighted music and reducing legitimate sales of such music to that extent. Most Napster and Grokster users understood this and primarily used those systems to purloin copyrighted music. Further, the Grokster operators explicitly targeted then-current users of the Napster program by sending them ads for its OpenNap program. In contrast, Perfect 10 does not allege that Defendants created or promote their payment systems as a means to break laws. Perfect 10 simply alleges that Defendants generally promote their cards and payment systems but points to no "clear expression" or "affirmative acts" with any specific intent to foster infringement. ...

Finally, we must take as true the allegations that Defendants lend their names and logos to the offending websites and continue to allow their cards to be used to purchase infringing images despite actual knowledge of the infringement-and perhaps even bending their association rules to do so. But we do not and need not, on this factual basis, take as true that Defendants "induce" consumers to buy pirated content with their cards. "Inducement" is a legal determination, and dismissal may not be avoided by characterizing a legal determination as a factual one. We must determine whether the facts as pled constitute a "clear expression" of a specific intent to foster infringement, and, for the reasons above noted, we hold that they do not.

2. Vicarious Copyright Infringement

Vicarious infringement is a concept related to, but distinct from, contributory infringement. Whereas contributory infringement is based on tort-law principles of enterprise liability and imputed intent, vicarious infringement's roots lie in the agency principles of *respondeat superior*. To state a claim for vicarious copyright infringement, a plaintiff must allege that the defendant has (1) the right and ability to supervise the infringing conduct and (2) a direct financial interest in the infringing activity. The Supreme Court has recently offered (in dictum) an alternate formulation of the test: "One ... infringes vicariously by profiting from direct infringement while declining to exercise a right to stop or limit it." *Grokster*, 545 U.S. at 930 (internal citations omitted). Perfect 10 alleges that Defendants have the right and ability to control the content of the infringing websites by refusing to process credit card payments to the websites, enforcing their own rules and regulations, or both. We hold that Defendants' conduct alleged in Perfect 10's first amended complaint fails to state a claim for vicarious copyright infringement.

a. Right and Ability to Supervise the Infringing Activity

In order to join a Defendant's payment network, merchants and member banks must agree to follow that Defendant's rules and regulations. These rules, among other things, prohibit member banks from providing services to merchants engaging in certain illegal activities and require the members and member banks to investigate merchants suspected of engaging in such illegal activity and to terminate their participation in the payment network if certain illegal activity is found. Perfect 10 has alleged that certain websites are infringing Perfect 10's copyrights and that Perfect 10 sent notices of this alleged infringement to Defendants. Accordingly, Perfect 10 has adequately pled that (1) infringement of Perfect 10's copyrights was occurring, (2) Defendants were aware of the infringement, and (3) on this basis, Defendants could have stopped processing credit card payments to the infringing websites. These allegations are not, however, sufficient to establish vicarious liability because even with all reasonable inferences drawn in Perfect 10's favor, Perfect 10's allegations of fact cannot support a finding that Defendants have the right and ability to control the infringing activity.

In reasoning closely analogous to the present case, the *Amazon.com* court held that Google was not vicariously liable for third-party infringement that its search engine facilitates. In so holding, the court found that Google's ability to control its own index, search results, and webpages does not give Google the right to control the infringing acts of third parties even though that ability would allow Google to affect those infringing acts to some degree. Moreover, and even more importantly, the *Amazon.com* court rejected a vicarious liability claim based on Google's policies with sponsored advertisers, which state that it reserves "the right to monitor and terminate partnerships with entities that violate others' copyright[s]." (alteration in original). The court found that

> Google's right to terminate an [sponsored advertiser] partnership does not give Google the right to stop direct infringement by third-party websites. An infringing third-party website can continue to reproduce, display, and distribute its infringing copies of

Perfect 10 images after its participation in the [sponsored advertiser] program has ended.

This reasoning is equally applicable to the Defendants in this case. Just like Google, Defendants could likely take certain steps that may have the indirect effect of reducing infringing activity on the Internet at large. However, neither Google nor Defendants has any ability to directly control that activity, and the mere ability to withdraw a financial "carrot" does not create the "stick" of "right and ability to control" that vicarious infringement requires. A finding of vicarious liability here, under the theories advocated by the dissent, would also require a finding that Google is vicariously liable for infringement—a conflict we need not create, and radical step we do not take. ...

Perfect 10 also argues that were infringing websites barred from accepting the Defendants' credit cards, it would be impossible for an online website selling adult images to compete and operate at a profit. While we must take this allegation as true, it still fails to state a claim because it conflates the power to stop profiteering with the right and ability to control infringement. Perfect 10's allegations do not establish that Defendants have the authority to prevent theft or alteration of the copyrighted images, remove infringing material from these websites or prevent its distribution over the Internet. Rather, they merely state that this infringing activity could not be *profitable* without access to Defendants' credit card payment systems. The alleged infringement does not turn on the payment; it turns on the reproduction, alteration and distribution of the images, which Defendants do not do, and which occurs over networks Defendants do not control.

The Supreme Court's recent decision in *Grokster* does not undermine the validity of this distinction. As we held in *Amazon.com*, *Grokster* does not stand for the proposition that just because the services provided by a company help an infringing enterprise generate revenue, that company is necessarily vicariously liable for that infringement. Numerous services are required for the third party infringers referred to by Perfect 10 to operate. In addition to the necessity of creating and maintaining a website, numerous hardware manufacturers must produce the computer on which the website physically sits; a software engineer must create the program that copies and alters the stolen images; technical support companies must fix any hardware and software problems; utility companies must provide the electricity that makes all these different related operations run, etc. All these services are essential to make the businesses described viable, they all profit to some degree from those businesses, and by withholding their services, they could impair—perhaps even destroy—the commercial viability of those business. But that does not mean, and *Grokster* by no means holds, that they are all potentially liable as vicarious infringers. Even though they have the "right" to refuse their services, and hence the literal power to "stop or limit" the infringement, they, like Defendants, do not exercise sufficient control over the actual infringing activity for vicarious liability to attach.

b. Obvious and Direct Financial Interest in the Infringing Activity

Because Perfect 10 has failed to show that Defendants have the right and ability to control the alleged infringing conduct, it has not pled a viable claim of vicarious liability. Accordingly, we need not reach the issue of direct financial interest.

[The court's discussion of trademark and state law claims is omitted.]

CONCLUSION

We decline to create any of the radical new theories of liability advocated by Perfect 10 and the dissent and we affirm the district court's dismissal with prejudice of all causes of action in Perfect 10's complaint for failure to state a claim upon which relief can be granted.

KOZINSKI, Circuit Judge, dissenting for the most part:[67]

Federal law gives copyright owners the exclusive right to "distribute copies [of their works] ... to the public by sale." 17 U.S.C. § 106(3). Plaintiff alleges that certain third parties it refers to as the "Stolen Content Websites" unlawfully copy its protected images and sell them to the public, using defendants' payment systems as financial intermediaries. ... Plaintiff has repeatedly notified defendants that they are abetting the sale of stolen merchandise by "knowingly providing crucial transactional support services for the sale of millions of stolen photos and film clips worth billions of dollars," but to no avail. Frustrated in its effort to protect the rights Congress has given it, plaintiff turns to the federal courts for redress. We should not slam the courthouse door in its face.

Accepting the truth of plaintiff's allegations, as we must on a motion to dismiss, the credit cards are easily liable for indirect copyright infringement: They knowingly provide a financial bridge between buyers and sellers of pirated works, enabling them to consummate infringing transactions, while making a profit on every sale. If such active participation in infringing conduct does not amount to indirect infringement, it's hard to imagine what would. By straining to absolve defendants of liability, the majority leaves our law in disarray.

Contributory Infringement

We have long held that a defendant is liable for contributory infringement if it "materially contributes to the infringing conduct." *A & M Records, Inc. v. Napster, Inc.,* 239 F.3d 1004, 1019 (9th Cir. 2001). Our recent opinion in *Perfect 10, Inc. v. Amazon.com, Inc.,* 487 F.3d 701 (9th Cir. 2007), canvasses the caselaw in this area and concludes that Google "could be held contributorily liable if it had knowledge that infringing Perfect 10 images were available using its search engine, could take simple measures to prevent further damage to Perfect 10's copyrighted works, and failed to take such steps." Substitute "payment systems" for

---

[67] [Footnote 1] I join part C of the "California Statutory and Common Law Claims" section of the opinion, dealing with plaintiff's libel and prospective economic advantage claims.

"search engine" in this sentence, and it describes defendants here: If a consumer wishes to buy an infringing image from one of the Stolen Content Websites, he can do so by using Visa or MasterCard, just as he can use Google to find the infringing images in the first place. My colleagues engage in wishful thinking when they claim that "Google's search engine itself assists in the distribution of infringing content to Internet users, while Defendants' payment systems do not" and that "[h]elping users to locate an image might substantially assist users to download infringing images, but processing payments does not."

The majority struggles to distinguish *Amazon* by positing an "additional step in the causal chain" between defendants' activities and the infringing conduct. According to the majority, "Google may materially contribute to infringement by making it fast and easy for third parties to locate and distribute infringing material, whereas Defendants make it easier for infringement to be *profitable,* which tends to increase financial incentives to infringe, which in turn tends to increase infringement." The majority is mistaken; there is no "additional step." Defendants participate in every credit card sale of pirated images; the images are delivered to the buyer only after defendants approve the transaction and process the payment. This is not just an economic incentive for infringement; it's an essential step in the infringement process.

In any event, I don't see why it matters whether there is an "additional step." Materiality turns on how significantly the activity helps infringement, not on whether it's characterized as one step or two steps removed from it. The majority recognizes that "Defendants make it easier for websites to profit from this infringing activity," that defendants' conduct "tends to increase infringement," that defendants "have the effect of increasing ... infringement," that "Defendants have the power to undermine the commercial viability of" the Stolen Content Websites and that they "make it easier for websites to profit from this infringing activity," that "Defendants could likely take certain steps that may have the indirect effect of reducing infringing activity on the Internet," and that defendants could "reduce the number of those [infringing] sales," Taking the majority at its word, it sounds like defendants are providing very significant help to the direct infringers.

My colleagues recognize, as they must, that helping consumers locate infringing content can constitute contributory infringement, but they consign the means of payment to secondary status. But why is *locating* infringing images more central to infringement than *paying* for them? If infringing images can't be found, there can be no infringement; but if infringing images can't be paid for, there can be no infringement either. Location services and payment services are equally central to infringement; the majority's contrary assertion is supported largely by disparaging use of "merely," "simply" and "only."

The majority dismisses the significance of credit cards by arguing that "infringement could continue on a large scale [without them] because other viable funding mechanisms are available." Of course, the same could be said about Google. As the majority admits, if Google were unwilling or unable to serve up infringing images, consumers could use Yahoo!, Ask.com, Microsoft Live Search, A9.com or AltaVista instead. Even if none of these were available, consumers could still locate websites with infringing images through e-mails from friends, messages on discussion forums, tips via online chat, "typo-squatting," peer-to-peer networking using BitTorrent or eDonkey, offline and online advertisements, disreputable search engines hosted on servers in far-off jurisdictions or even old-fashioned word of mouth. The majority's claim that search engines "could effectively cause a website to disappear by removing it from their search results" is quite a stretch. ...

The majority's concern that imposing liability on defendants here would implicate vast numbers of other actors who provide incidental services to infringers is unfounded. Line-drawing is always a bit tricky, but courts have shown themselves adept at dealing with it from time out of mind, in resolving such issues as proximate causation and reasonable suspicion. Contributory infringement requires *material* assistance to the infringing activity, and those the majority worries about would doubtless be absolved of liability because their contribution to the infringing activity is insufficiently material. ...

Were we to rule for plaintiff, as we should, I have every confidence that future courts would be able to distinguish this case when and if they are confronted with lawsuits against utility companies, software vendors and others who provide incidental services to infringers.

Vicarious Infringement

A party "infringes vicariously by profiting from direct infringement while declining to exercise a right to stop or limit it." *Amazon,* 487 F.3d at 729 (quoting *Grokster*). There is no doubt that defendants profit from the infringing activity of the Stolen Content Websites; after all, they take a cut of virtually every sale of pirated material. The majority does not dispute this point so I need not belabor it.

Defendants here also have a right to stop or limit the infringing activity, a right they have refused to exercise. As the majority recognizes, "Perfect 10 ... claims that Defendants' rules and regulations permit them to require member merchants to cease illegal activity-presumably including copyright infringement-as a condition to their continuing right to receive credit card payments from the relevant Defendant entities." Assuming the truth of this allegation, the cards have the authority, given to them by contract, to force the Stolen Content Websites to remove infringing images from their inventory as a condition for using defendants' payment systems. If the merchants comply, their websites stop peddling stolen content and so infringement is stopped or limited. If they don't comply, defendants have the right—and under copyright law the duty— to kick the pirates off their payment networks, forcing them to find other means of getting paid or go out of business. In that case, too, infringement is stopped or limited. The swap meet in *Fonovisa* was held vicariously liable precisely because it did not force the pirates to stop infringing or leave; there is no reason to treat defendants here differently. ...

The majority toils to resist this obvious conclusion but its arguments are not persuasive. For example, it makes no difference that defendants control only the means of payment, not the mechanics of transferring the material. In a commercial environment, distribution and payment are (to use a quaint anachronism) like love and marriage—you can't have one without the other. If cards don't process payment, pirates don't deliver booty. The credit cards, in fact, control distribution of the infringing material. ...

Finally, the majority dismisses the Supreme Court's opinion in *Grokster* by suggesting that the Court could not have meant what it said because the standard it announced (and which we adopted in *Amazon*) would sweep in too many goods and services that contribute to infringing activity. *See* maj. op. at 806 (listing hardware manufacturers, software engineers, technical support companies and utilities). The majority misreads the Court's opinion. Providing a crucial service to an infringer may give someone the practical ability to stop infringement, but that's only half of what it takes to be a vicarious infringer. The other half is a right, found in contract, to control the infringer's actions. Those third parties the majority worries about could not be held vicariously liable because they lack the legal right to stop the infringement. So far as I know, utilities are provided by public franchise, not by contract, and a utility has no right to stop providing electricity or phone service because it learns that its electrons are being put to illegal use. Computer manufacturers don't usually retain the right to reclaim computers they have sold because they are being used unlawfully. Ditto for software producers and repairmen. Having no contract that authorizes them to stop providing services on account of illegality, these actors do not meet the first prong of the test for vicarious infringement. ...

[Discussion of trademark and state law claims is omitted]

... The majority's refrain that imposing liability on defendants here would violate "the public policy of the United States," maj. op. at 795, 797, is equally off base. While the majority correctly identifies that policy as facilitating the development of electronic commerce, that solicitude does not extend to commerce in illegal merchandise. I am aware of no policy of the United States to encourage electronic commerce in stolen goods, illegal drugs or child pornography. When it comes to traffic in material that violates the Copyright Act, the policy of the United States is embedded in the FBI warning we see at the start of every lawfully purchased or rented video: Infringers are to be stopped and prosecuted. Preventing financial intermediaries from servicing such shady transactions is entirely consistent with that policy. If Congress believes that this places too heavy a burden on credit cards, it can grant the cards immunity (along with corresponding responsibilities), as it did for ISPs in passing the DMCA. ...

This is an easy case, squarely controlled by our precedent in all material respects. Fairly applying our cases to the facts alleged by Perfect 10, we should reverse the district court and give plaintiff an opportunity to prove its case through discovery and trial. In straining to escape the strictures of our caselaw, the majority draws a series of ephemeral distinctions that are neither required nor permitted; the opinion will prove to be no end of trouble.

Notes and Questions

1. Perfect 10 supported its case by citing a number of earlier decisions in which plaintiffs had successfully sued defendants for contributory or vicarious liability. In each of those cases, the defendant persisted in offering a product or service despite knowing that such behavior would help others infringe. Perfect 10 argued that Visa and MasterCard were no different from the swap meet operators, peer-to-peer providers and search engines that had previously been found liable, but the Ninth Circuit disagreed. What were the distinctions relied upon by the court, and do you find them persuasive? Judge Kozinski certainly did not find them persuasive and sharply criticized the majority in his dissent. Was Judge Kozinski right, and if so, can you explain why the *Perfect 10* majority insisted on making such unpersuasive distinctions?

2. Judge Kozinski's dissent also relied on some potentially slippery factual distinctions. As the majority pointed out, a decision in Perfect 10's favor would raise the possibility of liability against a wide range of potential defendants who knowingly support infringers, including "computer display companies, storage device companies, and software companies that make the software necessary to alter and view the pictures and even utility companies that provide electricity to the Internet." Kozinski acknowledged the challenges associated with line drawing and expressed confidence that courts could distinguish entities like software makers and utilities from credit card companies. If *Perfect 10* had been decided the other way, how would future courts have made the distinctions posited by Judge Kozinski? Did his dissent satisfactorily explain why his theory of the case would not hold utility companies liable for infringement committed by their customers?

3. Judge Kozinski's dissent suggests that the credit card companies deserved to be held vicariously liable. After all, they had the ability to influence whether infringement occurred, and they profited from the sale of infringing material. Is he right, or has he overlooked something crucial to the interpretation of vicarious liability?

4. The majority and dissent both claimed that federal policy supported their positions. The majority argued that the federal policy of encouraging e-commerce supported its decision, while the dissent claimed that the federal policy of stopping infringement took precedence. Both

sides seem to have a point. The majority's opinion does support e-commerce by assuring financial intermediaries that they are unlikely to be held liable for copyright infringement simply because they do business with infringers. At the same time, a decision in *Perfect 10*'s favor would have stopped at least some infringement of Perfect 10's images. Does this mean that the decision in *Perfect 10* came down to a choice between the relative importance of e-commerce and the prevention of infringement? In thinking about your response to this question, recall the rationale behind *Sony*. If the Supreme Court had decided against Sony, it surely would have prevented many people from infringing. Nevertheless, the Court chose not to hold Sony liable because it worried about the loss of noninfringing uses supported by videorecorders. Do similar concerns arise when considering the potential liability of credit card companies, software makers, and utility companies who facilitate infringement?

5. *Perfect 10* and *Grokster* may seem far removed from cases presented at the beginning of this chapter like *Shapiro* and *Abdallah*. However, it is also possible to understand *Perfect 10* and *Grokster* as illustrations of the basic problem raised by *Shapiro* and *Abdallah*, namely the proper scope of third party copyright liability. Looking back, what do you think about the judicial development of this area of law? Have courts applied third party copyright liability appropriately, too broadly, or too narrowly? Do you think that a different interpretation of the law could have avoided some of the difficulties encountered in *Grokster* and *Perfect 10*?

6. For what it is worth, a number of District Court opinions since *Grokster* and *Perfect 10* indicate that inducement has become a powerful weapon against who distribute filesharing software or provide other Internet services devoted primarily to infringement.[68] By contrast, copyright holders have not been successful suing defendants whose services or networks support a relatively broad range of behavior.[69] Although these cases understandably distinguish filesharing from other potentially less culpbable behavior, they do not significantly address the issues left open by *Sony*, *Grokster*, and *Perfect 10* about the kind of knowledge and material contribution that establish contributory liability and the kind of control and financial interest that establish vicarious liability.

---

[68] *See Arista Records v. Lime Group*, 784 F. Supp. 2d. 398 (S.D.N.Y. 2011) (granting summary judgment for inducement against distributor of filesharing program in part because of specific behavior to attract infringing users and facilitate their searches for infringing copies of recorded music); *Arista Records v. Usenet.com*, 633 F. Supp. 2d 124 (S.D.N.Y 2009) (granting summary judgment for inducement against defendant selling access to the USENET network because 94% of the content on defendants' music-related newsgroups was infringing or likely infringing, and because defendant purposefully courted subscribers interested in infringing music).

[69] *See Luvdarts v. AT & T Mobility*, 98 U.S.P.Q.2d 1277 (C.D. Cal. 2011) (defendant wireless carriers not liable simply because their networks enabled users to infringe plaintiff's multimedia messages).

Problem

Your client, an electronics manufacturer, has come to you for advice concerning the design of its best-selling tablets. The current tablets have many of the functions associated with laptop computers. The tablets can surf the Internet, receive and send email, and edit word processing and spreadsheet files. They also store and play music and video files.

Your client's engineers have developed an enhancement to these tablets that it believes will be popular, especially with its business customers. The enhancement in question will make it possible for users to share files quickly via infrared technology. Your client believes that business users will like this feature because they will now be able to transfer large files to other users in the same room without having to hook up to the Internet. Indeed, your client's new technology will transfer files many times faster than the typical wi-fi connection. Best of all, the technology can easily be installed on laptop computers.

Your client has decided to ask you for advice because it knows that people could also use its technology to make multiple unauthorized transfers of copyrighted music and movie files. The technology is so efficient that it would take approximately 3 seconds for a user to transmit an entire movie-length video file to another user.

Your client wonders if it should simply not sell the technology to avoid getting sued for facilitating infringement by others. Alternatively, it is considering re-designing the technology to block or slow the transfer of music and video files while leaving spreadsheet, word processing and other file transfers undisturbed. This "fix" would discourage infringement and be fairly easy to implement, but it would also decrease the value of the technology to business users who have noninfringing reasons to transfer music or video files (e.g., business people transferring company training videos or moviemakers carrying and sharing samples of their own work), and the re-design could, in rare cases, interfere with the transfer of files other than music and video.

What advice would you give your client about how to proceed?

SECTION D. DIGITAL MILLENNIUM COPYRIGHT ACT AND INTERNET SERVICE PROVIDER LIABILITY

The ambiguities associated with third party copyright liability frustrated copyright holders and Internet service providers a great deal. On one hand, Internet service providers feared that the threat of massive copyright damages would make it impossible for them to do business. On the other hand, copyright holders worried that failure to impose some degree of liability on ISPs would allow intermediaries of all kinds to unreasonably facilitate or tacitly encourage infringement. Not surprisingly, both turned to Congress in hopes of finding satisfaction.

Congress reacted to the concerns of copyright holders and Internet service providers by enacting the Digital Millennium Copyright Act (DMCA). The DMCA contains two parts of particular interest to us. The first, codified in section 512 of the Copyright Act, offers limited immunity from infringement committed by others to Internet service providers who comply with certain requirements that help copyright holders protect their interests. The second, codified in section 1201 *et seq.* of the Copyright Act, assists copyright holders by restricting the use and distribution of technology that defeats encryption and other methods of protecting digital content. This section deals with the first of these parts, while Chapter Eight will deal with the second.

The DMCA offers ISPs four basic types of immunity:

First, § 512(a) eliminates liability for *transitory digital network communications*. In the course of doing business, ISPs routinely pass tremendous amounts of data through their servers as customers send emails, browse websites, and download material. Some of this material may well be infringing, and ISPs could potentially be liable for facilitating infringement by passing this material along. This provision immunizes ISPs, under certain circumstances, for the the transmission of infringing material on a pass-through basis, thereby preventing lawsuits against ISPs simply because infringing material sometimes travels through their networks.

Second, § 512(b) exempts ISPs from liability for *system caching*. When users place or transmit material on, or request material through, an ISPs network, that network sometimes automatically stores the material on its servers for short periods of time to facilitate display or transmission. Such storage is necessary for the efficient operation of networks. Again, some of this material could be infringing, and absent immunity, ISPs could be liable simply because they designed their networks to operate efficiently. This provision immunizes ISPs from such liability, so long as ISPs comply with certain conditions.

Third, § 512(c) prevents liability arising from non-temporary *storage of material placed on their networks by users*. This provision applies to ISPs that host websites for users and to websites and services that allow users to upload and store or distribute material on their servers (e.g. Facebook, YouTube, etc.). Some of the material uploaded and stored by users on the ISPs servers may well be infringing, and absent immunity, such companies could be subject to massive liability for hosting and distributing this material. This provision immunizes ISPs from such liability under certain circumstances, which will be discussed in more detail below.

Fourth, § 512(d) blocks liability for ISPs who *link or otherwise direct users to infringing material*. When a search engine or other entity links to a website that contains infringing material, that entity could potentially be liable for helping others engage in infringement. This provision immunizes ISPs from such liability, as long as they do not know that the material in question is infringing, and so long as they act expeditiously to remove such links once notified of the infringing material.

The immunities provided by the DMCA exist only if ISPs comply with requirements found in § 512(i). First, ISPs must implement and inform their users about a policy for terminating access for repeat infringers. Second, ISPs must configure their networks so that they do not interfere with "standard technical measures" used by copyright holders to detect infringement. The foregoing shows that the DMCA operates by promising ISPs immunity from third party liability in return for cooperation in the fight against copyright infringement.

Of the four ISP "safe harbors" set forth above, the one for user-stored content has generated the most attention. This is because many of the largest Internet companies, such as Facebook and YouTube, rely upon this particular safe harbor. Accordingly, we now take a detailed look at the specific provisions of this safe harbor:

(c) INFORMATION RESIDING ON SYSTEMS OR NETWORKS AT DIRECTION OF USERS.—

(1) IN GENERAL. — A service provider shall not be liable for monetary relief, or, except as provided in subsection (j), for injunctive or other equitable relief, for infringement of copyright by reason of the storage at the direction of a user of material that resides on a system or network controlled or operated by or for the service provider, if the service provider —

(A)

(i) does not have actual knowledge that the material or an activity using the material on the system or network is infringing;

(ii) in the absence of such actual knowledge, is not aware of facts or circumstances from which infringing activity is apparent; or

(iii) upon obtaining such knowledge or awareness, acts expeditiously to remove, or disable access to, the material;

(B) does not receive a financial benefit directly attributable to the infringing activity, in a case in which the service provider has the right and ability to control such activity; and

(C) upon notification of claimed infringement as described in paragraph (3), responds expeditiously to remove, or disable access to, the material that is claimed to be infringing or to be the subject of infringing activity.

(2) DESIGNATED AGENT. — The limitations on liability established in this subsection apply to a service provider only if the service provider has designated an agent to receive notifications of claimed infringement described in paragraph (3), by making available through its service, including on its website in a location accessible to the public, and by providing to the Copyright Office, substantially the following information:

(A) the name, address, phone number, and electronic mail address of the agent.

(B) other contact information which the Register of Copyrights may deem appropriate.

The Register of Copyrights shall maintain a current directory of agents available to the public for inspection, including through the Internet, in both electronic and hard copy formats, and may require payment of a fee by service providers to cover the costs of maintaining the directory.

(3) ELEMENTS OF NOTIFICATION. —

(A) To be effective under this subsection, a notification of claimed infringement must be a written communication provided to the designated agent of a service provider that includes substantially the following:

(i) A physical or electronic signature of a person authorized to act on behalf of the owner of an exclusive right that is allegedly infringed.

(ii) Identification of the copyrighted work claimed to have been infringed, or, if multiple copyrighted works at a single online site are covered by a single notification, a representative list of such works at that site.

(iii) Identification of the material that is claimed to be infringing or to be the subject of infringing activity and that is to be removed or access to which is to be disabled, and information reasonably sufficient to permit the service provider to locate the material.

(iv) Information reasonably sufficient to permit the service provider to contact the complaining party, such as an address, telephone number, and, if available, an electronic mail address at which the complaining party may be contacted.

(v) A statement that the complaining party has a good faith belief that use of the material in the manner complained of is not authorized by the copyright owner, its agent, or the law.

(vi) A statement that the information in the notification is accurate, and under penalty of perjury, that the complaining party is authorized to act on behalf of the owner of an exclusive right that is allegedly infringed.

(B)

(i) Subject to clause (ii), a notification from a copyright owner or from a person authorized to act on behalf of the copyright owner that fails to comply substantially with the provisions of subparagraph (A) shall not be considered under paragraph (1)(A) in determining whether a service provider has actual knowledge or is aware of facts or circumstances from which infringing activity is apparent.

(ii) In a case in which the notification that is provided to the service provider's designated agent fails to comply substantially with all the provisions of subparagraph (A) but substantially complies with clauses (ii), (iii), and (iv) of subparagraph (A), clause (i) of this subparagraph applies only if the service provider promptly attempts to contact the person making the notification or takes other reasonable steps to assist in the receipt of notification that substantially complies with all the provisions of subparagraph (A).

(g) REPLACEMENT OF REMOVED OR DISABLED MATERIAL AND LIMITATION ON OTHER LIABILITY.—

(1) NO LIABILITY FOR TAKING DOWN GENERALLY. — Subject to paragraph (2), a service provider shall not be liable to any person for any claim based on the service provider's good faith disabling of access to, or removal of, material or activity claimed to be infringing or based on facts or circumstances from which infringing activity is apparent, regardless of whether the material or activity is ultimately determined to be infringing.

(2) EXCEPTION. — Paragraph (1) shall not apply with respect to material residing at the direction of a subscriber of the service provider on a system or network controlled or operated by or for the service provider that is removed, or to which access is disabled by the service provider, pursuant to a notice provided under subsection (c)(1)(C), unless the service provider —

(A) takes reasonable steps promptly to notify the subscriber that it has removed or disabled access to the material;

(B) upon receipt of a counter notification described in paragraph (3), promptly provides the person who provided the notification under subsection (c)(1)(C) with a copy of the counter notification, and informs that person that it will replace the removed material or cease disabling access to it in 10 business days; and

(C) replaces the removed material and ceases disabling access to it not less than 10, nor more than 14, business days following receipt of the counter notice, unless its designated agent first receives notice from the person who submitted the notification under subsection (c)(1)(C) that such person has filed an action seeking a court order to restrain the subscriber from engaging in infringing activity relating to the material on the service provider's system or network.

(3) CONTENTS OF COUNTER NOTIFICATION. — To be effective under this subsection, a counter notification must be a written communication provided to the service provider's designated agent that includes substantially the following:

(A) A physical or electronic signature of the subscriber.

(B) Identification of the material that has been removed or to which access has been disabled and the location at which the material appeared before it was removed or access to it was disabled.

(C) A statement under penalty of perjury that the subscriber has a good faith belief that the material was removed or disabled as a result of mistake or misidentification of the material to be removed or disabled.

(D) The subscriber's name, address, and telephone number, and a statement that the subscriber consents to the jurisdiction of Federal District Court for the judicial district in which the address is located, or if the subscriber's address is outside of the United States, for any judicial district in which the service provider may be found, and that the subscriber will accept service of process from the person who provided notification under subsection (c)(1)(C) or an agent of such person.

(4) LIMITATION ON OTHER LIABILITY. — A service provider's compliance with paragraph (2) shall not subject the service provider to liability for copyright infringement with respect to the material identified in the notice provided under subsection (c)(1)(C).

Together, § 512(c) and (g) establish what has become known as the DMCA's notice and take-down scheme. The general idea is simple. An ISP normally bears no liability for hosting infringing files posted by users as long as it does two things. First, it must establish a designated agent to receive official complaints about infringement from copyright holders. Second, it must respond to such complaints by taking down or disabling access to material complained of as infringing, notify the user of such action, and restore access to the material if the user objects. If a copyright holder should file suit against the user for infringement, then access to the material is not restored.

The notice and take-down provisions formalize a seemingly beneficial bargain between ISPs and copyright holders. In exchange for immunity from third-party liability, ISPs remove infringing material from the Internet upon the request of copyright holders. This gives copyright holders inexpensive and prompt relief from infringement without the fuss of having to go to court.

This does not mean, however, that all are satisfied with how notice and take-down work in practice. Some argue that the process creates opportunities for abuse because most people accused of copyright infringement do not understand their substantive rights (such as fair use) nor the process of counter notification. Accordingly, the vast majority of DMCA complaints about alleged infringement go unchallenged, and material disappears from the Internet with no impartial examination of whether infringement actually occurred.

Others argue that the process allows ISPs to knowingly facilitate and profit from infringement without taking responsibility for the damage done to copyright holders' interests. Granted, copyright holders can file official take-down requests, but the volume of infringement is so large that it is impossible to send enough complaints. Copyright holders have therefore sued a number of prominent ISPs like YouTube, claiming under § 512(c)(1) that the ISPs have lost their DMCA safe harbors because they know too much about infringement on their networks and have sufficient control to stop that infringement.

Our next case examines one of these suits and how it raises anew the fundamental question of who, if anyone, is responsible for copyright infringement on the Internet.

Viacom v. YouTube
676 F.3d 19 (2d Cir. 2013)

JOSE A. CABRANES, Circuit Judge:

This appeal requires us to clarify the contours of the "safe harbor" provision of the Digital Millennium Copyright Act (DMCA) that limits the liability of online service providers for copyright infringement that occurs "by reason of the storage at the direction of a user of material that resides on a system or network controlled or operated by or for the service provider." 17 U.S.C. § 512(c).

The plaintiffs-appellants in these related actions—Viacom International, Inc. ("Viacom"), The Football Association Premier League Ltd. ("Premier League"), and various film studios, television networks, music publishers, and sports leagues (jointly, the "plaintiffs")—appeal from an August 10, 2010 judgment of the United States District Court for the Southern District of New York, which granted summary judgment to defendants-appellees YouTube, Inc., YouTube, LLC, and Google Inc. (jointly, "YouTube" or the "defendants"). The plaintiffs alleged direct and secondary copyright infringement based on the public performance, display, and reproduction of approximately 79,000 audiovisual "clips" that appeared on the YouTube website between 2005 and 2008. ...

In a June 23, 2010 Opinion and Order, the District Court held that the defendants were entitled to DMCA safe harbor protection primarily because they had insufficient notice of the particular infringements in suit. In construing the statutory safe harbor, the District Court concluded that the "actual knowledge" or "aware[ness] of facts or circumstances" that would disqualify an online service provider from safe harbor protection under § 512(c)(1)(A) refer to "knowledge of specific and identifiable infringements." The District Court further held that item-specific knowledge of infringing activity is required for a service provider to have the "right and ability to control" infringing activity under § 512(c)(1)(B). ...

These related cases present a series of significant questions of statutory construction. We conclude that the District Court correctly held that the § 512(c) safe harbor requires knowledge or awareness of specific infringing activity, but we vacate the order granting summary judgment because a reasonable jury could find that YouTube had actual knowledge or awareness of specific infringing activity on its website. We further hold that the District Court erred by interpreting the "right and ability to control" provision to require "item-specific" knowledge. ...

BACKGROUND

...

B. Factual Background

YouTube was founded in February 2005 by Chad Hurley ("Hurley"), Steve Chen ("Chen"), and Jawed Karim ("Karim"), three former employees of the internet company Paypal. When YouTube announced the "official launch" of the website in December 2005, a press release described YouTube as a "consumer media company" that "allows people to watch, upload, and share personal video clips at www.YouTube.com." Under the slogan "Broadcast yourself," YouTube achieved rapid prominence and profitability, eclipsing competitors such as Google Video and Yahoo Video by wide margins. In November 2006, Google acquired YouTube in a stock-for-stock transaction valued at $1.65 billion. By March 2010, at the time of summary judgment briefing in this litigation, site traffic on YouTube had soared to more than 1 billion daily video views, with more than 24 hours of new video uploaded to the site every minute.

The basic function of the YouTube website permits users to "upload" and view video clips free of charge. Before uploading a video to YouTube, a user must register and create an account with the website. The registration process requires the user to accept YouTube's Terms of Use agreement, which provides, *inter alia*, that the user "will not submit material that is copyrighted ... unless [he is] the owner of such rights or ha[s] permission from their rightful owner to post the material and to grant YouTube all of the license rights granted herein." When the registration process is complete, the user can sign in to his account, select a video to upload from the user's personal computer, mobile phone, or other device, and instruct the YouTube system to upload the video by clicking on a virtual upload "button."

Uploading a video to the YouTube website triggers a series of automated software functions. During the upload process, YouTube makes one or more exact copies of the video in its original file format. YouTube also makes one or more additional copies of the video in "Flash" format, a process known as "transcoding." The transcoding process ensures that YouTube videos are available for viewing by most users at their request. The YouTube system allows users to gain access to video content by "streaming" the video to the user's computer in response to a playback request. YouTube uses a computer algorithm to identify clips that are "related" to a video the user watches and display links to the "related" clips....

DISCUSSION

A. Actual and "Red Flag" Knowledge: § 512(c)(1)(A)

The first and most important question on appeal is whether the DMCA safe harbor at issue requires "actual knowledge" or "aware[ness]" of facts or circumstances indicating "specific and identifiable infringements." We consider first the scope of the statutory provision and then its application to the record in this case.

1. The Specificity Requirement

... Under § 512(c)(1)(A), safe harbor protection is available only if the service provider:

(i) does not have actual knowledge that the material or an activity using the material on the system or network is infringing;

(ii) in the absence of such actual knowledge, is not aware of facts or circumstances from which infringing activity is apparent; or

(iii) upon obtaining such knowledge or awareness, acts expeditiously to remove, or disable access to, the material....

As previously noted, the District Court held that the statutory phrases "actual knowledge that the material ... is infringing" and "facts or circumstances from which infringing activity is apparent" refer to "knowledge of specific and identifiable infringements." For the reasons that follow, we substantially affirm that holding.

Although the parties marshal a battery of other arguments on appeal, it is the text of the statute that compels our conclusion. In particular, we are persuaded that the basic operation of § 512(c) requires knowledge or awareness of specific infringing activity. Under § 512(c)(1)(A), knowledge or awareness alone does not disqualify the service provider; rather, the provider that gains knowledge or awareness of infringing activity retains safe-harbor protection if it "acts expeditiously to remove, or disable access to, the material." 17 U.S.C. § 512(c)(1)(A)(iii). Thus, the nature of the removal obligation itself contemplates knowledge or awareness of specific infringing material, because expeditious removal is possible only if the service provider knows with particularity which items to remove. Indeed, to require expeditious removal in the absence of specific knowledge or awareness would be to mandate an amorphous obligation to "take commercially reasonable steps" in response to a generalized awareness of infringement. Such a view cannot be reconciled with the language of the statute, which requires "expeditious[ ]" action to remove or disable *the material* " at issue. 17 U.S.C. § 512(c)(1)(A)(iii) (emphasis added).

On appeal, the plaintiffs dispute this conclusion by drawing our attention to § 512(c)(1)(A)(ii), the so-called "red flag" knowledge provision. *See id.* § 512(c)(1)(A)(ii) (limiting liability where, "in the absence of such actual knowledge, [the service provider] is not aware of facts or circumstances from which infringing activity is apparent"). In their view, the use of the phrase "facts or circumstances" demonstrates that Congress did not intend to limit the red flag provision to a particular type of knowledge. The plaintiffs contend that requiring awareness of specific infringements in order to establish "aware[ness] of facts or circumstances from which infringing activity is apparent" renders the red flag provision superfluous, because that provision would be satisfied only when the "actual knowledge" provision is also satisfied. For that reason, the plaintiffs urge the Court to hold that the red flag provision "requires less specificity" than the actual knowledge provision.

This argument misconstrues the relationship between "actual" knowledge and "red flag" knowledge. It is true that "we are required to 'disfavor interpretations of statutes that render language superfluous.'" But contrary to the plaintiffs' assertions, construing § 512(c)(1)(A) to require actual knowledge or awareness of specific instances of infringement does not render the red flag provision superfluous. The phrase "actual knowledge," which appears in § 512(c)(1)(A)(i), is frequently used to denote subjective belief. By contrast, courts often invoke the language of "facts or circumstances," which appears in § 512(c)(1)(A)(ii), in discussing an objective reasonableness standard.

The difference between actual and red flag knowledge is thus not between specific and generalized knowledge, but instead between a subjective and an objective standard. In other words, the actual knowledge provision turns on whether the provider actually or "subjectively" knew of specific infringement, while the red flag provision turns on whether the provider was subjectively aware of facts that would have made the specific infringement "objectively" obvious to a reasonable person. The red flag provision, because it incorporates an objective standard, is not swallowed up by the actual knowledge provision under our construction of the § 512(c) safe harbor. Both provisions do independent work, and both apply only to specific instances of infringement. ... [W]e note that no court has embraced the contrary proposition—urged by the plaintiffs—that the red flag provision "requires less specificity" than the actual knowledge provision.

Based on the text of § 512(c)(1)(A), as well as the limited case law on point, we affirm the District Court's holding that actual knowledge or awareness of facts or circumstances that indicate specific and identifiable instances of infringement will disqualify a service provider from the safe harbor.

2.   The Grant of Summary Judgment

The corollary question on appeal is whether, under the foregoing construction of § 512(c)(1)(A), the District Court erred in granting summary judgment to YouTube on the record presented. For the reasons that follow, we hold that although the District Court correctly interpreted § 512(c)(1)(A), summary judgment for the defendants was premature.

i.   Specific Knowledge or Awareness

The plaintiffs argue that, even under the District Court's construction of the safe harbor, the record raises material issues of fact regarding YouTube's actual knowledge or "red flag" awareness of specific instances of infringement. To that end, the plaintiffs draw our attention to various estimates regarding the percentage of infringing content on the YouTube website. For example, Viacom cites evidence that YouTube employees conducted website surveys and estimated that 75–80% of all YouTube streams contained copyrighted material. The class plaintiffs similarly claim that Credit Suisse, acting as financial advisor to Google, estimated that more than 60% of YouTube's content was "premium" copyrighted content—and that only 10% of the premium content was authorized. These approximations suggest that the defendants were conscious that significant quantities of material on the YouTube website were infringing. But such estimates are insufficient, standing alone, to create a triable issue of fact as to whether YouTube actually knew, or was aware of facts or circumstances that would indicate, the existence of particular instances of infringement.

Beyond the survey results, the plaintiffs rely upon internal YouTube communications that do refer to particular clips or groups of clips. The class plaintiffs argue that YouTube was aware of specific infringing material because, *inter alia,* YouTube attempted to search for specific Premier League videos on the site in order to gauge their "value based on video usage." In particular, the class plaintiffs cite a February 7, 2007 e-mail from Patrick Walker, director of video partnerships for Google and YouTube, requesting that his colleagues calculate the number of daily searches for the terms "soccer," "football," and "Premier League" in preparation for a bid on the global rights to Premier League content. On another occasion, Walker requested that any "clearly infringing, official broadcast footage" from a list of top Premier League clubs—including Liverpool Football Club, Chelsea Football Club, Manchester United Football Club, and Arsenal Football Club—be taken down in advance of a meeting with the heads of "several major sports teams and leagues." YouTube ultimately decided not to make a bid for the Premier League rights—but the infringing content allegedly remained on the website.

The record in the *Viacom* action includes additional examples. For instance, YouTube founder Jawed Karim prepared a report in March 2006 which stated that, "[a]s of today[,] episodes and clips of the following well-known shows can still be found [on YouTube]: Family Guy, South Park, MTV Cribs, Daily Show, Reno 911, [and] Dave Chapelle

[sic]." Karim further opined that, "although YouTube is not legally required to monitor content ... and complies with DMCA takedown requests, we would benefit from *preemptively* removing content that is blatantly illegal and likely to attract criticism." He also noted that "a more thorough analysis" of the issue would be required. At least some of the TV shows to which Karim referred are owned by Viacom. A reasonable juror could conclude from the March 2006 report that Karim knew of the presence of Viacom-owned material on YouTube, since he presumably located specific clips of the shows in question before he could announce that YouTube hosted the content "[a]s of today." A reasonable juror could also conclude that Karim believed the clips he located to be infringing (since he refers to them as "blatantly illegal"), and that YouTube did not remove the content from the website until conducting "a more thorough analysis," thus exposing the company to liability in the interim.

Furthermore, in a July 4, 2005 e-mail exchange, YouTube founder Chad Hurley sent an e-mail to his co-founders with the subject line "budlight commercials," and stated, "we need to reject these too." Steve Chen responded, "can we please leave these in a bit longer? another week or two can't hurt." Karim also replied, indicating that he "added back in all 28 bud videos." Similarly, in an August 9, 2005 e-mail exchange, Hurley urged his colleagues "to start being *diligent* about rejecting copyrighted / inappropriate content," noting that "there is a cnn clip of the shuttle clip on the site today, if the boys from Turner would come to the site, they might be pissed?" Again, Chen resisted:

> but we should just keep that stuff on the site. i really don't see what will happen. what? someone from cnn sees it? he happens to be someone with power? he happens to want to take it down right away. he gets in touch with cnn legal. 2 weeks later, we get a cease & desist letter. we take the video down.

And again, Karim agreed, indicating that "the CNN space shuttle clip, I like. we can remove it once we're bigger and better known, but for now that clip is fine."

Upon a review of the record, we are persuaded that the plaintiffs may have raised a material issue of fact regarding YouTube's knowledge or awareness of specific instances of infringement. The foregoing Premier League e-mails request the identification and removal of "clearly infringing, official broadcast footage." The March 2006 report indicates Karim's awareness of specific clips that he perceived to be "blatantly illegal." Similarly, the Bud Light and space shuttle e-mails refer to particular clips in the context of correspondence about whether to remove infringing material from the website. On these facts, a reasonable juror could conclude that YouTube had actual knowledge of specific infringing activity, or was at least aware of facts or circumstances from which specific infringing activity was apparent. Accordingly, we hold that summary judgment to YouTube on all clips-in-suit, especially in the absence of any detailed examination of the extensive record on summary judgment, was premature.

... Accordingly, we vacate the order granting summary judgment and instruct the District Court to determine on remand whether any specific infringements of which YouTube had knowledge or awareness correspond to the clips-in-suit in these actions.

ii. "Willful Blindness"

The plaintiffs further argue that the District Court erred in granting summary judgment to the defendants despite evidence that YouTube was "willfully blind" to specific infringing activity. On this issue of first impression, we consider the application of the common law willful blindness doctrine in the DMCA context. ...

A person is "willfully blind" or engages in "conscious avoidance" amounting to knowledge where the person "'was aware of a high probability of the fact in dispute and consciously avoided confirming that fact.'" Writing in the trademark infringement context, we have held that "[a] service provider is not ... permitted willful blindness. When it has reason to suspect that users of its service are infringing a protected mark, it may not shield itself from learning of the particular infringing transactions by looking the other way."

The DMCA does not mention willful blindness. As a general matter, we interpret a statute to abrogate a common law principle only if the statute "speak[s] directly to the question addressed by the common law." The relevant question, therefore, is whether the DMCA "speak[s] directly" to the principle of willful blindness. The DMCA provision most relevant to the abrogation inquiry is § 512(m), which provides that safe harbor protection shall not be conditioned on "a service provider monitoring its service or affirmatively seeking facts indicating infringing activity, except to the extent consistent with a standard technical measure complying with the provisions of subsection (i)." 17 U.S.C. § 512(m)(1). Section 512(m) is explicit: DMCA safe harbor protection cannot be conditioned on affirmative monitoring by a service provider. For that reason, § 512(m) is incompatible with a broad common law duty to monitor or otherwise seek out infringing activity based on general awareness that infringement may be occurring. That fact does not, however, dispose of the abrogation inquiry; as previously noted, willful blindness cannot be defined as an affirmative duty to monitor. Because the statute does not "speak[ ] directly" to the willful blindness doctrine, § 512(m) limits—but does not abrogate—the doctrine. Accordingly, we hold that the willful blindness doctrine may be applied, in appropriate circumstances, to demonstrate knowledge or awareness of specific instances of infringement under the DMCA.

The District Court cited § 512(m) for the proposition that safe harbor protection does not require affirmative monitoring, but did not expressly address the principle of willful blindness or its relationship to the DMCA safe harbors. As a result, whether the defendants made a "deliberate effort to avoid guilty knowledge," remains a fact question for the District Court to consider in the first instance on remand.

B.   Control and Benefit: § 512(c)(1)(B)

Apart from the foregoing knowledge provisions, the § 512(c) safe harbor provides that an eligible service provider must "not receive a financial benefit directly attributable to the infringing activity, in a case in which the service provider has the right and ability to control such activity." 17 U.S.C. § 512(c)(1)(B). The District Court addressed this issue in a single paragraph, quoting from § 512(c)(1)(B), the so-called "control and benefit" provision, and concluding that "[t]he 'right and ability to control' the activity requires knowledge of it, which must be item-specific." *Viacom,* 718 F.Supp.2d at 527. For the reasons that follow, we hold that the District Court erred by importing a specific knowledge requirement into the control and benefit provision, and we therefore remand for further fact-finding on the issue of control.

1.   "Right and Ability to Control" Infringing Activity

On appeal, the parties advocate two competing constructions of the "right and ability to control" infringing activity. Because each is fatally flawed, we reject both proposed constructions in favor of a fact-based inquiry to be conducted in the first instance by the District Court.

The first construction, pressed by the defendants, is the one adopted by the District Court, which held that "the provider must know of the particular case before he can control it." The Ninth Circuit recently agreed, holding that "until [the service provider] becomes aware of specific unauthorized material, it cannot exercise its 'power or authority' over the specific infringing item. In practical terms, it does not have the kind of ability to control infringing activity the statute contemplates." *UMG Recordings, Inc. v. Shelter Capital Partners LLC,* 667 F.3d 1022, 1041 (9th Cir. 2011). The trouble with this construction is that importing a specific knowledge requirement into § 512(c)(1)(B) renders the control provision duplicative of § 512(c)(1)(A). Any service provider that has item-specific knowledge of infringing activity and thereby obtains financial benefit would already be excluded from the safe harbor under § 512(c)(1)(A) for having specific knowledge of infringing material and failing to effect expeditious removal. No additional service provider would be excluded by § 512(c)(1)(B) that was not already excluded by § 512(c)(1)(A). Because statutory interpretations that render language superfluous are disfavored, we reject the District Court's interpretation of the control provision.

The second construction, urged by the plaintiffs, is that the control provision codifies the common law doctrine of vicarious copyright liability. The common law imposes liability for vicarious copyright infringement "[w]hen the right and ability to supervise coalesce with an obvious and direct financial interest in the exploitation of copyrighted materials—even in the absence of actual knowledge that the copyright mono[poly] is being impaired." To support their codification argument, the plaintiffs rely on a House Report relating to a preliminary version of the DMCA: "The 'right and ability to control' language ... codifies the second element of vicarious liability.... Subparagraph (B) is intended to preserve existing case law that examines all relevant aspects of the relationship between the primary and secondary infringer." H.R.Rep. No. 105–551(I), at 26 (1998). In response, YouTube notes that the codification reference was omitted from the committee reports describing the final legislation, and that Congress ultimately abandoned any attempt to "embark[ ] upon a wholesale clarification" of vicarious liability, electing instead "to create a series of 'safe harbors' for certain common activities of service providers." S.Rep. No. 105–190, at 19.

Happily, the future of digital copyright law does not turn on the confused legislative history of the control provision. The general rule with respect to common law codification is that when "Congress uses terms that have accumulated settled meaning under the common law, a court must infer, unless the statute otherwise dictates, that Congress means to incorporate the established meaning of those terms." Under the common law vicarious liability standard, "'[t]he ability to block infringers' access to a particular environment for any reason whatsoever is evidence of the right and ability to supervise.'" *Arista Records LLC v. Usenet.com, Inc.,* 633 F.Supp.2d 124, 157 (S.D.N.Y. 2009) (alteration in original). To adopt that principle in the DMCA context, however, would render the statute internally inconsistent. Section 512(c) actually presumes that service providers have the ability to "block ... access" to infringing material. Indeed, a service provider who has knowledge or awareness of infringing material or who receives a takedown notice from a copyright holder is *required* to "remove, or disable access to, the material" in order to claim the benefit of the safe harbor. But in taking such action, the service provider would—in the plaintiffs' analysis—be admitting the "right and ability to control" the infringing material. Thus, the prerequisite to safe harbor protection under § 512(c)(1)(A)(iii) & (C) would at the same time be a disqualifier under § 512(c)(1)(B). ...

In any event, the foregoing tension—elsewhere described as a "predicament" and a "catch22"—is sufficient to establish that the control provision "dictates" a departure from the common law vicarious liability standard. Accordingly, we conclude that the "right and ability to control" infringing activity under § 512(c)(1)(B) "requires something more than the ability to remove or block access to materials posted on a service provider's website." The remaining—and more difficult—question is how to define the "something more" that is required.

To date, only one court has found that a service provider had the right and ability to control infringing activity under § 512(c)(1)(B). In *Perfect 10, Inc. v. Cybernet Ventures, Inc.,* 213 F.Supp.2d 1146 (C.D. Cal. 2002), the court found control where the service provider instituted a monitoring program by which user websites received "detailed instructions regard[ing] issues of layout, appearance, and content." The service provider also forbade certain types of content and refused access to users who failed to comply with its instructions. Similarly, inducement of copyright infringement under *Metro–Goldwyn–Mayer Studios Inc. v. Grok-*

ster, Ltd., 545 U.S. 913 (2005), which "premises liability on purposeful, culpable expression and conduct," might also rise to the level of control under § 512(c)(1)(B). Both of these examples involve a service provider exerting substantial influence on the activities of users, without necessarily—or even frequently—acquiring knowledge of specific infringing activity.

In light of our holding that § 512(c)(1)(B) does not include a specific knowledge requirement, we think it prudent to remand to the District Court to consider in the first instance whether the plaintiffs have adduced sufficient evidence to allow a reasonable jury to conclude that YouTube had the right and ability to control the infringing activity and received a financial benefit directly attributable to that activity. ...

Notes and Questions

1.   *YouTube* rejected the plaintiffs' argument that an ISP's general knowledge about infringement destroys safe harbor protection. Was this the correct thing to do? If § 512(c) gives ISPs protection against liability in exchange for ISPs behaving responsibly, does *YouTube*'s interpretation of the law upset this exchange by allowing irresponsible ISPs to profit from infringement with effective impunity? After all, YouTube surely knew that many of its users infringed, and that many viewers come to YouTube to view infringing posts. To the extent that YouTube did nothing to stop these infringements, YouTube profited from the existence of widespread infringement but owed copyright holders nothing because YouTube never gained knowledge about specific acts of infringement.

2.   Summary judgment plays an important role in understanding how § 512(c) works and the possible significance of *YouTube*. If ISPs can consistently win at summary judgment, then the safe harbors provide fairly strong protection from liability, because ISPs can dispose of third party liability claims quickly and without the expense of trial. If, however, ISPs cannot shield themselves at summary judgment, the expense and uncertainty of trial significantly diminish the value of the safe harbor because ISPs will feel significantly exposed to liability. In *YouTube*, the District Court granted summary judgment to the defendant, but the Second Circuit reversed. Was the court right to do so? Interestingly, on very similar facts, the Ninth Circuit affirmed summary judgment in favor of the defendant in *UMG Recordings, Inc. v. Shelter Capital Partners LLC*, 718 F.3d 1006 (9th Cir. 2013). And, on remand, the District Court in *YouTube* once again granted summary judgment in YouTube's favor. Are these decisions consistent with the reasoning adopted by the Second Circuit in *YouTube*?

3.   *YouTube* struggles with the issue of red flag liability. The DMCA clearly provides that ISPs lose safe harbor protection by failing to re-

move infringing material identified in official DMCA notices. If that were the only way for ISPs to lose such protection, ISPs would enjoy very secure safe harbors by making sure they handle DMCA compliant notices properly. The DMCA also clearly states, however, that an ISP can lose safe harbor protection by having certain kinds of knowledge developed independently from any DMCA compliant notice. *YouTube* tries to limit the kinds of knowledge that destroy safe harbor protection because a broad definition of such knowledge would effectively destroy the safe harbor by forcing ISPs to constantly monitor their networks for infringement. Do you think that *YouTube* has chosen an appropriate definition of knowledge that preserves meaningful safe harbors?

As you ponder this question, consider whether *any* definition of knowledge can meaningfully preserve safe harbors. Social media sites are full of user postings that infringe music, movies, and other works. If this is so, can an ISP possibly operate without developing knowledge that would destroy the DMCA safe harbor? For example, executives of YouTube probably view their websites for job-related reasons or watch their children surf the site at home. Do you think they can do this for long without seeing specific examples of obvious copyright infringement? If you believe that they will surely stumble across infringement, does that mean that most ISPs have red flag knowledge? Also, what happens when companies like YouTube receive complaints outside the DMCA process about specific instances of infringement?

4. The *YouTube* opinion only briefly addresses the question of willful blindness. Although the court clearly rejects the idea that ISPs have an affirmative duty to search for infringement, the court leaves open the possibility that an ISP could lose safe harbor protection by deliberately avoiding information that would create red flag knowledge. How easy is it for an ISP to run afoul of willful blindness? For example, a private citizen could send an email to YouTube with URLs of infringing material that he watches. Does an ISP who receives such a letter have an affirmative obligation to investigate on pain of losing safe harbor protection? If so, what would the consequences be for the viability of § 512(c)'s safe harbors and the value of the entire notice and take-down process?

5. *YouTube* leaves open the possibility that an ISP can lose safe harbor protection by having the "right and ability to control" a user's infringement. The court clearly stated that the mere ability to remove infringement from the Internet was not, in and of itself, sufficient manifestation of control to destroy safe harbor protection. Instead, "something more" would be required. How would you explain to a client what "something more" means?

6. If copyright owners cannot proceed against ISPs who take advantage of the safe harbor, they can still proceed against the individuals who upload the materials onto an ISP's website. In all of the cases involving third-party liability, the lack of such liability does not mean that the copyright owner is without remedy. It just means that the copyright owner must proceed against the direct infringer.

Filing individual lawsuits against each and every direct infringer, however, is extremely expensive and may have limited deterrent effect, given the large numbers of potential defendants and the small risk that any particular individual will be sued. The record industry for many years pursued lawsuits against specific individuals who offered copyrighted music to others over peer-to-peer file sharing networks, but has since largely abandoned these efforts.

Even if copyright owners wish to bring such actions, merely identifying a specific individual can be costly, given the relative anonymity of the Internet. The DMCA contains provisions that help copyright owners identify potential defendants by creating a streamlined procedure for getting subpoenas directing ISPs to disclose the identity of subscribers accused of infringement. § 512(h)(1)-(4). However, even with such streamlined procedures, the costs of identifying potential defendants remain high.

What policy conclusions, if any, should we draw from the relative difficulty of meaningfully proceeding against individual infringers on the Internet? Is this simply a cost that copyright owners must bear? Or should copyright law respond to this in some fashion, perhaps requiring ISPs to prevent or pay for infringement taking place on the Internet?

7. More generally, do you think the DMCA's notice and takedown structure, as interpreted in *YouTube*, strikes the appropriate balance between the interests of the ISPs, copyright owners, and users? On the one hand, the structure provides relatively clear rules to ISPs and insulates them from liability, while offering copyright owners a way to have the material quickly removed. On the other hand, copyright owners complain that they are constantly submitting thousands of DMCA takedown notices to YouTube every day, only to have the same material re-uploaded the next day, and that YouTube in the meantime profits handsomely from the material being available on its site. Can you think of a better way of balancing these interests?

Would your opinion change if YouTube had a cost-effective way to identify potentially infringing material? YouTube has in fact developed a technology called ContentID, which can identify with a good deal of accuracy whether video clips loaded onto its site correspond to particular copyrighted works. Indeed, YouTube works with certain copyright owners and shares revenue with some of them based on how often their video clips are viewed. Having developed such a technology, should YouTube be obligated to deploy it to help reduce unauthorized uploading? What happens when YouTube identifies a video clip that was uploaded without permission by the copyright owner?

Finally, what about the interests of users of sites like YouTube? What if users claim they have a fair use right to upload a particular video clip or use a particular music clip in their own videos? The DMCA's notice and takedown system gives users the right to file a counter-notification asserting a right to upload the material, and sites like

YouTube can then make the material available without liability. In practice, however, many users may not be aware of this ability. Given the above, what impact do you expect the notice and takedown system to have on the uploading of videos that are arguably privileged by fair use?

Chapter Eight

<hr>

ANTI-CIRCUMVENTION AND
ANTI-TRAFFICKING

<hr style="width:20%">

In this chapter, we will examine some of the ways in which copyright law has responded to digital technology. First, we examine the technologies—so-called "digital rights management" (DRM) technologies—that copyright owners are using to protect their works. Second, we will take a close look at the Digital Millennium Copyright Act of 1998 (DMCA), which Congress enacted in an attempt to provide support for these technologies.

As you read these materials, consider what effect recent changes in technology and the law have had on copyright and the realization of copyright's objectives. Some have argued that the DMCA provides the foundation for a new and far more efficient market for copyrighted works, one that harnesses digital technology's potential for increasing copyright's public benefits. Others argue that the DMCA will undercut the public's ability to exercise rights of access and use already provided by the Copyright Act. Which of these positions do you find more persuasive?

SECTION A. BACKGROUND

1. THE DIGITAL CHALLENGE

Technology has always challenged the adequacy of copyright. Over time, inventions like the phonorecord, the photocopier, the tape recorder, and the VCR have greatly reduced the cost of reproducing copyrighted works. Copyright owners have generally predicted that these technologies would lead to more infringement and undercut incentives to produce creative works. Yet in each of these cases, the supply of new creative works has remained abundant without an alteration in copyright's basic principles or structure.

The newest challenge to copyright comes from digital technology, and there are reasons to think that things may now be different. First, digital technology reduces the cost of copying certain works to nearly zero. Although earlier technologies like analog tape reduced the cost of reproducing works, the copying process proved slow and cumbersome, and the resulting copies were generally inferior to the quality of the original. This is not the case with digital works, which can be copied nearly effortlessly and perfectly with a click of a button.

Second, digital technology radically reduces the costs of distributing copyrighted works. Even if earlier technologies reduced the costs of copying, the costs of distributing physical copies (for example, infringing analog tapes), were still significant, thus limiting the extent of infringing activity. With modern communications networks and the rise of the Internet, infringing copies can be distributed literally around the world at essentially zero cost. Thus, the potential impact of unauthorized copying may be greater.

Some believe that digital technology presents a significant threat to copyright incentives. For them, the low cost of making and distributing unauthorized copies will increase the incidence of infringement. Moreover, the relative anonymity of Internet users may make it difficult for copyright owners to enforce their copyrights directly against infringers. As a result, some have argued that the threat of digital technology warrants legislative action.

Others, however, argue that existing laws are sufficient, just as they have been in the past, to deal with the new technology. Copyright owners have always had to deal with some level of infringement, but that has not unduly compromised the creation of new works. Moreover, digital technology may in some cases reduce the costs of enforcement, through technological self-help (described in more detail below). Finally, digital technology greatly reduces the costs of creating and distributing creative works. Works in digital form are extremely malleable. The flexibility of the medium makes it possible for more individuals to engage in creative activity and to distribute the fruits of that activity to others. Thus, it is possible that authors will continue to create works even if copyright holders face higher levels of infringement than ever before.

2. DIGITAL RIGHTS MANAGEMENT TECHNOLOGIES

In response to concerns about the potential negative effect of digital technology on copyright markets, copyright owners have used that very same technology in an attempt to restrict unauthorized copying. Although such technologies have been around for some time, particularly in the software industry, they are being deployed more frequently as other types of copyrighted works become distributed in digital form. We will refer to these technologies generally as "digital rights management technologies" or "DRM." An example of a DRM technology would be the technology that encrypts movies on DVD and prevents them from being easily copied.

DRM technologies typically use a number of methods to restrict access to works in digital form. One of the most common is encryption. Encryption technologies scramble digital information to prevent third parties from accessing or copying the information. Thus, for example, movies distributed on DVD are encrypted using a system called Content Scramble System (CSS). All properly-licensed DVD players have the decryption algorithm, which allows the digital information to be played on the television. Without the decryption algorithm, one cannot easily access the digital information.

Another technology is digital watermarking. Watermarking embeds digital information in a digital file in such a way as to be hidden from third-party observers. The information may include the identity of the copyright owner, terms of use, the year of creation, the identity of the purchaser, and other useful information. Programs and devices that access such works can be configured to provide access only when certain types of information are found in the watermarking. Watermarking can also facilitate enforcement, insofar as it can embed information that indicates where the original digital file came from or information that helps companies find infringing copies being distributed on the Internet. In order for watermarking to be successful, it must be difficult for third-parties to find and remove the watermarked information.

DRM technologies are widely deployed in many markets. The software industry has had a long history of using technological measures to prevent unauthorized copying. The movie industry has also widely deployed such technologies, most prominently in the case of DVDs, as mentioned above. The music industry has also used digital rights management technologies to limit the unauthorized copying and distribution of digital music. So, for example, music distributed by Apple's iTunes for many years employed a technology called FairPlay, which imposed some restrictions on accessing and copying music. Similarly, the Windows Media Player includes a DRM platform which allows those who distribute music and movies to limit copying and access.

It is important to note that these technologies can do more than simply help copyright owners enforce their copyrights. As we have seen in previous chapters, under some circumstances (e.g. fair use), third parties have the right to make copies of copyrighted works without permission of the copyright owner. DRM technologies, however, make no distinctions between different types of copying, and thus can be used to prevent both infringing and non-infringing copying. In addition, DRM technologies often control not just copying, but also access to copyrighted works. Even though copyright law does not, on its face, restrict the number of times that a person can play a song, read a book, or otherwise access a work, DRM can be used to limit a consumer to a single incident of access. Thus, DRM technology can, in some cases, offer copyright owners control over their works beyond the rights conferred by the Copyright Act.

At the same time, DRM technology is vulnerable. The problem, from the perspective of copyright owners, is that DRM technologies can be circumvented or cracked. It is, as a practical matter, impossible to create a perfect DRM system. And indeed, nearly all of the technologies mentioned above have been circumvented, sometimes within hours of their release. So, for example, CSS, the technology used by the movie industries to protect movies on DVDs, was circumvented by a Norwegian programmer, who created and distributed a decrypting program called DeCSS. With access to DeCSS, a third party could decrypt a movie on DVD and gain access to an unprotected file, which he or she could then distribute at will.

Similarly, attempts to perfectly protect digital music have been unsuccessful. The music industry has, on various occasions, attempted to copy-protect music distributed on compact discs (CDs). In a number of such cases, the attempts were easily circumvented (in one case by simply using a felt-tipped pen to color the edge of the CD). The technologies used to protect music distributed online, for example through iTunes or similar services, have also been cracked.

Because DRM technologies are vulnerable to circumvention, they cannot solve the problems facing copyright owners on their own. If end-users generally gain the ability to circumvent DRM, then DRM becomes essentially useless. Accordingly, DRM can help copyright owners only if users are somehow denied the ability to circumvent. Copyright holders therefore asked Congress to pass legislation that would restrict the circumvention of DRM, and Congress responded in 1998 with the Digital Millennium Copyright Act (DMCA).

SECTION B. THE DIGITAL MILLENNIUM COPYRIGHT ACT

Earlier chapters have already discussed the provisions of the DMCA that deal with liability for Internet service providers. In this chapter, we will focus on separate provisions of the DMCA that deal with circumvention of DRM. These provisions come in two forms: (1) liability for circumvention; and (2) liability for making and distributing technologies that circumvent. A separate provision, discussed in the following subsection, deals with copyright management information.

1. ANTI-CIRCUMVENTION

The DMCA makes it generally illegal to circumvent DRM. It allows "any person injured" by illegal circumvention to sue the circumventer for damages,[70] and it provides stiff criminal sanctions as well.[71] The relevant provision, now codified at § 1201 of the Copyright Act, is reproduced here:

§ 1201. Circumvention of copyright protection systems

(a) Violations Regarding Circumvention of Technological Measures.—

    (1)

        (A) No person shall circumvent a technological measure that effectively controls access to a work protected under this title....

    (3) As used in this subsection—

        (A) to "circumvent a technological measure" means to descramble a scrambled work, to decrypt an encrypted work, or otherwise to avoid, bypass, remove, deactivate, or impair a technological measure, without the authority of the copyright owner; and

        (B) a technological measure "effectively controls access to a work" if the measure, in the ordinary course of its operation, requires the application of information, or a process or a treatment, with the authority of the copyright owner, to gain access to the work.

To see how this works in practice, consider a motion picture distributed on a DVD. DVDs are encrypted and can only be accessed using a DVD player that uses the authorized decryption algorithm. If someone came along and found a way to decrypt the DVD without using an authorized player, that person could be liable under the DMCA if she did so without the permission of the copyright holder. The encryption algorithm is likely a "technological measure that effectively controls access to a work" and the decryption of the DVD would likely constitute "circumvent[ing] a technological measure."

Note that liability for an act of circumvention is separate and distinct from liability for copyright infringement. Sections 501-06 of the Copyright Act define liability for copyright infringement, while sections 1203-04 do so for circumvention. Additionally, liability for unauthorized circumvention does not, at least on the face of the statute, depend on committing infringement. The act of unpermitted circumvention alone is generally enough to raise the prospect of liability, even if the circumventer did so to make legal, noninfringing use of the encrypted work. So, using the example above, the person decrypting the DVD could be liable under the DMCA, regardless of whether she infringed upon the underlying copyrighted work.

The imposition of liability for unauthorized circumvention on those who do not commit infringement can, in at least some cases, restrict the ability of people to make legitimate uses of protected works. The DMCA therefore contains provisions designed to soften the hard edges of blanket illegality for unauthorized circumvention. However, these provisions are not comprehensive, for the DMCA does not contain a general defense like fair use that can be flexibly applied on a case by case basis. Instead,

---

[70] 17 U.S.C. § 1203.

[71] Section 1204 of the Copyright Act permits fines of up to $500,000 and imprisonment of not more than 5 years against anyone who illegally circumvents "willfully and for purposes of commercial advantage or private financial gain." Repeat offenders risk fines of up to $1,000,000 and imprisonment of not more than 10 years.

the DMCA contains a number of statutory exemptions that protect a relatively narrow range of circumventers from liability. These include exemptions for certain non-profit libraries and archives, § 1201(d); law enforcement activities, § 1201(e); reverse engineering to create compatible software programs, § 1201(f); encryption research, § 1201(g); and security testing, § 1201(j). Each of these exemptions contains specific limitations and requirements, which defendants must meet in order to fall within the exemption.

The DMCA also gives the Librarian of Congress the authority, every three years, to issue regulations that exempt certain classes of works from the anti-circumvention provisions, if the Librarian finds that individuals would be "adversely affected by virtue of such prohibition in their ability to make noninfringing uses of that particular class of works." 17 U.S.C. § 1201(a)(1)(C). Congress envisioned that this regulatory process would permit the Librarian of Congress to reasonably adapt the DMCA in response to changing circumstances.

The Librarian of Congress has thus far engaged in six rulemakings under the DMCA. In the most recent rulemaking in 2015, after a period of notice and comment, the Librarian exempted the following classes of works:

- Motion pictures (including television programs and videos):
  - For educational uses by college and university instructors and students
  - For educational uses by K-12 instructors and students
  - For educational uses in massive open online courses ("MOOCs")
  - For educational uses in digital and literacy programs offered by libraries, museums and other nonprofits
  - For multimedia e-books offering film analysis
  - For uses in documentary films
  - For uses in noncommercial videos
- Literary works distributed electronically (i.e., e-books), for use with assistive technologies for persons who are blind, visually impaired or have print disabilities
- Computer programs that operate the following types of devices, to allow connection of a used device to an alternative wireless network ("unlocking"):[72]
  - Cellphones
  - Tablets
  - Mobile hotspots
  - Wearable devices (e.g., smartwaches)
- Computer programs that operate the following types of devices, to allow the device to interoperate with or to remove software applications ("jailbreaking"):

---

[72] Note that in 2014, Congress passed a specific statutory exemption, to permit certain third parties to circumvent technological measures "at the direction of" a cellphone or device owner to enable its use on a different wireless network. This proposed exemption reflects regulatory adoption of the statutory provision.

- o Smartphones
- o Tablets and other all-purpose mobile computing devices
- o Smart TVs
- Computer programs that control motorized land vehicles, including farm equipment, for purposes of diagnosis, repair and modification of the vehicle (effective after 12-month delay)
- Computer programs that operate the following devices and machines, for purposes of good-faith security research (effective after 12-month delay or, for voting machines, immediately):
  - o Devices and machines primarily designed for use by individual consumers, including voting machines
  - o Motorized land vehicles
  - o Medical devices designed for implantation in patients and corresponding personal monitoring systems
- Video games for which outside server support has been discontinued, to allow individual play by gamers and preservation of games by libraries, archives and museums (as well as necessary jailbreaking of console computer code for preservation uses only)
- Computer programs that operate 3D printers, to allow use of alternative feedstock
- Literary works consisting of compilations of data generated by implanted medical devices and corresponding personal monitoring systems

Each of the above exemptions is subject to detailed limitations and qualifications, which can be found at 37 C.F.R. § 201.40.

Notes and Questions

1. Imagine that a copyright owner seeks to control access to a copyrighted novel using technology. The owner distributes the novel through her website. However, the distributed file is encrypted. Consumers can download the encrypted file, but must pay a fee in order to get a password that will enable the consumer to access the novel in unencrypted form. For a fee of $1, a consumer can get access to the novel for one month, after which the access will expire. Alternatively, a consumer can pay $10 and get a password that will provide unlimited access to the file. Imagine, now, that a consumer decrypts the copyrighted file and obtains access to the unencrypted novel without paying any fee. Has the consumer violated the DMCA?

2. Suppose that a movie reviewer wants to take a 10-second clip of a movie on DVD and post it on her website, as part of her review. Imagine that this reviewer uses a software program to circumvent the encryption to gain access to the DVD, in order to copy the 10-second clip. Finally, assume that the use would otherwise be a fair use under standard

copyright law. Would the movie reviewer nevertheless be liable under the DMCA?

3.   In enacting the DMCA, Congress quite clearly believed that copyright owners needed additional protection before they would provide copyrighted works to the public in digital form:

> Due to the ease with which digital works can be copied and distributed worldwide virtually instantaneously, copyright owners will hesitate to make their works readily available on the Internet without reasonable assurance that they will be protected against massive piracy. [The DMCA] provides this protection and creates the legal platform for launching the global digital on-line marketplace for copyrighted works. It will facilitate making available quickly and conveniently via the Internet the movies, music, software, and literary works that are the fruit of American creative genius.

S. Rep. No. 190, 105th Cong., 2d Sess., at 2 (1998). Congress thus viewed the DMCA as a necessary step to help copyright owners secure their existing rights. What do you think of Congress' reasoning and the level of protection given to DRM systems?

4.   To what extent does the DMCA grant copyright owners rights beyond what they traditionally had under the Copyright Act? For example, if a copyright owner uses DRM to control the number of times a consumer can access a DVD, does the DMCA effectively give copyright owners a right to control the use of their copyrighted works? If so, should we be concerned?

Alternatively, perhaps we should be pleased by such a development. Some commentators have argued that giving copyright owners a right to control access would actually have the effect of increasing both incentives to authors and access by consumers. Under such a view, DRM technology permits copyright owners to easily charge consumers differential prices, depending on how much access they wanted to a given work. Thus, a consumer could pay a lower price to view a movie on DVD a single time, and a higher price to view it many times or keep it permanently. This kind of price discrimination would maximize the return to copyright owners, while at the same time increasing access to consumers. *See* Robert Merges, *The End of Friction? Property Rights and Contract in the Newtonian World of OnLine Commerce*, 12 BERKELEY TECH. L.J. 115 (1997). Do you find this view persuasive?

2.   ANTI-TRAFFICKING

In addition to prohibiting unauthorized circumvention, the DMCA also forbids trafficking in anti-circumvention technologies. Two similar, but distinct, provisions define the relevant restrictions. The first, section 1201(a)(2) of the Copyright Act, prohibits the distribution or sale of certain technologies facilitating the circumvention of DRM that controls access to a copyrighted work:

§ 1201. Circumvention of copyright protection systems

(a) Violations Regarding Circumvention of Technological Measures.—

    (2) No person shall manufacture, import, offer to the public, provide, or otherwise traffic in any technology, product, service, device, component, or part thereof, that—

        (A) is primarily designed or produced for the purpose of circumventing a technological measure that effectively controls access to a work protected under this title;

        (B) has only limited commercially significant purpose or use other than to circumvent a technological measure that effectively controls access to a work protected under this title; or

        (C) is marketed by that person or another acting in concert with that person with that person's knowledge for use in circumventing a technological measure that effectively controls access to a work protected under this title.

The second provision, section 1201(b)(1), prohibits the distribution or sale of technology used to circumvent DRM protecting not access, but any "right of a copyright owner":

§ 1201. Circumvention of copyright protection systems

(b) Additional violations.—

    (1) No person shall manufacture, import, offer to the public, provide, or otherwise traffic in any technology, product, service, device, component, or part thereof, that -

        (A) is primarily designed or produced for the purpose of circumventing protection afforded by a technological measure that effectively protects a right of a copyright owner under this title in a work or a portion thereof;

        (B) has only limited commercially significant purpose or use other than to circumvent protection afforded by a technological measure that effectively protects a right of a copyright owner under this title in a work or a portion thereof; or

        (C) is marketed by that person or another acting in concert with that person with that person's knowledge for use in circumventing protection afforded by a technological measure that effectively protects a right of a copyright owner under this title in a work or a portion thereof.

Broadly speaking, the two provisions deal respectively with technologies that control access to copyrighted works and technologies that prevent copyrighted works from being copied or otherwise infringed.[73] In practice, a given technology may fall within one or both of these categories.

The dual anti-trafficking provisions of the DMCA are intended to support the use of DRM to prevent unauthorized uses of copyrighted

---

[73] Note that the DMCA bans both: (a) the sale of technologies that facilitate circumvention of a technology that *controls access* to a work, § 1201(a)(2); and (b) the act of circumventing a technology that *controls access* to a work, § 1201(a)(1). However, while the DMCA bans: (a) the sale of technologies that facilitate the circumvention of a technology that protects a *right of a copyright owner*, it does not contain a parallel provision banning (b) the act of violating a *right of a copyright owner*. The legislative history makes clear that Congress felt such a provision unnecessary, given that the violation of a right of a copyright owner would already give rise to ordinary copyright liability.

works. Standing alone, prohibitions against circumvention or infringement mean little if people can freely acquire circumvention technology, for people could use the technology to circumvent the DRM that prevents people from infringing or gaining unpermitted access. Thus, the anti-trafficking provisions bolster rights against circumvention and infringement by making it hard for people to flout the law.

At the same time, the DMCA's anti-trafficking provisions may have a more significant effect on copyright. Remember that the very DRM preventing unauthorized access or infringement also prevents perfectly legal behavior. As we have already seen, the DMCA itself gives certain people the right to circumvent, and the Librarian of Congress can do likewise via regulation. More importantly, a certain act may constitute infringement in one set of circumstances, but not another. For example, making an electronic copy of a single movie scene from a DVD may be infringement in one case, but fair use in another. In an ideal world, DRM would prevent only infringing behavior, but such technology does not exist. Accordingly, DRM that prevents people from copying sometimes hinders fair use or other noninfringing behavior. This might not be noteworthy if people could obtain circumvention technology to re-enable the exercise of those rights. However, if the DMCA makes such technology unavailable then people have arguably lost the ability to exercise certain rights in a digital setting.

So far, it is not completely clear whether the DMCA will or should affect copyright in this dramatic way. Section 1201(c)(1) of the Copyright Act provides that nothing in the basic anti-trafficking provisions "shall affect rights, remedies, limitations, or defenses to copyright infringement, including fair use..." Perhaps this language means that courts should interpret the anti-trafficking provisions in a way that permits the exercise of legal rights hindered by DRM. However, as our next cases show, courts have only begun working out the relationship between anti-circumvention, anti-trafficking, and infringement.

Universal City Studios v. Reimerdes
111 F. Supp. 2d 294 (S.D.N.Y. 2000), *aff'd sub nom.*
Universal City Studios v. Corley, 273 F.3d 429 (2d Cir. 2001)

KAPLAN, District Judge.

...

I. The Genesis of the Controversy

...

B. Parties

Plaintiffs are eight major motion picture studios. Each is in the business of producing and distributing copyrighted material including motion pictures. Each distributes, either directly or through affiliates, copyrighted motion pictures on DVDs. Plaintiffs produce and distribute a large majority of the motion pictures on DVDs on the market today.

Defendant Eric Corley is viewed as a leader of the computer hacker community. ... He and his company, defendant 2600 Enterprises, Inc., together publish a magazine called *2600: The Hacker Quarterly*, which Corley founded in 1984, and which is something of a bible to the hacker community. ... In addition, defendants operate a web site located at <http://www.2600.com> ("2600.com"), which is managed primarily by Mr. Corley and has been in existence since 1995. ...

C. The Development of DVD and CSS

The major motion picture studios typically distribute films in a sequence of so-called windows, each window referring to a separate channel of distribution and thus to a separate source of revenue. The first window generally is theatrical release, distribution, and exhibition. Subsequently, films are distributed to airlines and hotels, then to the home market, then to pay television, cable and, eventually, free television broadcast. The home market is important to plaintiffs, as it represents a significant source of revenue.

Motion pictures first were, and still are, distributed to the home market in the form of video cassette tapes. In the early 1990's, however, the major movie studios began to explore distribution to the home market in digital format, which offered substantially higher audio and visual quality and greater longevity than video cassette tapes. This technology, which in 1995 became what is known today as DVD, brought with it a new problem—increased risk of piracy by virtue of the fact that digital files, unlike the material on video cassettes, can be copied without degradation from generation to generation. In consequence, the movie studios became concerned as the product neared market with the threat of DVD piracy.

Discussions among the studios with the goal of organizing a unified response to the piracy threat began in earnest in late 1995 or early 1996. They eventually came to include representatives of the consumer electronics and computer industries, as well as interested members of the public, and focused on both legislative proposals and technological solutions. In 1996, Matsushita Electric Industrial Co. ("MEI") and Toshiba Corp., presented—and the studios adopted—CSS.

CSS involves encrypting, according to an encryption algorithm, the digital sound and graphics files on a DVD that together constitute a motion picture. A CSS-protected DVD can be decrypted by an appropriate decryption algorithm that employs a series of keys stored on the DVD and the DVD player. In consequence, only players and drives containing the appropriate keys are able to decrypt DVD files and thereby play movies stored on DVDs.

As the motion picture companies did not themselves develop CSS and, in any case, are not in the business of making DVD players and drives, the technology for making compliant devices, i.e., devices with CSS keys, had to be licensed to consumer electronics manufacturers. In order to ensure that the decryption technology did not become generally available and that compliant devices could not be used to copy as well as merely to play CSS-protected movies, the technology is licensed subject to strict security requirements. Moreover, manufacturers may not, consistent with their licenses, make equipment that would supply digital output that could be used in copying protected DVDs. Licenses to manufacture compliant devices are granted on a royalty-free basis subject only to an administrative fee. At the time of trial, licenses had been issued to numerous hardware and software manufacturers, including two companies that plan to release DVD players for computers running the Linux operating system.

With CSS in place, the studios introduced DVDs on the consumer market in early 1997. All or most of the motion pictures released on DVD were, and continue to be, encrypted with CSS technology. Over 4,000 motion pictures now have been released in DVD format in the United States, and movies are being issued on DVD at the rate of over 40 new titles per month in addition to re-releases of classic films. Currently, more than five million households in the United States own DVD players, and players are projected to be in ten percent of United States homes by the end of 2000.

DVDs have proven not only popular, but lucrative for the studios. Revenue from their sale and rental currently accounts for a substantial percentage of the movie studios' revenue from the home video market. Revenue from the home market, in turn, makes up a large percentage of the studios' total distribution revenue.

D.   The Appearance of DeCSS

In late September 1999, Jon Johansen, a Norwegian subject then fifteen years of age, and two individuals he "met" under pseudonyms over the Internet, reverse engineered a licensed DVD player and discovered the CSS encryption algorithm and keys. They used this information to create DeCSS, a program capable of decrypting or "ripping" encrypted DVDs, thereby allowing playback on non-compliant computers as well as the copying of decrypted files to computer hard drives. Mr. Johansen then posted the executable code on his personal Internet web site and informed members of an Internet mailing list that he had done so. Neither Mr. Johansen nor his collaborators obtained a license from the DVD CCA.

Although Mr. Johansen testified at trial that he created DeCSS in order to make a DVD player that would operate on a computer running the Linux operating system, DeCSS is a Windows executable file; that is, it can be executed only on computers running the Windows operating system. Mr. Johansen explained the fact that he created a Windows rather than a Linux program by asserting that Linux, at the time he created DeCSS, did not support the file system used on DVDs. Hence, it was necessary, he said, to decrypt the DVD on a Windows computer in order subsequently to play the decrypted files on a Linux machine. Assuming that to be true, however, the fact remains that Mr. Johansen created DeCSS in the full knowledge that it could be used on computers running Windows rather than Linux. Moreover, he was well aware that the files, once decrypted, could be copied like any other computer files. ...

E.   The Distribution of DeCSS

In the months following its initial appearance on Mr. Johansen's web site, DeCSS has become widely available on the Internet, where hundreds of sites now purport to offer the software for download. A few other applications said to decrypt CSS-encrypted DVDs also have appeared on the Internet.

In November 1999, defendants' web site began to offer DeCSS for download. It established also a list of links to several web sites that purportedly "mirrored" or offered DeCSS for download. ...

II. The Digital Millennium Copyright Act

...

B.   Posting of DeCSS

1.   Violation of Anti-Trafficking Provision

Section 1201(a)(2) of the Copyright Act, part of the DMCA, provides that:

> "No person shall ... offer to the public, provide or otherwise traffic in any technology ... that-
> "(A)is primarily designed or produced for the purpose of circumventing a technological measure that effectively controls access to a work protected under [the Copyright Act];
> "(B)has only limited commercially significant purpose or use other than to circumvent a technological measure that effectively controls access to a work protected under [the Copyright Act]; or
> "(C)is marketed by that person or another acting in concert with that person with that person's knowledge for use in circumventing a technological measure that effectively controls access to a work protected under [the Copyright Act]."

In this case, defendants concededly offered and provided and, absent a court order, would continue to offer and provide DeCSS to the public by making it available for download on the 2600.com web site. DeCSS, a computer program, unquestionably is "technology" within the meaning of the statute. "[C]ircumvent a technological measure" is defined to mean descrambling a scrambled work, decrypting an encrypted work, or "otherwise to avoid, bypass, remove, deactivate, or impair a technological measure, without the authority of the copyright owner," so DeCSS clearly is a means of circumventing a technological access control measure.[74] In consequence, if CSS otherwise falls within paragraphs (A), (B) or (C) of Section 1201(a)(2), and if none of the statutory exceptions applies to their actions, defendants have violated and, unless enjoined, will continue to violate the DMCA by posting DeCSS.

a. Section 1201(a)(2)(A)

(1) CSS Effectively Controls Access to Copyrighted Works

During pretrial proceedings and at trial, defendants attacked plaintiffs' Section 1201(a)(2)(A) claim, arguing that CSS, which is based on a 40-bit encryption key, is a weak cipher that does not "effectively control" access to plaintiffs' copyrighted works. They reasoned from this premise that CSS is not protected under this branch of the statute at all. Their post-trial memorandum appears to have abandoned this argument. In any case, however, the contention is indefensible as a matter of law.

First, the statute expressly provides that "a technological measure 'effectively controls access to a work' if the measure, in the ordinary course of its operation, requires the application of information or a process or a treatment, with the authority of the copyright owner, to gain access to a work." One cannot gain access to a CSS-protected work on a DVD without application of the three keys that are required by the software. ... One cannot lawfully gain access to the keys except by entering into a license with the DVD CCA under authority granted by the copyright owners or by purchasing a DVD player or drive containing the keys pursuant to such a license. In consequence, under the express terms of the statute, CSS "effectively controls access" to copyrighted DVD movies. It does so, within the meaning of the statute, whether or not it is a strong means of protection. ...

[T]he interpretation of the phrase "effectively controls access" offered by defendants at trial—viz., that the use of the word "effectively" means that the statute protects only successful or efficacious technological means of controlling access—would gut the statute if it were adopted. If a technological means of access control is circumvented, it is, in common parlance, ineffective. Yet defendants' construction, if adopted, would limit the application of the statute to access control measures that thwart circumvention, but withhold protection for those measures that can be circumvented. In other words, defendants would have the Court construe

---

[74] [Footnote 137] Decryption or avoidance of an access control measure is not "circumvention" within the meaning of the statute unless it occurs "without the authority of the copyright owner." Defendants posit that purchasers of a DVD acquire the right "to perform all acts with it that are not exclusively granted to the copyright holder." Based on this premise, they argue that DeCSS does not circumvent CSS within the meaning of the statute because the Copyright Act does not grant the copyright holder the right to prohibit purchasers from decrypting. As the copyright holder has no statutory right to prohibit decryption, the argument goes, decryption cannot be understood as unlawful circumvention. The argument is pure sophistry. The DMCA proscribes trafficking in technology that decrypts or avoids an access control measure without the copyright holder consenting to the decryption or avoidance.

the statute to offer protection where none is needed but to withhold protection precisely where protection is essential. The Court declines to do so. Accordingly, the Court holds that CSS effectively controls access to plaintiffs' copyrighted works.

(2) DeCSS Was Designed Primarily to Circumvent CSS

As CSS effectively controls access to plaintiffs' copyrighted works, the only remaining question under Section 1201(a)(2)(A) is whether DeCSS was designed primarily to circumvent CSS. The answer is perfectly obvious. By the admission of both Jon Johansen, the programmer who principally wrote DeCSS, and defendant Corley, DeCSS was created solely for the purpose of decrypting CSS—that is all it does. Hence, absent satisfaction of a statutory exception, defendants clearly violated Section 1201(a)(2)(A) by posting DeCSS to their web site. ...

c.   The Linux Argument

Perhaps the centerpiece of defendants' statutory position is the contention that DeCSS was not created for the purpose of pirating copyrighted motion pictures. Rather, they argue, it was written to further the development of a DVD player that would run under the Linux operating system, as there allegedly were no Linux compatible players on the market at the time. The argument plays itself out in various ways as different elements of the DMCA come into focus. But it perhaps is useful to address the point at its most general level in order to place the preceding discussion in its fullest context.

As noted, Section 1201(a) of the DMCA contains two distinct prohibitions. Section 1201(a)(1), the so-called basic provision, "aims against those who engage in unauthorized circumvention of technological measures.... [It] focuses directly on wrongful conduct, rather than on those who facilitate wrongful conduct...." Section 1201(a)(2), the anti-trafficking provision at issue in this case, on the other hand, separately bans offering or providing technology that may be used to circumvent technological means of controlling access to copyrighted works. If the means in question meets any of the three prongs of the standard set out in Section 1201(a)(2)(A), (B), or (C), it may not be offered or disseminated.

As the earlier discussion demonstrates, the question whether the development of a Linux DVD player motivated those who wrote DeCSS is immaterial to the question whether the defendants now before the Court violated the anti-trafficking provision of the DMCA. The inescapable facts are that (1) CSS is a technological means that effectively controls access to plaintiffs' copyrighted works, (2) the one and only function of DeCSS is to circumvent CSS, and (3) defendants offered and provided DeCSS by posting it on their web site. Whether defendants did so in order to infringe, or to permit or encourage others to infringe, copyrighted works in violation of other provisions of the Copyright Act simply does not matter for purposes of Section 1201(a)(2). The offering or provision of the program is the prohibited conduct—and it is prohibited irrespective of why the program was written, except to whatever extent motive may be germane to determining whether their conduct falls within one of the statutory exceptions. ...

2. Statutory Exceptions

    a. Reverse engineering

Defendants claim to fall under Section 1201(f) of the statute, which provides in substance that one may circumvent, or develop and employ technological means to circumvent, access control measures in order to achieve interoperability with another computer program provided that doing so does not infringe another's copyright and, in addition, that one may make information acquired through such efforts "available to others, if the person [in question] ... provides such information solely for the purpose of enabling interoperability of an independently created computer program with other programs, and to the extent that doing so does not constitute infringement...." They contend that DeCSS is necessary to achieve interoperability between computers running the Linux operating system and DVDs and that this exception therefore is satisfied. This contention fails.

First, Section 1201(f)(3) permits information acquired through reverse engineering to be made available to others only by the person who acquired the information. But these defendants did not do any reverse engineering. They simply took DeCSS off someone else's web site and posted it on their own.

Defendants would be in no stronger position even if they had authored DeCSS. The right to make the information available extends only to dissemination "solely for the purpose" of achieving interoperability as defined in the statute. It does not apply to public dissemination of means of circumvention, as the legislative history confirms. These defendants, however, did not post DeCSS "solely" to achieve interoperability with Linux or anything else.

Finally, it is important to recognize that even the creators of DeCSS cannot credibly maintain that the "sole" purpose of DeCSS was to create a Linux DVD player. DeCSS concededly was developed on and runs under Windows—a far more widely used operating system. The developers of DeCSS therefore knew that DeCSS could be used to decrypt and play DVD movies on Windows as well as Linux machines. They knew also that the decrypted files could be copied like any other unprotected computer file. Moreover, the Court does not credit Mr. Johansen's testimony that he created DeCSS solely for the purpose of building a Linux player. Mr. Johansen is a very talented young man and a member of a well known hacker group who viewed "cracking" CSS as an end it itself and a means of demonstrating his talent and who fully expected that the use of DeCSS would not be confined to Linux machines. Hence, the Court finds that Mr. Johansen and the others who actually did develop DeCSS did not do so solely for the purpose of making a Linux DVD player if, indeed, developing a Linux-based DVD player was among their purposes.

Accordingly, the reverse engineering exception to the DMCA has no application here. ...

d. Fair use

Finally, defendants rely on the doctrine of fair use. Stated in its most general terms, the doctrine, now codified in Section 107 of the Copyright Act, limits the exclusive rights of a copyright holder by permitting others to make limited use of portions of the copyrighted work, for appropriate purposes, free of liability for copyright infringement. For example, it is permissible for one other than the copyright owner to reprint or quote a suitable part of a copyrighted book or article in certain circumstances. The doctrine traditionally has facilitated literary and artistic criticism, teaching and scholarship, and other socially useful forms of expression. It has been viewed by courts as a safety valve that accommodates the exclusive rights conferred by copyright with the freedom of expression guaranteed by the First Amendment.

The use of technological means of controlling access to a copyrighted work may affect the ability to make fair uses of the work. Focusing specifically on the facts of this case, the application of CSS to encrypt a copyrighted motion picture requires the use of a compliant DVD player to view or listen to the movie. Perhaps more significantly, it prevents exact copying of either the video or the audio portion of all or any part of the film. This latter point means that certain uses that might qualify as "fair" for purposes of copyright infringement—for example, the preparation by a film studies professor of a single CD-ROM or tape containing two scenes from different movies in order to illustrate a point in a lecture on cinematography, as opposed to showing relevant parts of two different DVDs—would be difficult or impossible absent circumvention of the CSS encryption. Defendants therefore argue that the DMCA cannot properly be construed to make it difficult or impossible to make any fair use of plaintiffs' copyrighted works and that the statute therefore does not reach their activities, which are simply a means to enable users of DeCSS to make such fair uses.

Defendants have focused on a significant point. Access control measures such as CSS do involve some risk of preventing lawful as well as unlawful uses of copyrighted material. Congress, however, clearly faced up to and dealt with this question in enacting the DMCA.

The Court begins its statutory analysis, as it must, with the language of the statute. Section 107 of the Copyright Act provides in critical part that certain uses of copyrighted works that otherwise would be wrongful are "not ... infringement[s] of copyright. Defendants, however, are not here sued for copyright infringement. They are sued for offering and providing technology designed to circumvent technological measures that control access to copyrighted works and otherwise violating Section 1201(a)(2) of the Act. If Congress had meant the fair use defense to apply to such actions, it would have said so. Indeed, as the legislative history demonstrates, the decision not to make fair use a defense to a claim under Section 1201(a) was quite deliberate.

Congress was well aware during the consideration of the DMCA of the traditional role of the fair use defense in accommodating the exclusive rights of copyright owners with the legitimate interests of noninfringing users of portions of copyrighted works. It recognized the contention, voiced by a range of constituencies concerned with the legislation, that technological controls on access to copyrighted works might erode fair use by preventing access even for uses that would be deemed "fair" if only access might be gained. And it struck a balance among the competing interests.

The first element of the balance was the careful limitation of Section 1201(a)(1)'s prohibition of the act of circumvention to the act itself so as not to "apply to subsequent actions of a person once he or she has obtained authorized access to a copy of a [copyrighted] work...." Judiciary Comm. Rep. 18. By doing so, it left "the traditional defenses to copyright infringement, including fair use, ... fully applicable" provided "the access is authorized." *Id.*

Second, Congress delayed the effective date of Section 1201(a)(1)'s prohibition of the act of circumvention for two years pending further investigation about how best to reconcile Section 1201(a)(1) with fair use concerns. Following that investigation, which is being carried out in the form of a rule-making by the Register of Copyright, the prohibition will not apply to users of particular classes of copyrighted works who demonstrate that their ability to make noninfringing uses of those classes of works would be affected adversely by Section 1201(a)(1).

Third, it created a series of exceptions to aspects of Section 1201(a) for certain uses that Congress thought "fair," including reverse engineering, security testing, good faith encryption research, and certain uses by nonprofit libraries, archives and educational institutions.

Defendants claim also that the possibility that DeCSS might be used for the purpose of gaining access to copyrighted works in order to make fair use of those works saves them under *Sony Corp. v. Universal City Studios, Inc.* But they are mistaken. *Sony* does not apply to the activities with which defendants here are charged. Even if it did, it would not govern here. *Sony* involved a construction of the Copyright Act that has been overruled by the later enactment of the DMCA to the extent of any inconsistency between *Sony* and the new statute. ...

Notes and Questions

1. *Reimerdes* illustrates the challenge of determining how the DMCA's anti-trafficking rules affect the public's ability to engage in legal behavior. The court acknowledged the possibility that the DMCA could

interfere with the exercise of fair use rights. The court decided that Congress had already resolved the conflict between anti-trafficking and fair use in the general favor of copyright holders, so it refused to interpret any of the potentially relevant exceptions in ways that would allow the continued distribution of DeCSS. Did you find the court's reasoning persuasive, and do you think that the *Reimerdes* result serves the public interest?

In its most recent rulemaking, the Librarian of Congress addressed, to some extent, the example that troubled the court in *Reimerdes*, exempting from anti-circumvention liability "Motion pictures" used for various purposes, including educational uses, commentary and criticism, certain nonprofit uses, etc. Does this suggest that the court in *Reimerdes* was right in deciding the case the way it did? If a film professor wanted to take advantage of the exemption, where would he or she find the technology to do so?

Although the DMCA gives the Librarian of Congress the power to craft exemptions to the anticircumvention provisions, it does not give the Librarian power to craft exceptions to the anti-trafficking provisions. Thus, beneficiaries of the regulatory exemptions may have practical difficulties practically exercising their ability to engage in circumvention. In the most recent rulemaking, the Register of Copyrights noted this potential difficulty and suggested that "Congress may wish to consider clarifications to section 1201 to ensure that the beneficiaries of exemptions are able to take full advantage of them even if they need assistance from third parties."

2. The court in *Reimerdes* rejected the argument that DeCSS was not designed primarily to facilitate circumvention, but in order to allow individuals running the Linux operating system on their computers to view movies on DVD. Assume you represented a client who was interested in creating a program that would enable individuals to play DVDs on their Linux machines but that would not run afoul of the DMCA as interpreted in *Reimerdes*. What would you advise that client?

3. What is left of the *Sony* doctrine after the DMCA? In *Reimerdes*, the court expressly noted that *Sony* did not apply to liability under § 1201. Thus, even if a technology was capable of substantial non-infringing uses, it might still run afoul of the anti-trafficking provisions. Does this mean that *Sony* was effectively repealed, at least with respect to works protected by DRM?

4. Even if digital works are encrypted, at some point the works must be decrypted in order for consumers to access them. Thus, for example, the movies on DVDs must be decrypted by the DVD player and sent via an analog signal to the television. It is thus always possible for third parties to intercept the unprotected analog signal and re-digitize the work. Even if the signal from the DVD player to the TV is digitally encrypted, it will eventually have to be displayed on screen, and could therefore be re-recorded from the screen display. This so-called "analog

hole" ultimately makes it impossible for the copyright owners to completely lock up their works and keep them from being copied. And indeed, despite the use of CSS, movies can still be illegally downloaded on the Internet. What follows from this? Does this mean that the efforts of the copyright industries are ultimately futile and the DMCA is therefore of no use? Or is the DMCA nevertheless serving a useful purpose?

5. On appeal, the Second Circuit affirmed the result in *Reimerdes*. The appellate decision dealt primarily with the constitutional arguments that were omitted from the above excerpts.

Problem

DVDs are region-coded. That is, nearly every legitimate DVD sold on the market is encoded with a specific geographic region. This means that those DVDs can only be played by players that are sold in that particular region. So, for example, a DVD with a region code of North America can only be played on machines sold in North America, and will not be playable on a machine sold in Asia. The purpose of region coding is to allow the motion picture companies to price discriminate, i.e. to charge different prices to consumers in North America as compared to Asia, and thereby increase their overall profits.

Assume that you have a client who sells a program that allows DVDs to be played on a computer, but that disregards the region coding. The program does not permit copies to be made of the DVD. All it does is allow it to be played. Does this program violate the DMCA? Should there be liability for this sort of activity?

Chamberlain Group v. Skylink Technologies
381 F.3d 1178 (Fed. Cir. 2004)

GAJARSA, Circuit Judge.

BACKGROUND

The technology at issue involves Garage Door Openers (GDOs). A GDO typically consists of a hand-held portable transmitter and a garage door opening device mounted in a homeowner's garage. The opening device, in turn, includes both a receiver with associated signal processing software and a motor to open or close the garage door. In order to open or close the garage door, a user must activate the transmitter, which sends a radio frequency (RF) signal to the receiver located on the opening device. Once the opener receives a recognized signal, the signal processing software directs the motor to open or close the garage door.

When a homeowner purchases a GDO system, the manufacturer provides both an opener and a transmitter. Homeowners who desire replacement or spare transmitters can purchase them in the aftermarket. Aftermarket consumers have long been able to purchase "universal transmitters" that they can program to interoperate with their GDO system regardless of make or model. Skylink and Chamberlain are the only significant distributors of universal GDO transmitters. Chamberlain places no explicit restrictions on the types of transmitter that the homeowner may use with its system at the time of purchase. Chamberlain's customers therefore assume that they enjoy all of the rights associated with the use of their GDOs and any software embedded therein that the copyright laws and other laws of commerce provide.

This dispute involves Chamberlain's Security+ line of GDOs and Skylink's Model 39 universal transmitter. Chamberlain's Security+ GDOs incorporate a copyrighted "rolling code" computer program that constantly changes the transmitter signal needed to open the garage door. Skylink's Model 39 transmitter, which does not incorporate rolling code, nevertheless allows users to operate Security+ openers. Chamberlain alleges that Skylink's transmitter renders the Security+ insecure by allowing unauthorized users to circumvent the security inherent in rolling codes. Of greater legal significance, however, Chamberlain contends that because of this property of the Model 39, Skylink is in violation of the anti-trafficking clause of the DMCA's anticircumvention provisions, specifically § 1201(a)(2). ...

Skylink began marketing and selling universal transmitters in 1992. Skylink designed its Model 39, launched in August 2002, to interoperate with common GDOs, including both rolling code and non-rolling code GDOs. Although Chamberlain concedes that the Model 39 transmitter is capable of operating many different GDOs, it nevertheless asserts that Skylink markets the Model 39 transmitter for use in circumventing its copyrighted rolling code computer program. Chamberlain supports this allegation by pointing to the Model 39's setting that operates only Chamberlain's rolling code GDOs. ...

These facts frame the dispute now before us on appeal. Though only Chamberlain's DMCA claim is before us, and though the parties dispute whether or not Skylink developed the Model 39 independent of Chamberlain's copyrighted products, it is nevertheless noteworthy that Chamberlain has not alleged either that Skylink infringed its copyright or that Skylink is liable for contributory copyright infringement. What Chamberlain has alleged is that because its opener and transmitter both incorporate computer programs "protected by copyright" and because rolling codes are a "technological measure" that "controls access" to those programs, Skylink is prima facie liable for violating § 1201(a)(2). In the District Court's words, "Chamberlain claims that the rolling code computer program has a protective measure that protects itself. Thus, only one computer program is at work here, but it has two functions: (1) to verify the rolling code; and (2) once the rolling code is verified, to activate the GDO motor, by sending instructions to a microprocessor in the GDO...."

DISCUSSION

...

D. The Statute and Liability under the DMCA

The essence of the DMCA's anticircumvention provisions is that §§ 1201(a),(b) establish causes of action for liability. They do not establish a new property right. The DMCA's text indicates that circumvention is not infringement, and the statute's structure makes the point even clearer. This distinction between property and liability is critical. Whereas copyrights, like patents, are property, liability protection from unauthorized circumvention merely creates a new cause of action under which a defendant may be liable. ...

The anticircumvention provisions convey no additional property rights in and of themselves; they simply provide property owners with new ways to secure their property. Like all property owners taking legitimate steps to protect their property, however, copyright owners relying on the anticircumvention provisions remain bound by all other relevant bodies of law. Contrary to Chamberlain's assertion, the DMCA emphatically did not "fundamentally alter" the legal landscape governing the reasonable expectations of consumers or competitors. ...

What the DMCA did was introduce new grounds for liability in the context of the unauthorized access of copyrighted material. The statute's plain language requires plaintiffs to prove that those circumventing their technological measures controlling access did so "without the authority of the copyright owner." Our inquiry ends with that clear language. ...

F. Access and Protection

Though as noted, circumvention is not a new form of infringement but rather a new violation prohibiting actions or products that facilitate infringement, it is significant that virtually every clause of § 1201 that mentions "access" links "access" to "protection." ... Chamberlain urges us to read the DMCA as if Congress simply created a new protection for copyrighted works without any reference at all either to the protections that copyright owners already possess or to the rights that the Copyright Act grants to the public. Chamberlain has not alleged that Skylink's Model 39 infringes its copyrights, nor has it alleged that the Model 39 contributes to third-party infringement of its copyrights. Chamberlain's allegation is considerably more straightforward: The only way for the Model 39 to interoperate with a Security+ GDO is by "accessing" copyrighted software. Skylink has therefore committed a per se violation of the DMCA. Chamberlain urges us to conclude that no necessary connection exists between access and copyrights. Congress could not have intended such a broad reading of the DMCA.

Chamberlain derives its strongest claimed support for its proposed construction from the trial court's opinion in *Reimerdes*, a case involving the same statutory provision. Though Chamberlain is correct in considering some of the *Reimerdes* language supportive, it is the differences between the cases, rather than their similarities, that is most instructive in demonstrating precisely what the DMCA permits and what it prohibits.

The facts here differ greatly from those in *Reimerdes*. There, a group of movie studios sought an injunction under the DMCA to prohibit illegal copying of digital versatile discs (DVDs). The plaintiffs presented evidence that each motion picture DVD includes a content scrambling system (CSS) that permits the film to be played, but not copied, using DVD players that incorporate the plaintiffs' licensed decryption technology. The defendant provided a link on his website that allowed an individual to download DeCSS, a program that allows the user to circumvent the CSS protective system and to view or to copy a motion picture from a DVD, whether or not the user has a DVD player with the licensed technology. The defendant proudly trumpeted his actions as "electronic civil disobedience." The court found that the defendant had violated 17 U.S.C. § 1201(a)(2)(A) because DeCSS had only one purpose: to decrypt CSS.

Chamberlain's proposed construction of the DMCA ignores the significant differences between defendants whose accused products enable copying and those, like Skylink, whose accused products enable only legitimate uses of copyrighted software. ...

Chamberlain relies upon the DMCA's prohibition of "fair uses ... as well as foul," to argue that the enactment of the DMCA eliminated all existing consumer expectations about the public's rights to use purchased products because those products might include technological measures controlling access to a copyrighted work. But Chamberlain appears to have overlooked the obvious. The possibility that § 1201 might prohibit some otherwise noninfringing public uses of copyrighted material arises simply because the Congressional decision to create liability and consequent damages for making, using, or selling a "key" that essentially enables a trespass upon intellectual property need not be identical in scope to the liabilities and compensable damages for infringing that property; it is, instead, a rebalancing of interests that "attempt[s] to deal with special problems created by the so-called digital revolution...."

Furthermore, though the severance of access from protection appears plausible taken out of context, it would also introduce a number of irreconcilable problems in statutory construction. The seeming plausibility arises because the statute's structure could be seen to suggest that § 1201(b) strengthens a copyright owner's abilities to protect its recognized rights, while § 1201(a) strengthens a copyright owner's abilities to protect access to its work without regard to the legitimacy (or illegitimacy) of the actions that the accused access enables. Such an interpretation is consistent with the Second Circuit's description: "[T]he focus of subsection 1201(a)(2) is circumvention of technologies designed to prevent access to a work, and the focus of subsection 1201(b)(1) is circumvention of technologies designed to permit access to a work but prevent copying of the work or some other act that infringes a copyright."

It is unlikely, however, that the Second Circuit meant to imply anything as drastic as wresting the concept of "access" from its context within the Copyright Act, as Chamberlain would now have us do. Were § 1201(a) to allow copyright owners to use technological measures to block all access to their copyrighted works, it would effectively create two distinct copyright regimes. In the first regime, the owners of a typical work protected by copyright would possess only the rights enumerated in 17 U.S.C. § 106, subject to the additions, exceptions, and limitations outlined throughout the rest of the Copyright Act—notably but not solely the fair use provisions of § 107.[75] Owners who feel that technology has put those rights at risk, and who incorporate technological measures to protect those rights from technological encroachment, gain the additional ability to hold traffickers in circumvention devices liable under § 1201(b) for putting their rights back at risk by enabling circumventors who use these devices to infringe.

Under the second regime that Chamberlain's proposed construction implies, the owners of a work protected by both copyright and a technological measure that effectively controls access to that work per § 1201(a) would possess unlimited rights to hold circumventors liable under § 1201(a) merely for accessing that work, even if that access enabled only rights that the Copyright Act grants to the public. This second implied regime would be problematic for a number of reasons. First, as the Supreme Court recently explained, "Congress' exercise of its Copyright Clause authority must be rational." Chamberlain's proposed construction of § 1201(a) implies that in enacting the DMCA, Congress attempted to "give the public appropriate access" to copyrighted works by allowing copyright owners to deny all access to the public. Even under the substantial deference due Congress, such a redefinition borders on the irrational.

That apparent irrationality, however, is not the most significant problem that this second regime implies. Such a regime would be hard to reconcile with the DMCA's statutory prescription that "[n]othing in this section shall affect rights, remedies, limitations, or defenses to copyright infringement, including fair use, under this title." 17 U.S.C. § 1201(c)(1). A provision that prohibited access without regard to the rest of the Copyright Act would clearly affect rights and limitations, if not remedies and defenses. ... Chamberlain's proposed construction of § 1201(a) would flatly contradict § 1201(c)(1)—a simultaneously enacted provision of the

---

[75] [Footnote 14] We do not reach the relationship between § 107 fair use and violations of § 1201. We leave open the question as to when § 107 might serve as an affirmative defense to a prima facie violation of § 1201. For the moment, we note only that though the traditional fair use doctrine of § 107 remains unchanged as a defense to copyright infringement under § 1201(c)(1), circumvention is not infringement.

same statute. We are therefore bound, if we can, to obtain an alternative construction that leads to no such contradiction.

Chamberlain's proposed severance of "access" from "protection" in § 1201(a) creates numerous other problems. Beyond suggesting that Congress enacted by implication a new, highly protective alternative regime for copyrighted works; contradicting other provisions of the same statute including § 1201(c)(1); and ignoring the explicit immunization of interoperability from anticircumvention liability under § 1201(f); the broad policy implications of considering "access" in a vacuum devoid of "protection" are both absurd and disastrous. Under Chamberlain's proposed construction, explicated at oral argument, disabling a burglar alarm to gain "access" to a home containing copyrighted books, music, art, and periodicals would violate the DMCA; anyone who did so would unquestionably have "circumvent[ed] a technological measure that effectively controls access to a work protected under [the Copyright Act]." § 1201(a)(1). The appropriate deterrents to this type of behavior lie in tort law and criminal law, not in copyright law. Yet, were we to read the statute's "plain language" as Chamberlain urges, disabling a burglar alarm would be a per se violation of the DMCA.

In a similar vein, Chamberlain's proposed construction would allow any manufacturer of any product to add a single copyrighted sentence or software fragment to its product, wrap the copyrighted material in a trivial "encryption" scheme, and thereby gain the right to restrict consumers' rights to use its products in conjunction with competing products. In other words, Chamberlain's construction of the DMCA would allow virtually any company to attempt to leverage its sales into after-market monopolies—a practice that both the antitrust laws and the doctrine of copyright misuse normally prohibit. ...

Finally, the requisite "authorization," on which the District Court granted Skylink summary judgment, points to yet another inconsistency in Chamberlain's proposed construction. The notion of authorization is central to understanding § 1201(a). Underlying Chamberlain's argument on appeal that it has not granted such authorization lies the necessary assumption that Chamberlain is entitled to prohibit legitimate purchasers of its embedded software from "accessing" the software by using it. Such an entitlement, however, would go far beyond the idea that the DMCA allows copyright owner to prohibit "fair uses ... as well as foul." Chamberlain's proposed construction would allow copyright owners to prohibit exclusively fair uses even in the absence of any feared foul use. It would therefore allow any copyright owner, through a combination of contractual terms and technological measures, to repeal the fair use doctrine with respect to an individual copyrighted work—or even selected copies of that copyrighted work. Again, this implication contradicts § 1201(c)(1) directly. Copyright law itself authorizes the public to make certain uses of copyrighted materials. Consumers who purchase a product containing a copy of embedded software have the inherent legal right to use that copy of the software. What the law authorizes, Chamberlain cannot revoke.[76]

Chamberlain's proposed severance of "access" from "protection" is entirely inconsistent with the context defined by the total statutory structure of the Copyright Act, other simultaneously enacted provisions of the DMCA, and clear Congressional intent. ... The statutory structure and the legislative history both make it clear that the DMCA granted copyright holders additional legal protections, but neither rescinded the basic bargain granting the public noninfringing and fair uses of copyrighted materials, § 1201(c), nor prohibited various beneficial uses of circumvention technology, such as those exempted under §§ 1201(d),(f),(g), (j).

We therefore reject Chamberlain's proposed construction in its entirety. We conclude that 17 U.S.C. § 1201 prohibits only forms of access that bear a reasonable relationship to the protections that the Copyright Act otherwise affords copyright owners. While such a rule of reason may create some uncertainty and consume some judicial resources, it is the only meaningful reading of the statute. Congress attempted to balance the legitimate interests of copyright owners with those of consumers of copyrighted products. The courts must adhere to the language that Congress enacted to determine how it attempted to achieve that balance.

As we have seen, Congress chose to create new causes of action for circumvention and for trafficking in circumvention devices. Congress did not choose to create new property rights. That is the choice that we have identified. Were we to interpret Congress's words in a way that eliminated all balance and granted copyright owners carte blanche authority to preclude all use, Congressional intent would remain unrealized.

Congress chose words consistent with its stated intent to balance two sets of concerns pushing in opposite directions. The statute lays out broad categories of liability and broad exemptions from liability. It also instructs the courts explicitly not to construe the anticircumvention provisions in ways that would effectively repeal longstanding principles of copyright law. The courts must decide where the balance between the rights of copyright owners and those of the broad public tilts subject to a fact-specific rule of reason. Here, Chamberlain can point to no protected property right that Skylink imperils. The DMCA cannot allow Chamberlain to retract the most fundamental right that the Copyright Act grants consumers: the right to use the copy of Chamberlain's embedded software that they purchased.

---

[76] [Footnote 17] It is not clear whether a consumer who circumvents a technological measure controlling access to a copyrighted work in a manner that enables uses permitted under the Copyright Act but prohibited by contract can be subject to liability under the DMCA. Because Chamberlain did not attempt to limit its customers use of its product by contract, however, we do not reach this issue.

G. Chamberlain's DMCA Claim

The proper construction of § 1201(a)(2) therefore makes it clear that Chamberlain cannot prevail. A plaintiff alleging a violation of § 1201(a)(2) must prove: (1) ownership of a valid copyright on a work, (2) effectively controlled by a technological measure, which has been circumvented, (3) that third parties can now access (4) without authorization, in a manner that (5) infringes or facilitates infringing a right protected by the Copyright Act, because of a product that (6) the defendant either (i) designed or produced primarily for circumvention; (ii) made available despite only limited commercial significance other than circumvention; or (iii) marketed for use in circumvention of the controlling technological measure. A plaintiff incapable of establishing any one of elements (1) through (5) will have failed to prove a prima facie case. A plaintiff capable of proving elements (1) through (5) need prove only one of (6)(i), (ii), or (iii) to shift the burden back to the defendant. At that point, the various affirmative defenses enumerated throughout § 1201 become relevant.

The District Court analyzed Chamberlain's allegations in precisely the appropriate manner—a narrow focus on Skylink's behavior, intent, and product within the broader context of longstanding expectations throughout the industry. The District Court assumed that Chamberlain met the first element, copyright ownership, and for the purposes of its summary judgment motions accepted Chamberlain's evidence of the second element, technological access control. The District Court granted Skylink's motion for summary judgment because Chamberlain failed to meet its burden on the fourth element, the lack of authorization. Chamberlain emphatically contests this conclusion on appeal, though mostly by reiterating arguments that the District Court correctly rejected.

Chamberlain, however, has failed to show not only the requisite lack of authorization, but also the necessary fifth element of its claim, the critical nexus between access and protection. Chamberlain neither alleged copyright infringement *nor explained how the access provided by the Model 39 transmitter facilitates the infringement of any right that the Copyright Act protects*. There can therefore be no reasonable relationship between the access that homeowners gain to Chamberlain's copyrighted software when using Skylink's Model 39 transmitter and the protections that the Copyright Act grants to Chamberlain. The Copyright Act authorized Chamberlain's customers to use the copy of Chamberlain's copyrighted software embedded in the GDOs that they purchased. Chamberlain's customers are therefore immune from § 1201(a)(1) circumvention liability. In the absence of allegations of either copyright infringement or § 1201(a)(1) circumvention, Skylink cannot be liable for § 1201(a)(2) trafficking. The District Court's grant of summary judgment in Skylink's favor was correct. Chamberlain failed to allege a claim under 17 U.S.C. § 1201.

Notes and Questions

1.   Where does the court get the requirement that circumvention must "infringe[] or facilitate[] infringing a right protected by the Copyright Act"? Unlike the other elements of the court's test, this element appears nowhere in the text of the DMCA. Are you persuaded by the court's reasoning, especially its decision not to apply *Reimerdes* to the facts at hand? Is the court correct that Congress never intended to create a right to control access to a copyrighted work?

2.   What does it mean for an act of circumvention to "facilitate[] infringing a right protected by the Copyright Act"? How do we tell when an act of circumvention facilitates infringement? Take, for example, the facts in *Reimerdes*. Did the DMCA claim there satisfy the test laid out in *Chamberlain*? Couldn't it be argued that consumers using the circumvention technology are merely gaining access to the work in a way that does not infringe any copyrights? Can the decision in *Chamberlain* be squared with *Reimerdes*? What about the hypothetical about region coding in the earlier problem? Would a program that disregarded DVD region-coding violate the DMCA under *Chamberlain*?

3.   Could a party avoid the result in *Chamberlain* by imposing restrictive licensing terms on the end-user? For example, if *Chamberlain* had required purchasers of their garage door openers to agree to a license barring them from using third-party remote controls, would the result have been different? The *Chamberlain* court itself avoided addressing this question.

4.   The Federal Circuit's decision in *Chamberlain* was clearly motivated by a strong sense that Congress did not intend for the DMCA to be applied to these kinds of cases. Other circuits have used other doctrinal avenues to avoid such results.

For example, in *Lexmark Int'l v. Static Control Components*, 387 F.3d 522 (6th Cir. 2004), the laser printer manufacturer Lexmark used a technological measure to ensure that only approved toner cartridges would function with its printers. Static Control Components manufactured computer chips that allowed third-parties to make compatible toner cartridges. Lexmark brought at DMCA claim against Static Control, arguing that its technological measure controlled access to the software used to operate the laser printer, and that Static Control's chips circumvented this technological measure.

The Sixth Circuit rejected Lexmark's claim on two grounds. First, the court held that Lexmark's technological measure did not effectively control access to the laser printer software, since the software resided unprotected and unencrypted on the laser printer memory. Thus, purchasers of the printer could freely access the copyrighted work. Second, the court held that Static Control fell within the scope of the reverse engineering exception to the DMCA.

In its most recent proposed rulemaking, the Register of Copyrights noted that "[w]hile it is clear that section 1201 has played a critical role in the development of secure platforms for the digital distribution of copyrighted works, it is also the case that the prohibition on circumvention impacts a wide range of consumer activities that have little to do with the consumption of creative content or the core concerns of copyright." The Register then suggested that this was an area for Congress to revisit.

MDY Industries v. Blizzard Entertainment
629 F.3d 928 (9th Cir. 2010)
As amended on den. of reh'g, __ F.3d __ (9th Cir. 2011)

CALLAHAN, Circuit Judge.

Blizzard Entertainment, Inc. ("Blizzard") is the creator of World of Warcraft ("WoW"), a popular multiplayer online roleplaying game in which players interact in a virtual world while advancing through the game's 70 levels. MDY Industries, LLC and its sole member Michael Donnelly ("Donnelly") (sometimes referred to collectively as "MDY") developed and sold Glider, a software program that automatically plays the early levels of WoW for players....

I.

A. World of Warcraft

In November 2004, Blizzard created WoW, a "massively multiplayer online roleplaying game" in which players interact in a virtual world. WoW has ten million subscribers, of which two and a half million are in North America. The WoW software has two components: (1) the game client software that a player installs on the computer; and (2) the game server software, which the player accesses on a subscription basis by connecting to WoW's online servers. WoW does not have single-player or offline modes.

WoW players roleplay different characters, such as humans, elves, and dwarves. A player's central objective is to advance the character through the game's 70 levels by participating in quests and engaging in battles with monsters. As a player advances, the character collects rewards such as in-game currency, weapons, and armor. WoW's virtual world has its own economy, in which characters use their virtual currency to buy and sell items directly from each other, through vendors, or using auction houses. Some players also utilize WoW's chat capabilities to interact with others....

C. Development of Glider and Warden

Donnelly is a WoW player and software programmer. In March 2005, he developed Glider, a software "bot" (short for robot) that automates play of WoW's early levels, for his personal use. A user need not be at the computer while Glider is running. As explained in the Frequently Asked Questions ("FAQ") on MDY's website for Glider:

> Glider ... moves the mouse around and pushes keys on the keyboard. You tell it about your character, where you want to kill things, and when you want to kill. Then it kills for you, automatically. You can do something else, like eat dinner or go to a movie, and when you return, you'll have a lot more experience and loot.

Glider does not alter or copy WoW's game client software, does not allow a player to avoid paying monthly subscription dues to Blizzard, and has no commercial use independent of WoW. Glider was not initially designed to avoid detection by Blizzard....

In September 2005, Blizzard launched Warden, a technology that it developed to prevent its players who use unauthorized third-party software, including bots, from connecting to WoW's servers. Warden was able to detect Glider, and Blizzard immediately used Warden to ban most Glider users. MDY responded by modifying Glider to avoid detection and promoting its new antidetection features on its website's FAQ. It added a subscription service, Glider Elite, which offered "additional protection from game detection software" for five dollars a month....

IV.

[The court rejected Blizzard's claim that MDY committed contributory or vicarious copyright infringement by selling Glider.]

V.

... Blizzard claims that MDY is liable under DMCA § 1201(a)(2) and (b)(1) because it ... programmed Glider to avoid detection by Warden.

A. The Warden technology

Warden has two components. The first is a software module called "scan.dll," which scans a computer's RAM prior to allowing the player to connect to WoW's servers. If scan.dll detects that a bot is running, such as Glider, it will not allow the player to connect and play. After Blizzard launched Warden, MDY reconfigured Glider to circumvent scan.dll by not loading itself until after scan.dll completed its check. Warden's second component is a "resident" component that runs periodically in the background on a player's computer when it is connected to WoW's servers. It asks the computer to report portions of the WoW code running in RAM, and it looks for patterns of code associated with known bots or cheats. If it detects a bot or cheat, it boots the player from the game, which halts the computer's copying of copyrighted code into RAM.

B. The Digital Millennium Copyright Act

Congress enacted the DMCA in 1998 to conform United States copyright law to its obligations under two World Intellectual Property Organization ("WIPO") treaties, which require contracting parties to provide effective legal remedies against the circumvention of protective technological measures used by copyright owners. In enacting the DMCA, Congress sought to mitigate the problems presented by copyright enforcement in the digital age. The DMCA contains three provisions directed at the circumvention of copyright owners' technological measures. The Supreme Court has yet to construe these provisions, and they raise questions of first impression in this circuit.

The first provision, 17 U.S.C. § 1201(a)(1)(A), is a general prohibition against "circumventing a technological measure that effectively controls access to a work protected under [the Copyright Act]." The second prohibits trafficking in technology that circumvents a technological measure that "effectively controls access" to a copyrighted work. 17 U.S.C. § 1201(a)(2). The third prohibits trafficking in technology that circumvents a technological measure that "effectively protects" a copyright owner's right. 17 U.S.C. § 1201(b)(1).

C. The district court's decision

The district court assessed whether MDY violated DMCA § 1201(a)(2) and (b)(1) with respect to three WoW components. First, the district court considered the game client software's literal elements: the source code stored on players' hard drives. Second, the district court considered the game client software's individual non-literal elements: the 400,000+ discrete visual and audible components of the game, such as a visual image of a monster or its audible roar. Finally, it considered the game's dynamic nonliteral elements: that is, the "real-time experience of traveling through different worlds, hearing their sounds, viewing their structures, encountering their inhabitants and monsters, and encountering other players."...

D. Construction of § 1201

One of the issues raised by this appeal is whether certain provisions of § 1201 prohibit circumvention of access controls when access does not constitute copyright infringement....

We begin by considering the scope of DMCA § 1201's three operative provisions, §§ 1201(a)(1), 1201(a)(2), and 1201(b)(1)....

2. Our harmonization of the DMCA's operative provisions

For the reasons set forth below, we believe that § 1201 is best understood to create two distinct types of claims. First, § 1201(a) prohibits the circumvention of any technological measure that effectively controls access to a protected work and grants copyright owners the right to enforce that prohibition. Second, and in contrast to § 1201(a), § 1201(b)(1) prohibits trafficking in technologies that circumvent technological measures that effectively protect "a right of a copyright owner." Section 1201(b)(1)'s prohibition is thus aimed at circumventions of measures that protect the copyright itself: it entitles copyright owners to protect their existing exclusive rights under the Copyright Act. Those exclusive rights are reproduction, distribution, public performance, public display, and creation of derivative works. 17 U.S.C. § 106. Historically speaking, preventing "access" to a protected work in itself has not been a right of a copyright owner arising from the Copyright Act.

Our construction of § 1201 is compelled by the four significant textual differences between § 1201(a) and (b). First, § 1201(a)(2) prohibits the circumvention of a measure that "effectively controls access to a work protected under this title," whereas § 1201(b)(1) concerns a measure that "effectively protects a right of a copyright owner under this title in a work or portion thereof." We read § 1201(b)(1)'s language—"right of a copyright owner under this title"—to reinforce copyright owners' traditional exclusive rights under § 106 by granting them an additional cause of action against those who traffic in circumventing devices that facilitate infringement. Sections 1201(a)(1) and (a)(2), however, use the term "work protected under this title." Neither of these two subsections explicitly refers to traditional copyright infringement under § 106. Accordingly, we read this term as extending a new form of protection, i.e., the right to prevent circumvention of access controls, broadly to works protected under Title 17, i.e., copyrighted works....

[Another] significant difference between the subsections is that § 1201(a)(1)(A) prohibits circumventing an effective access control measure, whereas § 1201(b) prohibits trafficking in circumventing devices, but does not prohibit circumvention itself because such conduct was already outlawed as copyright infringement. The Senate Judiciary Committee explained:

> This ... is the reason there is no prohibition on conduct in 1201(b) akin to the prohibition on circumvention conduct in 1201(a)(1). The prohibition in 1201(a)(1) is necessary because prior to this Act, the conduct of circumvention was never before made unlawful. The device limitation on 1201(a)(2) enforces this new prohibition on conduct. The copyright law has long forbidden copyright infringements, so no new prohibition was necessary.

S.Rep. No. 105–90, at 11 (1998). This difference reinforces our reading of § 1201(b) as strengthening copyright owners' traditional rights against copyright infringement and of § 1201(a) as granting copyright owners a new anti-circumvention right....

Our reading of § 1201(a) and (b) ensures that neither section is rendered superfluous. A violation of § 1201(a)(1)(A), which prohibits circumvention itself, will not be a violation of § 1201(b), which does not contain an analogous prohibition on circumvention. A violation of § 1201(a)(2), which prohibits trafficking in devices that facilitate circumvention of access control measures, will not always be a violation of § 1201(b)(1), which prohibits trafficking in devices that facilitate circumvention of measures that protect against copyright infringement. Of course, if a copyright owner puts in place an effective measure that both (1) controls access and (2) protects against copyright infringement, a defendant who traffics in a device that circumvents that measure could be liable under both § 1201(a) and (b). Nonetheless, we read the differences in structure between § 1201(a) and (b) as reflecting Congress's intent to address distinct concerns by creating different rights with different elements....

4. The Federal Circuit's decisions

The Federal Circuit has adopted a different approach to the DMCA. In essence, it requires § 1201(a) plaintiffs to demonstrate that the circumventing technology infringes or facilitates infringement of the plaintiff's copyright (an "infringement nexus requirement"). *See Chamberlain Group, Inc. v. Skylink Techs., Inc.,* 381 F.3d 1178, 1203 (Fed.Cir.2004); *Storage Tech. Corp. v. Custom Hardware Eng'g & Consulting, Inc.,* 421 F.3d 1307 (Fed.Cir.2005).

The seminal decision is *Chamberlain,* 381 F.3d 1178 (Fed.Cir.2004). In *Chamberlain,* the plaintiff sold garage door openers ("GDOs") with a "rolling code" security system that purportedly reduced the risk of crime by constantly changing the transmitter signal necessary to open the door. Customers used the GDOs' transmitters to send the changing signal, which in turn opened or closed their garage doors.

Plaintiff sued the defendant, who sold "universal" GDO transmitters for use with plaintiff's GDOs, under § 1201(a)(2). The plaintiff alleged that its GDOs and transmitters both contained copyrighted computer programs and that its rolling code security system was a technological measure that controlled access to those programs. Accordingly, plaintiff alleged that the defendant—by selling GDO transmitters that were compatible with plaintiff's GDOs—had trafficked in a technology that was primarily used for the circumvention of a technological measure (the rolling code security system) that effectively controlled access to plaintiff's copyrighted works.

The Federal Circuit rejected the plaintiff's claim, holding that the defendant did not violate § 1201(a)(2) because, *inter alia,* the defendant's universal GDO transmitters did not infringe or facilitate infringement of the plaintiff's copyrighted computer programs. The linchpin of the *Chamberlain* court's analysis is its conclusion that DMCA coverage is limited to a copyright owner's rights under the Copyright Act as set forth in § 106 of the Copyright Act. Thus, it held that § 1201(a) did not grant copyright owners a new anti-circumvention right, but instead, established new causes of action for a defendant's unauthorized access of copyrighted material when it infringes upon a copyright owner's rights under § 106. Accordingly, a § 1201(a)(2) plaintiff was required to demonstrate a nexus to infringement—i.e., that the defendant's trafficking in circumventing technology had a "reasonable relationship" to the protections that the Copyright Act affords copyright owners....

Accordingly, the Federal Circuit held that a DMCA § 1201(a)(2) action was foreclosed to the extent that the defendant trafficked in a device that did not facilitate copyright infringement.

5. We decline to adopt an infringement nexus requirement

While we appreciate the policy considerations expressed by the Federal Circuit in *Chamberlain*, we are unable to follow its approach because it is contrary to the plain language of the statute. ..

i. Statutory inconsistencies

Were we to follow *Chamberlain* in imposing an infringement nexus requirement, we would have to disregard the plain language of the statute. Moreover, there is significant textual evidence showing Congress's intent to create a new anticircumvention right in § 1201(a) distinct from infringement. As set forth supra, this evidence includes: (1) Congress's choice to link only § 1201(b)(1) explicitly to infringement; (2) Congress's provision in § 1201(a)(3)(A) that descrambling and decrypting devices can lead to § 1201(a) liability, even though descrambling and decrypting devices may only enable non-infringing access to a copyrighted work; and (3) Congress's creation of a mechanism in § 1201(a)(1)(B)-(D) to exempt certain non-infringing behavior from § 1201(a)(1) liability, a mechanism that would be unnecessary if an infringement nexus requirement existed....

The *Chamberlain* court reasoned that if § 1201(a) creates liability for access without regard to the remainder of the Copyright Act, it "would clearly affect rights and limitations, if not remedies and defenses." 381 F.3d at 1200. This perceived tension is relieved by our recognition that § 1201(a) creates a new anti-circumvention right distinct from the traditional exclusive rights of a copyright owner. It follows that § 1201(a) does not limit the traditional framework of exclusive rights created by § 106, or defenses to those rights such as fair use.[77] We are thus unpersuaded by *Chamberlain's* reading of the DMCA's text and structure.

ii. Additional interpretive considerations

Though we need no further evidence of Congress's intent, the parties, citing *Chamberlain*, proffer several other arguments, which we review briefly in order to address the parties' contentions. *Chamberlain* relied heavily on policy considerations to support its reading of § 1201(a). As a threshold matter, we stress that such considerations cannot trump the statute's plain text and structure. Even were they permissible considerations in this case, however, they would not persuade us to adopt an infringement nexus requirement. *Chamberlain* feared that § 1201(a) would allow companies to leverage their sales into aftermarket monopolies, in tension with antitrust law and the doctrine of copyright misuse. Concerning antitrust law, we note that there is no clear issue of anticompetitive behavior in this case because Blizzard does not seek to put a direct competitor who offers a competing roleplaying game out of busi-

---

[77] [Footnote 12.] Like the *Chamberlain* court, we need not and do not reach the relationship between fair use under § 107 of the Copyright Act and violations of § 1201. MDY has not claimed that Glider use is a "fair use" of WoW's dynamic non-literal elements. Accordingly, we too leave open the question whether fair use might serve as an affirmative defense to a prima facie violation of § 1201.

ness and the parties have not argued this issue. If a § 1201(a)(2) defendant in a future case claims that a plaintiff is attempting to enforce its DMCA anti-circumvention right in a manner that violates antitrust law, we will then consider the interplay between this new anti-circumvention right and antitrust law.

Chamberlain also viewed an infringement nexus requirement as necessary to prevent "absurd and disastrous results," such as the existence of DMCA liability for disabling a burglary alarm to gain access to a home containing copyrighted materials. In addition, the Federal Circuit was concerned that, without an infringement nexus requirement, § 1201(a) would allow copyright owners to deny all access to the public by putting an effective access control measure in place that the public is not allowed to circumvent. Both concerns appear to be overstated, but even accepting them, *arguendo*, as legitimate concerns, they do not permit reading the statute as requiring the imposition of an infringement nexus. As § 1201(a) creates a distinct right, it does not disturb the balance between public rights and the traditional rights of owners of copyright under the Copyright Act. Moreover, § 1201(a)(1)(B)-(D) allows the Library of Congress to create exceptions to the § 1201(a) anticircumvention right in the public's interest. If greater protection of the public's ability to access copyrighted works is required, Congress can provide such protection by amending the statute.

In sum, we conclude that a fair reading of the statute (supported by legislative history) indicates that Congress created a distinct anti-circumvention right under § 1201(a) without an infringement nexus requirement.... We now consider whether MDY has violated § 1201(a)(2) and (b)(1).

E. Blizzard's § 1201(a)(2) claim

1. WoW's literal elements and individual non-literal elements

We agree with the district court that MDY's Glider does not violate DMCA § 1201(a)(2) with respect to WoW's literal elements and individual non-literal elements, because Warden does not effectively control access to these WoW elements. First, Warden does not control access to WoW's literal elements because these elements—the game client's software code—are available on a player's hard drive once the game client software is installed. Second, as the district court found:

> [WoW's] individual nonliteral components may be accessed by a user without signing on to the server. As was demonstrated during trial, an owner of the game client software may use independently purchased computer programs to call up the visual images or the recorded sounds within the game client software. For instance, a user may call up and listen to the roar a particular monster makes within the game. Or the user may call up a virtual image of that monster.

Since a player need not encounter Warden to access WoW's individual non-literal elements, Warden does not effectively control access to those elements.

Our conclusion is in accord with the Sixth Circuit's decision in *Lexmark International v. Static Control Components*, 387 F.3d 522 (6th Cir. 2004). In *Lexmark*, the plaintiff sold laser printers equipped with an authentication sequence, verified by the printer's copyrighted software, that ensured that only plaintiff's own toner cartridges could be inserted into the printers. The defendant sold microchips capable of generating an authentication sequence that rendered other manufacturers' cartridges compatible with plaintiff's printers.

The Sixth Circuit held that plaintiff's § 1201(a)(2) claim failed because its authentication sequence did not effectively control access to its copyrighted computer program. Rather, the mere purchase of one of plaintiff's printers allowed "access" to the copyrighted program. Any purchaser could read the program code directly from the printer memory without encountering the authentication sequence. The authentication sequence thus blocked only one form of access: the ability to make use of the printer. However, it left intact another form of access: the review and use of the computer program's literal code....

Here, a player's purchase of the WoW game client allows access to the game's literal elements and individual non-literal elements. Warden blocks one form of access to these elements: the ability to access them while connected to a WoW server. However, analogously to the situation in *Lexmark*, Warden leaves open the ability to access these elements directly via the user's computer. We conclude that Warden is not an effective access control measure with respect to WoW's literal elements and individual non-literal elements, and therefore, that MDY does not violate § 1201(a)(2) with respect to these elements.

2. WoW's dynamic non-literal elements

We conclude that MDY meets each of the six textual elements for violating § 1201(a)(2) with respect to WoW's dynamic non-literal elements. That is, MDY (1) traffics in (2) a technology or part thereof (3) that is primarily designed, produced, or marketed for, or has limited commercially significant use other than (4) circumventing a technological measure (5) that effectively controls access (6) to a copyrighted work. *See* 17 U.S.C. § 1201(a)(2).

The first two elements are met because MDY "traffics in a technology or part thereof"—that is, it sells Glider. The third and fourth elements are met because Blizzard has established that MDY markets Glider for use in circumventing Warden, thus satisfying the requirement of § 1201(a)(2)(C). Indeed, Glider has no function other than to facilitate the playing of WoW. The sixth element is met because, as the district court held, WoW's dynamic non-literal elements constitute a copyrighted work.

The fifth element is met because Warden is an effective access control measure. To "effectively control access to a work," a technological measure must "in the ordinary course of its operation, require[ ] the application of information, or a process or a treatment, with the authority of the copyright owner, to gain access to the work." 17 U.S.C. § 1201(a)(3)(B). Both of Warden's two components "require[ ] the application of information, or a process or a treatment ... to gain access to the work." For a player to connect to Blizzard's servers which provide access to WoW's dynamic non-literal elements, scan.dll must scan the player's computer RAM and confirm the absence of any bots or cheats. The resident component also requires a "process" in order for the user to continue accessing the work: the user's computer must report portions of WoW code running in RAM to the server. Moreover, Warden's provisions were put into place by Blizzard, and thus, function "with the authority of the copyright owner." Accordingly, Warden effectively controls access to WoW's dynamic non-literal elements.[78] We hold that MDY is liable under § 1201(a)(2) with respect to WoW's dynamic non-literal elements. Accordingly, we affirm the district court's entry of a permanent injunction against MDY to prevent future § 1201(a)(2) violations.[79]

F. Blizzard's § 1201(b)(1) claim

Blizzard may prevail under § 1201(b)(1) only if Warden "effectively protect[s] a right" of Blizzard under the Copyright Act. Blizzard contends that Warden protects its reproduction right against unauthorized copying. We disagree.

First, although WoW players copy the software code into RAM while playing the game, Blizzard's EULA and ToU authorize all licensed WoW players to do so. We have explained that ToU § 4(B)'s bot prohibition is a license covenant rather than a condition. Thus, a Glider user who violates this covenant does not infringe by continuing to copy code into RAM. Accordingly, MDY does not violate § 1201(b)(1) by enabling Glider users to avoid Warden's interruption of their authorized copying into RAM.

Second, although WoW players can theoretically record game play by taking screen shots, there is no evidence that Warden detects or pre-

---

[78] [Footnote 17.] The statutory definition of the phrase "effectively control access to a work" does not require that an access control measure be strong or circumvention-proof. Rather, it requires an access control measure to provide some degree of control over access to a copyrighted work. As one district court has observed, if the word "effectively" were read to mean that the statute protects "only successful or efficacious technological means of controlling access," it would "gut" DMCA § 1201(a)(2), because it would "limit the application of the statute to access control measures that thwart circumvention, but withhold protection for those measures that can be circumvented." See *Universal City Studios v. Reimerdes*, 111 F.Supp.2d 294, 318 (S.D.N.Y.2000).

[79] [Footnote 19.] For the first time in its petition for rehearing, MDY raises the applicability of Section 1201(f) and the question whether Glider is an "independently created computer program" under that subsection and thus exempt from the coverage of Section 1201(a). Because this argument was not raised to the district court or presented in the parties' briefs on appeal, we decline to reach it.

vents such allegedly infringing copying. This is logical, because Warden was designed to reduce the presence of cheats and bots, not to protect WoW's dynamic non-literal elements against copying. We conclude that Warden does not effectively protect any of Blizzard's rights under the Copyright Act, and MDY is not liable under § 1201(b)(1) for Glider's circumvention of Warden.

Notes and Questions

1. Another part of the DMCA, § 1201(c), provides: "Nothing in this section shall affect rights, remedies, limitations, or defenses to copyright infringement, including fair use, under this title." Given this provision, what do you think of the court's reasoning about Congressional intent and its reliance on the "plain language" of the statute? Does the *MDY* opinion adequately deal with §1201(c)?

2. The Ninth Circuit panel in *MDY* clearly rejected the Federal Circuit's rule from *Chamberlain*, which required a copyright infringement "nexus" for liability under §1201(a)(1). Which view do you find more persuasive? Under the Ninth Circuit's rule, would the manufacturers of the garage door openers in *Chamberlain* have been liable? Why or why not?

3. In footnote 18 of the *MDY* opinion, the court notes that MDY had failed earlier to argue that its program fell under the exemption in § 1201(f) for reverse engineering in order to make a compatible piece of software. Do you think this argument would have been successful, if timely raised?

3. COPYRIGHT MANAGEMENT INFORMATION

The DMCA contains a separate provision that deals with so-called copyright management information. Copyright management information refers generally to information accompanying a copyrighted digital file, such as the copyright owner, terms of use, date of publication, etc. The DMCA imposes liability for knowingly stripping such information from digital files and for knowingly distributing files from which such information has been stripped.

> § 1202. Integrity of copyright management information
> (a) False Copyright Management Information.— No person shall knowingly and with the intent to induce, enable, facilitate, or conceal infringement—
> (1) provide copyright management information that is false, or
> (2) distribute or import for distribution copyright management information that is false.
> (b) Removal or Alteration of Copyright Management Information.— No person shall, without the authority of the copyright owner or the law—
> (1) intentionally remove or alter any copyright management information,

    (2) distribute or import for distribution copyright management information knowing that the copyright management information has been removed or altered without authority of the copyright owner or the law, or

    (3) distribute, import for distribution, or publicly perform works, copies of works, or phonorecords, knowing that copyright management information has been removed or altered without authority of the copyright owner or the law,

knowing, or, with respect to civil remedies under section 1203, having reasonable grounds to know, that it will induce, enable, facilitate, or conceal an infringement of any right under this title.

These provisions have received comparably less attention to date.

Chapter Nine

REMEDIES

If a copyright plaintiff succeeds in proving infringement, the next question is: what can that plaintiff get? In this chapter, we will explore the law of copyright remedies. Although the issue of remedies sometimes gets short shrift, this is a mistake for at least two reasons. First, remedies are of enormous practical importance—indeed, the availability of certain remedies (or lack thereof) may be the single most important issue to a particular party or client. Second, copyright remedies raise interesting theoretical issues regarding the proper scope and structure of the copyright entitlement, and these issues have received even more attention in recent years with changes in the law.

In general, copyright plaintiffs can get remedies similar to those available to other civil plaintiffs, such as injunctive relief, damages, and in some cases attorney's fees. Copyright differs somewhat from some other civil areas, however, in that actual damages can sometimes be difficult to measure with accuracy. Perhaps as a result, injunctive relief has in the past been more easily available in copyright cases (although this may be changing, as we will soon see). Moreover, unlike other areas of intellectual property, copyright also offers an alternative, statutory measure of damages. Finally, certain copyright infringers may be subject to criminal penalties.

The remedial structure of copyright law raises a number of interesting policy issues. For example, some have questioned whether injunctive relief in copyright cases best serves the broader purposes of copyright law. Particularly in cases where an author incorporates a preexisting work into his or her own creative work, might damages be preferable? Statutory damages are justified as a way of providing relief in cases where actual damages are difficult to calculate, but what happens when statutory damage awards become too disconnected from any plausible measure of harm? Finally, because copyrighted works contain speech, the availability of injunctive relief may raise First Amendment issues.

An inquiry into copyright remedies can thus shed some interesting light on rather fundamental issues of copyright policy.

SECTION A. INJUNCTIVE RELIEF

The Copyright Act gives courts a wide range of potential injunctive options. Courts can issue both preliminary and permanent injunctions. They can also order impoundment and destruction of infringing goods.

1. PERMANENT INJUNCTIONS

Section 502 of the Copyright Act gives courts the power to issue permanent injunctive relief after a successful judgment in favor of the copyright owner. Such relief commonly takes the form of a court order, directing the defendant to stop the infringing activity. Thus, for example, a losing defendant may be ordered to stop selling infringing copies of recorded music, stop distributing an unauthorized movie based on an underlying book, or stop performing a musical work without permission. Defendants who fail to obey these injunctions may be subject to contempt proceedings.

For many years, courts routinely issued permanent injunctions against losing defendants, without any meaningful inquiry into whether an injunction was an appropriate remedy, or whether simply awarding damages would be sufficient. The Copyright Act, like many other areas of federal law, gives trial courts broad discretion in setting remedies, and federal courts hearing copyright cases used this discretion to grant permanent injunctive relief largely as a matter of course.

In recent years, however, this routine granting of permanent injunctions has come under some scrutiny. In 2006, the U.S. Supreme Court decided *eBay v. MercExchange*, 547 U.S. 388 (2006). In that case, the Supreme Court confronted a similar practice in the field of patent law, under which courts often presumed permanent injunctive relief was appropriate. The Court overturned that practice in the context of permanent injunctions in patent cases. Federal courts have since attempted to adapt that ruling to both permanent and preliminary injunctions in copyright cases.

Metro-Goldwyn-Mayer Studios v. Grokster
518 F. Supp.2d 1197 (C. D. Cal. 2007)

STEPHEN V. WILSON, District Judge.

[The facts from this case can be found in the U.S. Supreme Court's opinion in Chapter Seven, *supra*. After the Supreme Court's decision, the case was remanded to the District Court, which found the remaining defendant StreamCast Networks, liable for inducement based on its distribution of the peer-to-peer file sharing software Morpheus. In this opinion, the District Court addresses plaintiffs' motion for a permanent injunction, barring StreamCast from directly or indirectly infringing upon plaintiffs' copyrighted works.]

III. ANALYSIS

A. Legal Standard

Under 17 U.S.C. § 502(a), this Court is empowered to grant a permanent injunction "as it may deem reasonable to prevent or restrain infringement of a copyright." ...

As recently confirmed by the Supreme Court, Plaintiffs must meet their burden with respect to the traditional four-part test. Plaintiffs "must demonstrate: (1) that it has suffered an irreparable injury; (2) that remedies available at law, such as monetary damages, are inadequate to compensate for that injury; (3) that, considering the balance of hardships between the plaintiff and defendant, a remedy in equity is warranted; and (4) that the public interest would not be disserved by a permanent injunction." *eBay Inc. v. MercExchange, L.L.C.*, 547 U.S. 388 (2006). "[T]he decision whether to grant or deny injunctive relief rests within the equitable discretion of the district courts." *Id.* at 1841. Further, the Supreme Court "has consistently rejected invitations to replace traditional equitable considerations with a rule that an injunction automatically follows a determination that a copyright has been infringed." *Id.* at 1840.

B. Application of the Four–Part Test

...

1. Irreparable Harm

The first question to address is whether Plaintiffs "ha[ve] suffered an irreparable injury." *eBay*, 126 S.Ct. at 1839. "The concept of irreparable harm, unfortunately, 'does not readily lend itself to definition.'" *Prairie Band of Potawatomi Indians v. Pierce*, 253 F.3d 1234, 1250 (10th Cir. 2001) (citation omitted). According to the Fifth Circuit, "[b]y definition, 'irreparable injury' is that for which compensatory damages are unsuitable." *Wildmon v. Berwick Universal Pictures*, 983 F.2d 21, 24 (5th Cir. 1992). Or, as alternatively stated by the Seventh Circuit, "[o]nly harm that the district court cannot remedy following a final determination on the merits may constitute irreparable harm." *Am. Hosp. Ass'n v. Harris*, 625 F.2d 1328, 1331 (7th Cir. 1980)....

a. There is no Presumption of Irreparable Harm

The parties dispute whether, in light of *eBay*, irreparable harm can be presumed.

Pre-eBay and Post-eBay Permanent Injunction cases: Other courts have in the past presumed the existence of irreparable injury upon the establishment of liability in copyright cases. *See, e.g., Twentieth Century Fox Film Corp. v. Streeter*, 438 F.Supp.2d 1065, 1072 (D.Ariz. 2006) ("Accordingly, when seeking a permanent injunction in copyright cases, irreparable harm is presumed on a showing of success on the merits."); *Elektra Entertainment Group, Inc. v. Bryant*, 2004 WL 783123, at *6 (C.D.Cal. Feb.13, 2004) ("Copyright infringement is presumed to give rise to irreparable injury. Accordingly, when seeking a permanent injunction in copyright cases, irreparable harm is presumed on a showing of success on the merits.") (internal citation omitted). As pointed out by Plaintiffs, this Court once essentially agreed with this analysis. *See Warner Bros. Entertainment Inc. v. Caridi*, 346 F.Supp.2d 1068, 1073 (C.D. Cal. 2004) (Wilson, J.) (entering a permanent injunction after a default judgment in a copyright action).

Yet, these cases were all decided prior to the Supreme Court's decision in *eBay*. The *eBay* Court held that it is Plaintiffs who "must demonstrate" (meaning, have the burden of proof) that the traditional factors favor a permanent injunction. 126 S.Ct. at 1839. The Supreme Court also highlighted that it has "consistently rejected" the rule that "an injunction automatically follows" an infringement holding. *Id.* at 1840....

This Court agrees with StreamCast ... that the presumption of irreparable harm no longer inures to the benefit of Plaintiffs. The *eBay* Court plainly stated that Plaintiffs "must demonstrate" the presence of the traditional factors, and therefore have the burden of proof with regard to irreparable harm. If this Court adopted a presumption of irreparable harm in favor of Plaintiffs, then StreamCast would effectively have the burden of proving the contrary. Such a rule would contravene the Supreme Court's intent that Plaintiffs establish not merely that infringement causes "harm," but how it amounts to irreparable harm....

b. Irreparable Harm has been Established

Irreparable harm cannot be established solely on the fact of past infringement. Additionally, it must also be true that the mere likelihood of future infringement by a defendant does not by itself allow for an inference of irreparable harm. As to the latter, future copyright infringement can always be redressed via damages, whether actual or statutory. To the extent that future infringement is relevant to the analysis, the onus is on Plaintiffs to explain why future infringements resulting from StreamCast's inducement would cause irreparable harm. It cannot be presumed. ...

"[I]rreparable harm may not be presumed[, but] [i]n run-of-the-mill copyright litigation, such proof should not be difficult to establish...." 6 Patry, supra, § 22:74. Thus, Plaintiffs may establish an irreparable harm stemming from the infringement (e.g., loss of market share, reputational harm). It is also possible that some qualitative feature about the infringement itself, such as its peculiar nature, could elevate its status into the realm of "irreparable harm."

StreamCast accepts that certain harms caused by infringement, such as loss of brand recognition and market share, can amount to irreparable harm. However, StreamCast rejects the argument that copyright infringement can itself ever represent irreparable harm. StreamCast asserts that "[i]f damages can be calculated, the injury is not irreparable ...—the Copyright Act specifically provides for statutory damages, which are calculable assuming Plaintiffs can prove direct infringement of their works, and a basis for the range requested." This Court has doubts regarding StreamCast's position. In *eBay*, Chief Justice Roberts indicated that irreparable harm can result from the infringement itself, depending upon the circumstances of the case:

> From at least the early 19th century, courts have granted injunctive relief upon a finding of infringement in the vast majority of patent cases. This "long tradition of equity practice" is not surprising, given the difficulty of protecting a right to exclude through monetary remedies that allow an infringer to use an invention against the patentee's wishes—a difficulty that often implicates the first two factors of the traditional four-factor test.

126 S.Ct. at 1841 (Roberts, C.J., concurring); see also *MercExchange*, 500 F.Supp.2d at 568 ("[T]he court is not blind to the reality that the nature of the right protected by a patent, the right to exclude, will frequently result in a plaintiff successfully establishing irreparable harm in the wake of establishing validity and infringement."); .... And "[l]ike a patent owner, a copyright holder possesses 'the right to exclude others from using his property.'" *eBay*, 126 S.Ct. at 1840 (citation omitted); see also *Grokster*, 454 F.Supp.2d at 997 ("The right to exclude is inherent in the grant of a copyright."). ...

In light of this authority, the Court concludes that certain qualities pertaining to the nature of StreamCast's inducement of infringement are relevant to a finding of irreparable harm. ...

The irreparable harm analysis centers on two basic themes: (1) StreamCast has and will continue to induce far more infringement than it could ever possibly redress with damages; and (2) Plaintiffs' copyrights (especially those of popular works) have and will be rendered particularly vulnerable to continuing infringement on an enormous scale due to StreamCast's inducement. The Court agrees with both arguments, and each is independently sufficient to support of finding of irreparable harm in this case.

First, the Court must ask whether a particular defendant's probable inability to pay damage constitutes irreparable harm. In the ordinary case, "merely alleging an opponent's inability to pay damages does not constitute irreparable harm." *Rosewood Apartments Corp. v. Perpignano*, 200 F.Supp.2d 269, 278 (S.D.N.Y. 2002). But "[i]n some limited circumstances, parties have demonstrated such a strong likelihood that their opponent will be unable to pay that courts have awarded them equitable relief." *Id.* ... The rationale in such cases must be that an award of monetary damages will be meaningless, and the plaintiff will have no substantive relief, where it will be impossible to collect an award for past and/or future infringements perpetrated by a defendant.

Plaintiffs have not yet sought an award of statutory damages. Additionally, Plaintiffs have not provided this Court with specific evidence as part of this motion demonstrating that StreamCast would be unable to pay damages for the infringements it has induced in the past, and could continue to induce in the future. But such evidence is not necessary here. Based on the undisputed evidence at summary judgment of massive end-user infringement, it is highly likely that the award of statutory damages that ultimately befalls StreamCast in this case will be enormous (especially considering the potential relationship between inducement and a finding of willfulness), and would far outstrip the amount of revenue the company has garnered in recent years. This Court's conclusion would also be the same even if Plaintiffs chose to forgo a damages award as part of this lawsuit. This is because the amount of infringement that StreamCast could induce in the future is so staggering that the recoverable statutory damages would very probably be well beyond StreamCast's anticipated resources. Because it is extremely unlikely that StreamCast will be able to compensate Plaintiffs monetarily for the infringements it has induced in the past, or the infringements it could induce in the future through Morpheus, Plaintiffs have and will continue to suffer irreparable harm.

Second, the Court agrees with Plaintiffs' claim that a substantial number of their copyrighted works have and would continue to become irreparably exposed to infringement on a tremendous scale due to StreamCast's inducement. This inducement greatly erodes Plaintiffs' ability to enforce their exclusive rights. It also promises no realistic mechanism through which statutory damages can be collected for all of the inevitable subsequent infringements occurring outside of the Morpheus System and Software. ...

Importantly, the inducement of infringement via the internet and other digital pathways represents no ordinary infringement. ...

When StreamCast induces infringement, Morpheus end-users obtain "perfect copies" of Plaintiffs' work that can be inexpensively reproduced and distributed *ad nauseam*. In fact, through StreamCast's inducement, an entire universe of copyrighted content has been, and can continue to be, made available for unending infringement outside of the Morpheus System and Software. And given the volume of infringement caused by StreamCast's inducement in this particular case, the assault on Plaintiffs' intellectual property rights through further digital transfers by members of the public—Plaintiffs' customer base—is difficult to overstate. StreamCast's inducement has eviscerated Plaintiffs' ability to protect and enforce their statutorily-created property rights.

StreamCast has submitted to this Court an article in which it is claimed that internet file sharing has had a "statistically indistinguishable" effect on music sales. However, this argument misses the mark because it does not matter whether file sharing affects record company sales or not. It would also make no difference if StreamCast's inducement was demonstrated to increase Plaintiffs' sales. The Court is not concerned with whether end-users are now less likely, or more likely, to buy Plaintiffs's music or movies as a result of their infringement. This is a policy rationale for a legislature to consider, if it should choose to do so.

As copyright owners, Plaintiffs have the exclusive right to decide when and how their material should be reproduced and/or distributed, regardless of whether their decisions make good business sense. When StreamCast induces infringement, Plaintiffs' copyrighted works can be unstoppably and near-instantaneously infringed throughout the computer-literate world with the files obtained by Morpheus endusers. Plaintiffs' power to control their rights has been so compromised by the means through which StreamCast encouraged end-users to infringe (digital files plus the internet) that the inducement amounts to irreparable harm. This is especially true considering the amount of infringement that occurs on the Morpheus System and Software. Morpheus users have the continued ability to pillage a tremendous quantity of Plaintiffs' intellectual property, and to spread this capacity elsewhere with additional file sharing.

The Court is aware that Plaintiffs can seek an award of statutory damages from StreamCast for infringements occurring through the Morpheus System and Software (ignoring for now the likely reality regarding StreamCast's ability to pay). However, Plaintiffs cannot recover damages from StreamCast for the inevitable derivative infringements that will occur outside of Morpheus, with copyrighted content originally acquired within it, as a consequence StreamCast's inducement. Even numerous lawsuits against direct infringers will necessarily prove to be insufficient under these conditions. Indeed, the very need to file multiple lawsuits as a consequence of StreamCast's inducement is itself supportive of an irreparable harm finding. ...

2. Adequate Remedy at Law

The Court must now consider whether there is an adequate remedy at law for the harm that has or could be caused by StreamCast's inducement. ... As should be expected, this Court's adequate remedy at law analysis parallels that performed for irreparable harm.

First, as discussed above, there is a substantial possibility that StreamCast will be unable to pay a statutory damages award for the infringement it has induced (or will continue to induce). "Damages are no remedy at all if they cannot be collected, and most courts sensibly conclude that a damage judgment against an insolvent defendant is an inadequate remedy." Douglas Laycock, *The Death of the Irreparable Injury Rule*, 103 Harv. L.Rev. 687, 716 (1990). For this reason, Plaintiffs lack an adequate remedy at law.

Second, "[a] legal remedy is inadequate if it would require a 'multiplicity of suits.'" *Id.* at 714. In this case, Plaintiffs will only be entitled to a statutory recovery of those infringements induced through the Morpheus System. However, this award will not compensate Plaintiffs when these same files are subsequently shared outside Morpheus. And it would simply be untenable for Plaintiffs to track and proceed against every infringer who continues to illegally reproduce and distribute elsewhere the files originally obtained through StreamCast's inducement. The only realistic method for remedying such future harm resulting from StreamCast's inducement is by way of a permanent injunction.

Therefore, the second equitable factor weighs in Plaintiffs' favor.

3. Balance of Hardships

As to the third factor, the Court must consider the hardships that might afflict the parties by the grant or denial of Plaintiffs' motion for a permanent injunction. The Court has already described in detail the substantial costs exacted by StreamCast's inducement, whether in the past or in the future, and need not recapitulate them here in detail....

StreamCast has its own claims of hardship. First, StreamCast complains that it will suffer undue harm because Plaintiffs' proposed injunction would "wipe[ ] out" the non-infringing aspects of the Morpheus System and Software. Essentially, StreamCast is concerned that Plaintiffs' proposed injunction would be technologically impossible to comply with and would result in the shutdown of the company. However, as discussed *infra* Part III.D.5, the injunction imagined by this Court alleviates such concerns.

In relation to this argument, StreamCast cites to Abe*nd v. MCA, Inc.*, 863 F.2d 1465 (9th Cir. 1988), where the Ninth Circuit denied an injunction as to further showings of the Alfred Hitchcock film "Rear Window." The Court held that "[i]t would cause a great injustice for the owners of the film" because the "success of the movie resulted in large part from factors completely unrelated to the underlying story." *Id.* at 1479. No such special circumstances are present in this case. StreamCast's inducement of infringement has no separate legitimate business purpose whatsoever. The injunction will be limited to restraining future infringement resulting from StreamCast's inducement, rendering *Abend* inapplicable.

Second, StreamCast argues that it no longer has the intent to induce infringement through its distribution of Morpheus, and that there is no risk that such intent will return. ... StreamCast's self-serving statements, and its actions taken post-September 27, 2006, do not change this Court's conclusion. ... The Court is inherently suspicious of StreamCast's statements, as it is entirely too easy for an adjudicated infringer to claim a reformation once the specter of a permanent injunction looms near.

The Court is persuaded that StreamCast would likely engage in further inducement of infringement in the absence of a permanent injunction. ... Even if this Court gave some credence to StreamCast's alleged reform, it could immediately return to its prior ways after the motion for a permanent injunction is denied. ... Because StreamCast is likely to induce further infringements without an injunction, the balance of hardships necessarily shifts further in Plaintiffs' favor. The Court therefore holds that the third equitable factor strongly supports a permanent injunction.

4. The Public Interest

The Court finally agrees that the public interest will be served with a permanent injunction, since it will protect Plaintiffs' copyrights against increased infringement. The public interest in receiving copyrighted content for free is outweighed by the need to incentivize the creation of original works. Certainly, the public does not benefit from StreamCast's inducement of infringement.

StreamCast claims the public will be harmed because Plaintiffs' proposed permanent injunction is so broad that: (1) StreamCast will be forced to discontinue the Morpheus System and Software (including all non-infringing aspects); and (2) StreamCast will not be able to update the non-filtering legacy versions of its software, which are still apparently used by a large number of end-users. However, as discussed *infra*, the injunction in this case will not require StreamCast to immediately shut down. StreamCast will be empowered to update legacy versions of its software as far as it is technologically feasible to do so.

Thus, the Court finds that the four-factor test favors the imposition of an injunction to restrain StreamCast's inducement of infringement. In its discretion, the Court deems it appropriate for a permanent injunction to issue.

Notes and Questions

1. What more, beyond establishing past infringement, must a plaintiff prove in order to establish irreparable harm? The district court in *Grokster* suggests that mere past infringement is not enough, but does it give clear guidance about what more need be proven? At one point, the *Grokster* court supported irreparable harm by pointing to the fact that plaintiffs in this case have lost their ability to control their exclusive right to reproduce the work. But isn't this usually the case in a copyright case?

2. The district court in *Grokster* refused to consider evidence presented by the defendants that purported to establish that the plaintiffs had suffered no harm from the infringing activity. Indeed, the court writes that "it does not matter whether file sharing affects record company sales or not." Why, according to the court, does this not matter? Isn't this exactly what courts should be considering when determining whether a plaintiff is entitled to relief? Can you think of any reasons why actual damages might not matter?

3. Many intellectual property rights are enforced through a property rule regime. Under such a regime, courts commonly award injunctive relief to enforce the right. Thus, the intellectual property owner has the absolute right to prevent others from using the intellectual property. This is in contrast to a liability rule regime, such as contract, under which courts award compensatory damages rather than an injunction. Under a liability rule regime, a party may infringe upon the legal right so long as he or she is willing to pay damages.

One justification for intellectual property law's preference for injunctive relief is that it is often quite difficult for courts to assess precisely how much a particular patent or copyright is worth, since valuation depends on many factors and there may be no easy substitutes in the market. An injunction forces parties to bargain and set the price for the work in the market. The preference for injunctive relief can be seen as an institutional allocation of responsibility for valuing the intellectual property right.

Do you think such an approach is warranted in all copyright cases?

4. In his concurrence in *eBay*, Chief Justice Roberts noted that, even though successful patent plaintiffs would not in the future be automatically entitled to permanent injunctive relief, such plaintiffs might in fact often obtain such relief even under the Court's new standard. Copyright cases decided since *eBay* appear to bear this observation out, as many district courts have continued to award permanent injunctive relief upon a finding of irreparable harm. *See, e.g., Warner Bros. Records v. Walker*, 704 F.Supp.2d 460 (W.D. Pa. 2010) (music file sharer); *Warner Bros. Entertainment v. RDR Books*, 575 F.Supp.2d 513 (S.D.N.Y. 2008) (encyclopedia based on Harry Potter fictional universe). *But see Phelps & Associates v. Galloway*, 492 F.3d 532, 543 (4th Cir. 2007) (refusing to issue permanent injunction in case involving an infringing house built from a copyrighted architectural plan).

5. What factors might make an award of permanent injunctive relief less likely? On this note, consider the pre-*eBay* case *Abend v. MCA*, 863 F.2d 1465 (9th Cir. 1988), *aff'd sub nom. Stewart v. Abend*, 495 U.S. 207 (1990), mentioned by the district court in *Grokster*. Even prior to the *eBay* case, courts on rare occasions refused to award permanent injunctive relief.

Abend involved a copyright claim based on the story, "It Had to be Murder," written by Cornell Woolrich. Woolrich assigned the initial copyright term to a movie production studio, which subsequently made and distributed a movie based on the story. The resulting movie, "Rear Window," was directed by Alfred Hitchcock and starred Grace Kelly and Jimmy Stewart. Many years later, Woolrich's estate renewed the copyright in the story and thus effectively ended the assignment of the copyright to the movie studio. Nevertheless, the movie studio continued to distribute the movie. The court in *Abend* held that the movie studio's continued exploitation of the movie infringed upon the estate's copyright in the story. However, the court refused to award a permanent injunction:

> The "Rear Window" film resulted from the collaborative efforts of many talented individuals other than Cornell Woolrich, the author of the underlying story. The success of the movie resulted in large part from factors completely unrelated to the underlying story, "It Had To Be Murder." It would cause a great injustice for the owners of the film if the court enjoined them from further exhibition of the movie. An injunction would also effectively foreclose defendants from enjoying legitimate profits derived from exploitation of the "new matter" comprising the derivative work, which is given express copyright protection by section 7 of the 1909 Act. Since defendants could not possibly separate out the "new matter" from the underlying work, their right to enjoy the renewal copyright in the derivative work would be rendered meaningless by the grant of an injunction. We also note that an injunction could cause public injury by denying the public the opportunity to view a classic film for many years to come...

> The district court is capable of calculating damages caused to the fair market value of plaintiff's story by the re-release of the film. Any impairment of Abend's ability to produce new derivative works based on the story would be reflected in the calculation of the damage to the fair market value of the story. ...

> In addition to actual damages suffered, Abend would be entitled to profits attributable to the infringement. Defendants' fear that Abend could receive 100% of their profits is unfounded. Abend can receive only the profits attributable to the infringement. Should the court find infringement because defendants have failed to establish any affirmative defenses, on remand it must apportion damages.

Do you think the *Abend* case represents a good example of a case where injunctive relief would be inappropriate? What do you think would have happened if the court in *Abend* had awarded injunctive relief? Would the public have been deprived of the opportunity to view the movie, as the Court of Appeals predicted?

6. More generally, should courts in copyright cases, after *eBay*, be more willing to award only damages and refuse to issue permanent injunctions, particularly in cases involving infringing derivative works or cases where a fair use defense just barely fails? Some have argued that awarding compensation to plaintiffs in such cases better balances the policies underlying copyright law, insofar as this compensates the copyright owners while permitting others to build upon the works and receive a reward for their own creativity. Do you agree with this? Can you think of any counterarguments?

––––––––––

Problem

A movie producer makes a movie based very loosely on a popular novel. Although the basic idea of the movie and its overall plot are similar to those of the novel, the dialogue and characters are quite different. The movie is produced and is extremely popular. The copyright owner of the novel sues the movie studio for copyright infringement. At summary judgment, the federal district court holds for the plaintiff, finding: (1) that the defendant took more than merely the idea; and (2) that the defendant's use was not fair use. However, in reaching the conclusion, the court said that this was an extremely close case on both issues.

The district court is now hearing arguments on the remedy. What arguments could the defendant make that the court should only award damages? What arguments could the plaintiff make that the court should also issue an injunction? How do you think a court would decide this issue? What is the correct result, as a matter of copyright policy?

2. PRELIMINARY INJUNCTIONS

As noted above, courts often award permanent injunctions to copyright owners who successfully establish infringement. Even before trial, however, courts can grant preliminary injunctions to prevent defendants from engaging in allegedly infringing activity during litigation. Indeed, many copyright cases are, in practice, resolved by the issuance of a preliminary injunction, for a preliminary injunction often puts the defendant out business for however long it takes to bring the case to trial. This creates tremendous pressure for defendants to settle.

In a typical civil case, a trial court will issue a preliminary injunction if the plaintiffs establish: (1) a likelihood of success on the merits; (2) irreparable harm if an injunction is not issued; (3) the balance of hardships favor the plaintiff; and (4) the public interest would be served by the issuance of an injunction. In the past, courts in copyright cases routinely issued preliminary injunctions in favor of copyright plaintiffs who established a likelihood of success on the merits. This happened because courts presumed that copyright infringement caused irreparable harm.

Just as with permanent injunctions, courts deciding whether to issue preliminary injunctions have had to consider whether such a presumption is warranted after the Supreme Court's decision in *eBay*. Such courts have generally concluded that the result in *eBay* applies equally to both permanent and preliminary injunctions. For example, in *Salinger v. Colting*, 607 F.3d 68 (2d Cir. 2010), the Second Circuit heard an appeal from a district court decision awarding a preliminary injunction to the author J.D. Salinger. The injunction barred the sale and distribution of a book, *60 Years Later: Coming Through the Rye*, based on characters and events from Salinger's famous novel *Catcher in the Rye*. The Second

Circuit held that, after *eBay*, courts could no longer presume irreparable harm upon a showing of likelihood of success on the merits. Rather, the plaintiff bore the burden of affirmatively establishing irreparable harm.

Notes and Questions

1.   How do you think the change in the law will affect the dynamics of copyright litigation in the future? Under what circumstances would a preliminary injunction be more likely? Less likely? How does this change affect the advice you would give to either a plaintiff or defendant in a copyright infringement case?

2.   Preliminary injunctions in copyright cases potentially raise First Amendment concerns, as they can arguably result in a prior restraint. For example, in the *Colting* case, the district court issued an order banning the publication and distribution of a book. Under standard First Amendment jurisprudence, prior restraints are heavily disfavored. *See, e.g., Nebraska Press Ass'n v. Stuart*, 427 U.S. 539, 559 (1976) ("prior restraints on speech and publication are the most serious and the least tolerable infringement on First Amendment rights"). Thus, for example, if the book at issue in *Colting* had involved sensitive government secrets, and the government had sought the same injunctive relief, the order would have been subject to extensive First Amendment analysis. In copyright cases, by contrast, courts have generally been far less concerned about any potential First Amendment concerns.

Is there something about copyright law that lessens the First Amendment concerns about prior restraints on speech? Or should preliminary injunctions in copyright cases be subject to the same kind of First Amendment scrutiny? *See, e.g., Suntrust Bank v. Houghton Mifflin Co.*, 252 F.3d 1165 (11th Cir. 2001) (preliminary injunction banning distribution of books was an unlawful restraint), *vacated by* 252 F.3d 1165 (11th Cir. 2001) (deciding issue on fair use grounds instead).

3.   IMPOUNDMENT AND DESTRUCTION

The Copyright Act authorizes courts to order the impoundment and/or destruction of infringing copies of a copyrighted work. This authority extends to "all plates, molds, matrices, masters, tapes, film negatives, or other articles by means of which such copies ... may be reproduced." 17 U.S.C. § 503(a). Thus, at the end of a successful trial, the plaintiff may seek the destruction of such infringing copies and the means of producing such copies. In practice, courts may, instead of ordering the destruction of such goods, order that they be transferred to the plaintiff in order to avoid needless waste.

SECTION B. DAMAGES

In addition to injunctive relief, § 504 of the Copyright Act authorizes courts to award damages at the conclusion of a successful copyright infringement lawsuit. Plaintiffs may elect to recover either: (1) actual damages and defendant's profits; or (2) statutory damages, in which the court fixes damages within a statutorily-set range, without proof of harm to the plaintiff or profits by the defendant. Plaintiffs can make this choice at any time prior to the final judgment in the case. As noted above, calculating damages can sometimes raise difficult issues.

1. ACTUAL DAMAGES AND PROFITS

Actual damages are measured by the actual harm the copyright owner suffered as a result of the infringing activity. In other words, actual damages are the usual civil measure of compensatory damages. So, for example, if the plaintiff can establish that he or she would have sold additional copies of the copyrighted work in the absence of infringement, then damages would be measured by the profit he or she would have made from those additional sales. Actual damages could also be measured as lost licensing revenue. For example, the owner of a copyrighted literary work that was turned into an unauthorized motion picture could obtain, in damages, the amount he or she would have received from a licensing agreement.

The Copyright Act also allows the copyright owner to receive the defendant's profits from the infringing activity. This removes the incentive to commit infringement. It also advances the equitable concern that a defendant should be required to disgorge its ill-gotten gains.

In some cases, there may be actual damages but no profits. For example, say that a defendant sells infringing copies at a loss (i.e. for less than it cost to make the copies). In this case, there would be no profits, but there might well be damages if the infringing copies substituted for sales that the plaintiff would have made. Conversely, there could be cases where there are defendant's profits, but no damages. For example, say that the defendant sold infringing copies in a region of the U.S. that plaintiff had not yet begun selling in. Technically, there would be no actual damages, since the infringing copies did not displace any of plaintiff's sales. Nevertheless, plaintiff would be entitled to defendant's profits. In still other cases, there may be neither profits nor damages. For example, say that a defendant sells infringing copies at a loss in a region of the U.S. not served by the plaintiff. In this case, the plaintiff could be limited to injunctive relief and statutory damages, as discussed below.

Plaintiffs can obtain *both* actual damages and defendant's profits, so long as there is no double counting. For example, assume that a defendant sells infringing copies and makes profit from those copies. In such a case, any given copy sold might constitute both damages and profits. The sale might have substituted for a sale by plaintiff and, at the same time, resulted in profit to the defendant. In such a case, the plaintiff would be entitled to recover its damages from the sale (i.e. the amount it would have profited from the sale), plus any of defendant's profits above and beyond the amount recovered in damages. However, the plaintiff would not be entitled to recover both its damages and defendant's profits in full, since this would amount to double-counting.

Although the theory behind damages and profits is relatively straightforward, there are often difficult questions in calculating damages and profits. In part, this is due to the difficulty of accurately valuing copyrighted works. How much, precisely, is a given copyrighted work worth? This may depend on complex issues, such as the quality of the work, the demand for the work, and the existence of substitutes. In addition, precisely how do plaintiffs establish a defendant's profits? Who bears the burden of proof, and how much evidence must be offered? Finally, what about cases where the original work is incorporated into a larger derivative work with independent original material?

Frank Music Corp. v. Metro-Goldwyn-Mayer
886 F.2d 1545 (9th Cir. 1989)

FLETCHER, Circuit Judge.

...

I. FACTS

... Plaintiffs are the copyright owners and authors of *Kismet*, a dramatico-musical work. MGM, Inc. under license produced a musical motion picture version of *Kismet*. Beginning April 26, 1974, MGM Grand presented a musical revue entitled *Hallelujah Hollywood* in the hotel's Ziegfeld Theatre. *Hallelujah Hollywood* was largely created by an employee of MGM Grand, Donn Arden, who also staged, produced and directed the show. The show comprised ten acts, four billed as "tributes" to MGM motion pictures. Act IV was entitled "Kismet", and was a tribute to the MGM movie of that name. It was based almost entirely on music from *Kismet*, and used characters and settings from that musical. Act IV "Kismet" was performed approximately 1700 times, until July 16, 1976, when, under pressure resulting from this litigation, MGM Grand substituted a new Act IV.

Plaintiffs filed suit, alleging copyright infringement, unfair competition, and breach of contract. In *Frank Music I*, we affirmed the district court's conclusion that the use of *Kismet* in *Hallelujah Hollywood* was beyond the scope of MGM Grand's ASCAP license and infringed plaintiffs' copyright. In this appeal, the parties focus on the adequacy of damages and attorney's fees.

II. DISCUSSION

A. Apportionment of Profits

   1.   Direct Profits

   ... [T]he district court calculated MGM Grand's net profit from *Halle-lujah Hollywood* at $6,131,606, by deducting from its gross revenues the direct costs MGM Grand proved it had incurred. Neither party challenges this calculation.

   In apportioning the profits between Act IV and the other acts in the show, the district court made the following finding:

>   Act IV of "Hallelujah Hollywood" was one of ten acts, approximately a ten minute segment of a 100 minute revue. On this basis, the Court concludes that ten percent of the profits of "Hallelujah Hollywood" are attributable to Act IV.

   Plaintiffs assert that this finding is in error in several respects. First, they point out that on Saturdays *Hallelujah Hollywood* contained only eight acts, not ten, and that on Saturdays the show ran only 75 minutes, not 100. Second, Act IV was approximately eleven and a half minutes long, not ten. Because the show was performed three times on Saturdays, and twice a night on the other evenings of the week, the district court substantially underestimated the running time of Act IV in relation to the rest of the show.

   If the district court relied exclusively on a quantitative comparison and failed to consider the relative quality or drawing power of the show's various component parts, it erred. However, the district court's apportionment based on comparative durations would be appropriate if the district court implicitly concluded that all the acts of the show were of roughly equal value. While a more precise statement of the district court's reasons would have been desirable, we find support in the record for the conclusion that all the acts in the show were of substantially equal value.

   The district court went on to apportion the parties' relative contributions to Act IV itself:

>   The infringing musical material was only one of several elements contributing to the segment. A portion of the profits attributable to Act IV must be allocated to other elements, including the creative talent of the producer and director, the talents of performers, composers, choreographers, costume designers and others who participated in creating Act IV, and the attraction of the unique Ziegfeld Theatre with its elaborate stage effects.... While no precise mathematical formula can be applied, the Court concludes that ... a fair approximation of the value of the infringing work to Act IV is twenty-five percent.

   The district court was correct in probing into the parties' relative contributions to Act IV. Where a defendant alters infringing material to suit its own unique purposes, those alterations and the creativity behind them should be taken into account in apportioning the profits of the infringing work. However, the district court appears to have ignored its finding in its previous decision that defendants used not only the plaintiffs' music, but also their lyrics, characters, settings, and costume designs, recreating to a substantial extent the look and sound of the licensed movie version of *Kismet*.

While it was not inappropriate to consider the creativity of producers, performers and others involved in staging and adapting excerpts from *Kismet* for use in *Hallelujah Hollywood*, the district court erred in weighing these contributions so heavily. In performing the apportionment, the benefit of the doubt must always be given to the plaintiff, not the defendant. And while the apportionment may take into account the role of uncopyrightable elements of a work in generating that work's profits, the apportionment should not place too high a value on the defendants' staging of the work, at the expense of undervaluing the plaintiffs' more substantive creative contributions. Production contributions involving expensive costumes and lavish sets will largely be taken into account when deducting the defendants' costs. Indeed, defendants concede that had they produced *Kismet in toto*, it would have been proper for the district court to award 100% of their profits, despite their own creative efforts in staging such a production.

The district court found that defendants' staging of the *Kismet* excerpts was highly significant to Act IV's success. While we believe that a defendant's efforts in staging an infringing production will generally not support more than a *de minimis* deduction from the plaintiff's share of the profits, we cannot say the district court's conclusion that the defendants' contributions were substantial in this case is clearly erroneous. We recognize that there will be shows in which the attraction of the costumes, scenery or performers outweighs the attraction of the music or dialogue. On the other hand, a producer's ability to stage a lavish presentation, or a performer's ability to fill a hall from the drawing power of her name alone, is not a license to use freely the copyrighted works of others.

We conclude that apportioning 75% of Act IV to the defendants grossly undervalues the importance of the plaintiffs' contributions. Act IV was essentially *Kismet*, with contributions by the defendants; it was not essentially a new work incidentally plagiarizing elements of *Kismet*. A fairer apportionment, giving due regard to the district court's findings, attributes 75% of Act IV to elements taken from the plaintiffs and 25% to the defendants' contributions.

2.   Indirect Profits

In *Frank Music I*, we held that the plaintiffs were entitled to recover, in addition to direct profits, a proportion of ascertainable indirect profits from defendants' hotel and gaming operations attributable to the promotional value of *Hallelujah Hollywood*. The district court considered the relative contributions of *Hallelujah Hollywood* and other factors contributing to the hotel's profits, including the hotel's guest accommodations, restaurants, cocktail lounges, star entertainment in the "Celebrity" room, the movie theater, Jai Alai, the casino itself, convention and banquet facilities, tennis courts, swimming pools, gym and sauna, and also the role of advertising and general promotional activities in bringing customers to the hotel. The district court concluded that two percent of MGM Grand's indirect profit was attributable to *Hallelujah Hollywood*. In light of the general promotion and the wide variety of attractions available at MGM Grand, this conclusion is not clearly erroneous. ...

III. CONCLUSION

We vacate the damages award. We conclude that the proper apportionment entitles plaintiffs to 9% of the direct profits from Hallelujah Hollywood. We affirm the district court's finding as to the percentage of indirect profits attributable to *Hallelujah Hollywood*. We correct the award however for a mathematical error. Accordingly, plaintiffs are entitled to $551,844.54 as their share of direct profits and $699,963.10 as their share of indirect profits. ...

Notes and Questions

1. The calculation of a defendant's profits contains two variables. First, the court must determine the defendant's gross revenues attributable to the infringement. Second, the court must subtract any expenses the defendant incurred. Section 504(b) of the Copyright Act allows a plaintiff to make her case by setting forth the defendant's gross revenues derived from infringement. The burden then shifts to the defendant to present evidence of any noninfringing explanations for his profits and the costs to be subtracted from the gross revenues.

2. What does it mean for profits to be "attributable to the infringement"? To get you started, consider these possibilities. First, the court could have been deciding that certain profits would not have occurred "but for" the defendant's infringement. Such a determination involves, at least in theory, a factual assessment of what was actually caused by the infringement. Second, the court might have been equitably calculating profits that were actually caused by infringement, but were equally caused by one or more noninfringing factors. These noninfringing factors could have been operative at the time of the infringement (e.g. noninfringing works that were part of *Hallelujah Hollywood*) or operative after the infringement but before revenue was realized (e.g. a customer came to see the show, stayed because he liked the menu at MGM's restaurant, and decided to patronize the casino that night because it was convenient to do so). Are either of these methods, or any other, sufficiently certain to avoid the imposition of speculative damages?

3. As mentioned earlier, sometimes plaintiffs will claim lost licensing revenue as a measure of actual damages. For example, if the plaintiff would have been willing to license the use to the defendant for a certain amount, but the defendant proceeded to use the work without the license, then the lost licensing revenue might serve as a good measure of actual damage. However, courts have generally required the plaintiff to establish a reasonable market value for the license, and have rejected speculative or unreasonable claims of licensing fees ex post.

For example, in *Davis v. The Gap*, 246 F.3d 152 (2d Cir. 2001), the plaintiff Davis brought a successful copyright infringement claim against the clothing retailer The Gap, based on the latter's unauthorized use of one of Davis's copyrighted pieces of sculptural eyewear in a print advertisement. Davis claimed that he was entitled to a licensing fee of $2.5 million. The Second Circuit affirmed the district court's conclusion that the amount of the fee was unreasonable and wildly inflated. Rather, the available evidence supported, at most, a fair market value of closer to $50, in light of the evidence that Davis had in fact licensed a similar use of his work for that amount in the past.

After reaching this conclusion, the Second Circuit had this to say more generally about the availability of potential licensing revenue as a measure of actual damages:

> The question is as follows: Assume that the copyright owner proves that the defendant has infringed his work. He proves also that a license to make such use of the work has a fair market value, but does not show that the infringement caused him lost sales, lost opportunities to license, or diminution in the value of the copyright. The only proven loss lies in the owner's failure to receive payment by the infringer of the fair market value of the use illegally appropriated. Should the owner's claim for "actual damages" under § 504(b) be dismissed? Or should the court award damages corresponding to the fair market value of the use appropriated by the infringer?

> Neither answer is entirely satisfactory. If the court dismisses the claim by reason of the owner's failure to prove that the act of infringement cause economic harm, the infringer will get his illegal taking for free, and the owner will be left uncompensated for the illegal taking of something of value. On the other hand, an award of damages might be seen as a windfall for an owner who received no less than he would have if the infringer had refrained from the illegal taking. In our view, the more reasonable approach is to allow such an award in appropriate circumstances....

> If a copier of protected work, instead of obtaining permission and paying the fee, proceeds without permission and without compensating the owner, it seems entirely reasonable to conclude that the owner has suffered damages to the extent of the

infringer's taking without paying what the owner was legally entitled to exact a fee for. We can see no reason why, as an abstract matter, the statutory term "actual damages" should not cover the owner's failure to obtain the market value of the fee the owner was entitled to charge for such use....

It is important to note that under the terms of § 504(b), unless such a foregone payment can be considered "actual damages," in some circumstances victims of infringement will go uncompensated. If the infringer's venture turned out to be unprofitable, the owner can receive no recovery based on the statutory award of the "infringer's profits." And in some instances, there will be no harm to the market value of the copyrighted work. The owner may be incapable of showing a loss of either sales or licenses to third parties. To rule that the owner's loss of the fair market value of the license fees he might have exacted of the defendant do not constitute "actual damages," would mean that in such circumstances an infringer may steal with impunity. We see no reason why this should be so.

Problem

A songwriter writes a song and distributes, for free, a digital recording of her song on the Internet. It is not terribly successful. After several months, the song is recorded by a major pop star. The song is placed on an album of 10 songs. The album is immensely successful, selling nearly a million copies and netting the record label nearly $5 million in profits. The songwriter is considering a lawsuit against the pop star. You represent the songwriter. She asks you to estimate roughly how much money she can expect from the lawsuit, if she is successful. How would you answer her question?

2. STATUTORY DAMAGES

As an alternative to actual damages and profits, a copyright plaintiff may instead elect to receive statutory damages from infringement. In general, a court may award between $750 and $30,000 in statutory damages for infringement of a given work. If the infringement is willful, then the court can, in its discretion, award up to $150,000. On the other hand, if the infringement is innocent, then the court may reduce the award to as low as $200. In general, courts have broad discretion to set amounts within these ranges.

It is important to note that statutory damages are awarded per copyrighted work infringed, not per act of infringement. So, for example, if a defendant made a single infringing copy or a million infringing copies, there would be only a single statutory damage award for that work. Of course, a court may take into account the extent of the infringement when setting an amount within the applicable range. However, the fact remains that each statutory damage award is issued for a given work. Conversely, imagine that a defendant made one infringing copy each of 200 separate works. That defendant would subject to 200 separate statutory damage awards, one for each work.

The plaintiff may elect the kind of damage reward (i.e. actual damages and profits or statutory damages) at any time prior to the final judgment. And in practice, some plaintiffs may well wait until after trial but before entry of judgment in order to decide which of these avenues to take. Note also that, as indicated in prior chapters, statutory damages are only available for acts of infringement occurring after the work has been registered with the Copyright Office. Thus, for non-registered works, copyright owners are limited to actual damages and profits.

The Copyright Act makes statutory damages available for a number of reasons. To some extent, statutory damages are an attempt to account for the fact that actual damages and profits can sometimes be difficult to prove. The Act thus provides copyright owners with a more easily-calculable damage remedy. In the materials that follow, consider how well statutory damages serve the above purpose.

Columbia Pictures Television v. Krypton Broadcasting
106 F.3d 284 (9th Cir. 1997)

BRUNETTI, Circuit Judge

C. Elvin Feltner is the owner of Krypton International Corporation, which in turn owns three television stations in the southeast. Columbia Pictures Television licensed several television shows to the three stations, including "Who's the Boss?," "Silver Spoons," "Hart to Hart," and "T.J. Hooker." After the stations became delinquent in paying royalties, Columbia attempted to terminate the licensing agreements. The stations continued to broadcast the programs, and Columbia filed suit. During the course of the litigation, Columbia dropped all causes of action except its copyright claims against Feltner. The district court found Feltner vicariously and contributorily liable for copyright infringement on the part of the Krypton defendants, granted summary judgment in favor of Columbia on liability, and, after a bench trial, awarded Columbia $8,800,000 in statutory damages and over $750,000 in attorneys fees and costs. In this appeal, Feltner and Krypton International challenge several of the district court's rulings. ...

IV. COURT TRIAL ON STATUTORY DAMAGES

Section 504(c)(1) of the Act allows a copyright holder to elect statutory damages in lieu of actual damages. If statutory damages have been elected, and a defendant is found to have infringed, damages are to be awarded "in a sum of not less than $500 or more than $20,000 as the court considers just."[80] 17 U.S.C. § 504(c)(1). Additionally, if the "court finds ... that infringement was committed willfully, the court in its discretion may increase the award of statutory damages to a sum of not more than $100,000,"[81] and if the court finds that the infringement was committed innocently " the court [in] its discretion may reduce the award of statutory damages to a sum of not less than $200." *Id.* § 504(c)(2). Columbia elected statutory damages. Over Feltner's objection, the district court held a bench trial on damages, found Feltner's infringement to be willful, and fixed the statutory damages at $20,000 per violation. ...

VII. CALCULATION OF THE NUMBER OF INFRINGEMENTS

...

B. Each Episode Was a Separate Work.

... § 504(c)(1) of the Act provides that statutory damages may be awarded "for all infringements involved in the action, with respect to any one work." Section 504(c)(1) further provides that "for purposes of this subsection, all the parts of a compilation or derivative work constitute one work." The district court found that each infringed episode of the television series constituted a separate work for purposes of § 504(c)(1). Feltner argues that each series, and not each episode, constitutes a work.

The two courts to have addressed whether each episode of a television series constitutes a separate work have both held in the affirmative. *Gamma Audio & Video, Inc. v. Ean-Chea*, 11 F.3d 1106, 1116-17 (1st Cir. 1993); *Twin Peaks Prods., Inc. v. Publications Int'l, Ltd.*, 996 F.2d 1366, 1380-81 (2d Cir. 1993). Feltner attempts to distinguish these cases by arguing that the episodes at issue are not separate works because they do not have independent economic value.

While Feltner correctly states the proper test to apply in analyzing whether each episode is a separate work, *see Gamma Audio*, 11 F.3d at 1117 (focusing on whether each television episode " has an independent economic value and is, in itself, viable"); *Walt Disney Co. v. Powell*, 897 F.2d 565, 569 (D.C. Cir. 1990) (stating that "separate copyrights are not distinct unless they can 'live their own copyright life' ") (*quoting Robert Stigwood Group Ltd. v. O'Reilly*, 530 F.2d 1096, 1105 (2d Cir.), *cert. denied*, 429 U.S. 848 (1976)), the facts upon which Feltner bases his argument—that the episodes are licensed as a series—were addressed and rejected in *Gamma Audio*.

In *Gamma Audio*, the district court found that the episodes were a single work because the copyright holder sold only complete sets of the series to video stores. The First Circuit found this unpersuasive. Instead, the court found significant "the fact that (1) viewers who rent the tapes from their local video stores may rent as few or as many tapes as they

---

[80] Editors' Note—these amounts have since been changed to $750 and $30,000.
[81] Editors' Note—now $150,000.

want, may view one, two, or twenty episodes in a single setting, and may never watch or rent all of the episodes; and (2) each episode in the ... series was separately produced."

In this case, the different episodes were broadcast over the course of weeks, months, and years. From this fact, it was reasonable for the district court to conclude that, as in *Gamma Audio*, viewers may watch as few or as many episodes as they want, and may never watch all of the episodes. Additionally, it was clear from the record that the episodes could be repeated and broadcast in different orders. Nor does Feltner contest that the episodes were separately written, produced, and registered. Thus, this case comes squarely within the holdings of *Gamma Audio* and *Twin Peaks*.

Feltner also contends that each series was an anthology, a type of "compilation" under § 504(c). Feltner argues that the question of whether the episodes amounted to a "collective whole" was a factual one. Thus, argues Feltner, the district court's refusal to allow Feltner to produce evidence on the issue, which would have consisted of a license agreement and expert testimony that "programs of this nature are considered to be anthologies," was error.

Even were Feltner allowed to prove that the programs were considered to be "anthologies," he would still have to show that they consisted of "separate and independent works ... assembled into a collective whole." As mentioned, the evidence was uncontroverted that the episodes were broadcast over the course of weeks, months, or even years, and could be repeated and rearranged at the option of the broadcaster. Because this evidence supports the conclusion that the episodes were not "assembled into a collective whole," it was not error for the district court to reject Feltner's contention that each series was a "compilation" under § 504(c). ...

Notes and Questions

1. In measuring statutory damages, parties often dispute the definition of a "work." As the *Columbia Pictures* case above indicates, the answer is not always entirely clear. The Copyright Act itself establishes that, for derivative works and compilations, all parts of the derivative work or compilation consist of a single work. 17 U.S.C. § 504(c)(1). Thus, for example, courts have held that the copying of several songs from a music CD constitutes infringement of a single work, entitling the plaintiff to a single award of statutory damages. *UMG Recordings, Inc. v. MP3.com,* 92 F. Supp. 2d 349 (S.D.N.Y. 2000).

2. As a general matter, courts have broad discretion to set statutory damages within the range set forth by the statute. In practice, courts in setting the amount will often consider a wide range of factors, including:

the magnitude of the infringement, the harm to the plaintiff, the knowledge of the defendant.

If a court finds that the defendant infringed upon the work willfully, then it may award up to $150,000 in statutory damages. Courts generally look to the defendant's state of mind and will find willfulness if the defendant knew it was infringing, had reason to know that it was infringing, or recklessly disregarded the fact that it was infringing. The most typical case is when a defendant ignores a plaintiff's warning that it is engaging in infringing activity.

If a court finds that the defendant infringed upon the work innocently, then the statutory damage award may be set as low as $250. The defendant bears the burden of proving innocent infringement. Courts will find innocent infringement when the defendant in good faith did not believe that it was infringing upon a copyrighted work.

3.   Are statutory damages always a good proxy for actual damages? Consider the case of Internet file sharing. Imagine a college student who uses a peer-to-peer file sharing software and makes available to other file sharers her extensive collection of copyrighted songs in MP3 format. Imagine that this student has 500 songs on her computer. Finally, imagine that the RIAA files a lawsuit against the student, alleging massive copyright infringement. If the RIAA succeeds in its lawsuit, the student is potentially subject to statutory damages ranging anywhere from a minimum of $375,000 (500 works x $750/work) to a maximum of $15 million (500 works x $30,000/work) in statutory damages.

If statutory damages are too disproportionate to actual harm suffered, would such an award run into problems under the Due Process Clause? In the example above, the student could be potentially liable for up to $15 million, when the cost of actually purchasing those songs was closer to $500. *See Sony BMG Music Entertainment v. Tenenbaum*, 721 F. Supp. 2d 85 (D. Mass. 2010) (reducing statutory damage award against student for file-sharing 30 songs from $675,000 to $67,500, because original award was grossly excessive and therefore violated the Due Process clause); *Capitol Records, Inc. v. Thomas-Rasset*, 680 F. Supp. 2d 1045 (D. Minn. 2010) (in similar file-sharing case involving 24 songs, reducing statutory damage award of $1,920,000 to $54,000).

4.   The availability of statutory damages in copyright cases also has implications for businesses that engage in mass digitization of copyrighted works on the Internet. For example, consider the activities of companies like Google (with respect to its Google Book Search), YouTube, or any other companies that rely upon storage and dissemination of large numbers of digital files. As discussed in prior chapters, these companies rely variously upon fair use and the safe harbors under the DMCA. But if they were to fall outside the scope of fair use or the safe harbors, they would be potentially subject to staggering liability for statutory damages, given the sheer number of copyrighted works at issue. *See, e.g., UMG Recordings v. MP3.com*, 92 F. Supp. 2d 349 (S.D.N.Y.

2000) (awarding more than $100 million in statutory damages against company that permitted users to upload recorded music onto a virtual on-line music locker, from which they could stream music). This dynamic dramatically increases the financial risks faced by companies engaged in such businesses, and places enormous pressure on the doctrines that govern whether liability attaches in these areas.

5.   What purpose do statutory damages serve in copyright infringement lawsuits? How well do they serve this purpose? Can you think of ways that you would amend the Copyright Act's treatment of statutory damages to better serve this role?

SECTION C. COSTS AND ATTORNEYS FEES

The Copyright Act also permits "prevailing parties" to recover costs and attorneys fees. 17 U.S.C. § 505. Can a successful copyright defendant be a "prevailing party?" The answer is clearly yes. The U.S. Supreme Court in *Fogerty v. Fantasy*, 510 U.S. 517, 534 (1994) held that both successful plaintiffs and defendants can be "prevailing parties" within the meaning of the Act. Thus, attorney's fees are not limited to just successful copyright owners, but are equally available to successful defendants.

Whether to award such fees in any given case is left to the discretion of the district court. In exercising this discretion, the court may consider a wide range of factors, including: the good or bad faith of the party; the strength or frivolousness of the claim; whether such an award would further the purposes of the Copyright Act; the identity of the parties and their ability to pay; the need to encourage parties to litigate meritorious claims or defenses.

For example, in *Fantasy v. Fogerty*, 94 F.3d 553 (9th Cir. 1996), the Ninth Circuit Court of Appeals affirmed an award of attorney's fees to John Fogerty, former lead singer and songwriter for the band Creedence Clearwater Revival. The plaintiff Fantasy brought suit against Fogerty, alleging that Fogerty's song "The Old Man Down the Road" infringed upon the copyright in one of Fogerty's own earlier songs "Run Through the Jungle," which Fantasy owned. After Fogerty successfully defended against the suit, the district court awarded him $1,347,519.15 in attorney's fees as the "prevailing party."

The district court based the award on several factors. The court found that the result furthered the broad purposes of the Copyright Act, insofar as it enabled Fogerty and others to compose and distribute new works in the "Swamp Rock" style. The court also found that Fogerty had prevailed on the merits of his defense, and not on a technicality like laches or statute of limitations. The court also noted that Fantasy was not an impecunious party and would not be deterred in the future from bringing meritorious claims.

Notes and Questions

1.   Some observers of copyright have complained that the uncertain nature of copyright liability systematically disfavors individual copyright defendants, as they tend to have fewer resources than copyright owners and therefore cannot afford to litigate even frivolous claims made by copyright owners. How, if at all, does the above structure affect the incentives of potential plaintiffs or defendants? For example, imagine that you represent a client who has received a letter alleging that the client has infringed upon a copyright, but your client strongly believes she has a fair use defense. Is your advice affected at all by the above structure?

SECTION D. CRIMINAL PENALTIES

Individuals who infringe upon copyrighted works are potentially subject to criminal penalties. Criminal copyright actions are brought, not by the copyright owners, but by the federal government, though in practice with the cooperation and assistance of the copyright owners. In recent years, as a result of the increase in copyright infringement in the digital environment, criminal copyright enforcement has received more attention.

The Copyright Act, 17 U.S.C. § 506(a)(1) states:

Any person who willfully infringes a copyright shall be punished ... if the infringement was committed—
(A) for purposes of commercial advantage or private financial gain; [or]
(B) by the reproduction or distribution, including by electronic means, during any 180-day period, of 1 or more copies or phonorecords of 1 or more copyrighted works, which have a total retail value of more than $1,000.

The key element in criminal copyright prosecutions is willfulness. The government must establish beyond a reasonable doubt that the defendant committed the copyright infringement willfully. Because of the difficulty of establishing this element, criminal prosecutions are typically brought, in practice, against the most egregious examples of copyright infringement (e.g. large-scale, commercial pirating of valuable computer software).

Even if the government establishes willfulness, it must also establish either: (1) infringement for purposes of commercial advantage or private financial gain; or (2) distribution within 180 days of works with a total retail value of more than $1,000. The second basis of criminal liability was added in 1997 with passage of the No Electronic Theft Act. Prior to that Act, criminal liability required commercial advantage or private financial gain. In *U.S. v. LaMacchia*, 871 F. Supp. 535 (D. Mass. 1994), the government prosecuted a student who had uploaded large amounts of copyrighted software on the Internet, for free distribution. The case was dismissed when the government was unable to establish any commercial advantage or private financial gain. Congress in 1997 thus amended the criminal provisions of the Copyright Act to close this "loophole".

The penalties for criminal copyright liability are set forth in 18 U.S.C. § 2319, and vary depending on whether the offense is a misdemeanor or a felony. An offense will constitute a felony when, within a 180 day period, the defendant reproduces or distributes at least 10 copies of one or more copyrighted works with a retail value of more than $2,500. If convicted of a felony, the maximum penalty is up to five years of imprisonment and/or a fine of up to $250,000 for individuals who are repeat offenders (up to $500,000 for corporations). 18 U.S.C. § 3571(b).

Notes and Questions

1.   Why does the Copyright Act provide for criminal liability for certain acts of infringement? One possibility is that criminal liability provides an added deterrent against the most egregious and economically harmful forms of copyright infringement. If this is the case, how well do the criminal provisions map against this subset of copyright infringement cases?

Chapter Ten

STATE LAW AND PREEMPTION

Federal copyright law does not operate in a vacuum. Rather, it sits amidst, and coexists with, a patchwork of various state laws that affect the creation and use of copyrighted works. These laws include misappropriation, contract law, the right of publicity, and other statutes and common law doctrines. In some cases, state law appears to grant plaintiffs copyright-like rights that do not exist in the Copyright Act. When this happens, defendants often claim that the state law claims in question cannot be enforced because doing so conflicts with our federal copyright scheme.

The doctrines of preemption presented in this chapter control the viability and scope of state law claims related to copyright. As you will see, preemption claims rarely appear straightforward, and they raise complex questions about copyright policy and the exclusivity of federal intellectual property.

SECTION A. PREEMPTION OVERVIEW

1. BACKGROUND

Prior to the 1976 Act, state copyright law played a significant role in protecting creative works. As we saw in the chapter on formalities, the 1909 Act generally did not protect a work until after publication with notice. This left state copyright as the primary source of protection for unpublished works.

The 1976 Act changed things by protecting works from the moment of fixation. This brought both published and unpublished works under federal protection, and it greatly reduced the significance of state copyright law. Indeed, Congress made this explicit in § 301 of the 1976 Act, which preempted any state laws that purported to confer rights "equivalent to" the rights granted under the 1976 Act.

Despite the express preemption clause of the 1976 Act, a number of tricky questions remain regarding the relationship between the Copyright Act and state law. In particular, various state common law doctrines that are not "equivalent to" copyright can be applied in ways that augment or interfere with federal copyright. For example, state misappropriation laws may, in some cases, prohibit the taking of ideas. To what extent should these state laws be permitted to operate?

In answering this question, it may help to distinguish between two different types of preemption: (1) constitutional or conflict preemption, and (2) statutory preemption. Although not every federal court adopts this distinction expressly, it helps to make sense of some of the complicated case law on preemption.

2. CONSTITUTIONAL PREEMPTION

Constitutional or conflict preemption applies whenever Congress enacts a law. Under the Supremacy Clause of the U.S. Constitution, federal law prevails if a conflict with state law exists. In some cases, the existence of a conflict can be very clear. For example, imagine a state law that gave purchasers of ditigal sound recording files the unlimited right to make and sell copies of the sound recordings to third parties. Such a law would clearly conflict with federal copyright's exclusive right to make and publicly distribute copies, and would therefore be preempted. Cases involving such a direct conflict are rare.

More common are cases where state law does not conflict with an express provision of federal copyright law, but is inconsistent with federal copyright policy. For example, imagine a state law that gave an additional 10 years of protection to works whose federal copyright term had expired. Strictly speaking, there is no express conflict, as federal copyright law does not say that states may not do this. Yet it is clear that such a state law would conflict with Congress's clear intent that works with expired federal copyrights pass into the public domain. This policy would be frustrated if states could extend the copyright term. Accordingly, such a state provision would likely be preempted.

Cases involving potential conflicts between state law and copyright policy can be difficult to resolve. Copyright policy is often nebulous, especially when the Copyright Act and its legislative history are silent about their impact on state law. For example, consider a state law that protects facts and ideas, or one protecting unfixed works. Would these provisions conflict with federal copyright policy?

Not surprisingly, the answer to questions like this often turns on an inference about what Congress intended when it left something outside the scope of copyright law. In some cases, Congress may have wanted the material in the public domain, available to all. In other cases, Congress may have intended to give individual states discretion over how to treat the material. Possibilities like these have made it hard for courts to articulate a consistent approach to these questions of preemption.

3. STATUTORY PREEMPTION

In addition to constitutional or conflict preemption, the Copyright Act contains an express preemption clause, 17 U.S.C. § 301. Statutory preemption can apply even in the absence of any constitutional or conflict preemption. Section 301 represents an effort on the part of Congress to expressly set forth the preemptive scope of the Copyright Act. Unfortunately, despite this laudable goal, much confusion still surrounds the scope of statutory preemption. This is due, in part, to the confusing wording of the statute and the subsequent case law, which has grappled with this wording.

The relevant provision of the Copyright Act (§ 301(a)) states:

(a) [A]ll legal or equitable rights that are equivalent to any of the exclusive rights within the general scope of copyright as specified by section 106 in works of authorship that are fixed in a tangible medium of expression and come within the subject matter of copyright as specified by sections 102 and 103 ... are governed exclusively by this title. [N]o person is entitled to any such right or equivalent right in any such work under the common law or statutes of any State.

In interpreting this language, courts have held that a state law will be preempted if: (1) it involves a fixed work of authorship within the *subject matter* of copyright; and (2) it grants rights that are *equivalent* to rights conferred under copyright.

With respect to the first requirement, the subject matter of copyright is defined by sections 102 and 103 of the Copyright Act. Thus, the subject matter includes original works of authorship that are fixed in a tangible medium of expression. Unfixed works would be outside the subject matter, and are thus still potentially subject to state copyright protection.[82] It is important to note that a work could be within the subject matter of copyright, but not entitled to protection. So, for example, a novel whose copyright term had expired would be within the subject matter of copyright (since it is original and fixed), though it would not be protected by federal copyright law.

With respect to the second requirement, a state law right is equivalent if it is the same type of right as found in section 106 of the Copyright Act, which sets forth the exclusive rights that a copyright owner is entitled to. It is important to note that the right must be equivalent in

---

[82] *See, e.g.,* Cal Civil Code § 980 (protecting unfixed works).

type, not in scope. For example, a state law conferring an exclusive right to make copies for 3 years would be equivalent (and therefore preempted).

Together, these two elements define the field within which Congress has legislated, to the exclusion of state law. Within that field, Congress has set a particular balance of incentives, author's rights, and access. Under this view, the protection afforded by Congress is neither a ceiling nor a floor, but a particular balance, which states are not free to alter. Thus, it is just as improper for a state to expand protection within this field as it is for it to reduce protection. For works that fall outside the field, however, states are free set whatever balance they wish.

Although these two elements may seem straightforward when explained in the above fashion, they turn out to be rather difficult to apply, as we will see in more detail below.

SECTION B. STATE LAW CAUSES OF ACTION

This section surveys some of the most common state law causes of action that implicate copyrighted works and copyright policy. In this context, observe how courts apply the two different types of preemption analysis mentioned above.

1. MISAPPROPRIATION

One of the most common state law causes of action invoked in copyright-related cases is misappropriation. The tort of misappropriation is often invoked in cases where a plaintiff is not entirely certain that the work is entitled to copyright protection. Misappropriation can thus step in to afford protection from copying. Tricky questions arise, however, in determining whether and to what extent misappropriation survives preemption by the Copyright Act. We begin with the landmark case *International News Service v. Associated Press*, which sets forth the basic misappropriation tort.

International News Service v. Associated Press
248 U.S. 215 (1918)

MR. JUSTICE PITNEY delivered the opinion of the Court.

The parties are competitors in the gathering and distribution of news and its publication for profit in newspapers throughout the United States. The Associated Press, which was complainant in the District Court, is a co-operative organization, ... its members being individuals who are either proprietors or representatives of about 950 daily newspapers published in all parts of the United States. ... Complainant gathers in all parts of the world ... news and intelligence of current and recent events of interest to newspaper readers and distributes it daily to its members for publication in their newspapers. The cost of the service, amounting approximately to $3,500,000 per annum, is assessed upon the members and becomes a part of their costs of operation, to be recouped, presumably with profit, through the publication of their several newspapers. ...

Defendant [International News Service] is a corporation organized under the laws of the state of New Jersey, whose business is the gathering and selling of news to its customers and clients, consisting of newspapers published throughout the United States, under contracts by which they pay certain amounts at stated times for defendant's service. It has widespread news-gathering agencies; the cost of its operations amounts, it is said, to more than $2,000,000 per annum; and it serves about 400 newspapers located in the various cities of the United States and abroad, a few of which are represented, also, in the membership of the Associated Press.

The parties are in the keenest competition between themselves in the distribution of news throughout the United States; and so, as a rule, are the newspapers that they serve, in their several districts. ...

The only matter that has been argued before us is whether defendant may lawfully be restrained from appropriating news taken from bulletins issued by complainant or any of its members, or from newspapers published by them, for the purpose of selling it to defendant's clients. Complainant asserts that defendant's admitted course of conduct in this regard both violates complainant's property right in the news and constitutes unfair competition in business. ... As presented in argument, these questions are: (1) Whether there is any property in news; (2) Whether, if there be property in news collected for the purpose of being published, it survives the instant of its publication in the first newspaper to which it is communicated by the news-gatherer; and (3) whether defendant's admitted course of conduct in appropriating for commercial use matter taken from bulletins or early editions of Associated Press publications constitutes unfair competition in trade. ...

No doubt news articles often possess a literary quality, and are the subject of literary property at the common law; nor do we question that such an article, as a literary production, is the subject of copyright by the terms of the act as it now stands. ...

But the news element—the information respecting current events contained in the literary production—is not the creation of the writer, but is a report of matters that ordinarily are publici juris; it is the history of the day. It is not to be supposed that the framers of the Constitution, when they empowered Congress "to promote the progress of science and useful arts, by securing for limited times to authors and inventors the exclusive right to their respective writings and discoveries," intended to confer upon one who might happen to be the first to report a historic event the exclusive right for any period to spread the knowledge of it.

We need spend no time, however, upon the general question of property in news matter at common law, or the application of the copyright act, since it seems to us the case must turn upon the question of unfair competition in business. ... The peculiar value of news is in the spreading of it while it is fresh; and it is evident that a valuable property interest in the news, as news, cannot be maintained by keeping it secret. ... What we are concerned with is the business of making it known to the world, in which both parties to the present suit are engaged. That business consists in maintaining a prompt, sure, steady, and reliable service designed to place the daily events of the world at the breakfast table of the millions at a price that, while of trifling moment to each reader, is sufficient in the aggregate to afford compensation for the cost of gathering and distributing it, with the added profit so necessary as an incentive to effective action in the commercial world. The service thus performed for newspaper readers is not only innocent but extremely useful in itself, and indubitably constitutes a legitimate business. The parties are competitors in this field; and, on fundamental principles, applicable here as elsewhere, when the rights or privileges of the one are liable to conflict with those of the other, each party is under a duty so to conduct its own business as not unnecessarily or unfairly to injure that of the other.

Obviously, the question of what is unfair competition in business must be determined with particular reference to the character and circumstances of the business. The question here is not so much the rights of either party as against the public but their rights as between themselves. And, although we may and do assume that neither party has any remaining property interest as against the public in uncopyrighted news matter after the moment of its first publication, it by no means follows that there is no remaining property interest in it as between themselves. For, to both of them alike, news matter, however little susceptible of ownership or dominion in the absolute sense, is stock in trade, to be gathered at the cost of enterprise, organization, skill, labor, and money, and to be distributed and sold to those who will pay money for it, as for any other merchandise. Regarding the news, therefore, as but the material out of which both parties are seeking to make profits at the same time and in the same field, we hardly can fail to recognize that for this purpose, and as between them, it must be regarded as quasi property, irrespective of the rights of either as against the public. ...

The peculiar features of the case arise from the fact that, while novelty and freshness form so important an element in the success of the business, the very processes of distribution and publication necessarily occupy a good deal of time. Complainant's service, as well as defendant's, is a daily service to daily newspapers; most of the foreign news reaches this country at the Atlantic seaboard, principally at the city of New York, and because of this, and of time differentials due to the earth's rotation, the distribution of news matter throughout the country is principally from east to west; and, since in speed the telegraph and telephone easily outstrip the rotation of the earth, it is a simple matter for defendant to take complainant's news from bulletins or early editions of complainant's members in the eastern cities and at the mere cost of telegraphic transmission cause it to be published in western papers issued at least as early as those served by complainant. ...

Defendant insists that when, with the sanction and approval of complainant, and as the result of the use of its news for the very purpose for which it is distributed, a portion of complainant's members communicate it to the general public by posting it upon bulletin boards so that all may read, or by issuing it to newspapers and distributing it indiscriminately, complainant no longer has the right to control the use to be made of it; that when it thus reaches the light of day it becomes the common possession of all to whom it is accessible; and that any purchaser of a newspaper has the right to communicate the intelligence which it contains to anybody and for any purpose, even for the purpose of selling it for profit to newspapers published for profit in competition with complainant's members.

The fault in the reasoning lies in applying as a test the right of the complainant as against the public, instead of considering the rights of complainant and defendant, competitors in business, as between themselves. The right of the purchaser of a single newspaper to spread knowledge of its contents gratuitously, for any legitimate purpose not unreasonably interfering with complainant's right to make merchandise of it, may be admitted; but to transmit that news for commercial use, in competition with complainant—which is what defendant has done and seeks to justify—is a very different matter. In doing this defendant, by its very act, admits that it is taking material that has been acquired by complainant as the result of organization and the expenditure of labor, skill, and money, and which is salable by complainant for money, and that defendant in appropriating it and selling it as its own is endeavoring to reap where it has not sown, and by disposing of it to newspapers that are competitors of complainant's members is appropriating to itself the harvest of those who have sown. Stripped of all disguises, the process amounts to an unauthorized interference with the normal operation of complainant's legitimate business precisely at the point where the profit is to be reaped, in order to divert a material portion of the profit from those who have earned it to those who have not; with special advantage to defendant in the competition because of the fact that it is not burdened with any part of the expense of gathering the news. The transaction speaks for itself and a court of equity ought not to hesitate long in characterizing it as unfair competition in business. ...

The contention that the news is abandoned to the public for all purposes when published in the first newspaper is untenable. Abandonment is a question of intent, and the entire organization of the Associated Press negatives such a purpose. The cost of the service would be prohibited if the reward were to be so limited. No single newspaper, no small group of newspapers, could sustain the expenditure. Indeed, it is one of the most obvious results of defendant's theory that, by permitting indiscriminate publication by anybody and everybody for purposes of profit in competition with the news-gatherer, it would render publication profitless, or so little profitable as in effect to cut off the service by rendering the cost prohibitive in comparison with the return. The practical needs and requirements of the business are reflected in complainant's by-laws which have been referred to. Their effect is that publication by each member must be deemed not by any means an abandonment of the news to the world for any and all purposes, but a publication for limited purposes; for the benefit of the readers of the bulletin or the newspaper as such; not for the purpose of making merchandise of it as news, with the result of depriving complainant's other members of their reasonable opportunity to obtain just returns for their expenditures.

It is to be observed that the view we adopt does not result in giving to complainant the right to monopolize either the gathering or the distribution of the news, or, without complying with the copyright act, to prevent the reproduction of its news articles, but only postpones participation by complainant's competitor in the processes of distribution and reproduction of news that it has not gathered, and only to the extent necessary to prevent that competitor from reaping the fruits of complainant's efforts and expenditure, to the partial exclusion of complainant. and in violation of the principle that underlies the maxim "sic utere tuo," etc.[83] ...

[Opinion by Justice Holmes omitted.]

MR. JUSTICE BRANDEIS, dissenting.

... News is a report of recent occurrences. The business of the news agency is to gather systematically knowledge of such occurrences of interest and to distribute reports thereof. The Associated Press contended that knowledge so acquired is property, because it costs money and labor to produce and because it has value for which those who have it not are ready to pay; that it remains property and is entitled to protection as long as it has commercial value as news; and that to protect it effectively, the defendant must be enjoined from making, or causing to be made, any gainful use of it while it retains such value. ... But the fact that a product of the mind has cost its producer money and labor, and has a value for which others are willing to pay, is not sufficient to ensure to it this legal attribute of property. The general rule of law is, that the noblest of human productions—knowledge, truths ascertained, conceptions, and ideas—become, after voluntary communication to others, free as the air to common use. Upon these incorporeal productions the attribute of property is continued after such communication only in certain classes of cases where public policy has seemed to demand it. These exceptions are

---

[83] Editors' note: The phrase "sic utere tuo ut alienum non laedas" is a Latin maxim that means "use your property in a way that doesn't harm others."

confined to productions which, in some degree, involve creation, invention, or discovery. But by no means all such are endowed with this attribute of property. The creations which are recognized as property by the common law are literary, dramatic, musical, and other artistic creations; and these have also protection under the copyright statutes. The inventions and discoveries upon which this attribute of property is conferred only by statute, are the few comprised within the patent law. ...

The knowledge for which protection is sought in the case at bar is not of a kind upon which the law has heretofore conferred the attributes of property; nor is the manner of its acquisition or use nor the purpose to which it is applied, such as has heretofore been recognized as entitling a plaintiff to relief. ...

Plaintiff ... contended that defendant's practice constitutes unfair competition, because there is "appropriation without cost to itself of values created by" the plaintiff; and it is upon this ground that the decision of this court appears to be based. To appropriate and use for profit, knowledge and ideas produced by other men, without making compensation or even acknowledgment, may be inconsistent with a finer sense of propriety; but, with the exceptions indicated above, the law has heretofore sanctioned the practice. Thus it was held that one may ordinarily make and sell anything in any form, may copy with exactness that which another has produced, or may otherwise use his ideas without his consent and without the payment of compensation, and yet not inflict a legal injury; and that ordinarily one is at perfect liberty to find out, if he can by lawful means, trade secrets of another, however valuable, and then use the knowledge so acquired gainfully, although it cost the original owner much in effort and in money to collect or produce.

Such taking and gainful use of a product of another which, for reasons of public policy, the law has refused to endow with the attributes of property, does not become unlawful because the product happens to have been taken from a rival and is used in competition with him. The unfairness in competition which hitherto has been recognized by the law as a basis for relief, lay in the manner or means of conducting the business; and the manner or means held legally unfair, involves either fraud or force or the doing of acts otherwise prohibited by law. ...

He who follows the pioneer into a new market, or who engages in the manufacture of an article newly introduced by another, seeks profits due largely to the labor and expense of the first adventurer; but the law sanctions, indeed encourages, the pursuit. He who makes a city known through his product, must submit to sharing the resultant trade with others who, perhaps for that reason, locate there later.

The means by which the International News Service obtains news gathered by the Associated Press is also clearly unobjectionable. It is taken from papers bought in the open market or from bulletins publicly posted. ... The manner of use is likewise unobjectionable. No reference is made by word or by act to the Associated Press, either in transmitting the news to subscribers or by them in publishing it in their papers. Neither the International News Service nor its subscribers is gaining or seeking to gain in its business a benefit from the reputation of the Associated Press. They are merely using its product without making compensation. That they have a legal right to do, because the product is not property, and they do not stand in any relation to the Associated Press, either of contract or of trust, which otherwise precludes such use. The argument is not advanced by characterizing such taking and use a misappropriation.

It is also suggested that the fact that defendant does not refer to the Associated Press as the source of the news may furnish a basis for the relief. But the defendant and its subscribers, unlike members of the Associated Press, were under no contractual obligation to disclose the source of the news; and there is no rule of law requiring acknowledgment to be made where uncopyrighted matter is reproduced. The International News Service is said to mislead its subscribers into believing that the news transmitted was originally gathered by it and that they in turn mislead their readers. There is, in fact, no representation by either of any kind. Sources of information are sometimes given because required by contract; sometimes because naming the source gives authority to an otherwise incredible statement; and sometimes the source is named because the agency does not wish to take the responsibility itself of giving currency to the news. But no representation can properly be implied from omission to mention the source of information except that the International News Service is transmitting news which it believes to be credible. ...

The great development of agencies now furnishing country-wide distribution of news, the vastness of our territory, and improvements in the means of transmitting intelligence, have made it possible for a news agency or newspapers to obtain, without paying compensation, the fruit of another's efforts and to use news so obtained gainfully in competition with the original collector. The injustice of such action is obvious. But to give relief against it would involve more than the application of existing rules of law to new facts. It would require the making of a new rule in analogy to existing ones. ...

Courts are ill-equipped to make the investigations which should precede a determination of the limitations which should be set upon any property right in news or of the circumstances under which news gathered by a private agency should be deemed affected with a public interest. Courts would be powerless to prescribe the detailed regulations essential to full enjoyment of the rights conferred or to introduce the machinery required for enforcement of such regulations. Considerations such as these should lead us to decline to establish a new rule of law in the effort to redress a newly disclosed wrong, although the propriety of some remedy appears to be clear.

———————

Notes and Questions

1. *INS* does not discuss preemption explicitly, but the issues associated with preemption loom large. The majority seems untroubled by a state common law doctrine that gives the plaintiff rights not granted by the Copyright Act, while Brandeis's dissent limits the plaintiff to rights granted by the Act. Which approach do you prefer, and why?

2. It may be important to recognize that *INS* was decided before two major developments in modern copyright, passage of the 1976 Act and *Feist*. As discussed earlier, § 301 of the 1976 Act explicitly preempted "all legal or equitable rights that are equivalent to any of the exclusive rights within the general scope of copyright as specified by section 106 in works of authorship that are fixed in a tangible medium of expression and come within the subject matter of copyright as specified by sections 102 and 103." *Feist* clearly identified sweat of the brow as an invalid basis for copyright. Does either of these affect the vitality of *INS*?

3. How far does the misappropriation tort described in *INS v. AP* extend? For example, what if, instead of INS itself, a newspaper customer of INS took and used the news collected by AP and republished stories based on the news? Would this constitute actionable misappropriation? What if INS, instead of copying all of the news from AP, copied the news only from a single, but very important, article? What if INS waited one week, and then copied the news?

4. Justice Brandeis argues, among other things, that Congress is institutionally better equipped than the courts to decide whether and to what extent the information at issue in the case should be protected. Do you agree? Are there any benefits to courts being involved in these cases?

National Basketball Association v. Motorola
105 F.3d 841 (2d. Cir. 1997)

WINTER, Circuit Judge:

Motorola, Inc. and Sports Team Analysis and Tracking Systems ("STATS") appeal from a permanent injunction entered by Judge Preska. The injunction concerns a handheld pager sold by Motorola and marketed under the name "SportsTrax," which displays updated information of professional basketball games in progress. The injunction prohibits appellants, absent authorization from the National Basketball Association and NBA Properties, Inc. (collectively the "NBA"), from transmitting scores or other data about NBA games in progress via the pagers, STATS's site on America On-Line's computer dial-up service, or "any equivalent means." ...

I. BACKGROUND

The facts are largely undisputed. Motorola manufactures and markets the SportsTrax paging device while STATS supplies the game information that is transmitted to the pagers. The product became available to the public in January 1996, at a retail price of about $200. SportsTrax's pager has an inch-and-a-half by inch-and-a-half screen. ... SportsTrax displays the following information on NBA games in progress: (i) the teams playing; (ii) score changes; (iii) the team in possession of the ball; (iv) whether the team is in the free-throw bonus; (v) the quarter of the game; and (vi) time remaining in the quarter. The information is updated every two to three minutes, with more frequent updates near the end of the first half and the end of the game. There is a lag of approximately two or three minutes between events in the game itself and when the information appears on the pager screen.

SportsTrax's operation relies on a "data feed" supplied by STATS reporters who watch the games on television or listen to them on the radio. The reporters key into a personal computer changes in the score and other information such as successful and missed shots, fouls, and clock updates. The information is relayed by modem to STATS's host computer, which compiles, analyzes, and formats the data for retransmission. The information is then sent to a common carrier, which then sends it via satellite to various local FM radio networks that in turn emit the signal received by the individual SportsTrax pagers. ...

II. THE STATE LAW MISAPPROPRIATION CLAIM

...

B. Copyrights in Events or Broadcasts of Events

[The court concluded: (1) that the underlying games are not works of authorship subject to copyright protection; and (2) that the broadcasts of the games are subject to copyright protection, but the defendants took only the unprotectible facts from the broadcasts, and therefore did not commit infringement.]

C. The State-Law Misappropriation Claim

The district court's injunction was based on its conclusion that, under New York law, defendants had unlawfully misappropriated the NBA's property rights in its games. The district court reached this conclusion by holding: (i) that the NBA's misappropriation claim relating to the underlying games was not preempted by Section 301 of the Copyright Act; and (ii) that, under New York common law, defendants had engaged in unlawful misappropriation. We disagree.

1. Preemption Under the Copyright Act

a) Summary

When Congress amended the Copyright Act in 1976, it provided for the preemption of state law claims that are interrelated with copyright claims in certain ways. Under 17 U.S.C. § 301, a state law claim is preempted when: (i) the state law claim seeks to vindicate "legal or equitable rights that are equivalent" to one of the bundle of exclusive rights already protected by copyright law under 17 U.S.C. § 106—styled the "general scope requirement"; and (ii) the particular work to which the state law claim is being applied falls within the type of works protected by the Copyright Act under Sections 102 and 103—styled the "subject matter requirement."

The district court concluded that the NBA's misappropriation claim was not preempted because, with respect to the underlying games, as opposed to the broadcasts, the subject matter requirement was not met. The court dubbed as "partial preemption" its separate analysis of misappropriation claims relating to the underlying games and misappropriation claims relating to broadcasts of those games. ...

> b) "Partial Preemption" and the Subject Matter Requirement

The subject matter requirement is met when the work of authorship being copied or misappropriated "fall[s] within the ambit of copyright protection." *Harper & Row, Publishers, Inc. v. Nation Enter.*, 723 F.2d 195, 200 (1983), *rev'd on other grounds*, 471 U.S. 539 (1985). We believe that the subject matter requirement is met in the instant matter. ... Although game broadcasts are copyrightable while the underlying games are not, the Copyright Act should not be read to distinguish between the two when analyzing the preemption of a misappropriation claim based on copying or taking from the copyrightable work. We believe that:

> [O]nce a performance is reduced to tangible form, there is no distinction between the performance and the recording of the performance for the purposes of preemption under § 301(a). Thus, if a baseball game were not broadcast or were telecast without being recorded, the Players' performances similarly would not be fixed in tangible form and their rights of publicity would not be subject to preemption. By virtue of being videotaped, however, the Players' performances are fixed in tangible form, and any rights of publicity in their performances that are equivalent to the rights contained in the copyright of the telecast are preempted.

Baltimore Orioles, Inc. v. Major League Baseball Player's Assn., 805 F.2d 663, 675 (7th Cir. 1986) (citation omitted).

Copyrightable material often contains uncopyrightable elements within it, but Section 301 preemption bars state law misappropriation claims with respect to uncopyrightable as well as copyrightable elements. In *Harper & Row*, for example, we held that state law claims based on the copying of excerpts from President Ford's memoirs were preempted even with respect to information that was purely factual and not copyrightable. We stated:

[T]he [Copyright] Act clearly embraces "works of authorship," including "literary works," as within its subject matter. The fact that portions of the Ford memoirs may consist of uncopyrightable material ... does not take the work as a whole outside the subject matter protected by the Act. Were this not so, states would be free to expand the perimeters of copyright protection to their own liking, on the theory that preemption would be no bar to state protection of material not meeting federal statutory standards.

723 F.2d at 200 (citation omitted). ...

Adoption of a partial preemption doctrine—preemption of claims based on misappropriation of broadcasts but no preemption of claims based on misappropriation of underlying facts—would expand significantly the reach of state law claims and render the preemption intended by Congress unworkable. It is often difficult or impossible to separate the fixed copyrightable work from the underlying uncopyrightable events or facts. Moreover, Congress, in extending copyright protection only to the broadcasts and not to the underlying events, intended that the latter be in the public domain. Partial preemption turns that intent on its head by allowing state law to vest exclusive rights in material that Congress intended to be in the public domain and to make unlawful conduct that Congress intended to allow. ...

c)   The General Scope Requirement

Under the general scope requirement, Section 301 "preempts only those state law rights that 'may be abridged by an act which, in and of itself, would infringe one of the exclusive rights' provided by federal copyright law." *Computer Assoc. Int'l, Inc. v. Altai, Inc.*, 982 F.2d 693, 716 (2d Cir. 1992) (quoting *Harper & Row*, 723 F.2d at 200). However, certain forms of commercial misappropriation otherwise within the general scope requirement will survive preemption if an "extra-element" test is met. ...

We turn, therefore, to the question of the extent to which a "hot-news" misappropriation claim based on INS involves extra elements and is not the equivalent of exclusive rights under a copyright. Courts are generally agreed that some form of such a claim survives preemption. This conclusion is based in part on the legislative history of the 1976 amendments. The House Report stated:

"Misappropriation" is not necessarily synonymous with copyright infringement, and thus a cause of action labeled as "misappropriation" is not preempted if it is in fact based neither on a right within the general scope of copyright as specified by section 106 nor on a right equivalent thereto. For example, state law should have the flexibility to afford a remedy (under traditional principles of equity) against a consistent pattern of unauthorized appropriation by a competitor of the facts (i.e., not the literary expression) constituting "hot" news, whether in the traditional mold of *International News Service v. Associated Press* ... or in the newer form of data updates from scientific, business, or financial data bases.

H.R. No. 94-1476 at 132, *reprinted in* 1976 U.S.C.C.A.N. at 5748 (footnote omitted). ... The crucial question, therefore, is the breadth of the "hot-news" claim that survives preemption.

In *INS*, the plaintiff AP and defendant INS were "wire services" that sold news items to client newspapers. AP brought suit to prevent INS from selling facts and information lifted from AP sources to INS-affiliated newspapers. One method by which INS was able to use AP's news was to lift facts from AP news bulletins. Another method was to sell facts taken from just-published east coast AP newspapers to west coast INS newspapers whose editions had yet to appear. The Supreme Court held ... that INS's use of AP's information was unlawful under federal common law. It characterized INS's conduct as

> amount[ing] to an unauthorized interference with the normal operation of complainant's legitimate business precisely at the point where the profit is to be reaped, in order to divert a material portion of the profit from those who have earned it to those who have not; with special advantage to defendant in the competition because of the fact that it is not burdened with any part of the expense of gathering the news.

INS, 248 U.S. at 240.

The theory of the New York misappropriation cases relied upon by the district court is considerably broader than that of *INS*. For example, the district court quoted at length from *Metropolitan Opera Ass'n v. Wagner-Nichols Recorder Corp.*, 199 Misc. 786, 101 N.Y.S.2d 483 (N.Y. Sup.Ct. 1950). *Metropolitan Opera* described New York misappropriation law as standing for the "broader principle that property rights of commercial value are to be and will be protected from any form of commercial immorality"; that misappropriation law developed "to deal with business malpractices offensive to the ethics of [ ] society"; and that the doctrine is "broad and flexible." 939 F. Supp. at 1098-1110 (quoting *Metropolitan Opera*, 101 N.Y.S.2d at 492, 488-89).

However, we believe that *Metropolitan Opera*'s broad misappropriation doctrine based on amorphous concepts such as "commercial immorality" or society's "ethics" is preempted. Such concepts are virtually synonymous for wrongful copying and are in no meaningful fashion distinguishable from infringement of a copyright. The broad misappropriation doctrine relied upon by the district court is, therefore, the equivalent of exclusive rights in copyright law.

Indeed, we said as much in [*Financial Information, Inc. v. Moody's Investors Service, Inc.*, 808 F.2d 204 (2d Cir. 1986) ("*FII*")]. That decision involved the copying of financial information by a rival financial reporting service and specifically repudiated the broad misappropriation doctrine of *Metropolitan Opera*. We explained:

> We are not persuaded by FII's argument that misappropriation is not "equivalent" to the exclusive rights provided by the Copyright Act. ... Nor do we believe that a possible exception to the general rule of preemption in the misappropriation area-for claims involving "any form of commercial immorality,"... quoting *Metropolitan Opera Ass'n v. Wagner-Nichols Recorder Corp.*, 199 Misc. 786, 101 N.Y.S.2d 483, ... should be applied here. We believe that no such exception exists and reject its use here. Whether or not reproduction of another's work is "immoral" depends on whether such use of the work is wrongful. If, for example, the work is in the public domain, then its use would not be wrongful. Likewise, if, as here, the work is unprotected by federal law because of lack of originality, then its use is neither unfair nor unjustified.

FII, 808 F.2d at 208. In fact, *FII* only begrudgingly concedes that even narrow "hot news" *INS*-type claims survive preemption. ...

Our conclusion, therefore, is that only a narrow "hot-news" misappropriation claim survives preemption for actions concerning material within the realm of copyright. ...[84]

In our view, the elements central to an *INS* claim are: (i) the plaintiff generates or collects information at some cost or expense; (ii) the value of the information is highly time-sensitive; (iii) the defendant's use of the information constitutes free-riding on the plaintiff's costly efforts to generate or collect it; (iv) the defendant's use of the information is in direct competition with a product or service offered by the plaintiff; (v) the ability of other parties to free-ride on the efforts of the plaintiff would so reduce the incentive to produce the product or service that its existence or quality would be substantially threatened.

INS is not about ethics; it is about the protection of property rights in time-sensitive information so that the information will be made avail-

---

[84] [Footnote 7] Quite apart from Copyright Act preemption, *INS* has long been regarded with skepticism by many courts and scholars and often confined strictly to its facts. In particular, Judge Learned Hand was notably hostile to a broad reading of the case. He wrote:

> [W]e think that no more was covered than situations substantially similar to those then at bar. The difficulties of understanding it otherwise are insuperable. We are to suppose that the court meant to create a sort of common-law patent or copyright for reasons of justice. Either would flagrantly conflict with the scheme which Congress has for more than a century devised to cover the subject-matter.

Cheney Bros. v. Doris Silk Corp., 35 F.2d 279, 280 (2d Cir. 1929), *cert. denied*, 281 U.S. 728 (1930). See also Restatement (Third) of Unfair Competition § 38 cmt. c (1995):

> The facts of the INS decision are unusual and may serve, in part, to limit its rationale. ... The limited extent to which the INS rationale has been incorporated into the common law of the states indicate that the decision is properly viewed as a response to unusual circumstances rather than as a statement of generally applicable principles of common law. Many subsequent decisions have expressly limited the *INS* case to its facts.

able to the public by profit seeking entrepreneurs. If services like AP were not assured of property rights in the news they pay to collect, they would cease to collect it. The ability of their competitors to appropriate their product at only nominal cost and thereby to disseminate a competing product at a lower price would destroy the incentive to collect news in the first place. The newspaper-reading public would suffer because no one would have an incentive to collect "hot news."

We therefore find the extra elements—those in addition to the elements of copyright infringement-that allow a "hot-news" claim to survive preemption are: (i) the time-sensitive value of factual information, (ii) the free-riding by a defendant, and (iii) the threat to the very existence of the product or service provided by the plaintiff.

2.   The Legality of SportsTrax

We conclude that Motorola and STATS have not engaged in unlawful misappropriation under the "hot-news" test set out above. To be sure, some of the elements of a "hot-news" *INS* claim are met. The information transmitted to SportsTrax is not precisely contemporaneous, but it is nevertheless time-sensitive. Also, the NBA does provide, or will shortly do so, information like that available through SportsTrax. It now offers a service called "Gamestats" that provides official play-by-play game sheets and half-time and final box scores within each arena. It also provides such information to the media in each arena. In the future, the NBA plans to enhance Gamestats so that it will be networked between the various arenas and will support a pager product analogous to SportsTrax. SportsTrax will of course directly compete with an enhanced Gamestats.

However, there are critical elements missing in the NBA's attempt to assert a "hot-news" *INS*-type claim. As framed by the NBA, their claim compresses and confuses three different informational products. The first product is generating the information by playing the games; the second product is transmitting live, full descriptions of those games; and the third product is collecting and retransmitting strictly factual information about the games. The first and second products are the NBA's primary business: producing basketball games for live attendance and licensing copyrighted broadcasts of those games. The collection and retransmission of strictly factual material about the games is a different product: e.g., box-scores in newspapers, summaries of statistics on television sports news, and real-time facts to be transmitted to pagers. In our view, the NBA has failed to show any competitive effect whatsoever from SportsTrax on the first and second products and a lack of any free-riding by SportsTrax on the third.

With regard to the NBA's primary products—producing basketball games with live attendance and licensing copyrighted broadcasts of those games—there is no evidence that anyone regards SportsTrax or the AOL site as a substitute for attending NBA games or watching them on television. In fact, Motorola markets SportsTrax as being designed "for those times when you cannot be at the arena, watch the game on TV, or listen to the radio ..."

The NBA argues that the pager market is also relevant to a "hot-news" *INS*-type claim and that SportsTrax's future competition with Gamestats satisfies any missing element. We agree that there is a separate market for the real-time transmission of factual information to pagers or similar devices, such as STATS's AOL site. However, we disagree that SportsTrax is in any sense free-riding off Gamestats.

An indispensable element of an *INS* "hot-news" claim is free riding by a defendant on a plaintiff's product, enabling the defendant to produce a directly competitive product for less money because it has lower costs. SportsTrax is not such a product. ... Appellants are in no way free-riding on Gamestats. Motorola and STATS expend their own resources to collect purely factual information generated in NBA games to transmit to SportsTrax pagers. They have their own network and assemble and transmit data themselves. ...

For the foregoing reasons, the NBA has not shown any damage to any of its products based on free-riding by Motorola and STATS, and the NBA's misappropriation claim based on New York law is preempted. ...

Notes and Questions

1. The court above makes the important point that, once a work falls within the subject matter of copyright for purposes of preemption, it satisfies this requirement even as to elements of the work that copyright leaves unprotected. So, taking the example of a literary work, we know from earlier sections that the facts in a literary work are not protected by copyright. However, the work as a whole falls within the subject matter of copyright and this includes the facts contained in the work. The court makes clear above that this is a matter of congressional intent. With respect to works falling within the subject matter, the lack of protection is an intended feature of the copyright act. With respect to these works, congress not only sets the minimum level of protection, but also the maximum.

2. Even if a work falls within the subject matter of copyright, state law can still apply to the work so long as it does not purport to grant rights that are "equivalent to" the rights granted by the Copyright Act. In determining whether a work is equivalent, courts typically examine whether the state law claim contains an "extra element." Thus, for example, state trade secret law is generally not preempted by copyright since a trade secret case requires more than simply unauthorized copying. Note that in examining whether state law requires an "extra element," courts will look qualitatively at the claim, as the court did in the

above case when it rejected the argument that an allegation of unethical behavior was sufficient to constitute an extra element.

3.   The *Motorola* court took great pains to divide the NBA's business into three parts. This ultimately proved important to the outcome of the case, as it prevented a finding of free riding. Do you agree with the court's division? After all, Motorola clearly depended on licensed broadcasts to produce SportsTrax. Wasn't this a form of free riding?

4.   What remains of the misappropriation tort after the above case? For example, reports about stock market trades generally increase in value as the time lag between the actual trade and the reports decreases. Many websites charge subscribers a fee to see stock market quotes in "real time." Could a provider of real time stock quotes successfully sue a subscriber who immediately posted those quotes to another website? If so, how long of a delay would shield the subscriber from such a claim?

5.   Misappropriation-like claims are sometimes brought under the doctrine of implied contract. The classic example is a purloined idea. A party brings an uncopyrightable idea to another party. The course of conduct leads the first party to believe that a contract exists. However, the second party goes ahead and uses the idea without compensation. Some states recognize a cause of action for an implied contract.

Are such claims preempted? In *Wrench LLC v. Taco Bell*, 256 F.3d 446 (6th Cir. 2001), the court held no. In that case, the owners of a copyright in the character Psycho Chihuahua approached Taco Bell with the idea of using a Chihuahua in Taco Bell commercials. Taco Bell later employed a separate advertising agency and used a Chihuahua in its commercials. The plaintiffs sued for breach of implied contract, and the court held that, although the claim fell within the subject matter of copyright, it required additional elements beyond mere copying, and therefore was not preempted.

2. CONTRACT LAW

Increasingly, copyright owners are using contract law to restrict the activities of individuals who purchase copyrighted works. The computer software industry was one of the first industries to use contracts in this fashion. Because of concerns about the applicability of copyright law to computer software, such companies began selling software with so-called "shrinkwrap" licenses attached to them. Such licenses purported to bind purchasers of software once they opened and used the software.

Today, with the advent of the Internet, such contracts are more ubiquitous than ever. In many cases, shrinkwrap agreements have been replaced by so-called "clickwrap" agreements, which require individuals to click their assent to contractual terms before being allowed to access the software. Moreover, such agreements are being applied not only to computer software, but also to other copyrighted works such as recorded music, audio visual works, etc.

Such agreements raise tricky questions about contract enforceability, which some of you may be familiar with from your contract law class. For example, when a consumer purchases a piece of software from a store, who is making the offer? What constitutes acceptance? And is there sufficient consideration? Is the contract a contract of adhesion, and are there terms that are unconscionable?

Although we will discuss enforceability here briefly, of more relevant concern is the impact of these arrangements on copyright policy. To what extent does the ubiquity of such private contracts undermine the careful balance of rights and responsibilities set by copyright law? Should copyright law be concerned with these developments? What about the enforceability of specific terms? For example, if a shrinkwrap contract contains a no-criticism clause, is this enforceable? Specifically, are certain such contracts or contractual terms preempted by copyright law?

ProCD v. Zeidenberg
86 F.3d 1447 (7th Cir. 1996)

EASTERBROOK, Circuit Judge.

Must buyers of computer software obey the terms of shrinkwrap licenses? The district court held not, for two reasons: first, they are not contracts because the licenses are inside the box rather than printed on the outside; second, federal law forbids enforcement even if the licenses are contracts. The parties and numerous amici curiae have briefed many other issues, but these are the only two that matter-and we disagree with the district judge's conclusion on each. Shrinkwrap licenses are enforceable unless their terms are objectionable on grounds applicable to contracts in general (for example, if they violate a rule of positive law, or if they are unconscionable). Because no one argues that the terms of the license at issue here are troublesome, we remand with instructions to enter judgment for the plaintiff.

I

ProCD, the plaintiff, has compiled information from more than 3,000 telephone directories into a computer database. We may assume that this database cannot be copyrighted. ... ProCD sells a version of the database, called SelectPhone, on CD-ROM discs. (CD-ROM means "compact disc-read only memory." The "shrinkwrap license" gets its name from the fact that retail software packages are covered in plastic or cellophane "shrinkwrap," and some vendors, though not ProCD, have written licenses that become effective as soon as the customer tears the wrapping from the package. Vendors prefer "end user license," but we use the more common term.) A proprietary method of compressing the data serves as effective encryption too. Customers decrypt and use the data with the aid of an application program that ProCD has written. This program, which is copyrighted, searches the database in response to users' criteria (such as "find all people named Tatum in Tennessee, plus all firms with 'Door Systems' in the corporate name"). The resulting lists (or, as ProCD prefers, "listings") can be read and manipulated by other software, such as word processing programs.

The database in SelectPhone cost more than $10 million to compile and is expensive to keep current. It is much more valuable to some users than to others. The combination of names, addresses, and SIC codes enables manufacturers to compile lists of potential customers. Manufacturers and retailers pay high prices to specialized information intermediaries for such mailing lists; ProCD offers a potentially cheaper alternative. People with nothing to sell could use the database as a substitute for calling long distance information, or as a way to look up old friends who have moved to unknown towns, or just as an electronic substitute for the local phone book. ProCD decided to engage in price discrimination, selling its database to the general public for personal use at a low price (approximately $150 for the set of five discs) while selling information to the trade for a higher price. It has adopted some intermediate strategies too: access to the SelectPhone database is available via the America Online service for the price America Online charges to its clients (approximately $3 per hour), but this service has been tailored to be useful only to the general public.

If ProCD had to recover all of its costs and make a profit by charging a single price-that is, if it could not charge more to commercial users than to the general public-it would have to raise the price substantially over $150. The ensuing reduction in sales would harm consumers who value the information at, say, $200. They get consumer surplus of $50 under the current arrangement but would cease to buy if the price rose substantially. If because of high elasticity of demand in the consumer segment of the market the only way to make a profit turned out to be a price attractive to commercial users alone, then all consumers would lose out-and so would the commercial clients, who would have to pay more for the listings because ProCD could not obtain any contribution toward costs from the consumer market.

To make price discrimination work, however, the seller must be able to control arbitrage. An air carrier sells tickets for less to vacationers than to business travelers, using advance purchase and Saturday-night-stay requirements to distinguish the categories. A producer of movies segments the market by time, releasing first to theaters, then to pay-per-view services, next to the videotape and laserdisc market, and finally to cable and commercial tv. Vendors of computer software have a harder task. Anyone can walk into a retail store and buy a box. Customers do not wear tags saying "commercial user" or "consumer user." Anyway, even a commercial-user-detector at the door would not work, because a consumer could buy the software and resell to a commercial user. That arbitrage would break down the price discrimination and drive up the minimum price at which ProCD would sell to anyone.

Instead of tinkering with the product and letting users sort themselves-for example, furnishing current data at a high price that would be attractive only to commercial customers, and two-year-old data at a low price-ProCD turned to the institution of contract. Every box containing its consumer product declares that the software comes with restrictions stated in an enclosed license. This license, which is encoded on the CD-ROM disks as well as printed in the manual, and which appears on a user's screen every time the software runs, limits use of the application program and listings to non-commercial purposes.

Matthew Zeidenberg bought a consumer package of SelectPhone in 1994 from a retail outlet in Madison, Wisconsin, but decided to ignore the license. He formed Silken Mountain Web Services, Inc., to resell the information in the SelectPhone database. The corporation makes the database available on the Internet to anyone willing to pay its price-which, needless to say, is less than ProCD charges its commercial customers. Zeidenberg has purchased two additional SelectPhone packages, each with an updated version of the database, and made the latest information available over the World Wide Web, for a price, through his corporation. ProCD filed this suit seeking an injunction against further dissemination that exceeds the rights specified in the licenses (identical in each of the three packages Zeidenberg purchased). The district court held the licenses ineffectual because their terms do not appear on the outside of the packages. The court added that the second and third licenses stand no different from the first, even though they are identical, because they might have been different, and a purchaser does not agree to—and cannot be bound by—terms that were secret at the time of purchase.

II

Following the district court, we treat the licenses as ordinary contracts accompanying the sale of products, and therefore as governed by the common law of contracts and the Uniform Commercial Code. Whether there are legal differences between "contracts" and "licenses" (which may matter under the copyright doctrine of first sale) is a subject for another day. ... Zeidenberg does argue, and the district court held, that placing the package of software on the shelf is an "offer," which the customer "accepts" by paying the asking price and leaving the store with the goods. In Wisconsin, as elsewhere, a contract includes only the terms on which the parties have agreed. One cannot agree to hidden terms, the judge concluded. So far, so good—but one of the terms to which Zeidenberg agreed by purchasing the software is that the transaction was subject to a license. Zeidenberg's position therefore must be that the printed terms on the outside of a box are the parties' contract—except for printed terms that refer to or incorporate other terms. But why would Wisconsin fetter the parties' choice in this way? Vendors can put the entire terms of a contract on the outside of a box only by using microscopic type, removing other information that buyers might find more useful (such as what the software does, and on which computers it works), or both. The "Read Me" file included with most software, describing system requirements and potential incompatibilities, may be equivalent to ten pages of type; warranties and license restrictions take still more space. Notice on the outside, terms on the inside, and a right to return the software for a refund if the terms are unacceptable (a right that the license expressly extends), may be a means of doing business valuable to buyers and sellers alike. Doubtless a state could forbid the use of standard contracts in the software business, but we do not think that Wisconsin has done so.

Transactions in which the exchange of money precedes the communication of detailed terms are common. Consider the purchase of insurance. The buyer goes to an agent, who explains the essentials (amount of coverage, number of years) and remits the premium to the home office, which sends back a policy. On the district judge's understanding, the terms of the policy are irrelevant because the insured paid before receiving them. Yet the device of payment, often with a "binder" (so that the insurance takes effect immediately even though the home office reserves the right to withdraw coverage later), in advance of the policy, serves buyers' interests by accelerating effectiveness and reducing transactions costs. Or consider the purchase of an airline ticket. The traveler calls the carrier or an agent, is quoted a price, reserves a seat, pays, and gets a ticket, in that order. The ticket contains elaborate terms, which the traveler can reject by canceling the reservation. To use the ticket is to accept the terms, even terms that in retrospect are disadvantageous. Just so with a ticket to a concert. The back of the ticket states that the patron promises not to record the concert; to attend is to agree. A theater that detects a violation will confiscate the tape and escort the violator to the exit. One could arrange things so that every concertgoer signs this promise before forking over the money, but that cumbersome way of doing things not only would lengthen queues and raise prices but also would scotch the sale of tickets by phone or electronic data service.

Consumer goods work the same way. Someone who wants to buy a radio set visits a store, pays, and walks out with a box. Inside the box is a leaflet containing some terms, the most important of which usually is the warranty, read for the first time in the comfort of home. By Zeidenberg's lights, the warranty in the box is irrelevant; every consumer gets the standard warranty implied by the UCC in the event the contract is silent; yet so far as we are aware no state disregards warranties furnished with consumer products. Drugs come with a list of ingredients on the outside and an elaborate package insert on the inside. The package insert describes drug interactions, contraindications, and other vital information—but, if Zeidenberg is right, the purchaser need not read the package insert, because it is not part of the contract.

Next consider the software industry itself. Only a minority of sales take place over the counter, where there are boxes to peruse. A customer may place an order by phone in response to a line item in a catalog or a review in a magazine. Much software is ordered over the Internet by purchasers who have never seen a box. Increasingly software arrives by wire. There is no box; there is only a stream of electrons, a collection of information that includes data, an application program, instructions, many limitations ("MegaPixel 3.14159 cannot be used with BytePusher 2.718"), and the terms of sale. The user purchases a serial number, which activates the software's features. On Zeidenberg's arguments, these unboxed sales are unfettered by terms—so the seller has made a broad warranty and must pay consequential damages for any shortfalls in performance, two "promises" that if taken seriously would drive prices through the ceiling or return transactions to the horse-and-buggy age.

According to the district court, the UCC does not countenance the sequence of money now, terms later. ...

What then does the current version of the UCC have to say? We think that the place to start is § 2-204(1): "A contract for sale of goods may be made in any manner sufficient to show agreement, including conduct by both parties which recognizes the existence of such a con-tract." A vendor, as master of the offer, may invite acceptance by con-duct, and may propose limitations on the kind of conduct that constitutes acceptance. A buyer may accept by performing the acts the vendor pro-poses to treat as acceptance. And that is what happened. ProCD pro-posed a contract that a buyer would accept by using the software after having an opportunity to read the license at leisure. This Zeidenberg did. He had no choice, because the software splashed the license on the screen and would not let him proceed without indicating acceptance. So although the district judge was right to say that a contract can be, and often is, formed simply by paying the price and walking out of the store, the UCC permits contracts to be formed in other ways. ProCD proposed such a different way, and without protest Zeidenberg agreed. Ours is not a case in which a consumer opens a package to find an insert saying "you owe us an extra $10,000" and the seller files suit to collect. Any buyer finding such a demand can prevent formation of the contract by return-ing the package, as can any consumer who concludes that the terms of the license make the software worth less than the purchase price. Noth-ing in the UCC requires a seller to maximize the buyer's net gains.

Section 2-606, which defines "acceptance of goods", reinforces this understanding. A buyer accepts goods under § 2-606(1)(b) when, after an opportunity to inspect, he fails to make an effective rejection under § 2-602(1). ProCD extended an opportunity to reject if a buyer should find the license terms unsatisfactory; Zeidenberg inspected the package, tried out the software, learned of the license, and did not reject the goods. We refer to § 2-606 only to show that the opportunity to return goods can be important; acceptance of an offer differs from acceptance of goods after delivery; but the UCC consistently permits the parties to structure their relations so that the buyer has a chance to make a final decision after a detailed review. ...

III

The district court held that, even if Wisconsin treats shrinkwrap licenses as contracts, § 301(a) of the Copyright Act, 17 U.S.C. § 301(a), prevents their enforcement. The relevant part of § 301(a) preempts any "legal or equitable rights [under state law] that are equivalent to any of the exclusive rights within the general scope of copyright as specified by section 106 in works of authorship that are fixed in a tangible medium of expression and come within the subject matter of copyright as specified by sections 102 and 103". ProCD's software and data are "fixed in a tangible medium of expression", and the district judge held that they are "within the subject matter of copyright". The latter conclusion is plainly right for the copyrighted application program, and the judge thought that the data likewise are "within the subject matter of copyright" even if, after *Feist*, they are not sufficiently original to be copyrighted. One function of § 301(a) is to prevent states from giving special protection to works of authorship that Congress has decided should be in the public domain, which it can accomplish only if "subject matter of copyright" includes all works of a type covered by sections 102 and 103, even if federal law does not afford protection to them.

But are rights created by contract "equivalent to any of the exclusive rights within the general scope of copyright"? ... Rights "equivalent to any of the exclusive rights within the general scope of copyright" are rights established *by law*—rights that restrict the options of persons who are strangers to the author. Copyright law forbids duplication, public performance, and so on, unless the person wishing to copy or perform the work gets permission; silence means a ban on copying. A copyright is a right against the world. Contracts, by contrast, generally affect only their parties; strangers may do as they please, so contracts do not create "exclusive rights." Someone who found a copy of SelectPhone on the street would not be affected by the shrinkwrap license—though the federal copyright laws of their own force would limit the finder's ability to copy or transmit the application program.

Think for a moment about trade secrets. One common trade secret is a customer list. After *Feist*, a simple alphabetical list of a firm's customers, with address and telephone numbers, could not be protected by copyright. Yet *Kewanee Oil Co. v. Bicron Corp.*, 416 U.S. 470 (1974), holds that contracts about trade secrets may be enforced—precisely because they do not affect strangers' ability to discover and use the information independently. ... Think, too, about everyday transactions in intellectual property. A customer visits a video store and rents a copy of *Night of the Lepus*. The customer's contract with the store limits use of the tape to home viewing and requires its return in two days. May the customer keep the tape, on the ground that § 301(a) makes the promise unenforceable?

A law student uses the LEXIS database, containing public-domain documents, under a contract limiting the results to educational endeavors; may the student resell his access to this database to a law firm from which LEXIS seeks to collect a much higher hourly rate? Suppose ProCD hires a firm to scour the nation for telephone directories, promising to pay $100 for each that ProCD does not already have. The firm locates 100 new directories, which it sends to ProCD with an invoice for $10,000. ProCD incorporates the directories into its database; does it have to pay the bill? Surely yes. ...

Although Congress possesses power to preempt even the enforcement of contracts about intellectual property, ... courts usually read preemption clauses to leave private contracts unaffected. ... Section 301(a) ... prevents states from substituting their own regulatory systems for those of the national government. Just as § 301(a) does not itself interfere with private transactions in intellectual property, so it does not prevent states from respecting those transactions. ... [W]e think it prudent to refrain from adopting a rule that anything with the label "contract" is necessarily outside the preemption clause: the variations and possibilities are too numerous to foresee. ...

Everyone remains free to copy and disseminate all 3,000 telephone books that have been incorporated into ProCD's database. Anyone can add SIC codes and zip codes. ProCD's rivals have done so. Enforcement of the shrinkwrap license may even make information more readily available, by reducing the price ProCD charges to consumer buyers. To the extent licenses facilitate distribution of object code while concealing the source code (the point of a clause forbidding disassembly), they serve the same procompetitive functions as does the law of trade secrets. Licenses may have other benefits for consumers: many licenses permit users to make extra copies, to use the software on multiple computers, even to incorporate the software into the user's products. But whether a particular license is generous or restrictive, a simple two-party contract is not "equivalent to any of the exclusive rights within the general scope of copyright" and therefore may be enforced.

———————

Notes and Questions

1. Although *ProCD* finds the particular shrinkwrap at issue enforceable, other circuits have been somewhat more reluctant to enforce such agreements. *See, e.g., Step-Saver Data Systems, Inc. v. Wyse Technology,* 939 F.2d 91 (3d Cir. 1991) (software license disclaiming all warranties held unenforceable); *Vault Corp. v. Quaid Software Ltd.,* 847 F.2d 255, 268-70 (5th Cir. 1988) (license held unenforceable because state statute authorizing license preempted by federal law). Thus, despite their ubiquity, the enforceability of shrinkwrap licenses remains unclear.

2. *ProCD* emphasizes the desirability of enforcing licenses in order to support price discrimination. This suggests that price discrimination is consistent with federal copyright policy. Is that so? You may recall

having seen courts consider the relationship between copyright and price discrimination before. In *Kirtsaeng v. John Wiley & Sons* (Chapter Five, *supra*) the plaintiff tried to stop the low cost importation of textbooks because the lower cost of imported textbooks might undercut the higher prices charged by the plaintiff in the United States. In short, to use Judge Easterbrook's language, the *Kirtsaeng* plaintiff was trying "to control arbitrage." In *Sega Enters. v. Accolade* (Chapter Six, *supra*), the plaintiff sued because the defendant's reverse engineering enabled creation of competing games for the Sega console, which in turn disrupted the differential pricing strategy used to engage in price discrimination. In both of those cases, the court ruled against supporting price discrimination. Does this mean that federal copyright policy is, at least some of the time, hostile to price discrimination? If so, was Judge Easterbrook correct to support price discrimination in *ProCD*? Or, were *Kirtsaeng* and *Sega* wrongly decided in light of Judge Easterbrook's explanation of benefits of price discrimination and the DMCA's apparent support of price discrimination?

3. The shrinkwrap agreement in *ProCD* appears to be a contract of adhesion, insofar as there is no opportunity for the purchaser to meaningfully bargain over terms. Adhesion contracts often face challenges in formation and enforceability. With respect to formation, how easy do you think it should be for a purchaser to bind himself by opening a package or clicking "I accept" on the Internet? The *ProCD* court seemed comfortable with this sort of contract formation. Nevertheless, what would happen if a purchaser of software or data on a CD wanted to reject the terms of a shrinkwrap license? *ProCD* suggests that she could return her purchase for a refund, but is that truly possible? What would you expect to happen if you returned an open package to a store? Is it possible to "return" a product downloaded over the Internet?

With respect to enforceability, courts generally enforce adhesion contracts so long as their terms are not unconscionable. What types of shrinkwrap terms might be considered unconscionable, and therefore unenforceable?

4. Even if the contract in *ProCD* is enforceable, there is a separate question about the impact of contracts on copyright policy. The *ProCD* court is undoubtedly correct that negotiated contracts concerning copyrighted materials are generally enforceable, otherwise all copyright licensing would be preempted. This appears to follow quite directly from the court's analysis of § 301.

But what do we make of the fact that the particular contracts at issue in *ProCD* were all non-negotiated? Does this change our analysis? For example, imagine that in the future, every copyrighted work distributed in digital form comes with an enforceable shrinkwrap, under which the copyright owner dictates terms of use that vary from federal copyright legislation and policy. Could one argue that such contracts should be preempted under conflict preemption? Note that *ProCD* considers only statutory preemption. Could one argue that ubiquitous use of shrinkwrap agreements represents an improper variance of the balance struck by Congress, and thus must be preempted? What flaws, if any, do you see in this argument?

Bowers v. Baystate Technologies
320 F.3d 1317 (Fed. Cir. 2003)

RADER, Circuit Judge.

... Harold L. Bowers (Bowers) created a template to improve computer aided design (CAD) software, such as the CADKEY tool of Cadkey, Inc. ...

Since the early 1980s, CAD programs have assisted engineers to draft and design on a computer screen. George W. Ford, III, a development engineer and supervisor of quality control at Heinemann Electric, envisioned a way to improve Mr. Bowers' template and CAD software. Specifically, Mr. Ford designed Geodraft, a DOS-based add-on program to operate with CAD. Geodraft allows an engineer to insert technical tolerances for features of the computer-generated design. ...

In 1989, Mr. Ford offered Mr. Bowers an exclusive license to his Geodraft software. Mr. Bowers accepted that offer and bundled Geodraft and Cadjet together as the Designer's Toolkit. Mr. Bowers sold the Designer's Toolkit with a shrink-wrap license that, *inter alia*, prohibited any reverse engineering.

In 1989, Baystate also developed and marketed other tools for CADKEY. One of those tools, Draft-Pak version 1 and 2, featured a template. ... In 1988 and 1989, Mr. Bowers offered to establish a formal relationship with Baystate, including bundling his template with Draft-Pak. Baystate rejected that offer, however, telling Mr. Bowers that it believed it had "the in-house capability to develop the type of products you have proposed."

In 1990, Mr. Bowers released Designer's Toolkit. By January 1991, Baystate had obtained copies of that product. Three months later, Baystate introduced the substantially revised Draft-Pak version 3, incorporating many of the features of Designer's Toolkit. Although Draft-Pak version 3 operated in the DOS environment, Baystate later upgraded it to operate with Microsoft Windows. ...

On May 16, 1991, Baystate sued Mr. Bowers for declaratory judgment [on a number of patent claims]. Mr. Bowers filed counterclaims for copyright infringement, patent infringement, and breach of contract. ...

Baystate contends that the Copyright Act preempts the prohibition of reverse engineering embodied in Mr. Bowers' shrink-wrap license agreements. ... This court holds that, under First Circuit law, the Copyright Act does not preempt or narrow the scope of Mr. Bowers' contract claim.

Courts respect freedom of contract and do not lightly set aside freely-entered agreements. Nevertheless, at times, federal regulation may preempt private contract. The Copyright Act provides that "all legal or equitable rights that are equivalent to any of the exclusive rights within the general scope of copyright ... are governed exclusively by this title." 17 U.S.C. § 301(a) (2000). The First Circuit does not interpret this language to require preemption as long as "a state cause of action requires an extra element, beyond mere copying, preparation of derivative works, performance, distribution or display." *Data Gen. Corp. v. Grumman Sys. Support Corp.*, 36 F.3d 1147, 1164 (1st Cir. 1994). Nevertheless, "[n]ot every 'extra element' of a state law claim will establish a qualitative variance between the rights protected by federal copyright law and those protected by state law." *Id.* ...

The First Circuit has not addressed expressly whether the Copyright Act preempts a state law contract claim that restrains copying. This court perceives, however, that *Data General*'s rationale would lead to a judgment that the Copyright Act does not preempt the state contract action in this case. Indeed, most courts to examine this issue have found that the Copyright Act does not preempt contractual constraints on copyrighted articles. ...

This court believes that the First Circuit would follow the reasoning of *ProCD* and the majority of other courts to consider this issue. This court, therefore, holds that the Copyright Act does not preempt Mr. Bowers' contract claims.

In making this determination, this court has left untouched the conclusions reached in *Atari Games v. Nintendo* regarding reverse engineering as a statutory fair use exception to copyright infringement. *Atari Games Corp. v. Nintendo of America, Inc.*, 975 F.2d 832 (Fed. Cir. 1992). In *Atari*, this court ... held "reverse engineering object code to discern the unprotectable ideas in a computer program is a fair use." Application of the First Circuit's view distinguishing a state law contract claim having additional elements of proof from a copyright claim does not alter the findings of *Atari*. ...

The First Circuit recognizes contractual waiver of affirmative defenses and statutory rights. ... Thus, case law indicates the First Circuit would find that private parties are free to contractually forego the limited ability to reverse engineer a software product under the exemptions of the Copyright Act. ...

DYK, Circuit Judge, concurring in part and dissenting in part.

I join the majority opinion except insofar as it holds that the contract claim is not preempted by federal law. ...

A state is not free to eliminate the fair use defense. Enforcement of a total ban on reverse engineering would conflict with the Copyright Act itself by protecting otherwise unprotectable material. If state law provided that a copyright holder could bar fair use of the copyrighted material by placing a black dot on each copy of the work offered for sale, there would be no question but that the state law would be preempted. A state law that allowed a copyright holder to simply label its products so as to eliminate a fair use defense would "substantially impede" the public's right to fair use and allow the copyright holder, through state law, to protect material that the Congress has determined must be free to all under the Copyright Act.

I nonetheless agree with the majority opinion that a state can permit parties to contract away a fair use defense or to agree not to engage in uses of copyrighted material that are permitted by the copyright law, if the contract is freely negotiated. A freely negotiated agreement represents the "extra element" that prevents preemption of a state law claim that would otherwise be identical to the infringement claim barred by the fair use defense of reverse engineering.

However, state law giving effect to shrinkwrap licenses is no different in substance from a hypothetical black dot law. Like any other contract of adhesion, the only choice offered to the purchaser is to avoid making the purchase in the first place. State law thus gives the copyright holder the ability to eliminate the fair use defense in each and every instance at its option. In doing so, as the majority concedes, it authorizes "shrinkwrap agreements ... [that] are far broader than the protection afforded by copyright law." ...

There is, moreover, no logical stopping point to the majority's reasoning. The amici rightly question whether under our original opinion the first sale doctrine and a host of other limitations on copyright protection might be eliminated by shrinkwrap licenses in just this fashion. If by printing a few words on the outside of its product a party can eliminate the fair use defense, then it can also, by the same means, restrict a purchaser from asserting the "first sale" defense, embodied in 17 U.S.C. § 109(a), or any other of the protections Congress has afforded the public in the Copyright Act. That means that, under the majority's reasoning, state law could extensively undermine the protections of the Copyright Act. ...

I conclude ... that state law authorizing shrinkwrap licenses that prohibit reverse engineering is preempted; and that the First Circuit would so hold because the extra element here "merely concerns the extent to which authors and their licensees can prohibit unauthorized copying by third parties." I respectfully dissent.

Notes and Questions

1.   Under the majority's view, are there any limits on the ability of copyright owners to use shrinkwrap agreements to contract away baseline entitlements granted by copyright law? For example, imagine that a copyright owner wrapped a law school casebook in shrinkwrap, along with a license that barred the re-sale or lending of the book. Would this be enforceable under the majority's view? What about a clause on a shrinkwrapped book or movie DVD that limited the ability of the purchaser to publish unfavorable reviews?

2.   Do you share the dissent's concern about the power of copyright owners to use shrinkwrap agreements to supplant the careful balance set by copyright law? Imagine that sometime in the near future, all copyrighted works distributed in digital form come with a click-wrap agreement, under which copyright owners drastically limit the extent of fair use. Is this a concern for copyright policy?

3.   RIGHT OF PUBLICITY

Many states recognize a common law or statutory right of publicity, under which individuals have the right to control commercial exploitation of their names, images, and likenesses. So, for example, under California law, individuals have the right to prevent unauthorized uses of their names and images in association with the sale of goods or services.

State law rights of publicity are not generally preempted by copyright law, since they deal with subject matters outside the scope of copyright law and often involve different kinds of rights (e.g. the right to prevent the use of one's image as an endorsement in an advertisement). However, in a number of cases, individuals have sought to assert state publicity rights to control uses of their images appearing in copyrighted works, such as movies or television broadcasts. Accordingly, in these cases, courts have had to determine whether the application of state publicity laws is preempted by federal copyright law.

Laws v. Sony Music Entertainment
448 F.3d 1134 (9th Cir. 2006)

BYBEE, Circuit Judge.

Plaintiff Debra Laws ("Laws") brought suit against defendant Sony Music Entertainment, Inc. ("Sony") for misappropriating her voice and name in the song "All I Have" by Jennifer Lopez and L.L. Cool J. The district court found that Sony had obtained a license to use a sample of Laws's recording of "Very Special" and held that Laws's claims for violation of her common law right to privacy and her statutory right of publicity were preempted by the Copyright Act, We agree with the district court that the Copyright Act preempts Laws's claims, and we affirm.

I. FACTS AND PROCEEDINGS

In 1979, professional vocalist and recording artist Debra Laws and Spirit Productions ("Spirit") entered into a recording agreement with Elektra/Asylum Records ("Elektra") to produce master recordings of Laws's vocal performances for Elektra. The agreement gave Elektra the "sole and exclusive right to copyright such master recordings" and "the exclusive worldwide right in perpetuity ... to lease, license, convey or otherwise use or dispose of such master recordings." Elektra also secured the right "to use and to permit others to use your name, the Artist's name ... likeness, other identification, and biographical material concerning the Artist ... in connection with such master recordings." ... In 1981, Laws recorded the song "Very Special," which was released on Laws's album on the Elektra label. Elektra copyrighted the song that same year.

In November 2002, Elektra's agent, Warner Special Products, Inc., entered into an agreement with Sony Music Entertainment, Inc. ("Sony") to grant Sony a non-exclusive license to use a sample of Debra Laws's recording of "Very Special" in the song "All I Have," performed by recording artists Jennifer Lopez and L.L. Cool J. The agreement required Sony to include a credit stating, "Featuring samples from the Debra Laws recording 'Very Special'" in any reproduction. Warner, Elektra's agent, did not seek permission from Laws or Spirit before it released the disc and video, and neither Laws nor Spirit was compensated.

Sony subsequently released a Jennifer Lopez compact disc and music video incorporating brief samples of "Very Special" into her recording of "All I Have." The sampled portions include a segment approximately ten seconds in length at the beginning of "All I Have," and shorter segments repeated in the background throughout the song. Sony included the required credit in the booklet accompanying the compact disc. The song and Lopez's album, "This is Me ... Then," became a huge commercial success, netting over forty-million dollars. At one time "All I Have" was the number one song in the United States.

In February 2003, Laws brought an action ... alleging multiple claims. The two claims relevant to this appeal were: (1) a common law claim for invasion of privacy for the misappropriation of Laws's name and voice and (2) a claim for misappropriation of Laws's name and voice for a commercial purpose under California Civil Code § 3344 ....

III. ANALYSIS

.... We have adopted a two-part test to determine whether a state law claim is preempted by the Act. We must first determine whether the "subject matter" of the state law claim falls within the subject matter of copyright as described in 17 U.S.C. §§ 102 and 103. Second, assuming that it does, we must determine whether the rights asserted under state law are equivalent to the rights contained in 17 U.S.C. § 106, which articulates the exclusive rights of copyright holders.

Laws alleges two causes of action. First, she asserts a claim for protection of her voice, name and likeness under California's common law right of privacy. To sustain this action, Laws must prove: "(1) the defendant's use of the plaintiff's identity; (2) the appropriation of plaintiff's name or likeness to defendant's advantage, commercially or otherwise; (3) lack of consent; and (4) resulting injury." Second, Laws asserts a statutory misappropriation or "right of publicity" claim under California Civil Code § 3344(a), which provides that:

> Any person who knowingly uses another's name, voice, signature, photograph, or likeness, in any manner, on or in products, merchandise, or goods, or for purposes of advertising or selling, or soliciting purchases of, products, merchandise, goods or services, without such person's prior consent ... shall be liable for any damages sustained by the person or persons injured as a result thereof.

We have observed that "[t]he remedies provided for under California Civil Code § 3344 complement the common law cause of action; they do not replace or codify the common law." Nevertheless, for purposes of our preemption analysis, section 3344 includes the elements of the common law cause of action. For convenience's sake, we will refer to Laws's claims as "right of publicity" claims.

Sony does not argue that common law privacy actions and statutory claims under section 3344 are preempted generally by section 301; rather, it argues that they are preempted as applied to the facts of this case. We thus turn to (1) whether the subject matter of Laws's right of publicity claims comes within the subject matter of copyright, and (2) whether the rights Laws asserts under California law are equivalent to those created under the Copyright Act.

A. The "Subject Matter" of Copyright

We first consider whether the subject matter of Laws's misappropriation claim is within the subject matter of the Copyright Act. We conclude that it is. Sections 102 and 103 of the Act identify the works of authorship that constitute the "subject matter" of copyright. Section 102 of the Act extends copyright protection to "original works of authorship fixed in any tangible medium of expression ... from which they can be ... reproduced, ... either directly or with the aid of a machine or device." That section defines a "work of authorship" to include "sound recordings." "A work is 'fixed' in a tangible medium of expression when its embodiment in a copy or phonorecord, by or under the authority of the author, is sufficiently permanent or stable to permit it to be perceived, reproduced, or otherwise communicated for a period of more than transitory duration." Laws's master recordings held by Elektra are plainly within these definitions.

Laws nevertheless contends that the subject matter of a copyright claim and a right of publicity claim are substantively different. She argues that a copyright claim protects ownership rights to a work of art, while a right of publicity claim concerns the right to protect one's persona and likeness. Sony, by contrast, contends that the subject matter of a right of publicity in one's voice is not different from a copyright claim when the voice is embodied within a copyrighted sound recording. Sony argues that once a voice becomes part of a sound recording in a fixed tangible medium it comes within the subject matter of copyright law.

Our jurisprudence provides strong guidance to the resolution of this question. In *Sinatra v. Goodyear Tire & Rubber Co.*, 435 F.2d 711 (9th Cir. 1970), Nancy Sinatra filed suit against Goodyear Tire on the basis of an advertising campaign that featured "These Boots Are Made for Walkin'," a song that Sinatra made famous. Goodyear Tire had obtained a license from the copyright proprietor for the use of music, lyrics, and arrangement of the composition. Goodyear Tire subsequently used the music and lyrics in its ads, which were sung by unknown vocalists. She alleged the song had taken on a "secondary meaning" that was uniquely injurious to her. We rejected her claim:

> [A]ppellant's complaint is not that her sound is uniquely personal; it is that the sound in connection with the music, lyrics and arrangement, which made her the subject of popular identification, ought to be protected. But as to these latter copyrightable items she had no rights. Presumably, she was required to obtain permission of the copyright owner to sing "Boots", and to make an arrangement of the song to suit her own tastes and talents. Had she desired to exclude all others from use of the song so that her "secondary meaning" with the song could not be imitated she could have purchased those rights from the copyright proprietor. One wonders whether her voice ... would have been identifiable if another song had been presented, and not "her song," which unfortunately for her was owned by others and licensed to the defendants.

Although Sinatra was decided prior to passage of the modern-day preemption provision in section 301, we nonetheless ruled that the Copyright Act impliedly preempted Sinatra's state law claim. We later confirmed this holding in *Midler v. Ford Motor Co.*, 849 F.2d 460, 462 (9th Cir. 1988), when we observed that "[t]o give Sinatra damages for [defendants'] use of the song would clash with federal copyright law."

In *Midler*, recording and performing artist Bette Midler filed suit against an advertising agency and its client when a professional "sound alike" was used to imitate Midler's voice from her hit song "Do You Want to Dance." The agency did not acquire a license to use Midler's recording; instead, it had obtained a license from the song's copyright holder and then attempted to get Midler to do the commercial. When Midler's agent advised the agency that she was not interested, the agency hired someone who had been a backup singer for Midler and could imitate her voice and style. Indeed, the singer was instructed to sound as much like Bette Midler as possible. We held that Midler's common law misappropriation claim was not preempted by copyright law because the "thing" misappropriated, her voice, was not copyrightable in that instance. We explained:

> Midler does not seek damages for [the defendant's] use of "Do You Want To Dance," and thus her claim is not preempted by federal copyright law. Copyright protects "original works of authorship fixed in any tangible medium of expression." A voice is not copyrightable. The sounds are not "fixed." What is put forward as protectible here is more personal than any work of authorship.

What Midler sought was relief from an unauthorized vocal imitation for advertising purposes, and that was not the subject of copyright....

In this case, Laws's voice misappropriation claim is plainly different from the claims in *Midler* ... and falls within the subject matter of copyright. In contrast to *Midler* ..., where the licensing party obtained only a license to the song and then imitated the artist's voice, here Sony obtained a license to use Laws's recording itself. Sony was not imitating "Very Special" as Laws might have sung it. Rather, it used a portion of "Very Special" as sung by Debra Laws.

Laws does not dispute Sony's contention that the recording of "Very Special" was a copyrighted sound recording fixed in a tangible medium of expression. Laws's right of publicity claim is based exclusively on what she claims is an unauthorized duplication of her vocal performance of the song "Very Special." Although California law recognizes an assertable interest in the publicity associated with one's voice, we think it is clear that federal copyright law preempts a claim alleging misappropriation of one's voice when the entirety of the allegedly misappropriated vocal performance is contained within a copyrighted medium. Our conclusion is consistent with our holdings in *Midler* and *Waits*, where we concluded that the voice misappropriation claim was not preempted, because the alleged misappropriation was the imitation of the plaintiffs' voices. Neither of those imitations was contained in a copyrighted vocal performance. Moreover, the fact that the vocal performance was copyrighted demonstrates that what is put forth here as protectible is not "more personal than any work of authorship." *Midler*, 849 F.2d at 462.

Laws points to two cases for support. Both cases, however, involve photographs used in advertising, and are distinguishable from this case. In *Downing*, 265 F.3d 994, we held that a claim based on the right of publicity was not preempted by the Copyright Act. In *Downing*, retailer Abercrombie & Fitch was developing a surfing theme—"Surf Nekkid"— for its subscription catalog. Abercrombie published a photo of the plaintiffs, who were participants in a surf championship in Hawaii in 1965. Abercrombie ran the photo, which it had purchased from the photographer (who held the copyright), and it identified the plaintiffs by name.

Abercrombie went well beyond mere republication of the photograph. Without obtaining plaintiffs' consent to use their names and images, it also offered t-shirts exactly like those worn by the plaintiffs in the photo. We noted that the photograph itself was within the subject matter protected by the Copyright Act. But Abercrombie had not merely published the photograph. Rather, it published the photo in connection with a broad surf-themed advertising campaign, identified the plaintiffs-surfers by name, and offered for sale the same t-shirts worn by the plaintiffs in the photo. By doing so, it had suggested that the surfers had endorsed Abercrombie's t-shirts. Accordingly, we concluded that "it is not the publication of the photograph itself, as a creative work of authorship, that is the basis for [plaintiffs'] claims, but rather, it is the use of the [plaintiffs'] likenesses and their names pictured in the published photograph." *Id.* at 1003. We thus concluded that the claim was not within the subject matter of copyright because "[a] person's name or likeness is not a work of authorship within the meaning of 17 U.S.C. § 102."

Laws also relies on a second case, *Toney v. L'Oreal USA, Inc.*, 406 F.3d 905 (7th Cir. 2005), in which the Seventh Circuit held that a claim under the Illinois Right of Publicity Act was not preempted by the Copyright Act. Toney was a model who had posed for photographs used to promote hair-care products on packaging and in national advertisements. Defendants owned the copyright for the photograph of Toney that was used, and had a right to use it from November 1995 to November 2000; any other use would be negotiated separately. In apparent violation of their understanding, defendants continued to use the photographs in their advertising beyond 2000. Toney alleged that this use violated her right of publicity under Illinois law. The Seventh Circuit concluded that

> Toney's identity is not fixed in a tangible medium of expression. There is no "work of authorship" at issue in Toney's right of publicity claim. A person's likeness—her persona—is not authored and it is not fixed. The fact that an image of the person might be fixed in a copyrightable photograph does not change this.... The fact that the photograph itself could be copyrighted, and that defendants owned the copyright to the photograph that was used, is irrelevant to the [right of publicity] claim.... The defendants did not have her consent to continue to use the photograph....

The fact that the photograph was copyrighted could not negate the fact that Toney had reserved artistic control over her image for any period beyond the contractual time frame. The Seventh Circuit concluded that Toney's claim was not preempted.

In contrast, Jennifer Lopez's song "All I Have" incorporated samples of Deborah Laws's "Very Special" and gave her the attribution negotiated by Elektra and Sony. Sony did not use Laws's image, name, or the voice recording in any promotional materials. Her state tort action challenges control of the artistic work itself and could hardly be more closely related to the subject matter of the Copyright Act.

We find more to the point, and quite persuasive, the California Court of Appeal's decision in *Fleet v. CBS, Inc.*, 58 Cal.Rptr.2d 645 (1996). There, defendant CBS owned the exclusive rights to distribute a motion picture in which plaintiffs performed. A third party who financed the operation of the movie refused to pay plaintiffs their previously agreed-to salaries. Plaintiffs brought suit against CBS alleging, *inter alia*, that by airing the motion picture using their names, pictures, and likenesses without their consent, CBS had violated their statutory right of publicity. The Court of Appeal held that the Copyright Act preempted the action. As the court observed, "it was not merely [plaintiffs'] likenesses which were captured on film—it was their dramatic performances which are ... copyrightable." "[O]nce [plaintiffs'] performances were put on film, they became 'dramatic work[s]' 'fixed in [a] tangible medium of expression....' At that point, the performances came within the scope or subject matter of copyright law protection," and the claims were preempted. In effect, the plaintiffs' right of publicity claim was a question of control over the distribution, display or performance of a movie CBS owned. Since CBS's use of plaintiffs' likenesses did not extend beyond the use of the copyrighted material it held, there was no right of publicity at issue, aside from the actors' performances. Had the court held otherwise, each actor could claim that any showing of the film violated his right to control his image and persona....

In sum, we hold that Laws's cause of action is within the subject matter of copyright.

B. Equivalent Rights

We must next determine whether the rights she asserts under California law are equivalent to the rights protected under the Copyright Act. We conclude that they are. In *Del Madera Props. v. Rhodes & Gardner*, 820 F.2d 973 (9th Cir.1987), *overruled on other grounds*, *Fogerty v. Fantasy, Inc.*, 510 U.S. 517 (1994), we outlined the test for determining whether state rights were "equivalent" to those under the Copyright Act:

> To satisfy the "equivalent rights" part of the preemption test ... the ... alleged misappropriation ... must be equivalent to rights within the general scope of copyright as specified by section 106 of the Copyright Act. Section 106 provides a copyright owner with the exclusive rights of reproduction, preparation of derivative works, distribution, and display. To survive preemption, the state cause of action must protect rights which are qualitatively different from the copyright rights. The state claim must have an extra element which changes the nature of the action.

... Laws contends that her right of publicity claim under California Civil Code § 3344 requires proof of a use for a "commercial purpose," which is not an element of a copyright infringement claim. She concedes that a right which is the "equivalent to copyright" is one that is infringed by the mere act of reproduction; however, she argues that her claim is not based on Sony's mere act of reproduction, but "is for the use of ...

Laws'[s] voice, the combination of her voice with another artist, and the commercial exploitation of her voice and name in a different product without her consent."

Sony argues that Laws's claims are based exclusively on the reproduction of "Very Special" in "All I Have." It asserts that the rights protected under Laws's voice misappropriation claim are not qualitatively different from the rights protected under copyright law because the sole basis for her voice misappropriation claim is the unauthorized reproduction of her copyrighted vocal performance.

The essence of Laws's claim is, simply, that she objects to having a sample of "Very Special" used in the Jennifer Lopez–L.L. Cool J recording. But Laws gave up the right to reproduce her voice—at least insofar as it is incorporated in a recording of "Very Special"—when she contracted with Elektra in 1981 and acknowledged that Elektra held the "sole and exclusive right to copyright such master recordings," including the right "to lease, license, convey or otherwise use or dispose of such master recordings." At that point, Laws could have either retained the copyright, or reserved contractual rights in Elektra's use of the recording. Indeed, Laws claims that the latter is precisely what she did. But if Elektra licensed "Very Special" to Sony in violation of its contract with Laws, her remedy sounds in contract against Elektra, not in tort against Sony.

The mere presence of an additional element ("commercial use") in section 3344 is not enough to qualitatively distinguish Laws's right of publicity claim from a claim in copyright. The extra element must transform the nature of the action. Although the elements of Laws's state law claims may not be identical to the elements in a copyright action, the underlying nature of Laws's state law claims is part and parcel of a copyright claim. Under the Act, a copyright owner has the exclusive right "to reproduce the copyrighted work." Laws's claims are based on the premise that Sony reproduced a sample of "Very Special" for commercial purposes without her permission. But Sony obtained a limited license from the copyright holder to use the copyrighted work for the Lopez album. The additional element of "commercial purpose" does not change the underlying nature of the action.

IV. CONCLUSION

... We sense that, left to creative legal arguments, the developing right of publicity could easily supplant the copyright scheme. This, Congress has expressly precluded in § 301. Were we to conclude that Laws's voice misappropriation claim was not preempted by the Copyright Act, then virtually every use of a copyrighted sound recording would infringe upon the original performer's right of publicity. We foresaw this distinct possibility in *Sinatra*:

An added clash with the copyright laws is the potential restriction which recognition of performers' "secondary meanings" places upon the potential market of the copyright proprietor. If a proposed licensee must pay each artist who has played or sung the composition and who might therefore claim unfair competition-performer's protection, the licensee may well be discouraged to the point of complete loss of interest.

Sinatra, 435 F.2d at 718. It is hard to imagine how a copyright would remain meaningful if its licensees were potentially subject to suit from any performer anytime the copyrighted material was used.

To be clear, we recognize that not every right of publicity claim is preempted by the Copyright Act. Our holding does not extinguish common law or statutory rights of privacy, publicity, and trade secrets, as well as the general law of defamation and fraud (or any other similar causes of action), so long as those causes of action do not concern the subject matter of copyright and contain qualitatively different elements than those contained in a copyright infringement suit. Elektra copyrighted Laws's performance of "Very Special" and licensed its use to Sony. If Laws wished to retain control of her performance, she should (and may) have either retained the copyright or contracted with the copyright holder, Elektra, to give her control over its licensing. In any event, her remedy, if any, lies in an action against Elektra, not Sony.

We therefore agree with the district court's conclusion that Laws's right of publicity claims are preempted by the Copyright Act.

Notes and Questions

1. In *Laws*, the Ninth Circuit makes a number of fine distinctions between cases where the right of publicity is preempted and cases where it is not. In *Laws*, the court addressed the case where the defendant had licensed the actual sound recording with the plaintiff's voice and used it in another work, finding the right of publicity claim preempted. The court contrasted *Midler*, where the defendant had licensed the underlying musical work and then hired someone to mimic the plaintiff's voice. In *Midler*, the same circuit held the publicity claim was not preempted. Does this distinction make sense?

Similarly, the court in *Laws* drew a distinction between the use of a person's voice in a sound recording and the use of a person's image in a copyrighted photograph. In *Downs* and *Toney*, the defendants had licensed the copyright in photographs of the plaintiffs in those cases and used those photographs in advertising. In both of those cases, the courts held that the right of publicity claims were not preempted. What distinguishes those cases from the facts of *Laws*? More generally, can you derive a rule for when right of publicity claims will be preempted in such cases?

2. In *Baltimore Orioles v. Major League Baseball Players Association*, 805 F.2d 663 (7th Cir. 1986), the Major League Baseball Players

Association claimed that the major league baseball clubs violated the publicity rights of the players when it broadcast baseball games on television. The court held that these publicity rights claims were preempted under § 301. The court first concluded that the rights fell within the subject matter of copyright, insofar as the performances were original and fixed in the copyrighted broadcast. The court then concluded that the rights were equivalent to the rights granted to copyright owners, insofar as the players were seeking to control the public performance of the broadcast.

The court in *Baltimore Orioles* took pains to emphasize that it was only preempting the players' publicity rights claims insofar as they sought to enjoin the copyrighted broadcasts. Copyright law would not preempt publicity claims that did not seek to control the use of a copyrighted work. On this score, consider *Wendt v. Host International*, 125 F.3d 806 (9th Cir. 1997), in which one of the actors in the popular sitcom *Cheers* sued the creators of animatronic robots that resembled the actor and that were placed in airport *Cheers*-themed bars. The court in that case held that the claim was not preempted, insofar as it did not seek to control a copyrighted work.

Chapter Eleven

INTERNATIONAL COPYRIGHT LAW

The international aspects of copyright law are becoming increasingly important as international trade in copyrighted works becomes ever more common. A long time ago, when international trade in copyrighted works was more limited, U.S. lawyers did not have to worry as much about the international dimensions of copyright practice. Today, however, that is no longer the case. The copyright industries are responsible for an increasingly significant portion of the U.S. economy and an even greater portion of U.S. exports.

More and more attention is being paid to the enforcement of copyrights outside the U.S. As U.S. companies have become net exporters of copyrighted works to other countries, they have become more concerned about unauthorized copying in these other countries. They have thus sought ways to enforce their copyrights more effectively in other countries, with mixed success. The challenges of enforcement will only increase as communications networks become faster and more efficient.

More attention is also being paid to international copyright treaties. For a long time, the U.S. paid little attention to such treaties and refused to join the major international copyright treaty, the Berne Convention. Today, the U.S. is far more involved in the international copyright treaty-making process. As we have already seen, and will study in more detail, treaty obligations have had an increasing impact on U.S. domestic copyright law and policy.

In this chapter, we begin exploring some of the international dimensions of copyright law. A full exploration of this complex topic would require a separate entire casebook. Accordingly, this chapter does not attempt to be comprehensive. Instead, the goal is to introduce you to the basic structure of international copyright law and some of the main issues that arise in practice.

SECTION A. TREATIES

Copyright law is, at bottom, territorial. Each country can choose to pass its own copyright laws, and the laws, roughly speaking, apply to conduct that occurs within that country's borders. So, for example, if a U.S. author is concerned about unauthorized copying of her book in China and wishes to enforce her copyright in China, that author must look to Chinese copyright law and the Chinese legal system.

International treaties, however, can affect the copyright laws of signatory countries by requiring certain minimum protection levels. In addition, some treaties may provide for remedies outside the scope of a given country's domestic legal system. In this section, we will explore some of the major international copyright treaties and their impact on copyright owners.

1. BERNE CONVENTION

First established in 1886, the Berne Convention is the major international treaty on copyright law. Approximately 140 countries have joined the Berne Convention, including all major western countries, many major Asian countries (including China), and Russia. Today, the Berne Convention is administered by the World Intellectual Property Organization (WIPO), an inter-governmental organization headquartered in Switzerland.

The U.S. did not join Berne until 1988, more than 100 years after Berne was first established.[85] The delay was due, in part, to philosophical differences regarding the basis for copyright protection. As we have seen, U.S. copyright law is based largely (though not exclusively) on an instrumental, incentive-based theory of copyright. Berne, however, adopts a more Continental tradition of copyright based on the recognition of authors' rights (*droit d'auteur*). Berne thus required certain changes to U.S. law (discussed below), which the U.S. was unwilling to accept until relatively recently.

The Berne Convention contains two major principles: (1) national treatment and (2) substantive minima. National treatment means that Berne signatory countries will treat foreign works no worse than domestic works. Thus, for example, the U.S. cannot give preferential copyright treatment to its own domestic authors and copyrighted works. However, Berne does permit countries to treat their own works worse than foreign works, a point that we will return to later.

---

[85] The U.S. signed on to the Universal Copyright Convention (U.C.C.) in 1955. The U.C.C. was designed primarily as a vehicle for inducing the U.S. to enter into a copyright treaty with other countries, and as a bridge to the U.S.'s eventual entry into Berne. The U.C.C.'s provisions are broadly similar to those of Berne, although the substantive minima are in general lower.

With respect to the second of these two principles, Berne signatory countries agree to provide a basic minimum level of copyright protection. Berne defines the substantive minima with respect to the types of works that must be covered (e.g. literary and artistic works, whether published or not, etc.); types of rights that copyright owners must be given (e.g. exclusive rights to reproduce, perform, etc.); the minimum length of protection (currently the life of the author plus 50 years for most works); and a set of minimum privileges that must be afforded to third parties (analogous to fair use, though generally more limited in scope).

Although pre-1988 U.S. Copyright law met many of these substantive minima, it did not meet all of them. In particular, Berne required that works be copyrightable immediately upon fixation, without any further formalities. This directly conflicted with the pre-1988 requirements of notice and registration found in U.S. law. Berne also required that signatory countries afford authors certain non-economic moral rights of attribution and integrity, which pre-1988 U.S. copyright law did not provide. Both of these requirements reflected Berne's conception of copyright as a right inherent in the author, a conception that stood at odds with U.S. copyright law's more instrumental stance.

As already noted in previous chapters, Congress amended the Copyright Act to address the above concerns after the U.S. signed the Berne Convention. In the 1988 Berne Convention Implementation Act, Congress largely eliminated formalities as a prerequisite to copyright. Moreover, although registration is required for domestic works before an infringement lawsuit can be brought, it is not required for works from other Berne signatory countries. Similarly, in 1990, Congress enacted the Visual Artists Rights Act, which gave authors of certain types of works some limited rights of attribution and integrity.[86]

Since the U.S.'s accession to Berne, there have been additional international treaties entered into under Berne's auspices. In 1996, many states (including the U.S.) signed the WIPO Copyright Treaty, which required, among other things, signatory countries to provide copyright protection to computer software and certain data compilations. Also in 1996, many states (including the U.S.) signed the WIPO Performance and Phonograms Treaty, which required, among other things, signatory countries to increase recognition of the rights of performers in sound recordings. These provisions obligated member states to enact legislation supporting attempts to protect copyrighted works through technology and to recognize copyright management information. These provisions led, in the U.S., to the passage of the Digital Millennium Copyright Act of 1998, which was discussed in Chapter Eight, *supra*.

---

[86] The U.S. also amended the Copyright Act to include architectural works in 1990, in order to comply with Berne.

Notes and Questions

1.   The enactment of the DMCA in the fashion described above raised critiques from some commentators. Prior to the WIPO treaties mentioned above, anti-circumvention legislation had been introduced in Congress and defeated. Supporters of the legislation, including members of the Clinton Administration, went to WIPO and succeeded in lobbying for similar protections to be written into the WIPO treaties. Once those treaties were signed, implementing legislation was re-introduced in the U.S. and passed in the form of the DMCA. Some commentators have critiqued this as an "end-run" around the domestic law-making process.

2.   GATT-TRIPS AND NAFTA

Copyright obligations have also, in recent years, found their way into international treaties regarding trade. This should come as little surprise, as international trade in copyrighted works becomes more ubiquitous. Increasingly, the failure to protect intellectual property is being seen as an unfair trade practice, potentially triggering enforcement through international tribunals such as the World Trade Organization (WTO).

In 1992, the U.S. signed the North American Free Trade Agreement (NAFTA) with Canada and Mexico. NAFTA required signatory countries to provide some minimum level of copyright protection for certain types of works like software, and effective enforcement mechanisms such as injunctive relief. Both U.S. and Canadian copyright law already met many of these requirements, so the impact of NAFTA was felt largely in increased copyright protection and enforcement under Mexican copyright law.

In 1994, many countries, including the U.S., signed onto the General Agreement on Tariffs and Trade–Trade Related Aspects of Intellectual Property (GATT-TRIPS). The GATT is a multi-lateral free-trade treaty structure, which involves the efforts of more than 100 countries in reducing barriers to trade. Conducted in "rounds," the Uruguay round of GATT resulted in TRIPS, which dealt with trade in intellectual property. Under TRIPS, intellectual property enforcement (or, more specifically, the lack thereof), is potentially considered a non-tariff barrier to trade. TRIPS thus includes provisions dealing with copyright law.

Some of the copyright provisions in TRIPS merely echo the requirements in Berne and indeed incorporate the requirements of Berne expressly. So, for example, TRIPS includes a similar principle of national treatment. At the same time, TRIPS goes beyond Berne in a number of important ways. In particular, TRIPS requires copyright protection for computer software, which Berne originally did not. Perhaps more importantly, TRIPS comes with a built-in enforcement mechanism that was lacking in Berne. Failure to live up to the TRIPS requirements could trigger an enforcement proceeding before the WTO, resulting in potential sanctions against the violating country.

Although U.S. law was already largely consistent with GATT-TRIPS, Congress amended the Copyright Act in a number of ways to fulfill its obligations. Among other things, the amendments made permanent the ban against rental of computer software. They also added a provision to the Copyright Act that banned bootlegging of music performances (i.e. unauthorized live recordings of performances). The amendments also, perhaps most controversially, restored the copyrights in certain foreign works that had passed into the public domain prior to 1988 as a result of failure to comply with formalities.[87] The last two changes have been subject to constitutional challenges, as discussed in prior chapters.

Notes and Questions

1. Does uniform recognition and enforcement of copyrights provide equal benefits to all countries? Certainly, the U.S., as a net exporter of copyrighted materials, benefits from stronger enforcement in other countries. But what about countries that are net importers of copyrighted materials? How might these treaties affect developing countries? Does Ghana, for example, benefit from strong copyright protection? If you were a trade representative for a developing country, would you support high minimum protection requirements? What kinds of considerations would you look at? On this score, note that for many years after independence, the U.S. routinely failed to recognize foreign copyrights, leading to many complaints that the U.S. was a lawless, pirate nation.

In partial recognition of the potentially differing positions of developing countries, such countries were given a five-year grace period within which to implement the TRIPS requirements. For certain "least developed countries" the grace period was initially ten years (subsequently extended until 2013).

SECTION B. ENFORCEMENT

Although the treaty structure above lays down the basic requirements that signatory countries must meet, it says little about the practicalities of international enforcement of copyrights. True, a U.S. author is, under Berne, entitled to a minimum level of protection of her copyright under Chinese law. However, enforcing that right is quite a different matter, as the software and movie industries have learned.

---

[87] Similar provisions were enacted after NAFTA for Canadian and Mexican motion pictures that had passed into the public domain for failure to comply with formalities.

The actual enforcement of copyrights in foreign jurisdictions under foreign law is beyond the scope of this casebook, as they involve the particulars of the law and legal systems of other countries. However, we consider here a number of issues that come up involving attempts to reach foreign activity through lawsuits brought within the U.S.

1. CROSS-BORDER ENFORCEMENT

Subafilms v. MGM Pathe Communications
24 F.3d 1088 (9th Cir. 1994)

D.W. NELSON, Circuit Judge:

In this case, we consider the "vexing question" of whether a claim for infringement can be brought under the Copyright Act when the assertedly infringing conduct consists solely of the authorization within the territorial boundaries of the United States of acts that occur entirely abroad. We hold that such allegations do not state a claim for relief under the copyright laws of the United States.

Factual and Procedural Background

In 1966, the musical group The Beatles, through Subafilms, Ltd., entered into a joint venture with the Hearst Corporation to produce the animated motion picture entitled "Yellow Submarine" (the "Picture"). Over the next year, Hearst, acting on behalf of the joint venture (the "Producer"), negotiated an agreement with United Artists Corporation ("UA") to distribute and finance the film. Separate distribution and financing agreements were entered into in May, 1967. Pursuant to these agreements, UA distributed the Picture in theaters beginning in 1968 and later on television.

In the early 1980s, with the advent of the home video market, UA entered into several licensing agreements to distribute a number of its films on videocassette. Although one company expressed interest in the Picture, UA refused to license "Yellow Submarine" because of uncertainty over whether home video rights had been granted by the 1967 agreements. Subsequently, in 1987, UA's successor company, MGM/UA Communications Co. ("MGM/UA"), over the Producer's objections, authorized its subsidiary MGM/UA Home Video, Inc. to distribute the Picture for the domestic home video market, and, pursuant to an earlier licensing agreement, notified Warner Bros., Inc. ("Warner") that the Picture had been cleared for international videocassette distribution. Warner, through its wholly owned subsidiary, Warner Home Video, Inc., in turn entered into agreements with third parties for distribution of the Picture on videocassette around the world.

In 1988, Subafilms and Hearst ("Appellees") brought suit against MGM/UA, Warner, and their respective subsidiaries (collectively the "Distributors" or "Appellants"), contending that the videocassette distribution of the Picture, both foreign and domestic, constituted copyright infringement and a breach of the 1967 agreements. The case was tried before a retired California Superior Court Judge acting as a special master. The special master found for Appellees on both claims, and against the Distributors on their counterclaim for fraud and reformation. Except for the award of prejudgment interest, which it reversed, the district court adopted all of the special master's factual findings and legal conclusions. Appellees were awarded $2,228,000.00 in compensatory damages, split evenly between the foreign and domestic home video distributions. In addition, Appellees received attorneys' fees and a permanent injunction that prohibited the Distributors from engaging in, or authorizing, any home video use of the Picture.

A panel of this circuit, in an unpublished disposition, affirmed the district court's judgment on the ground that both the domestic and foreign distribution of the Picture constituted infringement under the Copyright Act. With respect to the foreign distribution of the Picture, the panel concluded that it was bound by this court's prior decision in *Peter Starr Prod. Co. v. Twin Continental Films, Inc.*, 783 F.2d 1440 (9th Cir. 1986), which it held to stand for the proposition that, although "'infringing actions that take place entirely outside the United States are not actionable' [under the Copyright Act, an] 'act of infringement within the United States' [properly is] alleged where the illegal *authorization* of international exhibitions *t[akes] place in the United States*," *Subafilms*, slip op. at 4917-18 (quoting *Peter Starr*, 783 F.2d at 1442, 1443 (emphasis in original) (alterations added)). Because the Distributors had admitted that the initial authorization to distribute the Picture internationally occurred within the United States, the panel affirmed the district court's holding with respect to liability for extraterritorial home video distribution of the Picture.

We granted Appellants' petition for rehearing *en banc*. ...

Discussion

I. The Mere Authorization of Extraterritorial Acts of Infringement does not State a Claim under the Copyright Act

As the panel in this case correctly concluded, *Peter Starr* held that the authorization within the United States of entirely extraterritorial acts stated a cause of action under the "plain language" of the Copyright Act. Observing that the Copyright Act grants a copyright owner "the exclusive rights to do and to authorize" any of the activities listed in 17 U.S.C. § 106(1)-(5), and that a violation of the "authorization" right constitutes infringement under section 501 of the Act, the *Peter Starr* court reasoned that allegations of an authorization within the United States of extraterritorial conduct that corresponded to the activities listed in section 106 "allege[d] an act of infringement within the United States." Accordingly, the court determined that the district court erred "in concluding that 'Plaintiff allege[d] only infringing acts which took place outside of the United States,'" and reversed the district court's dismissal for lack of subject matter jurisdiction.

The *Peter Starr* court accepted, as does this court, that the acts *authorized* from within the United States themselves could not have constituted infringement under the Copyright Act because "[i]n general, United States copyright laws do not have extraterritorial effect," and therefore, "infringing actions that take place entirely outside the United States are not actionable." *Peter Starr*, 783 F.2d at 1442. The central premise of the *Peter Starr* court, then, was that a party could be held liable as an "infringer" under section 501 of the Act merely for authorizing a third party to engage in acts that, had they been committed within the United States, would have violated the exclusive rights granted to a copyright holder by section 106.

Since *Peter Starr*, however, we have recognized that, when a party authorizes an activity *not* proscribed by one of the five section 106 clauses, the authorizing party cannot be held liable as an infringer. In *Lewis Galoob*, we rejected the argument that "a party can unlawfully authorize another party to use a copyrighted work even if that party's use of the work would not violate the Copyright Act," *Lewis Galoob*, 964 F.2d at 970, and approved of Professor Nimmer's statement that "'to the extent that an activity does not violate one of th[e] five enumerated rights [found in 17 U.S.C. § 106], authorizing such activity does not constitute copyright infringement.'" *id*. ...

The apparent premise of *Lewis Galoob* was that the addition of the words "to authorize" in the Copyright Act was not meant to create a new form of liability for "authorization" that was divorced completely from the legal consequences of authorized conduct, but was intended to invoke the preexisting doctrine of contributory infringement. We agree.

Contributory infringement under the 1909 Act developed as a form of third party liability. Accordingly, there could be no liability for contributory infringement unless the authorized or otherwise encouraged activity itself could amount to infringement. ...

[U]nder the 1909 Act courts differed over the degree of involvement required to render a party liable as a contributory infringer. Viewed with this background in mind, the addition of the words "to authorize" in the 1976 Act appears best understood as merely clarifying that the Act contemplates liability for contributory infringement, and that the bare act of "authorization" can suffice [to create such liability]. ...

Although the *Peter Starr* court recognized that the addition of the authorization right in the 1976 Act "was intended to remove the confusion surrounding contributory ... infringement," it did not consider the applicability of an essential attribute of the doctrine identified above: that contributory infringement, even when triggered solely by an "authorization," is a form of third party liability that requires the authorized acts to constitute infringing ones. We believe that the *Peter Starr* court erred in not applying this principle to the authorization of acts that cannot themselves be infringing because they take place entirely abroad. As Professor Nimmer has observed:

> Accepting the proposition that a direct infringement is a prerequisite to third party liability, the further question arises whether the direct infringement on which liability is premised must take place within the United States. Given the undisputed axiom that United States copyright law has no extraterritorial application, it would seem to follow necessarily that a primary activity outside the boundaries of the United States, not constituting an infringement cognizable under the Copyright Act, cannot serve as the basis for holding liable under the Copyright Act one who is merely related to that activity within the United States.

3 Nimmer, *supra*, § 12.04[A][3][b], at 12-86 (footnotes omitted).

Appellees resist the force of this logic, and argue that liability in this case is appropriate because, unlike in *Lewis Galoob* ..., in which the alleged primary infringement consisted of acts that were entirely outside the purview of 17 U.S.C. § 106(1)-(5) (and presumably lawful), the conduct authorized in this case was precisely that prohibited by section 106, and is only uncognizable because it occurred outside the United States. Moreover, they contend that the conduct authorized in this case would have been prohibited under the copyright laws of virtually every nation.

Even assuming *arguendo* that the acts authorized in this case would have been illegal abroad, we do not believe the distinction offered by Appellees is a relevant one. Because the copyright laws do not apply extraterritorially, each of the rights conferred under the five section 106 categories must be read as extending "no farther than the [United States'] borders." 2 Goldstein, *supra*, § 16.0, at 675. In light of our above conclusion that the "authorization" right refers to the doctrine of contributory infringement, which requires that the authorized act itself could violate one of the exclusive rights listed in section 106(1)-(5), we believe that "[i]t is simply not possible to draw a principled distinction" between an act that does not violate a copyright because it is not the type of conduct proscribed by section 106, and one that does not violate section 106 because the illicit act occurs overseas. In both cases, the authorized conduct could not violate the exclusive rights guaranteed by section 106. In both cases, therefore, there can be no liability for "authorizing" such conduct.

To hold otherwise would produce the untenable anomaly, inconsistent with the general principles of third party liability, that a party could be held liable as an infringer for violating the "authorization" right when the party that it authorized could not be considered an infringer under the Copyright Act. Put otherwise, we do not think Congress intended to hold a party liable for merely "authorizing" conduct that, had the authorizing party chosen to engage in itself, would have resulted in no liability under the Act. ...

II. The Extraterritoriality of the Copyright Act

Appellees additionally contend that, if liability for "authorizing" acts of infringement depends on finding that the authorized acts themselves are cognizable under the Copyright Act, this court should find that the United States copyright laws do extend to extraterritorial acts of infringement when such acts "result in adverse effects within the United States." Appellees buttress this argument with the contention that failure to apply the copyright laws extraterritorially in this case will have a disastrous effect on the American film industry, and that other remedies, such as suits in foreign jurisdictions or the application of foreign copyright laws by American courts, are not realistic alternatives.

We are not persuaded by Appellees' parade of horribles. More fundamentally, however, we are unwilling to overturn over eighty years of consistent jurisprudence on the extraterritorial reach of the copyright laws without further guidance from Congress. ...

Furthermore, we note that Congress chose in 1976 to expand one specific "extraterritorial" application of the Act by declaring that the unauthorized importation of copyrighted works constitutes infringement even when the copies lawfully were made abroad. *See* 17 U.S.C.A. § 602(a) (West Supp. 1992). Had Congress been inclined to overturn the preexisting doctrine that infringing acts that take place wholly outside the United States are not actionable under the Copyright Act, it knew how to do so. ...

At the time that the international distribution of the videocassettes in this case took place, the United States was a member of the Universal Copyright Convention ("UCC"), and, in 1988, the United States acceded to the Berne Convention for the Protection of Literary and Artistic Works ("Berne Conv."). The central thrust of these multilateral treaties is the principle of "national treatment." A work of an American national first generated in America will receive the same protection in a foreign nation as that country accords to the works of its own nationals. Although the treaties do not expressly discuss choice-of-law rules, it is commonly acknowledged that the national treatment principle implicates a rule of territoriality. ...

[W]e think it inappropriate for the courts to act in a manner that might disrupt Congress's efforts to secure a more stable international intellectual property regime unless Congress otherwise clearly has expressed its intent. The application of American copyright law to acts of infringement that occur entirely overseas clearly could have this effect. Extraterritorial application of American law would be contrary to the spirit of the Berne Convention, and might offend other member nations by effectively displacing their law in circumstances in which previously it was assumed to govern. Consequently, an extension of extraterritoriality might undermine Congress's objective of achieving "'effective and harmonious' copyright laws among all nations." House Report, *supra*, at 20. Indeed, it might well send the signal that the United States does not believe that the protection accorded by the laws of other member nations is adequate, which would undermine two other objectives of Congress in joining the convention: "strengthen[ing] the credibility of the U.S. position in trade negotiations with countries where piracy is not uncommon" and "rais[ing] the like[li]hood that other nations will enter the Convention." S. Rep. 352, 100th Cong., 2d Sess. 4-5.

Moreover, although Appellees contend otherwise, we note that their theory might permit the application of American law to the distribution of protected materials in a foreign country conducted exclusively by citizens of that nation. ... Of course, under the Berne Convention, all states must guarantee minimum rights, and it is plausible that the application of American law would yield outcomes roughly equivalent to those called for by the application of foreign law in a number of instances. Nonetheless, extending the reach of American copyright law likely would produce difficult choice-of-law problems, dilemmas that the federal courts' general adherence to the territoriality principle largely has obviated. ...

Conclusion

We hold that the mere authorization of acts of infringement that are not cognizable under the United States copyright laws because they occur entirely outside of the United States does not state a claim for infringement under the Copyright Act. *Peter Starr* is overruled insofar as it held to the contrary. Accordingly, we vacate Part III of the panel's disposition, in which it concluded that the international distribution of the film constituted a violation of the United States copyright laws. We also vacate that portion of the disposition that affirmed the damage award based on foreign distribution of the film and the panel's affirmance of the award of attorneys' fees. Finally, we vacate the district court's grant of injunctive relief insofar as it was based on the premise that the Distributors had violated the United States copyright laws through authorization of the foreign distribution of the Picture on videocassettes.

The cause is remanded to the panel for further proceedings consistent with the mandate of this court.

Notes and Questions

1. How, if at all, could the plaintiffs in *Subafilms* have reached the infringing overseas activity? As the *Subafilms* court indicates, the application of copyright laws is generally territorial. U.S. copyright law, generally speaking, applies only to infringing activity that occurs within the geographic boundaries of the U.S. Thus, the plaintiffs in *Subafilms* would have had to sue the defendants in a foreign jurisdiction to enforce their copyrights there under foreign law.

2. Do you find the arguments made by the *Subafilms* court persuasive? After all, the plaintiffs in *Subafilms* were, strictly speaking, target-

ing behavior that occurred in the United States, namely the express authorization of sale and distribution of copies of plaintiff's work internationally. If it turned out that the activity was infringing under the law of the foreign jurisdictions, why shouldn't the plaintiffs have been entitled to collect in the U.S.?

3. Could the plaintiffs in *Subafilms* have successfully asserted causes of action under foreign law in the U.S. courts? For example, could plaintiffs have argued in U.S. federal court that the distribution of the work in France violated French copyright law? Presumably, the courts had personal jurisdiction over the defendants, and subject matter jurisdiction could be found under diversity jurisdiction. Does anything prevent a U.S. court from applying foreign copyright law?

In some cases, federal courts have in fact been willing to apply foreign copyright law. For example, in *London Film Productions v. Intercontinental Communications*, 580 F. Supp. 47 (S.D.N.Y. 1984), a British copyright owner sued a U.S. corporation for allegedly infringing activity occurring in various Latin American countries. The court in that case held that it had jurisdiction over the defendant and could pass on the application of foreign law.

In other cases, some federal courts have dismissed such cases under the doctrine of *forum non conveniens*. Although the court might have both personal and subject matter jurisdiction over such a case, it may still dismiss the case if the cause of action could be more effectively and conveniently heard in another jurisdiction. This depends on a balancing of various factors, including the location of the parties, location of witnesses, access to proof, etc.

Problem

Imagine that an individual sets up a website with a server in a country that is not a member of the Berne Convention and has very lax copyright laws. The individual makes available for download a high-quality digital copy of every sound recording ever made, for a low price of 5 cents per song. This website is enormously popular among college students around the world.

Imagine that you represent the record industry in the U.S. What, if any, steps can you take to remedy the above situation? What if you learn that the individual is a U.S. resident? Can you file suit against him here in the U.S.? What if the individual resides in a foreign jurisdiction? What, if any, options do you have to attempt to reduce unauthorized copying?

2. CHOICE OF LAW

In most cases, U.S. copyright law applies rather straightforwardly to causes of action brought in the U.S. Thus, an action brought by a U.S. author against a U.S. defendant for infringement of a work created in the U.S. is wholly governed by U.S. law. The choice of which law to apply is, accordingly, rarely an issue.

Complications can arise, however, when foreign works and parties are involved. For example, what if a work was first created in France and then infringed upon in the U.S.? Under the Berne Convention, the U.S. would be obligated to protect the French work here in the U.S. But would a court apply U.S. law or French law to the case? If infringement of the work occurred in the U.S., then U.S. law would generally apply under the doctrine *lex loci delicti* (law of the place where the infringing activity occurred).

But what if there is a dispute over the ownership of the foreign work? Say, for example, that there is a dispute over whether two French authors are joint authors. In an infringement suit brought in the U.S., should the federal district court apply U.S. copyright law to determine ownership? Or French copyright law?

Itar-Tass Russian News Agency v. Russian Kurier
153 F.3d 82 (2d Cir. 1998)

JON O. NEWMAN, Circuit Judge:

This appeal primarily presents issues concerning the choice of law in international copyright cases and the substantive meaning of Russian copyright law as to the respective rights of newspaper reporters and newspaper publishers. The conflicts issue is which country's law applies to issues of copyright ownership and to issues of infringement. The primary substantive issue under Russian copyright law is whether a newspaper publishing company has an interest sufficient to give it standing to sue for copying the text of individual articles appearing in its newspapers, or whether complaint about such copying may be made only by the reporters who authored the articles. Defendants-appellants Russian Kurier, Inc. ("Kurier") and Oleg Pogrebnoy (collectively "the Kurier defendants") appeal from the March 25, 1997, judgment of the District Court for the Southern District of New York (John G. Koeltl, Judge) enjoining them from copying articles that have appeared or will appear in publications of the plaintiffs-appellees, mainly Russian newspapers and a Russian news agency, and awarding the appellees substantial damages for copyright infringement.

On the conflicts issue, we conclude that, with respect to the Russian plaintiffs, Russian law determines the ownership and essential nature of the copyrights alleged to have been infringed and that United States law determines whether those copyrights have been infringed in the United States and, if so, what remedies are available. We also conclude that Russian law, which explicitly excludes newspapers from a work-for-hire doctrine, vests exclusive ownership interests in newspaper articles in the journalists who wrote the articles, not in the newspaper employers who compile their writings. We further conclude that to the extent that Russian law accords newspaper publishers an interest distinct from the copyright of the newspaper reporters, the publishers' interest, like the usual ownership interest in a compilation, extends to the publishers' original selection and arrangement of the articles, and does not entitle the publishers to damages for copying the texts of articles contained in a newspaper compilation. We therefore reverse the judgment to the extent that it granted the newspapers relief for copying the texts of the articles. However, because one non-newspaper plaintiff-appellee is entitled to some injunctive relief and damages and other plaintiffs-appellees may be entitled to some, perhaps considerable, relief, we also remand for further consideration of this lawsuit.

Background

The lawsuit concerns *Kurier*, a Russian language weekly newspaper with a circulation in the New York area of about 20,000. It is published in New York City by defendant Kurier. Defendant Pogrebnoy is president and sole shareholder of Kurier and editor-in-chief of *Kurier*. The plaintiffs include corporations that publish, daily or weekly, major Russian language newspapers in Russia and Russian language magazines in Russia or Israel; Itar-Tass Russian News Agency ("Itar-Tass"), formerly known as the Telegraph Agency of the Soviet Union (TASS), a wire service and news gathering company centered in Moscow, functioning similarly to the Associated Press; and the Union of Journalists of Russia ("UJR"), the professional writers union of accredited print and broadcast journalists of the Russian Federation.

The Kurier defendants do not dispute that *Kurier* has copied about 500 articles that first appeared in the plaintiffs' [newspaper] publications or were distributed by Itar-Tass. The copied material, though extensive, was a small percentage of the total number of articles published in *Kurier*. The Kurier defendants also do not dispute how the copying occurred: articles from the plaintiffs' publications, sometimes containing headlines, pictures, bylines, and graphics, in addition to text, were cut out, pasted on layout sheets, and sent to *Kurier*'s printer for photographic reproduction and printing in the pages of *Kurier*.

Most significantly, the Kurier defendants also do not dispute that, with one exception, they had not obtained permission from any of the plaintiffs to copy the articles that appeared in *Kurier*. ...

Discussion

I.   Choice of Law

The threshold issue concerns the choice of law for resolution of this dispute. That issue was not initially considered by the parties, all of whom turned directly to Russian law for resolution of the case. Believing that the conflicts issue merited consideration, we requested supplemental briefs from the parties and appointed Professor William F. Patry as Amicus Curiae. Prof. Patry has submitted an extremely helpful brief on the choice of law issue.

Choice of law issues in international copyright cases have been largely ignored in the reported decisions and dealt with rather cursorily by most commentators. Examples pertinent to the pending appeal are those decisions involving a work created by the employee of a foreign corporation. Several courts have applied the United States work-for-hire doctrine, without explicit consideration of the conflicts issue. Other courts have applied foreign law. In none of these cases, however, was the issue of choice of law explicitly adjudicated. ...

Source of conflicts rules. Our analysis of the conflicts issue begins with consideration of the source of law for selecting a conflicts rule. ...

We start our analysis with the Copyrights Act itself, which contains no provision relevant to the pending case concerning conflicts issues. We therefore fill the interstices of the Act by developing federal common law on the conflicts issue. ...

The choice of law applicable to the pending case is not necessarily the same for all issues. We consider first the law applicable to the issue of copyright ownership.

Conflicts rule for issues of ownership. Copyright is a form of property, and the usual rule is that the interests of the parties in property are determined by the law of the state with "the most significant relationship" to the property and the parties. *See* Restatement (Second) Conflict of Laws § 222. The Restatement recognizes the applicability of this principle to intangibles such as "a literary idea." *id*. Since the works at issue were created by Russian nationals and first published in Russia, Russian law is the appropriate source of law to determine issues of ownership of rights. ...

Conflicts rule for infringement issues. On infringement issues, the governing conflicts principle is usually *lex loci delicti*, the doctrine generally applicable to torts. We have implicitly adopted that approach to infringement claims, applying United States copyright law to a work that was unprotected in its country of origin. In the pending case, the place of the tort is plainly the United States. To whatever extent *lex loci delicti* is to be considered only one part of a broader "interest" approach, United States law would still apply to infringement issues, since not only is this country the place of the tort, but also the defendant is a United States corporation.

The division of issues, for conflicts purposes, between ownership and infringement issues will not always be as easily made as the above discussion implies. If the issue is the relatively straightforward one of which of two contending parties owns a copyright, the issue is unquestionably an ownership issue, and the law of the country with the closest relationship to the work will apply to settle the ownership dispute. But in some cases, including the pending one, the issue is not simply who owns the copyright but also what is the nature of the ownership interest. Yet as a court considers the nature of an ownership interest, there is some risk that it will too readily shift the inquiry over to the issue of whether an alleged copy has infringed the asserted copyright. Whether a copy infringes depends in part on the scope of the interest of the copyright owner. Nevertheless, though the issues are related, the nature of a copyright interest is an issue distinct from the issue of whether the copyright has been infringed. The pending case is one that requires consideration not simply of who owns an interest, but, as to the newspapers, the nature of the interest that is owned.

II. Determination of Ownership Rights Under Russian Law

[The court subsequently held that under Russian Copyright Law, the wire service Itar-Tass owned the copyrights in the articles it published. However, the court held that the newspapers did not own the copyrights in the articles they published because Russian law specifically excluded newspapers from the Russian version of the work made for hire doctrine. Accordingly, the copyrights for articles published by Russian newspapers were retained by the writers. The newspapers only had a copyright in the selection and arrangement of the articles.]

Conclusion

Accordingly, we affirm the judgment to the extent that it granted relief to Itar-Tass, we reverse to the extent that the judgment granted relief to the other plaintiffs, and we remand for further proceedings.

Notes and Questions

1. The case above lays out a seemingly straightforward distinction between issues of ownership and issues of infringement. Generally speaking, the law of the country where the work was created applies to issues of ownership, whereas the law of the country where the infringement occurred applies to issues of infringement.

Note, however, that some issues may not fit neatly into those two categories. For example, what about issues concerning the types of rights that the copyright encompasses? The case above suggests that these are determined by the law of the country in which infringement occurs. What about a dispute arising out of a licensing agreement negotiated in another country? Typically, the courts in such cases apply the law of the country in which the contract was executed.

2. Although the above rules are generally applicable, as in most choice of law cases, a court may choose to depart from the rules if there are strong reasons of public policy dictating such a departure. For example, if application of foreign law would have a significant negative impact on the public policy of the jurisdiction, a court would, consistent with general conflict of laws rules, be free to apply local law instead.

What about a case involving a work that would not satisfy the originality requirement in the U.S., but would be protectable under foreign law? Would a U.S. court be obligated to enforce the copyright here in the U.S.? This issue came up in *Bridgeman Art Library v. Corel*, 36 F. Supp. 2d 191 (S.D.N.Y. 1999), which involved a copyright claim for color transparencies of paintings that were in the public domain. The court held that such literal reproductions did not satisfy the originality requirement under U.S. law. However, the plaintiff argued that the transparencies created in the United Kingdom would have been protected under U.K. law.

The *Bridgeman* court held that the U.S. was not obligated to apply U.K. law. The court pointed specifically to language in 17 U.S.C. § 104(c), which provides that "[n]o right or interest in a work eligible for protection under this title may be claimed by virtue of, or in reliance upon, the provisions of the Berne Convention ...." The court thus looked to U.S. copyright law and found that the works did not satisfy the originality requirement set forth in § 102.

Index

References are to pages.